Controversies in Constitutional Law

Collections of Documents and Articles on Major Questions of American Law

General Editor

Paul Finkelman
University of Tulsa School of Law

A ROUTLEDGE SERIES

Contents of the Collection

Children and the Law

Volume 2

The State and the Schooling of Children

Edited with introductions by

Janet W. Steverson
Northwestern School of Law
of Lewis and Clark College

ROUTLEDGE
New York/London

Published in 2002 by
Routledge
29 West 35th Street
New York, NY 10001

Published in Great Britain by
Routledge
11 New Fetter Lane
London EC4P 4EE

Routledge is an imprint of the Taylor & Francis Group.

Printed in the United States of America on acid-free paper.

10 9 8 7 6 5 4 3 2 1

Library of Congress Cataloging-in-Publication Data

Children and the law / edited with introductions by Janet W. Steverson.
p. cm. — (Controversies in constitutional law)
Includes bibliographical references.
Contents: v. 1. The State as Child Protector — v. 2. The State and the Schooling of Children — v. 3. Child vs. State.
ISBN 0-415-93803-1 (set : alk paper) — ISBN 0-415-93804-X (vol. 1 : alk. paper) — ISBN 0-415-93805-8 (vol. 2 : alk. paper) — ISBN 0-415-93806-6 (vol. 3 : alk. paper)
1. Children—Legal status, laws, etc.—United States. 2. Parent and child (Law)—United States. 3. Juvenile justice, Administration of—United States. I. Steverson, Janet W. II. Series.
KF479.A75 C478 2002
346.7301'35—dc21 2002020626

Contents

Series Introduction

This ongoing series, *Controversies in Constitutional Law,* provides teachers, scholars, and students convenient access to the debates and scholarly literature surrounding major questions of constitutional law. Each set of books—from two to four volumes—consists of four elements: an extended introduction to the issue by the editor; reprints of the significant cases and briefs on the subject; congressional testimony, and other primary documents on the issue; and a selection of the best scholarly articles on the subject. By conveniently gathering all this material in one place, each set of volumes allows users to become familiar quite quickly with the arguments and positions surrounding a particular constitutional controversy.

Scholars and students interested in constitutional law and public policy are often overwhelmed by the sheer amount of material published on controversial subjects. The topics in *Controversies in Constitutional Law* are timely, politically significant, and intellectually compelling. They are the issues that bring the legal academy, courts, politicians, and general public together—although not always in harmony.

Many scholars are barely able to keep up with the material in their own fields. Yet there is a need to learn about issues beyond our own specialties. A new course may require an introduction to a problem; our own research may lead us to a new issue. The series *Controversies in Constitutional Law* is designed to meet these needs, enabling scholars and teachers to come up to speed quickly on the topics in each volume.

This series also serves students at all levels of higher education. Students often encounter controversial topics without the background in how the problem developed. These volumes provide such a background. The important cases are reprinted in full; the introductions provide students with a map of the issues; the briefs, congressional testimony, and scholarly articles give convenient access to the arguments and debates.

The volumes bring together in one place a wide variety of sources and materials that are unlikely to be found in any one library. The primary documents include cases, briefs, testimony from legislative committee hearings, and, on occasion, executive branch publications. Few law libraries, university libraries, or public libraries will have all these materials. The secondary literature comes from the scholarly literature of law, history, political science, economics, criminology, and other relevant fields. Some of the articles also may be from serious nonacademic journals.

The related government publications, briefs, and congressional testimony are particularly important. Too often scholars overlook them. There is a tendency to focus on court opinions—what the Supreme Court said. Obviously this is important for understanding doctrine, but briefs, especially amicus briefs, are also an important source of information about the larger constitutional controversy the case represents. The politics of a case are often more apparent in these briefs than in either the oral arguments or the Court's opinion. Similarly, congressional hearings illustrate the social, philosophical, and political dimensions of these questions.

The goal of limiting each collection—two to four focused volumes—and the occasional inability to secure a reasonable copyright permission fee for some important articles often forces hard and judicious choices. Important articles that are not reprinted here are listed in the further reading sections at the end of the introductions.

The ongoing series *Controversies in Constitutional Law* provides in one single place comprehensive introductions to topics that will satisfy most lawyers, scholars, and students. By combining cases, briefs, legislative debates, and testimony from committee hearings with secondary articles, it is hoped to facilitate access to the issue presented in each set of volumes.

Paul Finkelman

Volume Introduction

Given that a democratic society depends upon an educated populace for its survival, the question of how our children are to be educated has been, and is currently, an area of hot debate. In addition, because children spend a great deal of time in school, an important issue for them is whether their constitutional rights will be respected while they are in the school building. Both of these issues are the subject of this second volume.

Although it is generally recognized that the existence of harm to the child may justify the state's intervention in the parent-child relationship, the question still remains as to when the state may interfere in the parent-child relationship when no harm *per se* to the child is present. Part one delves into the question of when, and to what extent, the state may exercise control over the education of children. In this area we again see a tension between the parents' desire to educate their children free from state intervention and the state's interest in ensuring the "proper" education of its youth. Interestingly, however, here the state's interest in intervening is not only (or even mainly) for the direct benefit of the child, but also for the direct benefit of the state. The state desires to have a hand in molding its future leaders and voters. The materials explore the question of what is the proper balance between these competing interests. The first article delineates the nature of the competing interests in this area, while the next two articles disagree as to whether the state's interests (and peripherally the children's) or the parents' rights should predominate in this area. Part two then takes a look at both sides of the school voucher issue. Although there is no U.S. Supreme Court decision in this area, the constitutionality of an Ohio school voucher system is currently before the U.S. Supreme Court.

Part three explores how the Court has grappled with the question of what impact, if any, a minor's status as a child in need of guidance and support, should have on the scope of a child's constitutional rights. Part three specifically limits its purview to schoolchildren, while volume three explores the rights of children outside of school. With regard to the constitutional rights of schoolchildren, in the *Tinker v. Des Moines* case the Supreme Court opined the following: "In our system, state-operated schools may not be enclaves of totalitarianism. School officials do not possess absolute authority over their students. Students in school as well as out of school are 'persons' under our Constitution. They are possessed of fundamental rights which the State must respect, just as they themselves must respect their obligation to the State." Thus, the materials in part three focus upon how the Court does, and should, balance the interests of the state in maintaining orderly and safe schools with the constitutional rights of the schoolchildren. The two articles in part three provide a general overview of the rights of children in this area.

Part four focuses upon the specific question of whether a school may corporally punish a child. In general, the Supreme Court has held that a school's use of corporal punishment does not violate the child's constitutional right against cruel and unusual punishment, nor does it deprive a child of liberty without due process of law. The Court has further held that a school may inflict corporal punishment on a child even if a parent of that child objects. The materials in part four provide information and opposing viewpoints concerning the constitutional issues in this area. Such is done through an overview article, a position paper against corporal punishment in schools, and an article that does a nice job of presenting the various legal arguments on both sides of the issue.

Part five provides a fairly in-depth discussion of the free speech rights of minors. In this area the Supreme Court has espoused the view that students have free speech rights, but at the same time has placed some fairly substantial limits upon the students' exercise of that right. Because this is an issue on which there has been an extensive amount of writing, with a variety of viewpoints, the five articles present are designed to give the reader some insight into the flavor of the debate.

Part six then moves into the question of whether a student's right to be free from unreasonable searches and seizures extends to the school context and if so, what is the best way in which to protect the students' rights. This question has become increasingly pertinent in light of the increased incidence of seriously violent acts in the schools and the states' attempts to forestall future such occurrences. On this question the Supreme Court has held that the Fourth "Amendments prohibition on unreasonable searches and seizures applies to searches conducted by public school officials."[1] However, it has recognized that "[a]gainst the child's interest in privacy must be set the substantial interest of teachers and administrators in maintaining discipline in the classroom and on school grounds."[2] The article in this section examines the different positions taken with regard to how best to protect students' privacy rights, and then proposes an approach that the author claims will better meet the competing concerns of promoting student safety and protecting student privacy.

Finally, the materials in part seven discuss the applicability of the Due Process Clause to school discipline. In 1975, the Supreme Court held that the due process clause required that, prior to suspension, a student be given "notice of the charges against him and, if he denies them, an explanation of the evidence the authorities have and an opportunity to present his side of the case."[3] The Court declined, however, to require the use of hearings prior to suspension. A question that was not decided by the Court was whether expulsion from school requires more in the way of due process. The two articles in part eight examine these issues and debate the relative merits of applying the right to procedural due process to school discipline.

Janet W. Steverson

Notes

1 *New Jersey v. T.L.O.*, 469 U.S. 325 (1985).
2 *Ibid.*
3 *Goss v. Lopez*, 419 U.S. 565, 581 (1975).

Children and the Law

Volume 2

The State and the Schooling of Children

"The Right to Direct the Upbringing of a Child." Parent as Sovereign and the State as Educator: A Balance of Vital Interests

Todd A. DeMitchell
Associate Professor of Administration and Supervision
Associate Chair, Department of Education
University of New Hampshire
Durham, NH 03824-3595

"A Popular Government, without popular information, or the means of acquiring it, is but a Prologue to a Farce or a Tragedy; or perhaps both. Knowledge will forever govern ignorance: a people who mean to be their Governors, must arm themselves with the power which knowledge gives."

—James Madison
Writings of James Madison

"In our system, state-operated schools may not be enclaves of totalitarianism. School officials do not possess absolute authority over their students." *Tinker v. Des Moines School District,* 89 S.Ct.733, 739 (1969)

"Plaintiffs right to direct Annie's education is not absolute, nothing in the Constitution, federal or state, grants [parents] the right to control public education on an individual basis." *Swanson v. Guthrie Independent School District, No. I-1,* 942 F.Supp. 511, 515 (W.D. Okl. 1996)

Educating youth is of prime importance to parents and the State. The United States Supreme Court echoed this principle when it wrote: "The American people have always regarded education and the acquisition of knowledge as matters of supreme importance which should be diligently promoted" (*Meyer v. Nebraska,* 1923, p. 393). In many ways, educating a child is the essence of parenting. "The history and culture of Western civilization reflect a strong tradition of parent concern for the nurture and upbringing of their children. This primary role of the parents in the upbringing of their children is now established beyond debate as an enduring American tradition" (*Wisconsin v. Yoder,* 1972, p. 232). For the State, education is perhaps the most important function of government *(Brown v. Board of Education,* 1954). Both parenting and the teaching power of the State[1] have an inculcative function. But, when parents assert their right to make educational decisions regarding their children, this can trench on the state's educational processes, programs, and goals of promoting the general welfare by preparing students for the broader society. Conversely, educational decisions made in the public schools may contradict values taught at home and encroach on parental sovereignty of parents over their children.

This conflict between parents' wishes and the decisions of school authorities has historically occurred in several areas including compulsory education, placement in special education classes, and most notably in curriculum decisions, to name a few.[2] The tension between the purposes of our majoritarian government and the desires of individuals to live their lives unrestricted readily clash in the area of education, "where our nation has enjoyed a long history of encouraging families to take responsibility for the instruction of their own children, while at the same time, making school attendance compulsory and granting control of the curriculum to state and local officials" (*Immediato by Immediato v. Rye Neck School District,* 1995, p. 849). An intense debate about the proper balance of power that parents and the government should exercise over the education and futures of children in our society is being heard in the halls of various legislative bodies and in numerous courtrooms. Both sides to the debate have conjured up visions of the other side using children as the unwitting tools of adults' agendas for the direction of society.

This column will focus on that part of the debate that intersects the right of the parent to direct the education of their child and the State's compelling interest in educating its citizenry. The discussion will start with a review of the legal precedents for parental rights, explore some current court cases involving the proper balance of parental rights and the State's educational authority, and finish with a critique of some of the recent legislation regarding parents' rights. Parental free exercise claims and privacy claims under the First Amendment, although important, are beyond the limited space available for this discussion.

Parents' Rights: The Legal Precedents

Advocates for strengthening parental rights regarding the education of their children often cite two major United States Supreme Court decisions as legal precedent for their position. The two cases are *Meyer v. Nebraska* (1923) and *Pierce v. Society of Sisters* (1925). Prior to these two cases, the "courts tended to rely on a common law presumption of the soundness of parental judgment in making educational decisions pertaining to their children" (Mawdsly and Drake, 1992, p. 301). An Illinois court reflected this presumption in favor of parents by stating that even if parental decisions represented a misfortune for their child, the parents' decision would be upheld if it did not "affect the government of the school or incommode the other students or the teachers" (*The Trustees of Schools v. The People ex. rel. Martin Van Allen*, 1877, p. 309).

Meyer v. Nebraska

After World War I, Nebraska passed a statute imposing criminal penalties on public or private school teachers who taught languages other than English to students below high school level or who taught in any language except English. This legislation "was born of the animosity against alien groups aroused by World War I; in Nebraska, the target was Germans generally and the German language in particular" (Yudof, Kirp, and Levin, 1992, p. 23).[3] The stated purpose of the legislation was to promote civic development by teaching students the American ideals through the English language before exposing them to foreign languages and cultures. The avowed purpose of the legislation was that English would be the "mother tongue" of all children reared in Nebraska. A teacher in Zion Parochial School was convicted under this statute for teaching German to children before they passed the eighth grade.

In the resulting court case, the United States Supreme Court upheld the power of the State to impose compulsory education, to regulate all schools, to "conduct its schools as to 'foster a homogenous people' " (*Meyer v. Nebraska*, 1923, p. 402), and to prescribe a curriculum for the public schools. It also held that the Nebraska law was arbitrary and unreasonably infringed the plaintiff's liberty guaranteed by the Due Process Clause of the Fourteenth Amendment. The Court, in much quoted language defining the contours of the liberty interest protected by the Fourteenth Amendment, wrote:

> Without doubt, it denotes not merely freedom from bodily restraint, but also the right of the individual to contract, to engage in any of the common occupations of life, to acquire useful knowledge, to marry, establish a home and bring up children, to worship God according to the dictates of his own conscience, and generally, to enjoy those privileges long recognized at common law as essential to the orderly pursuit of happiness of free men. (p. 399)

After establishing the general parameters of the liberty interest, the Court referring to the teaching of German, stated: "His right thus to teach and the right of parents to engage him so to instruct their children, we think are within the liberty of the Amendment" (p. 402). The Court found that the statute was "arbitrary and without reasonable relation to any end within the competency of the State" (p. 403).

Thus, the High Court found that parents had the right to contract for teaching services that they wanted for their children. Parents' rights were upheld, but so were the rights of the State to establish its public school curriculum and to compel students to attend school. It would appear that according to *Meyer*, parents had the right to contract for the educational services they deemed important for their child. This case cannot be read to mean that parents' right to contract for educational services trumps the right of the public school to prescribe its curriculum. There is nothing in the language of the case to suggest that parents have the right to control the public school curriculum to meet their wishes. Parents simply have the right to contract for educational services without reasonable interference from the state. Clearly, the power of the State over its curriculum is not diminished by *Meyer*.

Pierce v. Society of Sisters

On November 7, 1922, the voters of Oregon passed an initiative that changed its Constitution. The result was the passage of the Compulsory Education Act of 1922.[4] The law required that all of Oregon's children attend public schools between the ages of eight and sixteen. This law effectively closed down parochial schools of which Catholic schools were the most numerous. The referendum campaign was organized and promoted primarily by the Ku Klux Klan and the Oregon Scottish Rite Masons (Yudof, Kirp, and Levin, 1992). The strategy was to "Americanize" the schools in response to a wave of immigration. One Klansman succinctly stated the underlying rationale for the referendum: "Somehow these mongrel hordes must be Americanized; failing that, deportation is the only remedy" (Yudof, Kirp, and Levin, 1992, p. 13). The referendum narrowly carried.

Suit was brought by two plaintiffs. The first appellee, Society of Sisters, was an Oregon corporation organized in 1880 with the power to "care for orphans, educate and instruct the youth, establish and maintain academies and schools, and acquire necessary real and personal property" (*Pierce v. Society of Sisters*, 1925, p. 512). The schools run by the Society of Sisters taught the subjects usually pursued in the public schools and provided systematic religious instruction according to the tenets of the Roman Catholic Church. The passage of the Compulsory Education Act of 1922 resulted in the withdrawal of students and the decline of the Society of Sister's income.

The second plaintiff in *Pierce* was the Hill Military Academy, a private school operated for profit. The Academy owned and operated an elementary, college preparatory, and military training school for boys from ages five to twenty-one. It, too, was losing money with the institution of the compulsory education act.

Both plaintiffs argued that the state had deprived them of property—without the due process of law guaranteed by the Fourteenth Amendment. The inevitable outcome of instituting the Act would be the destruction of the plaintiffs' schools. The Society of Sisters and the Hill Military Academy also argued that the law compelling attendance at public schools also interfered with parents' and guardians' rights as a part of their liberty to "direct the education of children by selecting reputable teachers and places" (p. 513). This liberty right of parents to engage individuals to teach their children was discussed and affirmed in *Meyer v. Nebraska* (1923).

The United States Supreme Court's ruling was similar to its holding in *Meyer*. In both cases, the Court upheld the right of the State to mandate compulsory attendance for a specified period of time. Broad powers of the State to determine the content of a public school education was also upheld. The High Court's language was quite unequivocal about the extent of the State's teaching power. The Court wrote:

> No question is raised concerning the power of the State reasonably to regulate all schools, to inspect, supervise and examine them, their teachers and pupils; to require that all children of proper age attend some school, that teachers shall be of good moral character and patriotic disposition, that certain studies plainly essential to good citizenship must be taught, and that nothing be taught which is manifestly inimical to the public welfare. (p. 515)

Although the Supreme Court afforded the State extensive teaching powers as educator, that right to educate youth was not without limits. Writing for the Court, Justice McReynolds enunciated an often quoted statement: "The child is not the mere creature of the State; those who nurture and direct his destiny have the right, coupled with the high duty, to recognize and prepare him for additional duties" (p. 535). The High Court found that the Oregon Act of 1922 unreasonably interfered with "the liberty of parents and guardians to direct the upbringing and education of children under their control" (p. 534). On one hand, the Court found that the State had broad powers to establish and direct the public schools. On the other hand, the Court also found that parents had the right and "high duty" to direct the upbringing and education of their children. Two legitimate interests were identified by the Supreme Court, but how to balance those competing interests became part of the legacy of *Pierce*.

In trying to build an understanding of the contours of the rights enumerated by the Supreme Court in *Pierce*, the issues before the Court in 1925 must be kept uppermost in the minds of the reader. One issue was the property rights of the plaintiffs. The other issue, important for our discussion, dealt with where to send children to be educated: do parents have the right to decide whether to send their child to a public school or to a private school, or can the State force children to only attend public schools was the essential question. The Act of 1922 took that right of deciding where a child will be educated away from parents when it compelled attendance at a public school exclusively. Therefore, when the Court ascribed a right to direct the upbringing and education of a child, it is within the context of the issue before the Court. The High Court enumerated extensive teaching power to the State to reasonably regulate all schools; it did not enumerate a concomitant power to parents. For example, parents were not given the right or authority to control the curriculum that their child would receive in a public school, nor could parents decide not to educate their child. That authority was clearly left to the State. The United States Supreme Court merely resolved the issue of whether it is reasonable for the State to compel a student to attend only a public school. The High Court found that parents have the liberty to choose whether to educate their child at a public school or a private school such as ones maintained by the Society of Sisters and the Hill Military Academy. The decision did not exempt parents and their children from reasonable regulations that the State might promulgate.

Selected Court Cases and Parental Rights

Several current court cases in which the plaintiff parents asserted a right to direct the upbringing of their child will be reviewed. The list of cases selected for review is not exhaustive, but it is representative of how the courts are balancing issues involving an asserted parental right to direct the upbringing and the state's efforts to educate children in their public schools.

Mandatory Community Service Programs

Rye Neck School District in New York established a mandatory community service requirement for graduation from its high school. The program required students in grades nine through twelve to perform forty hours of community service during the four years of high school as a condition of graduation. According to the regulations, students may not receive pay for their services and the service must be performed for people in need. Daniel Immediato, a student at Rye Neck High School, and his parents brought suit against the school district challenging the constitutionality of the program (*Immediato by Immediato v. Rye Neck School District*, 1995). For our purposes, only the plaintiff's assertion that the program violated their parental rights will be explored; all other claims will not be discussed.

The plaintiff parents alleged that they possessed a Constitutional right to "have their children opt out of programs that are contrary to the beliefs and values they seek to impart" (p. 852). Their objections were secular and not religious. This distinction is important because parental objections based on the free exercise clause[5] call for a different level of review of state regulations. There are three recognized tests that are used when a governmental statute or regulation is challenged. The most difficult test of the three for government to pass is strict scrutiny analysis. This is the test that plaintiffs normally assert the court should use in resolving their dispute. Under strict scrutiny, the challenged legislation is held unconstitutional unless government can show that the legislation is justified by a compelling state interest and is narrowly drawn to meet that interest. Heightened scrutiny, the middle level test, is a relatively new standard. It is still being developed. It is generally applied when a regulation impacts on a "sensitive" classification such as gender, age, and undocumented aliens. Under this standard, a rule or regulation is invalid unless it can be shown that it serves an important state interest and that the classification is substantially related to that interest. The last test is rational basis. This is the most permissive of the three tests. It is considered the standard test. As opposed to strict scrutiny, the rational basis test places the burden of proof on the person challenging the classification. In order for the state to pass the rational basis test, the state action must only serve a legitimate state interest and be rationally related to that purpose. Legislation examined under the rational basis test "carries with it a presumption

Table 1.

	Strict Security	Heightened Scrutiny	Rational Basis
Classification of the plaintiff	Suspect class[6] Fundamental right	Sensitive class Gender Undocumented aliens Age	All other
State objective for the rule or law must be:	Compelling	Important	Legitimate
Means used to attain the objective are:	Necessary to meet the objective	Substantially related to the objective	Rationally related to the objective

of rationality that can only be overcome by a clear showing of arbitrariness and irrationality" (*Hodel v. Indiana,* 1981, pp. 331–332). The challenger of legislation under rational basis has a heavy burden. Table 1 shows the comparative difficulties for government under each test.

The plaintiff, Immediato, cited *Meyer* and *Pierce* for the proposition that the right to direct the upbringing of a child is fundamental, thus, strict scrutiny analysis would be employed when governmental laws or regulations infringed on that fundamental right. The court in *Immediato* disagreed. Referring to both *Meyer* and *Pierce*, District Court Judge Brieant found that both cases used rational basis instead of strict scrutiny. *Meyer* discussed the *reasonable* relationship of the disputed law and noted the "power of the State to make *reasonable* regulations for all schools," and to "prescribe a curriculum for institutions which it supports" (*Meyer,* 1923, p. 402, emphasis added). In *Pierce,* the Court found that the state regulation unreasonably interfered with the liberty of parents. Judge Brieant wrote that the issue is whether the community service program "has a reasonable relation to an end within the competency of the state" (*Immediato,* 1995, p. 852). Thus, the parental right was not a fundamental right calling for strict scrutiny analysis, but rather rational basis.

Using the rational basis test, the District Court found that the program had a reasonable relation to purposes within the competency of the State. Because the service program was rationally related to a legitimate state interest, the plaintiffs lost. The court's analysis did not stop there as it could have once the issue was resolved. The court went beyond the rational basis test to discuss the impact on public policy if the courts allowed parents to seek intervention by the courts whenever an educational decision clashed with a value held by the parents. The court found that no public policy allowing such redress of grievances which bypassed the duly elected board of education would be served by the courts "usurping the legitimate authority of school officials to perform their duties in educating citizens" (Immediato, 1995, p. 852). The court concluded its analysis of the parental rights assertion with the following: "Plaintiff parents may not use this Court to interpose their own way of life or their own philosophy, however laudable, as a barrier to reasonable state and local regulation of the educational curriculum" (p. 853).

The defendant school district was granted summary judgment and the plaintiffs appealed. The Second Circuit Court of Appeals heard the appeal on October 10, 1995, and rendered a decision on January 2, 1996 (*Immediato v. Rye Neck School District,* 1996). The plaintiffs reargued their parental rights claims asserted during the District Court proceedings. The Court of Appeals reviewed the summary judgment of the lower court *de novo.* The appellate court reviewed *Meyer, Pierce,* and *Yoder* and found that parents have a cognizable liberty interest in the upbringing of their children. The court also found that the proper standard of review was rational basis for parents who seek, for secular reasons, to exempt their child from an educational requirement. The court opined that the "Supreme Court has never expressly indicated whether this 'parental right,' when properly invoked against a state regulation, is fundamental, deserving strict scrutiny, or earns only rational basis review. Our reading of the appropriate case law convinces us that rational basis review is appropriate" (p. 461).

The Second Circuit Court of Appeals quickly dispatched the plaintiffs' argument under a rational basis review. The court concluded that Rye Neck School District's mandatory community service program was "reasonably related to the state's legitimate function of educating its students" (p. 462).

Rye Neck School District was not the only school district to institute a mandatory community service program. The Chapel Hill-Carrboro City Board of Education in North Carolina adopted a similar program to Rye Neck School District requiring fifty hours of unpaid community service as a graduation requirement. Some students and parents brought suit in federal court to declare the practice unconstitutional (*Herndon v. Chapel Hill-Carrboro City Board of Education,* 1995). The students and parents did not allege a religious basis for their complaint. As with *Immediato,* the district court in North Carolina used the rational basis test. The court argued that the Supreme Court's treatment of the parental right to direct the upbringing of their child does not fashion a right for individual parents to "exert pre-emptive control over the curriculum of public schools [and] is not a 'fundamental' one subject to 'strict scrutiny' " (p. 1450). Judge Bullock concluded that the plaintiffs did not meet their "heavy burden of clearly showing that the program is arbitrary and irrational" (p. 1453).

The plaintiffs appealed arguing that the service requirement violated their right to direct the upbringing and education of their child (*Herndon by Herndon v. Chapel Hill-Carrboro City Board of Education,* 1996). The Fourth Circuit Court of Appeals heard their appeal. Once again, the court recognized the existence of the right of parents to direct their children's education. Citing another Supreme Court case *Runyon v. McCrary* (1976),[7] the court of appeals concluded that rational basis rather than strict scrutiny should be used. The court quoted the

Runyon opinion as authority for its decision: "The Court has repeatedly stressed that while parents have a constitutional right to send their children to private schools and a constitutional right to select private schools that offer specialized instruction, they have no constitutional right to provide their children with private education unfettered by reasonable government regulation" (p. 179). All of the pertinent Supreme Court cases used rational basis language. The Fourth Circuit followed suit and using the rational basis test concluded that the service requirement is rationally related to the school district's interest in teaching the value of service.

All four courts reviewed the case law on the issue of parental rights and all four were unanimous in holding that the most deferential test to government, rational basis, was the appropriate tool to be used. It is important to note that these cases found that the parental right to direct the upbringing of a child is not considered a fundamental right. We will look at a few other cases to see if this trend of using rational basis and not strict scrutiny continues.

Condom Availability Policies

The New York City School Board of Education approved a condom availability program as part of an AIDS education program. The condom availability program was not mandatory, unlike the service programs discussed above. Students who wanted to participate could obtain condoms from the health resource room located within the school building. Students were not required to obtain parental permission before obtaining a condom. No student was required to request or obtain a condom. Parents brought suit arguing, among other arguments, that the program violated their due process rights to raise their children (*Alfonso v. Fernandez*, 1992).[8]

The trial court found that parents had a constitutional right to direct the upbringing of their children, but that right was not absolute. The court argued that a corollary, or restraining factor, in this right is the constitutional rights of the children "which must be protected by all, including parents" (p. 412). The court concluded that the voluntary nature of the condom availability program did not infringe upon the parents' rights to raise their children. There was no coercive effect to the program and that the existence of the program is mere exposure to other ideas. Even if an opt out provision was adopted, the exposure would still be present since the program would still continue in school. The plaintiffs appealed (*Alfonso v. Fernandez*, 1993).

The New York appellate court reversed the lower court's holding. The appellate court distinguished this case from those in which parents were complaining solely about having their child exposed to ideas or points of view with which they disagree. The court argued if this were the case, "such opposition would falter in the face of the public school's role in preparing students for participation in a world replete with complex and controversial issues" (p. 266). The condom availability program, the majority opined, was different from situations in which parents disagree with school authorities on what should be taught. Because parents are compelled to send their children "into an environment where they will be permitted even encouraged to obtain a contraceptive device" (p. 265), "[s]tudents are not just exposed to talk or literature on the subject of sexual behavior; the school offers the means for students to engage in sexual activity at a lower risk of pregnancy and contracting sexually transmitted diseases" (p. 266). This is a curious argument. Boiled down, the statement of the appellate court reads: instruction/content that parents may object to cannot form the basis for parental veto unless the students can actually use the material to affect their lives.

With this background on the vitality of the parental right to direct upbringing, the court looked at what test to employ in balancing the competing rights. The court concluded that strict scrutiny analysis was the proper test because of the compulsion surrounding the condom availability program. Strict scrutiny analysis asks whether a compelling state interest is involved and whether this program is necessary to meet it. The court easily found that there is a compelling interest in controlling AIDS. But, are the means used by the condom availability program necessary to meet the compelling state interest? The court argued that they are not. If the program did not exist, students would still be able to acquire condoms without difficulty, thus the program in the public schools is not necessary. The court concluded that the condom availability program violated the parents' right to direct the upbringing of their children. "We do not find that the policy is essential. No matter how laudable its purpose, by excluding parental involvement, the condom availability component of the program impermissibly trespasses on the parental rights by substituting the respondents in loco parentis, without a compelling necessity" (p. 265).

It is interesting to note that the majority did not specifically find that the parental right was fundamental. Its closest point to finding a fundamental right is found in the following passage: "Intrusion into the relationship between parent and child requires a showing of overriding necessity" (p. 265). The problem with this assertion is that the majority cites *Wisconsin v. Yoder* (1972) as authority for this conclusion, and *Wisconsin v. Yoder* involved a free exercise claim which gave it an additional value which necessitated a greater inquiry into state action. In *Alfonso*, there was no free exercise claim made by the plaintiffs which would call for the increased analysis.

Judge Eiber offered an interesting dissent. He disagreed with the majority that the condom distribution program "unreasonably" interfered with the parents' liberty interest. The judge found, unlike the majority, that because students are compelled to attend school that does not "vest the condom distribution program with the aura of 'compulsion' necessary to make out a viable claim of deprivation of a fundamental constitutional right" (p. 272). If there is no fundamental right involved in the controversy, then rational basis is the correct analytical tool to use. This is counter to the majority which used strict scrutiny analysis, the least deferential test to government. Because there is no compulsion associated with the program, the dissent argued, parents were free to impart their religious and moral values to their children in the privacy of their own homes and direct their children not to participate in the condom distribution program.

The majority in *Alfonso* (1993) used strict scrutiny analysis to strike down the condom availability program. The dissent used rational basis to uphold the program. The dissent's position was consistent with all four courts reviewed in the previous section on mandatory community service programs. The dissent in *Alfonso* made a point about the voluntariness of the program. It is possible that the dissent may have reached a different conclusion if the program had been mandatory. This raises the question of whether the vitality of the parental right to direct the upbringing may be more vigorous in certain areas that have historically been more sensitive, such as sexuality. We will briefly review the only other published opinion on this issue of condom availability programs and parental rights for comparison purposes.

The School Committee of Falmouth on January 2, 1992, instituted a condom availability program for its junior and senior high schools. The program was voluntary, did not require parental permission nor provide parental notification, and was coupled with a message that abstinence was the most effective method for avoiding sexually transmitted diseases. Parents sued. The trial court granted summary judgment for the defendant arguing that the plaintiffs did not demonstrate that the program placed a coercive burden on their rights. The plaintiffs appealed (*Curtis v. School Committee of Falmouth,* 1995).

The Supreme Judicial Court of Massachusetts agreed that parents possess a "fundamental liberty interest, protected by the Fourteenth Amendment, to be free from unnecessary governmental intrusion in the rearing of their children" (p. 585). But, they found that the plaintiff parents failed to demonstrate how their interests were burdened by the program. The type of interference necessary to support the plaintiffs' complaint was that which causes a coercive or compulsory effect on the claimants' rights. The plaintiffs argued unsuccessfully that the appropriate standard was infringement and not the higher standard of coercion. This standard of coercion/compulsion is the same as that articulated in *Alfonso* in which the majority found "compulsion on parents to send their children into an environment where they had unrestricted access to free contraceptives" (*Alfonso,* 1993, p. 266) and the dissent did not.

The court argued that coercion exists where the State mandates action and there is no outlet for refusal and such refusal results in sanctions. The plaintiffs asserted that the condom availability program is coercive because it is implemented in a compulsory setting. The plaintiffs relied on the ruling in *Alfonso* (1993). The Massachusetts court disagreed with the holding in *Alfonso,* thus its reasoning was found not to be persuasive. The Supreme Judicial Court agreed with the view expressed in the dissent. Specifically, the court cited the *Alfonso* dissent's argument that compulsory education does not vest the condom availability program with an "aura of compulsion." Students in Falmouth, the court held, are free to decline to avail themselves of condoms and parents remain free to instruct their children not to participate. The court concluded because "the program lacks any degree of coercion or compulsion in violation of the plaintiffs' parental liberties, or their familial privacy, we conclude also that neither an opt-out provision nor parental notification is required by the Federal constitution" (p. 587).

The *Alfonso* majority in the appeal used the strict scrutiny test, but did not find that parents had a fundamental right. If the parental right is not fundamental and there is no assertion that a suspect classification is involved, it is difficult to see the legal basis upon which the majority employed strict scrutiny analysis. On the other hand, the dissent and the court in *Curtis* (1995) used the rational basis test. This was the same test used by all four courts in the mandatory service program cases.

Our last court cases also took place in Massachusetts, but have a different, but related issue involving school assemblies and the school's programs involving AIDS.

Brown v. Hot, Sexy and Safer Productions, Inc.

Chelmsford High School sponsored a mandatory school-wide assembly. The assembly consisted of a ninety-minute presentation characterized as an AIDS awareness program. Plaintiff students and their parents brought suit in federal court seeking declaratory and monetary relief. They alleged a violation of parents' right to direct and control the upbringing of their children.[9] The district court granted the defendant's motion to dismiss the complaint for failure to state a claim upon which relief could be granted. The plaintiffs appealed (*Brown v. Hot, Sexy and Safer Productions, Inc.,* 1995).

The First Circuit Court of Appeals heard the appeal from the district court's dismissal of the plaintiffs' claim. On the issue of the right to rear children, the plaintiffs argued, using the *Alfonso* (1993) decision as authority, that the right to direct the upbringing of a child is "fundamental" and can only be infringed upon a showing of a compelling state interest that cannot be achieved by any less restrictive means (strict scrutiny analysis). The Court of Appeals, similar to the Supreme Judicial Court in *Curtis,* skirted the issue of whether the right is fundamental and held that "even if it were, the plaintiffs have failed to demonstrate an intrusion of constitutional magnitude on this right" (p. 533). Referring to the seminal cases of *Meyer* and *Pierce,* the First Circuit Court wrote:

> [W]e think [they] evince the principle that the state cannot prevent parents from choosing a specific educational program—whether it be religious instruction at a private school or instruction in a foreign language. That is, the state does not have the power to "standardize its children" or "foster a homogenous people" by completely foreclosing the opportunity of individuals and groups to choose a different path of education. (p. 533)

Having stated the principles of *Meyer* and *Pierce,* which undergird the parental right to direct the upbringing of children, the appellate court found that parents do not possess a "fundamental constitutional right to dictate the curriculum at the public school to which they have chosen to send their children" (p. 533).

Interestingly, after concluding the plaintiffs did not have a fundamental right, thus strict scrutiny analysis would not be appropriate, the court did not do a rational basis analysis. Instead, the court made some conclusory general remarks regarding the extent of the parental right to direct the upbringing of their child. These remarks are the strongest ones concerning the balance of competing interests found in this section of the paper. The court concluded the section on parental rights with the following policy statement:

If all parents had a fundamental constitutional right to dictate individually what the schools teach their children, the schools would be forced to cater a curriculum for each student whose parents had genuine moral disagreements with the school's choice of subject matter. We cannot see that the Constitution imposes such a burden on state educational systems, and accordingly find that the rights of parents as described in *Meyer* and *Pierce* do not encompass a broad-based right to restrict the flow of information in the public schools. (p. 534)

Recent Legislation on Parental Rights

Parental claims in the courts regarding the vitality and scope of parental rights have largely been unsuccessful. While the courts have been willing to recognize the rights of parents to direct the upbringing of their children, for the most part, they have been unwilling to consider it a fundamental right deserving of strict scrutiny analysis protection. Parents and advocacy groups, such as the Christian Coalition and the Family Research Council, have turned from the courtroom to the halls of legislative bodies to push for the strengthening of the parental right to direct the upbringing of their children. Scott Willis (1997) noted that this "nationwide movement to write 'parental rights' into law has raised questions about how big a role parents should play in determining what happens in public schools" (p. 1). Proponents of parental rights legislation cite instances "where schools have violated parents' wishes by making condoms available, exposing students to sexually explicit materials, and giving counseling without their parents' consent" (Willis, 1997, p. 6). Parental rights legislation has been advanced in both state and federal venues, so far without much success.

One of the most visible national parental rights bills is Senate Bill 984 of the 104th Congress. The bill, known by its short title as the "Parental Rights and Responsibilities Act of 1995" was written to protect the "fundamental right of a parent to direct the upbringing of a child, and for other purposes" (p. 1). The bill, in its Findings and Purposes section, cites both *Meyer* and *Pierce* as recognizing the "right of parents to direct the upbringing of their children as a fundamental right" (p. 1). From the analysis of court cases in the previous section, this finding of a fundamental right is highly suspect. With the exception of *Alfonso* (1993), the various courts have consistently held that the parental right is not fundamental. The court in *Alfonso* did not specifically find that the parental right is fundamental. Instead, the court merely asserted that the parental right to direct the upbringing of his/her child was constitutionally protected and then flatly stated that it would use strict scrutiny analysis without a showing that it was a fundamental right or that it involved a suspect class, the two triggers for strict scrutiny analysis. The court's only offered reasoning for using this most stringent test is found in its statement that the compulsory nature of the education foisted upon the plaintiffs an environment where the children "will be permitted, even encouraged to obtain a contraceptive device, which the parents disfavor as a matter of personal belief" (*Alfonso,* 1993, p. 265). Therefore, the Senate Bill's assertion that the parental right is fundamental is not supported by the weight of case law. Apparently, parental rights proponents are trying to have Congress recognize that the right is fundamental when the courts have refused to do so.

Senate Bill 984 defines the right of a parent to direct the upbringing of a child as encompassing but not limited to (1) directing or providing for the education of the child; (2) making a health care decision for the child,. . .; (3) disciplining the child, including reasonable corporal discipline. . .; and (4) directing or providing for the religious teaching of the child" (pp. 5–6). Any action by the state usurping or interfering with these rights, according to the bill, shall be reviewed by strict scrutiny analysis. The looseness of the language invites mischief because the definition of what it means to "direct" the education of a child is vague. For example, since the right to direct the education of a child is fundamental, that right could legitimately be viewed as robust and expansive. Teachers direct the education of their pupils through the selection, pacing, and sequencing of lessons. Since the parents' right to direct is fundamental, it would supersede a teacher's right, which is not a fundamental constitutional right, to direct the education of a particular child. If a parent disagreed with a teacher's curricular decision, under S. 984, the school district would have to demonstrate that the teacher's decision was "essential to accomplish a compelling governmental interest and is narrowly drawn or applied in a manner that is the least restrictive means of accomplishing the compelling interest" (p. 7). Given the myriad educational decisions that a teacher makes daily, it would be difficult to characterize all of them as essential. Most pedagogical decisions involve the exercise of professional judgment in light of various options. Very seldom is there one bright, illuminated pedagogical path; some may be better than others, but then agreement as to what is best is often difficult to reach. The debate over phonics and whole language is indicative of how difficult it is for the profession to arrive at the one-best instructional strategy. It is doubtful that any pedagogical decision could meet the high standard of "essential." What happens then if educators cannot show that their contested pedagogical decisions are not essential? Must classroom instruction be balkanized to meet the wishes of every parent?

It is difficult, if not impossible, to see how this type of legislation could be implemented in our public schools. Which master does the teacher serve if parents are given the fundamental right to direct the education of their child—the parent or the school board? Also, what happens when one parent's concept of directing the education of their child clashes with the express wishes of another parent; how is the issue resolved? Even in private schools, parents are not given the ability to "direct" the education of their child. Senate Bill 984 is unworkable.

The voters in Colorado in November of 1996 were asked to vote on Amendment 17. This ballot measure, similar to S. 984, would have added to the bill of rights in the Colorado Constitution the "inalienable right of parents 'to direct and control the upbringing, education, values, and discipline of their children' " (White, 1996, p. 1). Opponents of the amendment argued that one of the primary targets of the ballot was the public school system. Education officials feared that the amendment would stunt curricula. Deborah Fallin, a spokesperson for the Colorado Association of School Boards said it would precipitate ideological battles in the schools "with individual parents pushing for their child's individual needs" (p. 24). Public education as a public good and a private benefit would have been reduced to only a private benefit. The public would have been taken out of public education.

The measure was rejected by 57 percent of the voters. If it would have passed, proponents of the measure stated that they were prepared to launch similar proposals in more than twenty states (White, 1996).

A third piece of legislation pushing parental rights is found in New Hampshire. In 1996, the New Hampshire legislature debated SB 653-FN the Parent and Pupil Rights Act. The bill was written to protect the privacy of parents and pupils and stated that "under federal legislation and court decisions, as well as New Hampshire law, parents have the primary responsibility for their children's education and pupils have certain rights which the schools may not deny" (p. 2). It called for protections already guaranteed by the Family Rights and Privacy Act and enforced by the Family Policy Compliance Office. Outside of restating rights already guaranteed, the bill mandated that all parents/guardians of public school students receive a letter which allowed them to exercise their right under New Hampshire law that their "child NOT be involved with any of the school activities or materials listed below" (p. 2, emphasis in original) without written consent for their participation or use. In other words, parents, under this proposed legislation, could pick and choose from a laundry list of topics what their child will be taught or not taught. A partial list of topics needing written consent to be taught to their child included: "auto criticism strategies designed for self-disclosure, including the keeping of a diary, journal, or log book; curricula pertaining to drugs and alcohol; nuclear war and nuclear policy; globalism and one-world government; education in sexuality including population control; and organic evolution" (pp. 2–3). The Department of Education at the University of New Hampshire passed a motion opposing the bill. The motion, sent to the Senate and House Education Committees, argued that the bill restricted the access to ideas in the very place that should be the marketplace of ideas—the public school classroom, would chill classroom discussions on important topics such as nuclear policy, and would be unworkable because how could a teacher keep track of which students could discuss what topics or answer questions pertaining to a guarded topic, and what would be done with the students who opted out of a topic. The main argument advanced by the faculty was that this type of legislation aimed at strengthening the control that parents have over education had an unacceptable trade-off restricting the flow of information in our public schools. The general welfare of the State of New Hampshire is served best by an educated citizenry. The bill did not pass.

Conclusion

There has been a rise in the advocacy of the parents' right to direct the upbringing and education of their children. This advocacy has occurred in the courts and in the legislative halls. Finding the proper balance between parents as sovereign over the lives of their minor children and the State as educator is important. Both have a legitimate and necessary function and both do not possess absolute power over minor children. The State cannot turn children into "mere appendages" and parents' power over children is checked by the concept of *parens patriae* (parent of the country), in which government may make decisions in order to protect the interests of children that overrule the express wishes of their parents. Parents must be active participants in their child's education, but that participation cannot turn the public school into a private tutor. The court's recognition of parental rights is appropriate. That recognition, though, is limited by most courts to choosing public or private education. Setting aside the parental right, parents are free to influence school board decisions through the democratic process.

Advocates of expanded parental rights have not been successful in getting legislation passed. If all parental rights legislation is similar to that reviewed in this discussion, our society has benefited from their lack of success. The legislation is vague, overbroad, and unworkable. The parental right to direct a child's education is important, but it should not encompass the ability of a parent to control one of our most important democratic processes—public education. A proper balance currently exists.

Endnotes

1. Joseph Tussman, in *Government and Mind* (1977), defined the teaching power of the state as "the inherent constitutional authority of the state to establish and direct the teaching activity and institutions needed to ensure its continuity and further its legitimate, general and special purposes. . . . The teaching power is a peer to the legislative, the executive, and the judicial powers, if it is not, indeed, the first among them" (quoted in Yudof, Kirp, and Levin, 1992, p. 15).
2. For a discussion of the conflict between parents' rights and school discretion, see, *Mozert v. Hawkins County Board of Education*, 827 F.2d 1058 (6th Cir. 1987); M. M. McCarthy, 1993, "Challenges to the Public School Curriculum: New Targets and Strategies," *Phi Delta Kappan*, 75:55–60; T. A. DeMitchell, 1994, "Witches, Cauldrons, and 'Wicca' in the Public School Curriculum: Is Government Establishing a Religion? The Courts Think Not," *International Journal of Educational Reform*, 3:474–480; and D. Stern, 1975, "Challenging Ideological Exclusion of Curriculum: Rights of Students and Parents," *Harvard Civil Rights, Civil Liberties Law Review*, 14:485.
3. Similar to the legislation in *Meyer v. Nebraska*, (1923), Hawaii, in 1920, passed a law aimed at the many foreign language schools (163 in number) that served the large and growing immigrant population. Students, according to the regulations, could not attend foreign language schools unless they regularly attended a public school or approved private school. The Hawaiian legislation and regulations were held to be unconstitutional by the United States Supreme Court in *Farrington v. Tokushige*, 273 U.S. 284 (1927). The Court held that "the Japanese's parent has the right to direct the education of his own child without unreasonable restrictions" (p. 298).
4. It is interesting to note that The Compulsory Education Act of 1922 allowed for home-schooling up to the eighth grade by a parent or private teacher if the county school superintendent gave written permission. The permission was valid for one school year [Section 5259(d)]. When the legislation was struck down as unconstitutional, this authority for home-schooling was also struck down. For a discussion of the *Pierce* decision and compulsory education see: Tyack, D. 1968. "The Perils of Pluralism: The Background of the *Pierce* Case." *American History Review*, 74:74–92; Tyack, D. 1976. "Ways of Seeing: An Essay on the History of Compulsory Schooling." *Harvard Education Review*, 46:355–375. For a review of state courts that upheld compulsory education laws, see *State v. Hoyt*, 84 N.H.38 (1929) and *State v. Bailey*, 157 Ind. 324 (1901).
5. *Wisconsin v. Yoder* is the authority for reviewing religious objections to educational decisions. This case involved compulsory

education of Amish children beyond the eighth grade. The general applicability of this holding has not been extensive due in large part to the uniqueness of the Amish religion and way of life. In this case, the High Court combined the interests of parenthood with the free exercise claim and found that a higher standard of review than rational basis must be used. Plaintiffs try to use this case as authority for their claims against governmental action because of the higher standard that the state must meet in order to withstand the challenge.

6. A classification is "inherently suspect" if it is based upon race, national origin, or religion. A suspect class has the following characteristics:
   - immutable characteristics
   - highly visible characteristics
   - historical disadvantage
   - relative lack of political representation

   A suspect class is a group that has been "saddled with such disabilities, or subjected to such a history of purposeful unequal treatment, or relegated to such position of political powerlessness as to command extraordinary protection from the majoritarian process." *San Antonio Independent School District v. Rodriguez*. 411 U.S. 1 (1973). Race has been considered a suspect class since the 1944 case *Korematsu v. United States*, 212 U.S. 214.

   Strict scrutiny analysis is also triggered when state action affects the exercise of a fundamental right such as the right to speech, press, association, religion, marriage, access to the courts, interstate travel, or the right to vote.

   For an insightful recent discussion of equal protection, see J. Dayton and A. P. Dupre. 1997. Equal Protection of the Laws: Recent Judicial Decisions and Their Implications for Public Educational Institutions. 114 *Ed. law Rep.* [1] (Jan. 9).

7. Runyon addressed racial segregation in private schools. The Supreme Court found that the parental right to direct the upbringing of their child was not infringed upon by a prohibition against segregation, because the law restricted admission policies rather than the curriculum or choice of schools.

8. One of the plaintiffs' arguments was that the condom availability program was health related, but did not qualify as a health service. The appellate court reached an opposite conclusion. What is instructive for our discussion was Judge Eiber's dissenting opinion. Judge Eiber argued, rather persuasively in my opinion, that the availability of condoms was analogous to the child's constitutional rights regarding procreating. The judge discussed the United States Supreme Court decision in *Carey v. Population Services International*, 431 U.S. 678 (1977) in which the Court overturned on constitutional grounds a New York statute that made it a crime to sell or distribute contraceptive devices to minors under the age of sixteen. Minors, the Supreme Court argued, possessed constitutional rights in connection with decisions affecting procreation. The plurality wrote: "Since the State may not impose a blanket prohibition, or even a blanket requirement of parental consent, on the choice of a minor to terminate her pregnancy, the constitutionality of a blanket prohibition of the distribution of contraceptives is a fortiori foreclosed (p. 694)."

   It seemed quite clear to the dissent in *Alfonso* (1993) that if minors can obtain contraceptives, abortions, and treatment for sexually transmitted diseases without parental permission, surely their access to condoms at school cannot be conditioned to a greater degree than what it is outside the schoolhouse gate. Essentially, the dissent advanced the argument that parental rights to direct the upbringing of their child are not augmented by exercising those rights inside the schoolhouse gate.

9. The plaintiffs alleged that the skits and monologues involved profane, lewd, and lascivious language; told the group that they were going to have a group sexual experience; advocated and approved oral sex, masturbation, homosexual activity, and condom use during promiscuous premarital sex; simulated masturbation; characterized the loose pants worn by one student as 'erection wear'; referred to being in 'deep sh__' after anal sex; had a minor lick an oversized condom with her, after which she had a female student pull it over a male students head and blow it up; encouraged a male student to display his orgasm face for the camera; informed a male student that he was not having enough orgasms; closely inspected a minor and told him that he had a "nice butt"; and made eighteen references to orgasms, six references to male genitals, and eight references to female genitals (p. 529).

References

Alfonso v. Fernandez. 584 N.Y.S.2d 406 (Sup. 1992).

Alfonso v. Fernandez. 606 N. Y. S.2d 259 (A.D.2 Dept. 1993).

Brown v. Board of Education. 347 U.S. 483 (1954).

Brown v. Hot, Sexy and Safer Productions, Inc., 68 F.3d 525 (1st Cir. 1995).

Curtis v. School Committee of Falmouth, 652 N.E.2d 580 (Mass. 1995).

Herndon v. Chapel Hill-Carrboro City Board of Education, 899 Fsupp. 1443 (MD.N.C 1995).

Herndon by Herndon v. Chapel Hill-Carrboro City Board of Education, 89 F.3d 174 (4th Cir. 1996).

Hodel v. Indiana, 452 U.S. 314 (1981).

Immediato v. Rye Neck School District, 73 F.3d 454 (2nd Cir. 1996).

Immediato by Immediato v. Rye Neck School District. 873 F.Supp. 846 (S.D.N.Y. 1995).

Mawdsley, R. D. and D. Drake. 1992. "Involving Parents in the Public Schools: Legal and Policy Issues." 76 *Ed. Law Rep.* [299] (Oct. 8).

Meyer v. Nebraska, 262 U.S. 390 (1923).

Pierce v. Society of Sisters, 268 U.S. 510 (1925).

Runyon v. McCrary, 427 U.S. 160 (1976).

The Trustees of Schools v. The People ex. rel. Martin Van Allen, 87 Ill. 303 (1877).

White, K. A 1996. "Colo. Voters Reject Parent-Rights Measure." *Education Week*, 1:24–25, November 13.

Wisconsin v. Yoder, 406 U.S. 205 (1972).

Willis, S. 1997. "Parental Rights: Proposed Laws Would Affect Parent-School Relationships." *Education Update* (Association for Supervision and Curriculum Development) 39:1, 6–7 (January).

Yudof, M. G., D. L. Kirp and B. Levin. 1992. *Educational Policy and the Law, Third Edition*. New York: West Publishing Company.

SYMPOSIUM

TAKING *PIERCE* SERIOUSLY: THE FAMILY, RELIGIOUS EDUCATION, AND HARM TO CHILDREN

*Richard W. Garnett**

Most people believe in the power of prayer, and many try to orient and direct their lives in accord with this and other religious beliefs.[1] To many scholars and theorists, this persistence of faith and piety is a bit mysterious; to some, it is even cause for concern.[2] True, many of those who pray likely think of what they are doing in New Age, psycho-oncological, therapeutic, "power of positive thinking" terms and so are less worrisome.[3] For many others, though, prayer is more than "having a good thought" about something or participating

---

* Assistant Professor, Notre Dame Law School, Notre Dame, Indiana. J.D., Yale Law School, 1995; B.A., Duke University, 1990. This Article is (loosely) based on a talk given on January 9, 2000 at the Joint Program of the Sections on Law, Religion & Family and Juvenile Law during the Annual Meeting of the Association of American Law Schools in Washington, D.C. I am grateful to Fred Marczyk for his help and advice with this and other projects; to the Notre Dame Law School for research assistance; to A.J. Bellia, Paolo Carozza, Nicole Garnett, Steffen Johnson, William Kelley, John Nagle, David Petron, Charles Rice, Howard Sklamberg, Steven Smith, and Eric Treene for their comments and criticism; and to the editors and staff of the *Notre Dame Law Review* for their patience. This Article is dedicated, warts and all, to my teacher and friend, Joseph Goldstein, who died this past year. The author can be contacted at rick.garnett.4@nd.edu.

1 *See, e.g.*, David Whitman, *More Moral*, THE NEW REPUBLIC, Feb. 22, 1999, at 18, 18 (citing a 1997 Gallup Poll showing that ninety percent of Americans pray).

2 As Michael Paulsen has noted, many in the academy "believe that religious faith is crazy (or . . . put more gently, 'irrational') and its adherents are the functional equivalent of lunatics." Michael Stokes Paulsen, *God Is Great, Garvey Is Good: Making Sense of Religious Freedom*, 72 NOTRE DAME L. REV. 1597, 1613 (1997) (book review); *see, e.g.*, Suzanna Sherry, *The Sleep of Reason*, 84 GEO. L.J. 453 (1996).

3 *See* James G. Dwyer, *Spiritual Treatment Exemptions to Child Medical Neglect Laws: What We Outsiders Should Think*, 76 NOTRE DAME L. REV. 147, 149 (2000) (discussing "the usefulness of positive thinking, . . . the ability of the mind to support physical

in a moment of warm or hopeful feeling at the invitation of a politician. It is, instead, a mysterious, yet miraculously efficacious, form of participation in and cooperation with God's creative activity, His providence, and "His plan of love for men."[4] Indeed, for many, prayer is not optional; they regard themselves as called—as *commanded*—to pray "in everything"[5] and "without ceasing."[6]

Moreover, many people believe that prayer is a perfectly appropriate response to physical illness, pain, and injury.[7] They have no problem with medical science, hospitals, drugs, and doctors, but they also believe that God hears and answers prayers. They know that He cures the sick, comforts the suffering, and heals the injured. To paraphrase the old saying, these believers pray as if everything depends on God, but are quite willing to act as if everything depends on medicine.

For still others—Christian Scientists, for example—prayer is, in times of sickness, not only appropriate, it is the response *required* by their faith.[8] Those under such religious obligations often refuse conventional and even emergency medical treatment for themselves and—more controversially—for their children. But for their religious motivation, these refusals could be viewed as culpably negligent, as abusive, or perhaps even as criminal.[9]

---

responses to disease and injury, and . . . the possibility of using prayer and religious teaching as one form of such positive thinking").

4 U.S. CATHOLIC CONFERENCE, CATECHISM OF THE CATHOLIC CHURCH §§ 2565, 2738 (2000) (relating prayer to "the living relationship of the children of God with their Father who is good beyond measure" and to our "cooperation with [God's] providence [and] his plan of love for men"); *see id.* § 2568 ("Prayer is bound up with human history, for it is the relationship with God in historical events.").

5 *Philippians* 4:6 ("Do not be anxious about anything, but in everything, by prayer and petition, with thanksgiving, present your requests to God.").

6 1 *Thessalonians* 5:16–18 ("Rejoice always, pray without ceasing, give thanks in all circumstances; for this is the will of God in Christ Jesus for you.").

7 *See, e.g.*, *James* 5:15–16 ("And the prayer offered in faith will make the sick person well; the Lord will raise him up . . . . Therefore confess your sins to each other and pray for each other so that you may be healed. The prayer of a righteous man is powerful and effective.").

8 *See, e.g.*, Children's Healthcare Is a Legal Duty, Inc. v. Min De Parle, 212 F.3d 1084, 1088 (8th Cir. 2000) (noting that Christian Scientists "object to medical care and embrace prayer as the sole means of healing"). *See generally* MARY BAKER EDDY, SCIENCE AND HEALTH WITH KEY TO THE SCRIPTURES (First Church of Christ, Scientist 1994) (1875). For a discussion of other religious groups that opt for spiritual healing over medical treatment, see, for example, Jennifer L. Hartsell, Comment, *Mother May I . . . Live? Parental Refusal of Life-Sustaining Medical Treatment for Children Based on Religious Objections*, 66 TENN. L. REV. 499, 503–06 (1999).

9 *See, e.g.*, State v. Williams, 484 P.2d 1167 (Wash. Ct. App. 1971) (affirming manslaughter conviction where husband and wife failed to supply their young child with necessary medical attention).

Most states, however, exempt religious parents from prosecution, or limit their exposure to criminal liability, when their failure to seek medical care for their sick or injured children is motivated by religious belief.[10] These spiritual-healing exemptions are both common and controversial, and they raise important questions, including: How ought we to reconcile what sometimes appear to be the competing demands of a Constitution that protects religious liberty and family integrity by disabling government,[11] our moral commitments to the full personhood and equal dignity of children,[12] and a *parens patriae* tradition in which the health and welfare of children are thought to be the proper objects of government concern and activity?[13]

Although the topic for this symposium is "Children, Spiritual Healing, and Religious Exercise," I am not going to discuss whether spiritual-healing exemptions from otherwise generally applicable child-welfare and criminal laws are constitutional, sensible, or morally justifiable.[14] Instead, I will ask what, if anything, the debate about

10 On spiritual-treatment exemptions generally, see James G. Dwyer, *The Children We Abandon: Religious Exemptions to Child Welfare and Education Laws as Denials of Equal Protection to Children of Religious Objectors*, 74 N.C. L. REV. 1321 (1996); Eric W. Treene, *Prayer-Treatment Exemptions to Child Abuse and Neglect Statutes, Manslaughter Prosecutions, and Due Process of Law*, 30 HARV. J. ON LEGIS. 135 (1993).

11 This is *precisely why* the Framers disabled—or refused to enable—the federal government. *See, e.g.*, United +States v. Lopez, 514 U.S. 549, 552 (1995).

12 *See, e.g.*, POPE JOHN PAUL II, THE APOSTOLIC EXHORTATION ON THE ROLE OF THE CHRISTIAN FAMILY IN THE MODERN WORLD [*Familiaris consortio*] No. 26 (St. Paul Editions 1981) ("[S]pecial attention must be devoted to the children by developing a profound esteem for their personal dignity, and a great respect and generous concern for their rights."); James G. Dwyer, *Parents' Religion and Children's Welfare: Debunking the Doctrine of Parents' Rights*, 82 CAL. L. REV. 1371, 1446 (1994) ("[T]he child is . . . not the mere creature of the parent . . . [but is rather] his or her own person.").

13 *Parens patriae*—"parent of the country"—is the "principle that the state must care for those who cannot take care of themselves." BLACK'S LAW DICTIONARY 1114 (6th ed. 1990). As one court has observed, "[I]t is well-settled that the State as *parens patriae* has a special duty to protect minors and, if necessary, make vital decisions as to whether to submit a minor to necessary treatment where the condition is life threatening, as wrenching and distasteful as such actions may be." *In re* E.G., 549 N.E.2d 322, 327 (Ill. 1989) (internal quotation marks and citation omitted). *See generally* Douglas R. Rendleman, Parens Patriae*: From Chancery to the Juvenile Court*, 23 S.C. L. REV. 205 (1971).

14 I believe that spiritual-treatment exemptions *can* be crafted to be both constitutional and morally justified and that such exemptions are not inconsistent with court-ordered medical care over parents' religion-based objections when such care is likely to succeed and is clearly necessary to avoid death or serious physical harm to a young child. *See* JOSEPH GOLDSTEIN ET AL., THE BEST INTERESTS OF THE CHILD: THE LEAST DETRIMENTAL ALTERNATIVE 128–38 (1996) (discussing situations where court-ordered medical care over parents' objections is appropriate).

these exemptions says about the State's authority to override parents' decisions about education, particularly religious education.[15] What can the questions surrounding spiritual-treatment exemptions tell us about who should decide what, where, for what purpose, and from whom children will learn? If we accept, for example, that the State may in some cases require medical treatment for a child, over her parents' objections, to avoid serious injury or death, should it follow that it may regulate, or even forbid, a child's religious training or religious-school education to prevent an analogous, though perhaps less tangible, "harm"? What is the extent of the Government's power to interfere—whether to protect children's "temporal well-being,"[16] to inculcate majoritarian values, or to "bolster the preconditions of liberal democracy"[17]—with parents' education-related decisions and, in particular, with their decisions to provide religious training to their children and to send them to authentically religious schools?[18] The Supreme Court has said, over and again, in a long line of cases from *Pierce v. Society of Sisters*[19] to last summer's *Troxel v. Granville*,[20] that parents enjoy a "fundamental" right to direct and control the education of their children, but do we *really* accept, or even understand, the premises, foundations, and implications of these repeated pronouncements?[21]

---

15 My fellow contributor, Professor James Dwyer, has highlighted the connection between the medical-treatment and education issues. *See* JAMES G. DWYER, RELIGIOUS SCHOOLS v. CHILDREN'S RIGHTS (1998); Dwyer, *supra* note 3, at 168–70, 172–73; Dwyer, *supra* note 10, at 1329–53.

16 Dwyer, *supra* note 10, at 1407 ("The state itself must determine what children's fundamental interests are and, in doing so, may only consider children's temporal well-being.").

17 William A. Galston, *Expressive Liberty, Moral Pluralism, Political Pluralism: Three Sources of Liberal Theory*, 40 WM. & MARY L. REV. 869, 869 (1999).

18 By "authentically" religious schools, I mean simply schools whose religiosity goes beyond mere institutional affiliation or historical tradition, schools whose "overriding religious mission . . . permeates their teaching," Mitchell v. Helms, 120 S. Ct. 2530, 2582 (2000) (Souter, J., dissenting), schools that the Supreme Court has until recently too often branded disapprovingly as "pervasively sectarian," *id.* at 2552 (plurality opinion) (rejecting the Court's "pervasively sectarian" test as a doctrine "born of bigotry").

19 268 U.S. 510, 535 (1925).

20 120 S. Ct. 2054, 2060 (2000).

21 Some think the Court has yet to come up with a good *theory* to explain its holding in *Pierce* and to make it cohere with the autonomy-centered individualism that seems generally to animate its constitutional jurisprudence. *See, e.g.*, Planned Parenthood v. Casey, 505 U.S. 833 (1992). As a result, parents' educational rights "are both ill defined and vulnerable to unduly deferential judicial review of state educational regulation." Stephen G. Gilles, *On Educating Children: A Parentalist Manifesto*, 63 U. CHI. L. REV. 937, 938 (1996).

Now, it has been argued powerfully that parents in a liberal state do not and should not have a "right" to control their children's education—after all, it is said, no one has a *right* to control anyone.[22] Children are not slaves; they are no one's property.[23] It follows, then, that decisions about children's education should, like all child-related decisions, be "child centered"; they should be guided entirely by children's interests, *as determined by the State*, and not by appeals to the liberties, rights, interests, or preferences of parents.[24] But again, the Supreme Court said in *Pierce*, and still purports to believe,[25] that our Constitution guarantees the "liberty of parents and guardians to direct the upbringing and education of children."[26] Can this statement be defended?

I think so.[27] I certainly *hope* so. Recent calls for a "thicker" liberalism and for the harnessing of education to create truly liberal citizens make it all the more important that we take *Pierce* seriously. And

---

22 *See, e.g.*, Dwyer, *supra* note 12, at 1405 ("[A]s a general rule, our legal system does not recognize or bestow on individuals rights to control the lives of other persons."). *But see* Stephen G. Gilles, *Hey, Christians, Leave Your Kids Alone!*, 16 CONST. COMMENT. 149, 187–90 (1999) (arguing that there is nothing "anomalous" about permitting parents, rather than the State, to balance children's spiritual and temporal interests).

23 *See, e.g.*, Barbara Bennett Woodhouse, *"Who Owns the Child?"* Meyer *and* Pierce *and the Child as Property*, 33 WM. & MARY L. REV. 995 (1992).

24 *See, e.g.*, Dwyer, *supra* note 3, at 160–61; Dwyer, *supra* note 12, at 1374 ("I propose that children's rights, rather than parents' rights, be the legal basis for protecting the interests of children."). Then again, many who endorse parental control do so *precisely* because they think it well serves the best interests of children. *See, e.g.*, Parham v. J.R., 442 U.S. 584, 602 (1979) (noting that the concept of the "family as a unit with broad parental authority over minor children" is rooted in the recognition that the "natural bonds of affection lead parents to act in the best interests of their children"); Gilles, *supra* note 22, at 951 n.53 (1996) ("The human flourishing of adult parents, which is highly bound up with the education of their children, matters too, as does society's interest in good citizens. Nonetheless, no justification is persuasive if it fails to give great weight to the child's best interest.").

25 *See Troxel*, 120 S. Ct. at 2060 (plurality opinion) ("[I]t cannot now be doubted that the Due Process Clause of the Fourteenth Amendment protects the fundamental right of parents to make decisions concerning the care, custody, and control of their children."); Washington v. Glucksberg, 521 U.S. 702, 720 (1997) ("[T]he 'liberty' specially protected by the Due Process Clause includes the right . . . to direct the education and upbringing of one's children . . . .").

26 Pierce v. Soc'y of Sisters, 268 U.S. 510, 534–35 (1925).

27 *See* Stephen L. Carter, *Parents, Religion, and Schools: Reflections on* Pierce, *70 Years Later*, 27 SETON HALL L. REV. 1194, 1195 (1997) ("I want to speculate . . . on the possibility that *Pierce* is both rightly decided and rightly reasoned, and thus that parents really do possess a fundamental constitutional right to direct the upbringing of their children."). *See generally, e.g.*, Stephen G. Gilles, *Liberal Parentalism and Children's Educational Rights*, 26 CAP. U. L. REV. 9 (1997); Gilles, *supra* note 22.

so, I will try to outline some reasons why it *does* make sense to talk in *Pierce*-like terms, not only about parental control over education, but also about the intrinsic dignity of the family—the "first and vital cell of society"[28]—and its role in civil society. Given the nature and format of this symposium, my suggestions and thoughts on these matters are unavoidably preliminary. I will not be able in this Article to flesh out completely my own arguments or to respond fully to other and opposing views. Still, I will suggest that, if we *do* resolve to take *Pierce* seriously, we should then say that state functionaries, guided and restrained by a proper humility about their authority and competence, should meddle with parents' educational decisions only to prevent *harm*, very carefully defined, to a child. That is, they should *not* intervene simply whenever they think intrusion or oversight would serve the Government's notion of the child's "best interests" or its own perceived need and claimed prerogative to create a certain kind of citizen.[29]

The problem is, how do we define "harm." We have a good idea what physical abuse and medical neglect look like, but when are parents' educational decisions, and particularly their decisions about religious training, "harmful"? This is a difficult question, but I will propose, as a start, that the content of religious instruction, traditions, or beliefs should not be viewed as harmful in the sense necessary to justify government second-guessing or "supervention"[30] of parents' decisions about such instruction. In a free society, one that values religious freedom, the State should not entertain, let alone enforce, a belief that children would be better off without religious faith.

II. The Question Presented—Why we Outsiders Agree

Almost every state exempts religious parents who opt for prayer over medical treatment for their children from criminal prosecution

28 Pope John Paul II, *supra* note 12, No. 42, at 67 (quoting Second Vatican Ecumenical Council, Decree on the Apostolate of the Laity [*Apostolicam actuositatem*] No. 11 (1965)).

29 In my view, government "intervention" in the family *is* intervention. *But see* Dwyer, *supra* note 3, at 167 ("[T]he reality is that the family is not a separate, primordial sphere that is or can be cordoned off from the power of the state. Quite the opposite. The law creates the family, and things could not be otherwise."); Frances E. Olsen, *The Myth of State Intervention in the Family*, 18 U. Mich. J.L. Reform 835, 838 (1985). But this is *not* "the reality." The law no more "creates" the family than the Rule Against Perpetuities "creates" dirt.

30 Joseph Goldstein, *Medical Care for the Child at Risk: On State Supervention of Parental Autonomy*, 86 Yale L.J. 645, 647 (1977).

and from liability under neglect, abuse, and endangerment laws.[31] These exemptions, and the conflict between religious views and children's healthcare generally, have been examined thoroughly in the law reviews,[32] the courts,[33] and the public square.[34] And it is safe to say, as my co-panelist Professor James Dwyer observes, that we "outsiders"—"we who are not members of a religious group with beliefs opposed to medical care and who therefore have no personal stake in the issue"[35]—disagree among ourselves about the wisdom, constitutionality, and morality of such exemptions. Some take the position that exemptions reflect attempts to balance free-exercise values and the State's interest in protecting children, that it is appropriate to balance these interests, and that while blanket exemptions might reflect excessive deference to the religious beliefs of parents, some limitation

---

31 *See* Hermanson v. State, 604 So. 2d 775, 776–77 n.1 (Fla. 1992) (listing statutes); Hartsell, *supra* note 8, at 509–10.

32 *See generally, e.g.*, Dwyer, *supra* note 10; Ann MacLean Massie, *The Religion Clauses and Parental Healthcare Decisionmaking for Children: Suggestions for a New Approach*, 21 HASTINGS CONST. L.Q. 725 (1994); Rita Swan, *On Statutes Depriving a Class of Children of Rights to Medical Care: Can This Discrimination Be Litigated?*, 2 QUINNIPIAC HEALTH L.J. 73 (1998); LaDonna DiCamillo, Comment, *Caught Between the Clauses and the Branches: When Parents Deny Their Child Non-emergency Medical Treatment for Religious Reasons*, 19 J. JUV. L. 123 (1998); Hartsell, *supra* note 8; Anne D. Lederman, Note, *Understanding Faith: When Religious Parents Decline Conventional Medical Treatment for Their Children*, 45 CASE W. RES. L. REV. 891 (1995).

33 *See, e.g.*, Children's Healthcare Is a Legal Duty, Inc. v. Min De Parle, 212 F.3d 1084, 1088 (8th Cir. 2000); Lybarger v. People, 807 P.2d 570, 571 (Colo. 1991); *Hermanson*, 604 So. 2d at 776; Commonwealth v. Twitchell, 617 N.E.2d 609, 612 (Mass. 1993); State v. McKown, 475 N.W.2d 63, 64 (Minn. 1991); State v. Hays, 964 P.2d 1042, 1044 (Or. Ct. App. 1998); Commonwealth v. Nixon, 718 A.2d 311, 312 (Pa. Super. Ct. 1998).

34 *See, e.g.*, Ellen Barry & Elisa Crouch, *Probe Asks if Faith Put Children at Risk*, BOSTON GLOBE, Nov. 16, 1999, at B1; Mark Larabee, *Balancing Rights Makes Faith-Healing Bills Thorny*, PORTLAND OREGONIAN, June 28, 1999, at E8; Mark Larabee, *Christian Scientists Promote Legal Shields for Faith Healers*, CLEVELAND PLAIN DEALER, Jan. 9, 1999, at 3F; Nancy Lofholm, *A Matter of Faith, Justice: Is Withholding Care a Crime?*, DENVER POST, Mar. 15, 1999, at A1; Patricia G. Miller, *Parents Hold Major Role in Minors' Decisions*, PITTSBURGH POST-GAZETTE, Apr. 20, 2000, at B2. For more information on religion-based exemptions from neglect and abuse statutes, from an advocacy group that opposes such exemptions, see http://www.childrenshealthcare.org/legal.htm (last visited Aug. 31, 2000).

35 Dwyer, *supra* note 3, at 148. I disagree with the claim that those of us "outsiders" who are not required by our faith to rely solely on spiritual healing therefore "have no personal stake" in questions about spiritual-healing exemptions. The exemptions debate implicates broader questions about religious freedom, family integrity, and parental control, questions in whose correct resolution a great many "outsiders" have a significant "stake."

on exposure to criminal liability is probably appropriate.[36] Others insist, though, that any appropriate balancing of interests must weigh heavily against spiritual-healing exemptions, or that it is simply wrong to "balance" children's health against parents' faith.[37] Professor Dwyer, for example, objects to exemptions because they privilege the religious views and interests of parents over the Government's view of children's temporal interests.[38] Although "extremely limited" exemptions might be justified by reasons "tied to the interests of the children of insiders, as the State sees them" and by "general principles regarding treatment of individuals in light of their personhood," the sweeping provisions that exist in many states are, he thinks, unconstitutional, illiberal, and—put bluntly—"immoral."[39]

I am not entirely sure how we should strike the balance between parents' religion-based preferences for prayer over doctors' and the Government's interest in protecting the physical well-being of chil-

36 *See, e.g.*, DiCamillo, *supra* note 32, at 124; Hartsell, *supra* note 8, at 528–30; Lederman, *supra* note 32, at 894–95. Professor David Steinberg, for example, offers such a moderate view. He recognizes both the First Amendment right of religious parents to follow the dictates of their faith when treating a child's illness *and* the State's interest in protecting the health and welfare of its citizens, particularly children, who, he observes, cannot care for themselves. Given these competing values, he concludes that the Government may require parents to obtain medical care, and punish them for not obtaining such care, only when the failure to seek treatment poses a serious threat of permanent harm to a child's health. *See* David E. Steinberg, *Children and Spiritual Healing: Having Faith in Free Exercise*, 76 NOTRE DAME L. REV. 179, 207 (2000).

37 *See, e.g.*, Janna C. Merrick, *Christian Science Healing of Minor Children: Spiritual Exemption Statutes, First Amendment Rights, and Fair Notice*, 10 ISSUES L. & MED. 321, 341 (1994); Jennifer L. Rosato, *Putting Square Pegs in a Round Hole: Procedural Due Process and the Effect of Faith Healing Exemptions on the Prosecution of Faith Healing Parents*, 29 U.S.F. L. REV. 43, 116 (1994); Elizabeth A. Lingle, Comment, *Treating Children by Faith: Colliding Constitutional Issues*, 17 J. LEGAL MED. 301, 329 (1996).

38 *See* Dwyer, *supra* note 3, at 166–68. Professor Dwyer has developed his "child centered" approach to child rearing, his arguments against *Pierce*-style notions of parents' rights, and his criticisms of religious education in a number of books and articles, including DWYER, *supra* note 15; James G. Dwyer, *Children's Interests in a Family Context—A Cautionary Note*, 39 SANTA CLARA L. REV. 1053 (1999); Dwyer, *supra* note 10; Dwyer, *supra* note 12.

39 Dwyer, *supra* note 3, at 166. The latter charge—that spiritual-treatment exemptions are "immoral to the extent they cannot be justified in terms of what is best, from the state's perspective, for the children whose welfare is at stake"—seems too harsh, at least with respect to exemptions from criminal prosecution. Even accepting child-centered premises—that is, that children's interests, not parents' wishes, control and that the State's views about children's temporal best interests are privileged—we might morally still refuse to treat a religious parent's state of mind as sufficiently blameworthy to merit criminal punishment.

dren.[40] It should be noted that, exemptions from prosecution aside, courts often order medical treatment for children, on a case-by-case basis, even over those children's parents' religion-based objections. These orders implicate First Amendment and religious-freedom values, but I think most of us would agree that they can be, if done right, consistent with a proper respect for parental prerogatives, religious freedom, and limited government.[41]

This is because we generally *agree*—insiders and outsiders with each other, and outsiders among themselves—that the "harm" to the

40 A careful examination of the constitutionality of spiritual-treatment exemptions and a response to the claim that they violate the Establishment Clause because they privilege the religious beliefs of "insiders" are beyond the scope of this Article. *See* Dwyer, *supra* note 3, at 152 ("[S]upporters of exemptions cannot appeal to religious beliefs, since the State may not assume that any particular religious beliefs are true. . . . [A]lso . . . [they] cannot expect the State itself to *adopt* the insiders' perspective, insofar as it is based on religious beliefs."). Assuming, though, that exemptions are denomination-neutral, *see* Larson v. Valente, 456 U.S. 228, 244–47 (1982), why should they be regarded as anything other than run-of-the-mill "accommodations" of religion? *See generally* Children's Healthcare Is a Legal Duty, Inc. v. Min De Parle, 212 F.3d 1084 (8th Cir. 2000) (upholding certain Medicare-related exemptions for Christian Science facilities); Treene, *supra* note 10, at 160–64 (analyzing spiritual-healing exemptions in light of the Establishment Clause). The First Amendment permits the Government to pursue the valid secular purpose of accommodating religious belief and practice. *See, e.g.*, Corp. of the Presiding Bishop v. Amos, 483 U.S. 327, 335 (1987); Lynch v. Donnelly, 465 U.S. 668, 673 (1984) ("Nor does the Constitution require complete separation of church and state; it affirmatively mandates accommodation, not merely tolerance, of all religions, and forbids hostility toward any."); Zorach v. Clauson, 343 U.S. 306, 315 (1952) (rejecting argument that "public institutions can make no adjustments . . . to accommodate the religious needs of the people"). *See generally* William K. Kelley, *The Primacy of Political Actors in Accommodation of Religion*, 22 U. HAW. L. REV. (forthcoming 2000); Michael W. McConnell, *Accommodation of Religion: An Update and a Response to the Critics*, 60 GEO. WASH. L. REV. 685, 695–96 (1992). The claim that exemptions are unconstitutional because they take account of religious belief, recognize that insiders have religious interests, or respond to those beliefs by lifting a government-imposed burden is simply wrong. *All* accommodations take account of religious beliefs. That is why they exist. It is not true that government may only accommodate religion by accident. *See, e.g.*, *Amos*, 483 U.S. at 338 ("[This Court] has never indicated that statutes that give special consideration to religious groups are *per se* invalid. That would run contrary to the teaching of our cases that there is ample room for accommodation of religion under the Establishment Clause.").

41 *But see* Dwyer, *supra* note 3, at 166.

> Curiously, though, most proponents of this sort of "spheres of authority" position allow for state control over child rearing at the margins. The State may step in to prevent death. But they provide no real explanation for this qualification of the separate spheres position, for ceding some authority to the State.

Id.

child that is used to justify supervention of parents' religion-based health-care decisions *really is* a harm. We know what physical or medical harm looks like. And, whoever we think is the best decision-maker when it comes to children's health-care, and whether or not we think the religious beliefs of parents and children may be considered by that decision-maker, and whatever our general views about the competing claims of religious believers and governments, *none of us* wants a child to die or to suffer serious physical harm. Certainly, few spiritual-healing believers are oblivious of or indifferent to their children's temporal well-being.[42] They simply believe that prayer, religious faith, and spiritual-healing practices are more likely to avert that harm, and to do so via more acceptable (to them, and to God) means, than is medical treatment.

This helps to explain why outsiders who disagree strongly about the power of the State and the child-rearing rights of parents actually *agree* as much as they do about the propriety of court-ordered emergency medical treatment. It is not because parents' moral claims evaporate in the health-care context, but rather because, *first,* no one thinks these claims include an entitlement to do or cause real harm to a child; *second,* we all agree that death or physical injury is a real harm; and *third,* we are less worried, because of this agreement, than we might be in other contested contexts about the dangers of statist second-guessing.

Can this point of consensus be put to any use in the education debate? Again, the Court tells us that part of the "liberty" protected by the Fourteenth Amendment is parents' "fundamental" right to direct their children's education[43] and, in particular, given the First Amendment's religious-freedom guarantee, to control their children's *religious* training.[44] Still, the debate goes on. On one side, there are those who contend that the State has the duty and right to regulate children's education, to decide what they must and should not be

---

42 *Cf.* Dwyer, *supra* note 3, at 150 ("I doubt that members of the Church of Christ Scientist watch their children suffer and die with equanimity, and the children themselves might be terrified, in addition to suffering physical pain.").

43 *See* Troxel v. Granville, 120 S. Ct. 2054, 2060 (2000) (plurality opinion) ("In light of this extensive precedent, it cannot now be doubted that the Due Process Clause of the Fourteenth Amendment protects the fundamental right of parents to make decisions concerning the care, custody, and control of their children.").

44 *See* Wisconsin v. Yoder, 406 U.S. 205, 229 (1972). Indeed, the Court in *Yoder* seemed to think that *only* those educational decisions that are rooted in religious belief enjoy the protection afforded "fundamental" rights. *See id.* at 215–16; *see also* Steven D. Smith, Wisconsin v. Yoder *and the Unprincipled Approach to Religious Freedom,* 25 CAP. U. L. REV. 805, 807 (1996).

taught in schools,[45] and to do so solely on the basis of its *own* assessment of the child's best interests. On the other side are those who maintain that parents are not only entitled but obligated to make these decisions, based on their *own* assessments of the competing values, informed perhaps by their faith, subject to state second-guessing only to prevent clear harm to a child.

So far, it looks like the education debate maps fairly closely onto the health-care debate, and it appears that there is agreement at least on the point that the State may justifiably override parents' education-related decisions to prevent "harm" to a child. But when, if ever, is education "harmful"? What about *religious* education and instruction? Again, in the health-care context, notwithstanding important disagreements, we agree, by and large, that the State may override parents' wishes in order to prevent harm, that physical injury or death *is* a harm, and that the purpose of medical care is to avoid such harm. But when it comes to government regulation of education, the disagreement between statists and "parentalists"[46] turns not only on the rights/privileges distinction, the scope of the State's *parens patriae* and police powers, and the relevance of religion to decision-makers' calcu-

45 Less common, I think, is the bolder claim that the *parens patriae* power of the liberal state permits or requires it to regulate what is "taught" to children *outside* school—say, at the dinner table. *See, e.g.*, DWYER, *supra* note 15, at 158 ("[P]arents . . . may be required to give up some measure of their personal liberty as a condition for enjoying the privilege of participating in the children's upbringing . . . . For example, they might justifiably be proscribed from expressing sexist views in the presence of children in a way that damages children's self-esteem . . . ."). This is a remarkable—and, to many, repellent—assertion. *See, e.g.*, Bowen v. Gilliard, 483 U.S. 587, 632 (1987) (Brennan, J., dissenting).

> In *The Republic* and in *The Laws*, Plato offered a vision of a unified society, where the needs of children are met not by parents but by the government, and where no intermediate forms of association stand between the individual and the state. The vision is a brilliant one, *but it is not our own.*

Id. (emphasis added) (citations omitted). Then again, if the State is authorized, and perhaps obligated, to look after the best temporal interests of children as it sees them, and if parents' authority to direct and control their children's education is more in the nature of a privilege than a right, and if the liberal state believes that it is *not* in the best interests of children to be taught certain views, opinions, and beliefs, then I am not sure what principled basis there is for liberal statists to assure us that the dinner table, car pool, and bedtime story, unlike the traditional school day, are teaching moments beyond the State's power. As Rousseau once recommended, the "newlyborn infant, upon first opening his eyes, must gaze upon the fatherland, and until his dying day should behold nothing else." J. ROUSSEAU, THE GOVERNMENT OF POLAND 21 (W. Kendall trans., 1972), *quoted in* Cass R. Sunstein, *Beyond the Republican Revival*, 97 YALE L.J. 1539, 1572 (1988).

46 *See generally* Gilles, *supra* note 27, at 11 (defending "liberal parentalism").

lations, but also on the basic problem of identifying "harm."[47] If the State may, in some cases, require medical treatment to prevent serious physical harm, may it also protect children from the "harm" of being taught, for example, that Genesis is true, that extra-marital sexual activity is a sin, or that unbelievers are damned? Are such teachings harmful? Some say "yes"; many say "no." But it is precisely this kind of inevitable and intractable disagreement that makes it all the more important to examine carefully, and to cabin closely, the Government's asserted authority to second-guess parents and supervise their educational choices.

III. Taking *Pierce* Seriously

Here, one might object: "You say that the Government must stay its hand, because 'harm' is hard to define when it comes to education. So what if it is? Your standard is too demanding, and it is inconsistent with the importance of education to the public good and with the State's *parens patriae* obligations. It is enough if the experts decide that a particular course of study is or is not, all (non-religious) things considered, in the best interests of children and the community." No, it is not—not if we take *Pierce* seriously.

We have probably all heard the story about Benjamin Franklin being asked by a Philadelphia woman during the Constitutional Convention, "Well, Doctor, what have we got?," and responding, "A republic, if you can keep it."[48] I suspect that many political theorists wish that a colonial Chris Matthews or Tim Russert had been there to ask the now-obvious follow-up question, "And *how* exactly do we keep it?"

Today, some argue that one of the things we have to do to "keep" our republic (or, our liberal democracy) is to quite self-consciously create—specifically, to educate—republicans (or, liberal democrats).[49] After all, citizens capable of self-government do not just *happen*; "[L]iberal democratic citizens are made, not born . . . ."[50] As George Will puts it, statecraft, properly understood, is soulcraft: "[M]en and women are biological facts, but . . . ladies and gentlemen

47 *See* Dwyer, *supra* note 3, at 150–51 (listing reasons for disagreement).

48 *See* 3 The Records of the Federal Convention of 1787, at 85 (Max Farrand ed., 1966).

49 *Cf.* Galston, *supra* note 17, at 872 ("Within the civic republican tradition, state intrusion to foster good citizens poses no threshold issues; not so for liberal democracy, whose core commitments place limits on the measures the state legitimately may employ."). The lines between today's "neo-republicans," "republican revivalists," and civil-society liberals are often hard to identify, and I will not try to find them here.

50 Galston, *supra* note 17, at 870.

fit for self-government are social artifacts, creations of the law."[51] And so, Amy Gutmann argues, "conscious social reproduction"—citizen creation—is both a "core value" of, and a requirement for, "deliberative democracy."[52] Even liberal societies, if they hope to thrive and survive, must inculcate values and promote "contested views of the good"; they must orient their governments and citizen-shaping processes in a way likely to produce agreement on those views.[53] A society that aspires to meaningful democracy, the argument goes, must take care that it makes—again, that it *educates*—citizens capable of valuing and achieving that end.[54]

In other words, it looks like the emerging consensus in political theory is that the poet, William Ross Wallace, was right (as was the creepy movie): The hand that rocks the cradle rules the world. In other words, those who decide what children may and should learn thereby shape, if not determine, those children's character and commitments, as well as those of the community.[55] This is why many political theorists have answered the "who should decide" question by "subordinating the authority of individual parents to overriding conceptions of liberal democratic values or to the decisions of political majorities."[56] This is why leading liberal statists[57] like Gutmann and, more recently, Stephen Macedo insist candidly that "public schools

51 George F. Will, Statecraft as Soulcraft: What Government Does 90–91 (1983).

52 Amy Gutmann, Democratic Education 39, 42 (1987) ("We are committed to collectively re-creating the society that we share . . . . The substance of this core commitment is conscious social reproduction.").

53 Abner S. Greene, *Government of the Good*, 53 Vand. L. Rev. 1, 2 (2000).

54 *See* Gutmann, *supra* note 52, at 39 ("[A] society that supports conscious social reproduction must educate all educable children to be capable of participating in collectively shaping their society.").

55 *See* Scott W. Somerville, *Education Reform at the Crossroads: The History and Politics of School Choice*, 10 Geo. Mason U. Civ. Rts. L.J. 121, 123 (1999/2000) ("It slowly dawned on me that schools are the most powerful possible instruments for gaining long-term control over a democracy.").

56 Gilles, *supra* note 22, at 937.

57 "Liberal statism" is, for present purposes, the view that the needs of liberal democracy and the demands of liberal citizenship authorize or require the State to supervise, regulate, and dictate the content of education. *See* Stephen L. Carter, *Religious Freedom as if Religion Matters: A Tribute to Justice Brennan*, 87 Cal. L. Rev. 1059, 1065 (1999) ("When I say statism, . . . I have in mind a sense of the state's rightness, or goodness—an empirical belief that the state is less likely than the individual to make a moral error. Since the Enlightenment, the entire liberal political project has rested on this idea."); Dwyer, *supra* note 3, at 172–73 (rejecting "liberal statis[m]" and insisting that "only children themselves have any moral claim or entitlement in connection with their upbringing"); Gilles, *supra* note 27, at 10 ("The main alternative to liberal parentalism is what I call liberal statism—the view that parental educational authority

are instruments for the most basic and controversial of civic ends," the "project of forming citizens . . . ."[58] And this is why, more than seventy-five years ago, Oregon voters enacted by initiative the Compulsory Education Act, making it a crime to send one's child to a Catholic school.[59]

It is clear that this Act, and others like it, were animated largely by substantive opposition to and suspicion toward the teachings and institution of the Roman Catholic Church.[60] In this sense, of course, the Act was nothing new: anti-Catholicism is, some say, our nation's oldest prejudice,[61] and the early history of American public education, starting in the early-mid-nineteenth century, is in large part the story of the efforts of America's "*de facto* [Protestant] establishment,"[62] and later the self-styled Progressive vanguard, to respond to perceived threats to the national character posed by massive immigration and by the religion of the immigrants.[63] After the Civil War, wild-eyed de-

---

must ordinarily yield to the state's authority to define what constitutes children's best interests and its interest in educating children to be good citizens.").

58 STEPHEN MACEDO, DIVERSITY AND DISTRUST, at ix (2000). Macedo claims that while "[o]ur central aims are the protection of individual freedom and preservation of stable, limited, and orderly government, . . . to plan for these great political goods we need to think very broadly about how liberal citizens become capable of their great office." *Id.* at 275. *See generally* Amy Gutmann, *Religious Freedom and Civic Responsibility,* 56 WASH. & LEE L. REV. 907 (1999); Stephen Macedo, *Constituting Civil Society: School Vouchers, Religious Nonprofit Organizations, and Liberal Public Values,* 75 CHI.-KENT L. REV. 417 (2000). For a powerful critique of such and similar claims, see Michael W. McConnell, *The New Establishmentarianism,* 75 CHI.-KENT L. REV. 453 (2000).

59 *See* Pierce v. Soc'y of Sisters, 268 U.S. 510, 530–31 (1925). The Act "require[d] every . . . person having control or charge or custody of a child between 8 and 16 years to send him 'to a public school' . . . and failure to do so [was] declared a misdemeanor." *Id.* at 530 (citing the Compulsory Education Act, 1922 Or. Laws 5259).

60 *See* Carter, *supra* note 27, at 1203 ("[*Pierce*] must be understood in a historical context in which the Justices knew as well as anybody that the Oregon law was, in large part, an effort to destroy Roman Catholicism."). For a "revisionist"—and, in my judgment, mistaken—reading of *Pierce* and its context, see MACEDO, *supra* note 58, at 99 ("We should . . . also take account of legitimate considerations advanced on behalf of the Oregon law, for it was not simply motivated by anti-Catholic prejudice."); *id.* at 303 n.38.

61 *See* JOHN TRACY ELLIS, AMERICAN CATHOLICISM 151 (2d ed. 1969) (quoting Arthur Schlesinger, Sr.).

62 MARK DEWOLFE HOWE, THE GARDEN AND THE WILDERNESS 31 (1965). As Henry Adams observed, in the elite society of his boyhood, "[s]ocial perfection was . . . sure, because human nature worked for Good, and three instruments were all she asked—Suffrage, Common Schools, and Press. On these points doubt was forbidden." THE EDUCATION OF HENRY ADAMS 33 (Modern Library ed. 1996).

63 Thomas Jefferson once expressed his hope that a system of public schools would bring about "a quiet euthanasia of the heresies of bigotry and fanaticism which have so long triumphed over human reason . . . ." Letter from Thomas Jefferson to

nunciations of the "sectarian" schools were a regular staple in Republican organs like *Harper's Weekly* and in the illustrations of Thomas Nast. "It must be remembered," *Harper's* warned, "that the primary object of the Roman party is not the education of the children, but the maintenance and extension of the Roman sect. The plan is to make the schools nurseries of Roman Catholicism—a plan which every good citizen should strenuously oppose."[64]

In a similar vein, for the evidently quite progressive majority of Oregon citizens, egged on by the Ku Klux Klan and other anti-Catholic organizations,[65] the tasks of "social reproduction" and assimilation demanded that students attend public, not "sectarian," schools. These tasks required that children receive what Macedo calls a "civic education"[66] consistent with common American values and that they be protected from the influence of foreign superstition or authoritarian religion.[67] In other words, Oregon's law appears to have been

---

William Short (Oct. 31, 1819), *in* THE LIFE AND SELECTED WRITINGS OF THOMAS JEFFERSON 694 (Adrienne Koch & William Peden eds., 1972). *See generally* CHARLES LESLIE GLENN, JR., THE MYTH OF THE COMMON SCHOOL (1988); LLOYD P. JORGENSON, THE STATE AND THE NON-PUBLIC SCHOOL 1825–1925 (1987); JOSEPH P. VITERITTI, CHOOSING EQUALITY: SCHOOL CHOICE, THE CONSTITUTION, AND CIVIL SOCIETY 145–79 (1999); John T. McGreevy, *Thinking on One's Own: Catholicism in the American Intellectual Imagination, 1928–1960*, 84 J. AM. HIST. 97 (1997).

64 *The Parochial Schools*, HARPER'S WKLY., Apr. 10, 1875, at 294.

65 *See* MACEDO, *supra* note 58, at 98–103 (noting, for instance, that "the Oregon mandatory public school attendance law . . . had gained substantial support in other states . . . [and] was supported by populists"); Jay S. Bybee, *Substantive Due Process and Free Exercise of Religion:* Meyer, Pierce, *and the Origins of* Wisconsin v. Yoder, 25 CAP. U. L. REV. 887, 891 (1996) (noting that the Oregon Act was "the result of complex forces, uniting groups as disparate as the Ku Klux Klan and the progressives, both of which advocated the 'Americanization' of the state's young people"); McConnell, *supra* note 58, at 461 ("Who would guess that this argument was made on behalf of a hateful law passed at the urging of the Ku Klux Klan for the purpose of closing Catholic schools?" (citing David B. Tyack, *The Perils of Pluralism: The Background of the* Pierce *Case*, 74 AMER. HIST. REV. 74 (1968))).

66 MACEDO, *supra* note 58, at 149–228.

67 *See* Pierce v. Soc'y of Sisters, 268 U.S. 510, 526 (1925) (arguments of counsel) ("It would . . . be both unjust and unreasonable to prevent [the states] from taking the steps which each may deem necessary and proper for Americanizing its new immigrants and developing them into patriotic and law-abiding citizens."); *id.* at 525 (arguments of counsel) (contending that "religious suspicions" in America were attributable to "the separation of children along religious lines during the most susceptible years of their lives, with the inevitable awakening of a consciousness of separation, and a distrust and suspicion of those from whom they were so carefully guarded"). *See generally* MACEDO, *supra* note 58, at 88–109; Carter, *supra* note 27, at 1200–03 (describing *Pierce*'s historical context).

motivated less by a desire to do right by poor children than by a fear that Catholic schools would *do wrong* to them.[68]

Given that the Compulsory Education Act was comfortably consonant with the smart-set views of the day,[69] it is perhaps surprising that the Supreme Court, without dissent, struck down the law. The Court relied on its earlier decision in *Meyer v. Nebraska*,[70] where it had struck down a nativist but not uncommon law against teaching in any language other than English, insisting, in *Lochner*-esque terms, that the Constitution protects, "[w]ithout doubt, . . . not merely freedom from bodily restraint but also . . . those privileges long recognized at common law as essential to the orderly pursuit of happiness by free men."[71] The *Meyer* Court closed by emphasizing: "That the state may do much, go very far, indeed, in order to improve the quality of its citizens, physically, mentally, and morally, is clear; but the individual has certain fundamental rights which must be respected."[72]

Two years later, turning back Oregon's aggressively assimilationist effort to homogenize children's values, the *Pierce* Court insisted that, notwithstanding the "power of the state reasonably to regulate all schools,"[73]

> the Act of 1922 unreasonably interferes with the liberty of parents and guardians to direct the upbringing and education of children under their control. . . . The fundamental theory of liberty upon which all governments in this Union repose excludes any general

---

68 Oregon was also concerned, apparently, that, just as surely as pool leads to Trouble, Catholic schools could lead to schools run by "bolshevists, syndicalists, and communists." *Pierce*, 268 U.S. at 526 (arguments of counsel). Interestingly, although he seems embarrassed by the Klannish underbelly of the arguments for the Oregon Act, Stephen Macedo nonetheless insists that the Act's supporters were on to something.

> Reasonable measures to promote civic virtues are to be distinguished from the extremism of those who tried to force Catholic children to read the Protestant Bible . . . and the Klan. Prejudice against Catholics is also to be distinguished from perhaps reasonable fears that those educated in relatively authoritarian religious doctrines may be more prone than others to reject liberal democratic political norms and institutions.

MACEDO, *supra* note 58, at 130.

69 John Dewey, for example, insisted that parents should not be permitted to "innoculate" their children with the outdated and useless religious beliefs that they "happen[ed] to have found serviceable to themselves." STEVEN C. ROCKEFELLER, JOHN DEWEY: RELIGIOUS FAITH AND DEMOCRATIC HUMANISM 260 (1991); *see also* JOHN DEWEY, A COMMON FAITH (1934).

70 262 U.S. 390 (1923).

71 *Id.* at 399.

72 *Id.* at 401.

73 *Pierce*, 268 U.S. at 534.

> power of the State to standardize its children by forcing them to accept instruction from public teachers only. The child is not the mere creature of the State; those who nurture him and direct his destiny have the right, coupled with the high duty, to recognize and prepare him for additional obligations.[74]

I suspect that many law professors and political philosophers do not like this passage.[75] And although the Supreme Court keeps reaffirming that the "primary role of the parents in the upbringing of their children is now established beyond debate as an enduring American tradition,"[76] the federal courts tend generally to treat *Pierce* like a

---

74 *Id.* at 534–35; *cf.* SECOND VATICAN COUNCIL, DECLARATION ON CHRISTIAN EDUCATION, at No. 3 (1965) ("[S]ince parents have conferred life on their children, they have a most solemn obligation to educate their offspring. Hence, parents must be acknowledged as the first and foremost educators of their children.").

75 *See* Carter, *supra* note 27, at 1194 ("When scholars meet to discuss the great pantheon of constitutional rights, . . . we are not much concerned with the right to direct the upbringing of children; indeed, I suspect that many scholars disbelieve in it . . . ."); *see also* Dwyer, *supra* note 12, at 1447 (concluding that "[c]ourts should acknowledge the illegitimacy of the parents' rights doctrine and decline to recognize claims of parents rights in the future" and that "[t]he evolution of our social attitudes [provides sufficient ground] for overruling . . . *Pierce*"); Abner S. Greene, *Why Vouchers Are Unconstitutional, and Why They're Not*, 13 NOTRE DAME J.L. ETHICS & PUB. POL'Y 397, 406–08 (1999) (arguing that *Pierce* be "reconsidered" and for "requir[ing] public schooling, ensuring that children are exposed to multiple sources of value"); *cf.* MACEDO, *supra* note 58, at 101 ("I do not . . . want to go so far as to argue that *Meyer* and *Pierce* were wrongly decided . . . .").

76 Wisconsin v. Yoder, 406 U.S. 202, 232 (1972); *see also* Troxel v. Granville, 120 S. Ct. 2054, 2060 (2000) (citing cases); Santosky v. Kramer, 455 U.S. 745, 753 (1982) (affirming "[t]he fundamental liberty interest of natural parents in the care, custody, and management of their child"); Smith v. Org. of Foster Families for Equal. and Reform, 431 U.S. 816, 845 (1977) (holding that parents' child-rearing rights are "intrinsic human rights, as they have been understood in this Nation's history and tradition"); *Yoder*, 406 U.S. at 232 (affirming the "fundamental interest of parents, as contrasted with that of the State, to guide the religious future and education of their children"). In *Prince v. Massachusetts*, 321 U.S. 158 (1944), the court noted:

> It is cardinal with us that the custody, care and nurture of the child reside first in the parents, whose primary function and freedom include preparation for obligations the state can neither supply nor hinder. . . . And it is in recognition of this that . . . decisions have respected the private realm of family life which the state cannot enter.

Id. at 166. True, the Court has, from the beginning, hedged its pronouncements on parental control. Even in *Pierce*, the Court was careful to acknowledge the "power of the State reasonably to regulate all schools." *Pierce*, 268 U.S. at 534. And, in *Prince*, the Court insisted that neither parents' prerogatives nor "the family itself" is beyond all police-power regulation. 321 U.S. at 166 ("[T]he family itself is not beyond regulation in the public interest. . . . [The] rights of parenthood are [not] beyond limitation."); *see also, e.g.*, Stanley v. Illinois, 405 U.S. 645, 649 (1972) ("The State's right—

quirky aged relative who, although she is still invited to Thanksgiving dinner, is watched nervously for fear she will embarrass the family and start tossing mashed potatoes.[77]

In my view, though, the above-quoted passage from *Pierce* is no dusty anachronism but is instead one of the more inspiring and truly liberating statements in the *United States Reports.* The "fundamental theory of liberty" it endorses is, rightly understood, all the more to be embraced for being today so widely challenged.[78] And *Pierce is* widely challenged, despite having been (sort of) re-affirmed just last summer in *Troxel.*[79] In *Troxel,* the Supreme Court of Washington had struck down, as a violation of fundamental *Pierce* rights, a "breathtakingly

indeed, duty—to protect minor children through a judicial determination of their interests in a neglect proceeding is not challenged here.").

77 The *Pierce* Court's reference to "reasonable regulation," 268 U.S. at 534, has caused many courts to treat the freedom vindicated in that case as a "poor relation" which must ride piggy-back on some *other* right in order to enjoy meaningful constitutional protection. *See* Dolan v. City of Tigard, 512 U.S. 374, 392 (1994) ("We see no reason why the Takings Clause of the Fifth Amendment, as much a part of the Bill of Rights as the First Amendment or Fourth Amendment, should be relegated to the status of a poor relation in these comparable circumstances."). These courts have failed to employ the "strict scrutiny" usually required in "fundamental rights" cases. *See* Herndon v. Chapel Hill-Carrboro City Bd. of Educ., 89 F.3d 174, 179 (4th Cir. 1996) (concluding that because parents' "interest is not religious, . . . we must reject their position if the [challenged regulation] bear[s] some rational relationship to legitimate state purposes"); Immediato v. Rye Neck Sch. Dist., 73 F.3d 454, 462 (2d Cir. 1996) ("[W]here, as here, parents seek for secular reasons to exempt their child from an educational requirement and the basis is a claimed right to direct the 'upbringing' of their child, rational basis review applies."); Ohio Ass'n of Indep. Sch. v. Goff, 92 F.3d 419, 423 (6th Cir. 1996) (stating that "rational basis review, not strict scrutiny," governs "wholly secular limitations on private school education"); Brown v. Hot, Sexy, and Safer Prods., Inc., 68 F.3d 525, 533 (1st Cir. 1995) ("We need not decide here whether the right to rear one's children is fundamental . . . .").

78 Which is not necessarily to endorse the opinion's substantive-due-process reasoning. *See Troxel,* 120 S. Ct. at 2074 (Scalia, J., dissenting) (noting that *Pierce* was decided in "an era rich in substantive due process holdings that have since been repudiated"); MACEDO, *supra* note 58, at 98–103 (discussing connections between *Pierce* and *Lochner*-style substantive due process).

79 120 S. Ct. at 2060 (plurality opinion). I say that *Pierce* was "sort of" re-affirmed in *Troxel* because the Court did not appear to apply, nor did it give any indication that it would apply in the future, the kind of strict scrutiny that laws touching "fundamental" rights are usually thought to require. *See id.* at 2068 (Thomas, J., concurring).

> Our decision in [*Pierce*] holds that parents have a fundamental constitutional right to rear their children, including the right to determine who shall educate and socialize them. The opinions of the plurality, Justice Kennedy, and Justice Souter recognize such a right, but curiously none of them articulates the appropriate standard of review. I would apply strict scrutiny to infringements of fundamental rights.

broad"[80] third-party-visitation law, which authorized courts to award visitation rights to third parties, over parents' objections, whenever visitation is in the child's best interests. Although the four-Justice plurality opinion was careful to avoid prejudicing the case of third-party-visitation laws generally,[81] it objected strongly to the fact that, under the Washington statute, "a parent's decision that visitation would not be in the child's best interest is accorded no deference"—that, "should the judge disagree with the parent's estimation of the child's best interests, the judge's view necessarily prevails."[82] Because "the Due Process Clause does not permit a State to infringe on the fundamental right of parents to make childrearing decisions simply because a state judge believes a 'better' decision could be made,"[83] the Court invalidated the application of the visitation law.[84]

Troxel and the Supreme Court aside, the challenges to *Pierce* come on (at least) two fronts.[85] First, there are those who insist that parents' educational preferences must yield to the public need to produce citizens of a certain ideological cast and deliberative temperament and that both children and society are harmed if parents transmit misguidedly illiberal views and beliefs to their children. Stephen Macedo in particular has grown impatient with what he regards as hand-wring-

Id. I should add that I drafted *amicus curiae* briefs for the Society of Catholic Social Scientists and the Christian Legal Society in support of the respondents in the *Troxel* case.

80 120 S. Ct. at 2061 (plurality opinion) ("[The] language effectively permits any third party seeking visitation to subject any decision by a parent concerning visitation of the parent's children to state-court review.").

81 *See id.* at 2064 (plurality opinion) ("Because much state-court adjudication in this context occurs on a case-by-case basis, we would be hesitant to hold that specific nonparental visitation statutes violate the Due Process Clause as a *per se* matter."). *See generally* Joan C. Bohl, *Grandparent Visitation Law Grows Up: The Trend Toward Awarding Visitation Only When the Child Would Otherwise Suffer Harm*, 48 DRAKE L. REV. 279 (2000); Joan C. Bohl, *The "Unprecedented Intrusion": A Survey and Analysis of Selected Grandparent Visitation Cases*, 49 OKLA. L. REV. 29 (1996). For a recent state-court decision involving a more carefully crafted grandparent-visitation statute in which the court nonetheless insisted that the Constitution limits states' power to authorize visitation over parents' objections, see generally *Hampton v. Hampton*, 17 S.W.3d 599 (Mo. Ct. App. 2000).

82 120 S. Ct. at 2061 (plurality opinion).

83 *Id.* at 2064 (plurality opinion).

84 *See id.* at 2065 (plurality opinion) ("We therefore hold that the application of [the visitation law] to Granville and her family violated her due process right to make decisions concerning the care, custody, and control of her daughters.").

85 There is at least one more line of attack—the argument that, whatever we think about parental liberty as a moral matter, the Due Process Clause of the Fourteenth Amendment simply does not confer on federal judges the power to strike down duly enacted state laws that restrict that liberty. *See, e.g., id.* at 2074–75 (Scalia, J., dissenting).

ing versions of liberalism, versions whose ability to justify using government to shape civic life and public values—in *Pierce*'s words, to "standardize" children—is, he thinks, hamstrung by their undue focus on "the boundaries and limits of individual rights."[86] As Michael McConnell has observed, "it is difficult or impossible for a liberal state to engage in the direct inculcation of public virtue without compromising its liberal commitment to neutrality among the different and competing reasonable worldviews of the society."[87] Macedo responds to this difficulty by calling unabashedly for a "more judgmental liberalism," one that is wary of and aggressive in opposing "religious enthusiasm" and that—*Pierce* notwithstanding—uses not only the public schools, but "all of the instruments of public policy," to "shape [the] social norms and meanings that mold individual choices and character."[88]

There are also those who claim that *Pierce*-style notions of parental control are inconsistent with a proper focus on the present and future interests of children and who contend that children have a right to be exposed to a sufficiently wide range of ideas and ways of life and to be assisted in developing the capacities necessary to exercise and enjoy meaningful autonomy.[89] Professor Dwyer argues, for example, that parents' child-rearing rights—as opposed to their legal

---

86 MACEDO, *supra* note 58, at 278.

87 McConnell, *supra* note 58, at 455.

88 MACEDO, *supra* note 58, at 278, 276, 277. *But see, e.g.*, W. Va. State Bd. of Educ. v. Barnette, 319 U.S. 624, 642 (1943) ("If there is any fixed star in our constitutional constellation, it is that no official, high or petty, can prescribe what shall be orthodox . . . ."). Professor Abner Greene has suggested a related, but distinct, critique of *Pierce*. In Greene's view, "[o]ur constitutional structure is one of multiple repositories of power . . . ." *Pierce*'s "assumption that parents must have the right to school their children as they wish" violates this key structural principle, because it "ensures that children will get their basic education not from multiple sources, but rather from their parents or their parents' agents alone . . . . " Greene, *supra* note 75, at 406–07. It seems unlikely that even the most robust reading and vigorous implementation of *Pierce* could, in today's society, do anything to prevent children from being influenced substantially by a wide variety of sources other than their parents. Nor am I convinced that our constitutional strategy of protecting liberty by dividing and limiting state power points toward *restrictions* on parents' traditional authority to educate their children.

89 *See generally* Joel Feinberg, *The Child's Right to an Open Future*, *in* WHOSE CHILD? CHILDREN'S RIGHTS, PARENTAL AUTHORITY, AND STATE POWER 124 (William Aiken & Hugh LaFollette eds., 1980); Goldstein, *supra* note 30, at 645 ("The law is designed to assure for each child an opportunity to meet and master the developmental crises on the way to adulthood—to that critical age when he or she is presumed by the state to be qualified to determine what is 'best' for oneself."); Laurence D. Houlgate, *Three Concepts of Children's Constitutional Rights: Reflections on the Enjoyment Theory*, 2 U. PA. J. CONST. L. 77 (1999).

privilege to act in accord with their own moral duties and their children's rights[90]—are unjustifiable, but not so much because parental control of education compromises the task of social reproduction or undermines the workings of civic education. Rather, he views *Pierce* rights as inconsistent with bedrock liberal commitments to the individual autonomy and self-determination rights of children. After all, he insists, "no one is *entitled* to control the life of another person in accord with their own preferences . . . ."[91]

These are serious objections, but I will stick with *Pierce* and try to take it seriously.[92] As I will try to show next, neither the perceived demands of political soulcraft, nor an appropriate respect for the dignity and personhood of children, undermines *Pierce* or supplies the liberal state with the legal power or moral right to standardize the thoughts and values of children over the objection of their parents.

First, the liberal-statist objection: According to "judgmental liberalism,"[93] liberal citizens are made, not born, and they are made carefully, through a certain kind of civic education. Parents have a role to play, but they should not determine the fundamental values and ideals toward which a child should be trained to aspire. And so, the objection from this camp to *Pierce* is its lack of fit with the State's need to engage in the kind of values inculcation it requires to maintain itself. After all, if given free rein, parents could obstruct or garble the State's messages, or perhaps even convey contrary ones.

This argument is as old as *The Republic*. It will not likely be settled any time soon, and I cannot do justice to it here. I am tempted to say, with the Supreme Court in *Meyer*, only that while the Spartans might

---

90 *See* Dwyer, *supra* note 10, at 1374–76 (contrasting "rights" with "privileges" and arguing that parents enjoy the privilege, but not the right, of making child-rearing decisions). Although I share many of Professor Glendon's reservations about the atomizing tendencies of "rights talk," I am confident that parents enjoy more than a mere positive-law "privilege" to decide how best to raise and educate their children. *See generally* Mary Ann Glendon, Rights Talk: The Impoverishment of Political Discourse (1991).

91 Dwyer, *supra* note 3, at 173.

> In my view, neither parents *nor* the State have any moral claim on their own behalf, any *entitlement* to decide what the ends of a child's life are. Rather, only children themselves have any moral claim or entitlement in connection with their upbringing, and we adults should be deliberating about how best to fulfill our obligation to them, not about which adults are entitled to determine how children's lives will go.

Id.

92 *See* Carter, *supra* note 27, at 1195 ("I want to speculate . . . on the possibility that *Pierce* is both rightly decided and rightly reasoned . . . .").

93 Macedo, *supra* note 58, at 278.

well have seen fit to "submerge the individual and develop ideal citizens, . . . their ideas touching the relation between individual and State were wholly different from those upon which our institutions rest."[94] Or, as Justice Brennan put it, "Plato offered a vision of a unified society, where the needs of children are not met by parents but by the government, and where no intermediate forms of association stand between the individual and the State. The vision is a brilliant one, *but it is not our own.*"[95] Perhaps not. Still, as Oregon's Compulsory Education Act and the common-school movement vividly illustrate, when it comes to educating children and forming citizens, "our own" tradition has often been tempted by the ideals of the "Spartans." And in failing to reject these ideals, our tradition has, at times, fallen short.[96]

This is not to say that we should ignore the dangers of an overly atomistic public philosophy or an uncritical celebration of pluralism in morality.[97] It is true, we cannot take for granted the cultural conditions of democracy and self-government.[98] But as Professor McConnell has pointed out, "a liberal society is always at risk. One can hope that the free institutions of civil society will produce virtuous citizens, each in its own way . . . . But there is no guarantee."[99] By humbling government, and by respecting parents, families, and other "free institutions of civil society," we take a chance. And we tie our own hands[100] when we swear off using government to indoctrinate other

94 Meyer v. Nebraska, 262 U.S. 390, 402 (1923).

95 Bowen v. Gilliard, 483 U.S. 587, 632 (1987) (Brennan, J., dissenting) (emphasis added).

96 *See generally, e.g.*, McConnell, *supra* note 58.

97 *See generally* GLENDON, *supra* note 90; MICHAEL J. SANDEL, DEMOCRACY'S DISCONTENT: AMERICA IN SEARCH OF A PUBLIC PHILOSOPHY (1996).

98 *See* MACEDO, *supra* note 58, at 279 ("Our good fortune in having developed institutions that foster . . . shared civic values must neither lull us into complacency nor encourage reforms that rashly overlook the advantages of the system we have."). Still, as Michael McConnell has reminded us, "in the liberal tradition, it is thought that citizens of a political community need not share common values regarding the nature of the good life . . . . All must agree to live and let live. We need not agree on much more than that." McConnell, *supra* note 58, at 454.

99 McConnell, *supra* note 58, at 457.

100 *See* Richard W. Garnett, *Why Informed Consent? Human Experimentation and the Ethics of Autonomy*, 36 CATH. LAW. 455, 499–502 (1996) (discussing the "self-paternalism" inherent in our Constitution); Michael W. McConnell, *Why Is Religious Liberty the "First Freedom"?*, 21 CARDOZO L. REV. 1243, 1254 (2000) ("Disestablishment of religion meant that democratic politics in America was deprived of a key instrument for social reproduction.").

people's children—and they are *other people's* children[101]—in those contested views of the good that a particular majority happens to find most conducive to the development of judgmental liberalism's values.[102]

The second, child-centered, critique of *Pierce* concedes that children are not the mere creatures of the State, but insists that they are not the mere creatures of their parents, either.[103] According to this view, *Pierce*-style child-rearing rights are inconsistent with the dignity and personhood of children because they, in effect, reduce children to property.[104] And it is said that the parental-control idea is inconsistent with the best interests of children, both because it rests on the dubious presumption that parents will always perceive and act in accord with the best interests of their children,[105] and because it limits the ability of state officials and other experts to correctly identify and advance those interests. What is more, parental control over education is said to be inconsistent with children's *future* best interests, that is, in their interests in growing up to have certain capacities, experiences, and dispositions that are, in the State's view, associated with autonomy and necessary for flourishing.[106]

---

101 As Justice Scalia remarked during oral argument in *Troxel*, "The child does not belong to the courts. The child belongs to the parents." *Visitation Rights Challenged*, CHI. SUN-TIMES, Jan. 13, 2000, at 22. *But see, e.g.*, Jessica C. Cox, *Parental Rights and Responsibilities of Control Over Children's Education*, 26 J.L. & EDUC. 179, 179 (1997) ("In the debate over who controls the education of our nation's children, it is the lives of these natural resources that are at stake . . . .").

102 *But see* Greene, *supra* note 53, at 2. It is worth noting here that many believe that parental control in education and, more particularly, religious education, serves quite well the civic needs of liberalism. *See, e.g.*, James W. Caeser & Patrick J. McGuinn, *Civic Education Reconsidered*, 133 THE PUB. INT. 84 (1998) (arguing that religious schools are teaching the values upon which civic education is based); McConnell, *supra* note 58, at 473 (citing research showing that "religious Americans are more democratically engaged than most of their fellow citizens"); Christian Smith & David Sikkink, *Is Private School Privatizing?*, 92 FIRST THINGS 16 (1999) (noting that families whose children attend home schools or private religious or private non-religious schools are more likely to participate in civic life); Richard Boyd, *Including Us Out*, COMMONWEALTH, Sept. 22, 2000, at 25, 26 (noting that "ostensibly 'illiberal' institutions like the family, church, and parochial schools may offer just the values that liberal democratic institutions themselves are incapable of providing").

103 *See* Dwyer, *supra* note 12, at 1446 ("[T]he child is . . . not the mere creature of the parent . . . [but is rather] his or her own person.").

104 *See* MACEDO, *supra* note 58, at 100 (discussing connection between *Pierce* and opposition to child-labor laws). *See generally* Woodhouse, *supra* note 23, at 1059–68.

105 *See* Dwyer, *supra* note 3, at 169–70.

106 *See generally* DWYER, *supra* note 15, at 148–77 (arguing that regulation of religious schools is required in order to insure that children in those schools are given equal opportunity to develop self-esteem, self-respect, and self-determination).

These objections are misplaced. It is not enough—though it is surely right—to affirm the human dignity of children. There is still no avoiding the fact that *someone* is going to make decisions about children's lives, their education, and their religious training; saying it should be parents rather than bureaucrats or activists in no way makes chattel out of children, and saying it should be the State rather than parents shows no greater respect for children's dignity and autonomy.[107] Thus, *Pierce* and parental control in education generally are grounded not on archaic and patriarchal prejudices, but on the common-sense, *truly* child-centered belief that, in Professor Stephen Gilles's words, "parents are more likely to pursue the child's best interest as they define it than is the State to pursue the child's best interest as the state defines it."[108]

And there is more to *Pierce* than Gilles's hard-to-dispute predictive judgment. Surely, the attitude toward a child that best reflects an appreciation for her dignity as a human person is not the disembodied paternalism of a government functionary, or even the genuine concern of a well-meaning case-worker, but the *love* of a parent. A parent loves *this child*; the Government, its experts, and well-meaning third parties, try as they might, most likely do not. A parent has a moral obligation to nurture and protect *this child*,[109] this child who can only be, to the Government, simply a particular manifestation of an abstraction—"children"—whose best interests the State has charged itself with advancing. Parental control is a *this-child-centered*, truly personalist, value, while state control, it seems to me, respects the personhood of children only if one believes that there is something dignified about being regarded by a hubristic state as a policy datum to be manipulated by third parties in accord with best-interests generalities.[110]

---

107 *See, e.g.*, U.S. CATHOLIC CONFERENCE, *supra* note 4, §§ 2221–22 (noting both that "the right and the duty of parents to educate their children are primordial and inalienable" and that "parents must regard their children as children of God and respect them as human persons").

108 Gilles, *supra* note 21, at 940. *See generally id.* at 951–60; Goldstein, *supra* note 30, at 654 ("No one has a greater right or responsibility and no one can be presumed to be in a better position . . . than a child's parents to decide.").

109 *See, e.g.*, Prince v. Massachusetts, 321 U.S. 158, 166 (1944) ("[T]he custody, care and nurture of the child reside first in the parents, whose primary function and freedom include preparation for obligations the state can neither supply nor hinder."); Pierce v. Soc'y of Sisters, 268 U.S. 510, 535 (1925) ("[T]hose who nurture [the child] and direct his destiny have the right, *coupled with the high duty*, to recognize and prepare him for additional obligations." (emphasis added)).

110 *See* C.S. Lewis, *The Humanitarian Theory of Punishment*, 6 RES JUDICATAE 224, 228 (1952) ("Of all tyrannies a tyranny sincerely exercised for the good of its victims may

As I read the decision, *Pierce* is not really about the power of parents *over* children but about the State's lack of power over its citizens generally.[111] *Pierce* is a rejection of state omnipotence, not children's personhood.[112] *Pierce* affirms, not that the child is the property of the parent, but that the child is *not* the property of the State.[113] On this reading, child-rearing authority and family integrity are not anachronistically despotic licenses to control the lives of others, but rather illustrate "first principles" of limited, liberal government.[114] And nothing in *Pierce*, so read, at all undermines the human dignity of the child, nor contravenes her moral right to be assisted in her human development and to be the focus of any debate about her treatment.[115]

In fact, the parental authority and family integrity recognized and defended in *Pierce* are genuinely *liberating* for children. After all, we think of ourselves as free when, among other things, decisions about our best interests are made by us or our agents and not by the Government. What reason is there for thinking that, in contested matters of education, values, and faith, a child's dignity is more respected, and her autonomy better served, when her "best interests" in those matters are determined by the State, rather than by her family? *Pierce* promises children that decisions about their best interests will be made by those who, generally speaking, are most likely to work conscientiously, motivated by love and moral obligation, to advance their

---

be the most oppressive. . . . [T]hose who torment us for our own good will torment us without end for they do so with the approval of their own conscience.").

111 *See In re* Custody of Smith, 969 P.2d 21, 28 (Wash. 1998) ("In answering whether the state visitation statutes at issue serve a compelling state interest we must understand the sources of state power to intrude on family life."), *aff'd sub nom.* Troxel v. Granville, 120 S. Ct. 2054 (2000).

112 *Cf.* McConnell, *supra* note 100, at 1247 ("If the state does not have power over the church, it follows that the power of the state is limited.").

113 Thus, *Pierce* seems to be in accord with Professor Dwyer's claim that "the child is . . . not the mere creature of the parent . . . [; rather, the child is] his or her own person." Dwyer, *supra* note 12, at 1446; *see also* Dwyer, *supra* note 3, at 177 ("There are widely shared moral beliefs and legal rules about how we should treat people simply by virtue of their personhood.").

114 United States v. Lopez, 514 U.S. 549, 552 (1995) (emphasizing "first principles" of constitutionally limited government). As William Galston put it, the *Pierce* line establishes and stands for two propositions. "First, in a liberal democracy, there is . . . a division of authority between parents and the state. . . . Second, there are some things the liberal state *may not do*, even in the name of forming good citizens." Galston, *supra* note 17, at 874 (emphasis added).

115 *See* Bellotti v. Baird, 443 U.S. 622, 638 (1979) ("Properly understood . . . the tradition of parental authority is not inconsistent with our tradition of individual liberty; rather, the former is one of the basic presuppositions of the latter.").

best interests.[116] Dean John Garvey has shown that this is a promise of real *freedom* to children, a promise to respect their liberty by respecting the decisions of their best agents, rather than by taking them into government wardship.[117] It appears that to the extent the child-centered critique rejects *Pierce* rights as inconsistent with the personhood and dignity of children, it fails to appreciate the best rationale for that decision.

In sum, *Pierce* makes moral sense. We need not apologize for talking about and defending parents' rights to control their children's education. Such talk *is* appropriately child-centered; it is personalist, not statist. *Pierce* does not mean parents have *dominion* over their children and their children's education; it *does* mean that popular majorities and well-meaning third parties—however confident they might be in their own virtue or powers of perception—lack the moral authority to override parents' child-rearing decisions on the basis of what they believe to be the "best interests" of other people's children.[118]

---

116 *Cf.* Calabretta v. Floyd, 189 F.3d 808, 820 (9th Cir. 1999) ("The government's interest in the welfare of children embraces not only protecting children from physical abuse, but also protecting children's interest in the privacy and dignity of their homes and in the lawfully exercised authority of their parents.").

117 *See* JOHN GARVEY, WHAT ARE FREEDOMS FOR? 97–122 (1996). Garvey notes, *inter alia,* that the "problem" with "allow[ing] the government to override a parent's choice about her child's proper education . . . is that, in the effort to make children more free vis-à-vis their parents, the government makes children less free in their relations with the state." *Id.* at 122. Although the child-centered critique of *Pierce* aims at creating and protecting children's self-determination, children "are not free when the government represents them . . . . [T]heir actions are not free because they are directed by the government." *Id.* at 121. It is worth adding, with respect to the autonomy-based objections to *Pierce,* Garvey's observations, *first,* that, even if the point of state supervention of parental educational control is to "keep choices open" for children, so that they can "self-determine" when they grow up, the choices those children make will be "guided by values, talents, and propensities that are themselves largely the result of parental influences"; and *second,* that,

> [e]ven if parents could promote self-determination by offering [their children] a smorgasbord, it is not objectively clear that they should. Autonomy is an ideal just as knowledge, power, virtue, and the service of God are ideals. Each states a certain view of what people ought to be like, of how they can best live their lives. Adults do not all subscribe to the same ideal, and courts should not require children to.

Id. at 117.

118 *See In re* Custody of Smith, 969 P.2d 21, 30–31 (Wash. 1998).

> Short of preventing harm to the child, the standard of "best interest of the child" is insufficient to serve as a compelling state interest overruling a parent's fundamental rights . . . . It is not within the province of the state to make significant decisions concerning the custody of children merely because it could make a "better" decision.

IV. Religion and (as?) Harm to Children

If we take *Pierce* seriously, state supervention of parents' educational authority is justified only to prevent *harm* to a child and not to inculcate those values that the State believes will best serve its own, or the child's, "best interests."[119] The Supreme Court had a chance in *Troxel* to emphasize this point, but it dropped the ball.[120] The Washington Supreme Court, though, put it at the center of its decision. That court's objection to the third-party-visitation statute was not merely that it was applied heavy-handedly, but that it permitted visitation orders, over parents' objection, *whenever* "visitation may serve the best interest of the child . . . ."[121] Because "it is undisputed that parents have a fundamental right to autonomy in child rearing decisions,"[122] interference with those decisions "is justified only if the state can show that it has a compelling interest and such interference is narrowly drawn to meet only the compelling state interest involved."[123]

In that court's view, pursuing the "best interests" of children, as seen by particular trial-court judges and in opposition to the parents' wishes, is *not* a compelling state interest. Rather, traditional police and *parens patriae* powers authorize the State to "intrude on a family's autonomy" only "where a child has been harmed or where there is a threat of harm to a child."[124] Of course, there are all kinds of situations where children might be better off, in a third party's view, or perhaps even in fact, if a particular parental decision—say, to encourage or permit the child to play soccer rather than baseball, prefer Britney Spears to Willie Dixon, or read law-review articles rather than the Narnia chronicles—were overridden. But then, as the court ob-

---

Id.

119 This statement is consistent with the "minimum state intervention" model set out in Goldstein et al., *supra* note 14. *See also* Goldstein, *supra* note 30, at 648–51.

120 *See* Troxel v. Granville, 120 S. Ct. 2054, 2064 (2000).

> Because we rest our decision on the sweeping breadth of [the statute] and the application of that broad, unlimited power in this case, we do not consider the primary constitutional question passed on by the Washington Supreme Court—whether the Due Process Clause requires all nonparental visitation statutes to include a showing of harm or potential harm to the child as a condition precedent to granting visitation. We do not, and need not, define today the precise scope of the parental due process right in the visitation context.

Id.

121 969 P.2d at 24.

122 *Id.* at 27.

123 *Id.* at 28; *cf. Troxel*, 120 S. Ct. at 2068 (Thomas, J., concurring).

124 969 P.2d at 28.

served, "the authority to raise the child as the parents see fit, except when the State thinks another choice would be better, is . . . no authority at all."[125] And, moving from visitation orders to decisions about education and religious training, a right to direct the education of one's children that is subject to best-interests ratification or veto by the State is an empty and ineffectual right.[126]

Am I suggesting that we should be cavalier about children's best interests? Of course not. Still, taking *Pierce* seriously does require us to tolerate the fact that some parents will, in the opinion of most "outsiders," incorrectly perceive and inadequately promote their children's best interests. But the world is full of second-bests. We tolerate imperfection and imprecision all the time, because the "costs" of eliminating them—here, the costs of statist perfectionism—are too great.[127] A demanding harm requirement reflects a trade-off; we *risk* the chance that some parents, sometimes, will fail to act in their child's best interests to insure that the State does not simply intervene to re-educate children whenever parents' (or children's) decisions

125 *Id.* at 30 (quoting Kathleen Bean, *Grandparent Visitation: Can the Parent Refuse?*, 24 U. LOUISVILLE J. FAM. L. 393, 441 (1985–86)); *see also* Hawk v. Hawk, 855 S.W.2d 573, 580 (Tenn. 1993) ("The requirement of harm is the sole protection that parents have against pervasive state interference in the parenting process."); Bean, *supra*, at 31 ("Short of preventing harm to the child, the standard of 'best interest of the child' is insufficient to serve as a compelling state interest overruling a parent's fundamental rights.").

126 None of this calls into question the black-letter family-law rule that courts assign custody on the basis of the "best interests of the child." This is what courts called to adjudicate family and custodial disputes *should* do. But the question, "what is in the best interests of [some other person's] child?," is *not* the right standard for identifying those situations when the Government may, *as an initial matter*, interfere with or intrude upon the family. Custody cases leave courts with little choice other than to engage in fantastically elaborate balancing exercises in order to identify that elusive arrangement that will serve the child's "best interests." *See* Carl E. Schneider, *Religion and Child Custody*, 25 U. MICH. J.L. REFORM 879, 904 (1992) ("Courts *have* to make custody decisions, and to make them as well as possible. . . . Courts must do what courts must do; they should avoid doing what they can do only badly."). In the educational context, unlike the child-custody context, the "costs" of intervention in the family—and these *are* costs—are not already sunk.

127 *See* Goldstein, *supra* note 30, at 670 ("[I]t is the absence of a substantial societal consensus about the legitimacy of state intrusion on parental autonomy . . . which is the best evidence for holding in check the use of state power to impose highly personal values on those who do not share them."); Schneider, *supra* note 126, at 904 ("Children will sometimes suffer because of their parents' disputes over religion. But we live with such disputes . . . all the time.").

conflict with the ideological commitments, or "rescue fantasies," of government functionaries.[128]

So, what "counts" as "harm"? I suggested earlier that the required-medical-treatment cases and questions about spiritual-treatment exemptions are made somewhat less difficult (though certainly not easy) by the fact that everyone agrees that the harm in question really is a harm.[129] People might strike differently the balance between the competing interests, in keeping with their different philosophical commitments, but there is still this agreement. What children should be taught to believe, however, is simply not a question of fact; it is an inescapably ideological, political, moral, and religious question. Reasonable pluralism is a given which, as I have tried to show, directs us in the debate over educational control away from a "best interests" focus and toward a "prevent harm" standard. But the education debate is not like the spiritual-treatment controversies in that people disagree not only about "best interests," but about "harm," too.

One way to reduce the range of possible disagreements about educational harm is to rule out of court the perspectives of insiders, opinions based on religious commitments, or otherwise illiberal views. If we stipulate that the State may not privilege religious views, and should not privilege illiberal ones, we can limit the permissible range of disagreement about harm to those disagreements that persist among those who subscribe to the secular ideology of the current political majority.[130] Coming at the problem another way, rather than limiting the kinds of interests and beliefs that may be considered, and ruling out religious or illiberal ones, we could narrow *ex ante* the kinds of things that can "count" as harm justifying government intervention.

---

128 Goldstein, *supra* note 30, at 651; *see also* Hillary Rodham, *Children Under the Law*, 43 Harv. Educ. Rev. 487, 513 (1973) (noting that the best-interests standard is "a rationalization by decision-makers justifying their judgments about a child's future, like an empty vessel into which adult perceptions and prejudices are poured").

129 If someone were to assert, though, that serious physical injury or death to a child were *not* a harm to be avoided (as opposed to claiming that, even though harmful, it must be accepted reluctantly), that view could, I think, be ruled out of the conversation as simply unreasonable. But again, it is not that religious objectors, generally speaking, do not think that death is a "harm" to be avoided. They simply disagree, in some cases, with the State about the best way to avoid that harm and about the morally permissible ways to avoid that harm. After all, even those "outsiders" who disagree with spiritual-healing advocates would concede, I suppose, that not *all* means of avoiding medical harm to children are permitted. *Cf.* Galston, *supra* note 17, at 872 (noting that, in the liberal tradition, not all means of achieving desirable ends are at a state's disposal).

130 *See generally* Dwyer, *supra* note 3, at 148.

For example, we might say that only *physical* harm counts, effectively ruling out all government supervention of education-related decisions.[131] After all, what conduct is "abusive" is, outside the physical-harm context, unavoidably contested.[132] But a physical-abuse-only limitation would likely unduly restrict the State's ability to respond to serious psychological and emotional abuse, abuse that is real notwithstanding the difficulty of defining it precisely. Are there any other categorical limits that we can place on what counts as "harm" to children?

I submit the (fairly modest) suggestion that religious education, the transmission of religious beliefs and traditions, and the religious or religion-based content of education should not be a permissible basis for government intervention or second-guessing. That is, the Government should neither come to nor act on the conclusion that religious teaching (as opposed to religiously inspired conduct) or religious education is harmful, at least not in a sense analogous to the physical harm that we all agree the Government may act to prevent. It does not matter if a child's best interests, as the State sees them, are ill-served by a particular religious teaching or set of beliefs, nor does it matter if the State thinks that a child would be a better liberal citizen, or that the preconditions of liberal democracy would be better served, or that liberalism generally would, in Gutmann's words, be better "reproduced," if the child were not exposed to that teaching or those beliefs.

Is such a rule defensible? I think so, and I have tried to outline such a defense here, inspired by the Court's warning that "[t]hose who begin coercive elimination of dissent soon find themselves exterminating dissenters. Compulsory unification of opinion achieves only

131 *See, e.g.*, GOLDSTEIN ET AL., *supra* note 14, at 111–27.

132 *Compare* DWYER, *supra* note 15, at 7–44 (arguing that many children are abused by traditional religious education), *and* Greene, *supra* note 75, at 406 ("Parental choice regarding their children is subject to state intervention when the parent abuses or neglects the child, and this can involve . . . educational abuse or neglect."), *with* GOLDSTEIN ET AL., *supra* note 14, at 114 ("In the face of . . . uncertainties and imprecise definitions of 'emotional neglect' and 'serious emotional damage,' neither concept should be used as a ground for modifying parent-child relationships."), *and* Mich. Ass'n Special Educ. Admin. v. Dep't Soc. Servs., 526 N.W.2d 36, 37, 39 (Mich. Ct. App. 1994) (refusing, for purposes of the State's abuse and neglect laws, to treat "parents' failure to act in conformity with petitioners' opinions regarding . . . children's educational needs" with abuse or "mental injury"). *See generally* Natalie Abrams, *Problems in Defining Child Abuse and Neglect*, *in* WHOSE CHILD? CHILDREN'S RIGHTS, PARENTAL AUTHORITY, AND STATE POWER 289 (William Aiken & Hugh LaFollette eds., 1980) (arguing that child abuse may be defined as a failure to respect children as autonomous individuals).

the unanimity of the graveyard. . . . If there is any fixed star in our constitutional constellation, it is that no official, high or petty, can prescribe what shall be orthodox . . . ."[133] "But seriously," one might complain, "is there *really* any danger of religious education, or the passing on of religious faith, being treated as sufficiently harmful to justify government intervention?"

Of course there is. The view that traditional or minority religious beliefs, religious beliefs not adequately re-formed by the premises of modernity, or religious beliefs that are taken seriously and not treated as a hobby, are "harmful" to children, both in their personal development and in their development as citizens, has been around and influential for a long time. It was, as I noted earlier, the view of many in the common-school movement and of many right-thinking twentieth century "progressives." *Harper's* was not alone in wondering "whether cruelty is not taught or necessarily infused in the doctrines of the Romish Church; whether the triumph of the Jesuits has not condemned the great body of its adherents to become the blind instruments of a persecuting creed. . . . [It cannot] be doubted that such inhuman teaching must fill with savage aspirations the ignorant and fanatical—must arouse the worst instincts of man."[134]

The "religion can be harmful to children" argument has at times even enjoyed a respectful hearing in at least some of the chambers of the United States Supreme Court. Justice Douglas, for example, dissenting in *Wisconsin v. Yoder*, complained that a child "harnessed to the Amish way of life" could suffer great harm; her "entire life may be stunted and deformed," and she could "be forever barred from entry into the new and amazing world of diversity that we have today."[135] If the child is not equipped to "break from the Amish tradition," Justice Douglas asked, how will she "be a pianist or an astronaut or an oceanographer[?]"[136]

---

133 W. Va. State Bd. of Educ. v. Barnette, 319 U.S. 624, 641–42 (1943); *see also* Lee v. Weisman, 505 U.S. 577, 594 (1992) ("[T]he government may no more use social pressure to enforce orthodoxy than it may use more direct means.").

134 Eugene Lawrence, *Hunter's Point—Compulsory Education*, HARPER'S WKLY., Dec. 23, 1871, at 1197.

135 Wisconsin v. Yoder, 406 U.S. 205, 245–46 (Douglas, J., dissenting).

136 *Id.* It seems unlikely that Justice Douglas was concerned that most children educated in public schools are poorly equipped by their education to "break from the [modernist] tradition" and become devout Amish believers. Similarly, Justice Stevens, in his *Kiryas Joel* concurrence, questioned the value of "a religious sect's interest in segregating itself and preventing its children from associating with their neighbors" and was concerned that the state law at issue in that case—which authorized an all-Hasidic village to have its own public-school district—"unquestionably increased the likelihood that they would remain within the fold, faithful adherents of their parents'

At times, some Justices' hostility toward religious instruction has degenerated from concerns about children's future opportunities to ugly assertions about the nature and aims of Catholic education. Recall the concurring opinion of Justices Black and Douglas in *Lemon v. Kurtzman*,[137] where they observed, quoting from a once-popular anti-Catholic tract:

> In the parochial schools Roman Catholic indoctrination is included in every subject. History, literature, geography, civics, and science are given a Roman Catholic slant. The whole education of the child is filled with propaganda. That, of course, is the very purpose of such schools, the very reason for going to all of the work and expense of maintaining a dual school system. Their purpose is not so much to educate, but to indoctrinate and train, not to teach Scripture truths and Americanism, but to make loyal Roman Catholics. The children are regimented, and are told what to wear, what to do, and what to think.[138]

Even today, there are those who echo such sentiments and who believe that Catholic schools—or, more generally, traditional religious education—are, or can be, harmful to children, both as citizens and in their development, and that this purported harm warrants govern-

---

religious faith." Bd. of Educ. of Kiryas Joel Vill. Sch. Dist. v. Grumet, 512 U.S. 687, 711 (1994) (Stevens, J., concurring). Why, one wonders, is this a bad thing—that children should "remain within the fold"? Does Justice Stevens believe it a proper function of the liberal State to *decrease* the likelihood that children remain "faithful adherents of their parents' religious faith"? Maybe so. Michael McConnell describes a University of Nebraska study that reported—evidently approvingly—that on-campus residency reduces the likelihood that college students will retain religious preferences. "Apparently, the University viewed abandonment of moral and religious upbringing as a liberating and enlightening development in the lives of students." McConnell, *supra* note 58, at 463 (discussing Rader v. Johnson, 924 F. Supp. 1540 (D. Neb. 1996)).

137 403 U.S. 602 (1971).

138 *Id.* at 635 (Douglas, J., concurring) (quoting LORAINE BOETTNER, ROMAN CATHOLICISM 360 (1962)). Justice Douglas continued, "One can imagine what a religious zealot, as contrasted to a civil libertarian, can do with the Reformation or with the Inquisition." *Id.* at 635–36. And in Justice Black's mind, Catholic schools posed more than a danger of slanted curricula.

> The same powerful sectarian religious propagandists who have succeeded in securing passage of the present law to help religious schools carry on their sectarian religious purposes can and doubtless will continue their propaganda, looking toward complete domination and supremacy of their particular brand of religion. And it nearly always is by insidious approaches that the citadels of liberty are most successfully attacked.

Bd. of Educ. v. Allen, 392 U.S. 236, 251–52 (1968) (Black, J., dissenting).

ment action and restrictions.[139] This is reason enough, it seems to me, for concern, and for retrieving and re-affirming *Pierce.*

Another cause for reasonable concern is the mountain of cases dealing with the treatment of religious beliefs in the context of child-custody disputes, cases where courts must decide whether and how the religious beliefs of parents (and children) should be factored into the "best interests" inquiry employed in custody matters.[140] Now, these

139 In Professor Dwyer's view, for example, the world of evangelical Christian, Catholic, Orthodox Jewish, and other traditional religious schools is heavily populated by neglected and abused children, who are being harmed as a result of their parents' decisions and the State's inaction just as surely as a child who is injured or dies because her parent refuses medical care on religious grounds. *See* DWYER, *supra* note 15, at 62–101 (exploring parents' rights to determine medical treatment for children, among other aspects of child-rearing). My own view, though, is that Professor Dwyer's claims about the harm to children from religious education reflect more his disagreement with Catholic, Orthodox Jewish, and evangelical Christian doctrine than a demonstration of "harm" sufficient to justify the kind of regulation he proposes. Although Professor Dwyer's arguments against parents' rights and his defense of children's welfare, as he sees it, are passionate and powerful, his tendentious portrait of Catholic schools, and his claim that these schools—and, evidently, Catholicism generally—are often harmful to children are seriously undermined by his reliance on highly polemical accounts of Catholic education and the Catholic Church. *See* JOANNE H. MEEHL, THE RECOVERING CATHOLIC: PERSONAL JOURNEYS OF WOMEN WHO LEFT THE CHURCH 69–98 (1995); *see also* Carter, *supra* note 27, at 1209 ("[S]uch arguments as these rest on questionable empirical propositions about what values children learn, and where, supported principally by anti-religious stereotypes rather than by any hard analysis of how religions operate."). For a detailed and, in my view, convincing response to Professor Dwyer's claim about the "sexist" and otherwise damaging nature of Catholic and other traditional religious schools, see Gilles, *supra* note 21, at 199–210.

140 For a *small* sampling of these cases, see, for example, *In re Marriage of Short*, 698 P.2d 1310, 1313 (Colo. 1985) (noting that unless religious beliefs are likely to result in physical or emotional harm, they are not relevant to custody); *Osteraas v. Osteraas*, 859 P.2d 948 (Idaho 1993) (pointing out that absent compelling reasons, custody proceedings may not favor religion over non-religion); *Osier v. Osier*, 410 A.2d 1027, 1031–32 (Me. 1980) (vacating custody order on the ground that the trial court granted custody to the father after giving undue weight to the mother's religious beliefs as a Jehovah's Witness); *Kendall v. Kendall*, 687 N.E.2d 1228 (Mass. 1997) (holding that a divorce judgment limiting defendant from sharing certain aspects of his "fundamentalist" Christian faith with child is constitutional); *Harris v. Harris*, 343 So. 2d 762, 763 (Miss. 1977) (commenting that the court has no authority to dictate what religion a parent teaches her child, unless it involves exposing him to physical danger or to "immoral" practices); *Zummo v. Zummo*, 574 A.2d 1130, 1157 (Pa. Super. Ct. 1990) (holding that an order prohibiting parent from taking children to non-Jewish religious services was unconstitutional); *Burrows v. Brady*, 605 A.2d 1312, 1316–17 (R.I. 1992) (holding that consideration of religious beliefs or disbeliefs are appropriate when determining what is in the best interests of the child); *Larson v. Larson*, 888 P.2d 719, 723–25 (Utah Ct. App. 1994) (holding that a parent's "religious compatibility"

are *custody* cases, cases where, generally speaking, the State has been called in, most likely by the parents, to adjudicate custody questions and has not intruded into the sphere of family association. A demanding threshold "harm" standard is probably not necessary to protect family integrity or to act as a check on government overreaching, because the family has, in effect, submitted itself to the Government for supervision and adjustment.[141] Still, courts in these cases often engage in "weighing the relative value" of parents' religious beliefs (or lack of beliefs) in light of their own sense of what is best for the parents' children.[142] This kind of weighing strikes me as a task for which courts are dangerously unsuited, and these custody cases caution strongly against endorsing, in the education context, a government prerogative to police for "harmful" elements the content of religious training.[143]

I cannot emphasize enough that my claim here is *not* that religion absolves parents who actually harm their children or that the Constitu-

with a child is an appropriate factor for a court to consider in determining custody); *Varnum v. Varnum*, 586 A.2d 1107, 1111–12 (Vt. 1990) (holding that religious practice must have a direct impact on a child's mental or physical health to be relevant to custody determination). *See also* Walker v. Johnson, 891 F. Supp. 1040, 1045–51 (M.D. Pa. 1995) (discussing limits on parents' control over a child's religious training generally). For more detailed discussions of the religion-and-custody issue, and of the many cases in which it arises, see generally Donald L. Beschle, *God Bless the Child?: The Use of Religion as a Factor in Child Custody and Adoption Proceedings*, 58 FORDHAM L. REV. 383 (1989); Barbara Handschu & Mary Kay Kisthardt, *Religion as a Custody Issue*, NAT'L L.J., Feb. 21, 2000, at A17 (examining "parameters for consideration of religious factors in both custody and visitation disputes"); Rebecca Korzec, *A Tale of Two Religions: A Contractual Approach to Religion as a Factor in Child Custody and Visitation Disputes*, 25 NEW ENG. L. REV. 1121 (1991); Schneider, *supra* note 126, at 879, 879–906 (surveying recent child custody decisions involving parents' religious disputes); Jennifer Benning, Note, *A Guide for Lower Courts in Factoring Religion into Child Custody Disputes*, 45 DRAKE L. REV. 733 (1997); Jennifer Ann Drobac, Note, *For the Sake of the Children: Court Consideration of Religion in Child Custody Cases*, 50 STAN. L. REV. 1609 (1998) (including survey of "over fifty state child custody cases since 1988"); Note, *The Establishment Clause and Religion in Child Custody Disputes: Factoring Religion into the Best Interest Equation*, 82 MICH. L. REV. 1702 (1984); Robyn E. Blumner, *Custody Rulings on Religion Flawed*, CLEVELAND PLAIN DEALER, Oct. 30, 1999, at 1F.

141 That said, "[t]o balance the competing rights of parents and children" in custody cases, "many courts have adopted a 'harm' standard. . . . [This] allows a court to examine parental religious practices in determining custody only if the practice causes the child a threshold level of harm." Lauren D. Freeman, *The Child's Best Interests vs. The Parent's Free Exercise of Religion*, 32 COLUM. J.L. & SOC. PROBS. 73, 78 (1998).

142 Beschle, *supra* note 140, at 400.

143 *See* Schneider, *supra* note 126, at 904 ("Courts *have* to make custody decisions, and to make them as well as possible. . . . Courts must do what courts must do; they should avoid doing what they can only do badly.").

tion entitles them to do so (though it certainly protects their liberty in a manner that enables parents, sometimes, to do badly by their children), but only that we should resist the temptation to treat as harmful the transmission of unpopular or illiberal religious beliefs. And I agree, as I hope I have made clear, that children's best interests are, in the end, the moral criteria for evaluating legal rules in this area. I am claiming, though, that children's best interests, and freedom generally, are best served when the State's ability to second-guess parents' decisions—especially in areas involving religion and education—is carefully limited, as it was in *Pierce,* to prevent those who happen to hold power and whose views happen to hold sway from imposing their own orthodoxy on other people's children in the name of advancing those children's best interests.[144]

Maybe traditional religious education, or a particular brand of religion itself, really does harm children by undermining their future capacities for choice, their future freedom and options and opportunities in life, their future autonomy. Maybe these children are deprived of the required grounding in shared values and deliberative skills and habits that being a good citizen in a liberal society requires. But I doubt it. In any event, in the face of uncertainty, it seems to me that we ought to require the Government to stay its hand and defer to parents' incentives, obligations, and love when it comes to deciding what children should learn, especially what they should learn, if anything, about faith. And who knows? Perhaps constraining the State, and clearing out space for families and for the "little platoons" of civil society to do their work,[145] would have the happy effect of encouraging and nurturing the development of precisely those other-regarding virtues that we are told liberal democracies cannot do without.

Conclusion: Families, Subsidiarity, and Subversion

There is no avoiding the fact that the Supreme Court's statements, in *Pierce* and elsewhere, about parental *control,* and about parents' *rights* to *direct* their children's upbringing and education, are jarring to many modern ears. It is easy to hear in such statements outdated and unappealing assertions of ownership and dominion over children. But this is not how we should read *Pierce* today. We should regard the case as a ringing endorsement of religious freedom and of limited government dominion over citizens. The French Revolution-

144 *See* Goldstein, *supra* note 30, at 664 ("[A] prime function of law is to prevent one person's truth . . . from becoming another person's tyranny.").

145 *See* Edmund Burke, Reflections on the Revolution in France 41 (J.G.A. Pocock ed., Hackett Pub. Co. 1987) (1790).

aries asserted the "right" not to be free from any authority that did *not* emanate from the State,[146] but we have learned to be wary of such atomizing freedoms. In *A Man for All Seasons,* Thomas More warns his son-in-law Will Roper—who boasts that he would "cut down every law in England" to "get after the Devil"—that "when the last law was down, and the Devil turned round," few of us "could stand upright in the winds that would blow."[147] Substitute the liberal state for the Devil, and mediating institutions, like the family, for the laws of England.

We can defend *Pierce* and at the same time recognize that parents are blessed with the opportunity to raise, nurture, and educate their children more than they are "entitled" to "control" them. Parents' rights and obligations flow from their *vocation,* not from their store of individual entitlements.[148] We are called to nurture, love, and educate children; we are not merely required or privileged by law to do so. In so doing, we participate, in a sense, in the creation of a human person whose dignity, I think we all agree, is inestimable.

I wonder, though, if *Pierce* is unavoidably anomalous in an intellectual and legal culture that views families more as contractual arrangements between autonomous individuals, or as dangerous seedbeds of oppression, inequality, and patriarchy—as "school[s] of despotism"[149]—instead of as the "first and vital cell[s] of society."[150] Perhaps *Pierce* and the cluster of values and maxims for which it is thought to stand are best defended not in terms of parents' individual "rights" against government, and certainly not in terms of ownership and property, but instead in terms of subsidiarity.[151] Maybe we should

---

146 *See* DECLARATION OF THE RIGHTS OF MAN AND CITIZEN, art. 3 (Fr. 1789).

147 Robert Bolt, *A Man for All Seasons* (1960), *reprinted in* PLAYS OF OUR TIME 631, 669 (Bennet Cerf ed., 1967).

148 This notion of parenthood as "vocation" is emphasized in my own religious tradition. *See* POPE JOHN PAUL II, LETTER TO FAMILIES, at No. 16 (U.S. Catholic Conference Pub'g Servs. 1994) ("*Parents are the first and most important educators* of their own children, and they also possess a *fundamental competence* in this area: they are *educators because they are parents.*" (emphasis added)); POPE JOHN PAUL II, *supra* note 12, at No. 36 ("The task of giving education is rooted in the primary vocation of married couples to participate in God's creative activity . . . .").

149 John Stuart Mill, *The Subjection of Women in* A VINDICATION OF THE RIGHTS OF WOMEN 217, 217 (Neill H. Alford, Jr. et al. eds., 1993).

150 POPE JOHN PAUL II, *supra* note 12, at No. 42 (quoting SECOND VATICAN ECUMENICAL COUNCIL, APOSTOLICAM ACTUOSITATEM [DECREE ON THE APOSTOLATE OF THE LAITY], at No. 11 (1965)); *cf.* Parham v. J.R., 442 U.S. 584, 602 (1979) ("Our jurisprudence historically has reflected Western civilization concepts of *the family as a unit* with broad parental authority over minor children." (emphasis added) (citations omitted)).

151 Subsidiarity is, in twentieth-century Catholic social thought, the principle according to which

think of the family, as it appears in *Pierce* and in contemporary debates about civic education, parental authority, and religious freedom, as the original "mediating institution." On this view, the State properly refrains from second-guessing families on matters of education and the transmission of religious tradition not only out of respect for the religious freedom and parental authority of the individuals situated within those families, but also out of wise regard for those families' integrity and health, precisely because the integrity and freedom of these "vital cells" is important to the common good.[152]

On the other hand, not only are families constitutive elements of civil society, supporting the entirely legitimate "higher" associations, including the State, they are also, and should be, *subversive.* Like the Church, the family is an organic "community of persons"[153] and an independent (from the State) source of meaning and value.[154] At their best, families can provide, for their members, their neighbors, and society, a prophetic counter-weight to the State, just as, at its best, religious faith challenges and subverts the State's claims to virtue and competence. This is precisely why statists understandably seek to atomize the family and to minimize religion's influence through perse-

> a community of a higher order should not interfere in the internal life of a community of a lower order, depriving the latter of its functions, but rather should support it in case of need and help to co-ordinate its activity with the activities of the rest of society, always with a view to the common good.

U.S. CATHOLIC CONFERENCE, *supra* note 4, § 1883; *see also* Mary Ann Glendon, *Civil Service,* THE NEW REPUBLIC, Apr. 1, 1996, at 39, 40 (describing "subsidiarity" as "the principle of leaving social tasks to the smallest social unit that can perform them adequately"). "Subsidiarity" is also a more technical term in international and European Community law. *See generally* George A. Bermann, *Taking Subsidiarity Seriously: Federalism in the European Community and the United States,* 94 COLUM. L. REV. 331 (1994).

152 *See, e.g.,* Pope Pius XI, *Quadragesimo anno* [On Reconstructing the Social Order] ¶ 79, *in* CONTEMPORARY CATHOLIC SOCIAL TEACHING 47, 71 (National Conference of Catholic Bishops ed., 1991) ("[I]t is an injustice and at the same time a grave evil and disturbance of right order to assign to a greater and higher association what lesser and subordinate organizations can do.").

153 POPE JOHN PAUL II, *supra* note 12, at Nos. 18, 26; *see also* SECOND VATICAN ECUMENICAL COUNCIL, DECLARATION ON RELIGIOUS LIBERTY [*Dignitatis humanae*], at No. 5, *in* VATICAN COUNCIL II 803 (Austin Flannery, O.P. ed., rev. ed. 1992) ("Every family . . . is a society with its own basic right.").

154 *See* Greene, *supra* note 75, at 406–07; *see also* Marci Hamilton, *Power, The Establishment Clause, and Vouchers,* 31 CONN. L. REV. 807, 808 (1999) ("[T]he entire Constitution is governed by the overarching principle that society is best served when centers of power are kept separate.").

cution, suppression, or co-option,[155] or perhaps through the milder methods of civic education.[156]

I have argued that *Pierce* points to ideals that should be taken seriously, that do not conflict with personalist ideals regarding children's dignity, and that are—especially in the context of education and religious training—worth defending vigorously. In *Pierce*, the integrity of the family, the educational rights of parents, the limits on the State's power to standardize thought, and the rightful demands of the common good are all grounded firmly, as child-centered liberals would insist they must be, in the dignity of the human person.[157] Still, it could be that defenses of *Pierce* that fail to move beyond parents'-rights terms to discussions about the family *as a* society, and about its supportive and subversive role *in* society, will not be able to respond as powerfully as they must to the increasingly confident claims made for government intervention in the name of civic education.

155 George Weigel provides a wonderful account of communist Poland's efforts in this regard in his recent biography of Pope John Paul II. *See* GEORGE WEIGEL, WITNESS TO HOPE: THE BIOGRAPHY OF POPE JOHN PAUL II 140–41, 300–25 (1999).

156 As Stephen Carter has observed, "[q]uite simply, religion in its subversive mode provides the believer with a transcendent reason to question the power of the state. That is the reason that the state will always try to domesticate religion: to avoid being subverted." Carter, *supra* note 57, at 1060; *see also id.* ("Often the willingness of the religious to be subversive in the face of official and unofficial pressures has made the nation better.").

157 *See, e.g.*, Dwyer, *supra* note 3, at 177 ("There are widely shared moral beliefs and legal rules about how we should treat people simply by virtue of their personhood.").

THE CONTEMPORARY SIGNIFICANCE OF *MEYER* AND *PIERCE* FOR PARENTAL RIGHTS ISSUES INVOLVING EDUCATION

by

William G. Ross*

The appropriate relationship between government and parents in the education of children is an issue that has created recorded controversy since Plato advocated the communal rearing of children. The U.S. Supreme Court first addressed this issue in two landmark decisions during the 1920s in which the Court forcefully declared that the Due Process Clause of the Fourteenth Amendment protects the right of parents to direct the education of their offspring.[1]

In the first case, *Meyer v. Nebraska* in 1923, the Court held that several state statutes prohibiting the teaching of German to elementary school children interfered with "the power of parents to control the education of their own."[2] The statutes, enacted in the wake of the First World War for the stated purpose of ensuring the assimilation of German-Americans who lived in isolated ethnic enclaves, were motivated in large measure by the nativism and xenophobia that swept the nation in the years immediately following the war.[3] The Court's opinion observed that the Platonic guardianship of children was at odds with American concepts of liberty.[4] In its earliest recognition that due process embraces human rights as well as economic rights, the Court in *Meyer* observed in *dictum* that "the individual has certain fundamental rights which must be respected."[5] Although the Court explained that the meaning of liberty within the Fourteenth Amendment cannot be defined "with exactness," the Court declared that these liberties include, but are not necessarily limited to, "the right to marry, establish a home, and bring up children."[6]

---

* Professor, Cumberland School of Law, Samford University. A.B., Stanford, 1976; J.D., Harvard, 1979. Professor Ross is the author of a book about the *Meyer* and *Pierce* decisions, FORGING NEW FREEDOMS: NATIVISM, EDUCATION AND THE CONSTITUTION, 1917-1927 (1994).

[1] Meyer v. Nebraska, 262 U.S. 390 (1923); Pierce v. Society of the Sisters, 268 U.S. 510 (1925).

[2] *Meyer*, 262 U.S. at 401.

[3] *See* WILLIAM G. ROSS, FORGING NEW FREEDOMS: NATIVISM, EDUCATION, AND THE CONSTITUTION, 1917-1927, at 57-95 (1994).

[4] 262 U.S. at 401-02.

[5] *Id.* at 401.

[6] *Id.* at 399.

These are moving words – among the most eloquent in the Court's canon. Their meaning, however, remains enigmatic.

In the second case, *Pierce v. Society of the Sisters* in 1925, the Court struck down an Oregon statute that required all children to attend public elementary school. The law, which was part of a national campaign for compulsory public elementary education, was animated by anti-Catholicism and probably would have resulted in the closing of all comprehensive non-public schools since few parents would have sent their children to both full-time public and private schools.[7] The Court held that the statute "unreasonably interfere[d] with the liberty of parents and guardians to direct the upbringing and education of children under their control."[8] The Court explained that:

> [t]he fundamental theory of liberty upon which all governments in this Union repose excludes any general power of the State to standardize its children by forcing them to accept instruction from public teachers only. The child is not the mere creature of the State; those who nurture him and direct his destiny have the right, coupled with the high duty, to recognize and prepare him for additional obligations.[9]

Despite their ringing declarations about human rights, *Meyer* and *Pierce* were both formally decided largely on the basis of property rights — the liberty of the schools to conduct a business, the right of private school teachers to follow their occupation, and the freedom of the schools and the parents to enter into contracts.[10] Although the Court easily could have decided the cases on the bases of freedom of religion or freedom of speech,[11] the Court had not yet incorporated any part of the Bill of Rights into state law, and it was not prepared to begin the process of incorporation in these cases.[12]

---

[7] *See* ROSS, *supra* note 3, at 134-59.

[8] 268 U.S. at 534-35.

[9] *Id.* at 535.

[10] *See* ROSS, *supra* note 3, at 186-87.

[11] As Justice Kennedy recently observed, "*Pierce* and *Meyer*, had they been decided in recent times, may well have been grounded upon First Amendment principles protecting freedom of speech, belief, and religion." Troxel v. Granville, 120 S. Ct. 2054, 2076 (2000) (Kennedy, J., dissenting).

[12] ROSS, *supra* note 3, at 189-91. *Meyer* and *Pierce* may be seen as a bridge to incorporation, however, insofar as they were, for all practical purposes, the first decisions in which the Court struck down state legislation that interfered with

The Court's reliance upon substantive due process was consistent with its suspicion of social and economic regulatory legislation. But while the Court rejected the arguments of the states that only public education could instill democratic values in children, the Court did not deny that the states had a compelling need to foster such values in youth. This accommodation of the rights of the parents and the needs of the state seemed to strike an appropriate balance at the time, and the decisions received widespread popular approval, for they seemed to offer something to everyone.[13] Ethnic Americans hailed the decision as a strike against nativism,[14] liberals welcomed the Court's defense of human rights,[15] and economic conservatives correctly perceived that the decisions would discourage growing efforts by progressives to curb the Court's power.[16] Coming at a time when the nativism that had motivated the statutes was waning, the decisions abruptly terminated a widespread compulsory public education movement.

The decisions may therefore be more controversial today than they were 75 years ago. Like many other judicial decisions, *Meyer* and *Pierce* have had unforeseen and indeed strange doctrinal consequences. Beginning almost immediately after *Pierce*, the Court suspended its use of substantive due process in personal liberties cases in favor of selective incorporation of the Bill of Rights. Although, after 1937, the Court rejected even in economic cases the substantive due process theory upon which *Meyer* and *Pierce* are based, the decisions provided the cornerstone for the Court's revival of substantive due process in the context of personal liberties during the 1960s and 1970s.[17] The conservative Lutherans

---

personal liberties. The Court began the process of incorporation only seven days after it decided *Pierce* when it stated in *dictum* in *Gitlow v. New York*, 268 U.S. 652 (1925), that the First Amendment's protection of free speech and the press is incorporated into state law. *See* ROSS, *supra* note 3, at 191-97.

[13] Although *Pierce* was unanimously decided, Oliver Wendell Holmes, Jr., and George Sutherland dissented in *Meyer* on the ground that the statutes did not unduly restrict the freedom of either the teachers or the students because the laws were a reasonable and perhaps necessary means of achieving the desirable state interest of having citizens use a common language. Meyer v. Nebraska, 262 U.S. 3990, 412-13 (1923). For a discussion of these dissents, see ROSS, *supra* note 3, at 130-32.

[14] *See* ROSS, *supra* note 3, at 172-73.

[15] *Id.* at 195-96.

[16] *Id.* at 193-95. *See also* WILLIAM G. ROSS, A MUTED FURY: POPULISTS, PROGRESSIVES AND LABOR UNIONS CONFRONT THE COURTS, 1890-1937, at 246-49, 286-87 (1994).

[17] *See, e.g.*, Roe v. Wade, 410 U.S. 113 (1973) (invalidating anti-abortion statute); Griswold v. Connecticut, 381 U.S. 479 (1965) (invalidating statute that prohibited use of contraceptives).

and Roman Catholics who challenged the laws that the Court struck down in *Meyer* and *Pierce* might not have hailed the Court so heartily for saving their schools if they could have known that these decisions would provide the foundation for the Court's enunciation of a right to privacy that culminated in *Roe v. Wade.* Cultural conservatives today may disdain the use of these decisions in support of abortion rights, but they hail *Meyer* and *Pierce* as the cornerstone of parental rights.[18] Meanwhile, many liberals who may approve of the privacy doctrines for which *Meyer* and *Pierce* provide the foundation believe that the decisions unduly diminish the rights of children. From a feminist perspective, some scholars have criticized the decisions for reinforcing patriarchy.[19]

Few critics of *Meyer* and *Pierce* today are motivated by the antagonism against ethnic Americans and Roman Catholicism that animated the legislation that *Meyer* and *Pierce* nullified. Like the proponents of that legislation, however, some people today continue to view non-public schooling with suspicion because they believe that non-public education tends to promote racial, economic, and cultural divisiveness that contravenes the interest of both the state and the child.

Some critics of private education have even gone so far as to revive the prospect of compulsory public education. These critics point out that the decisions were based in part upon a now-discredited theory of economic due process. Moreover, they remind us that there may have been more latitude for parental control over education during the 1920s,

---

[18] For example, while this paper was being revised after the conference, courts relied upon *Pierce* in two major decisions involving parental rights. In *Troxel v. Granville,* 120 S. Ct. 2054 (2000), the U.S. Supreme Court cited *Meyer* and *Pierce* to support its decision to invalidate a state law that allowed a court to permit grandparents to visit a grandchild more than the parent wished to authorize. *See also infra* note 72 and accompanying text. In another recent decision, the Eleventh Circuit cited *Pierce's* recognition of the importance of the parent-child relationship in support of its decision affirming the dismissal of a claim that the Immigration and Naturalization Service denied due process to a six-year-old alien by dismissing his asylum application as void on the ground that the minor lacked the capacity to seek asylum without his father's consent. Gonzalez v. Reno, 212 F.3d 1338 (11th Cir. 2000), *cert. denied,* 120 S. Ct. 2737 (2000). *See also* PHILIP BOBBITT, CONSTITUTIONAL FATE 239-40 (1982); ROSS, *supra* note 3, at 190-91.

[19] *See, e.g.,* Barbara Bennett Woodhouse, *"Who Owns the Child?":* Meyer *and* Pierce *and the Child as Property,* 33 WM. & MARY L. REV. 995, 996-1001, 1112-22 (1992). Professor Woodhouse has argued that the decisions aggrandize private rights at the expense of community values and constitutionalized "a patriarchal notion of parental rights" that "interrupted the trend of family law moving toward children's rights." *Id.* at 1113.

when education was less important than it is today. Stricter enforcement of truancy laws, racial integration of schools, and abolition of child labor are all expressions of changed attitudes toward education's importance. Mark Tushnet has suggested that the shaky substantive due process grounds on which *Pierce* is based might permit Congress, pursuant to Section Five of the Fourteenth Amendment, to prohibit private schools on the ground that they unduly interfere with "society's ability to reach a point of integration where judgments about people's worth are made solely on the basis of individual merit."[20] Similarly, Abner Greene has stated that compulsory public education "would ensure that all children are exposed to multiple sources of authority and knowledge" and "would free up funds used for private schooling and would direct parental energies at improving the public schools."[21] And James S. Liebman has suggested that public education be compulsory to the extent that parents who have religious objections could elect to remove their children.[22]

These criticisms of *Pierce* are part of a broader assault on parental rights. Professor James G. Dwyer has argued that parental child-rearing rights are illegitimate and that parents should enjoy only a "legal privilege to care for and make decisions on behalf of children in ways that are not contrary to the children's best interests."[23]

Contemporary criticisms of *Meyer* and *Pierce*, however, do not diminish the enduring significance of the decisions for human rights. Even though the Court abandoned economic due process after 1937, the Court's growing solicitude for personal liberties indicates that the Court

---

[20] Mark Tushnet, *Public and Private Education: Is There a Constitutional Difference?*, 1991 U. CHI. LEGAL F. 43, 54 (1991). Professor Tushnet contends that "[t]hat justification is more substantial than the one offered in *Pierce*, and it might be sufficient to overcome the weakened protection given substantive due process rights by the Court's analysis" in *Bowers v. Hardwick*, 478 U.S. 186 (1986) (upholding state statute prohibiting sodomy).

[21] Abner S. Greene, *Why Vouchers are Unconstitutional, and Why They're Not*, 13 NOTRE DAME J.L. ETHICS & PUB. POL'Y 397, 407 (1999).

[22] James S. Liebman, *Voice Not Choice*, 101 YALE L.J. 259, 307 (1991) (reviewing JOHN E. CHUBB & TERRY M. MOE, POLITICS, MARKETS, AND AMERICA'S SCHOOLS (1990)). Professor Liebman explains that "[b]y curtailing exit from public schools except by the few citizens whose religious beliefs require them to exit organized society, the states could stem enough . . . escape to promote genuine voice-activated educational reform and simultaneously extend a civic education to all young people whose coming participation in the larger society requires it." *Id.*

[23] James G. Dwyer, *Parents' Religion and Children's Welfare: Debunking the Doctrine of Parents' Rights*, 82 CAL. L. REV. 1371, 1447 (1994). *See also* JAMES G. DWYER, RELIGIOUS SCHOOLS V. CHILDREN'S RIGHTS (1998).

would reach the same result today. Now, however, a court would probably hold that the First Amendment's Free Exercise Clause compels the state to permit parents to have the option to send their children to a sectarian school. To the extent that the right of parents to prefer a sectarian school to a public school is now presumably guaranteed by the Free Exercise Clause, that right is probably more secure than it was at the time of *Pierce*. Insofar as a parent's right to send his child to a private, non-sectarian school must remain grounded in generic due process, however, the right is vulnerable to complaints against the non-textual vagueness of substantive due process. In contrast to Meyer's attorney, who in his autobiography hailed the *Meyer* decision for its vision of a "fenceless land of liberty,"[24] many critics of the opinion would prefer to confine liberty within at least some fences, particularly if the Supreme Court is going to be the ultimate surveyor of liberty's terrain.

Although substantive due process invites excessive judicial activism, and even though courts during the past twenty years have exhibited little willingness to expand the parameters of substantive due process, the doctrine that there are certain rights that are not specifically mentioned in the Constitution seems likely to remain secure because there are certain unwritten rights that most Americans believe to exist. If indeed there are any fundamental rights that are not spelled out in the Constitution, then many persons – myself included – would count among these the right of a parent to exercise a high level of control over a child's education, for child-rearing involves the most intimate aspects of one's life and is a critical expression of personal autonomy.

The Supreme Court recently re-affirmed the vitality of *Meyer* and *Pierce* in its decision in *Troxel v. Granville*, which nullified a Washington statute that permitted state courts to exercise broad discretion to override parental decisions concerning the visits of third parties with their children.[25] Citing *Meyer* and *Pierce*, Justice O'Connor's plurality opinion declared that "[t]he liberty interest at issue in this case – the interest of parents in the care, custody, and control of their children – is perhaps the oldest of the fundamental liberty interests recognized by this Court."[26]

But while *Troxel* demonstrates the continuing significance of *Meyer* and *Pierce*, it also illustrates the continuing enigma of those decisions. Although Justice Kennedy correctly pointed out in his dissent that all of the Justices seemed to agree that a "custodial parent has a constitutional right to determine, without undue interference by the state, how best to

---

[24] ROSS, *supra* note 3, at 192 (citing ARTHUR F. MULLEN, WESTERN DEMOCRAT 226 (1940)).

[25] Troxel v. Granville, 120 S. Ct. 2054, 2060 (2000).

[26] *Id.*

raise, nurture and educate the child,"[27] various members of the Court interpreted this right in different ways. Both the four-justice plurality opinion and Justice Souter's concurring opinion relied heavily upon *Meyer* and *Pierce* to argue that parents have a powerful interest in controlling their children's personal associations.[28] As Justice Souter acknowledged in his concurring opinion, however, the Court's decisions "have not set out exact metes and bounds to the protected interest of a parent in the relationship with his child."[29] Therefore, it is not surprising, as Justice Thomas pointed out in his concurrence, in which he argued in favor of strict scrutiny, that the opinions of the Court and of Justice Souter did not articulate a standard of review for legislation that interferes with the parental rights enunciated by *Meyer* and *Pierce*.[30]

Although Justice Scalia's dissent acknowledges that parents have fundamental rights to "direct the upbringing of their children," Justice Scalia contends that the Court lacks power to nullify legislation that infringes on those rights.[31] Pointing out that *Meyer*, *Pierce*, and *Wisconsin v. Yoder*[32] are the only decisions in which the Court had relied "in whole or in part upon a substantive constitutional right of parents to direct the upbringing of their children," Justice Scalia contends that the "sheer diversity" of the opinions in *Troxel* persuaded him that "the theory of unenumerated parental rights underlying [*Meyer*, *Pierce*, and *Yoder*] has

---

[27] *Id.* at 2076 (Kennedy, J., dissenting).

[28] *Id.* at 2060; *id.* at 2066 (Souter, J., concurring). As Justice Souter stated:

> *Meyer's* repeatedly recognized right of upbringing would be a sham if it failed to encompass the right to be free of judicially compelled visitation by "any party" at "any time" a judge believed he "could make a 'better' decision" than the objecting parent had done. The strength of a parent's interest in controlling a child's associates is as obvious as the influence of personal associations on the development of the child's social and moral character.

Id. at 2066-67. Souter also concluded that *Pierce* implied that "parental choice in such matters is not merely a default rule in the absence of either governmental choice or the government's designation of an official with the power to choose for whatever reason and in whatever circumstances." *Troxel*, 120 S. Ct. at 2067.

[29] *Id.* at 2066 (Souter, J., concurring).

[30] *Id.* at 2068 (Thomas, J., concurring).

[31] *Id.* at 2074 (Scalia, J., dissenting).

[32] 406 U.S. 205 (1972) (holding that enforcement of state law requiring school attendance past the eighth grade violated the free exercise rights of the Amish).

small claim to stare decisis protection. A legal principle that can be thought to produce such diverse outcomes in the relatively simple case before us here is not a legal principle that has induced substantial reliance."[33] Similarly, Justice Kennedy's dissent argues that, while the principle of parental rights as articulated by *Meyer* and *Pierce* exists "in broad formulation," the "courts must use considerable restraint, including careful adherence to the incremental instruction given by the precise facts of particular cases, as they seek to give further and more precise definition to the right."[34]

While *Pierce* therefore clearly provides a constitutional foundation for some type of parental rights, the scope of those rights remains unclear. Certainly parental rights are far from absolute. Clearly there are some limits on a parent's right to control a child's education, or else, as one court has observed, "a truant's parent could plausibly proclaim that he or she was exercising his or her right while 'home-schooling' the child to be a safe-cracker or prostitute."[35] Moreover, the language in *Pierce* stating that "the child is not the mere creature of the state"[36] may withhold more parental autonomy than it confers, for the use of the word "mere"could be read to suggest that the child is primarily the creature of the state. If the Court had believed that parental powers were generally paramount to governmental powers, the Court might have stated that "the child is not primarily the creature of the state."[37] The Court's decision in *Pierce* also declared that the state had the right to regulate non-public schools,[38] a right that the non-public schools that op-

---

[33] *Troxel*, 120 S. Ct. at 2074 (Scalia, J., dissenting). Scalia also observed that *Meyer* and *Pierce* were "from an era rich in substantive due process holdings that have since been repudiated." *Id.*

[34] *Id.* at 2076.

[35] Hubbard v. Buffalo Indep. Sch. Dist., 20 F. Supp. 2d 1012, 1015 (W.D. Tex. 1998) (holding that a school district's policy of requiring students who transferred from non-accredited or home schools to pass proficiency tests at their own expense did not burden free exercise of religion).

[36] Pierce v. Society of the Sisters, 268 U.S. 510, 535 (1925).

[37] If the Court had regarded the rights of the parent as paramount, the Court likewise might have stated that "the child is not the mere creature of the parent," although there would have been little point in using this language since the decision was directed against the power of the state rather than the power of the parent. The Court's use of the word "mere," however, must be read in the context of the Court's seemingly broad declaration of parental rights: "those who nurture [the child] and direct his destiny have the right, coupled with the high duty, to recognize and prepare him for additional obligations." 268 U.S. at 535.

[38] The Court stated that:

posed compulsory education had acknowledged and indeed emphasized in support of their position.[39]

Furthermore, the U.S. Supreme Court has never specifically stated that the right of parents to direct the education of their children is actually a "fundamental" right that would trigger strict judicial scrutiny of legislation that affects that right. The determination of the scope of the parental right to educate children is further complicated because the Court has refused to categorize education itself as a fundamental right.[40] Accordingly, there is no clear standard of review that a federal court must apply in reviewing legislation that affects the rights of parents to direct the education of their children.[41] The First Circuit has recently pointed out that the Supreme Court "has yet to decide whether the right to direct the upbringing and education of one's children is among those fundamental rights whose infringement merits heightened scrutiny."[42] Accordingly, the Second Circuit has held that parents lack a fundamental right to direct their children's education and that "rational basis review is appropriate" in cases in which parents seek to exempt their children from educational procedures.[43] Although legislation presumably

---

> [n]o question is raised concerning the power of the State reasonably to regulate all schools, to inspect, supervise and examine them, their teachers and pupils; to require that all children of proper age attend some school, that teachers shall be of good moral character and patriotic disposition, that certain studies plainly essential to good citizenship be taught, and that nothing be taught which is manifestly inimical to the public welfare.

268 U.S. at 534.

[39] ROSS, *supra* note 3, at 163 (citing oral argument in the *Pierce* case). Opponents of a compulsory public education movement in Michigan during the early 1920s tried to discourage campaigns against non-public schools by promoting legislation to require closer state supervision of non-public schools. *Id.* at 140-41.

[40] *See* Plyler v. Doe, 457 U.S. 202, 221 (1982); San Antonio Indep. Sch. Dist. v. Rodriguez, 411 U.S. 1 (1973).

[41] As one commentator recently observed, "[c]onfusion and inconsistency reign as to the proper standards for judicial review." Eric W. Schulze, *The Constitutional Right of Parents to Direct the Education of Their Children*, 138 EDUC. L. REP. 583, 587 (1999).

[42] Brown v. Hot, Sexy, and Safer Productions, Inc., 68 F.3d 525, 533 (1st Cir. 1995).

[43] Immediato v. Rye Neck Sch. Dist., 73 F.3d 454, 461 (2d Cir. 1996).

is subject to a heightened standard of review when parents claim that public school practices infringe upon their religious rights as well as their parental rights, the level of scrutiny even here is unclear.[44] The situation is further complicated by a number of state court decisions that indicate that education is a fundamental right under state constitutions.[45]

Since both federal and state courts have generally refused to read *Pierce* as conferring a fundamental right upon parents that would trigger strict scrutiny of legislation affecting parental rights, parental rights advocates recently have unsuccessfully sponsored parental-rights amendments in Congress and in numerous states. A parental-rights amendment was defeated in a 1996 initiative in Colorado by a margin of 58 to 42 percent.[46] These proposed amendments typically track the language of *Pierce* by asserting the liberty of parents and guardians to direct the upbringing and education of children under their control. Although advocates of amendments based on the language of *Pierce* contend that an amendment would merely codify *Pierce*, such amendments would interfere with the subtle balance between parental rights and the rights of the state which have been worked out since *Pierce* by impeding efforts to curtail child abuse and providing more impetus for school vouchers.[47] A parental-rights amendment also would be superfluous since many statutes already contain parental-rights provisions.[48]

Moreover, such amendments might unduly interfere with the power of school officials to make curriculum decisions and provide parents with a virtual veto over curriculum that they find objectionable. This would allow a minority of parents the power to overrule the decisions of

---

[44] As one commentator has pointed out, when courts are "faced with hybrid claims asserting violations of both parental and religious constitutional rights, another layer of inconsistency and confusion is added to the judicial mix." Schulze, *supra* note 41, at 596.

[45] *See* Kelly Thompson Cochran, Comment, *Beyond School Financing: Defining the Constitutional Right to an Adequate Education*, 78 N.C. L. REV. 399, 401-02 (2000).

[46] Jean Hellwege, *Parents Seek Control Over Children's Lives in Legislatures, Courts*, TRIAL, May 1999, at 15.

[47] Judith Schaeffer, Deputy Legal Director for People for the American Way, has stated that "[a] blanket constitutional amendment that says parents have a constitutional right to direct the upbringing of their children sounds innocuous, but it's a wolf in sheep's clothing. Good parents don't need it, and bad parents would abuse it." *Id.* at 13-14.

[48] For example, Texas law provides specific rights to parents, including the right to review all teaching materials used in the classroom, the right to file a grievance to be heard by the school board, and a limited right of prior consent before a child may be videotaped by a school employee. TEX. EDUC. CODE ANN. §26.001-26.012 (West 1995).

elected officials, thereby substituting a crude form of direct democracy for republican government. Such a veto power would interfere with the curricular preferences of a majority of parents, thereby interfering with their right to direct their children's education by sending them to public schools.[49] These amendments also might violate the constitutional rights of teachers to teach and students to learn.[50]

Similarly, the amendments would pose a perennial threat of litigation that would tend to encourage school administrators to dilute the curriculum, reaching for the lowest common denominator of public sensibilities.[51] The danger of more litigation might be particularly potent because a parental-rights amendment might shift the standard of judicial scrutiny of governmental interference with parental rights from the "rational basis" standard that is presently used in most cases to an intermediate standard, or even to a compelling-interest test.

In the absence of a more compelling standard of review of government action that affects parental rights, *Pierce* has generally not enabled public school parents to persuade courts to permit them to remove their children from practices and programs to which they object.[52] The Supreme Court's anomalous decision in *Wisconsin v. Yoder* is the only education decision in which *Pierce* has been successfully invoked. In one much publicized case in which parents objected to a sexually-explicit AIDS awareness assembly that their children were required to attend, the First Circuit stated that *Pierce* does not provide "a fundamental constitutional right to dictate the curriculum at the public school to which they have chosen to send their children . . . . If all parents had a fundamental constitutional right to dictate individually what the schools teach their children, the schools would be forced to cater a curriculum for each student whose parents had genuine moral disagreements with the school's choice of subject matter."[53] In other similar decisions, federal courts have

---

[49] *See* Jennifer L. Sabourin, Note, *Parental Rights Amendments: Will a Statutory Right to Parent Force Children to " 'Shed Their Constitutional Rights' at the Schoolhouse Door?,"* 44 WAYNE L. REV. 1899, 1917, 1920, (1999). As Ms. Sabourin has pointed out, "[p]arents only have a constitutional right in directing their own children and not the children of other parents." *Id.* at 1920.

[50] *Id.* at 1923.

[51] *Id.* at 1920.

[52] As one commentator has observed, "[t]he federal courts narrowly have restricted *Meyer, Pierce,* and *Yoder* to the facts of those cases. The courts are unwilling to grant parents any general power to select the educational requirements with which they will or will not comply, under the rubric of the constitutional right of parents to direct the education of their children." Schulze, *supra* note 41, at 596.

[53] Brown v. Hot, Sexy and Safer Productions, Inc., 68 F.3d 525, 533-34 (1st Cir.

held that parents of public school children had no constitutional basis for objecting to the administration of psychological counseling to a third grader;[54] the imposition of corporal punishment on a sixth grader;[55] a mandatory sex education program;[56] a compulsory community service program;[57] mandatory academic achievement testing;[58] and a period for silent meditation or prayer not exceeding one minute.[59]

Courts also have rejected parental objections to public school practices and curriculum even in cases in which parents have relied both on parental rights and the free exercise of religion. In its controversial decision in *Mozert v. Hawkins County Board of Education*, the Sixth Circuit, for example, rejected efforts by parents to have their children opt out of reading a textbook that contained passages that were deeply offensive to fundamentalist Christians. The Court held that mere exposure to this curriculum did not unconstitutionally burden the free exercise of religion.[60]

One of the most troubling aspects of *Mozert* is that the curriculum that the parents challenged may have marginalized the religious beliefs of the parents because its numerous references to religion virtually ignored Christianity, particularly Protestantism. Two of the judges on the panel aptly expressed regret that the school board could not have done more to accommodate the needs of the parents who objected to the curriculum. Nevertheless, they rather ruefully acknowledged that the parents' remedy was political rather than judicial. As one of the judges explained, "[a] constitutional challenge to the content of instruction . . . is a challenge to the notion of a politically-controlled school system."[61]

It is not difficult to collect examples of public school curricula to which reasonable parents might object. To one degree or another, many schools have succumbed to the latest trends in political correctness and/

1995). The Court declared that "[w]e cannot see that the Constitution imposes such a burden on state educational systems, and accordingly find that the rights of parents as described by *Meyer* and *Pierce* do not encompass a broad-based right to restrict the flow of information in the public schools." *Id.* at 534.

[54] Newkirk v. East Lansing Pub. Sch., 57 F.3d 1070 (6th Cir. 1995).

[55] Baker v. Owen, 395 F. Supp. 294, 299 (M.D.N.C. 1975), *aff'd without opinion*, 423 U.S. 907 (1975).

[56] Cornwell v. State Bd. of Educ., 314 F. Supp. 340, 344 (D.C. Md. 1969), *aff'd*, 428 F.2d 471, 472 (4th Cir. 1970) (per curiam).

[57] Immediato v. Rye Neck Sch. Dist., 73 F.3d 454, 461-62 (2d Cir. 1996).

[58] Hubbard v. Buffalo Indep. Sch. Dist., 20 F. Supp. 2d 1012, 1017 (W.D. Tex. 1998).

[59] Gaines v. Anderson, 421 F. Supp. 337, 346 (D. Mass. 1976).

[60] Mozert v. Hawkins County Bd. of Educ., 827 F.2d 1058, 1058 (6th Cir. 1987).

[61] *Id.* at 1079 (Boggs, J., concurring).

or to promoting sexual license. All too many criticisms of the public schools, however, begin with an anecdote about a loony curriculum and conclude with the *non sequitur* that public schools as a class are irredeemably depraved. Curricular abuses are inevitable when tens of millions of children attend tens of thousands of public schools. While many parents clearly have legitimate objections to public school curriculum, the ability of the political system to accommodate parental concerns about public school curriculum is demonstrated by the fact that the percentage of students enrolled in private schools has decreased among all economic groups during the past twenty years. As one commentator recently observed, "[i]f Americans now vote with their feet, they typically do so by moving toward public schools, not away from them."[62] The continued strength of the public school is all the more remarkable since the burgeoning prosperity of the past two decades has made parents more capable than ever before of paying for non-public education.

In some ways, the public schools have been the victims of their own success, for their increasing ability to draw and hold children of all abilities and social classes has created cultural tensions. As Professor Minow has observed, "the disillusionment with the public schools began at just about the same time that these schools took on the task of educating all children, including those with disabilities and limited English proficiency, non-citizens, the homeless, and migrants."[63] Critics of the public schools should beware the danger of succumbing to the "Miniver Cheevey syndrome" by romanticizing a golden age of public education that never existed. The public schools of yore were not necessarily more orderly or educationally efficient than are today's institutions, and their classrooms were segregated by race and were devoid of the physically and mentally challenged as well as many of the poor, particularly those children who sacrificed formal education to labor in factories, farms, and mines.

The argument that parents lack sufficient control over the education that their children receive in public schools is quite ironic since the public school is probably more amenable to grassroots democracy than is any other arm of government. Parents obviously could assert more control over the public schools if they became more involved in parent-teacher organizations or school board elections. At the very least they could vote in school board elections – a right that only approximately ten percent of all parents now exercise.[64] Since parents constitute a nu-

---

[62] Richard Rothstein, *Lessons; An Allegiance to Public Schools*, N.Y. TIMES, Mar. 15, 2000, at B11.

[63] Martha Minow, *Choice or Commonality: Welfare and Schooling After the End of Welfare as We Knew It*, 49 DUKE L.J. 493, 503 (1999).

[64] Hellwege, *supra* note 45, at 15.

merically large and generally prosperous segment of the electorate, they obviously are no discrete and insular minority. Although parents therefore have the power to influence political decisions concerning school curriculum, they also have vast ability to influence legal proceedings involving curricular issues.[65]

Moreover, the ability of parents to influence the schools that their children attend may be expanding. Educators have long since rejected the model of centralization in the hands of educational experts, the so-called "one best system." Some schools are now using so-called school-based management initiatives, which delegate decision-making authority over budget, personnel, and curriculum to councils of teachers, parents, and administrators at the local level.[66] Other reformers have suggested the creation of a so-called community engagement dialogic model, analogous to the process of alternative dispute resolution, in which a mediator would attempt to engage parents in a deliberative process that would work out compromises that would be broadly acceptable to various competing factions of parents, administrators, teachers, and students.[67] Throughout the nation, local school districts seem increasingly willing to hear and, when possible, accommodate the needs and concerns of parents. Charter schools, despite some drawbacks, also offer exciting possibilities for improving public education through initiatives that allow parents to exercise more control over their childrens' education.[68]

Indeed, the ability of parents to influence public school boards may, in many instances, actually provide parents with more control over their children's education than they would have if they sent their children to private schools. The burgeoning of the home-school movement suggests in part that many parents believe that even private schools do not provide parents with sufficient control over their children's education. At the very minimum, parents who send children to private schools must acquiesce at least in part to practices or curricula of which they do not wholly approve. To the extent that parents are not able to effect changes in the public schools, they retain the right under *Pierce* to remove their children from the public schools even though the exercise of this right has obvious costs.

---

[65] Stephen E. Gottlieb, *The Passing of the Cardozo Generations*, 34 AKRON L. REV. (in this volume).

[66] Michael A. Rebell & Robert L. Hughes, *Schools, Communities, and the Courts: A Dialogic Approach to Education Reform*, 14 YALE L. & POL'Y REV. 99, 102 (1996).

[67] *Id.* at 114-68.

[68] *See* Molly O'Brien, *Free at Last? Charter Schools and the "Deregulated" Curriculum*, 34 AKRON L. REV. (in this volume).

In addition to ignoring the political rights of parents, discussions of parental rights to direct their children's education also tend to overlook the rather obvious fact that parents have a vast opportunity to educate their children when school is out of session – as it is most of the time. American children attend school only approximately six hours per day, five days per week, 36 weeks per year. This means that more than 80 percent of a child's waking hours is spent away from school. During this time, parents have almost complete control over the company in which their children will spend their time and the type of influences to which the child will be exposed. Moreover, parents have full control of a child's education during the first five years of a child's life – the years that presumably are the most formative in a child's life. It is a misnomer to equate education with institutional schooling; most schooling is home schooling. The home especially provides a forum for transmitting cultural values that is at least as effective as the school, since so much of the time of public and non-public schools is taken up with technical learning that lacks any specific value content – for example, phonics and arithmetic. To the extent that parents object to the public school curriculum (without objecting so much that they wish to remove their children from public school), they have ample opportunity to provide antidotes at home and in their religious institutions during evenings, weekends, holidays, and summers.

The opportunities of parents to instill values in their children at home and in their religious institutions has long been recognized by persons who have defended the Supreme Court's decision prohibiting prayer in the public schools[69] against critics who alleged that it would subvert the religious and moral training of youth. As President John F. Kennedy stated in defense of that decision, "we can pray a good deal more at home, we can attend our churches with a good deal more fidelity, and we can make the true meaning of prayer much more important in the lives of our children. That power is very much open to us. And I hope that, as a result of this decision, . . . all American parents will intensify their efforts at home."[70]

One cannot, of course, deny that schools have a very powerful influence in shaping the values of children. Students obviously react to peer pressure, and they naturally tend to respect their teachers. Even though public school children spend most of their time outside of school, they obviously spend a very significant amount of their time in the custody of the state. The power of the state to communicate its values to public school children has influenced Stephen Gilles's interesting

---

[69] Engel v. Vitale, 370 U.S. 421 (1962).

[70] JOHN HERBERT LAUBACH, SCHOOL PRAYERS: CONGRESS, THE COURTS, AND THE PUBLIC 2 (1969).

argument that public school instruction is a form of parental speech that is protected by the First Amendment and that the laws that the Court nullified in *Meyer* and *Pierce* constituted restrictions on such speech.[71] Although *Meyer* and *Pierce* obviously recognize that parents have constitutional rights to exercise control over the content of their childrens' education, these decisions do not support the theory that parents do not delegate some of their autonomy to the state when they send their children to public school. Because it is impossible for the public schools to accommodate all parental opinions, a theory that the schools are direct agents of the state would permit parents to interfere with public school curricula in a manner that might create a chaotic cacophony in public school classrooms.

Although some parents might argue that they are unable to counter the baneful influence of teachers and peers in the public schools, I suspect that most objections to public school curricula involve what is *omitted* rather than what is *taught.* In other words, the principal objection of parents is not that their children are learning anything harmful, but that they are not sufficiently exposed to much that is helpful and healthy.

For example, I have heard some parents complain that the American history curriculum of many public schools devotes so much attention to women and racial minorities that it ignores many of the white men who once virtually monopolized the curriculum. Not one of these persons, however, has expressed any objection to having children learn about the contributions of women and racial minorities to American history. Indeed, they are happy that the schools are finally teaching about the contributions of persons and groups whom the public schools unfairly ignored for so long. Their quarrel is strictly one of emphasis. They do not feel that their children are learning too much about George Washington Carver, but they wish that they would learn more about

---

[71] Stephen G. Gilles, *On Educating Children: A Parentalist Manifesto,* 63 U. CHI. L. REV. 937, 1016-22 (1996). Professor Gilles argues that "[p]arents are no less 'speakers' for First Amendment purposes when they communicate indirectly with their children through the speech of schools, teachers, home tutors, or other educational intermediaries." *Id.* at 1016. Professor Gilles points out that while "[p]arents remain free to teach what they like when their child is in school . . . there are only so many hours in the day. Six hours a day, five days a week, nine months a year, only the public school's values may be communicated to one's child" *Id.* at 1022. He believes that "[t]his de facto prohibition unquestionably constitutes a major curtailment of dissenting parental . . . speech." *Id.* Gilles cites *Meyer* and *Pierce* in support of his argument. *Id.* at 1020-23. For discussions of other theories on how these decisions can be interpreted in terms of free speech, see *supra,* notes 11-13 and accompanying text.

George Washington. To the extent that these parents are unwilling or unable to persuade the school boards to effect the balance that they prefer, they have a rather easy remedy: provide instruction at home that fills in the gaps left by the public school curriculum. I suspect, however, that many of the parents who complain the most vociferously about the deficiencies of the public schools fail to provide their children with salubrious supplements when their children are at home. Several months ago, the Arts and Entertainment Network aired a splendid new film, *The Crossing*, about Washington's crossing of the Delaware River to fight the battle that turned the tide of the American Revolution. The film celebrated patriotic values in a manner that would warm the most conservative of hearts. But I would guess that the number of children who were tuned into smutty and vacuous TV and video programs was greater than the number who watched *The Crossing*.

Moreover, the lamentable decline in the standards of instruction for youth at many religious institutions during recent decades provides an example of how many religious parents fail to take advantage of opportunities to educate their children outside of the public schools. It is difficult to sympathize with complaints about the cultural deficiencies of the public schools when all too many religious institutions fail to adequately instruct young people in the morals, doctrines, history, and liturgies of their faith.

The abundant opportunities for education at home and in private religious institutions may explain why many public schools seem to emphasize multi-culturalism rather the cultures of the numerically dominant groups in the community. The schools naturally expect the parents to teach the children about their own traditions at home. If the child does not learn about other cultures at school however, she probably will not learn about them at home. For example, the parents in *Mozert* presumably had considerable opportunity to expose their children at home and at church to their Protestant heritage, if they had been willing to take the time and make the effort. It is unlikely, however, that the parents would have taught the children much about other traditions if the children had not been exposed to these at school. Although the school's neglect of the children's own religion may have made the children feel marginalized, the parents presumably could have made their children understand that the schools were emphasizing the culture of other groups because it was the duty of the parents to instill in them knowledge and pride about their own heritage, while the schools had the ability to teach about cultures with which their parents were unfamiliar.

Indeed, the ability of schools to teach students about a wide spectrum of cultures was at the heart of *Meyer* and *Pierce*, for the proponents of the nativistic legislation in both of those cases argued that the parochial schools instilled impressionable youth with alien values. The Court's decision in *Meyer* explicitly held that the teaching of German in parochial schools did not necessarily promote political subversion or exclude instruction in "American" values.[72] Similarly, the Court in *Pierce* implicitly found that religion-based schools did not necessarily fail to provide a sound education in secular subjects or neglect the inculcation of patriotism.[73] As a Nebraska judge quipped at Robert T. Meyer's trial when the state's attorney asked a pastor whether parochial school graduates could recite the national anthem, bilingual children "probably beat us in that. They can repeat it in two languages."[74]

Contrary to the widespread popular assumption that parents surrender to the schools most control over children, courts have recognized that parents retain primary control over their children in decisions that have refused to find that public schools have an affirmative duty to protect children from harm.[75] As the court explained in one decision that the parents of public schoolchilren:

> still retain primary responsibility for feeding, clothing, sheltering, and caring for the child. By mandating school attendance for children under the age of sixteen, the state of Illinois has not assumed responsibility for their entire personal lives; these children and their parents retain substantial freedom to act. The analogy of a school yard as a prison may be a popular one for school-age children, but we cannot recognize constitutional duties on a child's lament.[76]

In addition to their relevance to current struggles over parental rights amendments and curriculum issues, *Meyer* and *Pierce* also may be germane to the present controversy over school vouchers. Voucher advocates appear eager to bring vouchers within the umbrella of the parental rights enunciated by *Meyer* and *Pierce*.[77] For example, the Milwaukee

---

[72] Meyer v. Nebraska 262 U.S. 390, 400, 402 (1923).

[73] Pierce v. Society of the Sisters 268 U.S. 510, 534 (1925).

[74] ROSS, *supra* note 3, at 133 (citing *Transcript of Proceedings, Nebraska District v. Evangelical Lutheran Synod, et al., District Court of Dodge County, Sept. 1, 1921*).

[75] D.R. v. Middle Bucks Area Vocational Technical Sch., Nos. 91-1136, 91-1137, 1991 WL 276292, at *6 (3rd Cir. Dec. 31, 1991), *vacated*, 972 F.2d 1364 (3rd Cir. 1992); J.O. v. Alton Community Unit Sch. Dist. 11, 909 F.2d 267, 272 (7th Cir. 1990). Courts in both decisions dismissed lawsuits by parents whose children allegedly suffered sexual abuse in a public school.

[76] 909 F.2d at 272. Accordingly, the court concluded that "[s]choolchildren are not like mental patients and prisoners such that the state has an affirmative duty to protect them." *Id.* at 272-73.

[77] As one commentator has argued, *Pierce* "clearly recognizes the right of choice

school voucher program that was recently sustained by a Wisconsin court[78] is formally called "the Milwaukee Parental Choice program," thereby perhaps suggesting that vouchers permit parents to exercise a constitutional right to choose the school that their child attends. Some voucher proponents argue that economically disadvantaged parents are unable to avail themselves of the right to direct their childrens' education insofar as they cannot afford to send their children to a parochial school.[79] But while *Pierce* indeed permits parents to choose where to send their children to school, the Constitution does not compel the state to pay for any form of private education, and it may actually prohibit the state from paying for parochial education.

Although the Supreme Court has, in several instances, removed financial impediments to the exercise of rights,[80] the Court has held that the government has no obligation to provide funding to facilitate the exercise of a fundamental right.[81] Similarly, the Court has established that the failure to subsidize a fundamental right does not constitute a penalty on the exercise of that right. [82]

In particular, the Supreme Court has repeatedly held that there is no right to abortion funding.[83] The constitutional argument in favor of vouchers for private education is weaker than any argument in favor of public funding of abortion insofar as the Court has denied (however un-

---

implicit in the school vouchers system." Jill Jasperson, *Renaissance in Education: The Constitutionality and Viability of an Educational Choice or Voucher System,* 1993 B.Y.U. EDUC. & L.J. 126, 130.

[78] Jackson v. Benson, 578 N.W.2d 602 (Wis. 1998), *cert. denied,* 525 U.S. 997 (1998).

[79] As one commentator has argued, the only parents "who have a meaningful capacity to exercise their right of choice are those who have the financial means to afford private schooling (or the time to invest in home schooling) . . . . The public education system thus poses a great danger of infringing on the liberty of parents to direct the religious upbringing of their children." Andrew A. Cheng, *The Inherent Hostility of Secular Public Education Toward Religion: Why Parental Choice Best Serves the Core Values of the Religion Clauses,* 19 U. HAW. L. REV. 697, 733-34 (1997).

[80] *See, e.g.,* Boddie v. Connecticut, 401 U.S. 371 (1971) (invalidating fee for filing divorce petition).

[81] Regan v. Taxation With Representation of Washington, 461 U.S. 540, 545 (1983).

[82] Rust v. Sullivan, 500 U.S. 173, 193 (1991); Harris v. McRae, 448 U.S. 297, 317-18 & n.19 (1980).

[83] *See* Rust v. Sullivan, 500 U.S. 173; Webster v. Reproductive Health Serv., 492 U.S. 490 (1989); 448 U.S. 297; Maher v. Roe, 432 U.S. 464 (1977).

fortunately) that education is a fundamental right.[84] Moreover, a parent who receives no funds for private schooling is nevertheless able to secure public schooling for her child, while denial of public funding for a woman's abortion may completely foreclose the exercise of her right.

Vouchers have only an attenuated connection to the parental rights and interests that *Meyer* and *Pierce* – and *Yoder* – were intended to protect. Even though *Meyer* and *Pierce* did not directly address the free exercise implications of these cases, the laws that the Court nullified in those decisions interfered with the freedom of parents to provide a religious education for their children.[85] Since religious education was inextricably tied to ethnic heritage, the statutes struck at the very heart of parental efforts to preserve their cultural identity.[86] Indeed, the compelling desire of Lutheran and Roman Catholic parents to educate their children in schools that propagated their religious faith was what motivated the parents to establish those schools and to challenge the statutes. Likewise, this is what sustained them in their long, difficult, and expensive struggle to overturn the laws. The Court's ruling that parents had a fundamental right to choose the schools that their children attended and the subjects that they studied constituted a critical landmark in judicial respect for religious freedom and cultural pluralism.

In contrast, the so-called "choice" that the voucher movement is ostensibly intended to promote has no apparent direct relation to the

[84] *See* Plyler v. Doe, 457 U.S. 202 (1982); San Antonio Indep. Sch. Dist. v. Rodriguez, 411 U.S. 1 (1973).

[85] In *Meyer* and its companion cases, the parents challenged the constitutionality of the statutes because instruction in the German language was necessary to enable children to participate in German-language Lutheran services. *See* ROSS, *supra* note 3, at 4, 62, 100. The opponents of the laws based their challenges in state court largely on the ground of religious freedom, *id.* at 100-01, but largely ignored religious issues in their arguments before the U.S. Supreme Court, presumably because they held little hope for the success of these arguments in the absence of the incorporation of the First Amendment into state law. *See id.* at 117-19. Similarly, the Roman Catholic opponents of the Oregon compulsory public education statute did not emphasize religious freedom issues in their argument before the Court, even though religious liberty was the issue that animated most Catholic opposition to the statute. *Id.* at 169. Like the opponents of the language laws in *Meyer,* the Catholics correctly perceived that the Court would have little sympathy for religiously-based arguments. *Id.* at 169, 189-91.

[86] *See id.* at 1-5, *passim.* Robert T. Meyer explained to his attorney that he had openly defied the Nebraska statute prohibiting the teaching of German because he had a "'duty to uphold my religion. Teaching the children the religion of their fathers in the language of their fathers is part of that religion.'" ROSS, *supra* note 3 at 4 (citing MULLEN, *supra* note 24, at 218).

protection of any religious beliefs or the preservation of any cultural identity. Indeed, many parents who are using vouchers insist that they would much prefer to send their children to neighborhood public schools.[87] Rather, the announced goal of the voucher movement is to enable parents whose children attend sub-standard schools to obtain a better education for their children by providing them with the option to transfer to a non-public school. In other words, vouchers are intended to provide economic relief rather than to protect religion or culture.

Of course, it is not always possible to neatly distinguish between economic and non-economic issues. Indeed, the *Meyer* and *Pierce* decisions themselves nicely illustrate this point by blurring the distinction between the economic and the non-economic rights of the plaintiffs.[88] The economic desire of parents to provide a quality education for their children has a moral component that perhaps permits it in part to transcend economics. One might even argue that the goal of parents to provide a quality education for their children is morally equivalent to the desire of parents to educate their children in a school that will properly transmit their religious and cultural heritage. One also might argue that the violence and lewdness that presumably pervade some public schools grossly offend the cultural and spiritual traditions of many of the parents whose children attend these schools. Moreover, school vouchers may help to promote the type of individual autonomy that *Pierce* facilitated.[89] Constitutionally, however, there is a gaping difference between affirmatively forcing parents to send a child to a public school to which the parents have religious objections and merely denying economically impoverished parents public funds to send their children to a non-public school when the doors of the public school house are wide open and welcoming.

Although the non-sectarian schools that were saved by *Pierce* may not have served as similar conduits for cultural identity, the abolition of non-public schools would have given the state a complete monopoly over elementary education, thereby truly depriving parents of a significant choice about how to educate their children. In contrast, parents who seek to rescue their children from sub-standard schools and who cannot pay for private schools have a number of public options, such as inter-district transfers, charter schools, and political reform. Moreover, parents

---

[87] Lynette Clemetson & Joan Raymond, *A Ticket to Private School*, NEWSWEEK, Mar. 27, 2000, at 32.

[88] *See* ROSS, *supra* note 3, at 186-88.

[89] *See* Michael Heise, *Equal Educational Opportunity and Constitutional Theory: Preliminary Thoughts on the Role of School Choice and the Autonomy Principle*, 14 J. L. & POL. 411, 451-58 (1998).

whose children attend under-funded schools may obtain relief through equity funding lawsuits.

Because school vouchers involve economic issues rather than the questions of religious freedom that were at least tacitly present in *Meyer* and *Pierce*, advocates of school vouchers cannot avail themselves of any of the free exercise elements that are implicit in those decisions and on which the Court might have based it rulings if it had been ready to incorporate the First Amendment into state law.[90] Moreover, since some commentators have argued that prohibitions against public funding of sectarian schools violates the Equal Protection Clause,[91] it might not be wholly implausible to argue that vouchers interfere with the free exercise of religion since parental disapproval of the religious practices of parochial schools might present a wrenching dilemma for parents whose children attend poor schools and are eligible for school vouchers. In such a situation, the parent could face the cruel choice of leaving her child in a materially inferior public school or sending the child to a spiritually objectionable parochial school.[92] Moreover, vouchers for sectarian schools would also impose disadvantages for parents and children who resided in communities in which their own religion did not maintain a sectarian school.[93]

In addition to interference with free exercise of religion by the persons for whom vouchers were intended to assist, vouchers also could have a deleterious impact on the religious organizations that received vouchers insofar as vouchers might enable the government to increase its regulation of private and sectarian schools. The fear of increased public control of private education has caused the Home School Legal Defense Association to oppose government payments for private education. As an attorney for the Association has explained, "vouchers have a terrible po-

---

[90] *See supra* note 12 and accompanying text.

[91] Toby J. Heytens, Note, *School Choice and State Constitutions*, 86 VA. L. REV. 117, 140-52 (2000); Joseph P. Viteritti, *Blaine's Wake: School Choice, the First Amendment, and State Constitutional Law*, 21 HARV. J.L. & PUB. POL'Y 657, 660-61 (1998).

[92] *See* Minow, *supra* note 63, at 536. In discussing contracts between government and religious organizations for the provision of welfare services pursuant to 42 U.S.C. § 604(a), Professor Minow observes that "[v]oucher programs may directly burden the right of the destitute and desperate individuals to exercise freely their own religion or nonreligion, as the case may be." *Id.*

[93] *See* Kimberly M. DeShano, Note, *Educational Vouchers and the Religion Clauses Under* Agostini*: Resurrection, Insurrection and a New Direction*, 49 CASE W. RES. L. REV. 747, 784 (1999). As Ms. DeShano points out, exclusion of sectarian schools from a voucher program would enable the state to remain religiously neutral "as not all religions have community support to operate their own schools." *Id.* at 795.

tential to disrupt existing free market education."[94] The availability of government funds also might diminish the willingness of parents to support private and parochial schools.[95] Proponents of parochial education should not permit vouchers to debilitate the schools that parents and churches of the 1920s fought so valiantly to protect in *Meyer* and *Pierce*.

Vouchers also may violate the First Amendment's Establishment Clause.[96] In particular, vouchers seem vulnerable under the second prong of the Supreme Court's so-called "*Lemon* test," which requires that legislation challenged under the Establishment Clause have "a primary or principal effect . . . that neither advances nor inhibits religion."[97] The Court's recent relaxation of the *Lemon* test in decisions involving aid to parochial education[98] have caused some commentators to suggest that the Court might be sympathetic toward vouchers for attendance at sectarian schools.[99] Other commentators believe that the adherence to the Court's existing doctrines would make vouchers for sectarian schools unconstitutional.[100] The situation is further complicated because the Court

---

[94] Scott W. Somerville, *The History and the Politics of School Choice*, 10 GEO. MASON U. CIV. RTS. L.J. 121, 124 (1999-2000).

[95] *See* Marci A. Hamilton, *Power, the Establishment Clause, and Vouchers*, 31 CONN. L. REV. 807, 840-41 (1999).

[96] *See generally* Lisa H. Thurau-Gray, *Trojan Ponies: Undermining the Establishment Clause in the Name of 'Child Benefit Theory,'* 27 J.L. & EDUC. 435 (1998).

[97] Lemon v. Kurtzman, 403 U.S. 602, 612-13 (1971). The other prongs of the *Lemon* test require that the legislation have a secular purpose and that it not create excessive entanglement between government and religion. *Id.*

[98] *See* Mitchell v. Helms, 120 S. Ct. 2530 (2000) (permitting state and federal school aid programs to provide material and equipment to parochial schools); Agostini v. Felton, 521 U.S. 203 (1997) (allowing public school teachers to provide remedial education to parochial school students pursuant to federal statute); Zobrest v. Catalina Foothills Sch. Dist., 509 U.S. 1 (1993) (allowing public school district to provide sign-language interpreter to deaf student in parochial school); Witters v. Washington Dep't of Serv. for the Blind, 474 U.S. 481 (1984) (permitting state to aid blind students at sectarian college); Mueller v. Allen, 463 U.S. 388 (1983) (sustaining state statute providing tax deduction to parents for parochial school tuition, textbooks, and transportation).

[99] *See* Ira C. Lupu, *The Increasingly Anachronistic Case Against School Vouchers*, 13 NOTRE DAME J.L. ETHICS & PUB. POL'Y 375, 392-97 (1999); Minow, *supra* note 63, at 518; Greg Todd, *Fully Participating Voucher Programs and the Wisconsin Template: A Brick or a Breach in the Wall of Church-State Separation?*, 2 U. PA. J. CONST. L. 710, 729-39 (2000).

[100] *See* Hamilton, *supra* note 95; Danielle Jess Latham, Note, *Wall of Separation or Path to Interaction: The Uncertain Constitutional Future of School Vouchers in Light of Inconsistent Developments in Judicial Neutrality Between Church and State*, 48 DRAKE L.

has been closely divided in recent decisions in which it has upheld aid to parochial schools, with four justices adhering to a strict interpretation of the second prong of the *Lemon* test. The voucher issue hinges in part upon the precise manner in which voucher plans are framed, particularly since this could determine whether the Court would regard vouchers as a form of direct aid to parochial schools or as indirect aid to the extent that parents had the discretion to decide whether to use the voucher for a sectarian or a non-sectarian school.[101]

Although the Supreme Court of Wisconsin held in 1998 that Milwaukee's voucher program did not violate the Establishment Clause,[102] a federal court in 1999 held that Ohio's voucher program contravened the Establishment Clause,[103] and the Supreme Judicial Court of Maine in 1999 sustained Maine's exclusion of religious schools from a voucher

---

REV. 403, 432 (2000).

[101] *See* David S. Petron, Note, *Finding Direction in Indirection: The Direct/Indirect Aid Distinction in Establishment Clause Jurisprudence*, 75 NOTRE DAME L. REV. 1233, 1257-68 (2000); Laura S. Underkuffler, *Vouchers and Beyond: The Individual as Causative Agent in Establishment Clause Jurisprudence*, 75 IND. L.J. 167, 185-91 (2000); Martha McCarthy, *Religion and Education: Whither the Establishment Clause?*, 75 IND. L.J. 123, 160 (2000).

[102] Jackson v. Benson, 578 N.W.2d 602 (Wis.), *cert. denied*, 525 U.S. 997 (1998).

[103] Simmons-Harris v. Zelman, 72 F. Supp. 2d 834 (N.D. Ohio 1999). In its decision, the court rejected several of the arguments that voucher proponents commonly make in support of the constitutionality of vouchers. First, the court found that the program was not unconstitutional merely because the program did not directly fund schools, but rather because it merely provided vouchers to parents for use mainly at sectarian schools. *Id.* at 863. The court explained that students had "no meaningful choice" between religious or secular schools because 82 percent of the schools that participated in the voucher program were sectarian. *Id.* The court stated that it had not been influenced in this conclusion by the fact that 96 percent of participating students had enrolled in religious schools. *Id.* at 865. The court distinguished *Witters*, 474 U.S. 484 (1996), on the ground that "nearly all state aid under the Voucher program will flow to religious institutions. It cannot be said that this aid flows to those institutions as a result of the choice of the Program beneficiaries since nearly all the schools participating are religious." 72 F. Supp. 2d at 855-56.

The court in *Zelman* also distinguished the Supreme Court's 1992 decisions in *Zobrest v. Catalina Foothills Sch. Dist.*, 509 U.S. 1 (1993), and *Agostini v. Felton*, 521 U.S. 203 (1997), on the ground that the Ohio program, unlike the federal programs in *Agostini* and *Zobrest*, resulted in the receipt of actual funds by the sectarian schools. 72 F. Supp. 2d at 857-60. Moreover, the court emphasized that the Ohio program imposed no limits on the manner in which the funds were to be used. *Id.*

program on the ground that their inclusion would violate the Establishment Clause.[104]

Even if vouchers are found to be constitutional under the Establishment Clause, many state constitutions present impediments to vouchers. The Supreme Court of Vermont has held that a state voucher program violated the state's equivalent of the Establishment Clause.[105] A Florida court recently held that Florida's voucher plan violated a state constitutional provision that requires the state to provide "a uniform, efficient, safe, secure and high quality system of free public schools that allows students to obtain a high quality education."[106] According to the Florida decision, the voucher program "supplants the system of free public schools mandated by the constitution."[107] Other state constitutions contain significant prohibitions against public funding of sectarian schools,[108] and many states enforce their own establishment clauses more restrictively than the federal clause is enforced by the federal courts.[109] One study has concluded that the states are roughly equally divided into three groups: those that have a supportive constitutional environment for school vouchers, those that have an unsupportive climate, and those in which the outcome would be uncertain.[110] The Supreme Court's growing emphasis on federalism indicates that the Court would defer to state prohibitions on vouchers if the issue were framed primarily in terms of the Establishment Clause rather than the Free Exercise Clause.[111]

A state could, of course, exclude sectarian schools from a voucher program. Although some commentators have suggested that such an exclusion might run afoul of the Equal Protection or Free Exercise Clauses,[112] the invalidation of such a statute on either ground

---

[104] Bagley v. Raymond Sch. Dep't, 728 A.2d 127 (Me. 1999), *cert. denied,* 120 S. Ct. 364 (1999).

[105] Chittenden Town Sch. Dist. v. Department of Educ., 738 A.2d 539 (Vt. 1999), *cert. denied sub nom.* Andrews v. Vermont Dep't of Educ., 120 S. Ct. 626 (1999).

[106] Holmes v. Bush, No. CV99-3370, 2000 WL 526364 at *1 (Fla. Cir. Ct. Mar. 14, 2000) (citing to FLA. CONST. art. IX § 1).

[107] *Id.* at *7.

[108] Frank R. Kemerer, *The Constitutional Dimension of School Vouchers,* 3 TEX. F. ON CIV. LIB. & CIV. RTS. 137, 162-71 (1998). For example, most state constitutions require that all "public mon[ey] . . . be spent for a public purpose," and several state constitutions specifically require that only public schools receive public money. *Id.* at 169; 168. *See also* Deshano, *supra* note 93, at 778.

[109] *See* DeShano, *supra* note 93; Kemerer, *supra* note 108.

[110] Kemerer, *supra* note 108, at 179.

[111] *Id.* at 151-53.

[112] *See* Stephen L. Carter, *Oliver Wendell Holmes Lecture: Parents, Religion, and Schools: Reflections on* Pierce, *70 Years Later,* 27 SETON HALL L. REV. 1194, 1218

"would reverse a trend by the present U.S. Supreme Court to give greater deference to state authority."[113] Moreover, the exclusion of sectarian schools from a voucher program would enable the state to avoid favoring those denominations that have community support for sectarian schools at the expense of those which lack such support.[114] In its recent decision striking down Cleveland's voucher program, the U.S. District Court for the Northern District of Ohio refused to address the state's contention that it would be unconstitutional to exclude religious schools from a voucher program.[115] Congress might try to circumvent such state impediments by enacting a federal school voucher statute. Such a statute might "trump the application of state constitutional anti-establishment provisions in state court under the federal Supremacy Clause."[116]

Vouchers are antithetical to the spirit of *Pierce* insofar as they interfere with the delicate balance between public and private education that lies at the core of that decision. The Court in *Pierce* tacitly rejected the contention of proponents of compulsory public education that private schools threatened the viability of public education. As opponents of compulsory public education pointed out during the school wars of the early 1920s, non-public schools helped the public schools insofar as they relieved the state from finding extra funds to educate large numbers of students.[117] Although *Pierce* implicitly recognized that the private and parochial schools posed no threat to the state that would justify the

---

(1997) ("if the state decides to give aid to any private schools at all, to exclude religious schools would be to do just what *Pierce* does not allow: to pressure parents (through the device of a financial penalty) to send their children to the religion-destroying schools rather than the religion-affirming ones."); Heytens, *supra* note 91, at 153-61 (arguing that exclusion of religious schools from a voucher system would violate equal protection); Mark Tushnet, *supra* note 20, at 51 ("[s]uch an exclusion appears to violate the fundamental principle of the religion clauses that a government may not discriminate in favor of or against religion in its provision of benefits.").

[113] Kemerer, *supra* note 108, at 152. Professor Kemerer believes that "past decisions suggest that the U.S. Supreme Court may allow states to apply their own constitutional provisions to challenged voucher programs in the interest of federalism." *Id.* at 179.

[114] *See* DeShano, *supra* note 93, at 795.

[115] Simmons-Harris v. Zelman, 72 F. Supp. 2d 834, 860-61 (1999).

[116] Kemerer, *supra* note 108, at 152.

[117] ROSS, *supra* note 3, at 144, 156. Opponents of the Oregon school law, for example, variously estimated that the state would need between 3.6 and 6 million dollars to construct new schools if the statute were upheld, and that the annual cost of educating the 12,000 new pupils would exceed one million dollars (about 30 million dollars in today's money). *Id.* at 156.

state's exercise of its police power to destroy these schools, the Court's opinion in no way denigrated public education. Indeed, even opponents of compulsory public education seemed to assume that public education represented the norm and non-public education the exception – a constitutionally protected and healthy exception, but an exception nonetheless.

In contrast, many proponents of vouchers seem hostile to the very concept of public education,[118] just as the advocates of the compulsory public education law that the Court nullified in *Pierce* were hostile to any form of private elementary education. Many voucher advocates accept the highly questionable premises that public schools tend to be inferior to private ones,[119] that poor public schools cannot be improved, and that vouchers would help raise educational standards.[120] In its decisions in *Meyer* and *Pierce*, the Court tacitly rejected similar arguments about private schools, for antagonists of the parochial schools had complained about low standards in such schools. Although some of these complaints were justified,[121] others were wildly exaggerated,[122] just as

---

[118] *See* Molly Townes O'Brien, *Private School Tuition Vouchers and the Realities of Racial Politics*, 64 TENN. L. REV. 359, 406-07, *passim* (1997).

[119] *See, e.g.*, DAVID C. BERLINER & BRUCE J. BIDDLE, THE MANUFACTURED CRISIS: MYTHS, FRAUDS, AND THE ATTACK ON AMERICA'S PUBLIC SCHOOLS 26 (1995); KEVIN B. SMITH & KENNETH J. MEIER, THE CASE AGAINST SCHOOL CHOICE: POLITICS, MARKETS, AND FOOLS 15-16 (1995).

[120] Lynn Olson, *New Studies on Private Choice Fan the Flames*, EDUC. WK., Sept. 4, 1996, at 1, 20 (citing conflicting studies regarding performance of students who used vouchers in Milwaukee program); Adam Cohen, *A First Report Card on Vouchers*, TIME, Apr. 26, 1999, at 36 (discussing Indiana University study that concluded that students who used vouchers to attend established private schools slightly outperformed comparable public school students, while students who attended schools that had been established for the purpose of accepting vouchers had performance levels inferior to public school counterparts).

[121] ROSS, *supra* note 3, at 48, 78, 102, 140-41. In Michigan, for example, where voters in 1920 and 1924 rejected compulsory public education laws, "[t]he Roman Catholic schools had no superintendent until 1918, and administration continued to be weak for many years thereafter since the superintendent had no office or staff and served also as a parish priest." *Id.* at 141. Deploring the deficiencies in some of the Lutheran schools in Michigan in 1918, a Lutheran "pastor remarked that it was 'small wonder' that public school officials were 'not always friendly towards our school system.' " *Id.* (quoting H. Grueber to Theodore Graebner, Oct. 2, 1918, Graebner Papers, Box 122, Concordia Historical Institute, Clayton, Missouri).

[122] In advocating compulsory public education during the early 1920s, a Florida public school teacher argued that any public savings produced by parochial

many of the criticisms of today's public schools may be overwrought. By emphasizing that the state had the power to regulate private education in order to require the maintenance of certain standards, the Court in *Pierce* implied that any deficiencies in private schools did not alone permit the state to require compulsory public education.

Moreover, some advocates of vouchers argue that public schools are presently so stratified by race and income that they no longer effectively transmit the civic values that the advocates of the common school movement foresaw during the nineteenth century. Analogous arguments about private schools were made before *Pierce* by advocates of compulsory public education, who argued that non-public schools created deleterious racial, religious, and economic stratifications.[123]

Despite the diversity of an increasingly heterogeneous society, it is still possible to identify core values to which the overwhelming majority of parents appear willing to subscribe.[124] To the extent that Americans disagree about values, they are more likely to disagree about the manner in which core values should be applied in specific situations rather than about the values themselves. For example, while nearly everyone would agree that children should respect their parents, there is considerable

---

schools were "more than counterbalanced by increased public spending for 'the children's homes, . . . charity hospitals, insane asylums, courts of justice and prisons' that were needed to accommodate parochial school alumni." ROSS, *supra* note 3, at 70 (quoting Walter B. Jernigan, *Public Schools in Florida*, NEW AGE, Jan. 1923, at 16).

[123] ROSS, *supra* note 3, at 71.

[124] Rosemary C. Salomone, *Common Schools, Uncommon Values: Listening to the Voices of Dissent*, 14 YALE L. & POL'Y REV. 169, 225 (1996). As Professor Salomone has explained:

> [a]lthough not intended to be exhaustive, a listing of common values might include a mix of character traits such as honesty, integrity, responsibility, delayed gratification, hard work, respect for authority, and civic virtue combined with more fundamental political principles, particularly justice and fairness, political and religious tolerance, and equality in the sense of equal dignity for all. As a source of these "shared values," we should look to our common history and particularly to the United States Constitution, as interpreted by the Supreme Court, and to federal statutory law with supporting administrative regulations as statements of majority consensus.

Id.

disagreement about the methods by which parents may discipline children who fail to respect their parents. Similarly, while nearly everyone values the virtue of hard work, reasonable persons may differ about the extent to which food stamps given to the poor or inheritance taxes imposed on the rich encourage or discourage this virtue.

Some critics of public education also contend that the public schools fail to instill virtues, even to the extent that it remains possible to identify such virtues. Notwithstanding their shortcomings, however, public schools still help to transmit basic values and to promote social cohesion.[125] Any deficiencies in fulfilling this mission does not mean that public schools are incapable of improvement. As one commentator has aptly stated: "The cry of 'Fire!' has been heard in the institution of public education. Exit should not be the only option. Instead of devoting all resources to finding an exit, the public should find a way to extinguish the fire and to preserve a worthy and venerable structure."[126]

Although advocates of vouchers contend that the transfer of money away from supposedly inferior public schools will encourage public schools to raise their standards, vouchers could have precisely the opposite effect. Vouchers could relieve public officials of political pressure to improve sub-standard schools since they would reduce the number of students attending substandard schools and remove from the public schools the very students whose parents would be the most likely to seek public school reform.[127] Moreover, the competition argument is flawed

---

[125] As Professor Dupre argued recently:

> [o]ne of the great strengths of the public school institution is its ability to encourage social integration. Indeed, this nation may have no other institution with the same potential of integrating rich and poor on a daily basis and inculcating our commitment to representative democracy while children are young and before they become set in their views. Learning to deal with, and perhaps even be friends with, children of a different economic, racial, or religious background can be an enriching experience for children.

Anne Proffitt Dupre, *A Study in Double Standards, Discipline, and the Disabled Student*, 75 WASH. L. REV. 1, 84 (2000).

[126] Note, *The Hazards of Making Public Schools a Private Business*, 112 HARV. L. REV. 695, 712 (1999). This commentator has likewise aptly pointed out that the possibility that "the public schools are not meeting the ideal" does not necessarily mean "that the ideal is a bad one." *Id.* at 710.

[127] As Professor Minow has pointed out, "[t]he immediate consequence of

insofar as private schools enjoy certain competitive advantages over public schools, particularly their far more arbitrary power over the selection and retention of students.[128]

Advocates of vouchers have also failed to explain what will become of public school systems that have lost the support of the parents who presumably care most about their childrens' education. As one leading sociologist of education has predicted, "In any choice plan, the families who have the least resources in terms of information, energy and money will be left behind."[129] Moreover, it is unlikely that states will have the means to fund vouchers for every parent who wishes to receive one.[130]

The slogan of the opponents of compulsory public education during the early 1920s was "Whose is the Child?," a question to which the Court in *Pierce* provided an answer that struck a somewhat ambiguous balance between the rights of the parents and the rights of the state. Perhaps the rallying cry of opponents of school vouchers should be "Education is not a commodity." It is erroneous to assume that education is amenable to normal market forces. As Professor Liebman has explained, "[o]ne thing markets are *not* good for is allocating public goods, and an

---

school-choice programs will most likely leave the most vulnerable children from the least-engaged and least-solid families in the worst schools." Minow, *supra* note 63, at 528. Likewise, one opponent of school vouchers has aptly expressed fear that public schools would be "left only with children with disabilities, children of parents who do not care if, or where, their children attend and children who have been kicked out of all the private schools." Jennifer A. Hendrikson, Comment, Jackson v. Benson*: School Vouchers – Offering an Apple to Private Schools; Creating a Serpent for Public Schools*, 75 CHI.-KENT L. REV. 259, 277 (1999) (quoting an opponent of an Oklahoma voucher proposal). *See also* James S. Liebman, *Voice, Not Choice*, 101 YALE L.J. 259, 277-93 (1991) (reviewing JOHN E. CHUBB & TERRY M. MOE, POLITICS, MARKETS, AND AMERICAN SCHOOLS (1990)).

[128] As one commentator has pointed out, the public choice theory is flawed because: the public and private schools are not equal in terms of public accountability. The public schools must not only adhere to curriculum standards and anti-discrimination practices, but public schools must also admit every student that wishes to attend. On the other hand, private schools are less accountable to the community. Thus, they have more power to choose who to educate. Hendrikson, *supra* note 127, at 277.

[129] Jill Jasperson, *Renaissance in Education: The Constitutionality and Viability of an Educational Choice or Voucher System*, 1993 B.Y.U EDUC. & L.J. 126, 146 (1993) (quoting Robert L. Crain, a professor of sociology and education at Columbia University Teachers College).

[130] *See* Timothy D. Lynch, Note, *Education as a Fundamental Right: Challenging the Supreme Court's Jurisprudence*, 26 HOFSTRA L. REV. 953, 969 (1998).

educated public is just that. Accordingly, exit and choice will never work well to allocate that good – unless working well means warehousing the poor, the less gifted, and the academically disinclined in educational facilities that make existing public schools look like the Institute for Advanced Studies."[131]

The use of *Meyer* and *Pierce* by both the proponents and opponents of school vouchers illustrates again that these decisions remain enigmatic, controversial, and vital. Both decisions compel significant restrictions on the power of the state to interfere with the autonomy of parents over the education of their children. Both decisions also recognize that the state has significant power to regulate the manner in which children are educated. The decisions therefore must remain controversial in the absence of pure communism or pure libertarianism, for there is no obvious or perfect way to balance the competing interests of the parents and the state in matters of education in a free, but statist, society. In trying to achieve this balance, one might recall W.H. Auden's observation that civilization is a function of "the degree of diversity attained and the degree of unity retained."[132] Parental rights involving the education of their children help to promote a diversity that is essential to a free society, but the retention of governmental authority in this process helps to assure a unity that is no less essential.

---

[131] Liebman, *supra* note 127, at 313. Decrying school vouchers as "recipe for disaster," Professor Liebman argues that voucher plans, regardless of how they are designed, "inevitably will turn the schools into new and more efficient machines for sorting educational consumers into numerous homogenized pools of parents and children with the same levels of wealth, intellectual ability, consumer sophistication, academic orientation, and ethnicity. That, after all, is what markets are good for." *Id.*

[132] W.H. AUDEN, FOREWARDS AND AFTERWARDS 9 (1973).

The Price of Vouchers for Religious Freedom

LAURA S. UNDERKUFFLER*

I. INTRODUCTION

In *Pierce v. Society of Sisters,*[1] the Supreme Court held that a state's role in the education of its citizens must yield to the right of parents to provide an equivalent education for their children in a privately operated school – including a religious school – of the parents' choice. The question that underlies this colloquium is what the fundamental principles of *Pierce* may mean for pressing social and political issues in the twenty-first century. My particular task is to address how the principles of individual volition or individual choice, which *Pierce* represents, intersect - as a constitutional matter - with proposals to establish or extend public voucher programs to religiously affiliated elementary and secondary schools.

The importance of this question, in human terms, is something that I have personally experienced. While in college, I had the opportunity to teach a class of fifteen sixth-grade girls attending Presentation Elementary School, a Roman Catholic institution located in the near west side of Chicago. The experience was one that will stay with me for the rest of my life. The sheer ebullience and creative power of those girls, and their willingness to welcome me - a stranger from another world - into their midst, taught me more about the indomitability of the human spirit than any other single experience.

I also knew then, as I know now, that the availability of that school for those students was a life-altering and life-giving experience for them. All of the students whom I taught had failed in the public schools. It is therefore with a divided heart that I write of what I see as dangers in the use of public vouchers in religiously affiliated schools. I know that there are real children whose opportunities depend upon the resolution of this issue. However, I have concluded that the serious constitutional concerns that voucher programs raise are too important to be ignored, even if there is a difficult cost involved in the defense of those principles.

---

* Ms. Underkuffler is a Professor of Law at the Duke University School of Law.

1. 268 U.S. 510 (1925).

The availability of public moneys through voucher programs for religiously sponsored education seems, on the surface, to be a victory for freedom of conscience and individual choice. I have concluded, however, that the enactment of such programs—and their necessary approval by courts—would require that important constitutional principles regarding religious freedom be jeopardized. The upholding of voucher p.ans would be, one might say, a Pyrrhic victory for those who value freedom of conscience—if it is a victory at all. For in winning the right to channel public money in this way to religious schools, religious communities will, in the long run, serve forces that will undermine religious tolerance and the constitutionally protected place of freedom of conscience in our constitutional scheme.

Our country has a long history of political and legal opposition to the payment of public tax monies to religious institutions. In *Everson v. Board of Education*,[2] the Supreme Court set forth what has become the doctrinal baseline in this area. No state can, "consistently with the 'establishment of religion' clause of the First Amendment[,] contribute tax-raised funds to the support of an institution which teaches the tenets and faith of any church."[3] If a religiously affiliated elementary or secondary school is a "religious institution", in this sense, the use of public money for the general support of that school violates this entrenched Establishment Clause principle. For the use of voucher money by such schools to be upheld, the Court must take one of two avenues. It must either: 1) hold that the fact that individual parents choose the religious schools *breaks the causal connection* between the state program and the religious recipients, eliminating Establishment Clause concerns – a theory which I have called the "theory of the individual as causative agent;"[4] or 2) repudiate the idea that the payment of tax dollars to religious institutions for religious activities presents an Establishment Clause violation, in the belief that *neutrality* and *equal treatment* require that tax dollars be given to religious institutions, on a par with secular institutions, for their support.[5] It is my belief that neither choice serves the constitutional goal of the preservation of religious freedom.

2. 330 U.S. 1 (1947).

3. *Id.* at 16.

4. *See* Laura S. Underkuffler, *Vouchers and Beyond: The Individual as Causative Agent in Establishment Clause Jurisprudence*, 75 IND. L.J. 167 (2000).

5. This position has been advanced by some scholars. *See, e.g.*, Eugene Volokh, *Equal Treatment Is Not Establishment*, 13 NOTRE DAME J.L. ETHICS & PUB. POL'Y 341 (1999).

II. PUBLIC AID TO RELIGIOUS SCHOOLS: DOCTRINAL CURRENTS

The tests that the Supreme Court has used to determine the constitutionality of state aid to religious elementary and secondary schools have remained, until quite recently, remarkably constant over the years. As the Court observed as recently as 1997, it has "continue[d] to ask whether the government acted with the purpose of advancing or inhibiting religion" and "whether the aid has the 'effect' of advancing or inhibiting religion."[6] It has also considered whether the program "result[s] in . . . an excessive entanglement" between church and state,[7] and whether, under the "endorsement" test, the state program "creates an impermissible 'symbolic link' between government and religion."[8]

The most important of these tests for school-aid cases has been whether the state-aid program has the impermissible effect of advancing religion. As a general rule, if the state program purchased equipment or services that were themselves secular in nature, and if the equipment or services conferred only incidental financial benefit upon religious schools, the program has been upheld. If, however, state money was used to purchase overtly religious goods or services, or if it provided substantial support to religious institutions, the program has been struck down as an "advancement" of religion under the Establishment Clause.

Following these guidelines, the Court has approved the spending of tax-raised funds to pay the bus fares of religious-school students as part of a general program that paid the fares of all students attending public and nonpublic schools.[9] It has also approved state programs that involved the lending of secular textbooks, the giving of standardized tests, and the provision of speech and hearing diagnostic services.[10] The Court reasoned that "[a]s with public provision of police and fire protection, sewage facilities, and streets and sidewalks, [such programs are] . . . of some value to the religious school, but . . . not such support of a religious institution as to be a prohibited establishment of religion within the meaning of the First Amendment."[11] Under such programs, primary financial benefit "is to parents and children, not to schools."[12] In addition, the funded

6. Agostini v. Felton, 521 U.S. 203, 222-23 (1997).

7. *Id.* at 232.

8. *Id.* at 224.

9. *See* Everson v. Board of Educ., 330 U.S. 1, 16-18 (1947).

10. *See* Wolman v. Walter, 433 U.S. 229, 239-40, 244 (1977) (plurality opinion) (standardized tests and scoring services, and speech and hearing diagnostic services), *overruled on other grounds by* Mitchell v. Helms, 120 S. Ct. 2530 (2000); Board of Educ. v. Allen, 392 U.S. 236, 242-48 (1968) (textbook loan program).

11. *Allen*, 392 U.S. at 242.

12. *Id.* at 244.

activities or materials – bus fares, secular textbooks, standardized tests, and so on – were, of themselves, of an entirely secular nature.

The giving of cash grants of state money to religious schools has been traditionally viewed by the Court as an entirely different matter. It is fair to say that the giving of *unrestricted* cash grants to religious elementary and secondary schools has been assumed by the Court for more than five decades to be an unconstitutional advancement of religion by government. If a religiously affiliated elementary or secondary school is a "pervasively sectarian" institution—if the school's secular educational function and its religious mission are "inextricably intertwined"[13] – then the use of public money for that school's general support has been viewed as the use of public money for religious purposes in violation of the Establishment Clause.[14] Although some scholars have speculated about the possible constitutionality of such grants if given to all schools, regardless of sectarian character, the Court's shifting majorities and pluralities have never—until the most recent school-aid case, discussed below—seriously considered this idea.[15] Indeed, many state-aid programs that involved *restricted* cash grants have been struck down over the years, on the ground that they could be "diverted" too easily by recipient institutions to religious purposes or activities.[16]

The core of the Court's objection to the giving of unrestricted cash grants to religious schools apparently has been the view that since such schools are religious institutions – since the education that they

---

13. Lemon v. Kurtzman, 403 U.S. 602, 657 (1971) (Brennan, J., concurring).

14. *See, e.g.*, School Dist. v. Ball, 473 U.S. 373, 395 (1985), *overruled on other grounds by* Agostini v. Felton, 521 U.S. 203 (1997); *Lemon*, 403 U.S. at 621; *Everson*, 330 U.S. at 15-16.

15. *See, e.g.*, Roemer v. Board of Pub. Works, 426 U.S. 736, 747 (1976) (opinion of Blackmun, J.) ("The State may not . . . pay for what is actually a religious education, even though it purports to be paying for a secular one, and even though it makes its aid available to secular and religious institutions alike.").

16. *See, e.g.*, Wolman v. Walter, 433 U.S. 229, 248-54 (1977) (invalidating state provision of movie projectors, tape recorders, and record players to religious schools, and the funding of field trips by religious school students, where the trips were chosen and conducted by religious school teachers), *overruled by* Mitchell v. Helms, 120 S. Ct. 2530 (2000); Meek v. Pittenger, 421 U.S. 349, 363-72 (1975) (invalidating the public provision of counseling, testing, speech and hearing therapy services, and instructional materials and equipment to religious schools), *overruled by Mitchell*, 120 S. Ct. at 2530; Committee for Pub. Educ. & Religious Liberty v. Nyquist, 413 U.S. 756, 774-80 (1973) (invalidating grants of state money to nonpublic schools for the maintenance and repair of school facilities and equipment); Levitt v. Committee for Pub. Educ. & Religious Liberty, 413 U.S. 472, 479-82 (1973) (invalidating grants of state money to nonpublic schools for "reimbursement" of the costs of performing state-mandated testing, grading, and record-keeping tasks); *Lemon*, 403 U.S. at 615-620 (invalidating state program that reimbursed nonpublic schools for their expenditures for teachers' salaries, textbooks, and instructional materials in "secular" subjects).

offer is "subsumed in the religious mission,"[17] with religious practices and the propagation of faith as integral parts of their programs and curricula[18] – there is no functional way to distinguish the giving of cash grants to these schools and the giving of cash grants to churches, synagogues, and mosques. The fact that education in secular subjects goes on while the schools conduct religious activities and fulfill their religious missions has not, in the Court's view, sufficiently distinguished these religious institutions.

Vouchers are clearly unrestricted cash grants of state funds and —if given directly to religious schools—they would, without doubt, violate traditional Establishment Clause prohibitions. In an attempt to avoid this problem, advocates of vouchers have made two different but related arguments. First, they argue that the prohibition on unrestricted cash grants to religious institutions is inapplicable to voucher programs, because the decision to use voucher money for religious-school education is made by students or their parents, not by state authorities. Second, they argue, *even if* the money that reaches religious schools is deemed to be the result of state action, the substance of the Establishment Clause does not prohibit these payments. In their view, the Establishment Clause does not prohibit the "substantial" funding of religious institutions and activities, as the Supreme Court has traditionally held; rather, it only prohibits state favoritism for or against particular religious sects, or for or against religion generally. Since voucher programs give public money to religious and secular institutions on an evenhanded or "neutral" basis, they present no violation of the Establishment Clause.

17. Hunt v. McNair, 413 U.S. 734, 743 (1973).

18. *See Meek*, 421 U.S. at 366 ("The very purpose of [these schools] is to provide an integrated secular and religious education"); Walz v. Tax Comm'n of New York, 397 U.S. 664, 671 (1970) (such schools exist, in important part, to "assure future adherents to [the sponsoring religious organization's] particular faith. . ."). In one case, the Court cited the following as evidence of "pervasively sectarian character": that the schools "include[d] prayer and attendance at religious services as a part of their curricul[a], [were] . . . run by churches or other organizations whose members must subscribe to particular religious tenets, [had] . . . faculties and student bodies composed largely of adherents of the particular denomination, and [gave] . . . preference in attendance to children belonging to the denomination." *Ball*, 473 U.S. at 384 n.6. If a religiously affiliated school could sufficiently avoid these characteristics, it might be the permissible recipient of public funds, much in the way that religious hospitals and post-secondary schools are now. *See, e.g.*, Bowen v. Kendrick, 487 U.S. 589, 608-13 (1988) (upholding public funding of teenage counseling services offered by religious organizations); Tilton v. Richardson, 403 U.S. 672, 679-82 (1971) (plurality opinion) (upholding public funding of religious institutions of higher education); Bradfield v. Roberts, 175 U.S. 291, 298-99 (1899) (upholding public funding of religiously affiliated hospitals). Accomplishing such changes would, however, destroy the reason for being of most religious elementary and secondary schools.

The first theory – that independent, individual decision making may be the "causative agent" for Establishment Clause jurisprudence – has its roots in a series of cases decided by the Supreme Court from the mid-1980s to the present. Using this theory, the Supreme Court upheld a state program that permitted tax deductions for religious elementary and secondary school expenses;[19] upheld the use of state vocational assistance funds to pay for the costs of a college student's concededly religious training;[20] and upheld the use of federal funds to provide an interpreter for a deaf student enrolled in a religious high school.[21] The theory of these cases was that "public funds become available to sectarian schools 'only as a result of numerous private choices of individual[s] . . . ,' thus distinguishing [these programs from those] . . . involving 'the direct transmission of assistance from the State to the schools themselves.'"[22] As a result, any advancement of religion that resulted from these programs "cannot be attributed [in a constitutional sense] to state decision making."[23]

Whether this theory has potentially *dispositive* power - or whether it is simply used in conjunction with traditional Establishment Clause tests - has been unclear. For instance, in *Agostini v. Felton*,[24] decided in 1997, the Court upheld the sending of public school teachers into religious schools to provide remedial education under Title I of the Federal Elementary and Secondary Education Act. In the course of this opinion, the Court noted that services were provided to the student rather than to the school[25] – with the student's decision to attend a religious school being an independent one.[26] This discussion seemed to echo the Court's use of the theory of the individual as causative agent as it had appeared in prior cases. The importance of this theory was obscured, however, when the Court proceeded in *Agostini* to consider traditional Establishment Clause

---

19. *See* Mueller v. Allen, 463 U.S. 388, 399 (1983).

20. *See* Witters v. Washington Dep't of Servs. for the Blind, 474 U.S. 481, 485-89 (1986).

21. *See* Zobrest v. Catalina Foothills Sch. Dist., 509 U.S. 1, 9-14 (1993).

22. *Id.* at 9 (quoting *Mueller*, 463 U.S. at 399).

23. *Zobrest*, 509 U.S. at 10. The theory of the individual as causative agent has appeared in the Court's opinions in other Establishment Clause contexts as well. *See, e.g.*, Rosenberger v. Rector & Visitors of the Univ. of Va., 515 U.S. 819 (1995) (upholding the payment of university-collected student-activity funds to a printing contractor who was independently retained by students to print religious materials); Capitol Square Review & Advisory Bd. v. Pinette, 515 U.S. 753 (1995) (plurality opinion) (upholding the decision of a private group to place a cross on a state-owned square that was used for public speeches and other activities traditionally associated with public fora).

24. 521 U.S. 203 (1997).

25. *Id.* at 229.

26. *See id.* at 225-27.

concerns.[27] For instance, the Court cited as important—when upholding this aid—that it did not "supplant" services offered in the religious school;[28] that it created no "financial incentive to undertake religious indoctrination";[29] that it was, of itself, of a secular character;[30] and that its secular character could be ensured without excessive entanglement of church and state.[31]

Thus, after *Agostini*, the theory of the individual as causative agent seemed to be a part of the Court's Establishment Clause jurisprudence, but its role vis-à-vis traditional Establishment Clause concerns was unclear. In all of the cases in which this theory was used, it seemed to be something which simply reinforced the conclusion - derived from traditional Establishment Clause tests - that the state-aid program presented no real Establishment Clause dangers.

In a very recent case, however, a plurality of the Court indicated a potentially far more reaching role for this theory. *Mitchell v. Helms*,[32] decided last June, involved a challenge to a federal program under which computers and other technical materials and services were purchased with federal money by local school districts, and distributed as "loans" to all schools within the district's geographic boundaries - public, private, and parochial. Six justices voted to uphold the constitutionality of this program. Using a blended theory of "neutrality" and "private choice", the plurality held that the federal program in *Mitchell* posed no Establishment Clause problem. Under this program, the amount of aid that a school received was based on enrollment, and enrollment was determined by parental choice. This scheme used "'neutral, secular criteria'" for aid decisions that neither favored nor disfavored religion.[33] In addition, the aid that the program provided - computers, computing software, and library books - was "'secular, neutral, and nonideological'", and used in public schools.[34]

The result in *Mitchell* was not, of itself, a revolutionary one. Although in two old cases - *Meek v. Pittenger*[35] and *Wolman v. Walter*[36] - the Court had struck down the provision of otherwise secular instructional materials and equipment to religious schools, those

27. *Id.* at 229.
28. *Id.*
29. *Id.* at 231.
30. *See Agostini*, 521 U.S. at 223-28.
31. *See id.* at 232-35.
32. 120 S. Ct. 2530 (2000).
33. *Id.* at 2552 (quoting *Agostini*, 521 U.S. at 231).
34. *Id.* at 2537 (quoting 20 U.S.C.§ 7372(a) (1)).
35. 421 U.S. 349 (1975), *overruled by* Mitchell v. Helms, 120 S. Ct. 2530 (2000).
36. 433 U.S. 229 (1977), *overruled by* Mitchell, 120 S. Ct. at 2530.

cases were generally considered to be outliers by most commentators. The materials and equipment that were prohibited under *Meek* and *Wolman* seemed, to most observers, to be functionally indistinguishable from the materials and equipment that the Court had approved in other cases, such as secular textbooks provided to religious schools under textbook loan programs.[37] The federal program in *Mitchell* could have been upheld, and the *Meek* and *Wolman* cases overruled, using the Court's traditional Establishment Clause principles. In all of these cases, state programs purchased equipment and services which were - of themselves - secular in nature, and which conferred only incidental financial benefit upon religious schools.

What made the *Mitchell* opinion a radical break with the past was the way in which this result was reached. First, the terms in which the plurality discussed the theory of the individual as causative agent granted this theory well-nigh dispositive power. The role of individual choice in Establishment Clause jurisprudence was summarized by Justice Thomas in the following terms: "If aid to schools, even 'direct aid,' is neutrally available and, before reaching or benefiting any religious school, first passes through the hands (literally or figuratively) of numerous private citizens who are free to direct the aid elsewhere, the government has not provided any 'support of religion.'"[38]

Indeed, this theory has dispositive power, in the plurality's view, because of the plurality's reduction of Establishment Clause concerns to a single principle: whether the government action can reasonably be said to involve "indoctrination" in religion generally or in a particular religious faith.[39] If the aid is "neutral" – if it is "offered to a broad range of groups or persons without regard to . . . religion" – then it is unreasonable to conclude that any indoctrination has been done at government behest.[40] And if private choices – rather than the single act of government – determine the identity of aid recipients, "a government cannot, or at least cannot easily, grant special favors that might lead to a religious establishment."[41] And granting special favors, a deviation from "neutrality," is *all* that the Establishment Clause prohibits.

What is important is what is missing from this approach. In particular, absent is any mention of the traditional requirement that the state aid provide only "incidental" benefit to religious schools.

37. *See, e.g.*, Board of Educ. v. Allen, 392 U.S. 236, 242-48 (1968).

38. *Mitchell*, 120 S. Ct. at 2544 (quoting Witters v. Washington Dep't of Servs. for the Blind, 474 U.S. 481, 489 (1986)).

39. *See id.* at 2541-43.

40. *Id.* at 2541.

41. *Id.*

Under the plurality's approach, aid that is "neutral" and distributed in accordance with "private choice" would presumably be constitutional, even if it provided all, or nearly all, of a religious school's funding.

Voucher advocates have heralded the plurality opinion in *Mitchell* as proof that four Supreme Court justices, at least, are poised to remove the Establishment Clause barrier to the use of voucher money in religious schools. The enthusiasm that those who support vouchers feel after *Mitchell* may be premature. Justice Thomas carefully distinguished cash grants, citing the "'special Establishment Clause dangers'" that they have traditionally been believed to present.[42] There is no doubt, however, but that *Mitchell* adds momentum to the idea that "private choice" and "neutrality" should be powerful ideas - indeed, potentially dispositive ideas - in our interpretation of Establishment Clause guarantees.

How should we evaluate these ideas? Should they be the touchstones – the *exclusive* touchstones – for Establishment Clause analysis?

III. PRIVATE CHOICE AND NEUTRALITY: HIDDEN DANGERS FOR RELIGIOUS FREEDOM

A. *The Dispositive Power Of Private Choice*

If one believes that the direct payment of public money to religious institutions for religious purposes raises Establishment Clause concerns – the position that the Supreme Court has traditionally taken—then the idea of private choice is a possible way to distinguish voucher plans. Voucher plans, it is argued, are not school-aid programs in the traditional sense, but rather general welfare programs for students and their parents. If, as Justice Thomas observed, a state can issue a paycheck to one of its employees, knowing that the employee may direct the funds to a religious institution,[43] there seems to be little obvious reason why a state cannot give vouchers to parents or students, who can, in turn, use that money for religious education. In both cases, state funds are given to individuals who may direct those funds to religious activities and religious institutions. If individual decision making eliminates Establishment Clause issues in the first context, it is argued, it should do so equally in the latter.

---

42. *Id.* at 2546 (quoting Rosenberger v. Rector & Visitors of the Univ. of Va., 515 U.S. 819, 842 (1995)).

43. *See Mitchell*, 120 S. Ct. at 2545.

This theory – which I have called the "theory of the individual as causative agent"[44] – assumes that intervening individual decision-making breaks any constitutionally cognizable connection between the state action and the religious use. Under this theory, one simply looks to see if there is a private individual or entity whose actions or choices are responsible – in a causal sense – for the religious result. If there is, any constitutionally cognizable connection between the state's action and the religious result is eliminated.

Granting this theory dispositive power is, in many ways, a very attractive idea. It is clean, simple, and eliminates the need for much of the complicated line drawing that has plagued the Supreme Court's Establishment Clause jurisprudence. It also vindicates, in a powerful way, the ideals of parental autonomy and private choice.

Should we, however, view constitutionally cognizable connections between state actions and their ultimate results in such limited terms? Let us take, for instance, the establishment of a state program that lends textbooks to all students, including those who attend private, all-white academies. Let us further assume that the use of textbooks in such racially discriminatory schools is a result which the legislature has anticipated and which it has – through this program – explicitly or implicitly authorized. Does the intervening individual decision making in this case eliminate any constitutionally cognizable connection between the state act and the discriminatory result?

This question was presented in *Norwood v. Harrison*,[45] decided by the Supreme Court in 1973. In that case, the state argued that the use of the textbooks in racially discriminatory schools was not something for which the state was responsible, because the decision to attend such schools was a matter of private parental choice.[46] The Supreme Court rejected this argument.[47] The Court held that when the private conduct simply operates in an anticipated and authorized way as a part of a state sponsored plan, the private actions – and their results – may be fairly attributed to government.[48] Private parties cannot be used to both *implement and insulate* state policies and conduct. In the Court's words, "'a state may not induce, encourage or promote private persons to accomplish'" what it is—as a constitutional matter—forbidden to accomplish itself.[49]

---

44. *See* Underkuffler, *supra* note 4.
45. 413 U.S. 455 (1973).
46. *See id.* at 463-64 & n.7.
47. *Id.* at 465.
48. *Id.*
49. *Id.* (quoting Lee v. Macon County Bd. of Educ., 267 F. Supp. 458, 475-76 (M.D. Ala. 1967)).

The use of the theory of the individual as causative agent in Establishment Clause cases is, of course, quite different. In Establishment Clause cases, there is no question about the existence of state action since it is the government's funding action (or other action) that is, itself, the potentially unconstitutional act. However, the attempt to use individual decision making as a way to break the constitutionally cognizable connection between the state funding act and the ultimate use of those funds is the same in both cases. In the case of voucher plans, should this attempt succeed?

In my view, there is no convincing basis on which to distinguish voucher plans. The key in such cases is whether the individual choices that are made are *anticipated* and *authorized* by the state funding scheme. We must ask, in each case, whether the state retains an interest in the use of state funds beyond the individual decisional act. And, if it does, we must determine whether the individual decision making in question is something that furthers that interest in an anticipated and authorized way.

Voucher plans are established because of the vital public function – the education of children – which private schools perform. The use of public money in private religious schools is anticipated and authorized *because* of the schools' discharge of this function. The individual parental decisions made under voucher plans are not unrelated and unanticipated actions that break the connection between state payment and ultimate recipient; they are not cases in which an individual - such as a state employee, spending a paycheck—uses the money for something in which the state retains no interest. Rather, the individual parental decisions made pursuant to these plans are anticipated and authorized actions which *accomplish the goal*—the public funding of (private and public) education—*which the government has previously identified.*

If, therefore, the direct payment of tax moneys to religious elementary and secondary schools is something which the Constitution forbids, the fact that money is laundered through "private choice" under a state voucher plan does not, and should not, alter that unconstitutional result. We cannot, through this mechanism, avoid the more fundamental question that voucher plans present: whether such state funding – *in itself* – violates Establishment Clause guarantees.

B. *The Principle Of Neutrality*

The idea of government neutrality as an important part of Establishment Clause analysis is well established in Supreme Court jurisprudence. State neutrality - in the sense of equal treatment of all persons before the law, regardless of religious affiliation or identity - was one of the cardinal principles of reformers during the American

Founding Era[50] and is a bedrock principle today.[51] As the Court's opinion in *Everson* famously intoned, "[t]he 'establishment of religion' clause of the First Amendment means at least this: [n]either a state nor the federal government can set up a church. Neither can pass laws which aid one religion, aid all religions, or prefer one religion over another."[52]

The critical issue is whether neutrality, in this sense, is *all* that the Establishment Clause requires. This is actually an old debate, which has gained momentum with the question of the use of voucher money in religious schools.[53] If our only concern is state neutrality—if our only concern is that government not endorse, reward, or otherwise favor institutions or citizens on the basis of religious (or nonreligious) identity or belief—then, it is argued, the Establishment Clause presents no obstacle to voucher plans. The core idea of vouchers is that money will be available to all students and to all schools. This fact, and the mechanism of parental choice, guarantee that vouchers will not involve endorsement or favoritism of any kind.

One might quibble with some of the factual premises of this argument. For instance, the fact that a voucher plan is neutral in form does not necessarily mean that it was neutral in intention, or that it will, in fact, be neutral in operation. One can certainly imagine cases in which a legislative intention to favor certain groups is so apparent, or under which certain groups are such disproportionate beneficiaries, that the presumption of neutrality that the plan's form generates is seriously undermined. However, most of the voucher plans now proposed will have the formal, intentional, and operational neutrality that this argument assumes;

---

50. *See* Laura Underkuffler-Freund, *The Separation of the Religious and the Secular: A Foundational Challenge to First Amendment Theory*, 36 WM. & MARY L. REV. 837, 928-29, 947-49 (1995) (discussing historical record).

51. *See, e.g.*, Epperson v. Arkansas, 393 U.S. 97, 104 (1968) ("The First Amendment mandates government neutrality between religion . . . and nonreligion."); School Dist. v. Schempp, 374 U.S. 203, 215 (1963) (holding that the Constitution requires "'absolute equality before the law, of all religious opinions and sects . . . .'").

52. Everson v. Board of Educ., 330 U.S. 1, 15 (1947).

53. For discussion of this debate, *see, e.g.*, JESSE H. CHOPER, SECURING RELIGIOUS LIBERTY: PRINCIPLES FOR JUDICIAL INTERPRETATION OF THE RELIGION CLAUSES 15-16, 41-53, 97-159 (1995); Daniel O. Conkle, *The Path of American Religious Liberty: From the Original Theology to Formal Neutrality and an Uncertain Future*, 75 IND. L.J. 1 (2000); Ira C. Lupu, *To Control Faction and Protect Liberty: A General Theory of the Religion Clauses*, 7 J. CONTEMP. L. ISSUES 357 (1996); William P. Marshall, *What Is the Matter with Equality?: An Assessment of the Equal Treatment of Religion and Nonreligion in First Amendment Jurisprudence*, 75 IND. L.J. 193 (2000); Michael A. Paulsen, *Religion, Equality, and the Constitution: An Equal Protection Approach to Establishment Clause Adjudication*, 61 NOTRE DAME L. REV. 311 (1986).

and it is those plans that we must use to consider the merits of this argument.

The idea of government neutrality (in this sense) as the sole and dispositive content for Establishment Clause guarantees seems, at first glance, to be a favorable outcome for religious freedom. Under this understanding, religious individuals and institutions suffer no disability as the result of their religious status; they are, in particular, the potentially equal beneficiaries of government tax-funded largesse. But is this really the positive development for religious freedom that is imagined?

This neutrality – or, more accurately, this *parity* – paradigm is, unfortunately, a two-edged sword. For what it gives to freedom of conscience and individual choice through eligibility of religious institutions for government largesse, it takes from these very same values in critical ways.

First, the Establishment Clause prohibition on the payment of tax money to religious institutions for religious activities has been grounded in the belief that forcing individuals to support the religious beliefs of others – through the power of taxation – involves a particularly difficult violation of conscience. The enmeshing of government and religious institutions in this way was one of the practices to which reformers in the American Founding Era most bitterly objected.[54] We can ignore this objection, and the prohibitions it involves, only if we believe that the particular violation of conscience that government funding presents is – for some reason – no longer true.

The idea that compelled taxpayer support of the religion of others presents no particular violation of conscience – that such compulsion inflames no particularly dangerous or divisive passions – might be plausible if the plan were to involve only the funding of mainstream religious groups. Most citizens in this country would probably not feel a tremendous violation of conscience if they were compelled, through taxation, to fund (for instance) mainstream Christian or Jewish religious institutions with which they feel familiar and culturally comfortable. Indeed, most voucher advocates, when asked about the operation of voucher plans, envision such institutions as the recipients of state funds.

However, voucher plans that are premised upon the principle of neutrality *cannot*, by their very nature, be limited to such schools. If neutrality is to govern the operation of these programs, then *all* religious institutions, no matter how unfamiliar or even abhorrent their views, must be the equal recipients of such funds. If we publicly fund parochial schools, Quaker schools, Jewish schools, and other

54. *See, e.g.*, Underkuffler-Freund, *supra* note 50, at 930-56.

mainstream institutions – actions which most citizens would, in all likelihood, find quite benign – then we must also fund the private religious schools that preach religious hatred, racial bigotry, the oppression of women, and other views. It is one thing to tolerate intolerance; it is another thing to fund it. The divisiveness that the compelled public funding of such schools would inevitably create would serve only to destroy the atmosphere of tolerance and freedom that we have, as a society, so carefully and deliberately constructed. Indeed, the fact that we even *consider* such schemes is a testament to the success of our two centuries of freedom from them.

In addition, the idea that compelled financial support of the religions of others involves no particular violations of conscience for those who must pay endangers religious freedom in another way. If one believes that religious issues pose no particular difficulties for freedom of conscience - if one believes that coerced funding of religion is no different from the coerced funding of social programs, or foreign policy, or other uses with which one disagrees - then the traditional disabilities under which religious institutions have labored are eliminated. But this advantage comes, for them, at a cost. For with the triumph of the neutrality or "parity" paradigm in Establishment Clause jurisprudence comes, inevitably, the triumph of the neutrality or "parity" paradigm in the Free Exercise context, as well.

The fundamental reason for the different treatment of religious and secular institutions, as reflected in traditional understandings of the Establishment Clause, is the belief that *religion is different,* and that religious institutions reflect that difference. We worry about the merger of religion and government – we worry about the endorsement of religion by government – we worry about the funding of religion by government – because of the *particular* value and resultant power that religion has in individual lives. The movement to a neutrality or "parity" paradigm in Establishment Clause jurisprudence is possible only if we shed this idea. To decide that religious institutions can be funded on a par with secular ones, we must decide, as an implicit matter, that religious institutions are no different from secular ones. To do this, we must first conclude that religion as a specially powerful—and a specially valuable—force in human lives is one to which we no longer subscribe.

If we take this step—if we reject the idea that religion or freedom of conscience has any special power or value which justifies the imposition of particular legal *prohibitions*—then we must also reject the idea that religion or freedom of conscience has any special power or value which justifies the extension of particular legal *protections.* The same special characteristics that justify special treatment in one context drive special treatment in the other. If religion claims no special value or power, requiring its institutional separation from the processes of government, then it can likewise claim no special value or power, requiring its protection from ordinary political processes and ordinary laws. Indeed, we find that—with the advance of the neutrality or "parity" paradigm in Establishment Clause cases—has come its advance in the Free Exercise context, as well. In a recent doctrinal shift, the Supreme Court held that free exercise claims (as a class) will generally lose to public interests expressed as a part of "religiously neutral" state laws.[55] Some commentators have agreed, arguing that free exercise rights should not mean that religious exercise be privileged, but that it simply be treated with the same regard as citizens' other concerns.[56] The rise of neutrality or "parity" as the operative paradigm in this context was a marked departure from the Supreme Court's traditional approach, under which religious beliefs and practices were protected, absent a compelling state interest, from the operation of "otherwise neutral" state laws. This development should not, however, be an unanticipated one: if religion is not special in one context, there is no obvious reason why it should be in the other.

The issue of vouchers has, unfortunately and paradoxically, raised an issue that has tremendous implications for our understanding of First Amendment guarantees. We must grapple with whether, as a fundamental matter, religion or freedom of conscience is a uniquely powerful force in human life and law. We must ask whether the *special power* which we ascribe to religion – and which is the basis for both constitutional protections and prohibitions – is empirically true and legally justified. Does religion have unique power, such that compelled taxpayer funding of religious activities and religious institutions is somehow more opprobrious, and more dangerous, than the funding of other activities and institutions? Does religion have unique power, such that protection of its practice, and its institutions, is uniquely justified? These are the questions that the neutrality or "parity" paradigm, in all of its facets, presents. And so—for all of the gains that this idea might yield for choice and freedom of conscience, in some ways—we must ask whether it is worth the cost.

55. *See* Lyng v. Northwest Indian Cemetery Protective Ass'n, 485 U.S. 439 (1988) and Employment Div. v. Smith, 494 U.S. 872 (1990) (holding that if a state law simply precludes religious conduct, that – in the absence of evidence of intent to discriminate against the religious – creates no cognizable claim under the First Amendment's Free Exercise Clause).

56. *See, e.g.*, Christopher L. Eisgruber & Lawrence G. Sager, *The Vulnerability of Conscience: The Constitutional Basis for Protecting Religious Conduct*, 61 U. CHI. L. REV. 1245, 1283 (1994).

IV. CONCLUSION

On its face, the idea of the constitutionality of the use of voucher money in religious schools seems to be a victory for religious freedom. However, it is, in the end, a Trojan horse. For while proclaiming the cause of religious freedom, it necessarily carries – through the destruction of religious tolerance, and the denial of religion's special power – forces that will undermine that very freedom, within it.

THE INCREASINGLY ANACHRONISTIC CASE AGAINST SCHOOL VOUCHERS

IRA C. LUPU*

My father spent the last ten weeks of his life in St. Peter's Hospital in Albany, New York. Neither he nor his family had directly selected this hospital; rather, he was there as a result of his physician's admitting privileges. A small Crucifix hung on the wall of every room in which he received treatment. Catholic priests, as well as clergy from other denominations, frequently dropped into rooms at St. Peter's to see if patients needed prayers or other words of comfort. My father was Jewish, and he had not led a religiously observant life, but his childhood experience had brought him close to Catholic clergy.[1] In my presence (and, to my knowledge, throughout his stay), he welcomed the prayers of the priests he encountered at St. Peter's. My father was Medicare-eligible, and the United States eventually paid a very substantial sum to the hospital for the medical care he received in the concluding period of his life.

No Religion Clause scholar or advocate of whom I am aware would argue that government payment to St. Peter's Hospital for the cost of medical service for my father's benefit violated the Establishment Clause. Yet, this expenditure obviously contributed to the financial well-being of a sectarian institution. My father's Medicare eligibility permitted him to utilize, without charge to him, the services of that institution, and those services were rendered in a sectarian religious environment. Indeed, his vulnerability at that moment made him unusually susceptible to the religious influences in that setting, although he was in no way compelled to respond to those stimuli.

---

* Louis Harkey Mayo Research Professor of Law, The George Washington University Law School. Thanks to Bob Tuttle for very helpful comments on an earlier version of this piece, and to Julia Lee, of the Class of 2000 at the Law School, and Chris Reed, of the Burns Law Library at George Washington, for research help in the preparation of this essay.

1. At the age of four, my father was misdiagnosed as having an incurable illness, and his impoverished Jewish parents sent him to a charity hospital run by an order of the Catholic Church. He spent the ages of four through seven in that hospital and was attended to each day by Catholic nuns. For the rest of his life, despite continuing Jewish family ties, he displayed little attachment to Judaism, but reacted with energy and enthusiasm whenever he encountered members of Catholic religious orders.

Why are these arrangements uncontroversially accepted in the community of Religion Clause scholars, while comparable arrangements involving elementary and secondary school students produce so much controversy? Why do many of our citizens think that school vouchers and medical vouchers are so different in their constitutional significance?

Impressionability alone cannot sustain the distinction; at the end of life, and in all times of grave illness, hospital patients may be quite as impressionable as young students. Either medical vouchers are constitutionally questionable when they may be used at sectarian hospitals, or the constitutional case against school vouchers cannot effectively be sustained.[2] After years of wrestling with the question, I have come to the conclusion that the constitutional case against school vouchers is extremely weak; indeed, in this article, I question the force of the constitutional case against direct state aid to sectarian elementary and secondary schools. The arguments against vouchers—usually characterized as indirect aid to sectarian schools because families are an intervening force between the state and these schools—and the arguments against direct aid rest on precedents and policies whose contemporary relevance has dwindled dramatically.

The anti-voucher case essentially rests on three legs, each of which is analyzed in separate parts of this essay. The first, discussed in Part I, emphasizes the difference between forbidden, direct aid and permissible, indirect aid by government to religious institutions,[3] and suggests that voucher arrangements are really direct aid in disguise. The second leg, probed in Part II, rests primarily on the asserted non-neutrality of voucher arrangements; that is, it rests on the argument that voucher programs favor religion. The third, building upon the first two, goes to the heart of the matter—it purports to explain precisely why direct aid by the government to religious institutions, performing functions of secular value, is forbidden even if that aid is part of a religion-neutral program. The core argument against direct aid, evaluated critically in Part III, stands upon the case law from *Everson v. Board of Education*[4] to *Lemon v. Kurtzman*[5] and their progeny in the 1970s, and rests heavily upon these twentieth-century deci-

2. The Wisconsin Supreme Court recently arrived at this conclusion in *Jackson v. Benson*, 578 N.W.2d 602 (Wis. 1998), *cert denied* 119 S. Ct. 466 (1998).

3. *See, e.g.*, Mueller v. Allen, 463 U.S. 388 (1983) (indirect assistance to sectarian schools, by way of state income tax deduction for tuition and other expenses, does not violate the Establishment Clause).

4. 330 U.S. 1 (1947).

5. 403 U.S. 602 (1971).

sions' account of the Virginia version of Establishment Clause history.

I. The Distinction Between Direct and Indirect Aid

Ever since the Supreme Court's decision in *Mueller v. Allen*,[6] upholding state income tax deductions for school expenses typically associated with private, sectarian schools, the distinction between direct and indirect aid has been crucial to the voucher battle. Direct aid, presumptively forbidden, involves a transfer of funds from the government treasury to the coffers of religious institutions without passing through the hands of any citizen-intermediaries. If a state or local government were simply to make an unrestricted cash distribution of $X per enrolled pupil to each accredited school within its jurisdiction, the payments to sectarian schools made under such a program would constitute violations of current Establishment Clause principles. In particular, such aid would be held to either (a) impermissibly advance the school's religious mission, or (b) impermissibly involve the state's agents in monitoring to be sure that no such state-supported religious advancement occurred.[7] If, on the other hand, state or local government makes available to families with children a benefit which may be deployed by the family in favor of a religious institution, *Mueller* suggests that such an arrangement would not violate the Clause. Family-directed aid, even if it has its source in state largesse, benefits religion as the result of private rather than government choice.[8]

---

6. 463 U.S. 388 (1983).

7. *See Lemon*, 403 U.S. at 616; *see also* Wolman v. Walter, 433 U.S. 229 (1977) (use of public monies for purchases of instructional materials and equipment for nonpublic schools unconstitutional); Meek v. Pittenger, 421 U.S. 349 (1975) (statute authorizing loan of materials to nonpublic schools violates Establishment Clause). None of these cases involved unrestricted cash grants to parochial schools; all of them assumed that such grants would present clear violations of the Establishment Clause.

8. The leading case to the contrary—upon which voucher opponents heavily rely—is *Committee for Public Education v. Nyquist*, 413 U.S. 756 (1973), a 5-4 decision in which New York's tax credits, rather than deductions, for parochial school tuition, were held to violate the Establishment Clause, based primarily on the argument that the tax credits were equivalent to tuition grants to a class narrowly defined and dominated by parents of parochial school students. There is real doubt as to whether *Nyquist* would be decided the same way today; the Wisconsin Supreme Court in *Jackson v. Benson* distinguished the New York program invalidated in *Nyquist* on the ground that the Milwaukee program was designed to expand school choices for children in public schools, and therefore did not aid children already in private schools when the program commenced. *See* 578 N.W.2d 602, 614 (Wis. 1998), *cert denied*, 114 S. Ct. 466 (1998).

Accordingly, all voucher plans involve some version of the mechanics of indirection. For example, in the Milwaukee program recently upheld by the Wisconsin Supreme Court,[9] checks to cover voucher payments are made payable to the parent-custodians of the students, but are physically transmitted to the school in which the voucher student is enrolled.[10] The custodian never gets possession of the check; upon enrollment of the student, the custodian simply endorses the check over to the school, which does have possession. Unsurprisingly, this arrangement, which effectively involves the joint consent of school and custodian to effectuate a transfer from state to school, has provoked argument over whether the transfer should be characterized as direct (and therefore forbidden) or indirect (and therefore permissible).

The Wisconsin Supreme Court rather quickly and easily disposed of the argument that "these precautionary provisions . . . amount[ed] to some type of 'sham' to funnel public funds to sectarian private schools."[11] The court emphasized the crucial question was "not to ascertain the path upon which public funds travel . . . but rather to determine who ultimately chooses that path . . . . [N]ot one cent flows from the State to a sectarian private school . . . except as a result of the necessary and intervening choices of individual parents."[12] Accordingly, the court concluded, the program cannot be reasonably viewed as an endorsement of religion.[13]

However convincing the direct-indirect distinction may be,[14] few members of the Supreme Court have ever been persuaded by

9. *See Jackson*, 578 N.W.2d at 602.

10. *See id.* at 609, 618.

11. *Id.* at 618.

12. *Id.*

13. *Id.*

14. As a matter of constitutional policy, there is definitely more to be said for the indirect-direct distinction than the narrow, precedent-oriented approach of the Wisconsin Supreme Court. Direct aid to religious institutions presents dangers less forcefully present than aid controlled by individual choice. First, direct aid tends to favor large religious organizations, with an existing structure of schools, over smaller and more decentralized sects. Second, direct aid is far more likely than its indirect counterpart to be "captured" by the institution's capital expenditure plans; when direct aid fuels capital spending, the likelihood of increased institutional dependence on the state grows. Third, aid funneled through individuals is more likely to produce dynamics of change. Certainly, in a generalized system in which vouchers are made available to all, new schools (sectarian and otherwise) are more likely over time to come into being. When parents can vote the state's money with their children's feet, pre-existing systems of religious education have no political advantage over the long term.

it. The *Mueller v. Allen*[15] Court was divided 5-4, and the dissenters (Justices Brennan, Marshall, Blackmun, and Stevens) opposed both direct and indirect aid to sectarian elementary and secondary schools.[16] A number of other Justices, including Chief Justice Rehnquist, have seemed approving of most forms of both direct and indirect aid.[17] At the time of *Mueller*, Justices Powell and Stewart, and Chief Justice Burger were the only members of the Court who found the distinction dispositive. On today's Court, there is reason to believe that four Justices (Stevens, Souter, Breyer, and Ginsburg) strenuously oppose direct aid, and have their doubts about indirect aid,[18] that Justices Scalia and Thomas,[19] and Chief Justice Rehnquist would permit many forms of both direct and indirect aid, and that only Justices O'Connor and Kennedy might be tempted to draw lines on this basis. Whatever the merits of this way of looking at these issues, few Justices (albeit those with swing votes) have ever believed that this was the key to the problem.

In the end, the argument about "directness" of voucher aid, frequently characterized in terms of form and substance (*i.e.*, the vouchers are "really" direct aid even though they have some of the form of indirect aid), cannot be resolved on its own terms.[20] This is so because the direct-indirect distinction is completely insensitive to the degree of state constraint on private choice. When the state pays its employees a wage, they can spend the money for any lawful purpose, including for the advancement of religion. In such circumstances, the state cannot be held responsible for any religious benefit arising from the unfettered spend-

---

15. 463 U.S. 388 (1983).

16. *Id.* at 404 (Marshall, J., joined by Brennan, Blackmun, and Stevens, JJ., dissenting).

17. *See, e.g.*, Wallace v. Jaffree, 472 U.S. 38, 91-107 (1985) (Rehnquist, J., dissenting); Committee for Pub. Educ. v. Nyquist, 413 U.S. 756, 813 (1973) (White, J., dissenting); Lemon v. Kurtzman, 403 U.S. 602, 660 (1971) (White, J., dissenting).

18. *See, e.g.*, Rosenberger v. Rectors & Visitors of the Univ. of Va., 515 U.S. 819, 863 (1995) (Souter, J., dissenting, joined by Stevens, Ginsburg, and Breyer, JJ.).

19. *Id.* at 852 (Thomas, J., concurring). Justice Scalia has repeatedly expressed his disagreement with *Lemon*. *See, e.g.*, Lamb's Chapel v. Center Moriches Union Free Sch. Dist., 508 U.S. 384, 397-401 (1993) (Scalia, J., concurring in judgment); Edwards v. Aguillard, 482 U.S. 578, 636-40 (1987) (Scalia, J., dissenting).

20. The voucher debate would not be the first in which distinctions concerning directness and indirectness proved constitutionally unhelpful. *See, e.g.*, NLRB v. Jones & Laughlin Steel Corp., 301 U.S. 1 (1937) (rejecting approach of direct vs. indirect consequences in measuring the reach of the federal Commerce power).

ing choices of its employees. By contrast, when the state constrains the benefit in certain ways—for example, a state income tax deduction for all charitable contributions—the probability and forseeability of a boost to religion are markedly increased. Contemporary voucher programs tend to constrain yet further, limiting parents to the mix of participating schools, in which sectarian institutions will be heavily represented, at least in the short run. Even with a private choice mechanism, this sectarian predominance among school choices presents a pressing question about the constitutionality of school vouchers.

II. The Search for Neutrality

As suggested at the end of Part I, aid to religious institutions is on safer constitutional footing when it is folded into a larger, more inclusive category of beneficiaries.[21] Aid to religious institutions alone, even if channeled through individuals, carries the strong appearance of government intent to advance the cause of religion qua religion. Aid to a more general group of private hospitals, post-secondary schools, or family service agencies, even if these classifications include religious enterprises, is much more readily viewed as government support for a social purpose independent of religion. This way of considering the problem is revealing; it suggests that government objectives, rather than policy consequences, are constitutionally controlling. Even in a religion-neutral scheme with a broad beneficiary class, tax exemptions, government subsidies, and government services will put religious institutions in a better position than they would be in the absence of such government largesse.

That the consequential advancement of religious institutions is not constitutionally fatal in and of itself creates several puzzles. First, it leaves unexplained why direct aid to sectarian elementary and secondary schools should be forbidden when that aid falls within a larger, neutral category of aid to all schools. Second, and closely related to the first, it leaves unasked a crucial question about the meaning of neutrality. The conception of neutrality upon which the pro-aid position depends is formal; so long as the category of beneficiary institutions is drawn to include non-religious and religious institutions, formal neutrality is satisfied. Critics of this approach, however, focus upon the substantive distribution achieved in fact by such programs; if the great bulk of beneficiaries are religious institutions, the critics believe we

21. Virtually all of the Justices seem to subscribe to this theme. *See, e.g.*, Board of Educ. of Kiryas Joel v. Grumet, 512 U.S. 687 (1994); *Rosenberger*, 515 U.S. at 819; Bowen v. Kendrick, 487 U.S. 589 (1988).

should pierce the veil of formality and view the program as substantively nonneutral and therefore forbidden.[22]

As some scholars have emphasized, constitutional neutrality might be understood in very different terms than those presented by a debate about the formal description of the beneficiary category. One alternative approach emphasizes the behavioral incentives created by state policy; its advocates argue that neutrality should entail that the state not create incentives for or against religious choice.[23] The combination of compulsory education and free public schools creates powerful incentives to parents to select a secular option.[24] An incentive-focused theory of neutrality suggests that aid to sectarian schools is constitutionally required, and at the very least, constitutionally permitted.

A third, quite contrary approach to neutrality proceeds by redescribing the baseline from which neutrality is calculated. Voucher opponents argue that the provision of free secular education, long established by custom and practice in the United States, should be viewed as the baseline condition, departures from which are seen as nonneutral. On this view, vouchers can be seen as creating new, impermissible incentives to choose religious education instead of the secular, baseline alternative.[25]

---

22. *See, e.g.*, Mueller v. Allen, 463 U.S. 388, 404 (1983) (Marshall, J., dissenting).

23. *See* Douglas Laycock, *Formal, Substantive, and Disaggregated Neutrality Towards Religion*, 39 DEPAUL L. REV. 993 (1990). For an unusual and provocative slice through the question of neutrality, see Michael W. McConnell, *The Selective Funding Problem: Abortions and Religious Schools*, 104 HARV. L. REV. 989 (1991).

24. If extended to fields beyond those in which participation is compelled, the incentive neutrality theory has radical consequences. To thus extend the theory's premises is to require state financing of the religious variant of every enterprise of which there is a free or lower-than-market cost option provided by government. Universities, mental hospitals, cemeteries, family service organizations, and many more enterprises have public sector and religious parallels. To go down this road is to burden government with multiple financing obligations, or to drive the government entirely out of various enterprises. A commitment to incentive neutrality thus might foster an odd and dramatic transformation from a state of affairs in which government could not aid religious institutions to one in which the obligation to avoid disincentives to religious choice proves so overwhelming as to usher in the night watchman state.

25. *See* Steven K. Green, *The Legal Argument Against Private School Choice*, 62 U. CIN. L. REV. 37, 72-73 (1993). A different approach to the problem is offered in Kathleen Sullivan, *Parades, Public Squares, and Voucher Payments: Problems of Government Neutrality*, 28 CONN. L. REV. 243 (1996). Professor Sullivan argues that elementary and secondary education are forms of government speech (even if privately delivered) because of compulsory attendance and state regulation of curriculum. From this premise, she

Because the substantial majority of participating schools in the Milwaukee system are sectarian schools,[26] the operation of the Milwaukee voucher system can be characterized as creating incentives to choose sectarian education over its secular counterparts, public or private.

Notice the difficulties of this latter argument for the nonneutrality of vouchers. Its measuring stick is laid against departures from free secular education. But why should existing institutions of this sort establish a state of affairs used to measure neutrality? The current system of property tax exemptions for charitable uses includes religious uses; if the current system did not, would we think that a system of tax exemptions for secular charity was constitutionally neutral toward religion? Or would we see what would seem plain—that is, that our existing structures sharply preferred the nonreligious to the religious? To put it differently, in such a world, the baseline would be pro-secular nonneutrality, and every attempt to equalize the benefits between religious and secular institutions would be viewed as a nonneutral favoring of religion.[27]

Moreover, if free secular education is to be accepted as the baseline, the question remains as to how to characterize the change of affairs implemented by a voucher system like Milwaukee's. In static terms, the current profile of private schools eligible to participate in the voucher program suggests that some voucher students are being moved toward religion; roughly three-quarters of the participating schools are sectarian.[28] Two additional elements of the story, however, need to be factored

---

concludes that government need not and may not finance religious education at the elementary and secondary level. For a comprehensive general statement of the view that secularity enjoys a constitutionally privileged position, see Kathleen Sullivan, *Religion and Liberal Democracy*, 59 U. CHI. L. REV. 195 (1992). For a sharp rejoinder to Professor Sullivan, see Michael McConnell, *Religious Freedom at a Crossroads*, 59 U. CHI. L. REV. 115, 133 (1992) ("To permit religious choices only at the cost of forfeiting an equal share in public goods is not freedom of religion.").

26. Of the 122 private schools eligible to participate in the Milwaukee program, eighty-nine are sectarian. *See* Jackson v. Benson, 578 N.W.2d 602, 619 n.17 (Wis. 1998). Nevertheless, the court in *Jackson* held the system as a whole to be neutral, because voucher-eligible students had a choice among sectarian voucher schools, nonsectarian voucher schools, and free public schools in Milwaukee. *See id.* at 617-19.

27. The United States Supreme Court's recent decisions in *Lamb's Chapel* and *Rosenberger* plainly reject this proposition in favor of its exact opposite—that is, the exclusion of religious perspectives from certain government subsidies is forbidden by the Constitution. *See Rosenberger*, 515 U.S. at 828-37; *Lamb's Chapel*, 508 U.S. at 393-95.

28. *See Jackson*, 578 N.W.2d at 619.

into the analysis. First, the possibility of dynamic change over time in the composition of participating schools may move the incentive effects back toward neutral. As the quantity and quality of secular private schools increase, the religious incentives in the scheme decrease; put differently, otherwise identical voucher programs will be more or less religiously neutral, depending upon the mix of available schools.[29]

Second, the incentive effects will differ depending upon the extent to which parents desire their children to participate in the program of religious instruction at a given sectarian school. The Milwaukee program forbids participating schools from requiring religious studies or activities by voucher students.[30] On the Milwaukee facts, the religious incentives (as compared to the educational incentives) to choose sectarian schools may be very weak, nonexistent, or even slightly negative, and the religious consequences may be slender indeed.[31]

In the end, arguments about neutrality are unsatisfying and unresolvable. Voucher proponents believe that free public schools represent non-neutral favoring of irreligion, and voucher opponents believe that vouchers nonneutrally favor religion. Both may be right, but only because they view the problem from their own, contested vantage point. What is undeniable, however, is that the current structure of Religion Clause law, which leads to the lingering constitutional doubts about vouchers, is asymmetrical. On the "rights side"—that is, with respect to issues

---

29. When aid is indirect, current law precludes this mix from affecting the constitutional outcome. *See* Mueller v. Allen, 463 U.S. 388, 401 (1983) ("We would be loath to adopt a rule grounding the constitutionality of a facially neutral law on annual reports reciting the extent to which various classes of private citizens claimed benefits under the law.").

30. *See Jackson*, 578 N.W.2d at 609.

31. A report on the Milwaukee program asserts that almost three-quarters of the participants have been African-American. *See LaFollette Public Affairs Report*, (visited Mar. 3, 1999) <http://www.lafollette.wisc.edu/outreach/pubs/fifthyear/report.htm>. Nationwide, one-quarter of Catholic school students are non-white (African-American, Hispanic-American, Asian-American) and one-half of these are non-Catholic. *See* David Baker & Cornelius Riordan, *The "Eliting" of the Common American Catholic School and the National Education Crisis*, PHI DELTA KAPPAN, Sept. 1998, at 16. Most of the Hispanic students in Catholic schools are Catholic; most of the African-American students in Catholic schools are not. *See* JOHN J. CONVEY, CATHOLIC SCHOOLS MAKE A DIFFERENCE: 25 YEARS OF RESEARCH 42 (1992); *see also* ANTHONY S. BRYK ET AL., CATHOLIC SCHOOLS AND THE COMMON GOOD 69 (1993); Douglas Laycock, *Toward a General Theory of the Religion Clauses: The Case of Church Labor Relations and the Right to Church Autonomy*, 81 COLUM. L. REV. 1373, 1387-88 n.119 (1981). To the extent that the Milwaukee program funneled Protestant African-Americans to Catholic schools, the religious disincentives may have outweighed the religious incentives for family choice of a particular school.

of leaving families free to choose among market alternatives for educating their children, the existing legal framework is scrupulously neutral between religious and nonreligious schools. If one can afford sectarian school, one can find and buy that option, and the state may not eliminate it.[32] On the "benefits side," however—that is, the body of Establishment Clause principles governing the distribution of state largesse—the current law favors secular institutions by its restrictiveness on state assistance to religious institutions performing comparable functions.

Moreover, this asymmetry has over time been narrowed almost entirely to the field of elementary and secondary education. The state may give grants to church programs for educating adolescents on matters of sexuality and pregnancy, so long as the programs are not religiously oriented.[33] The state may provide grants to colleges and universities, so long as they are not "pervasively sectarian," for secular educational purposes,[34] and the state may help finance buildings on the campuses of religiously affiliated colleges, so long as the school promises not to use these buildings for sectarian purposes.[35] Most recently and stunningly, the Supreme Court has held that state universities that finance journals of student opinion must include journals with a religious perspective.[36] Tuition vouchers at the college and university level have existed for years, and these programs routinely include sectarian schools.[37]

To put it more starkly, the area of financing elementary and secondary education is a constitutional anomaly, and growing more so with each Supreme Court term. The Supreme Court's recent ruling in *Agostini v. Felton,*[38] overruling its decade-old deci-

---

32. *See* Pierce v. Society of Sisters, 268 U.S. 510 (1925).

33. *See* Bowen v. Kendrick, 487 U.S. 589 (1988).

34. *See* Roemer v. Board of Pub. Works, 426 U.S. 736, 755 (1976). *Roemer* played a prominent part in the Fourth Circuit's recent decision to remand a lower court ruling, upholding a grant denial, for further findings on the issue of whether a particular college is "pervasively sectarian," a finding which will disqualify a post-secondary school from state assistance. *See* Columbia Union College v. Clarke, 159 F.3d 151 (4th Cir. 1998).

35. *See, e.g.,* Hunt v. McNair, 413 U.S. 734 (1973); Tilton v. Richardson, 403 U.S. 672 (1971).

36. *See Rosenberger*, 515 U.S. at 819.

37. *See* Witters v. Washington Dep't of Servs. for the Blind, 474 U.S. 481 (1986). New York State has for many years operated its Regents Scholarship program, which provides tuition vouchers to New York residents attending in-state colleges and universities, including religiously affiliated ones. *See* N.Y. EDUC. LAW §§ 601, 605a (McKinney 1998).

38. 521 U.S. 203 (1997) (overruling *Aguilar* and declaring the permissibility of providing remedial education delivered by public employees on site at sectarian schools). For a critique of *Agostini* and an attempt to

sion in *Aguilar v. Felton*,[39] has only exacerbated the confusion in the field, as any follower of lower court decisions on aid to sectarian schools can confirm.[40] Are there arguments from earlier precedent, or from original constitutional history, that may help explain this difference in treatment between these financing questions and others, which on the surface seem indistinguishable?

III. The Crumbling Argument from Precedent—*Everson, Lemon,* and Their Progeny

All of the doctrinal machinery, discussed above, that focuses on neutrality and indirectness of aid is driven by the strictures contained in the line of Supreme Court decisions from *Everson* (1948) to *Lemon v. Kurtzman* (1971) and their progeny from the 1970s. These cases, all of which but *Everson* involve direct aid to elementary and secondary schools, reflect state attempts to aid an overwhelmingly Catholic set of private schools.[41] Justice Jackson's dissenting opinion in *Everson*,[42] and Chief Justice Burger's opinion for the Court in *Lemon*,[43] are open and conspicuous tracts about the pervasive religious indoctrination thought to accompany the system of Catholic education. The principles generated by these two cases rest entirely upon judicial perceptions of the utter inseparability of religion from education in the settings of such schools. Catholic education is held out by Justice Jackson as the engine that fuels intergenerational transmission of the faith, and Chief Justice Burger similarly emphasizes the

---

rehabilitate a strong version of the no-aid principle, see Gary Mozer, Note, *The Crumbling Wall Between Church and State:* Agostini v. Felton, *Aid to Parochial Schools, and the Establishment Clause in the Twenty-First Century*, 31 CONN. L. REV. 337 (1998).

39. 473 U.S. 402 (1985) (holding that the provision of remedial education by public employees on site at sectarian schools violates the Establishment Clause).

40. For good illustrations of the difficulties lower courts have had in applying the conflicting welter of Supreme Court decisions in this area, see *Helms v. Picard*, 151 F.3d 347 (5th Cir. 1998); *Walker v. San Francisco Unified School District*, 46 F.3d 1449 (1995); see also *Columbia Union College v. Clarke*, 159 F.3d 151 (4th Cir. 1998). In each of these three cases, the courts of appeals struggled with questions arising from the Supreme Court's inconsistent precedents and recent but incomplete movement in the direction of the permissibility of aid.

41. The transportation assistance to families of schoolchildren, at issue in *Everson v. Board of Education*, 330 U.S. 1 (1947), was explicitly limited by local resolution to public school students and Catholic school students.

42. *See id.* at 18-28 (Jackson, J., dissenting).

43. *See* Lemon v. Kurtzman, 403 U.S. 602, 606-25 (1971). *See also id.* at 625-42 (Douglas, J., concurring).

degree, pervasiveness, and missionary sweep of Catholic elementary and secondary education. These are inquiries into the sociology of a particular faith, and arguably prejudiced ones at that, masquerading as an inquiry into the meaning of the Constitution.

The Protestant paranoia fueled by waves of Catholic immigration to the U.S., beginning in the mid-nineteenth century, cannot form the basis of a stable constitutional principle,[44] and the stability of the principle has been undermined by the amelioration of those concerns. From the advent of publicly supported, compulsory education until very recently, aid to sectarian schools primarily meant aid to Catholic schools as an enterprise to rival publicly supported, essentially Protestant schools. But the anti-Catholic prejudice that drove this aspect of separationism has been progressively undermined in the last forty years. The election of John Kennedy was among the key ingredients of the change, as was the increased consciousness of prejudice that the civil rights movement provoked. The pronouncement of the church itself, in Vatican II's Declaration of Religious Freedom, in favor of religious liberty for all and church-state separation in the modern world, helped reassure non-Catholics that the church was no longer engaged in a campaign to dominate secular institutions.[45]

The suburbanization and upward mobility of American Catholics has also been a major contributing force;[46] as Catholics have left inner cities, the bastions of parish schools, they have become less inclined toward traditional participation in the Church, including educating their children in the prescribed sectarian way.[47] As a result of this migration, Catholic schools in the inner cities have been forced to become more ecumenical in their approach in order to attract enough students, a significant

---

44. The best documentation and analysis of this phenomenon will soon be forthcoming in my colleague Philip Hamburger's work on separation of church and state. *See also* Steven K. Green, *The Blaine Amendment Reconsidered*, 36 AMER. J. LEG. HIST. 38 (1992).

45. BRYK ET AL., *supra* note 31, at 49-50.

46. On suburbanization of Catholics, see Rosalind Rossi, "*Success-Failure Story" of Catholic Schools*, CHI. SUN-TIMES, (Jan. 21, 1997) at 12; Steve Berg, *Catholic Education; How Do Catholic Schools Do It?*, MINNEAPOLIS STAR TRIB., April 1, 1997 at 1A. On upward mobility, see Baker & Riordan, *supra* note 31, at 16. For a wider-angle lens on changes in Catholic schools over the period from 1960 to 1990, see BRYK ET AL., *supra* note 31.

47. *See* Baker & Riordan, *supra* note 31, at 16. *See also* BRYK ET AL., *supra* note 31, at 33 (Catholic school enrollment fell from a high of 5.5 million, or 12% of the school-age population, in 1965, to 2.5 million, or 5.4% of the school-age population, in 1990.).

number of whom are non-Catholic, to survive.[48] When *Lemon* was decided in 1971, less than three percent of the students in Catholic elementary and secondary schools were not of the Roman Catholic faith;[49] by the late 1990s, that percentage had quadrupled.[50]

Simultaneously, the rise of evangelical Protestant movements in America, the tendency among many American Jews to choose sectarian education, and the inclination among various immigrant groups to emphasize parochial education all have stimulated the creation of non-Catholic sectarian schools and a corresponding demand among non-Catholics for government policies supportive of religious education. At the time of *Lemon,* 65% of all private schools and 75% of all sectarian schools in the United States were Roman Catholic schools, and these schools contained 90% of all the pupils then enrolled in sectarian schools.[51] In *Lemon,* the Court tells us, "more than 96% of [the Pennsylvania students who would have benefitted from the aid program] attend church-related schools, and most of these schools are affiliated with the Roman Catholic church."[52] In *Earley v. DiCenso,*[53] a case from Rhode Island decided as a companion to *Lemon,* 95% of the pupils benefitted by the aid program attended Roman Catholic schools.[54] In *Wolman v. Walter,*[55] the parties stipulated that, in 1974-75, 691 of 720 nonpublic schools in the state were sectarian, and "more than 92% [of the nonpublic school enrollment] attended Catholic schools."[56]

By sharp contrast, in 1995-96, Catholic schools represented only 29.8% of the private elementary and secondary schools in

48. Non-Catholic enrollment in Catholic schools quintupled between 1970 (2.6%) and 1983 (14.3%). *See* BRYK ET AL., *supra* note 31, at 69. *See also* CONVEY, *supra* note 31, at 41; MARY JO METZLER, NATIONAL CATHOLIC EDUC. ASSOC., U.S. CATHOLIC ELEMENTARY AND SECONDARY SCHOOLS, 1997-98, at 16 (1998). Laycock, *supra* note 31, at 1387-88 n.119.

49. *See* NATIONAL CATHOLIC EDUCATION ASSOCIATION, A STATISTICAL REPORT ON CATHOLIC ELEMENTARY AND SECONDARY SCHOOLS FOR THE YEARS 1967-68 TO 1969-70, at 10.

50. The most recent survey by the National Catholic Education Association puts non-Catholic enrollment in Catholic schools at 13.6%. *See* METZLER, *supra* note 48, at 16.

51. *See* DIANE GERTLER & LINDA A. BARKER, U.S. DEP'T OF HEALTH, EDUC. & WELFARE, STATISTICS OF NONPUBLIC ELEMENTARY SCHOOLS, 1970-71, at 5-10 (1973).

52. Lemon v. Kurtzman, 403 U.S. 602, 610 (1971).

53. 403 U.S. 602 (1971).

54. *Id.* at 608.

55. 433 U.S. 229 (1977).

56. *Id.* at 234.

the United States,[57] and their enrollment represented 50.1% of the students enrolled at such schools.[58] Because many students now enrolled at Catholic schools are non-Catholic,[59] non-Catholics probably now represent the majority of students enrolled in sectarian schools in the United States.

If the line of decisions from *Everson* to *Lemon* was driven substantially by the then-demographics of public and private education, coupled with anti-Catholic animus, what remains to justify principles forbidding direct aid to sectarian elementary and secondary schools? For me, the key to this inquiry lies in the Virginia history upon which Justices Black and Rutledge so famously and heavily relied in *Everson*. The historical episode that, according to the *Everson* Justices, crystallized the constitutional no-aid principle now embodied in the Establishment Clause, involved the 1784 proposal in Virginia for a "Bill Establishing a Provision for Teachers of the Christian Religion" (hereinafter "the Bill"). After the State of Virginia suspended the requirement of tithing to the formally established Anglican Church in 1777, the 1784 proposal was designed to broaden and reassert state authority to tax for the support of Christianity. The Bill provided:[60]

> Whereas the general diffusion of Christian knowledge hath a natural tendency to correct the morals of men, restrain their vices, and preserve the peace of society; which cannot be effected without a competent provision for learned teachers . . .;
>
> Be it therefore enacted . . . [T]hat for the support of Christian teachers . . . [a property tax] is hereby assessed . . . .
>
> . . . [and each taxpayer shall express to the tax collector] to what society of Christians [the taxpayer directs] the money to be paid . . . and [the tax collector shall pay to the appropriate representative] of each such society, the sum so stated to be due to that society . . . .
>
> And be it further enacted, That the money to be raised by virtue of this Act, shall be by the Vestries, Elders, or Directors of each religious society, appropriated to a provision for a Minister or Teacher of the Gospel of their

57. *See* STEPHEN P. BROUGHAM AND LENORE A. COLACIELLO, NATIONAL CENTER FOR EDUCATION STATISTICS, PRIVATE SCHOOL UNIVERSE SURVEY, 1995-96, at 5 tbl.1 (1998) [hereinafter NATIONAL CTR. FOR EDUC. STATISTICS].

58. *See id.* at 8 tbl.4.

59. *See* sources cited *supra* note 48.

60. The Bill is included as part of the Appendix to Justice Rutledge's dissent in *Everson*. 330 U.S. at 72-74.

> denomination, or to providing places of divine worship, and to none other use whatsoever; except in the denominations of Quakers and Menonists, . . . [who may dispose of the funds] in a manner which they shall think best calculated to promote their particular mode of worship.
>
> And be it enacted, That all sums [not earmarked for particular societies of Christians] shall be . . . disposed of . . . for the encouragement of seminaries of learning within the Counties whence such sums shall arise . . . .

Madison's famous Memorial and Remonstrance[61] vigorously advocated against the enactment of the Bill, and it was soon defeated. A key element in the Bill's failure, not apparent from its text or from the Memorial and Remonstrance, was its significance in the Virginia struggle to disestablish the Anglican Church. Viewed only on its face, however, the Bill had certain critical features which should be recalled in any attempt to generate first principles from the Virginia history.

First, and most obviously, the Bill was limited to support of the Christian religion. Even Chief Justice Rehnquist, writing in support of jettisoning the "wall of separation" metaphor, recognized that this feature of the Virginia history should be viewed as forever settling the proposition that the state may not enact sectarian preferences.[62]

Second, the tax proposed by the Bill was not designed to augment general revenues. Rather, the Bill included a tax earmarked for this particular purpose. Whether one was supporting a sect in which one was active or not, one's tax contribution was being segregated to particular sectarian use. This is a symbolically and psychologically important feature of the arrangement. If one were subject to the tax, one could not say (as modern taxpayers do) that one is supporting the government generally without necessarily approving of all of the government's programs. Rather, under an earmarked tax scheme, the feel of the arrangements is involuntary support of a religious sect, even if the taxpayer gets to designate which one. This aspect of the Virginia tax highlighted its establishmentarian character and clashed with theological presuppositions, shared by

---

61. The Memorial and Remonstrance is printed in the Appendix to the dissent of Justice Rutledge in *Everson*, 330 U.S. at 63-72.

62. *See* Wallace v. Jaffree, 472 U.S. 38, 106 (1985) (Rehnquist, J., dissenting).

Madison and others, that support for religion (not government) must be voluntary.[63]

Third, the Virginia scheme against which Madison protested was not aimed at supporting existing schools and their instructional personnel. Rather, the monies were to be spent by those in charge of religious communities for "provision of a Minister or Teacher of the Gospel of their denomination, or to providing places of divine worship."[64] The funds could thus be used to build churches, without any provision whatsoever for education of the young. To be sure, the scheme permitted taxpayers to designate their payments for "the encouragement of seminaries of learning within [their respective] Counties,"[65] but, despite this nod to Jeffersonian sentiment,[66] no such institutions existed at the time.[67] Taxpayers thus could devote their payments to religious sects or to a set of future institutions which might never come into being. As a consequence of the taxpayer choices for which there were the greatest and most immediate incentives, the Virginia assessment scheme would have directly and immediately aided sects and their clergy in their religious mission.

Fourth, the education expected in the arrangements that would have been subsidized by the Virginia Bill was rudimentary at best. The Bible would have been the text of central impor-

63. As Madison stated in the Memorial and Remonstrance: "We remonstrate against the said Bill, 1. Because we hold it for a fundamental and undeniable truth, that Religion or the duty which we owe to our Creator . . . can be directed only by reason and conviction, not by force or violence." 330 U.S. at 64 (quoting THE VIRGINIA DECLARATION OF RIGHTS art. XVI). In *Lemon v. Kurtzman*, 403 U.S. 602, 610 (1971), the Court remarked that the funds for the challenged aid to nonpublic schools, predominantly Catholic, were "originally derived from a new tax on horse and harness racing, but . . . now [are] financed by a portion of the state tax on cigarettes." This sort of "vice tax" may well have been designed to undercut claims that the scheme coerced involuntary support of religion, but the Court did not offer a view of the constitutional significance of the chosen taxing device.

64. 330 U.S. at 73. Quakers and Menonists were permitted to spend the funds "in a manner which they shall think best calculated to promote their particular mode of worship." *Id.*

65. *Id.* at 74.

66. *See* THOMAS JEFFERSON, NOTES ON THE STATE OF VIRGINIA 146-48 (William Peden ed., 1995) (proposing non-sectarian public schools in each Virginia county).

67. *See* WILLIAM LEE MILLER, THE FIRST LIBERTY: RELIGION AND THE AMERICAN REPUBLIC 26 (1986). Although wealthy Virginians hired private tutors for their children, and other, middle-class Virginians of the 1780s purchased some basic educational instruction for their children, there were no publicly supported, free elementary or secondary schools at that time. *See* ROBERT E. BROWN & B. KATHERINE BROWN, VIRGINIA 1705-1786: DEMOCRACY OR ARISTOCRACY? 271-83 (1964).

tance, and the educational emphasis would have been primarily on religious virtue, and secondarily on basic reading, writing and arithmetic.[68] Put in today's terminology, the "secular value" of such an education would have been fairly small, and the religious value large by comparison.

Our educational and legal circumstances in the twentieth century are dramatically different, in ways that cast enormous doubt on any principle barring direct financial assistance, for secular educational purposes, to state-accredited sectarian schools. First, as *Brown v. Board of Education*[69] emphasized, the role of education in the twentieth century is vastly different from what it was in the eighteenth. Education is the road to individual mobility and society-wide progress on every front. If long-entrenched and customary segregation yielded to such changes, why shouldn't the long-imposed restrictions on aid to sectarian schools similarly respond? Under *Plessy v. Ferguson*,[70] racially separate was at least supposed to be equal; under *Everson* and *Lemon*, separate inevitably means unequal with respect to possibilities of state support.

Second, as described above, the mix of sectarian schools in America bears absolutely no resemblance to the world of colonial Virginia, in which nothing resembling an elementary or secondary educational institution of today ever appeared. According to the most recent survey by the U.S. Department of Education,[71] sectarian schools now represent a wonderfully pluralistic assortment of religious affiliations. Although Catholic schools still represent a plurality, at slightly under 30%,[72] that percentage has dropped dramatically since the time of *Lemon*, when Catholic schools represented 75% of religiously affiliated schools.[73] Sectarian schools are now operated in substantial numbers by a wide variety of Protestant Christians, by Greek Orthodox, Islamic, and Jewish communities, and by many others.[74] This mix suggests that government aid to sectarian schools will not produce the

68. *See* MILLER, *supra* note 67, at 27-29 (explaining that religious virtue was the objective of the assessment bill); BROWN & BROWN, note 67, at 277-78 (describing the practical emphasis of education for most children in eighteenth-century Virginia).

69. 347 U.S. 483 (1954).

70. 163 U.S. 537 (1896).

71. *See* NATIONAL CTR. FOR EDUC. STATISTICS, *supra* note 57 *passim*.

72. *See id.* at 6 tbl.2.

73. In 1970-71, of the 14,270 religiously affiliated elementary and secondary schools, 10,770 were affiliated with the Roman Catholic Church. *See* GERTLER & BARKER, *supra* note 51, at 6 tbl.C.

74. *See* NATIONAL CTR. FOR EDUC. STATISTICS, *supra* note 57, at 6 tbl.2.

Protestant versus Catholic political divisions that so worried prior generations.[75]

Third, no contemporary proposal for school vouchers or direct subsidies to private schools would be likely to rely on earmarked taxes. Rather, the state would inevitably rely upon a portion of some more generally available source of revenue. As a consequence, taxpayers would not have the experience proposed for eighteenth-century Virginians of designating tax payments to a particular sect. Instead, today's taxpayers would make their payments and understand, as is always and everywhere the case, that some appropriated monies would be spent on purposes and projects with which some do not agree.

Fourth, contemporary regimes of education are inevitably characterized by processes and standards of government accreditation. Unlike the situation in early America, all states have compulsory education laws, and accreditation is the key to school survival; attendance at unaccredited schools will not satisfy those laws. Accordingly, government will retain control over the activities of sectarian schools. Voucher programs and any direct state financing will only serve to increase the demand for, and the likelihood of, such regulation.

The battle over state support for religion in late eighteenth-century Virginia makes a great story, but it has little to do with education in the United States in the next millennium. If a state were once again to expend monies for the support of the clergy and places of divine worship, such a measure would be clearly prohibited by the Establishment Clause. But the maintenance of such a prohibition on contemporary attempts at widening the choices available to parents of schoolchildren, through mechanisms of public finance, cannot be sustained for much longer.

IV. Issues for the Future.

In the Supreme Court, the pressures in the direction of undoing the regime of *Lemon* are unmistakable, though the steps have been incremental and the judicial arguments for rejecting *Lemon* have not been tied to the Virginia history and the distance we have come from it. But the key decisions moving away from the no-aid principle have frequently involved 5-4 splits,[76] and

75. For the argument that contemporary voucher programs will continue to produce an unhealthy dynamic of religious interest groups interacting with government officials, see Marci Hamilton, *Vouchers, The Establishment Clause, and Power*, 31 Conn. L. Rev. (forthcoming 1999).

76. *See* Agostini v. Felton, 521 U.S. 203 (1997); Rosenberger v. Rector & Visitors of the Univ. of Va., 515 U.S. 819 (1995). *Rosenberger* involved in-kind aid

have provoked passionate dissents.[77] So there is no promise, much less a guarantee, that the constitutional restrictions on direct funding of elementary and secondary education conducted by religious institutions are about to disappear. The recent denial of *certiorari* in the Milwaukee voucher case has only highlighted this uncertainty.[78]

Two key constitutional issues remain in the effort to remove the barriers to public funding of sectarian schools. The first, arising on the Establishment Clause side, involves the need for an adequate conception of severability of religious and secular components of sectarian education. The central premises in the regime of *Lemon* are (1) that elementary and secondary sectarian schools are pervasively religious, (2) that the minors being educated in them are highly vulnerable to indoctrination, and (3) that aid to such schools will inevitably advance the faith. And to some extent it will. But it will simultaneously advance the secular goals these schools achieve and upon which their accreditation depends.

Should the inevitably religious component of much of sectarian education serve to disqualify such schools from direct state assistance? *Lemon's* presumptions that it should, that state aid must therefore be monitored to ensure that the state pays for no religious instruction, and that such monitoring itself presents the constitutional problem of "excessive entanglement,"[79] lies at the heart of the current prohibition on direct aid. Several recent decisions, however, have begun to undermine rather directly some of these premises. In *Zobrest v. Catalina Foothills School District*,[80] the Supreme Court ruled that the Establishment Clause presents no bar to the provision of a state-provided hearing interpreter to a hearing-disabled boy in a pervasively sectarian Catho-

to students publishing a religious journal, but did not involve aid to a religious institution. *See Rosenberger*, 515 U.S. at 822-27. *Agostini* involved aid to a religious institution, but the aid was in the form of public employees teaching secular subjects. *See Agostini*, 521 U.S. at 209-13.

77. *Agostini*, 521 U.S. at 209 (Souter, J., dissenting); *Rosenberger*, 515 U.S. at 863 (Souter, J., dissenting).

78. *See* Jackson v. Benson, 578 N.W. 2d 602 (Wis. 1998), *cert. denied*, 119 S. Ct. 466 (1998). The lower courts, clinging to the ancient regime on these matters, appear not to be ready to predict and pioneer a breakthrough. *See* Columbia Union College v. Clarke, 159 F.3d 151 (4th Cir. 1998). Indeed, the Supreme Court in *Agostini* essentially ordered the lower courts not to anticipate yet unrealized changes in Establishment Clause law. 521 U.S. at 541.

79. Scholars have often and appropriately mocked this feature of the doctrine. *See, e.g.*, John Garvey, *Another Way of Looking at School Aid*, 1985 SUP. CT. REV. 61, 87-89.

80. 509 U.S. 1 (1993).

lic school. That the interpreter would translate religion class and pre-school Mass—both required elements of education at that school—as well as secular subjects did not alter the result. A severability requirement in such a setting, limiting the interpreter to translating secular subjects only, would have effectively made it impossible for the student to attend a school with a serious religion program. Accordingly, the incidental benefit to his religious training did not serve to disqualify him from the service of the interpreter and its obvious secular value.

More dramatically, the decision in *Rosenberger* to forbid a state university from excluding a journal of opinion with a Christian perspective from a group of state-subsidized student journals bespeaks an even firmer determination to reject a requirement of severability for state-aided enterprises with both secular and religious components. That the students in *Rosenberger* used their magazine as a tool to proselytize did not render it any less a vehicle for teaching students how to read, write, think, and edit an intellectual journal.

The approach to severability suggested by *Zobrest* and *Rosenberger* may go a long way toward the undoing of *Lemon* and its premises. When state efforts that incidentally advance religion involve activities that can readily be separated into secular and religious components, the state should be limited to support for the secular only. State sponsorship of the Ten Commandments, for example, is unconstitutional because the first several Commandments are entirely religious in their content;[81] if a state wants to promote those Commandments that form the backdrop of our criminal law and a number of our ethical commitments, those in Exodus 20:13-16 should suffice.[82] By contrast, state celebration of the birthday of Martin Luther King, Jr. is acceptable constitutionally because his secular achievements deserve their

81. *See* Stone v. Graham, 449 U.S. 39 (1980) (holding that the state may not require the posting of the Ten Commandments in public school classrooms). As a recent essay points out, the precise number and content of the Commandments is a matter of religious dispute. *See* Steven Lubet, *The Ten Commandments in Alabama*, 15 CONST. COMMENT 471 (1998). No matter how you assemble and count them, however, Commandments relating to God's identity and priority, the prohibition on making or bowing to graven images, the prohibition on taking the Lord's name in vain, and the obligation to honor and keep holy the Sabbath Day (*see Exodus* 20:4-9) cannot be understood as advancing secular objectives.

82. "You shall not murder. You shall not commit adultery. You shall not steal. You shall not bear false witness against your neighbor." The requirement of parent honoring, *see Exodus* 20:12, and the prohibition on coveting, *see Exodus* 20:14, perhaps can be defended as advancing secular as well as religious purposes.

own special attention, and we cannot separate his religious sentiments or vocation from his life and accomplishments. A similar attitude towards state assistance to accredited sectarian schools would put an end to the regime of *Lemon* and its concerns with non-secular effects; it would no longer matter if mathematics teachers in sectarian schools advance the faith while simultaneously teaching their secular subject.[83] And because such teaching efforts would no longer require monitoring, *Lemon*'s concern for "excessive entanglement" would disappear.

The second key issue will arise on the free exercise side—to what extent will legislatures be free to impose, and accrediting and funding agencies to enforce, requirements of a secular curriculum and nondiscrimination in student admissions or the hiring and retention of school personnel? This has been the inevitable tradeoff ultimately facing sectarian schools, forestalled by *Lemon*'s interdiction of the possibility of state assistance. Once the public begins to finance religious education, the regulatory concerns about design of curriculum, admissions, policy, and employment decisions will surface with a vengeance. It is not the case that financing will authorize such regulation where accreditation did not; rather, state financing will inevitably lead to more pressure for secular control and secular policies.

In particular, sectarian schools which accept government funding may well be required to reduce or eliminate discrimination based on faith commitments in selecting students, and perhaps in selecting faculty as well. In turn, a policy of nondiscrimination among students may lead to state pressure on schools to make participation in religious instruction and experience voluntary rather than compulsory. That these conditions are reasonable from the state's perspective, and considerably diluting of the religious character of the education from the school's perspective, can hardly be denied. The current shape of free exercise law, permitting burdens on religion so long as they are cast in religion-neutral terms,[84] suggests that such conditions

83. The mathematics taught would have secular value, and could be state-financed to that extent. Professor Choper made precisely such a suggestion on the eve of *Lemon*. *See* Jesse Choper, *The Establishment Clause and Aid to Parochial Schools*, 56 CALIF. L. REV. 260, 265-66 (1968) ("[G]overnmental financial aid may be extended directly or indirectly to support parochial schools . . . so long as such aid does not exceed the value of the secular educational service rendered by the school.").

84. *See* Employment Div. v. Smith, 494 U.S. 872 (1990).

may well be valid, although there is no shortage of plausible arguments to the contrary.[85]

The concern about regulatory control over religious schools of course is not limited to cases of direct aid. Voucher schemes already present such questions. The Milwaukee program, for example, forbade the schools from requiring religious instruction for voucher students.[86] Voucher schemes, however, permit tailoring of the conditions to the voucher students only; direct funding schemes would invite such conditions as umbrellas over the entire school enterprise. Such conditions, even when narrowly tailored to voucher students only, may discourage participation by some schools, but it should be obvious that conditions aimed only at publicly financed students will be more palatable and less intrusive than conditions that affect the school as a whole. For this reason, as well as reasons of lingering constitutional doubt, one should expect to see programs of aid to sectarian schools remain of the voucher type for a long time to come. What one should not similarly expect is perpetuation of insurmountable constitutional impediments to public financing of sectarian education.

85. A requirement that religious schools not discriminate on the basis of religion in choosing faculty and/or students has a profoundly different impact upon such schools than does the identical requirement imposed upon nonreligious institutions. For sectarian schools, such a requirement impedes their ability to create a religious community and advance a theological as well as educational mission. Theological missions, however, are precisely what the state should not be purposefully subsidizing.

Section 702 of the Civil Rights Act of 1964, as amended, exempts religious institutions from the ban on religious discrimination in hiring, and the Supreme Court unanimously upheld this provision against Establishment Clause challenge in *Corporation of Presiding Bishop v. Amos*, 483 U.S. 327 (1987). Whether such an exemption is required by the Free Exercise Clause or any other provision of the Constitution, however, especially after *Smith*, is of course another question. Moreover, leaving religious institutions free to so discriminate is one thing; subsidizing them financially while they continue to do so is quite another, because the discrimination may increase the religious value of the education at the expense of its secular value. The Milwaukee program prohibited participating voucher schools from engaging in any discrimination based on race, color, or national origin, and forbade compulsory religious activity for voucher students, but did not forbid religious selectivity by participating schools. *See Jackson*, 578 N.W.2d at 607-09.

86. *See Jackson*, 578 N.W.2d at 609.

Understanding the Constitutional Rights of School Children

Published in the March/April 1997 edition of the Houston Lawyer

Summary: This article summarizes legal developments with respect to student discipline, including student due process rights; free speech issues; religion in the schools; and sexual harassment and abuse of students.

By Lisa A. Brown and Christopher Gilbert[1]

In 1969, at the height of the Vietnam era, the United States Supreme Court declared in a free speech case that public school students "do not shed their constitutional rights ... at the schoolhouse gate."[1] During the last 25 years, the courts have had numerous opportunities to consider a variety of student issues, ranging from urinalysis of student athletes to censorship of the school paper. This article will spotlight four areas of continuing debate: student discipline; free speech; religion in the schools; and sexual harassment and abuse.

I. Student Discipline

School violence and student discipline remain critical issues for the nation's public schools. Schools are no more immune from violence than the surrounding neighborhoods in which they are located. Most Texas schools have adopted "zero tolerance" policies with respect to firearms and drugs, and many have hired full-time peace officers to patrol their campuses. As shown by the cases discussed below, achieving a balance between the rights of students and the needs of the educational environment remains a difficult one, and schools are often accused either of doing too little[2] or doing too much.[3] The Supreme Court has attempted to accommodate the competing interests of students and their schools. However, when no substantial rights are involved, the Court will not intervene, disdainful of jurisprudence that would turn the federal judiciary into a micromanager of the nation's public schools.[4]

---

[1] Lisa A. Brown and Christopher Gilbert practice school law at Bracewell & Patterson, L.L.P., in Houston. Ms. Brown is a 1989 graduate of the University of Texas School of Law. Mr. Gilbert is a 1993 graduate of the University of Michigan Law School.

A. *Fourth and Fifth Amendment issues*

May a public school principal search a student's pockets? Use a metal detector? Require drug testing? Question a student outside the presence of his parents? In recent years, each of these questions has been answered in the affirmative. Courts continue to recognize that school officials are not law enforcement officers and, accordingly, are not limited by the restrictions of the criminal law in investigating students for misconduct.

Searching a student. In *New Jersey v. T.L.O.*,[5] the U.S. Supreme Court upheld warrantless searches of students by school officials. The Court held that students do have Fourth Amendment rights, but that the need to maintain an orderly environment at school required an easing of the restrictions that ordinarily apply to government searches. Accordingly, the Court held that school employees need "reasonable cause" rather than "probable cause" to search a student. The Supreme Court established a two-prong test for judging the reasonableness of a search: (1) whether the search was justified at its inception, and (2) whether the search, as conducted, was reasonably related in scope to the circumstances that justified interference in the first place.

Ordinarily, a search by school officials will be justified when there are reasonable grounds for suspecting that the search will turn up evidence that the student has violated or is violating school rules or criminal laws. A search ordinarily will be permissible in scope when the measures adopted are reasonably related to the objectives of the search and are not excessively intrusive in light of the student's age, sex, and the nature of the infraction. Strip searches are disfavored but not absolutely forbidden.[6] If a school official finds contraband during an illegal search, the school may use the contraband against the student in a school disciplinary proceeding[7]; however, the individual official may be subject to a suit for damages under 42 U.S.C. § 1983 for a violation of the Fourth Amendment.

Drug testing. In 1995, in *Vernonia School District 47J v. Acton,*[8] the Supreme Court upheld a school district's policy that authorized random urinalysis testing of student athletes. The policy was upheld largely because the school district was able to establish the existence of a serious drug problem among its athletes. It is unclear from the decision whether random drug testing would be permissible in the absence of evidence of a widespread student drug problem. The Court has not yet considered the issue of drug testing of the entire student body.

Using metal detectors. A growing number of courts have upheld the use of metal detectors on students at school.[9] Expressing deep concern about the need to control violence in the schools, courts have upheld searches similar to those seen in airports. One of the first reported decisions from a federal appeals court is a recent case from the Eighth Circuit[10] in which a school had received reports that unidentified students had brought a knife and gun to campus. The principal subsequently searched all male students by asking students to empty their pockets, by using a metal detector, and by conducting pat downs. During the search for knives and guns, the plaintiff was found to be in possession of a match box that contained crack cocaine. He was expelled, and the mother sued, alleging that the expulsion was based on illegally seized evidence. The court held that the search was "sweeping, but minimally intrusive" in light of the concern about weapons on campus.[11] Citing *Vernonia*, the court determined that "individual suspicion" was not required under the circumstances.

Using drug dogs. The *sniffing* of student lockers and cars on school property by drug dogs does not constitute a search.[12] However, the subsequent search of the locker or car does implicate the Fourth Amendment. If the school can show that the dog has a history of being reasonably reliable, the dog's alert generally should constitute reasonable suspicion necessary to justify a search. In contrast, the sniffing of a student's person is a search; search of student's person requires reasonable suspicion independent of the dog's alert.[13]

Questioning a student. The courts have recognized that, for most types of misconduct, a quick trip to the principal's office is all that is required to resolve the situation. The courts thus far have refused to constitutionalize such meetings. Accordingly, students do not have a constitutional right to call their parents before being questioned or searched by schools officials.[14] Nor are *Miranda* warnings required.[15] A typical case is *Edwards v. Rees*,[16] in which a student was questioned and detained for 20 minutes regarding a bomb threat. The court assumed that the student had been "seized" but found the seizure to be reasonable in light of the magnitude of the offense being investigated.

B. *Expulsion and suspension procedures*

In the landmark case *Goss v. Lopez*,[17] the United States Supreme Court held that, before being suspended or expelled, a student is entitled to "notice" of the charges and an "opportunity" to tell his side of the story. Notice may be oral or written, and the timing, content, and nature of the notice and hearing will depend on the "appropriate accommodation of the competing interests involved."[18] The court observed that it is conceivable that both the notice and the hearing will occur within "minutes" of the misconduct.[19] The Court added that there are some emergency situations in which "prior notice and hearing cannot be insisted upon."[20]

For suspensions less than 10 school days, the due process clause requires only an informal "give-and-take" between the student and the school official.[21] For longer suspensions (including expulsions), students generally are entitled to notice of the charges, the names of witnesses who will testify at the hearing and a summary of their probable testimony, and the opportunity to present evidence or witnesses in rebuttal.[22] However, the technicalities of criminal procedure are inapplicable to student disciplinary hearings.[23] A long-term suspension or expulsion ultimately must be supported by "substantial evidence," which is more than a scintilla but less than a preponderance.[24] In contrast to both long-term and short-term suspensions, in-school suspensions generally do not implicate due process at all.[25] In addition to possessing certain constitutional protections, students have certain procedural protections under the Texas Education Code.[26]

C. *Corporal punishment*

Teachers are privileged to use reasonable force to compel student obedience.[27] In the words of the Fifth Circuit, "paddling of recalcitrant children has long been an accepted method of promoting good behavior."[28] Although concerns about child abuse and fear of litigation have caused many school boards to ban corporal punishment, many schools still authorize corporal punishment, provided the parent has given prior written consent. In *Ingraham v. Wright*,[29] the Supreme Court held that corporal punishment of school children does not violate the Eighth Amendment's proscription against cruel and unusual punishment or the Fourteenth Amendment's requirement of procedural due process. Since *Ingraham*, some federal courts have held that corporal punishment might violate *substantive* due process if the punishment is particularly brutal.[30]

II. Free Speech Rights of Students

The question of whether students possess First Amendment rights during the school day was addressed by the U. S. Supreme Court in *Tinker v. Des Moines Independent Community District,* the seminal case in which the Court declared that students do not "shed their constitutional rights to freedom of speech or expression at the schoolhouse gate."[31] *Tinker* was decided in 1969 and addressed whether administrators could prohibit the wearing of black armbands to protest the Vietnam War. Since *Tinker*, the Court has decided two other significant secondary school speech cases: *Bethel School District No. 403 v. Fraser,*[32] which involved the punishment of a student for making a sexually-suggestive nomination speech during a school assembly; and *Hazelwood School District v. Kuhlmeier,*[33] which involved the principal's alleged censorship of articles in the school-sponsored student newspaper. Although the cases would be appear to be irreconcilable, they involved different types of student speech and thus may be harmonized.

The *Tinker* Court noted the need for school officials to maintain order and discipline, but was concerned that there was no evidence that the armbands had actually caused any disorder or disruption of the educational process. The Court held that a school may regulate speech only where the speech will "materially and substantially interfere with the requirements of appropriate discipline in the operation of the school."[34]

Fraser and *Kuhlmeier* were decided almost 20 years later, and the discipline problems facing school officials had evolved considerably since the silent armbands worn in *Tinker*. The *Fraser* Court focused on what it called a "marked distinction" between the "political" nature of the armbands in *Tinker* and the "sexual" nature of Matthew Fraser's nominating speech. Stressing the importance of teaching students "the boundaries of socially appropriate behavior,"[35] the Court declared that even the most heated of political arguments requires a consideration "for the personal sensibilities of the other participants and audiences."[36] The Court held that the discipline of Matthew was appropriate. Although the Court did not state that Matthew's speech was "materially and substantially" disruptive, the Court was influenced by the fact that Matthew had apparently caused quite a stir at his school.

In *Kuhlmeier*, decided in 1988, the Supreme Court implicitly recognized that student speech, like adult speech, can cover a wide variety of topics and be delivered through a wide variety of means. At issue in *Kuhlmeier* was the decision of a high school principal to pull two articles from an upcoming issue of the school newspaper: an article on student pregnancy and an article on divorce. The principal articulated specific pedagogical reasons for his action. The Court determined that the principal's actions were appropriate. The Court found that the student newspaper was not an open public forum because the school by policy had given the journalism teacher and the principal final authority over what was printed.[37] In distinguishing *Tinker*, the *Kuhlmeier* Court established two different standards for dealing with two different types of speech. The Court noted that the armbands in *Tinker* were speech that simply happened to occur on school grounds. In contrast, the newspaper articles in *Kuhlmeier* constituted speech in a school-sponsored publication, which students, parents, and members of the public might reasonably perceive to bear the imprimatur of the school. Because educators are entitled to exercise control over this second form of student expression, the Court found the proper standard for judging restraints on school-promoted speech to be whether such "actions are reasonably related to legitimate pedagogical concerns."[38]

Applying Kuhlmeier, one appeals court upheld the right of school principals to decide what advertisements to accept for school yearbooks and to reject proposed advertisements that they felt might be too controversial, such as advertisements by Planned Parenthood.[39] *Another court rejected a group of students' claim that they had a collective first amendment right in their school's mascot and upheld the right of the principal to change his school's "Johnny Reb" mascot after he received complaints from black students and parents.[40] These were both instances of student speech promoted through school activities, and the schools could show reasonable pedagogical concerns that justified the restrictions. Courts have also upheld the right of schools to discipline students for cursing[41] and for threatening to shoot a counselor if the counselor did not change the student's schedule like the student wanted.[42]*

Dress Codes and Uniforms. Litigation over dress codes has now entered its third decade. Educators have viewed such codes as a means for combating gang violence and for promoting discipline and order in the schools, while students have bitterly protested what they see as infringements on their free speech right to wear whatever clothes they like. Most courts faced with dress code challenges have applied Tinker on the theory that the message conveyed by a student's clothes is the same sort of "incidental speech" as the armbands in Tinker. In Jeglin v. San Jacinto Unified School District,[43] a federal court upheld a school district policy forbidding the wearing of all clothing bearing sports insignia at the high school because the school could show that the policy was designed to combat the growing problem of gang violence. The court struck down the policy at the elementary and middle schools because there was no real evidence of a gang presence at either school.

School officials and fashion critics alike may take heart from the District Court of New Mexico, which has decided that students do not have a constitutionally-protected right to wear baggy or sagging pants.[44] The court ruled that for "non-verbal" clothing messages to be protected, a student must show both that he or she intends to convey a particularized message by the clothes worn, and that there is a great likelihood that the message would be understood by those who observe the clothing. Although the student was able to verbalize a particularized message conveyed by his sagging pants--

an attempt to show a link to his black identity and black culture--he could not show that others would understand the message. Indeed, his sagging pants were more likely to be seen as a sign of gang affiliation, and therefore wearing them was not protected speech.

III. Religion in the Schools

The question of religion in the schools remains one of the most contentious areas of litigation for students and schools. Surprisingly, there is no "typical school position" on religion. Similarly, some student groups favor an expanded role for religion in the schools, and some resist it. The Establishment Clause of the First Amendment forbids a school from favoring any one religion over other religions, or from favoring religion as a whole over nonreligion. At the same time, it requires a school to accommodate religious beliefs. Schools looking to find the straight and narrow line to walk between accommodation and promotion may find that the line is not very straight or, that in many cases, it disappears altogether.

The role that prayer should--or should not--play in the schools remains highly controversial. The courts have held that the First Amendment is violated when school officials sponsor or organize prayer activities for students.[45] A different issue is presented when students, without the involvement of school officials, wish to pray alone or in groups while at school. The issue of school-sponsored prayer versus student-initiated prayer is best illustrated by recent cases concerning graduation ceremonies. In 1992, the Supreme Court ruled in Lee v. Weisman[46] that a school violated the First Amendment by inviting a religious leader to deliver an invocation. In Jones v. Clear Creek Independent School District,[47] a case arising out of Texas, the Fifth Circuit upheld a school policy that allows graduation prayers where such prayers are student-initiated, student-led, student-controlled, and nonsectarian and nonproselytizing. (The Third Circuit recently criticized Jones as disingenuous.[48]) After Jones, the Mississippi legislature adopted a statute permitting student prayer at a wide variety of student activities. In 1995, in *Ingebretsen v. Jackson Public School District*, the Fifth Circuit struck down the Mississippi statute as unconstitutional; the court distinguished *Jones* on the ground that graduation is a once-in-a-lifetime event. [49] The Supreme Court refused to review either *Ingebretsen* or *Jones*.

The legality of prayer at sporting events also has been litigated. Long a staple of the Friday evening football game, opening invocations delivered over the loudspeaker have been declared unconstitutional by two courts of appeals.[50] One policy had permitted students, parents, and staff members to volunteer to give the invocations, but it was deemed constitutionally inadequate.[51] The Fifth Circuit has held that group prayers by a basketball team prior to games violated the Establishment Clause where the prayers were led by the coach.[52] Similarly, a federal court in Houston struck down the school song of a school district, which looked to the court suspiciously like a prayer.[53] In December 1996, however, a federal judge in Galveston upheld a policy that authorizes students to select a student volunteer to deliver a "pre-game message," which may include a prayer if the student so chooses.[54]

Another possible issue on the horizon is the new Texas moment of silence statute. In 1995, the Texas Education Code was amended to authorize school districts to "provide for a period of silence at the beginning of the first class of each school day during which a student may reflect or meditate."[55] As yet, no reported decision exists interpreting this provision, but a similar statute in Georgia was recently challenged in the courts as violating the Establishment Clause.[56] The Georgia statute was upheld, largely because of the documented secular purpose of the statute; it was passed as one of three bills designed to curb school violence. In contrast, the Supreme Court struck down an Alabama statute in 1985 that called for a moment of silence "for meditation or voluntary prayer."[57]

There, the Court ignored the statute's legislative history because it felt that the history was a sham designed to disguise the fact that the legislature was attempting to return prayer to the public schools.

One final issue of continuing inquiry is the scope of the right of students to distribute religious literature on school grounds. If a school has a general policy of allowing students to distribute literature, it may not discriminate against students who wish to distribute religious literature, as opposed to political literature or sports literature. While courts have rejected the argument that distribution of religious material on school grounds might cause people to believe that the school is endorsing the material and, hence, religion,[58] *the courts have ruled that schools may establish reasonable time, place, and manner restrictions on the distribution of the literature.*[59] *One court has upheld a policy that prohibited the distribution of more than ten pamphlets not written by students themselves, on the rationale that such a policy encouraged students to write their own material.*[60]

IV. Sexual harassment and abuse of students

Abuse of students by school employees. Students do not have a general constitutional right to a "safe" school environment.[61] They do, however, have a right *not* to be sexually molested by their teachers. This right flows from the Fourteenth Amendment's guarantee of due process. In *Doe v. Taylor Independent School District,*[62] the Fifth Circuit held that public school children have a liberty interest in being free from state-occasioned damage to their bodily integrity. In *Doe,* the Fifth Circuit held that a supervisory school official may be held liable for a subordinate's "physical, sexual abuse" of an elementary or secondary student if the plaintiff can establish that the supervisor learned of facts "plainly pointing to the conclusion that the subordinate was sexually abusing the student," that the supervisor demonstrated "deliberate indifference" by failing to take action that was obviously necessary to prevent or stop the abuse, and that the failure caused a constitutional injury to the student.[63]

In recent years, plaintiffs also have attempted to bring sexual abuse claims under Title IX of the Education Amendments of 1972, 28 U.S.C. § 1681,[64] which prohibits gender discrimination in educational programs. Although the Supreme Court has held that students may sue for money damages for intentional violations of Title IX, it has not yet defined the standard of liability to be applied in such cases. In November 1996, the Fifth Circuit rendered its first decision on this subject in a case involving the abuse of a second-grade girl by her male teacher.[65] The girl's family allegedly told a female teacher about the allegations, but no other school official was aware of the allegations. In rejecting the strict liability standard imposed by the district court, the Fifth Circuit acknowledged that child abuse is a "horrible" crime, but observed that "we do not live in a risk-free society." The court said that it "contorts 'public policy'" to make communities financially responsible for the criminal acts of teachers. The court held that a school district will not be held liable under such circumstances unless "someone in a management-level position" was on notice and failed to take sufficient remedial action. The court did not decide whether an "appropriate" management-level person would be a school board member, superintendent, or some other school official.

Abuse of students by other students. When a boy attacks another boy or molests a girl, may the victim sue the school district for failure to protect? Students have filed lawsuits urging such claims based on the due process clause and based on Title IX. The due process claims have been uniformly rejected, largely on the ground that the perpetrator (a fellow student) was a private actor, not a state actor.[66] With respect to claims brought under Title IX, the Fifth Circuit held in April 1996 that students may not sue for money damages unless they can show that the school district itself committed an act of intentional discrimination, such as treating complaints of girls less seriously than complaints of boys.[67] The students subsequently filed a petition for writ of certiorari, which the Supreme Court denied. A similar case was recently argued in the Eleventh Circuit and remains pending.[68]

V. Conclusion

Public school students possess certain fundamental constitutional rights even when they are at school. Because of the unique needs of the school environment, however, the rights of children are not coextensive with the rights of adults in all circumstances. Particularly in matters of student discipline, the courts have provided necessary breathing room to educators charged with the difficult and important task of educating students in a changing society. This accommodation of competing interests requires school personnel to be respectful of student rights but gives them the flexibility necessary to maintain an environment where learning may take place.

---

1. *Tinker v. Des Moines Indep. Comm. Sch. Dist.*, 393 U.S. 503, 89 S.Ct. 733 (1969).

2. *See, e.g., Rowinsky v. Bryan Indep. Sch. Dist.*, 80 F.3d 1006 (5th Cir. 1996) (female students alleged that discipline given to male students was inadequate), *cert. denied*, 117 S.Ct. 165 (1996).

3. *See, e.g., Cunningham v. Beavers,* 858 F.2d 269 (5th Cir. 1988), *cert. denied,* 109 S.Ct. 1343 (1989) (rejecting due process claim of kindergarten students who received bruises from corporal punishment); *Fisher v. Burkburnett Indep. Sch. Dist.*, 419 F.Supp. 1200 (N.D. Tex. 1976) (student alleged that suspension for drug offense was excessive).

4. *See, e.g., Wood v. Strickland,* 420 U.S. 308 (1975) ("it is not the role of the federal courts to set aside decisions of school administrators which the Court may view as lacking in wisdom or compassion"); *Board of Educ. v. Pico*, 457 U.S. 862, 864 (1982) ("public education in our Nation is committed to the control of state and local authorities" and the federal courts ordinarily should not intervene); *Hassan v. Lubbock Indep. Sch. Dist.*, 55 F.3d 1075 (5th Cir. 1995) ("That a better punishment may have been available does not establish that the punishment administered was unconstitutional.").

5. 469 U.S. 325, 105 S.Ct. 733 (1985).

6. *Jenkins v. Talladega City Bd. of Educ.*, 95 F.3d 1036 (11th Cir. 1996), *rehearing en banc granted and opinion vacated*, 1996 WL 606638 (11th Cir. Oct. 16, 1996); *Cornfield v. Consolidated High Sch. Dist.*, 991 F.2d 1316 (7th Cir. 1993).

7. *See Thompson v. Carthage Sch. Dist.*, 87 F.3d 979 (8th Cir. 1996) (exclusionary rule did not apply in expulsion hearing).

8. 115 S.Ct. 2386 (1995).

9. For a listing of cases, see *State v. J. A.*, 679 So.2d 316 (Fla. App. 1996).

10. *Thompson v. Carthage Indep. Sch. Dist.*, 87 F.3d 979 (8th Cir. 1996).

11. *Id.* at 983.

12. *Horton v. Goose Creek Indep. Sch. Dist.*, 690 F.2d 471 (5th Cir. 1982), *cert. denied*, 103 S.Ct. 3536 (1983).

13. *Id.*

14. *See Cason v. Cook*, 810 F.2d 188, 193 (8th Cir.), *cert. denied*, 482 U.S. 930 (1987); *Pollnow v. Glennon*, 594 F.Supp. 220, 224 (S.D.N.Y. 1984), *aff'd*, 757 F.2d 496 (2d Cir. 1985); *see also Osteen v. Henley*, 13 F.3d 221 (7th Cir. 1994) (college student not entitled to counsel at disciplinary hearing; cost to college of "judicializing" its proceedings would be high and real risk of unjust expulsion low).

15. *See In re Corey L.*, 203 Cal. App.3d 102, 250 Cal. Rptr. 359 (Cal. App. 1 Dist. 1988); *People in the Interest of P.E.A.*, 754 P.2d 383 (Colo. 1988); *Cason v. Cook*, 810 F.2d 188 (8th Cir. 1987), *cert. denied*, 482 U.S. 930 (1987); *Boynton v. Casey*, 543 F.Supp. 995 (D. Maine 1982).

16. 883 F.2d 882 (9th Cir. 1989).

17. 419 U.S. 565, 95 S.Ct. 729 (1975).

18. *Id.* at 738-39.

19. *Id.* at 740.

20. *Id.*

21. *Goss*, 95 S.Ct. at 741; *Keogh v. Tate County Bd. of Educ.*, 748 F.2d 1077, 1080 (5th Cir. 1984); *Broussard v. Sch. Bd. of City of Norfolk*, 801 F.Supp. 1526 (E.D. Va. 1992) (meeting with principal before one-day suspension).

22. *See Salazar v. Luty*, 761 F.Supp. 45, 47 (S.D. Tex. 1991); *William v. Dade County*, 441 F.2d 299 (5th Cir. 1971); *see also Keogh*, 748 F.2d at 1081 (due process not violated although student did not receive witness list until day of hearing).

23. *Brewer v. Austin Indep. Sch. Dist.*, 779 F.2d 260, 263 (5th Cir. 1985).

24. *Sanchez v. Huntsville Indep. Sch. Dist.*, 844 S.W.2d 286, 290 (Tex. App.--Houston [1st Dist.] 1992, no writ); *United Ind. Sch. Dist. v. Gonzalez*, 911 S.W. 2d 118 (Tex. App. -- San Antonio 1995), *writ denied per curiam*, 40 Tex. S. Ct. J. 62 (Tex. Oct. 18, 1996).

25. *See Wise v. Pea Ridge Sch. Dist.*, 855 F.2d 560, 563 (8th Cir. 1988); *Dickens v. Johnson County Bd. of Educ.*, 661 F.Supp. 155, 158 (E.D. Tenn. 1987); *see also Martinez v. Sch. Dist. No. 60*, 852 P.2d 1275, 1280 (Colo. App. 1992) (reassignment to another high school within the same district did not violate due process).

26. *See* Tex. Educ. Code, Chapter 37 (student discipline laws).

27. *See, e.g.,* Tex. Penal Code § 9.62 (educators immune from prosecution provided they do not use deadly force); Tex. Educ. Code § 21.055 (educators immune from civil suit provided they do not use excessive force). Corporal punishment litigation tends to focus on whether the punishment was "reasonable." *See, e.g., P.B. v. Koch*, 96 F.3d 1298 (9th Cir. 1996) (principal not immune from claim that he punched, slapped, and choked students); *Hogenson v. Williams*, 542 S.W.2d 456, 460 (Tex. Civ. App.--Texarkana 1976, no writ) (student suffered a cervical sprain and required hospitalization; coach's motion for summary judgment denied); *Wise*, 855 F.2d at 565 (summary judgment for educator who gave student two swats).

28. *Ingraham v. Wright*, 525 F.2d 909, 917 (5th Cir. 1976) (en banc), *aff'd*, 430 U.S. 651 (1977).

29. 430 U.S. 651, 97 S.Ct. 1401 (1977).

30. *Compare Garcia v. Miera*, 817 F.2d 650 (10th Cir. 1987), *cert. denied*, 485 U.S. 959 (1988) (student received welts, scars, and severe bruises; court held that "at some point of excessiveness or brutality," a government beating will violate substantive due process) *with Cunningham v. Beavers*, 858 F.2d 269 (5th Cir. 1988), *cert. denied*, 109 S.Ct. 1343 (1989) (little girls received bruises on their buttocks; federal substantive due process was not violated because the girls had other remedies available under state law).

31. *Tinker v. Des Moines Indep. Comm. Dist.*, 393 U.S. 503, 506, 89 S. Ct. 733, 736 (1969).

32. 475 U.S. 675, 106 S. Ct. 3159 (1986).

33. 484 U.S. 260, 108 S. Ct. 562 (1988).

34. *Tinker*, 89 S. Ct. at 738.

35. *Fraser,* 106 S. Ct. at 3163.

36. *Id.*

37. *Hazelwood*, 484 U.S. at 269-70, 108 S. Ct. at 569.

38. *Kuhlmeier*, 106 S. Ct. at 571.

39. *Planned Parenthood v. Clark Cnty Sch. Dist.*, 941 F.2d 817 (9th Cir. 1991).

40. *Crosby v. Holsinger*, 852 F.2d 801 (4th Cir. 1988).

41. *Heller v. Hodgin*, 928 F. Supp. 789 (S.D. Ind. 1996).

42. *Lovell v. Poway Unified Sch. Dist.*, 90 F.3d 367 (9th Cir. 1996).

43. 827 F.Supp. 1459 (C.D. Cal. 1993).

44. *Bivens v. Albuquerque Public Schools*, 899 F.Supp. 556 (D.N.M. 1995).

45. *Engel v. Vitale*, 370 U.S. 421, 424-25, 82 S. Ct. 1261, 1264 (1963).

46. 505 U.S. 577, 112 S. Ct. 2649 (1992).

47. 977 F.2d 963 (5th Cir. 1992), *cert. denied*, 508 U.S. 967 (1993).

48. *American Civil Liberties Union v. Black Horse Pike Regional Bd. of Educ.*, 84 F.3d 1471 (3rd Cir. 1996).

49. *Ingebretsen v. Jackson Public School District*, 88 F.3d 274 (5th Cir. 1996).

50. *See Jager v. Douglas Cnty. Sch. Dist.*, 862 F.2d 824 (11th Cir. 1989); *Doe v. Duncanville Indep. Sch. Dist.*, 70 F.3d 402 (5th Cir. 1995).

51. *Jager*, 862 F.2d at 829-31.

52. *Doe v. Duncanville Indep. Sch. Dist.*, 994 F.2d 160 (5th Cir. 1993).

53. *Doe v. Aldine Indep. Sch. Dist.*, 563 F. Supp. 883 (S.D. Tex. 1982).

54. *Jane Doe et al. v. Santa Fe Indep. Sch. Dist.*, C.A. 95-176, in the United States District Court for the Southern District of Texas.

55. TEX. EDUC. CODE § 25.082(b).

56. *Bown v. Gwinnett County School District*, 895 F. Supp. 1564 (N.D. Ga. 1995).

57. *Wallace v. Jaffree*, 472 U.S. 30, 105 S. Ct. 2479 (1985).

58. *Muller v. Jefferson Lighthouse Sch.*, 98 F.3d 1530 (7th Cir. 1996); *Hedges v. Wauconda Community Unit School Dist. No. 118*, 9 F.3d 1295 (7th Cir. 1993).

59. *Hedges*, 9 F.3d at 1301; *Muller*, 98 F.3d at 1540-42.

60. *Hedges*, 9 F.3d at 1301-02.

61. *See generally Collins v. City of Harker Heights, Tex.*, 503 U.S. 126, 112 S.Ct. 1061 (1992) (the due process clause acts a "limitation on the State's power to act, not as a guarantee of certain minimal levels of safety"); *Walton v. Alexander*, 44 F.3d 1297 (5th Cir. 1995); *Johnson v. Dallas Indep. Sch. Dist.*, 38 F.3d 198 (5th Cir. 1994), *cert. denied*, 115 S.Ct. 1361 (1995).

62. 15 F.3d 443 (5th Cir.), *cert. denied*, 115 S.Ct. 70 (1994).

63. *Id.* at 454. The *Doe v. Taylor* test applies to lawsuits against supervisors, not school boards. For cases against school boards, *see Jane Doe "A" v. Special Sch. Dist.*, 901 F.2d 642, 646 (8th Cir. 1990); *Gonzalez v. Ysleta Indep. Sch. Dist.*, 996 F.2d 749, 751 (5th Cir. 1993); *Gates v. Unified Sch. Dist.*, 996 F.2d 1035 (10th Cir. 1993).

64. The Supreme Court held in *Franklin v. Gwinnett County Pub. Schs.*, 503 U.S. 60 (1992), that monetary damages may be awarded for intentional violations of Title IX.

65. *Canutillo Indep. Sch. Dist. v. Leija*, 1996 WL 686116 (5th Cir., Nov. 27, 1996).

66. *See, e.g., Graham v. Indep. Sch. Dist.*, 22 F.3d 991 (10th Cir. 1994); *Dorothy J. v. Little Rock Sch. Dist.*, 7 F.3d 729 (8th Cir. 1993); *D.R. by L.R. v. Middlebucks Area Vocational Sch.*, 972 F.2d 1364 (3d Cir. 1992), *cert. denied*, 506 U.S. 107 (1993); *Walton v. Alexander*, 44 F.3d 1297 (5th Cir. 1995) (en banc).

67. *Rowinsky v. Bryan Indep. Sch. Dist.*, 80 F.3d 1006 (5th Cir. 1996).

68. *Davis v. Monroe County Pub. Sch. Bd.*, 74 F.3d 1186 (11th Cir. 1996), *opinion vacated and rehearing en banc granted*, 91 F.3d 1418 (11th Cir. 1996).

VIRGINIA LAW REVIEW

VOLUME 86 OCTOBER 2000 NUMBER 7

ARTICLES

THE SUPREME COURT AND PUBLIC SCHOOLS

*James E. Ryan**

INTRODUCTION

OVER the course of the last century, and especially in the last forty years, the Supreme Court has resolved a broad array of constitutional claims that have arisen in the context of public elementary and secondary schools. In so doing, the Court has created a body of rules that governs the constitutional rights that students (or their parents) can legitimately assert against state and local education officials.[1] This body of constitutional rules, curiously, has received almost no comprehensive study. Commentators have heaped attention upon particular decisions, such as *Brown v. Board of Education*[2] and *San Antonio Independent School District v. Rodriguez*.[3] They also have studied the application of particular constitutional provisions, such as the Establishment Clause and the Free Speech Clause, in the school context.[4] Almost no effort has

---

* Associate Professor, University of Virginia School of Law. I would like to thank Michael Heise, John C. Jeffries, Jr., Mike Klarman, Daryl Levinson, Elizabeth Magill, Crystal Gafford Muhammad, Bob O'Neil, Dan Ortiz, Doug Reed, Elizabeth Scott, Bill Stuntz, Amy Wax, and Ted White for helpful comments on earlier drafts of this Article. I would also like to thank the participants at a faculty retreat and a student-faculty workshop at the University of Virginia School of Law, and those at the 2000 Law & Society Conference, where I presented earlier versions of this Article. Thanks, finally, to Darcy Goddard and Luther Pilkinton for excellent research assistance.

[1] The Court has also decided a number of cases involving the rights of teachers, to which I will refer on occasion throughout the Article. I will not focus on these cases as a group, however, because I am primarily interested in explaining the rights that students and parents can assert against the government, rather than the rights of teachers as government employees.

[2] 347 U.S. 483 (1954).

[3] 411 U.S. 1 (1973). *Brown*, of course, declared intentional segregation unconstitutional, see 347 U.S. at 495, while *Rodriguez* held that education is not a fundamental right and that students are not entitled to equal educational expenditures, see 411 U.S. at 35. The literature on the two cases is immense. For discussion of the cases and citation to much of the commentary, see James E. Ryan, Schools, Race, and Money, 109 Yale L.J. 249, 258–72 & nn.23–91 (1999).

[4] See, e.g., Stephen Arons & Charles Lawrence III, The Manipulation of Consciousness: A First Amendment Critique of Schooling, 15 Harv. C.R.-C.L. L. Rev. 309 (1980); C. Thomas Dienes & Annemargaret Connolly, When Students Speak: Judicial Review in the Academic Marketplace, 7 Yale L. & Pol'y Rev. 343 (1989); Bruce C. Hafen, Developing Student Expression Through Institutional Authority: Public Schools As Mediating Institutions, 48 Ohio St. L.J. 663 (1987); Michael W. McConnell, Multiculturalism, Majoritarianism, and Educational Choice: What Does Our Constitutional Tradition Have to Say, 1991 U. Chi. Legal F. 123 (1991); Richard S. Myers, Reflections on the Teaching of Civic Virtue in the Public Schools, 74 U.

been made, however, to study the education cases as a whole—to examine what one might call the Court's public schools jurisprudence.[5] That is the purpose of this Article.

In my opinion, there is much to be gained from such a study. To begin, examining the cases comprehensively affords an opportunity to assess whether there are any unifying constitutional principles or educational theories that might tie these cases together. Specifically, it allows one to consider whether the Court has embraced, explicitly or implicitly, any overarching vision of public schooling. Searching for patterns among the decisions also offers unique insights into how some important constitutional issues, such as the

---

Det. Mercy L. Rev. 63 (1996); Richard L. Roe, Valuing Student Speech: The Work of the Schools as Conceptual Development, 79 Cal. L. Rev. 1269 (1991); Jacqueline A. Stefkovich, Students' Fourth and Fourteenth Amendment Rights After *Tinker*: A Half Full Glass?, 69 St. John's L. Rev. 481 (1995); Tyll van Geel, The Search for Constitutional Limits on Governmental Authority to Inculcate Youth, 62 Tex. L. Rev. 197 (1983); Mark G. Yudof, When Governments Speak: Toward a Theory of Government Expression and the First Amendment, 57 Tex. L. Rev. 863 (1979); James C. O'Brien, Note, The Promise of *Pico*: A New Definition of Orthodoxy, 97 Yale L.J. 1805 (1988).

[5] The only attempts to take a slightly more comprehensive view of the Court's public school cases that I discovered include: Anne Proffitt Dupre, Should Students Have Constitutional Rights? Keeping Order in the Public Schools, 65 Geo. Wash. L. Rev. 49, 53 (1996) (examining student speech, due process, and Fourth Amendment rights and arguing that the Court has recently adopted a "social reproduction model" of education, pursuant to which schools "must have the power to inculcate students with society's traditions and values"); Stephen G. Gilles, On Educating Children: A Parentalist Manifesto, 63 U. Chi. L. Rev. 937, 938 (1996) (arguing that the Constitution should provide broad protections to parents "to reject schooling that promotes values contrary to their own"); Betsy Levin, Educating Youth for Citizenship: The Conflict Between Authority and Individual Rights in the Public School, 95 Yale L.J. 1647, 1649 (1986) (examining student speech, due process, and Fourth Amendment rights and arguing that the failure to protect these rights more strenuously sends a message that schools care more about order than they do about democracy); Suzanna Sherry, Responsible Republicanism: Educating for Citizenship, 62 U. Chi. L. Rev. 131, 133, 157 (1995) (arguing that the Constitution should protect the right of "an education for republican citizenship," which would teach children "three things: moral character, critical thinking, and cultural literacy"); and William B. Senhauser, Note, Education and the Court: The Supreme Court's Educational Ideology, 40 Vand. L. Rev. 939, 941 (1987) (examining selected education cases and arguing that the Court has recently adopted a "cultural transmission" model of education, pursuant to which schools function "as the inculcator of fundamental values"). Although each of these articles examines more than a single education case or the application of a single constitutional right in the school setting, none attempts to address the entire range of constitutional issues that have arisen in public schools, nor do any offer a unifying theory that incorporates the entirety of the Court's public schools jurisprudence.

permissibility of voluntary racial integration, might be resolved.[6] Indeed, one might be able to generate a predictive theory about a wide range of future school cases not by studying in isolation the doctrinal rules regarding the various constitutional rights that are at issue in school conflicts, but rather by taking a broad and comprehensive look at all of the school cases.

Lurking among these cases is an intriguing puzzle, one that has gone unnoticed in the literature. The puzzle is that some constitutional rights are explicitly limited in the school context, while others are either no different or are slightly strengthened within the school setting.[7] Student free speech, Fourth Amendment, and due process rights are more limited in the school setting than they are outside of that setting.[8] With regard to this group of rights, the Court has characterized the government as acting in a special capacity—that of educator—and has accordingly given education officials greater leeway to bend constitutional rights in order to achieve certain educational goals. By contrast, student equal protection rights to be free of racial and gender discrimination, or to benefit from affirmative action programs, at the moment appear to be no different within the school setting than they are outside of that setting.[9] The same is true with regard to student free exercise rights.[10] Students' Establishment Clause rights, finally, are if any-

---

[6] Using race to assign students to public magnet or examination schools has been deemed unconstitutional in three cases decided by federal courts of appeals. See Eisenberg v. Montgomery County Pub. Schs., 197 F.3d 123 (4th Cir. 1999), cert. denied, 120 S. Ct. 1420 (2000); Tuttle v. Arlington County Sch. Bd., 195 F.3d 698 (4th Cir. 1999), cert. denied, 120 S. Ct. 1552 (2000); Wessman v. Gittens, 160 F.3d 790 (1st Cir. 1998). Given the importance of the issue, it seems likely that the United States Supreme Court will soon have to address it. See, e.g., Joan Biskupic, Bar on Race-Based Enrollment Stands; High Court Rejects Montgomery Co. Appeal in Dispute Over Student Transfer, Wash. Post, Mar. 21, 2000, at A1.

[7] A word of clarification about constitutional "rights" is in order. I recognize that a single constitutional right may mean different things in different contexts and thus that it may be nonsensical to speak of any particular right as being diluted in one context or another. In speaking of limited or diluted constitutional rights, I mean to refer only to the standards used by the Court to apply particular rights in the school context. As described in detail below, there can be no doubt that the Court has applied different constitutional standards—and ones more deferential to the government—in the school context.

[8] See infra notes 37–169 and accompanying text.

[9] See infra notes 171–224 and accompanying text.

[10] See infra notes 256–77 and accompanying text.

thing stronger than those possessed by citizens outside of the school context; put differently, the limitations on government support of religion are more stringent within public schools than outside of them.[11]

The central question that I would like to address is whether there is any way to tie these various rules together: Is there a unifying principle or theory that makes sense of the Court's decisions? Commentators who limit their study to a particular aspect of the Court's school cases typically suggest that the Court has been influenced by or has endorsed an overarching theory of education.[12] Little or no effort is made, however, to assess whether the theory allegedly endorsed explains the entire range of public school decisions. For example, commentaries on student speech rights all seem to agree that the Court has subscribed to an "inculcative model" of education, where teachers and administrators have broad authority to limit student speech in order to inculcate or indoctrinate students with community values.[13] But these commentaries do not attempt to explain whether this inculcative model is also consistent with, say, the Court's decisions regarding religion in public school or even the Court's earlier—and still applicable—student speech decisions.[14]

---

[11] See infra notes 226–56 and accompanying text.

[12] See, e.g., Dupre, supra note 5, at 53 (arguing that the Court has repudiated the view of schools as institutions to construct a new social order and accepted a view of schools as the transmitters of society's traditions and values); Senhauser, supra note 5, at 941–42 (arguing that the Court has adopted a philosophy of education pursuant to which schools function "as the inculcator of fundamental values").

[13] See, e.g., Dienes & Connolly, supra note 4, at 381–84; Dupre, supra note 5, at 85–86; Roe, supra note 4, at 1274 ("The Supreme Court currently views the work of the schools to be the inculcation of values."); Senhauser, supra note 5, at 973–78.

[14] For a recent example, see Mark D. Rosen, Our Nonuniform Constitution: Geographical Variations of Constitutional Requirements in the Aid of Community, 77 Tex. L. Rev. 1129, 1159–61 (1999). Rosen contends that the Court has altered constitutional standards in the school context in order to allow schools "to inculcate children with the values of the dominant culture," and he cites some of the Court's recent speech and Fourth Amendment decisions. Id. But he fails to consider the Establishment Clause cases and the Court's older student speech cases, most importantly West Virginia v. Barnette, 319 U.S. 624 (1943), which place significant limitations on the ability of schools to inculcate students with dominant cultural values. *Barnette* and the Court's Establishment Clause cases are discussed infra notes 37–48, 226–56 and accompanying text.

I would like to suggest that there is indeed a unifying (though limited) view of public education underlying the Court's school decisions, that it is quite different from those identified in the current literature, and that it is at least defensible. Contrary to suggestions in the literature, the Court's cases do not reveal an elaborate and comprehensive theory of education; there is nothing close to a precise or complete vision of the permissible goals of public schools or the means by which those goals should be pursued. Rather, the cases seem to rest on a pragmatic and necessarily rough distinction between two functions of education: academic and social.

A primary function of public schools, obviously, is academic: A chief goal of educating elementary and secondary students is to transmit knowledge about particular subjects, like math, science, history, and English, and to equip students with analytical and vocational skills. Public education, however, has always performed various social functions as well, including attempts to socialize students and to reform society. For example, schools have traditionally been considered places not only to teach students about particular bodies of knowledge, but also to teach them to be responsible and participatory members of society.[15] Schools have also been seen as places where society can be re-created in a more perfect image, where social ills—racial segregation is the most prominent example—can be addressed and ameliorated.[16]

One way to explain both the results and analytical approaches in the Court's school cases is to apply this divide—academic and social—to the decisions. It appears that the more a particular policy has to do with the academic function of schools, the more likely it is that the Court will uphold the policy, even if it means truncating a constitutional right.[17] Thus, the core principle that has survived in

[15] See, e.g., Lawrence A Cremin, The American Common School 28–82 (1951) (describing the history of early public schools); David B. Tyack, Ways of Seeing: An Essay on the History of Compulsory Schooling, 46 Harv. Educ. Rev. 355, 363–68 (1976) (describing the common school movement).

[16] See, e.g., Diane Ravitch, The Troubled Crusade: American Education, 1945–1980, at 323–24 (1983) (arguing that Americans have long viewed schools as "the best vehicle through which to change society").

[17] To avoid confusion, let me try to be as precise as I can in explaining what I mean by the "academic" and "social" function of schools. In using the phrase "academic function," I am referring to what the Court in Hazelwood School District v. Kuhlmeier, 484 U.S. 260 (1988), characterized as curricular activities, namely the

the free speech cases is that schools are free to limit speech that would disrupt the learning process.[18] Similarly, the Fourth Amendment cases can be understood as representing a belief, reasonable if contestable, that warrantless and even suspicionless searches are permissible in order to preserve an atmosphere that is safe and conducive to learning.[19] And the Due Process cases can be understood as resting on the view that teachers need to be able to maintain discipline in order to transmit academic knowledge.[20]

The further a policy moves away from the core academic function of schools, the more likely the Court will apply traditional constitutional rules to judge the policy and strike it down. Consider, for example, the cases involving religion in public schools: The Court has applied the Establishment Clause with just as much, if not more vigor in the school setting as elsewhere.[21] Allowing prayer or devotional Bible reading in schools may be thought quite important by a large number of parents, but it is certainly at least one step removed from the academic function of schools. And it may be just as likely to cause classroom disruptions as it would create an atmosphere conducive to learning.[22]

---

conveying of information or the teaching of academic or vocational skills to students by faculty members. See id. at 271. I do not mean to include within this function all activities that happen to occur on school grounds pursuant to which students actually learn something. By using the phrase "social function," by contrast, I am referring both to the efforts of schools to "socialize" students by teaching them particular values or standards of behavior and to the efforts to use schools to achieve particular social goals, such as increased racial tolerance or equality or increased gender equality.

[18] See *Hazelwood*, 484 U.S. at 271–73; Bethel Sch. Dist. No. 403 v. Fraser, 478 U.S. 675, 686 (1986); Tinker v. Des Moines Sch. Dist., 393 U.S. 503, 513 (1969). These cases are discussed infra notes 49–58, 80–108 and accompanying text.

[19] See Vernonia Sch. Dist. 47J v. Acton, 515 U.S. 646, 664–65 (1995); New Jersey v. T.L.O., 469 U.S. 325, 341 (1985). These cases are discussed infra notes 109–34 and accompanying text.

[20] See Ingraham v. Wright, 430 U.S. 651 (1977); Goss v. Lopez, 419 U.S. 565 (1975). These cases are discussed infra notes 130–69 and accompanying text.

[21] See Wallace v. Jaffree, 472 U.S. 38, 56 (1985); Stone v. Graham, 449 U.S. 39, 41 (1980); Abingdon Sch. Dist. v. Schempp, 374 U.S. 203, 223 (1963); Engel v. Vitale, 370 U.S. 421, 430 (1962). These cases are discussed infra notes226–56 and accompanying text.

[22] See McCollum v. Board of Educ., 333 U.S. 203, 231 (1948) (opinion of Frankfurter, J.) (suggesting, in the context of a case involving religion in public schools, that it is vitally important to keep "divisive forces" out of schools). It is instructive in this regard to contrast *Wallace*, *Stone*, *Schempp*, and *Engel*, which all prohibited religious exercises or displays in the classroom, with Board of Educ. of Westside Community Schs. v.

Consider the race cases as well. Although the Court in *Brown* justified racial desegregation as especially important in the education context, later decisions extending the prohibition against racial segregation to a host of other public settings (including beaches and golf courses) revealed that the Court viewed desegregation as also serving a broader societal goal.[23] In subsequent cases involving school desegregation and other race-based education policies, both the Supreme Court and lower federal courts have employed the same constitutional standard—the compelling interest test—that is used to judge race-based policies in other settings.[24] I suggest that one reason for this approach, which I will discuss in more detail below, is that racial mixing in schools has come to be seen by courts not as an academic goal—not as a policy that will improve the academic function of schools—but rather as a social goal, designed to increase interracial contact, improve race relations, or foster racial equality. That is, because racial integration is seen as a social rather than academic goal, the Supreme Court and lower courts have judged race-based school policies by the same constitutional standard that applies outside of schools.

In short, one way to understand why the Court treats the government as "educator" in some cases but not others is to recognize that school officials and teachers perform different roles within the school setting. Of these various roles, the Court has privileged the academic. To be sure, one could easily criticize the Court's approach on the ground that, as a matter of history or normative educational philosophy, the social functions performed by schools are just as important as the academic ones.[25] I will suggest, however, that the Court's approach is a defensible response to the real dilemma that public schools present—namely, the impossibility of fully protecting students' constitutional rights while simultaneously ensuring the effective operation of public schools. The academic function is both what all schools have in common and what makes

Mergens, 496 U.S. 226 (1990), which upheld the Equal Access Act on the ground that schools may permit private, religious speech in extracurricular activities.

[23] See cases cited infra at note 175.

[24] See Freeman v. Pitts, 503 U.S. 467 (1992); see also Eisenberg v. Montgomery County Pub. Schs., 197 F.3d 123, 123 (4th Cir. 1999), cert. denied, 120 S. Ct. 1420 (2000); Tuttle v. Arlington County Sch. Bd., 195 F.3d 698, 698 (4th Cir. 1999), cert. denied, 120 S. Ct. 1552 (2000); Wessman v. Gittens, 160 F.3d 790, 790 (1st Cir. 1998).

[25] See infra notes 407–10 and accompanying text.

schools unique as institutions. By privileging this function, the Court has selected a principle that simultaneously limits the degree to which students' constitutional rights are diluted and helps ensure that the rules created for schools will be confined to that context.

I will begin in Part I with an overview of the Court's public school cases, highlighting both how the Court has altered some constitutional rights but not others in the school context, and how and where the Court has privileged the academic function of public schools. In Part II, I will take a step back to consider whether there is a way to make sense of these cases—asking, in other words, if there are any principles, explicit or implicit in the decisions, that might tie these cases together in a coherent way. After suggesting that a number of factors seem to play an influential role in the Court's decisions, including the ages of the students and the nature of the constitutional rights themselves, I will argue that the key factor to understanding and explaining the cases is the distinction between social and academic functions explained above. In Part III, I will move from the positive to the normative and offer a general and limited defense of the Court's approach, as well as attempt to answer possible critiques of the approach. I conclude by suggesting how the analysis offered in the Article could be of use to academics and advocates alike, including those who disagree with my positive theory.

I. GOVERNMENT AS (OCCASIONAL) EDUCATOR: THE CASES

In *Healy v. James*,[26] a 1972 case involving the free speech rights of college students, then-Associate Justice William Rehnquist argued in a separate concurrence that the government should be treated differently for purposes of constitutional analysis when it acts in its capacity as educator.[27] Just as different constitutional

---

[26] 408 U.S. 169 (1972).

[27] See id. at 201–03 (Rehnquist, J., concurring). Rehnquist repeated this argument a decade later in his dissent in Board of Education v. Pico, 457 U.S. 853, 908–10 (1982), which was joined by Chief Justice Warren Burger and Justice Lewis Powell. See id. at 920 (Rehnquist, J., dissenting) ("I think the Court will far better serve the cause of First Amendment jurisprudence by candidly recognizing that the role of government as sovereign is subject to more stringent limitations than is the role of government as employer, property owner, or educator."); see also id., 457 U.S. at 921 (O'Connor, J., dissenting) ("As Justice Rehnquist persuasively argues [in a dissent that she did not

rules apply when the government acts as an employer rather than as a regulator of private behavior, Rehnquist reasoned, different (and more deferential) constitutional rules should apply when the government acts as a school administrator.[28] Rehnquist thus urged the Court to adopt the principle that "[t]he government as employer or school administrator may impose upon employees and students reasonable regulations that would be impermissible if imposed by the government upon all citizens."[29] Nearly a quarter of a century later, in *Vernonia School District 47J v. Acton,*[30] a majority of the Court, without much fanfare and without much notice from commentators, followed Rehnquist's advice.[31]

In *Acton*, the Court upheld a school district policy that authorized random drug testing of student athletes. The key factor in its analysis, the Court explained, was "that the policy was undertaken in furtherance of the government's responsibilities, under a public school system, as guardian and tutor of children entrusted to its care."[32] Hearkening back to, but not citing, Rehnquist's concurrence in *Healy*, the Court in *Acton* drew a connection between the government as employer and the government as educator. According to the Court,

> [j]ust as when the government conducts a search in its capacity as employer . . . the relevant question is whether that intrusion is one that a reasonable employer might engage in, so also when the government acts as guardian and tutor the relevant question is whether the search is one that a reasonable guardian and tutor might undertake.[33]

Although *Acton* itself only involved students' Fourth Amendment rights, the Court in dicta suggested that its government-as-educator rationale had broader scope, observing that "while children assuredly do not 'shed their constitutional rights . . . at the schoolhouse

---

join], the plurality's analysis overlooks the fact that in this case the government is acting in its special role as educator.").

[28] See *Healy*, 408 U.S. at 202 (Rehnquist, J., concurring).

[29] Id. at 203 (Rehnquist, J., concurring).

[30] 515 U.S. 646 (1995).

[31] The only limited discussion of this aspect of *Acton* that I have found appears in Dupre, supra note 5, at 86–93.

[32] *Acton*, 515 U.S. at 665.

[33] Id. (citation omitted).

gate,' the nature of those rights is what is appropriate for children in school."[34]

Despite the hint in *Acton* of a unified approach to school-related cases, the Court has not followed the same analytical path when applying constitutional rights in the school context. In the roughly twenty-five years between *Healy* and *Acton*, the Court has taken two divergent approaches in public school cases. In one set of cases, namely those involving student rights of expression, student Fourth Amendment rights, and student due process rights, the Court has adopted special constitutional standards for the school context. As the Court stated in *Acton*: "Fourth Amendment rights, no less than First and Fourteenth Amendment [due process] rights, are different in public schools than elsewhere."[35] In another set of cases, however, the Court has not explicitly altered constitutional standards to take account of the school context. Thus, the Establishment, Free Exercise, and Equal Protection Clauses appear—at the moment, anyway—not to operate differently in public schools than elsewhere. To the extent there are some slight differences, moreover, they cut in the opposite direction in this set of cases—for example, the Establishment Clause is applied more stringently in the public school context than elsewhere.

Before considering whether there is any way to explain the Court's seemingly disparate approaches in public school cases, it is necessary to set the table a bit by explaining the governing constitutional standards for public schools. I will begin with the set of rights that the Court has explicitly molded to fit the school context and then turn to those rights that do not seem to operate differently within school than outside of it. I will finish with a brief discussion of the cases involving fundamental rights and public schools.[36]

---

[34] Id. at 655–56 (alteration in original) (quoting Tinker v. Des Moines Sch. Dist., 393 U.S. 503, 506 (1969)).

[35] Id. at 656.

[36] I have separated these cases for discussion because each fundamental right is unique, and thus it is difficult to say whether a fundamental right recognized in the school context has or does not have an analogue outside of that context.

A. Speech, Searches, and Sanctions

1. Student Free Speech Rights

The Court has decided five cases involving the speech rights of students in elementary and secondary schools. Although the cases obviously have unique aspects, they are linked by the Court's efforts in each to classify either the nature of the student speech or the purpose of the speech restriction at issue. The categories that the Court employs track the academic/social distinction I have described, and they serve in my view to make these cases much more consistent than conventional wisdom supposes.

The Court's first pronouncement on the topic came in the 1942 case of *West Virginia State Board of Education v. Barnette.*[37] Overruling its 1939 decision in *Minersville School District v. Gobitis*,[38] the Court in *Barnette* struck down a statute that required students to salute the flag.[39] Although the Court was not entirely clear whether the statute violated the Free Speech Clause, Free Exercise Clause, or both, the Court did not limit its holding to those with religious objections and in subsequent cases has characterized the opinion as resting on free speech grounds—a characterization that is amply supported by the language and reasoning in the opinion itself.[40]

---

[37] 319 U.S. 624 (1943).

[38] 310 U.S. 586 (1940).

[39] See *Barnette*, 319 U.S. at 642.

[40] This is not to suggest that the issue is free from doubt. As mentioned above, later opinions by the Court describe *Barnette* as a free speech case, see, for example, Employment Division v. Smith, 494 U.S. 872, 882 (1990), and there is strong support in the *Barnette* opinion itself for that interpretation. See *Barnette*, 319 U.S. at 634 (explaining that the issue does not "turn on one's possession of particular religious views or the sincerity with which they are held"). There is also evidence pointing the other way. First, *Barnette* overruled *Gobitis*, 310 U.S. at 586, which held that a compulsory flag salute statute did not violate the Free Exercise Clause. See *Barnette*, 319 U.S. at 642. Second, two of the six Justices in the majority wrote a separate concurrence to explain that they believed the statute violated "the freedom of religion secured . . . by the First and Fourteenth Amendments." See id. at 643 (Black & Douglas, JJ., concurring). And third, Justice Frankfurter's lengthy dissent in *Barnette* is devoted solely to repudiating the argument that the flag law violates the Free Exercise Clause. See id. at 646–71 (Frankfurter, J., dissenting).

Although the proper classification of *Barnette* thus may be debatable, in light of the language in the opinion and the Court's subsequent characterization of the case as one involving free speech rights, it seems appropriate to consider it as a free speech case here. It seems even more appropriate when one considers that *Barnette* has been

Barnette's actual holding is fairly limited: Students cannot be compelled "to declare a belief."[41] More precisely, the Court held that students could not be forced to affirm their loyalty to the country through a compelled flag salute and recitation of the pledge of allegiance.[42] Importantly, the Court was careful to point out that the school board required the flag salute not "because it was claimed to have educational value," but rather to promote "national unity."[43] The Court also distinguished between teaching about democratic values and compelling students to accept and embrace those values. Thus, the Court did not seek to prohibit the teaching of democratic values and acknowledged that "the State may 'require teaching by instruction and study of all in our history and in the structure and organization of our government, including the guaranties of civil liberty, which tend to inspire patriotism.'"[44]

Having first classified the restriction on student speech rights in this case as serving a social rather than an academic goal, the Court proceeded to treat this restriction as a general government regulation of the speech of citizens. The Court refused to defer to education officials. School officials, the Court declared, had important and discretionary functions, "but none that they may not perform within the limits of the Bill of Rights."[45] The Court also refused to view the rights of students as somehow different or

---

prominently relied upon in cases articulating a free speech right against compelled speech. See, e.g., Wooley v. Maynard, 430 U.S. 705, 714 (1977) (relying on *Barnette* in concluding that the First Amendment protects "both the right to speak freely and the right to refrain from speaking at all").

[41] *Barnette*, 319 U.S. at 631.

[42] See id. at 631–33; see also Pruneyard Shopping Ctr. v. Robins, 447 U.S. 74, 88 (1980) (describing *Barnette* as involving "the compelled recitation of a message containing an affirmation of belief").

[43] *Barnette*, 319 U.S. at 631.

[44] Id. (quoting *Gobitis*, 310 U.S. at 604).

[45] Id. at 637. The Court's refusal to defer to school officials was one of the several points of contention between the majority and Justice Frankfurter, who authored *Gobitis* and wrote a long and passionate dissent in *Barnette*. See id. at 659–62 (Frankfurter, J., dissenting) (arguing that the Court should defer to school officials on decisions of education policy). Justice Frankfurter and the majority in *Barnette* were in a sense talking past one another, insofar as Frankfurter argued that the Court should defer on questions of education policy, while the majority suggested that this speech restriction did not really present a question of *education* policy.

separate from the rights of citizens in general.[46] Instead, the opinion spoke in general terms about the right of all citizens to dissent from prevailing views and to differ in their opinions and beliefs. The Court's oft-quoted and sweeping pronouncement about freedom of belief is a perfect example: "If there is any fixed star in our constitutional constellation, it is that no official, high or petty, can prescribe what shall be orthodox in politics, nationalism, religion, or other matters of opinion or force *citizens* to confess by word or act their faith therein."[47] The Court was obviously speaking here of a right that school children share with all other citizens; indeed, the only exception to this principle recognized by the Court was for those in military service.[48]

A similar structure is evident in the Court's next student speech opinion, issued in 1969, nearly three decades after *Barnette.* In *Tinker v. Des Moines Independent Community School District,*[49] the Court upheld the right of students to wear black armbands to school in a silent protest against the Vietnam War.[50] In an opinion conventionally thought to represent the high-water mark of judicial protection of student speech,[51] the Court ruled that student speech could not be suppressed unless it "materially and substantially interfere[d] with the requirements of appropriate discipline in the operation of the school."[52] The Court concluded that the wearing of

---

[46] See id. at 634 (describing the issue as whether the government can "force *an American citizen* publicly to profess any statement of belief or to engage in any ceremony of assent to one") (emphasis added).

[47] Id. at 642 (emphasis added).

[48] See id. at 642 n.19.

[49] 393 U.S. 503 (1969).

[50] See *Tinker*, 393 U.S. at 514. For some interesting perspectives on *Tinker* and its consequences, see Constitutional Law Symposium: The Constitution Inside the Schoolhouse Gate—Students' Rights Thirty Years After *Tinker v. Des Moines School District*, 48 Drake L. Rev. 433 (2000). For an equally interesting account of the history of the litigation and its participants, see John W. Johnson, The Struggle for Student Rights: *Tinker v. Des Moines* and the 1960s (1997).

[51] See, e.g., David A. Diamond, The First Amendment and Public Schools: The Case Against Judicial Intervention, 59 Tex. L. Rev. 477, 489 (1982); Dienes & Connolly, supra note 4, at 356; Dupre, supra note 5, at 72–74; Hafen, supra note 4, at 691–93; Roe, supra note 4, at 1282–83; Nadine Strossen, Keeping the Constitution Inside the Schoolhouse Gate—Students' Rights Thirty Years After *Tinker v. Des Moines Independent Community School District*, 48 Drake L. Rev. 445, 454 (2000).

[52] *Tinker*, 393 U.S. at 509 (quoting Burnside v. Byars, 363 F.2d 744, 749 (5th Cir. 1966)).

armbands in this case "was entirely divorced from actually or potentially disruptive conduct by those participating in it."[53] It then repeated this point over and again; indeed, in a short, ten-page opinion, the Court referred nine times to the ability of school officials to suppress speech that causes disruption.[54]

Notice that classifying the speech as nondisruptive served to separate that speech from curricular or academic concerns. Having characterized the speech as unrelated to legitimate academic concerns, the Court proceeded, as it had in *Barnette*, to suggest that school boards must operate within the boundaries of the Constitution.[55] The Court also suggested that the students' rights, under the circumstances, were not much different from the free speech rights possessed by all citizens.[56] The Court's opinion thus spoke eloquently about the rights of students, famously reminding readers that students do not "shed their constitutional rights . . . at the schoolhouse gate."[57]

At the same time, the Court quite clearly endorsed the authority of school officials to suppress student speech that substantially disrupts or interferes with "school activities."[58] Notwithstanding the paeans to free speech, the Court's holding is thus fairly circumscribed, as are the student speech rights recognized in the opinion. What *Tinker* establishes—and all that it establishes—is that students may express their views if such expression has neither the

---

[53] Id. at 505.

[54] The Court made this point once on page 505, three times on page 508, twice on page 509, once on page 513, and twice again on page 514. See, e.g., id. at 508 (noting that there was no evidence "whatever of petitioners' interference, actual or nascent, with the schools' work"); id. at 514 (noting that "the record does not demonstrate any facts which might reasonably have led school authorities to forecast substantial disruption of or material interference with school activities, and no disturbances or disorders on the school premises in fact occurred").

[55] See id. at 507 (recognizing that boards of education have "important, delicate, and highly discretionary functions, but none that they may not perform within the limits of the Bill of Rights") (quoting *Barnette*, 319 U.S. at 637).

[56] See, e.g., id. at 508-09 (noting that, "*in our system*, undifferentiated fear or apprehension of disturbance is not enough to overcome the right to freedom of expression") (emphasis added); see also id. at 514-15 (Stewart, J., concurring) (explaining that he does not "share the Court's uncritical assumption that, school discipline aside, the First Amendment rights of children are co-extensive with those of adults").

[57] Id. at 506.

[58] Id. at 514.

potential to disrupt class work nor actually causes disruption. In this limited context of non-disruptive speech, a context disassociated from the academic function of schools, the authority of school officials is no greater than the authority of other state officials; outside of this context, however, the authority of school officials expands and student speech rights contract. The notion expressed in *Tinker*—that school officials must act within the boundaries of the Constitution—is thus somewhat misleading, insofar as *Tinker* itself recognized that when acting to protect the academic function of schools, school officials clearly retain greater authority to regulate speech than that possessed by other state officials.

The Court's next student speech case, *Board of Education v. Pico*,[59] addressed the authority of school officials to remove books from school libraries. The Court fractured badly on the question. A majority of the Court agreed that a school board can remove library books, but no majority could agree on the appropriate governing standard. Although there were seven opinions in total, three groups emerged from the various opinions: (1) Four of the Justices believed that school boards could remove books provided that they did not do so simply because "they dislike[d] the ideas" contained in the books;[60] (2) four other Justices believed that school boards should have broad discretion to acquire and remove books;[61] and (3) Justice White simply punted by writing a separate concurrence that was "in effect a single vote to dismiss the writ of certiorari as improvidently granted."[62]

What separated the first two groups, in large measure, were their differing views about the nature and status of school libraries. Both

[59] 457 U.S. 853 (1982) (plurality opinion).

[60] Id. at 872 (plurality opinion); see id. at 879–80 (Blackmun, J., concurring in part and in the judgment).

[61] See *Pico*, 457 U.S. at 889 (Burger, C.J., dissenting); id. at 897 (Powell, J., dissenting); id. at 920 (Rehnquist, J., dissenting); id. at 921 (O'Connor, J., dissenting). This group of Justices also endorsed Justice Rehnquist's suggestion, repeated from his concurrence in Healy v. James, 408 U.S. 169, 201 (1972) (Rehnquist, J., concurring), that the Court should treat the government more deferentially when the government acts in the role of educator. See *Pico*, 457 U.S. at 909 (Rehnquist J., dissenting); see also supra note 27.

[62] Id. at 904 n.1 (Rehnquist, J., dissenting). Justice Rehnquist accused Justice White of essentially ignoring the Rule of Four, which provides that any case warranting consideration in the opinion of at least four Justices will be addressed on the merits. See id.

groups of Justices recognized that school authorities must have control over the curriculum, and both recognized that schools could seek to transmit and inculcate community values through the curriculum.[63] The plurality believed, however, that school libraries serve a function that is distinct from that served by regular classes. School libraries, in their view, are places of "voluntary inquiry," where students should be given the freedom to explore ideas on their own and school officials' authority to limit access to knowledge should be somewhat circumscribed.[64] The dissenting Justices, by contrast, did not see any material difference between the library and the classroom.[65] Given that the very nature of the elementary and secondary educational process requires the "selective presentation and explanation of ideas," these Justices saw no reason to limit school officials' authority to remove library books.[66]

Because of the importance of the issue, it is worth pausing here to consider the extensive discussion in *Pico* about the inculcation of values. By the time of *Pico*, the Court had already acknowledged that a legitimate goal of education is to inculcate democratic values.[67] The plurality went out of its way to indicate that schools have broad discretion to inculcate values *through the curriculum*, suggesting that school boards "might well defend their claim of absolute discretion in matters of curriculum by reliance upon their duty to inculcate community values."[68] However, if the inculcation

---

[63] See, e.g., id. at 869–70 (plurality opinion); id. at 876–78 (Blackmun, J., concurring); id. at 889 (Burger, C.J., dissenting); id. at 896 (Powell, J., dissenting); id. at 913–15 (Rehnquist, J., dissenting); id. at 921 (O'Connor, J., dissenting). See also van Geel, supra note 4, at 239 (lamenting the fact that "at least eight Justices agreed that school boards may engage in the inculcation of youth" and "assumed without analysis that this objective was to be given considerable weight").

[64] *Pico*, 457 U.S. at 869 (plurality opinion). I say "somewhat" because the plurality would allow books to be removed for a host of reasons, including if school officials found that they were "pervasively vulgar" or not educationally suitable. Id. at 871 (plurality opinion); see also id. at 880 (Blackmun, J., concurring) (listing reasons for which removal should be tolerated, including offensive language and ideas inimical to the public welfare).

[65] See, e.g., id. at 914–15 (Rehnquist, J., dissenting); id. at 921 (O'Connor, J., dissenting).

[66] Id. at 914 (Rehnquist, J., dissenting).

[67] See Ambach v. Norwick, 441 U.S. 68, 76–77 (1979).

[68] *Pico*, 457 U.S. at 869 (plurality opinion); see also id. at 864 (plurality opinion) (acknowledging "that there is a legitimate and substantial community interest in

of values were itself a constitutionally privileged goal (that is, a goal deemed sufficiently important to justify truncating student speech rights), it is hard to understand why the plurality would distinguish between the school library and the curriculum. As Justice Blackmun observed in a concurring opinion, "if schools may be used to inculcate ideas, surely libraries may play a role in that process."[69]

What the plurality may have been trying to establish, although it failed to do so explicitly, is that conveying and inculcating values is an inevitable aspect of teaching; teachers cannot select and transmit information without making some value choices and conveying those choices to students. The inculcation of values, when linked to an academic exercise, thus must be tolerated as a means of insulating academic decisions; if inculcating values were prohibited or closely regulated, curricular decisions, and indeed the day-to-day operation of classrooms would forever be open to attack and judicial oversight—something that all of the Justices in *Pico* seemed intent on avoiding.[70]

Although it may be difficult or impossible to conduct an academic exercise without inculcating values, it does not follow that inculcating values and academic exercises are co-extensive: Schools can attempt to inculcate values outside of academic, curricular exercises. *Pico* suggests (as does *Barnette*) that inculcating values may not be a privileged goal in itself, but rather that it is privileged *only* when linked to an academic exercise; when a school attempts to inculcate values independently of an academic exercise, its authority diminishes and becomes less distinguishable from the authority possessed by other government institutions and officials. Put differently, *Pico* indicates that schools do not possess unlimited discretion to inculcate values writ large; if they did, then it would be hard, as Justice Blackmun suggests, to understand why they cannot inculcate values by removing certain books from the library.

---

promoting respect for authority and traditional values be they social, moral, or political").

[69] Id. at 878 (Blackmun, J., concurring).

[70] See, e.g., id. at 862 (plurality opinion) (emphasizing that the Court's adjudication would not "intrude into the classroom").

The plurality viewed the school library as distinct from the classroom and curricular activities and accordingly was willing to interfere with the decisions made by school officials and with their attempts to inculcate values.[71] The dissenting Justices, by contrast, believed that overseeing the removal of library books would interfere too greatly with school officials' authority and discretion.[72] But of more significance for this Article, the dissenting Justices seemed to share the conception of inculcating values that was expressed, albeit somewhat obliquely, by the plurality. That is, the dissenting Justices seemed to view the inculcation of values as an inevitable consequence of the content-based decisions that educators must make in running schools.

Then-Justice Rehnquist's dissent conveys this point most clearly. After pointing out that inculcating values had long been recognized by the Court as an important goal of public schools, Rehnquist immediately argued that "[e]ducation consists of the selective presentation and explanation of ideas."[73] Educators must "of necessity . . . separate the relevant from the irrelevant, the appropriate from the inappropriate."[74] This inevitable "winnowing process necessarily leaves much information to be discovered by students at another time or another place."[75] Inculcation of values, in Rehnquist's view, was thus an unavoidable aspect of the nature of elementary and secondary schools, which of necessity must selectively organize, present, and explain information.[76] Where Justice Rehnquist differed from the plurality, and the only real difference between his views and those of the plurality, was in his conception of the school library: Rehnquist saw school libraries as "supplements to

[71] As Justice Blackmun noted in his concurrence, "library books on a shelf intrude not at all on the daily operation of a school." Id. at 878 n.1 (Blackmun, J., concurring) The plurality's desire to avoid interfering with the daily operations of schools may also explain why it limited its holding to the removal of library books, as regulating the acquisition of books would likely involve a greater amount of judicial oversight.

[72] See, e.g., id. at 894 (Powell, J., dissenting).

[73] Id. at 913–14 (Rehnquist, J., dissenting).

[74] Id. (Rehnquist, J., dissenting).

[75] Id. (Rehnquist, J., dissenting).

[76] See id. at 915 (explaining why "elementary and secondary schools are inculcative in nature") (Rehnquist, J., dissenting).

th[e] inculcative role" of secondary and elementary schools and "not designed for freewheeling inquiry."[77]

I have taken this detour in order to address a question that will likely nag readers throughout if left unattended. The question is this: How can it be that the Court has privileged academic over social goals if it has deemed the inculcation of values—which seems like a social as opposed to academic end—a legitimate educational objective? The answer I am suggesting is that the Court has not in fact *privileged* the inculcation of values as a goal in and of itself; it has not given school officials authority to truncate constitutional rights solely in order to inculcate values. Instead, the Court has tacitly recognized that schools must be allowed to inculcate values in academic exercises in order to preclude constant judicial oversight of such activities—but it is the academic exercises themselves that are being protected by the Court.[78] I will return to this point in later discussions of the speech and religion cases, but for now it may be sufficient to keep two thoughts in mind. First, all of the Justices in *Pico* seemed willing to allow schools to inculcate values when doing so was linked to the academic process; the plurality and dissenting Justices differed only on whether the school library was a part of that process or independent of it. Second, it is important to recall *Barnette*, which suggests that where values inculcation is *not* tied to an academic purpose, the authority of school officials

[77] Id. at 915. (Rehnquist, J., dissenting).

[78] Another objection that may occur to readers at this point deserves to be addressed. If academic exercises often entail some inculcation of values, does it really make sense to try to distinguish between academic and social functions—that is, are they not inextricably linked? The distinction does make sense, I believe, precisely because academic and social functions are not inextricably linked. Although academic exercises may contain some socializing elements, schools can try to socialize students outside of the context of academic exercises, via mandatory flag salutes or speech restrictions in the lunchroom as opposed to the classroom. What the Court's cases suggest is that efforts at socialization must be justified as linked to the academic process itself; where that link does not exist (or is not seen by the Court), socialization is not privileged in the same way that academic activities are. This is apparent not only in *Barnette* and *Pico*, but also in *Tinker*. The school in *Tinker* tried to justify the speech restriction as necessary to the goal of instilling respect for authority; although Justice Black in his dissent would have accepted this as a constitutionally privileged goal, the majority did not. See *Tinker*, 393 U.S. at 526 (Black, J., dissenting). Thus, despite the fact that the speech restriction in *Tinker* surely served the goal of socializing the students, because it did not also serve to protect the academic process, the Court found it unconstitutional. See supra notes 49–58 and accompanying text.

may be no greater than that possessed by other government officials.[79]

The Court's two most recent student speech cases were decided in the mid-1980s. The first, *Bethel School District v. Fraser*,[80] is a difficult decision to characterize, primarily because the Court took a scattershot approach to reach its holding. As the Court said in the opening line of its opinion, the case involved "whether the First Amendment prevents a school district from disciplining a high school student from giving a lewd speech at a high school assembly."[81] With the question phrased this way, it is perhaps not surprising that the Court answered: "No." Understanding why it answered the question this way is a bit more difficult to explain.

Matthew Fraser gave a speech at an assembly, which was "part of a school-sponsored educational program in self-government;" students either had to attend the assembly or report to study hall.[82] Fraser nominated a friend for student government and intentionally filled his speech with sexual innuendo, which the Court (through Chief Justice Burger) variously characterized as "obscene," "vulgar," "lewd," and "offensively lewd."[83] Some students reacted boisterously to the speech, by hooting and yelling; some made gestures that "graphically simulated the sexual activities pointedly alluded to in respondent's speech."[84] Others, some of whom were as young as fourteen, "appeared to be bewildered" by Fraser's speech.[85] The next day, at least one teacher had to forgo her scheduled lesson plan to "discuss the speech" with her class.[86]

---

[79] See supra notes 37–48 and accompanying text.

[80] 478 U.S. 675 (1986).

[81] Id. at 677.

[82] Id. at 677.

[83] Id. at 687 (Brennan, J., concurring). Justice Brennan's concurring opinion contains the full text of the speech. An excerpt suffices to convey its flavor: "Jeff Kuhlman is a man who takes his point and pounds it in. If necessary, he'll take an issue and nail it to the wall. He doesn't attack things in spurts—he drives hard, pushing and pushing until finally—he succeeds." Id. (Brennan, J., concurring). As Justice Brennan explained, one might reasonably take issue with the Court's characterization of this speech as "offensively lewd" or "obscene." Id. at 689 n.2 (Brennan, J., concurring) (suggesting that Fraser's speech was no more obscene or sexually explicit "than the bulk of programs currently appearing on prime time television or in the local cinema").

[84] Id. at 678.

[85] Id.

[86] Id.

Fraser was suspended for two days and prohibited from speaking at the school's commencement exercises.[87]

The Court failed to articulate a standard for assessing the school officials' actions and instead offered several justifications for it.[88] First, the Court distinguished *Tinker* on the grounds that the speech there was nondisruptive and involved a political (as opposed to a sexual) message.[89] Second, the Court reasoned that schools serve the purpose of inculcating "the habits and manners of civility essential to democratic society," and thus that schools can sanction speech that is uncivil and offensive.[90] Third, the Court pointed out that indecent and offensive speech is prohibited in Congress and asked rhetorically: "Can it be that what is proscribed in the halls of Congress is beyond the reach of school officials to regulate?"[91] Fourth, and finally, the Court reasoned that the government has an interest in protecting minors "from exposure to sexually explicit, indecent, or lewd speech," especially in schools where children are a captive audience.[92] Taken together, these justifications led the Court to conclude that "[t]he First Amendment does not prevent the school officials from determining that to permit a vulgar and lewd speech such as respondent's would undermine the school's basic educational mission."[93]

Notwithstanding the varied justifications for the school's sanction offered by the Court, there is a thread that ties *Bethel* to the earlier speech decisions. Notice that the Court did not purport to establish rules for student speech or conduct within all school settings; it did not suggest, for example, that Matthew Fraser could have been suspended for giving the same speech to a group of friends sitting in the cafeteria. The Court instead emphasized that the speech was given at a school assembly, which itself was part of a school-sponsored education program.[94] (In this sense, the opinion may be thought similar to *Pico*; whereas the plurality in *Pico* saw the school library

---

[87] Id.

[88] See Dupre, supra note 5, at 61 (observing that the Court in *Fraser* failed "to craft a principle that explained what power the school had").

[89] See *Fraser*, 478 U.S. at 680.

[90] Id. at 681, 683.

[91] Id. at 681–82.

[92] Id. at 684–85.

[93] Id. at 685.

[94] See id. at 677, 681, 685.

as distinct from the school classroom, the majority in *Bethel* saw the student assembly as an extension of the classroom.) Indeed, the Court explicitly linked the classroom and assembly in concluding that school officials were justified in determining the appropriate "manner of speech" for either "the classroom [or] school assembly."[95]

With the connection between Fraser's speech and an educational activity established, *Bethel* becomes consistent with *Tinker*, insofar as there was no doubt that the speech caused disruption. Thus, at the end of the day, Justice Brennan in his concurring opinion may have best captured the rule established by the Court's decision:

> [I]n light of the discretion school officials have to teach high school students how to conduct civil and effective public discourse, and to prevent disruption of school educational activities, it was not unconstitutional for school officials to conclude, under the circumstances of this case, that respondent's remarks exceeded permissible limits.[96]

Hazelwood School District v. Kuhlmeier[97] represents the Court's latest word on student speech rights and, unlike *Fraser*, establishes clear standards by which courts can assess restrictions on student speech. Importantly, these standards expressly distinguish between speech within curricular activities and speech outside of such activities.[98] The case involved a principal's decision to censor two articles from a student newspaper, produced as part of a journalism class, because the principal believed the articles treated their subjects un-

---

[95] Id. at 683.

[96] Id. at 687–88 (Brennan, J., concurring). It should be pointed out that Justice Brennan may have been unintentionally accurate, insofar as his concurring opinion seemed designed to limit the scope of the Court's holding. He failed to persuade many commentators, who read the decision more broadly. See, e.g., Roe, supra note 4, at 1284 ("The reasoning in *Fraser* left little room for freedom of student speech."); Senhauser, supra note 5, at 974–77 ("At a minimum, the Court articulated an educational philosophy supporting a low tolerance level for less than orthodox forms of student expression."). I obviously read the case more narrowly than these commentators and fail to see in it the expression of an educational philosophy intolerant of unorthodox methods of communication or the effective dismantling of free speech protections for students.

[97] 484 U.S. 260 (1988).

[98] See id. at 271–73.

fairly.[99] In upholding the principal's act of censorship, the Court established a taxonomy of student speech.[100] Student expression outside of curricular activities is to be governed by the *Tinker* standard, meaning that it cannot be suppressed unless it is demonstrated that school authorities have reason to believe that the expression "will substantially interfere with the work of the school or impinge upon the rights of other students."[101]

Student expression that occurs within the context of the school curriculum, by contrast, can be censored as to style and content so long as the suppression is "reasonably related to legitimate pedagogical concerns."[102] An activity is considered within the curriculum, in turn, if it is "supervised by faculty members and designed to impart particular knowledge or skills to student participants and audiences."[103] The Court justified this more deferential standard for speech in curricular activities in part on the ground that educators are entitled "to assure that participants learn whatever lessons the activity is designed to teach."[104] Because the principal's censorship occurred within the context of a curricular activity—here a news-

[99] See id. at 263–64. One article concerned three teenagers attending the school who were or had been pregnant, and the other concerned the impact of divorce on students attending the school. The principal testified that the pregnant students might be identifiable, even though the story used false names, and he also testified that he believed the story's references to sexual activity and birth control were inappropriate for some of the younger students. See id. at 263. The principal pulled the other story because he believed that one of the parents described in the article was characterized in unfavorable terms by his daughter and was never given an opportunity to respond to the remarks. See id.

[100] The Court also concluded that the school newspaper was not a public forum and thus school officials were entitled to regulate the contents of the paper in "any reasonable manner." Id. at 270. This conclusion in itself is both unremarkable and somewhat irrelevant for purposes of this Article. The determination of what constitutes a "reasonable manner" of regulation was the key to the case and the point at which the Court established the standards for assessing student speech restrictions.

[101] Id. at 266, 272 (quoting *Tinker*, 393 U.S. at 509).

[102] Id. at 273. Interestingly, this standard parallels the one adopted the prior year in a case involving prisoners' rights. In Turner v. Safley, 482 U.S. 78, 89 (1987), the Court held that "when a prison regulation impinges on inmates' constitutional rights, the regulation is valid if it is *reasonably related to legitimate penological interests*." Although the Court in a later case would deny that there is an equivalence between the constitutional rights of students and prisoners, see Vernonia Sch. Dist. 47J v. Acton, 515 U.S. 646, 664 n.3 (1995), there are more similarities (as the standards from *Hazelwood* and *Turner* indicate) than this denial suggests.

[103] *Hazelwood*, 484 U.S. at 271.

[104] Id.

paper produced in a journalism class—the Court applied the more deferential standard and concluded that the censorship advanced legitimate pedagogical concerns.[105]

In putting the pieces of these five cases together, several points bear emphasis. To begin, the Court's student speech cases explicitly establish standards for assessing speech restrictions that are uniquely tailored for the school environment. These standards are also more deferential to school authorities than are standards that apply in other contexts and to other government officials. Indeed, the Court itself recognized in *Hazelwood* that speech that could be censored in school could not be censored "outside of school."[106] At the same time, the standards themselves vary depending on whether the speech occurs within or outside of curricular activities, with greater authority given to school officials in the former context. This distinction, I will argue below, is telling and supports my suggestion that the Court privileges the academic function of schools and grants school officials leeway to protect and pursue classroom and curricular activities. Even with regard to student speech that occurs outside of curricular activities, the touchstone of the Court's analysis—that the speech should be allowed provided it does not "materially disrupt[] class work or involve[] substantial disorder"[107]—remains tethered to the academic function of schools. Finally, the sole student speech case that drew no distinction between the rights of students and the rights of adults, *Barnette*, itself involved a restriction on student "speech" that was not at all designed to promote an educational goal but a social one—that of enhancing national unity.[108]

---

[105] Id. at 276. As the Court stated, the principal

> could reasonably have concluded that the students who had written and edited these articles had not sufficiently mastered those portions of the Journalism II curriculum that pertained to the treatment of controversial issues and personal attacks, the need to protect the privacy of individuals whose most intimate concerns are to be revealed in the newspaper, and the 'legal, moral, and ethical restrictions imposed upon journalists within [a] school community' that includes adolescent subjects.

Id.

[106] Id. at 266.

[107] Id. at 265.

[108] See supra notes 37–48 and accompanying text; see also Sherry, supra note 5, at 190–93 (suggesting that the Court has been more willing to tolerate efforts to

2. Student Fourth Amendment Rights

The Court has decided two cases involving the right of students to be free from unreasonable searches. In *New Jersey v. T.L.O.*,[109] the Court upheld a school principal's search of the purse of a girl who had been caught smoking in the bathroom.[110] In fixing the appropriate standard to assess student searches, the Court balanced the students' "legitimate expectations of privacy and the school's equally legitimate need to *maintain an environment in which learning can take place*."[111] Because of the school's need to maintain an environment conducive to learning, the Court believed that it was inappropriate to impose either the warrant requirement or the probable cause standard that typically govern searches by state officials.[112] Instead, the Court held that school officials have the authority to search students when there is "reasonable suspicion" that the search would turn up evidence that the student had violated either the law or a school rule.[113] The Court explicitly left open the question of whether *individualized* suspicion was also required, as the principal in this case had reasonable grounds for suspecting that the particular student searched had violated a school rule against smoking in the bathroom.[114]

Justice Lewis Powell wrote a concurring opinion worth describing here because he drew a connection between the need for discipline and the academic function of schools that five other Justices, in concurring and dissenting opinions, explicitly endorsed.[115] Justice Powell argued that providing students the "full panoply of constitutional rules" would interfere with the "primary duty of school officials and teachers."[116] In Justice Powell's view, that duty

inculcate values when those efforts do not interfere with the "equally important educational task of teaching critical skills").

[109] 469 U.S. 325 (1985).

[110] See id. at 328–33.

[111] Id. at 340 (emphasis added).

[112] See id. at 340–42.

[113] See id.

[114] See id. at 342 n.8, 343–44.

[115] Those Justices were: Justice O'Connor, who joined Powell's opinion; Justice Blackmun, who concurred in the judgment; and Justices Brennan, Marshall, and Stevens, who concurred in part and dissented in part. See discussion infra note 119.

[116] *T.L.O.*, 469 U.S. at 350 (Powell, J., concurring).

was simple: "the education and training of young people."[117] The State, he argued, "has a compelling interest in assuring that the schools meet this responsibility. Without first establishing discipline and maintaining order, teachers cannot begin to educate their students."[118] Although Justices Harry Blackmun, William Brennan, Thurgood Marshall, and John Paul Stevens disagreed as to how much lower the standard for assessing student searches should be, they all agreed that school officials should be excused from the warrant requirement for precisely the rationale offered by Justice Powell—that is, they all concurred in Justice Powell's assessment that maintaining order was an essential prerequisite to educating students.[119]

The Court again drew a connection between maintaining order and protecting the "educational process" of schools in its most recent student search decision, *Vernonia School District 47J v. Acton.*[120] Described briefly above, in *Acton* the Court upheld ran-

---

[117] Id. (Powell, J., concurring).

[118] Id. (Powell, J., concurring). Powell also recognized that schools have a responsibility to keep students and teachers safe, and that this need also justifies the refusal to grant students the full panoply of constitutional rules that apply outside of school. See id. (Powell, J., concurring).

[119] Justice Blackmun, who wrote an opinion concurring in the judgment, agreed with Justice Powell's assertion that "[w]ithout first establishing discipline and maintaining order, teachers cannot begin to educate their students." Id. at 352 (Blackmun, J., concurring) (quoting Justice Powell's opinion). Justice Brennan, joined by Justice Marshall, agreed that warrants should not be required for student searches because they would interfere with the need to maintain an environment that is safe and conducive to learning and education. See id. at 357 (Brennan, J., concurring in part and dissenting in part). He disagreed, however, with the majority's abandonment of the probable cause requirement. See id. at 357–58 (Brennan, J., concurring in part and dissenting in part). Justice Stevens agreed that neither the warrant nor probable cause standards should be applied, because of the need for teachers and school officials to maintain safety and an atmosphere conducive to learning. See id. at 376–77 (Stevens, J., concurring in part and dissenting in part). Stevens simply disagreed with the Court's application of the reasonableness standard in this case. See id. at 377–78. (Stevens, J., concurring in part and dissenting in part).

[120] 515 U.S. 646, 662 (1995). For an interesting and largely favorable discussion of *Acton*, see Dupre, supra note 5, at 86–101. Professor Dupre suggests that the Court in *Acton* rightly rejected the "reconstruction" model of public schools, in which schools are seen as a "major force in reconstructing society's ills," and adopted the "reproduction" model of schools, in which schools are considered places where traditional values are inculcated and serious learning can take place. Id. at 64–69, 96. Although *Acton* does indeed help schools preserve order to enable "serious learning" to take place, I am less persuaded that the Court endorsed a particular model of

dom drug testing of student athletes in an Oregon school district.[121] The district adopted the drug testing policy in response to a sharp rise in drug use and attendant disciplinary problems among students.[122] The district targeted student athletes because they were "the leaders of the drug culture."[123] Pursuant to the policy, students wishing to participate on school sports teams had to consent to random drug testing; their parents had to consent to the testing as well.[124]

The key difference between *Acton* and *T.L.O.* was the lack of individualized suspicion in *Acton*.[125] The Court in *Acton* observed that individualized suspicion is not invariably required, citing prior decisions upholding suspicionless searches of railroad personnel involved in train accidents and certain federal customs officials.[126] To determine whether random drug testing in this instance was constitutional, the Court weighed the students' expectations of privacy, the nature of the search, and the importance of the government's interest.[127]

The Court concluded that students in general, and student athletes in particular, have a fairly low expectation of privacy and that the search was not very obtrusive.[128] As for the government's interest, the Court believed that it was important and "perhaps compelling."[129] Preventing drug use by students is important, the Court observed, not only to protect their safety but also to prevent "the educational process" from being "disrupted."[130] On the facts of

---

education in this decision. It is not entirely clear to me, for example, why *Acton* could not be characterized as endorsing the "reproduction" model of schools, insofar as it condoned the use of schools to "reconstruct[] society's ills" by deterring student drug use. For discussion of the ambiguous nature of the Court's holding in *Acton*, see infra note 403 and accompanying text.

[121] See *Acton*, 515 U.S. at 664–65; see also discussion supra notes 30–35 and accompanying text.

[122] See *Acton*, 515 U.S. at 648–49.

[123] See id. at 649.

[124] See id. at 650.

[125] Id. at 653 (observing that the school search approved in *T.L.O.* "was based on individualized *suspicion* of wrongdoing").

[126] See id. at 653–54 (citing, *inter alia*, Skinner v. Railway Labor Executives' Ass'n., 489 U.S. 602, 619 (1989); Griffin v. Wisconsin, 483 U.S. 868, 873 (1987); *T.L.O.*, 469 U.S. at 340–41).

[127] See id. at 654–65.

[128] See id. at 657–60.

[129] Id. at 661.

[130] Id. at 662.

this case, moreover, the Court accepted the district court's conclusion that drug use among students in general—and student athletes in particular—had created disciplinary problems of "epidemic proportions."[131]

The Court emphasized that its holding should not be construed to suggest that suspicionless drug testing would "readily pass constitutional muster in other contexts."[132] The key factor in the case was the role of the government "as guardian and tutor of children entrusted to its care."[133] Thus, where student searches are involved, the Court concluded, the relevant question to ask is "whether the search is one that a reasonable guardian and tutor might undertake."[134] Based on the factors described above, the Court answered this question affirmatively.

Like the student speech decisions, the Court's student search decisions establish constitutional standards that are explicitly tailored to take account of the school context. More importantly, the Court justified the standards and results as necessary to protect the educational process. The Court in both *T.L.O.* and *Acton* thus upheld the searches not on the ground that maintaining order is an inherently important goal, but rather on the theory that some semblance of order is a necessary means to achieve the "primary" goal of schools: educating students.[135]

3. Student Due Process Rights

The Court has decided two due process cases involving elementary and secondary school students, and a third involving a medical student that nonetheless is relevant to the elementary and secondary school setting. These three cases, together, are somewhat paradoxical for the purposes of my thesis. On the one hand, their immediate results seem easily explained by fairly mundane and his-

---

131 Id. at 662–63.

132 Id. at 665.

133 Id.

134 Id. at 665. Justice O'Connor, joined by Justices Stevens and Souter, dissented. See id. at 666 (O'Connor, J., dissenting). Importantly, she agreed that combating drug use is a compelling goal because maintaining order and discipline is necessary to protect the educational process. See id. at 685 (O'Connor, J., dissenting). But she believed this goal could be accomplished without dispensing with the requirement of individualized suspicion. See id. at 678–79 (O'Connor, J., dissenting).

135 *T.L.O.*, 469 U.S. at 350 (Powell, J., concurring).

torical contingencies. On the other hand, however, they fall into a pattern that is quite striking and supportive of the academic/social distinction I am urging as an explanation of the cases.

In *Goss v. Lopez,*[136] the Court held, by a 5-4 vote, that students have a right to receive "*some* kind of notice and *some* kind of hearing" before being suspended for disciplinary reasons.[137] In reaching this holding, the Court first concluded that students have a property interest in receiving an education.[138] The Court then followed its traditional methodology of forging due process rules on a practical, context-specific basis in order to accommodate "the competing interests involved."[139] On one side of the ledger stood the student's interest in avoiding "unfair or mistaken exclusion from the educational process, with all of its unfortunate consequences."[140] On the other side stood the government's interest in maintaining order and discipline, which the Court believed was "essential if the educational function [was] to be performed."[141] The Court balanced these interests by requiring that schools provide quite rudimentary protections: School officials or teachers must provide at least oral notice of the charges, present the evidence against the student, and then give the student a chance to respond.[142]

The Court emphasized the limited protection offered to students, and it stressed that the whole process could occur immediately after the incident.[143] In addition, the Court left undisturbed a school's authority to remove immediately, without any

---

136 419 U.S. 565 (1975).

137 Id. at 579.

138 See id. at 573–74. The Court also held that students had a liberty interest in protecting their "good name, honor, or integrity," see id. at 574–75, although this part of the Court's decision was cast into doubt by Paul v. Davis, 424 U.S. 693 (1975), where the Court held that the Due Process Clause does not protect reputational interests.

139 *Goss*, 419 U.S. at 579 (citing Morrisey v. Brewer, 480 U.S. 471, 481 (1982); Cafeteria Workers v. McElroy, 367 U.S. 886 (1961)).

140 Id.

141 Id. at 580. The Court also suggested, without much explanation, that "[s]uspension is considered not only to be a necessary tool to maintain order but a valuable educational device." Id.

142 See id. at 581.

143 See id. at 582 (noting that "[i]n the great majority of cases the disciplinarian may informally discuss the misconduct with the student minutes after it has occurred").

notice or hearing, "[s]tudents whose presence poses a continuing danger to persons or property or an ongoing threat of disrupting the academic process."[144] As the Court remarked, somewhat defensively but nonetheless accurately, it was imposing procedural requirements that were "if anything, less than a fair-minded school principal would impose upon himself in order to avoid unfair suspensions."[145]

Despite the limited nature of the protection offered to students, the dissenting Justices, through an opinion by Justice Powell, saw the sky falling.[146] Justice Powell, who took this occasion to issue his first verbal dissent from the bench, was especially worried that the due process rights of students would be limitless after *Goss*.[147] He suggested in his dissent that students might now be entitled to notice and a hearing before teachers gave them bad grades, failed to promote them to the next grade, placed them in a low-level track, or barred them from participating in extracurricular activities. After all, he reasoned, if students received notice and a hearing prior to being suspended for a single day, it would seem to follow that they should receive similar procedural protections before receiving these other types of sanctions.[148]

Only two years later, Justice Powell had the opportunity to limit the potential damage he believed that *Goss* could cause. In *Ingraham v. Wright*,[149] with Powell writing for a majority, the Court held that students have no right to notice or a hearing prior to receiving corporal punishment.[150] (The Court also held that the Eighth Amendment simply does not apply to school officials.[151]) The Court was again closely divided, 5-4, with Justice Stewart the only Justice to join both the *Goss* and *Ingraham* majorities. All of the other

[144] Id.

[145] Id. at 583.

[146] For an interesting and insightful discussion of Powell's dissent, see J. Harvie Wilkinson III, Goss v. Lopez: The Supreme Court as School Superintendent, 1975 Sup. Ct. Rev. 25, 45–52.

[147] See id. at 45–47.

[148] See *Goss*, 419 U.S. at 599–600 (Powell, J., dissenting).

[149] 430 U.S. 651 (1977).

[150] See id. at 683.

[151] See id. at 664–68.

Justices in the *Ingraham* majority had dissented in *Goss*, and all of the dissenters in *Ingraham* had joined the majority in *Goss*.[152]

Justice Powell acknowledged in *Ingraham* that students have a liberty interest in avoiding unjustified bodily restraint and punishment.[153] He rejected the notion that this case involved a property interest, because "[t]he purpose of corporal punishment [as opposed to suspension] is to correct a child's behavior without interrupting his education."[154] In holding that students have no due process rights to prior notice and a hearing before receiving physical punishment, the Court relied heavily on the common law privilege permitting teachers to inflict reasonable corporal punishment and the availability of civil and criminal penalties.[155] In addition, the Court believed that any incremental benefit from a notice and hearing requirement would be outweighed by the costs of such a requirement, which the Court felt would divert the time and attention of teachers and officials away from "normal school pursuits" and could undermine the teacher's ability to maintain discipline in the classroom.[156]

The majority attempted to distinguish *Goss* on the grounds that the suspension power was more likely to be abused and harder to confine than corporal punishment.[157] The dissenting Justices were not convinced. Justice White, author of *Goss*, pointed out that civil remedies would not allow recovery for good faith mistakes, and thus would not prevent such mistakes from occurring in the first place—which to him was the whole point of requiring notice and a hearing in *Goss*.[158] Justice White also pointed out that civil or criminal remedies would obviously occur after the infliction of

---

[152] Compare *Goss*, 419 U.S. at 565, with *Ingraham*, 430 U.S. at 651.

[153] See *Ingraham*, 430 U.S. at 674.

[154] Id. at 674 n.43.

[155] See id. at 675–78.

[156] See id. at 680–81.

[157] See id. at 678 n.46.

[158] See id. at 693–94 & nn. 10–11 (White, J., dissenting). Three other Justices (Brennan, Marshall, and Stevens) joined White's dissent. See id. at 683. (White, J., dissenting). Justice Stevens also wrote a separate and solo dissent. See id. at 700 (Stevens, J., dissenting).

physical punishment, and thus would come too late: Just as a bell cannot be unrung, a paddling cannot be undone.[159]

The last case in the due process trio, *Board of Curators v. Horowitz*,[160] arose in the context of a medical school: A student dismissed for failure to meet academic standards argued that she had not received sufficient procedural protections prior to her dismissal.[161] The Court unanimously held that the hearing and reviews that she received satisfied due process.[162] A majority of the Court proceeded to conclude, in what was clearly dicta, that academic dismissals should be distinguished from disciplinary actions.[163] In doing so, the Court sought to distinguish *Goss* and in effect answer the concerns raised by Justice Powell in his dissent in that case.

The Court reasoned, as had numerous state and lower federal courts before it, that a crucial difference exists "between decisions to suspend or dismiss a student for disciplinary purposes and similar actions taken for academic reasons."[164] Disciplinary action, the Court argued, requires sorting out factual claims—a process similar to traditional judicial or administrative fact-finding, which justifies a hearing before the relevant school officials.[165] Academic decisions, by contrast, often rest on subjective and expert, professional evaluations of a student's abilities, which are not easily adapted to judicial or administrative decisionmaking.[166] In addition, the Court expressed reluctance to "enlarge the judicial presence in the academic community" beyond that tolerated in *Goss*, signaling that Justice Powell's fear—that *Goss* would provide students due process rights to challenge academic decisions regarding grading, tracking, and promotion—would not be realized.[167] Accordingly,

---

[159] See id. at 695–96 (White, J., dissenting) ("The infliction of physical pain is final and irreparable; it cannot be undone in a subsequent proceeding."); id. at 701 (Stevens, J., dissenting).

[160] 435 U.S. 78 (1978).

[161] See id. at 79–80.

[162] See id. at 85; see also id. at 96 (White, J., concurring in part and dissenting in part); id. at 97 (Marshall, J., concurring in part and dissenting in part); id. at 108–09 (Blackmun, J., concurring in part and dissenting in part).

[163] See id. at 86–91 & n.3.

[164] Id. at 87.

[165] See id. at 88–89.

[166] See id. at 89–90.

[167] Id. at 90.

the Court concluded that a hearing is not required for academic dismissals.

Taken together, the due process cases establish that students have a right to notice and a hearing prior to being suspended from school for disciplinary reasons; they have no due process right to notice or a hearing before receiving corporal punishment; and they have no due process right when subjected to academic, as opposed to disciplinary, sanctions. As suggested above, the outcomes in these cases, at least in *Goss* and *Ingraham*, seem most immediately explained by the unremarkable fact that Justice Stewart switched sides between *Goss* and *Ingraham*.

At the same time, however, the distinctions drawn in the cases and the results are fairly striking: A student's due process rights are protected only when she is facing temporary expulsion, for disciplinary reasons, from the educational process itself. Requiring rudimentary protections in this instance is not likely to disrupt seriously the academic function of schools, if only because the student can presumably be immediately removed from the classroom and especially because seriously disruptive students can be suspended without any notice or hearing whatsoever. Allowing the immediate infliction of corporal punishment, by contrast, is at least arguably justified by the need of teachers to respond quickly to disruptions that occur within the classroom.[168] Thus, *Ingraham* can be reconciled with *Goss* by positing that the need to react swiftly to maintain order in the classroom justifies granting school teachers authority to impose punishment unilaterally.[169] *Horowitz*, finally, rests explicitly on a distinction between "academic" and "disciplinary" decisions, providing universities and schools (the Court did not limit its conclusion to the former) the utmost freedom to sanction students for academic reasons.

[168] See *Ingraham*, 430 U.S. at 657 (pointing out that many teachers, contrary to policy, inflicted corporal punishment without first seeking approval from a school official; the Court did not suggest that such approval was constitutionally required).

[169] But see Dupre, supra note 5, at 80 (arguing that the division between *Goss* and *Ingraham* is stark, and that *Ingraham* represented a victory for those who saw the purpose of schools as one of social reproduction).

4. Summary

In putting the Court's speech, search, and due process cases together, three points stand out as especially important. First, the Court has tailored the constitutional standards regarding these rights to fit the school context, and it has generally done so in a way that lends more authority to the government (here, school officials) and less protection to individuals (here, students) than exists outside of the school context. Second, the Court has justified adopting special standards for schools on the ground that school officials need sufficient authority to preserve and protect the "educational process." Third, the standards that the Court uses to apply different rights vary, as we might expect; it is thus not altogether surprising that the Court uses different standards to assess whether student First Amendment rights are violated than it uses to assess whether student Fourth Amendment rights are violated.[170] But the standards also vary with regard to the same right, depending on the context within the school in which the right is being asserted—students, for example, have stronger speech protection outside of curricular activities than they do within those activities; they also have greater procedural protections when facing suspension as opposed to facing in-school, corporal punishment.

It remains to be explained why the standards vary the way they do, which I will address in the next Part. But first the picture of the Court's cases must be completed. I turn next to the cases in which the Court has generally not altered constitutional standards to take account of the school context.

B. Race, Gender, and Religion

In applying the Equal Protection, Establishment, and Free Exercise Clauses in the school context, the Court has been far less willing to defer to school officials than it has been when student speech, privacy, or due process rights are at stake. In cases involv-

[170] It is also possible, however, to imagine the Court adopting a single standard to assess the exercise of constitutional rights in schools, just as it has done (ostensibly) in prisons. See Turner v. Safley, 482 U.S. 78 (1987). Thus, we might imagine the Court asking, with regard to all restrictions on students' constitutional rights, whether the restriction is reasonably related to a legitimate pedagogical objective. See Hazelwood Sch. Dist. v. Kuhlmeier, 484 U.S. 260 (1988).

ing race, gender, and religion, the Court typically employs the same constitutional standards in the school context that it applies outside of that context. Its application of those standards, moreover, is if anything more stringent in the school context. Indeed, while the school context in free speech, Fourth Amendment, and due process cases is used to justify diminishing student rights and increasing governmental authority, in race, gender, and religion cases, the Court often uses the school context to justify strengthening student rights and limiting governmental authority.

1. Race Cases

The Court's race cases in the elementary and secondary school context, at least those involving students, have revolved around a single issue: desegregation.[171] Because these cases are legion and discussed at length in the existing literature, I will dispense with plodding through each of the decisions.[172] Instead, I will identify the central liability and remedial principles established and applied by the Court in these cases and highlight how little deference the Court has granted education officials regarding desegregation issues.

[171] The Court has decided an affirmative action case involving the rights of teachers in secondary and elementary schools. See Wygant v. Jackson Bd. of Educ., 476 U.S. 267 (1986). In *Wygant*, the Court struck down a school system's affirmative action hiring plan, under which white teachers with more seniority could be laid off before black teachers with less seniority. In doing so, the Court rejected the argument that providing role models for students, through the retention of minority teachers, was a sufficient justification for the affirmative action plan. See id. at 275–76; see also id. at 288 (O'Connor, J., concurring). In addition, the Court decided one of its most famous (and enigmatic) affirmative action cases in the context of the university admissions process. See Regents of the Univ. of Cal. v. Bakke, 438 U.S. 265 (1978) (plurality opinion). As explained below, see infra note 206 and accompanying text, *Bakke* may have some bearing on the rights of elementary and secondary school students.

[172] The following discussion relies most heavily on the following sources within the voluminous *Brown* literature: John C. Jeffries, Jr., Justice Lewis F. Powell, Jr. 282–331 (1994); J. Harvie Wilkinson, From *Brown* to *Bakke*: The Supreme Court and School Integration: 1954–1978 (1979); Daryl J. Levinson, Rights Essentialism and Remedial Equilibration, 99 Colum. L. Rev. 857, 874–77 (1999); James S. Liebman, Desegregating Politics: "All-Out" School Desegregation Explained, 90 Colum. L. Rev. 1463 (1990); and Daniel R. Ortiz, The Myth of Intent in Equal Protection, 41 Stan. L. Rev. 1105 (1989).

In *Brown v. Board of Education*,[173] the Court appeared to tie the right to be free from state-imposed segregation to the school context by emphasizing the importance of education and suggesting that students have a right to equal educational opportunity.[174] In a series of per curiam decisions following *Brown*, however, it became clear that the right created in *Brown* would not be limited to the school context. Without explanation, the Court ruled that the segregation of beaches, bathhouses, golf courses, and buses, just like the segregation of schools, violated the Equal Protection Clause.[175] In so doing, the Court continued the trend it began in *Plessy v. Ferguson*[176] of viewing the schools as similar to other contexts when considering questions of race.[177] The only difference was whether segregation itself was constitutional. Whereas the *Plessy* Court suggested that segregating railroad cars was no more *unconstitutional* than segregating schools,[178] the Court in *Brown* and subsequent cases suggested that segregating schools was no more *constitutional* than segregating other public accommodations.

Since the first *Brown* decision, most of the Court's desegregation cases have concerned the remedial obligations of school districts that engaged in *de jure* segregation. Two of the Court's earliest remedial decisions, *Green v. County School Board*[179] and *Swann v. Charlotte-Mecklenberg Board of Education*,[180] led some to believe that the Court was creating a new constitutional right, applicable only in the school context, which would entitle all minority students to attend an integrated school.[181] The Court created this

---

[173] 347 U.S. 483 (1954).

[174] See id. at 493.

[175] See Gayle v. Browder, 352 U.S. 903 (1956) (municipal bus system); Holmes v. City of Atlanta, 350 U.S. 879 (1955) (municipal golf courses); Mayor of Baltimore v. Dawson, 350 U.S. 877 (1955) (public beaches and bathhouses).

[176] 163 U.S. 537 (1896).

[177] See id. at 550–52 (upholding a statute requiring separate but equal train accommodations).

[178] See id. at 550–51 (suggesting that just as laws requiring school segregation were obviously constitutional, so too were laws requiring segregated train cars).

[179] 391 U.S. 430 (1968).

[180] 402 U.S. 1 (1971).

[181] See *Swann*, 402 U.S. 1 (authorizing district courts, *inter alia*, to order busing as a remedy for school segregation); *Green*, 391 U.S. at 437–38 (striking down a "freedom-of-choice" plan and ordering school to take immediate action "necessary to convert to a unitary system in which racial discrimination would be eliminated root and branch."). On the suggestion that *Green* and *Swann* created an affirmative right to

impression by its emphasis in *Green* and *Swann* on the affirmative obligation of school districts to eliminate the vestiges of a dual school system, root and branch, and to take all steps practicable to ensure the "greatest possible degree of actual desegregation."[182]

The Court's subsequent decisions, however, demonstrated quite clearly that the affirmative obligation of school districts to desegregate was remedial and could only be triggered by a finding of liability; the obligation did not stem from a constitutional right of students to attend integrated schools.[183] A finding of liability, in turn, required proof of intent to segregate, just as equal protection claims outside of the school context required proof of intent to discriminate in order to succeed.[184] Thus, in *Keyes*, the Court made clear that the Constitution prohibited only *de jure* segregation and that the "differentiating factor between *de jure* segregation and so-called *de facto* segregation . . . is *purpose* or *intent* to segregate."[185] So, too, has the Court emphasized throughout its desegregation decisions that the existence of one-race schools does not in itself violate the Constitution, nor does the remedial obligation to desegregate require that every school in the community reflect the racial composition of the community as a whole.[186]

As the Court explained in *Freeman v. Pitts*,[187] in setting forth the conditions that justify releasing a school district from a desegregation decree, "[r]acial balance is not to be achieved for its own sake.

---

attend integrated schools, see, for example, Frank I. Goodman, *De facto* School Segregation: A Constitutional and Empirical Analysis, 60 Cal. L. Rev. 275 (1972); see also Owen M. Fiss, School Desegregation: The Uncertain Path of the Law, 4 Phil. & Pub. Aff. 3, 25 (1974) (arguing that *Swann* and Keyes v. School District No. 1, 413 U.S. 189 (1973), approached the "point where the segregated pattern itself is deemed a violation of the Equal Protection Clause").

[182] *Green*, 391 U.S. at 437–39; see *Swann*, 402 U.S. at 26. The implication that students had a right to attend integrated schools, in turn, led some to suggest that the Court embraced the notion that black students must attend school with white students in order to receive an "equal" education. See, e.g., Missouri v. Jenkins, 515 U.S. 70, 121–22 (1995) (Thomas, J., concurring).

[183] See, e.g., Dayton Bd. of Educ. v. Brinkman, 443 U.S. 526, 537 (1979); Columbus Bd. of Educ. v. Penick, 443 U.S. 449, 452, 463–64 (1979); *Keyes*, 413 U.S. at 208.

[184] See, e.g., Erwin Chemerinsky, Constitutional Law: Principles and Policies 580–81 (1997) (noting that school desegregation cases required proof of intent to discriminate (or segregate), as was "true in other areas of equal protection law").

[185] *Keyes*, 413 U.S. at 208 (emphasis in original).

[186] See, e.g., Freeman v. Pitts, 503 U.S. 467, 493–94 (1992); Pasadena City Bd. of Educ. v. Spangler, 427 U.S. 424, 435–37 (1976); *Swann*, 402 U.S. at 24, 26.

[187] 503 U.S. 467 (1992).

It is to be pursued when racial imbalance has been caused by a constitutional violation."[188] The remedial obligation terminates, in turn, once the racial imbalance caused by the de jure violation has been addressed to the extent practicable; school districts are not under an endless obligation to maintain racially balanced schools.[189] Again, as the Court stated in *Freeman*: "Once the racial imbalance due to the *de jure* violation has been remedied, the school district is under no duty to remedy imbalance that is caused by demographic factors."[190] After it has satisfied its remedial obligations, a school district is free from judicial supervision unless it again engages in intentional segregation.[191]

In simplest terms, then, the Court's desegregation cases established and applied the following principles: School districts that engaged in intentional segregation were required to take affirmative steps to desegregate.[192] The Court judged those steps by their effectiveness, namely, the degree to which they led to student integration and the elimination of a dual school system; racially neutral policies, which resulted in increased segregation, were not a sufficient response.[193] Once the school district has made as much effort as is practicable to eliminate the vestiges of past discrimination, the school district can be released from responsibilities imposed by desegregation decrees; the school district can then adopt racially neutral policies, even if they result in greater segregation.[194]

Although the operative standards governing the desegregation cases are similar to those governing equal protection claims in other contexts, it would be a mistake to suggest that there is noth-

---

[188] Id. at 494.

[189] See id.; see also *Jenkins*, 515 U.S. at 88 (emphasizing that "federal supervision of local school systems was intended as a temporary measure to remedy past discrimination") (quoting Board of Educ. v. Dowell, 498 U.S. 237, 247 (1991)); *Dowell*, 498 U.S. at 248 (noting that desegregation decrees "are not intended to operate in perpetuity"); *Spangler*, 427 U.S. at 434–35 (holding that district court could not continue to rearrange attendance zones in order to maintain racial balance).

[190] Freeman, 503 U.S. at 494.

[191] See *Dowell*, 498 U.S. at 250 (explaining that, once a school desegregation decree is terminated, school board actions are to be assessed under "appropriate equal protection principles," meaning that intentional discrimination must be proven).

[192] See, e.g., *Swann*, 402 U.S. at 26; *Green*, 391 U.S. at 437–39.

[193] See, e.g., *Brinkman*, 443 U.S. at 537; *Penick*, 443 U.S. at 452; *Keyes*, 413 U.S. at 200; *Green*, 391 U.S. at 437–39.

[194] See, e.g., *Freeman*, 503 U.S. at 494; *Dowell*, 498 U.S. at 250.

ing unique about school desegregation cases. Two features of these cases, in particular, differentiate them from other equal protection cases. First, as Professor Ortiz has demonstrated, the Court proved more willing to infer intent to segregate in the school context than it was willing to infer intent to discriminate in other contexts.[195] In *Swann* and *Keyes*, for example, the Court established presumptions regarding the lingering effects of past segregation and the scope of present segregation that functionally reduced the burden on plaintiffs to prove intentional segregation.[196] Second, although the remedial principles relied upon by the Court in school desegregation cases were not unique to those cases,[197] the remedial obligations of school districts have been quite extensive and long-running.[198] Local, state, and federal governments have incurred desegregation responsibilities in other contexts, such as prisons and public housing,[199] but it would be difficult to conclude as a general matter that these responsibilities have matched, in scope or length, the remedial obligations of school districts.

---

[195] See Ortiz, supra note 172, at 1132–33.

[196] See *Swann*, 402 U.S. at 18 (presuming that current racial imbalances are caused by prior *de jure* school segregation); *Keyes*, 413 U.S. at 208 (presuming that an entire school district is intentionally segregated if a substantial part of the district is proven to be). As Professor Jeffries has observed, the presumptions employed by the Court tended to blur the line between *de jure* and *de facto* segregation, insofar as they operated to require school districts to eliminate all segregation within a district (both *de jure* and *de facto*) upon a single finding of *de jure* segregation. See Jeffries, supra note 172, at 299–300; see also Levinson, supra note 172, at 875–76 (arguing that the presumptions established by *Swann* and *Keyes* served to blur the line between *de jure* and *de facto* segregation). Some members of the Court argued that the use of such presumptions was inconsistent with traditional equal protection principles. See, e.g., *Penick*, 443 U.S. at 481 (Powell, J., dissenting) (arguing that the presumptions established in *Keyes*, *Penick*, and *Brinkman* "are irreconcilable with principles of equal protection law applied in all other cases").

[197] See, e.g., Wendy Parker, The Supreme Court and Public Law Remedies: A Tale of Two Kansas Cities, 50 Hastings L.J. 475, 507 (1999) (arguing that the "Supreme Court's approach to public law remedies is generally transsubstantive—principles developed in one area of public law are applied in other areas as well"). Professor Parker also points out that the standards adopted by the Court for terminating school desegregation decrees have been applied by lower courts in other contexts, including cases involving prison conditions, employment discrimination, and institutions for the mentally retarded. See id. at 522 & n.210 (citing cases).

[198] See, e.g., *Jenkins*, 515 U.S. at 74–80 (describing the history of litigation and desegregation remedies).

[199] See, e.g., Hills v. Gautreaux, 425 U.S. 284 (1976) (desegregating public housing).

These unique features of school desegregation cases notwithstanding, the most crucial point for my purposes is that school officials in desegregation cases have not received much deference from the Court—certainly nothing like the deference displayed in the speech, search, and due process cases. Beginning with *Brown* itself, the Court rejected the notion that the decision as to whether students should be segregated, and the decision regarding the efforts that should be taken to desegregate, should be left to the discretion of school officials.[200] Part of the explanation, again, seems to be that the Court came quite quickly to view school desegregation as serving social rather than educational goals. Thus, the idea that segregation might be justified in educational terms, or that desegregation should be limited or expanded in light of other legitimate educational goals, is almost completely absent from the Court's opinions. The limited exception occurred in the context of *Swann*, where the Court indicated that schools may be able to limit the busing of students "when the time or distance of travel is so great as to either risk the health of the children or significantly impinge on the educational process."[201] Aside from this single comment and some lonely pleas from Justice Powell,[202] the impact of segregation or desegregation on the educational process was simply not discussed by the Court after *Brown*.[203] Rather than

[200] See, e.g., Richard Kluger, Simple Justice: The History of *Brown v. Board of Education* and Black America's Struggle for Equality 672 (1975) (describing how southern school districts argued that school segregation was beneficial to both white and black students).

[201] *Swann*, 402 U.S. at 30–31.

[202] Justice Powell often raised concerns about the impact of busing on the educational process. See, e.g., Estes v. Metropolitan Branches of Dallas NAACP, 444 U.S. 437, 450–52 (1980) (Powell, J., dissenting from dismissal of writ of certiorari as improvidently granted); *Penick*, 443 U.S. at 483–89 (Powell, J., dissenting); *Keyes*, 413 U.S. at 241–43 (Powell, J., concurring). For an insightful discussion of Justice Powell's views on desegregation, see Jeffries, supra note 172, at 280–327.

[203] There is a great deal of emphasis on limiting desegregation decrees in order to preserve or return to local control of schools. Local control is not really justified in educational terms, however, but rather as consistent with tradition and with principles of federalism; the notion, in other words, is that state and local governments, not federal courts, are the proper authorities to run public schools. See, e.g., *Dowell*, 498 U.S. at 248.

speaking in educational terms, the Court's desegregation decisions speak in terms of general constitutional and remedial principles.[204]

Before turning to the gender cases, brief mention must be made of the Court's statements regarding voluntary attempts to achieve racial integration, both because the statements appear to pose a challenge to my thesis and because the issue itself is one of increasing importance.[205] The Supreme Court has never ruled on this issue directly, although it has suggested in passing that the voluntary use of race in assigning students would be constitutional. In *Swann*, for example, the Court stated:

> School authorities are traditionally charged with broad power to formulate and implement educational policy and might well conclude, for example, that in order to prepare students to live in a pluralistic society each school should have a prescribed ratio of Negro to white students reflecting the proportion for the district as a whole. *To do this as an educational policy is within the broad discretionary powers of school authorities . . . .*[206]

[204] The Court, for example, has often repeated the principle that courts in desegregation cases should be guided by equitable principles and that, "as with any equity case, the nature of the violation determines the scope of the remedy." *Swann*, 402 U.S. at 16; see also, e.g., *Jenkins*, 515 U.S. at 88–89 (same). The Court has also indicated that, rather than achieving integration for its educational benefits, desegregation remedies should be designed "as nearly as possible to restore the victims of discriminatory conduct to the position they would have occupied in the absence of such conduct." Milliken v. Bradley, 433 U.S. 267, 280 (1977) (internal quotation omitted); see also *Jenkins*, 515 U.S. at 89, 109 (same).

[205] That the issue is one of increasing importance is demonstrated by the recent decisions by the First and Fourth Circuits, cited and discussed supra notes 6, 24, and infra notes 209–11.

[206] *Swann*, 402 U.S. at 16 (emphasis added); see also North Carolina Bd. of Educ. v. Swann, 402 U.S. 43, 45 (1971) (repeating this observation from *Swann*). The Court has touched on the issue in two other decisions. In *Bakke*, Justice Powell indicated in a footnote that voluntary efforts to achieve integration in public elementary and secondary schools might be on surer constitutional footing than similar efforts taken at the college or graduate school level. See *Bakke*, 438 U.S. 265, 300 n.39 (1978) (opinion of Powell, J.). In Washington v. Seattle School District No. 1, 458 U.S. 457, 472 (1982), the Court struck down a statute that required students to attend neighborhood schools, on the ground that the statute was racially based, insofar as it was designed to prohibit voluntary busing for the purpose of achieving racial integration. Although the legitimacy of the statute obviously rested in part on the legitimacy of voluntary, race-based busing, those defending the statute did not "challenge the propriety of race-conscious student assignments for the purpose of achieving integration, even absent a finding of prior *de jure* segregation." Id. at 472

At first glance, this passage will likely seem both surprising to modern eyes and inconsistent with my suggestion that the Court has been unwilling to defer to school officials on issues of race. There is strong reason, however, to doubt that the Court today would so casually conclude that school authorities have the power to take steps to achieve integration as a matter of educational policy. *Swann* arose before any of the Court's affirmative action decisions, including the most recent ones indicating that *all* racial classifications will be subject to heightened scrutiny.[207] At the time *Swann* was decided, it was unclear what constitutional restraints would encumber voluntary efforts to achieve integration or adopt affirmative action policies.[208]

The deference to school officials in *Swann* thus may have been no greater than the deference the Court would have afforded to any other government officials seeking to use race to achieve integration or undertake affirmative action. As I will discuss in more detail below, I would predict that today the Court would scrutinize voluntary efforts at school integration with the same intensity that it applies to all racial classifications, and that such efforts would stand the same slim chance of being upheld as do other race-based policies. The First and Fourth Circuits took precisely this tack in recent decisions;[209] indeed, the First Circuit specifically rejected the school district's argument that it should be granted discretion to pursue integration as an educational policy.[210] What appears likely to occur, interestingly, is similar to what occurred between *Plessy* and *Brown*: The general constitutional rules will change, and the

n.15. The Court therefore did not "specifically pass on that issue," although it did cite to the statements in *Swann* and *Bakke* cited above. See id.

[207] See Adarand Constructors v. Pena, 515 U.S. 200, 224 (1995) (plurality opinion) (concluding upon a review of the Court's precedents that the government must "justify any racial classification subjecting [a] person to unequal treatment under the strictest judicial scrutiny"); City of Richmond v. J.A. Croson Co., 488 U.S. 469, 494 (1989) (plurality opinion) (same).

[208] See, e.g., Chemerinsky, supra note 184, at 585–87 (describing how the Court struggled over the question of what level of scrutiny should be applied to "benign" racial classifications; only in 1989 did it expressly hold that strict scrutiny should be applied to all racial classifications).

[209] See Eisenberg v. Montgomery County Pub. Schs., 197 F.3d 123, 129 (4th Cir. 1999), cert. denied, 120 S. Ct. 1420 (2000); Tuttle v. Arlington County Sch. Bd., 195 F.3d 698, 704 (4th Cir. 1999), cert. denied, 120 S. Ct. 1552 (2000); Wessman v. Gittens, 160 F.3d 790, 794 (1st Cir. 1998).

[210] See *Wessman*, 160 F.3d at 797 n.3.

legality of the actions of school boards will change accordingly. Just as voluntary integration efforts were no *less* constitutional in the schools than outside of them at the time of *Swann*, now such efforts may be no *more* constitutional in schools than outside of them.[211]

2. Gender Cases

The issue of gender discrimination in public elementary and secondary schools revolves primarily around the question of whether it is constitutional to operate single-sex schools or single-sex classes within co-educational schools.[212] The Court has not squarely ruled on this question.[213] In the only case it has taken that raised this specific issue, the Court affirmed—without opinion and by an equally divided court—a Third Circuit decision allowing a single-sex high school.[214]

The Court has, however, decided two cases involving single-sex college programs. The first was *Mississippi University for Women v. Hogan*,[215] decided in 1982, in which the Court struck down the female-only admissions policy of a nursing school.[216] The second was the Court's recent decision in *United States v. Virginia*,[217] in which the Court struck down the male-only admissions policy of the Virginia Military Institute ("VMI").[218] In both cases, the Court applied

[211] Cf. id. at 797 (rejecting the argument that *Swann* provides school authorities broad discretion to adopt voluntary school integration plans).

[212] The equal treatment of athletic programs is another frequently litigated issue, but the claims are typically statutory, raised pursuant to Title IX. See, e.g., Earl C. Dudley, Jr. & George Rutherglen, Ironies, Inconsistencies, and Intercollegiate Athletics: Title IX, Title VII, and Statistical Evidence of Discrimination, 1 Va. J. Sports & L. 177 (1999).

[213] There have also been relatively few lower court decisions. According to one commentator, however, the popularity of single-sex schools and classes is rising and cases challenging single-sex schools are now beginning to wend their way through administrative processes and into federal courts. See Nancy Levit, Separating Equals: Educational Research and the Long-Term Consequences of Sex Segregation, 67 Geo. Wash. L. Rev. 451, 451–64 (1999) (discussing cases). The paucity of cases, of course, has not prevented a plethora of commentary. See id. at 451–70 & nn. 1–154 (citing and discussing commentary).

[214] See Vorchheimer v. School Dist. of Phila., 430 U.S. 703 (1977) (memorandum opinion).

[215] 458 U.S. 718 (1982).

[216] See id. at 723–27.

[217] 518 U.S. 515 (1996).

[218] See id. at 557–58.

the same standard—intermediate scrutiny—used to assess gender classifications outside of the school environment.[219] And in both cases, the Court left open the possibility that separate but truly equal schools for males and females could be established without violating the Constitution.[220] It would appear, however, that the fate of single-sex grade schools or classes will depend on whether they can survive intermediate scrutiny, as the Court gave no hint in *Virginia* or *Hogan* that constitutional standards would differ within the grade school setting.

Importantly, the VMI decision further indicates that whether single-sex schools or classes can survive intermediate scrutiny may depend on whether such programs offer demonstrable pedagogical benefits. This message is admittedly less than pellucid, as the opinion in VMI may charitably be described as difficult to decipher. But the Supreme Court did acknowledge that single-sex education is pedagogically beneficial to some students.[221] It refused, however, to pursue this inquiry to its logical conclusion by asking whether VMI's admissions policy could be upheld on this ground alone. Instead, the Court focused on the fact that VMI offered a unique educational opportunity and embraced the assertion that the admission of women would not destroy the mission of the school.[222]

The crucial question after VMI is whether the Court would similarly characterize most (or all) other single-sex schools as offering "unique" benefits that cannot justifiably be denied to members of

---

[219] See id. at 531–34; *Hogan*, 458 U.S. at 723–27;. In *Virginia*, the Court added a twist to the intermediate standard (and perhaps heightened it) by indicating that the State must provide an "exceedingly persuasive" justification for gender classifications. See *Virginia*, 518 U.S. at 531. But see United States v. Morrison, 120 S. Ct. 1740, 1755 (2000) (stating the intermediate scrutiny standard without mentioning the "exceedingly persuasive" requirement).

[220] See *Virginia*, 518 U.S. at 534 n.7 ("We do not question the Commonwealth's prerogative evenhandedly to support diverse educational opportunities."); see also id. at 535 n.8 (disputing Justice Scalia's suggestion, in his dissent, that the decision rendered single-sex education "functionally dead"); *Hogan*, 458 U.S. at 720 n.1 ("Mississippi maintains no other single-sex public university or college. Thus, we are not faced with the question of whether States can provide 'separate but equal' undergraduate institutions for males and females.").

[221] The *Virginia* Court did not deny that "[s]ingle-sex education affords pedagogical benefits to at least some students." *Virginia*, 518 U.S. at 535.

[222] See id. at 535–46. As the Court was careful to emphasize, the dispositive question was whether women could be justifiably excluded from "the training and attendant opportunities that VMI *uniquely* affords." Id. at 542 (emphasis added).

the excluded sex. Justice Scalia predicts that this is the path the Court will take in future cases, as he suggests that single-sex education is functionally dead after the Court's decision.[223] Although plausible, this prediction is inconsistent with the Court's acknowledgement of the pedagogical benefits of single-sex education and its suggestion that States can evenhandedly support single-sex schools. The Court's opinion seems intent on opening VMI to women without closing the door on all future single-sex schools and classes. It thus seems likely that the Court will be receptive to single-sex schools that do not have the unique characteristics or history of VMI, which will probably be true of many newly created single-sex colleges and will certainly be true of many single-sex elementary and secondary schools (or classes).[224] It also appears, given the discussion in the VMI opinion, that those advocating single-sex schools or classes may have to demonstrate that they are pedagogically beneficial before receiving approval from the Court.[225]

3. *Establishment Clause Cases*

The Supreme Court has applied no other constitutional provision as stringently in the school context as it has the Establishment Clause.[226] The constitutional standards that the Court has used in

---

[223] See id. at 596–97 (Scalia, J., dissenting).

[224] See Denise C. Morgan, Anti-Subordination Analysis After *United States v. Virginia*: Evaluating the Constitutionality of K–12 Single-Sex Public Schools, 1999 U. Chi. Legal F. 381, 383 (arguing that there is no "reason to believe that the 'exceeedingly persuasive justification' language in *Virginia* necessarily spells the end of the new generation of single-sex public schools"); Cass R. Sunstein, Foreword: Leaving Things Undecided, 110 Harv. L. Rev. 4, 75 (1996) (arguing that the Court, in the VMI decision, "left open the possibility that a new legislature, acting on the basis of a concern for the well-being of both men and women, could separate the sexes as long as it provided equal opportunity").

[225] For an elaboration of this point, see infra notes 351–59 and accompanying text.

[226] The Court's application of the Establishment Clause in the school context, it should be noted, is a relatively recent phenomenon. The Clause was not incorporated to apply against the states until 1947, see Everson v. Board of Educ., 330 U.S. 1 (1947), and it was not applied in the public school setting until the following year, see McCollum v. Board of Educ., 333 U.S. 203 (1948). Prior to 1948, the Court thus at least implicitly condoned the widespread use of prayer and Bible reading in public schools and, indeed, it was not until 1962 that the Court invalidated such religious exercises. See Engel v. Vitale, 370 U.S. 421 (1962); see also Abington Sch. Dist. v. Schempp, 374 U.S. 203, 267–78 (1963) (Brennan, J., concurring) (recounting the long

the school context over the last half-century are the same ones that it has used outside of that context. Prior to its 1971 decision in *Lemon v. Kurtzman*,[227] the Court relied on general principles of religious neutrality and separation of church and state, applicable within and outside of the school context, to invalidate religious classes held within public schools,[228] school prayer and Bible reading,[229] and a statute prohibiting the teaching of evolution.[230] Since *Lemon*, the Court has persistently, though not uniformly, applied the three-part test established in that opinion to cases within and outside of the schools context.[231]

At the same time, the Court has emphasized that the school context justifies applying the Establishment Clause with special vigilance. As the Court explained in a 1987 decision, such vigilance is required because parents entrust public schools to educate their children, but condition that trust on the understanding that the classroom will not be used to advance religious views.[232] Heightened vigilance is also required, the Court has stated, because

---

historical practice of using prayers and Bible readings at the opening of the school day).

[227] 403 U.S. 602, 612–13 (1971) (establishing that a government practice satisfies the Establishment Clause if it reflects a clearly secular purpose, has a primary effect that neither advances nor inhibits religion, and avoids excessive government entanglement with religion).

[228] See *McCollum*, 333 U.S. at 209–12 (1948).

[229] See *Engel*, 370 U.S. at 425 (school prayer); *Schempp*, 374 U.S. 203 (Bible reading).

[230] See Epperson v. Arkansas, 393 U.S. 97, 109 (1968).

[231] See, e.g., Lee v. Weisman, 505 U.S. 577, 603 n. 4 (1992) (Blackmun, J., concurring) (describing the Court's application of the *Lemon* test both within and outside of public schools). To be sure, the *Lemon* test has been criticized by commentators and a majority of sitting Justices alike, but it has thus far survived, albeit with some modifications. See, e.g., Chemerinsky, supra note 184, at 986. The Court has applied the test in all but one case involving religious activities in the schools, see *Lee*, including its most recent decision, Santa Fe Independent School District v. Doe, 120 S. Ct. 2267 (2000), in which the Court struck down a policy allowing for student-led prayers before high school football games. For discussion of the Court's application of the test, particularly in recent years, see, for example, Martha McCarthy, Religion and Education: Whither the Establishment Clause, 75 Ind. L.J. 123, 128–30 (2000).

[232] See Edwards v. Aguillard, 482 U.S. 578, 583–84 (1987). In *Edwards*, the Court invalidated a statute requiring that "creation science" be taught whenever evolution was taught, on the ground that the purpose of the statute was "to restructure the science curriculum to conform with a particular religious viewpoint." Id. at 593. This conclusion was vigorously challenged by the dissent. See id. at 619–26 (Scalia, J., dissenting).

children in school are young and impressionable, and they are likely to imitate teachers and be susceptible to peer pressure.[233] Lastly, the Court has justified heightened scrutiny of religious activities in schools on the ground that, because the public school is "the symbol of our democracy and the most pervasive means of promoting our common destiny," it is especially vital "to keep out divisive forces."[234] Thus, whereas the school context and the age of children are used in free speech cases to justify diluting student speech rights and granting teachers and school officials greater deference, in Establishment Clause cases the Court relies on these same factors to justify strengthening constitutional protections and depriving teachers and school officials of discretionary authority.[235]

The Court's record speaks for itself. It has decided ten cases involving religious activities in public schools. It has ruled for the school district and upheld the religious activity in only one, and that decision itself upheld the Equal Access Act, which grants students the right to form extracurricular religious clubs and to hold meetings on school grounds.[236] In the other nine cases, the Court has sided with the plaintiffs.[237] In doing so, the Court has struck down, in chronological order: voluntary religious classes held in public schools;[238] the recitation of a prayer at the beginning of each school day;[239] Bible reading and the recitation of the Lord's Prayer at the beginning of each school day;[240] a statute prohibiting the teaching of evolution;[241] the posting of the Ten Commandments on the walls of classrooms;[242] a statute authorizing a moment of silence

---

233 See id. at 584 & n.5 (citing cases). The Court in *Edwards* distinguished college students, whom the Court felt were less likely be unduly influenced by the presence of religion in the curriculum. See id. at 584 n.5.

234 Id. at 584 (quoting *McCollum*, 333 U.S. at 231 (opinion of Frankfurter, J.)).

235 In addition to *Edwards*, 482 U.S. at 584, see, for example, *Lee*, 505 U.S. at 592–93, 596–97 and Wallace v. Jaffree, 472 U.S. 38, 60–61 n.51 (1985).

236 See Westside Community Bd. of Educ. v. Mergens, 496 U.S. 226 (1989).

237 It is instructive to contrast the Court's record in these cases with its much more ambiguous record in cases involving aid to private religious schools. For discussion of these cases, see Chemerinsky, supra note 184 at 1005–15; see also infra notes 313–18.

238 See *McCollum*, 333 U.S. at 212.

239 See Engel v. Vitale, 370 U.S. 421, 436 (1962).

240 See Abington Sch. Dist. v. Schempp, 374 U.S. 203, 223 (1963).

241 See Epperson v. Arkansas, 393 U.S. 97, 109 (1968).

242 See Stone v. Graham, 449 U.S. 39, 43 (1980).

"for meditation or voluntary prayer;"[243] a statute prohibiting the teaching of evolution unless accompanied by instruction in "creation science;"[244] the use of clergy to deliver a prayer at graduation ceremonies;[245] and student-led prayer before football games.[246] That the Court's application of the Establishment Clause is more stringent within the schools than outside of them is well illustrated not only by this string of cases, but also by the fact that the Court has tolerated prayer in legislatures while invalidating it in schools.[247]

One of the overarching themes that emerges from these cases is a distinction between education and religious proselytizing. The Court has consistently made clear that it is constitutional to teach *about* religion.[248] Schools are thus free, the Court has emphasized, to educate students about the role of religion in American history, to use the Bible as a literary or historical text, and to teach courses

---

[243] Wallace v. Jaffree, 472 U.S. 38, 60–61 (1985).

[244] See Edwards v. Aguillard, 482 U.S. 578, 596–97 (1987).

[245] See Lee v. Weisman, 505 U.S. 577, 598–99 (1992). Although this case obviously did not actually involve religious activities during the regular school day, the Court nonetheless relied heavily on the school context to invalidate the use of clergy to deliver prayers at graduation. See id. at 592 (noting that prior decisions, such as *Engel* and *Schempp*, recognized "that prayer exercises in public schools carry a particular risk of indirect coercion").

[246] See Santa Fe Indep. Sch. Dist. v. Doe, 120 S. Ct. 2266 (2000).

[247] See Marsh v. Chambers, 463 U.S. 783, 792 (1983). A number of the concurring and dissenting opinions in school prayer cases have emphasized the apparent anomaly between invalidating school prayer and tolerating religious messages in other governmental contexts. See, e.g., *Engel*, 370 U.S. at 439 (Douglas, J., concurring) (noting that what the New York schools do, in beginning their days with prayer, "is what we do when we open Court"); id. at 446–50 & n.9 (Stewart, J., dissenting) (asking rhetorically whether "the Court [is] suggesting that the Constitution permits judges and Congressmen and Presidents to join in prayer, but prohibits school children from doing so"). Similar arguments appear in the dissenting opinions in *Wallace*. See *Wallace*, 472 U.S. at 84–85 (Burger, C.J., dissenting); id. at 113 (Rehnquist, J., dissenting).

[248] See, e.g., Abington Sch. Dist. v. Schempp, 374 U.S. 203, 225 (1963) ("Nothing we have said here indicates that . . . study of the Bible or of religion, when presented objectively as part of a secular program of education, may not be effected consistently with the First Amendment."); see also *Edwards*, 482 U.S. at 594 (explaining that schools are free to teach "a variety of scientific theories about the origins of humankind to schoolchildren" if done "with the clear secular intent of enhancing the effectiveness of science instruction"); Stone v. Graham, 449 U.S. 39, 42 (1980) (same); Epperson v. Arkansas, 393 U.S. 97, 106 (1968) (same).

on comparative religion.[249] Schools are not free, however, to promote religion.

The Court, moreover, has refused to defer to school officials' asserted secular justifications for ostensibly religious activities. The Court has instead determined for itself whether the purpose of such activities was to promote secular educational goals or religious viewpoints.[250] For example, the Court has rejected arguments that school prayers and Bible readings promote moral values and an appreciation of literature;[251] that the posting of the Ten Commandments educates students in the origins of the legal codes of Western Civilization;[252] and that requiring creationism to be taught whenever evolution is taught furthers academic freedom.[253] In each of these cases, the Court concluded that the actual purpose behind the activity was to promote religion and particular religious viewpoints.[254]

In short, the Establishment Clause cases reveal that the Court distinguishes between using religion for purposes of indoctrination, which is strictly forbidden, and studying religion for educational purposes, which is explicitly allowed. In this sense, the cases are quite similar to *Barnette*, in which the Court prohibited schools from compelling students to speak in order to promote the social goal of national unity, but explicitly acknowledged the authority of schools to teach about American history and democratic values.[255] Just like *Barnette*, the Establishment Clause cases demonstrate that

---

[249] See *Schempp*, 374 U.S. at 225.

[250] The Court's approach in *Stone* is illustrative. "The pre-eminent purpose for posting the Ten Commandments on schoolroom walls," the Court stated, "is plainly religious in nature. The Ten Commandments are undeniably a sacred text in the Jewish and Christian faiths, and no legislative recitation of a supposed secular purpose can blind us to that fact." *Stone*, 449 U.S. at 41 (footnote omitted).

[251] See *Schempp*, 374 U.S. at 223–24.

[252] See *Stone*, 449 U.S. at 42 (concluding that the "[p]osting of religious texts on the wall serves no [secular] educational function").

[253] See *Edwards*, 482 U.S. at 586–90 (explaining that, while normally deferential to a State's articulation of a secular purpose, the Court must determine for itself whether "the statement of such purpose [is] sincere and not a sham"); see also Wallace v. Jaffree, 472 U.S. 38, 56–60 (1985) (reviewing the legislative history of a statute authorizing a moment of silence for meditation or voluntary prayer and concluding that "the statute had *no* secular purpose") (emphasis in original).

[254] See *Edwards*, 482 U.S. at 590–93; *Stone*, 449 U.S. at 41–42; *Schempp*, 374 U.S. at 223–25.

[255] See supra note 44 and accompanying text.

school officials receive limited deference from the Court when they are acting to fulfill nonacademic goals.

4. Free Exercise Cases

The Court has explicitly applied the Free Exercise Clause to school disputes on only two occasions. The first decision was *Minersville School District v. Gobitis,*[256] in 1940, and it was short-lived.[257] The Court in *Gobitis* held that Jehovah's Witnesses did not have a free exercise right to be excused from saluting the flag and reciting the pledge of allegiance.[258] The Court's opinion was quite deferential to school authorities and emphasized the importance of forging national unity through the public schools.[259] At the same time, however, the opinion also suggested that as a general matter religious adherents did not have a free exercise right to be exempt from neutral laws of general applicability.[260] The Court did not purport, in other words, to be establishing a standard specifically for the school context, and the general principles applied in *Gobitis* were consistent with the Court's nascent free exercise jurisprudence.[261]

Gobitis, of course, was overruled three years later in *Barnette.*[262] In *Barnette*, however, the Court did not reject the analytical approach taken to the free exercise claim in *Gobitis*. To the contrary, the Court was careful to point out that it was not suggesting that religiously devout students had a free exercise right to be *exempt* from compulsory flag salutes.[263] Rather, the Court in *Barnette* concluded that legislatures could not compel *any* students to salute the

[256] 310 U.S. 586 (1940), overruled by West Virginia Bd. of. Educ. v. Barnette, 319 U.S. 624 (1943).

[257] See id.

[258] See id. at 594–95.

[259] See id. at 597–600.

[260] See id. at 594–95.

[261] The Court first incorporated the Free Exercise Clause earlier in the same Term in which *Gobitis* was decided. See Cantwell v. Connecticut, 310 U.S. 296 (1940). *Cantwell* involved restrictions on solicitation by Jehovah's Witnesses, and the Court made clear that general regulations of solicitation were "not open to any constitutional objection," even if the solicitation "be for a religious purpose." Id. at 305; see also Chemerinsky, supra note 184, at 987 (describing precedent).

[262] West Virginia Bd. of Educ. v. Barnette, 319 U.S. 624 (1943).

[263] See id. at 635–36 & n.16.

flag or recite the pledge of allegiance.[264] Thus the holding in *Barnette*, while broader than necessary to overrule *Gobitis*, nonetheless left undisturbed the conclusion that the Free Exercise Clause did not grant religious adherents (including students) a constitutional right to be exempt from laws of general applicability. *Barnette*'s treatment of *Gobitis* is interesting, and of enduring significance, not only because it is consistent with the current state of free exercise law, but also because it indicates that the Court in *Barnette* was wary of granting religious students liberty to exempt themselves from generally applicable and legitimate school policies—a reluctance that has resurfaced in lower court decisions, as I shall explain below.

The Court's second and only other application of the Free Exercise Clause in the school context occurred over thirty years later, in 1972, when the Court decided *Wisconsin v. Yoder*.[265] In between *Gobitis* and *Yoder*, the Court had established that free exercise claims should be subject to the compelling interest test; at least theoretically, free exercise claimants were thereby entitled to exemptions from generally applicable laws that burdened their religious exercises unless the laws were justified by a compelling governmental interest.[266] In *Yoder*, the Court applied this test to uphold the right of Amish parents to remove their children from state-sponsored education beyond the eighth grade.[267] The Amish

---

[264] As the Court in *Barnette* explained, *Gobitis* dealt with whether students had a right, based on religious beliefs, to be immune "from an unquestioned general rule." Id. at 635. In *Barnette*, by contrast, the Court addressed the legitimacy of the general rule itself. See id. ("It is not necessary to inquire whether non-conformist beliefs will exempt from the duty to salute unless we first find power to make the salute a legal duty.").

[265] 406 U.S. 205 (1972).

[266] See Sherbert v. Verner, 374 U.S. 398, 403 (1963). I say "theoretically" because the Court rarely sided with free exercise claimants despite purporting to apply a test that in theory was quite protective of their interests. For discussion of the Court's free exercise cases and its uneven application of the compelling interest test, see, e.g., Christopher L. Eisgruber & Lawrence G. Sager, Why the Religious Freedom Restoration Act Is Unconstitutional, 69 N.Y.U. L. Rev. 437, 446–47 (1994); James E. Ryan, Note, *Smith* and the Religious Freedom Restoration Act: An Iconoclastic Assessment, 78 Va. L. Rev. 1407, 1413–22 (1992).

[267] The case thus technically involved only the free exercise rights of parents, not those of students. However, the Court assumed that the students' wishes were in accord with the wishes of their parents, and explicitly reserved the question (raised by Justice Douglas in dissent) as to how to resolve a case where the interests of parents

plaintiffs believed "that their children's attendance at high school, public or private, was contrary to the Amish Religion and way of life."[268] The Court recognized that the State had a strong interest in ensuring that students were educated, but it held that this interest was not sufficiently compelling to override the free exercise rights of the Amish.[269]

The Court formally abandoned the compelling interest test in the later decision of *Employment Division v. Smith*,[270] ruling that facially neutral and generally applicable laws do not trigger strict scrutiny when free exercise claims are raised.[271] In doing so, however, the Court carved out an exception for so-called "hybrid" claims. This exception allows plaintiffs to challenge neutral and generally applicable laws when they raise a free exercise claim in conjunction with another constitutional claim—including, the Court was careful to point out, a claim asserting the right of parents "to direct the education of their children."[272] The Court in *Smith* thus preserved the holding in *Yoder*, and, indeed, some have argued that preserving *Yoder* may have been why the Court embraced the confounding and seemingly unjustified hybrid-rights exception in the first place.[273]

Given the paucity of school cases and the meandering nature of the Court's free exercise jurisprudence generally, it is difficult to draw hard and fast conclusions about the Court's application of the Free Exercise Clause in public schools. It seems fair to say that the Court's treatment of free exercise claims has itself been something of a hybrid between a general approach and one specifically tailored for the school context. Like its approach in Establishment

---

and children over attending school diverge. See *Yoder*, 406 U.S. at 230–32; see also id. at 237 (Stewart, J., concurring) (writing separately to emphasize that "there is no suggestion whatever in the record that the religious beliefs of the children here concerned differ in any way from those of their parents").

[268] Id. at 209.

[269] See id. at 213–15, 221–34. The religious rights of the Amish were augmented in this case, the Court reasoned, by the fundamental right of parents to direct the upbringing and education of their children, which the Court had recognized in 1925 in Pierce v. Society of Sisters, 268 U.S. 510 (1925). See *Yoder*, 406 U.S. at 214 (citing *Pierce*). *Pierce* is discussed infra at Section I.C.

[270] 494 U.S. 872 (1990).

[271] See id. at 884–85.

[272] Id. at 881–82 (discussing *Yoder*).

[273] See, e.g., Ira C. Lupu, *Employment Division v. Smith* and the Decline of Supreme Court-Centrism, 1993 BYU L. Rev. 259, 266–67.

Clause cases, the Court in free exercise cases has not adopted a standard that is explicitly tailored for the school context, and the current standard utilized by the Court renders the Free Exercise Clause virtually meaningless both within and outside of schools. At the same time, however, the school context does seem to have influenced the Court's application of general free exercise principles. For example, the Court relied on the school context in *Gobitis* to bolster its conclusion that religious adherents should not be excused from complying with general laws, and the Court used parental authority over schooling decisions in *Yoder* to bolster its conclusion that Amish children should be exempt from compulsory schooling beyond the eighth grade. Even the hybrid-rights exception to *Smith* is one that is applicable beyond the schools context but seems directed in particular at preserving the school-specific holding of *Yoder*.

Finally, just as important as what the Court has done with free exercise cases is what the Court has *not* done. Although the Court has made efforts to preserve the rights of parents to withdraw students from public schools for religious reasons, it has appeared uninterested in preserving the rights of parents to withdraw their children from particular classes or shield them from objectionable readings within public schools.[274] The Court has denied certiorari in at least two cases where lower courts rejected free exercise challenges to mandatory participation in particular classes or reading assignments within schools.[275] In each of these cases, as in others like them, the lower courts established a distinction—one that hearkens back to *Barnette* and *Gobitis* and is quite instructive for purposes of this Article—between the right of parents and students to exit the public school system and the right of parents to control

[274] See generally Nomi Maya Stolzenberg, "He Drew a Circle that Shut Me Out": Assimilation, Indoctrination, and the Paradox of a Liberal Education, 106 Harv. L. Rev. 581 (1993). Professor Stolzenberg uses the case of Mozert v. Hawkins County Board of Education, 827 F.2d 1058 (6th Cir. 1987), cert. denied, 484 U.S. 1066 (1988), to argue that neither courts nor commentators have responded adequately to complaints of fundamentalists that exposure to secular materials in public schools impinges their rights of free exercise.

[275] See Brown v. Hot, Sexy and Safer Prods., 68 F.3d 525 (1st Cir. 1995), cert. denied, 516 U.S. 1159 (1996) (refusing to exempt students from a sexually explicit AIDS awareness presentation); *Mozert*, 827 F.2d at 1070 (refusing to exempt students from their reading assignments).

the internal operations of the system.[276] Just as the Court in *Gobitis* and in *Barnette* was reluctant to recognize a free exercise right to be exempt from legitimate school policies, so too do lower courts today seem reluctant to do so. The limited exception is the free exercise right from *Yoder* to exit the school system altogether—an exception that makes the free exercise cases consistent with the due process cases, insofar as both acknowledge that schools have greater authority and leeway to control what occurs within the schools than they do to control who has access to the schools.

5. Summary

The Court's application of the Equal Protection, Establishment, and Free Exercise Clauses in the school context clearly differs from its application of the rights to free speech, Fourth Amendment privacy, and due process. On a more abstract level, the Court also appears to view the nature and purpose of public schools differently depending on the set of rights at stake. For example, in student speech, Fourth Amendment, and due process cases, the Court has voiced little worry that diluting constitutional protections in the school context might lead to a general dilution of such protections.[277] The Court's race, gender, and religion cases, by contrast, evince some concern that what happens in schools could easily happen elsewhere, and that weakening constitutional protections in schools could represent a dangerous first step toward weakening constitutional protections outside of school.[278] Thus, in the first set of cases discussed, schools are seen as unique institutions for which special rules can be created without setting

---

[276] See *Brown*, 68 F.3d at 533–34 (distinguishing between the right of parents to withdraw their children from public schools, which is recognized, and the right of parents to dictate the school curriculum, which is not); *Mozert*, 827 F.2d at 1067 (distinguishing *Yoder*); see also Fleischfresser v. Directors of Sch. Dist. 200, 15 F.3d 680 (7th Cir. 1994) (rejecting the free exercise claim of parents who argued that a supplemental reading program burdened the religious beliefs of their children by indoctrinating them contrary to their religious faith). The *Mozert* case drew a surprising amount of commentary, considering that it was decided by a lower federal court. In addition to the Stolzenberg article, supra note 274, see also George W. Dent, Jr., Religious Children, Secular Schools, 61 S. Cal. L. Rev. 863, 863–69 (1988); Gilles, supra note 5, at 992–1001; and Stanley Ingber, Religion or Ideology: A Needed Clarification of the Religion Clauses, 41 Stan. L. Rev. 233, 294–304 (1989).

[277] But see *Barnette*, 319 U.S. at 624.

[278] See supra notes 211, 234 and accompanying text.

precedent for other contexts. But in the second set of cases, schools are seen as representative institutions, where constitutional rights must, if anything, be more scrupulously observed lest the Court create a precedent in the school context that could be applied outside of it. Before returning to the Court's seemingly schizophrenic view of schools, one set of cases remains to be discussed.

C. *Public Schools and Fundamental Rights*

The Court's fundamental rights cases arising in the school context may usefully be divided into two groups: the right of parents to select private schools for their children, and the right of children to receive an education. The Court has upheld the right of parents to choose private schooling for their children, and it has recognized, somewhat obliquely, the right of all children to have access to public schools. It has refused, however, to recognize either that education is a fundamental right or that students have a right to equal educational expenditures.

1. The Fundamental Right to Attend Private Schools

One of the Court's earliest and most important decisions concerning public schools, *Pierce v. Society of Sisters*,[279] established the fundamental right of parents to exit the public school system and send their children to private schools.[280] At issue in the case was an Oregon law requiring attendance at public schools; the law was passed in an effort (supported by the Ku Klux Klan) to "Americanize" the children of newly-arrived immigrants.[281] The Supreme Court acknowledged the broad authority of the state to regulate all schools, public or private, and to compel all children to attend *a* school.[282] But the requirement that children attend a *public* school,

[279] 268 U.S. 510 (1925).
[280] See id. at 534–35.
[281] See id. at 529–30 & n.1. For discussion of the background of the Oregon statute, see David B. Tyack, The Perils of Pluralism: The Background of the *Pierce* Case, 74 Am. Hist. Rev. 74 (1968).
[282] See *Pierce*, 268 U.S. at 534. As the Court stated:

> No question is raised concerning the power of the State reasonably to regulate all schools, to inspect, supervise and examine them, their teachers and pupils; to require that all children of proper age attend some school, that teachers shall be of good moral character and patriotic disposition, that certain studies plainly

the Court held, "interfere[d] with the liberty of parents and guardians to direct the upbringing and education of children under their control."[283]

The Court struck a compromise in *Pierce* that is quite important for purposes of this Article. That compromise granted to the state the authority to compel attendance at "some" school, but granted to parents the right to choose for their children a private school—including a private, religious school. As Professor Mark Yudof has suggested, *Pierce* may be best understood as imposing limits on the power of the government to indoctrinate students.[284] Whether the Justices intended this or not, "*Pierce* may be understood as telling governments that they are free to establish public schools and to make education compulsory for certain age-groups, but they are not free to eliminate competing private sector institutions that promote heterogeneity in education."[285]

In addition, it is important to recognize that the Court implicitly acknowledged that the State has only limited authority to regulate private schools. The Court recognized that the State can require that certain classes be taught in private schools.[286] But the State, by negative implication, does not have the authority to control completely what transpires in private schools—including the transmission of cultural or religious values that differ from those transmitted in public schools; if it were otherwise, the right to attend a private school would be an empty shell.[287] Again, as Yudof explained, "[t]he state

---

> essential to good citizenship must be taught, and that nothing be taught which is manifestly inimical to the public welfare.

Id.

[283] Id. at 534–35. *Pierce* reaffirmed the position taken by the Court two years earlier in Meyer v. Nebraska, 262 U.S. 390 (1923), in which the Court struck down a law that prohibited public and private school teachers from instructing young students in German. The Court held that the statute interfered with the right of teachers to pursue a harmless occupation, the opportunities of students "to acquire knowledge," and the "power of parents to control the education of their own." Id. at 401.

[284] See Yudof, supra note 4, at 888–91.

[285] Id. at 890.

[286] In *Pierce*, the Court acknowledged that the state has authority to insist "that certain studies plainly essential to good citizenship must be taught, and that nothing be taught which is manifestly inimical to the public welfare." *Pierce*, 268 U.S. at 534. And in *Meyer*, the Court acknowledged the state's authority "to make reasonable regulations for all schools, including a requirement that they shall give instructions in English." *Meyer*, 262 U.S. at 402.

[287] In *Meyer*, for example, the Court stated that no challenge has "been made of the State's power to prescribe a curriculum for institutions *which it supports*," suggesting,

may promulgate its messages in the public school, and parents are free to choose private schools with different orientations."[288]

2. The Right of Access to Public Schools

In one of the Court's most famous school decisions, *San Antonio v. Rodriguez*,[289] the Court held—contrary to the strong suggestion in *Brown*—that education is not a fundamental right.[290] The Court accordingly upheld Texas's unequal school finance scheme, pursuant to which some schools were vastly better funded than others.[291] Two aspects of the Court's opinion are especially relevant here. First, the Court was clearly concerned that recognizing a fundamental right to an education would raise the possibility of having to recognize a fundamental right to other "necessities," such as housing, food, or employment. The Court thus refused to conceive of education as uniquely important to the welfare of citizens, and it rejected the argument that education is a fundamental right because it is essential to the effective exercise of other constitutional rights, such as the rights to speak and to vote. There was simply no logical way, the court reasoned, to distinguish education from food or shelter as being uniquely important to the exercise of constitutional rights.[292]

Second, the Court intimated that the complete denial of access to public schools might well be unconstitutional. Twice in the opinion, the Court emphasized that Texas was providing a basic education for all children and suggested that the case might be different were some children excluded from schools altogether.[293] As the Court stated, if the state made education available only to

---

of course, that the state's power to prescribe the curriculum of private schools may indeed be limited. 262 U.S. at 402 (emphasis added). See also Farrington v. Tokushige, 273 U.S. 284, 298 (1927) (striking down a Hawaiian act that strictly regulated foreign language schools on the ground that the act was "a deliberate plan to bring foreign language schools under a strict governmental control for which the record discloses no adequate reason").

[288] Yudof, supra note 4, at 890.

[289] 411 U.S. 1 (1973).

[290] See id. at 35–39. The Court also held that the Texas school finance scheme did not constitute impermissible wealth discrimination, strongly suggesting that poverty is not a suspect classification. See id. at 17–29.

[291] See id. at 29–40. On the expenditure disparities, see id. at 12–17.

[292] See id. at 37.

[293] See id. at 25 n.60.

those who could pay tuition, the "case would present a far more compelling set of circumstances for judicial assistance than the case before us today."[294] Less than a decade later, the Court would be faced with the set of circumstances hypothesized in *Rodriguez*, and the Court—in an opinion joined by Justice Powell, the author of *Rodriguez*—would indeed invalidate the law.

The case was *Plyler v. Doe*,[295] and it raised the question of whether Texas could deny a free public education to the children of illegal aliens.[296] Relying on the innocent nature of the children, whose parents were responsible for their presence in this country, and on the importance of education, the Court concluded that the discrimination against undocumented children could not be upheld unless it furthered a "substantial goal of the State."[297] Texas's justifications for the statute—that it preserved resources, deterred illegal immigration, and protected the state's school system—failed to meet this standard.[298]

The dissent believed that the Court had simply patched "together bits and pieces of what might be termed quasi-suspect class and quasi-fundamental-rights analysis" to "spin[] out a theory custom-tailored to the facts of these cases."[299] The dissent predicted that the opinion would ultimately stand for little, and that prediction has proved accurate. *Plyler* has never been extended, and the Court has indicated that it is not likely to do so. In *Kadrmas v. Dickinson Public Schools*,[300] for example, the Court upheld against an equal protection challenge a North Dakota law that allowed school districts to charge for bus service.[301] In holding that the bus fee survived rational basis scrutiny, the Court rejected the sugges-

294 Id.

295 457 U.S. 202 (1982).

296 See id. at 205.

297 See id. at 218–24.

298 See id. at 227–30.

299 Id. at 244 (Burger, C.J., dissenting).

300 487 U.S. 450 (1988).

301 See id. at 451. The fee did not actually prevent the student involved from attending school, as her family arranged for private transportation. See id. at 455; see also Martinez v. Bynum, 461 U.S. 321, 328 (1983) (upholding a state law that allowed school districts to charge students for their education if they lived apart from their parents solely for the purpose of attending school in the district, reasoning that the law represented a neutral and generally applicable residency requirement and was not aimed at aliens).

tion that *Plyler* required the use of heightened scrutiny.[302] "We have not extended [*Plyler*] beyond the 'unique circumstances' that provoked its 'unique confluence of theories and rationales,'" the Court observed, and it "decline[d] to extend the rationale of that decision to cover this case."[303]

Taken together, the fundamental rights cases establish some limited protections for students wishing to enter or exit the public school system. Students, however, possess no fundamental rights that can be exercised *within* the public school system. In this way, the fundamental rights cases are quite similar to the due process cases, which provide limited protection to those facing expulsion but not to those facing punishment within the school system.[304] They are also similar to the free exercise cases, at least if one adds the lower court decisions to *Yoder*, insofar as religious parents may have a limited right to remove their children from public schools but seem to possess no right to manage the education that occurs within the schools.[305] Despite these connections among lines of cases, serious discrepancies in approach and results remain to be explored. It is to that task that this Article now turns.

II. IS THERE A UNIFYING THEORY?

The Court's public school cases raise an intriguing question: Why are some constitutional rights but not others curtailed in the school setting? This question actually consists of two related parts. For ease of reference, I will call the first part the "wholesale question" and the second the "retail question." The wholesale question is simply this: Why has the Court altered some constitutional standards but not others to take account of the school setting? For example, in some student speech cases the Court, as described above, simply asks whether the challenged policy is reasonably related to legitimate pedagogical concerns. Why is this same standard not applied to all educational policies, regardless of the constitutional rights involved?

---

302 See *Kadrmas*, 487 U.S. at 459.

303 See id. at 459–60 (quoting *Plyler*, 457 U.S. at 239 (Powell, J., concurring) and *Plyler*, 457 U.S. at 243 (Burger, C.J., dissenting)).

304 See supra notes 163–67 and accompanying text.

305 See supra note 276 and accompanying text.

The retail question is why, with regard to those constitutional standards that have been altered, has the Court adopted the particular standards it has? The standards governing student speech and procedural rights, for example, are fairly deferential in general but also vary depending on particular contexts within the school setting. The Court thus provides more protection to student speech outside of rather than within the classroom; similarly, the Court has ruled that students have a due process right to be heard prior to a suspension but not prior to being physically struck by a teacher in the classroom. What I attempt to explain is why the Court has generally chosen deferential rather than stringent standards and why the degree of protection afforded to students' rights varies within the school context.

There appear to me to be at least four possible explanations of the cases. The first, which I would like to set aside as too easy, is that the Court is simply random and inconsistent, and that there is no discernible principle, rhyme, or reason to explain the cases. The second through fourth explanations, which I would like to consider in more detail, turn respectively on the nature of students (as children), the nature of the rights at stake, and the nature or function of public schools. I will suggest that it is the interaction of the last two factors—the nature of the rights at stake and the nature of public schools—that best explains the cases. I will also suggest, however, that the Court's conception of the function of public schools is the key to understanding the cases and predicting how future cases will likely be resolved.

A. *Students as Children*

One possible explanation of the school cases is that the Court is making special rules to govern children. Minors have traditionally had fewer legal rights than adults, constitutional rights included.[306] And the Court has occasionally cited this fact, as well as the immaturity of students in general, to justify its holdings. In a number of

[306] See, e.g., Vernonia Sch. Dist. 47J v. Acton, 515 U.S. 646, 654 (1995) (explaining that minors traditionally and currently lacked fundamental rights of self-determination); Ginsberg v. New York, 390 U.S. 629, 638 (1968) (acknowledging that children do not possess the same First Amendment rights as adults); Prince v. Massachusetts, 321 U.S. 158, 168 (1944) ("The state's authority over children's activities is broader than over like actions of adults.").

Establishment Clause cases, for example, the Court has explained that special vigilance is required in the school context because of the age of the students and their susceptibility to peer pressure and indoctrination.[307] Similarly, the Court in its free speech cases has justified imposing limits on student speech in light of the age of the students.[308] In *Acton*, finally, the Court characterized school officials as acting as guardians—as well as tutors—of minor children and used this status to justify granting the officials greater leeway to search students.[309]

There is also some evidence that the Court has been influenced in its decisions by whether most parents would support the school policy at issue. In *Acton*, for example, the Court pointed out that the parents attending a meeting regarding the school's drug policy uniformly supported it.[310] The different outcomes in *Tinker* and *Fraser* might also be explained on this rationale. In *Tinker*, the parents of the students wearing black armbands clearly supported (and indeed directed) their children's efforts, suggesting that there was at least some parental opposition to the school's policy of banning the armbands.[311] In *Fraser*, by contrast, it seems unlikely that most parents would have objected to prohibiting students from giv-

[307] See, e.g., Lee v. Weisman, 505 U.S. 577, 592–93 (1992); Edwards v. Aguillard, 482 U.S. 578, 584 (1987); Marsh v. Chambers, 463 U.S. 783, 792 (1983).

[308] *Fraser* is the best example. See Bethel Sch. Dist. v. Fraser, 478 U.S. 675, 677 (1986). There the Court upheld a sanction imposed on Fraser for giving a "lewd" speech at a student assembly in part on the ground that the audience included young children. Id; see also Hazelwood Sch. Dist. v. Kuhlmeier, 484 U.S. 260, 266 (1988) (affirming that the "rights of students in the public schools 'are not automatically coextensive with the rights of adults in other settings'") (quoting *Fraser*, 478 U.S. at 682).

[309] See *Acton*, 515 U.S. at 655–56 (stating that the nature of constitutional rights "is what is appropriate for children in school").

[310] See id. at 665 (noting that the parents of Vernonia's schoolchildren appeared to agree with the policy, and stating that, "The record shows no objection to this districtwide program by any parents other than the couple before us here—even though, as we have described, a public meeting was held to obtain parents' views").

[311] See Tinker v. Des Moines Indep. Comm. Sch. Dist., 393 U.S. 503, 504 (1969) (noting that the decision to wear armbands to protest the Vietnam war was made by a "group of adults and students" who met at one of the petitioner's homes). This is not to say that the protest was uncontroversial. For an account of the hostile reactions of other students to the protest, see John W. Johnson, Behind the Scenes in Iowa's Greatest Case: What is Not in the Official Record of *Tinker v. Des Moines Independent Community School District*, 48 Drake L. Rev. 473, 477–79 (2000).

ing lewd speeches at student assemblies.[312] In a sense then, some cases suggest that the Court itself might be acting *in loco parentis*, enforcing those policies that most parents would support and questioning those policies that a substantial number of parents would oppose.

Although the nature of students as children has some explanatory power, it is ultimately a problematic and incomplete explanation, for several reasons. First, the Court has not been consistent in its characterization of students and their level of maturity. In most Establishment Clause cases, for example, the Court has relied on the immaturity of students to justify keeping all religion out of the schools.[313] But in *Westside Community Board of Education v. Mergens*,[314] where the Court upheld the Equal Access Act, pursuant to which student religious clubs could meet on school grounds, the Court explicitly relied on the maturity of students in rejecting the suggestion that students would believe that the schools endorsed the religious message of the student clubs.[315] This inconsistency in itself suggests that the age of students might be more of a makeweight argument than a dispositive factor in the Court's analysis.

Second, the Court has explicitly rejected the notion that school officials act *in loco parentis* and thus should be infused with the same authority that parents have over their children. As the Court has explained, the idea that school officials should be granted parental authority is incompatible with compulsory school laws, which make it unreasonable to suppose that parents have voluntarily delegated all of their authority to schools.[316] Similarly, the Court itself has not always acted consistently with the apparent wishes of a majority of parents, making it unlikely that the Court is simply

[312] It is certainly true that Fraser's father, who filed the suit, objected to the punishment his son received. See *Fraser*, 478 U.S. at 679. But it nonetheless seems unlikely that there was a great deal of parental support for the notion that students should be free to give "lewd" speeches at student assemblies. See also *Hazelwood*, 484 U.S. at 263 (emphasizing that one of the stricken articles criticized a student's parent without giving the parent an opportunity to respond).

[313] See cases cited supra notes 227–55.

[314] 496 U.S. 226 (1989).

[315] See id. at 250 ("We think that secondary school students are mature enough and are likely to understand that a school does not endorse or support student speech that it merely permits on a nondiscriminatory basis.").

[316] See *Acton*, 515 U.S. at 655; Ingraham v. Wright, 430 U.S. 651, 662 (1977).

trying to fashion the rule or result any reasonable parent would make for his or her children. The school prayer cases are perhaps the best example of an area where the Court has diverged consistently from the wishes of a majority of parents, insofar as most parents (at the time of the decisions and still today) support some form of school prayer.[317] Another example is found in *Ingraham*, where the Court rejected the argument that parents should have the right to immunize their children from corporal punishment.[318]

Third, the Court has in some cases indicated that the same rules governing elementary and secondary student rights also apply in the college setting. For example, the Court has applied free speech precedents developed in elementary and secondary school cases, such as *Tinker*, to cases involving the speech rights of college students.[319] In addition, in its recent decision in *Rosenberger v. Rector and Visitors of the University of Virginia*,[320] which involved the free speech rights of college students, the Court suggested that *Hazelwood* would govern the speech rights of college students within curricular activities.[321] In the due process arena, the Court has also

---

[317] See Abington Sch. Dist. v. Schempp. 374 U.S. 203, 226–27 (1963) (striking down school prayer). The year that *Schempp* was decided, 1962, a Gallup poll of parents of students in public schools revealed that 79% approved of "religious observances" in public schools. See Dr. George H. Gallup, The Gallup Poll: Public Opinion 1935–1971, at 1779 (1972). Recent polls continue to show strong support for prayer in schools. See Public Opinion Online Surveys (revealing in a July 1999 poll that 65% of respondents believe that the government should allow prayer in school) (available in the Lexis Public Opinion database).

[318] See *Ingraham*, 430 U.S. at 662 n.22 (noting that "parental approval of corporal punishment is not constitutionally required") (citation omitted).

[319] See Papish v. University of Missouri Curators, 410 U.S. 667, 671 n.6 (1973) (per curiam) (applying *Tinker* to prohibit a university from expelling a student for selling an "underground" newspaper containing a lewd expression); Healy v. James, 408 U.S. 169, 174 (1972) (applying *Tinker* to hold that a university could not refuse to recognize a student group because of the group's political views and speech).

[320] 515 U.S. 819 (1995).

[321] See id. at 834. The Court distinguished between the broad authority of the university to make content-based decisions over the sort of "education" to provide and the university's limited authority to discriminate among types of student speech. In doing so, the Court stated: "A holding that the University may not discriminate based on the viewpoint of private persons whose speech it facilitates does not restrict the University's own speech, which is controlled by different principles." Id. (citing *Mergens*, 496 U.S. at 250 and *Hazelwood*, 484 U.S. at 270–72). *Mergens* and *Hazelwood*, of course, are both cases from the elementary and secondary school context.

suggested that similar rules apply in colleges and in secondary and elementary schools. The Court's decision in *Horowitz*, for example, establishing that a medical student does not have a right to due process before receiving an academic sanction, seems applicable in the elementary and secondary school context.[322] To be sure, the Court has also on occasion, particularly in Establishment Clause cases, suggested that the same rules applicable in secondary and elementary schools would not necessarily be applicable in the college setting.[323] But this differing treatment of the relevance of the age of students does not refute, and instead supports, the key point that the restrictions imposed on elementary and secondary school students cannot all be explained by the fact that they are children.

Finally, and most importantly, the Court has indicated that its decisions limiting the rights of students in school do not limit their rights outside of school. Thus, the Court has acknowledged in free speech cases that the restrictions on student speech upheld in the school context could not be constitutionally applied to these same students outside of the school setting. "A school need not tolerate student speech that is inconsistent with its basic educational mission," the Court stated in *Hazelwood*, "even though the government could not censor similar speech outside the school."[324] Similarly, there is no hint in *Acton*, and warnings to the contrary, that the Court would accept suspicionless searches of children outside of the school setting.[325] What these decisions suggest instead is

[322] See Board of Curators v. Horowitz, 435 U.S. 78, 89–90 (1978) (distinguishing *Goss*, which arose in the context of elementary and secondary schools).

[323] As the Court suggested in *Edwards*: "The potential for undue influence is far less significant with regard to college students who voluntarily enroll in courses. This distinction warrants a difference in constitutional results. Thus, for instance, the Court has not questioned the authority of state colleges and universities to offer courses on religion or theology." Edwards v. Aguillard, 482 U.S. 578, 584 (1987) (internal quotation and citations omitted). Note, however, that the Court may have overstated the difference between elementary and secondary schools and colleges in *Edwards*, given that the Court has acknowledged that elementary and secondary schools could constitutionally offer courses on "comparative religion or the history of religion." Abington Sch. Dist. v. Schempp, 374 U.S. 203, 225 (1963).

[324] *Hazelwood*, 484 U.S. at 266 (internal quotations and citations omitted); see also *Fraser*, 478 U.S. at 688 (Brennan, J., concurring) ("If respondent had given the same speech outside of the school environment, he could not have been penalized simply because government officials considered his language to be inappropriate; the Court's opinion does not suggest otherwise.") (internal citation omitted).

[325] See *Acton*, 515 U.S. at 665.

that the school setting, not the age of the students, justifies limiting students' rights.

B. The Nature of Constitutional Rights

Another potential explanation, which has a bit more traction than the preceding one, is that differences among the text, history, or Court interpretations of the various constitutional rights explain the differences in the cases. The notion here is that some rights might be more malleable or contingent than others, and thus it would follow that some rights but not others would be molded to fit the school context. The texts of the various constitutional provisions involved provide some, but not much, support for this theory. The texts of the Fourth Amendment and Due Process Clause suggest a certain flexibility in application, and the Court has indeed crafted special rules to govern the exercise of these rights within public schools. At the same time, however, the Equal Protection Clause, which is as textually ambiguous as the Due Process Clause and thus potentially as contingent, has been applied within the schools in largely the same manner that it is applied outside of them. Conversely, the First Amendment's prohibition on laws abridging speech is written in absolute terms, but this has not prevented the Court from creating special rules to govern student speech. As for the history surrounding these provisions, I am not aware of evidence supporting such a distinction among constitutional rights.

Whether supported by text and history or not, it is true that the Court has been more willing to adapt some constitutional rights than others to fit particular institutions. It is also largely true that the rights that have traditionally been more institution-dependent are the ones that the Court has altered in the school setting. The Free Speech Clause, for example, is not so much riddled with exceptions as it is a collection of them; different rules regarding the legitimacy of content- and viewpoint-based restrictions, prior restraint, and official discretion exist for a number of different institutions.[326] As Professors Schauer and Pildes point out, even

[326] See Robert Post, Subsidized Speech, 106 Yale L.J. 151, 164–65 (1996); Frederick Schauer & Richard C. Pildes, Electoral Exceptionalism and the First Amendment, 77 Tex. L. Rev. 1803, 1822–23 (1999).

with regard to political speech, the degree of protection provided is often institution-dependent: "There is one form of protection for political speech on government property, another for political speech on the broadcast media, another for political speech in the public schools, another for political speech by government employees, and so on."[327] Similarly, the Fourth Amendment has proven fairly flexible, perhaps in part because the Amendment literally guards against "unreasonable" searches.[328] And the Due Process Clause has traditionally been interpreted to require what the particular circumstances demand and hence to require a balancing of the government's interest in a particular context against the individual's interest in that same context.[329]

The standards for applying the Equal Protection and Establishment Clauses, on the other hand, have not been as malleable. This is not to say that the Court's application of these Clauses has been insensitive to institutional contexts. Institutional context has played an important role, for example, in both desegregation cases and in cases involving aid to religious institutions. Rather, the point is simply that the Court has rarely altered the constitutional standards for these rights to fit a particular context.[330] There is no suggestion in any of the Court's race cases, for example, that some institutions generally have greater leeway to employ race-based policies than others. To take one example, prison officials are given a great deal of authority over prisoners; policies restricting constitutional rights will generally be upheld if reasonably related to a

---

[327] Schauer & Pildes, supra note 326, at 1823.

[328] See U.S. Const. amend. IV ("The right of the people to be secure in their persons, houses, papers, and effects, against unreasonable searches and seizures, shall not be violated . . . ."); cf. *Acton*, 515 U.S. at 652 ("As the text of the Fourth Amendment indicates, the ultimate measure of the constitutionality of a government search is 'reasonableness.'").

[329] See, e.g., Goss v. Lopez, 419 U.S. 565, 578 (1974) (emphasizing "that the interpretation and application of the Due Process Clause are intensely practical matters and that [t]he very nature of due process negates any concept of inflexible procedures universally applicable to every imaginable situation") (internal quotation omitted).

[330] *Marsh*, where the Court approved prayer before legislative sessions without applying the *Lemon* test, is one exception. See supra note 247 and accompanying text for a discussion of *Marsh*. The presumptions regarding the lingering effects and scope of prior school segregation are arguably additional examples. See supra note 196 and accompanying text.

legitimate penological objective.[331] The Supreme Court, however, has never suggested that this same deferential standard would apply to race-based prison policies or actions, and lower courts have uniformly indicated that such policies and actions are to be judged by the traditional compelling interest test.[332]

The limited exception to this pattern is the Court's treatment of the Free Exercise Clause. Prior to *Smith*, the Court was willing to alter the standard used for assessing free exercise claims to fit particular institutions and thus refused to apply the compelling interest test in either the military or prison settings.[333] In *Yoder*, however, the Court applied the compelling interest test to a free exercise claim raised in the school setting, suggesting that schools, unlike prisons or the military, would not receive the benefit of a constitutional test tailored to accommodate institutional concerns.[334] After *Smith*, it is possible that the standard for assessing free exercise claims will no longer change depending on the institutional context, but this is because the standard is so low that it need not be diluted in order to take into account institutional concerns.

The Court's differential treatment of rights provides at least a partial answer to the wholesale question raised above: The Court has (generally) altered the same rights in the school setting that it alters in other settings as well, and it has applied a uniform standard to govern those rights that have traditionally not been institution-dependent. Thus, the standards for applying the Free Speech Clause, the Fourth Amendment, and the Due Process Clauses have been molded to fit the school context, just as they are molded to fit other institutional contexts. On the other hand, the standards for applying the Equal Protection and Establishment Clauses have not been altered, which is consistent with the Court's application of the Clauses in other contexts. The Free Exercise Clause, again, stands as something of an exception, as at least prior

[331] See Turner v. Safley, 482 U.S. 78, 89 (1987).

[332] See, e.g., Wittmer v. Peters, 87 F.3d 916, 918–19 (7th Cir. 1996) (discussing and then applying strict scrutiny to review a prison's decision to make a race-conscious effort to hire black guards to oversee "boot-camp" style prison for youthful offenders), cert. denied, 519 U.S. 1111 (1997).

[333] See O'Lone v. Estate of Shabazz, 482 U.S. 342 (1987) (prisons); Goldman v. Weinberger, 475 U.S. 503 (1986) (military).

[334] See Wisconsin v. Yoder, 406 U.S. 205, 213–15, 221–34 (1972).

to *Smith* the Court was willing to alter the constitutional standard for prisons and the military, but not for schools.

This explanation, however, leaves at least two important questions unanswered. First, that the Court has molded some rights but not others to fit different institutional contexts does not itself explain why some rights are more malleable than others. This simple observation does not tell us, for example, *why* free speech rights are more flexible than equal protection rights. Second, that some rights but not others have been bent to fit particular institutions does not answer the retail question—it does not explain why certain rights have been shaped the way that they have within the school context. The differential treatment of rights does not tell us, for example, why the Court has adopted the particular set of rules it has to govern student speech, the procedural rights of students facing punishment, or the Fourth Amendment rights of students facing searches by school officials. Nor does it tell us why, given that both rights are somewhat institution-dependent, the Free Speech Clause is truncated in the school setting but the Establishment Clause is not. One is still left to ponder, among other questions, why school authorities have ample authority to limit student speech, but almost no authority to encourage or lead students in religious exercises.

C. *The Nature of Public Schools*

This leaves the nature of public schools themselves as a potential explanation for the Court's public schools jurisprudence. And indeed it is from this vantage point that one can discern a unifying thread running through the Court's public school decisions. As I have suggested, the unifying theme is that the Court alters constitutional standards and upholds school policies or practices when doing so appears necessary to preserve the academic function of public schools. Put differently, the Court has throughout its public school cases privileged the academic function of schools over other possible functions, by designing analytical standards and reaching results that favor and protect the former.

This distinction was apparent in one of the Court's earliest cases, *Pierce*, and it is apparent in one of its most recent, *Hazelwood*. In *Pierce*, decided in 1925, the Court acknowledged the authority of the State to compel students to attend "some" school but prohibited the State from requiring students to attend a public school.[335] Prohibiting the State from requiring all students to attend public schools obviously limits the extent to which the State can control the socialization of students, while acknowledging the State's authority to require attendance at some school recognizes the State's important interest in ensuring that children obtain some education. If the Court considered the social function of schools as important as the academic function, one would have expected the Court to have been much more sympathetic to the requirement that students attend a public school, where the State would be able to control the socialization of students.[336]

Hazelwood, decided over sixty years after *Pierce*, evinces similar solicitude for the academic function of schools. In upholding the authority of a school principal to censor a student newspaper, which was produced as part of a journalism class, the Court distinguished between student speech that occurs within a curricular activity and that which occurs outside of it.[337] The Court defined a curricular activity as one "supervised by faculty members and designed to impart particular knowledge or skills to student participants and audiences."[338] And it explained that educators are entitled to exercise greater control over student expression occurring within a curricular activity in order "to assure that participants learn whatever lessons the activity is designed to teach."[339] Again, if the socialization of students were deemed as important as providing knowledge or imparting skills, it would have been odd for the Court to have distinguished between curricular and extracurricular activities—that is, if the primary point of the cases were to authorize schools to mold student behavior and shape values, it would

[335] Pierce v. Society of Sisters, 268 U.S. 510, 534–35 (1925).

[336] Cf. Stephen L. Carter, Parents, Religion, and Schools: Reflections On *Pierce*, 70 Years Later, 27 Seton Hall L. Rev. 1194, 1203 (1997) (noting that "by holding that parents could not be required to send their children to public schools, the Court [in *Pierce*] was holding that parents can decide what values should be inculcated in their children").

[337] See Hazelwood Sch. Dist. v. Kuhlmeier, 484 U.S. 260, 271–73 (1988).

[338] Id. at 271.

[339] Id.

have been odd to let students have freer reign to say obnoxious or offensive things in the lunchroom than in the classroom.[340]

To be sure, not all of the Court's public school cases neatly fit this pattern.[341] It would be surprising if they did. But the privileging of the academic function of schools is nonetheless a strong and recurring, if sometimes implicit, theme in the cases. And the distinction between academic and social functions helps answer both the wholesale and retail questions, as discussed below. It also helps reconcile some seemingly anomalous results in the cases, to which I will turn at the end of this section.

1. The Wholesale Question

As discussed above, the constitutional rights that are explicitly altered in the school context—those involving speech, searches, and discipline—are the same ones that are explicitly altered in other settings. Similarly, those rights that are applied with little or no adjustment for the school context—those involving race, gender, and religion—have traditionally (save for the Free Exercise Clause) been applied acontextually by the Court. Left unaddressed by this observation is the question of why these rights are treated differently. The academic and social distinction I am proposing may provide the answer.

[340] Interestingly, a similar distinction between curricular and extracurricular activities is suggested in the Establishment Clause cases and in a college speech case. The Court, as discussed above, will not tolerate the introduction of religion into curricular activities. But it will tolerate the religious activities of extracurricular clubs, see Westside Comm. Bd. of Educ. v. Mergens, 496 U.S.226, 247–53 (1989), and it has given some indication that such activities *must* be tolerated, see Rosenberger v. Rector and Visitors of the Univ. of Virginia, 515 U.S. 819, 834 (1995). Assuming that students do have a constitutional right, protected by the Free Speech or Free Exercise Clause, to form extracurricular religious clubs, then an instructive parallel arises between the student speech and religion cases. Schools could neither introduce religion into the classroom nor preclude it from being introduced into extracurricular offerings. Once one posits, as the Court has, see infra note 349 and accompanying text, that religious proselytizing is inconsistent with the academic function of schools, this state of affairs is sensible and consistent with the other speech cases: Schools do not have the authority to introduce religion into the classroom because doing so is not justified on academic grounds, and schools similarly may not have the authority to bar private religious speech, outside of the curriculum, again because doing so would not be related to an academic goal.

[341] See the discussion of the Court's Fourth Amendment cases, infra notes 378–81 and accompanying text.

To begin, the Court's decision not to alter particular constitutional rights to take account of different contexts obviously must rest on a judgment that the curtailment of certain rights will rarely, if ever, be related to legitimate governmental objectives. It is intuitive, for example, that government institutions will have to limit the speech rights of those associated with the institution—whether they are employees, students, prisoners, or soldiers—in order to accomplish legitimate institutional goals.[342] In particular, school officials and teachers will have to limit student speech rights to some extent in order to select courses, run classes, and grade tests. It is less intuitive, however, to suppose that the consideration of race, gender, or religion will ever be relevant to a legitimate institutional objective.

While less intuitive, it is not inconceivable that race, gender, or religion could be quite relevant to a legitimate objective of public schools. For example, one could plausibly argue that a legitimate objective of public schools is to foster racial equality, increase racial understanding, or simply increase interracial contact. Indeed, some of the Court's desegregation decisions suggest as much. One could similarly argue that a legitimate objective of public schools is to combat gender inequality. One might also argue (consistent with the earliest traditions of public schools)[343] that a legitimate objective of public schools is to inspire respect for this nation's religious heritage, instill virtue and morality in students, or perhaps even to encourage contemplation of a higher, religious authority.[344] If one or several of these objectives were accepted as important or compelling by the Court, it is easy to see how race, gender, and/or religion would be relevant to the achievement of the objective.

---

[342] See Post, supra note 326, at 164 (arguing that "[t]he state must be able to regulate speech within managerial domains so as to achieve explicit governmental objectives").

[343] See, e.g., Abington Sch. Dist. v. Schempp, 374 U.S. 203, 266–78 (1963) (Brennan, J., concurring) (describing the history of religion in public schools).

[344] I recognize that this last objective is illegitimate in the sense that the Court has indicated in its Establishment Clause cases that schools cannot seek to encourage the practice of religion. But this is really a difference of degree, insofar as the Court has not privileged such social goals as increasing racial tolerance or gender equality so as to allow schools deference to take race or gender into account in order to achieve those goals. The point of consistency is that, with regard to religion, race, and gender, if the Court were willing to privilege certain social goals within the school context, the use of religion, race, or gender could become directly relevant to the achievement of those goals.

For example, if the Court believed that a crucial function of schools was to increase racial understanding by increasing interracial contact, we would expect the Court to be much more deferential to race-based policies designed to foster racial diversity.[345] Similarly, if the Court believed that a crucial function of schools was to enhance the self-esteem and assertiveness of female students, we might expect the Court to be fairly deferential to all-female schools or classes. Lastly, if the Court believed it appropriate for schools to instill respect for or inspire contemplation of a higher, religious authority, we would expect the Court to be much more tolerant of the introduction of religion into public schools.

On the other hand, if the Court believed, as it apparently does, that the central function of schools is academic, it is not altogether surprising that the Court would take a closer look at policies that involve race, religion, and gender. The Court may understandably fear that schools will take religion, race, or gender into account not to further an academic goal, but rather to further a social goal divorced from academics, such as increased devotion to religion, or increased interracial contact, or greater racial or gender equality.[346] By contrast, policies that intrude upon the speech, due process, or privacy rights of students for the ostensible purpose of conveying necessarily selected knowledge, teaching particular skills, or maintaining order in the classroom or school may be less easily manipulated to achieve social goals that are unrelated to academic performance.

Several examples, one from past decisions and two involving issues that are likely to be decided by the Court in the near future, might help illustrate my point. The Court has twice prevented schools from adopting curricular policies that advanced a creation-

---

[345] Cf. Robert Post, Constitutional Domains: Democracy, Community, Management 324–29 (1995) (arguing that whether racist speech can constitutionally be regulated on public university campuses should turn on the educational purpose we attribute to universities).

[346] A version of this distrust is apparent in the Court's decision in the VMI case, where the Court seemed clearly suspicious of VMI's alleged educational justifications for excluding women, in part because of the long history of Virginia's denial of equal educational opportunities to women. See United States v. Virginia, 518 U.S. 515, 535–46 (1996). Similar skepticism pervades the Court's Establishment Clause cases, in which the Court closely scrutinizes the alleged secular benefits of introducing religion into the classrooms. See supra notes 250–56.

ist view of the origin of humans, on the ground that the purpose of the policies was to promote a religious viewpoint.[347] The Court rejected the schools' arguments in these cases that the policies were a legitimate means to enhance the academic experience of students.[348] At first glance, the cases are a little surprising: One might expect, given that the policies concerned what was taught in the classroom, that the Court would have deferred to the school officials.

But if we posit, as the Court has, that promoting religion is not a legitimate academic function, the results in these cases (as well as the Court's other religion cases) make sense. The Court in its creationism decisions examined the curricular policies closely to ascertain whether the curriculum and classroom were being used to promote a religious view of our origins; having reasonably (if controversially) concluded that they were, the Court understandably struck down the policies. As noted earlier, the Court was careful to emphasize in these and other cases that schools are free to teach *about* religion as an academic subject; they are not free, however, to *promote* religion under the guise of teaching about it.[349] This line of reasoning, as well as the results in the creationism decisions, suggest that the Court is intent on protecting what it conceives to be legitimate academic goals.

As for the issues on the Court's horizon, it seems reasonable to predict that the Court will fairly soon have to decide whether to allow the voluntary use of race in student assignments to elementary or secondary schools and whether to allow single-sex elementary or secondary schools. One can reasonably expect, based on relevant Supreme Court and lower court decisions, that the Court will not simply defer to school officials who argue that race- or gender-based attendance policies should be allowed because they promote legitimate educational goals. I would further expect that the Court would be especially interested in seeing convincing proof that such policies promote academic achievement.[350]

---

[347] See Edwards v. Aguillard, 482 U.S. 578, 596–97 (1987); Epperson v. Arkansas, 393 U.S. 97, 109 (1968).

[348] See *Edwards*, 482 U.S. at 587–88; *Epperson*, 393 U.S. at 107–08.

[349] See *Edwards*, 482 U.S. at 593–94; see supra notes 248–54 and accompanying text.

[350] Cf. Wygant v. Jackson Bd. of Educ., 476 U.S. 267, 314–15 (1986) (Stevens, J., dissenting) (suggesting, in an argument that obviously did not persuade the majority,

Consider first the issue of using race to determine assignment to examination or magnet schools. Such race-based assignment policies have been successfully challenged in each of the three cases decided by federal courts of appeal. In each case, the courts have applied strict scrutiny and asked whether the use of race is necessary to achieve a compelling interest, and in each case the interest asserted by the school district was the attainment of a diverse student body.[351] The courts have assumed that diversity might be a compelling interest but have struck down the programs on the ground that they were insufficiently tailored.[352] In so doing, one of the courts expressed deep skepticism that diversity, standing alone, is a compelling interest and suggested that school districts must demonstrate specifically how diversity enhances the educational process.[353]

It appears that the lower court's skepticism derives, at least in part, from a suspicion that diversity is simply too far removed from the academic function of schools to justify its use, at least in the absence of a stronger showing that a diverse student body furthers the educational environment of schools. The lower court's skepticism might in turn indicate that it would be impossible to convince a court (and especially the current Supreme Court) that racial integration carries with it academic benefits—particularly because it raises the specter that single-race schools could be potentially justified on the same ground. But I think this is the only hope that racially-based student assignment policies in secondary and elementary schools have of succeeding,[354] and I do not think it is

---

that a school board should have authority to determine "that an integrated faculty will be able to provide benefits to the student body that could not be provided by an all-white, or nearly all-white, faculty" such as promoting greater interracial understanding).

[351] See Eisenberg v. Montgomery County Pub. Schs., 197 F.3d 123 (4th Cir. 1999), cert. denied, 120 S. Ct. 1420 (2000); Tuttle v. Arlington County Sch. Bd., 195 F.3d 698 (4th Cir. 1999), cert. denied, 120 S. Ct. 1552 (2000); Wessman v. Gittens, 160 F.3d 790 (1st Cir. 1998).

[352] See *Eisenberg*, 197 F.3d at 130; *Tuttle*, 195 F.3d at 701.

[353] See *Wessman*, 160 F.3d at 796–800.

[354] It may well be that a diversity argument will fare better at the college level, given that the educational experience in college seems to rely more heavily on student interaction and discussion than does the experience in elementary or secondary schools. Indeed, the idea that a diverse student body enhances the educational environment in universities was one of the main reasons why Justice Powell in *Bakke* concluded that diversity was a compelling interest. See *Bakke*, 438 U.S. at 312–15

implausible to predict that, were it actually demonstrated in a particular case that racial integration would increase the academic performance of some students without decreasing that of others, a race-based admissions policy would be upheld.[355]

Whether single-sex schools or classes are deemed constitutional will also likely turn on the degree to which it can be demonstrated that such classes or schools enhance the academic performance of students. Recall the Court's treatment of the question, in *United States v. Virginia*, of whether VMI's all-male admissions policy could be justified on the ground that single-sex schools are pedagogically beneficial. The Court never adequately addressed this question.[356] But it did acknowledge that single-sex schools are pedagogically beneficial for some students and that a state can evenhandedly support single-sex schools.[357] Taken together, these somewhat cryptic suggestions at least point to the possibility that the Court would accept a state policy that provides for single-sex schools or single-sex classes if it could be demonstrated that such schools or policies provide pedagogical—in other words, academic—benefits.[358]

In short, it is possible to understand the religion cases as reflecting the Court's view that the promotion of religion is simply inconsistent with the academic function of schools; it follows that

---

(concluding that attaining a diverse student body is "a goal that is of paramount importance in the fulfillment of [a university's] mission") (opinion of Powell, J.).

[355] Cf. Wittmer v. Peters, 87 F.3d 916, 919–21 (7th Cir. 1996) (approving the race-based hiring of guards for a prison boot camp, on the ground that expert testimony and social science evidence indicated the importance of having black guards for black inmates in this setting).

[356] See supra notes 221–22 and accompanying text.

[357] See United States v. Virginia, 518 U.S. 515, 534 n.7, 535 (1996).

[358] Commentators on the topic also appear to assume that the fate of single-sex schools and classes will depend on proof that they improve the academic environment for students and lead to greater achievement. See, e.g., Levit, supra note 213, at 464 (arguing that "[t]he Supreme Court will be forced to inquire whether the asserted pedagogical benefits of single-sex schools and classes provide an 'exceedingly persuasive justification' for state-sponsored segregation of the sexes"); Carolyn B. Ramsey, Subtracting Sexism From the Classroom: Law and Policy in the Debate Over All-Female Math and Science Classes in Public Schools, 8 Tex. J. Women & L. 1, 7–14 (1998) (making a similar assumption and presenting social science evidence documenting academic benefits from all-girls math and science classes). But see Morgan, supra note 224, at 418–20 (suggesting that single-sex schools could be constitutionally justified on a number of alternative grounds, including the proposition that "they promote sex equality").

the Court will carefully scrutinize any introduction of religion in the schools. It is possible to understand the Supreme Court and lower court approaches to race and gender cases as reflecting the view that race and gender are unlikely to be relevant to academic goals, with the caveat that, should such a connection be demonstrated, race- or gender-based policies may well be approved.

At the same time, it is apparent that the constitutional rights themselves influence the Court's analysis, and thus the nature of the constitutional rights at stake remains an important part of the explanation of the Court's school cases. For example, the Court's scrutiny of any asserted connection between racial or gender classifications and academic goals has been and will likely remain quite intense. The Court's scrutiny of the asserted secular benefits of introducing religion into schools is also intense. But when student speech or Fourth Amendment rights are at stake, the Court seems much more willing to accept an asserted connection between the need to limit student speech or privacy rights and the achievement of academic goals. Thus, while the ultimate issue—does the policy or practice in question further or protect the academic function of schools—remains the same regardless of the constitutional right at issue, the Court's willingness to accept an asserted academic rationale for the policy or practice varies depending on the right at stake.

2. The Retail Question

As for the rights that have been explicitly altered to take account of the school context—namely speech, Fourth Amendment, and due process rights—the question to be answered is why the Court has adopted the particular standards it has. It is important to recognize at the outset that the Court has not simply deferred to school officials in every case involving these rights. Rather, at least with regard to speech and procedural rights, the Court has created different standards that apply to different circumstances within schools. Here, again, the academic and social distinction seems to do a good job of explaining the cases.

Consider first the Court's student speech cases. As described above, in one of its earliest student speech cases, *Tinker*, the Court upheld the right of students to wear black armbands to school in order to protest the Vietnam War.[359] The Court's opinion teems with eloquent statements about the importance of respecting constitutional rights within the school setting, but it also indicates that student First Amendment rights must be applied "in light of the special characteristics of the school environment."[360] And the opinion establishes a standard that allows schools to prohibit student speech on school grounds if the speech "materially disrupts classwork or involves substantial disorder or invasion of the rights of others."[361]

In the Court's two most recent student speech cases, *Fraser* and *Hazelwood*, the Court upheld policies that restricted student speech; in *Fraser* the Court upheld the suspension of a student who gave a sexually suggestive speech at a student assembly, and in *Hazelwood* it allowed a student newspaper, produced as part of a journalism class, to be censored by the school principal.[362] The Court also held in *Hazelwood* that school officials may restrict student speech in curricular activities "so long as their actions are reasonably related to legitimate pedagogical concerns."[363] Whereas *Tinker* emphasized the vitality of constitutional rights in the school setting, *Fraser* and *Hazelwood* emphasized the authority of school officials to inculcate certain values, including the "fundamental values necessary to the maintenance of a democratic political system."[364]

The conventional wisdom expressed in the literature is that these cases are in serious tension.[365] The Court in *Tinker*, it is said, endorsed a progressive model of education, under which students are allowed ample freedom to form ideas and challenge authority, while the Court in *Fraser* and *Hazelwood* endorsed a more conservative or inculcative model of education, under which students are considered passive recipients of community or democratic values.[366]

---

[359] Tinker v. Des Moines Indep. Sch. Dist., 393 U.S. 503, 514 (1969).
[360] Id. at 506.
[361] Id. at 513.
[362] See Hazelwood Sch. Dist. v. Kulhmeier, 484 U.S. 260, 276 (1988); Bethel Sch. Dist. v. Fraser, 478 U.S. 675, 685 (1986).
[363] *Hazelwood*, 484 U.S. at 273.
[364] See *Fraser*, 478 U.S. at 683; see also *Hazelwood* 484 U.S. at 272.
[365] See supra notes 80–105 and accompanying text.
[366] See id.

I think the cases are actually much more consistent than this conventional wisdom suggests and that they support the hypothesis I have advanced.

All three decisions are devoted to protecting the academic function of public schools. The different standards adopted depend on how closely connected the student speech is with that function; the closer the speech is to the academic function, the more diluted the student's speech rights become. When student speech "may fairly be characterized as part of the curriculum," schools are allowed greater control, in part to "assure that participants learn whatever lessons the activity is designed to teach."[367] By contrast, when student speech is not associated with a curricular activity, the school's authority is diminished—but it does not disappear. Schools retain the authority to quash speech that disrupts classwork.[368] What ties these cases together, again, is the recognition that school officials must be able to curtail student speech in order to protect the curricular activities—that is, the academic function—of schools.

That the protection of the academic function of schools lies at the heart of these cases is further demonstrated by *Barnette*, where the Court, in prohibiting schools from compelling students to salute the flag, made a point of indicating that the school board "did not adopt the flag salute because it was claimed to have educational value."[369] Distinguishing between core academic functions and other functions of schools also drives the plurality's opinion in *Pico*. There, the plurality distinguished between school officials' control over curriculum, which it recognized as nearly absolute, and control over the library, which it concluded must be more limited.[370] Rightly or wrongly, the Court characterized the library as outside of the teaching function of public schools and as a place where students should be able to explore ideas and arguments on their own.[371] As a consequence, the Court limited the authority of school officials to remove books from the library. One can question

[367] *Hazelwood*, 484 U.S. at 271.

[368] See *Tinker*, 393 U.S. at 513.

[369] West Virginia State Bd. of Educ. v. Barnette, 319 U.S. 624, 631 n.12 (1943).

[370] See Board of Education v. Pico, 457 U.S. 853, 869 (1982) (plurality opinion).

[371] See id. at 868–69 (plurality opinion) (observing that libraries are places where "a student can literally explore the unknown, and discover areas of interest and thought *not covered by the curriculum*") (emphasis added) (internal quotations omitted).

the Court's characterization of the library in this way, as the dissent did, but the more telling point for my purposes is that the Court was trying to distinguish between the core teaching function of schools, which it privileged, from other functions, in this case the function of providing the means and opportunity for self-exploration.[372]

The Court's due process cases, as largely explained above, also follow this general pattern.[373] Indeed, these cases are if anything more explicit about privileging the academic function of public schools. Recall that the Court in *Goss* provided that students have some right to a rudimentary hearing before being suspended for disciplinary reasons, but the Court in *Horowitz* established that students have no right to notice or a hearing prior to being dismissed or sanctioned for academic reasons. Students also, pursuant to *Ingraham*, have no right to prior notice or a hearing before being physically punished.[374]

The Court was willing to provide some protection to students facing exclusion from the academic process, but it was unwilling to interfere with that process itself. Thus, those facing dismissal for disciplinary reasons receive some procedural protections, but those facing dismissal for academic reasons do not, because providing such protections in the latter instance would require courts to oversee and interfere with the academic decisions of schools.[375] Likewise, the Court's unwillingness to hamper the ability of teachers or school officials to impose corporal punishment was justified, in part, by the need to provide teachers with sufficient authority to maintain order and discipline in the classroom.[376] What ties these cases together, like the free speech cases, is the Court's apparent

[372] Given that libraries contain books and that reading books may easily be characterized as an "academic" activity, it may seem odd to suggest that school libraries do not further the academic function of schools. But I am not suggesting, nor has the Court, that a school's academic function includes any activity through which a student participant learns something, but rather that the academic function refers to the actual conveying of information and teaching of skills to students by school faculty. See supra note 17.

[373] See supra notes 136–69 and accompanying text.

[374] See Board of Curators v. Horowitz, 435 U.S. 78, 88–90 (1978); Ingraham v. Wright, 430 U.S. 651, 682–83 (1977); Goss v. Lopez, 419 U.S. 565, 581–82 (1975).

[375] See *Horowitz*, 435 U.S. at 88–90 (explaining that the Court was reluctant to increase its involvement in the academic process beyond that contemplated by *Goss*).

[376] See *Ingraham*, 430 U.S. at 680–82.

desire to provide school officials and teachers sufficient authority to protect the academic process. This is apparent not only from the results in the three cases, but also from the fact that even students facing suspension for disciplinary reasons may be immediately removed if they present "an ongoing threat of disrupting the academic process."[377]

The Court's Fourth Amendment cases, finally, at the very least speak in the language of protecting the academic process. In both *T.L.O.* and *Acton*, a majority of Justices justified granting school officials fairly broad authority to conduct student searches on the ground that doing so was necessary to ensure a safe and orderly school atmosphere.[378] Significantly, protecting such an atmosphere was identified not as an end in itself, but rather as a means to ensure that learning could take place. Thus, in *T.L.O.*, five Justices agreed with Justice Powell's reasoning that fully protecting students' Fourth Amendment rights would impede the ability of school officials and teachers to fulfill their "primary duty" of ensuring "the education and training of young people."[379] Similarly, in *Acton*, the Court justified random drug testing of student-athletes in part on the ground that the disciplinary problems stemming from drug use had reached "epic" proportions, and that student-athletes were leaders in the burgeoning drug culture at the school. Drug testing, under these circumstances, the Court ruled, was justified as necessary to protect the "educational process."[380]

To be sure, one could argue that the connection between student searches and drug testing and academic goals is somewhat tenuous, and thus that the Fourth Amendment cases do not neatly fit within the framework I am proposing. I concede as much and recognize that the Court's decisions regarding student searches rest on the value-laden view that maintaining discipline is necessary to preserve the educational process of schools. But it is nonetheless important to recognize both that it is quite plausible to assert that discipline and academic goals are related and that the Court it-

---

[377] *Goss*, 419 U.S. at 582.

[378] Vernonia Sch. Dist. 47J v. Acton, 515 U.S. 646, 662 (1995); New Jersey v. T.L.O., 469 U.S. 325, 340–42 (1985).

[379] *T.L.O.*, 469 U.S. at 348–50 (Powell, J., concurring); see also supra notes 115–19 and accompanying text (describing statements of other concurring Justices).

[380] *Acton*, 515 U.S. at 662–64.

self—in these cases and others—has been quite intent on establishing this connection.

Indeed, in this regard it is instructive to consider that a number of dissenting opinions in school cases, beginning with Justice Black's rather shrill dissent in *Tinker*, have suggested that a primary function of schools is to inculcate discipline and respect for authority, and that pursuing this goal in itself justifies curtailing student rights.[381] This principle, however, has never made its way into a majority opinion. In *Goss*, for example, Justice Powell and those who joined him in dissent contended that the Due Process Clause should not protect students facing suspension because "[e]ducation in any meaningful sense includes the inculcation of an understanding in each pupil of the necessity of rules and obedience thereto. This understanding is no less important than learning to read and write."[382] This rationale, however, is completely absent from *Ingraham*, where Justice Powell and his fellow dissenters in *Goss* secured a majority to hold that the Due Process Clause does not require notice and a hearing before students receive corporal punishment.[383] While this is speculation, it is worth wondering whether this idea does not appear in *Ingraham* because Justice

[381] See, e.g., *Tinker*, 393 U.S. at 524 (Black, J., dissenting) ("School discipline, like parental discipline, is an integral and important part of training our children to be good citizens—to be better citizens."). Justice Black's dissent in *Tinker* is especially noteworthy given his self-proclaimed status as a free speech absolutist and his oft-repeated admonition that "'no law' means no law." See Roger K. Newman, Hugo Black: A Biography 512 (1994). In *Tinker*, however, it was the majority, not Justice Black, who stated: "The Constitution says that Congress (and the States) may not abridge the right to free speech. This provision means what it says." *Tinker*, 393 U.S. at 513. Justice Black's toleration of the suppression of student speech seemed influenced by the tumultuous times in which he wrote, when students, in Black's words, "all over the land are already running loose, conducting break-ins, sit-ins, lie-ins, and smash-ins." *Tinker*, 393 U.S. at 525 (Black, J., dissenting). Indeed, his dissent reads more like a crotchety grandfather's sermon to permissive parents on the importance of discipline rather than the product of a First Amendment absolutist. See, e.g., *Tinker*, 393 U.S. at 518 (Black, J., dissenting) ("I repeat that if the time has come when pupils of state-supported schools . . . can defy and flout orders of school officials to keep their minds on their own school work, it is the beginning of a new revolutionary era of permissiveness in this country fostered by the judiciary."). As Earl Warren reportedly said of Black's dissent: "Old Hugo really got hung up in his jock strap on that one." Newman, supra, at 592.

[382] *Goss*, 419 U.S. at 593 (Powell, J., dissenting).

[383] See *Ingraham*, 430 U.S. 651 (1977), discussed supra notes 149–59 and accompanying text.

Stewart, who voted with the majority in *Goss* but supplied the fifth vote in *Ingraham*, would not go along with the notion that a primary function of schools is to inculcate obedience to authority.

To put the two strands of my argument together: For one set of rights, involving the Free Speech Clause, Due Process Clause, and Fourth Amendment, the Court is willing to defer to education officials, with the caveat that policies that intrude upon these rights without furthering an academic goal will not be tolerated. For the second set of rights, involving the Equal Protection, Establishment, and Free Exercise Clauses, the Court is unwilling to defer to education officials, with the caveat that policies that intrude upon these rights in order to further an academic goal may well be tolerated. With regard to each set of rights, however, the dispositive question—does the challenged policy advance an academic goal—appears to remain the same.

3. Reconciling the Cases

The academic/social distinction also helps to reconcile school cases, involving different constitutional rights, that appear to be in some tension. These cases revolve around three recurring issues: the extent to which schools can engage in values inculcation; the protection of access to and exit from schools; and the characterization of schools as either unique or representative institutions. I will discuss each in turn.

Take first the issue of values inculcation: The Court in its recent student speech cases has seemingly endorsed values inculcation—qua values inculcation—as an important part of the mission of public schools.[384] At the same time, however, it has prohibited schools from inculcating religious values in its Establishment Clause cases.[385] The Court has also limited the *means* by which schools can inculcate values. Pursuant to *Barnette*, schools cannot compel students to affirm a belief with which they disagree, at least when doing so is not connected to an educational goal.[386] And pursuant to

[384] See, e.g., *Fraser*, 478 U.S. at 683 (inculcating "the fundamental values necessary to the maintenance of a democratic political system," the Court suggests, "is truly the work of the schools") (internal quotations omitted).

[385] See supra notes 226–56 and accompanying text.

[386] See *Barnette*, 319 U.S. at 631 & n.12

Tinker and *Hazelwood*, schools have a limited ability to censor student speech outside of curricular activities, regardless of whether doing so would help inculcate perfectly acceptable values.[387]

There thus exists some apparent tension both between the Court's speech and Establishment Clause cases and among the Court's speech cases themselves. The tension between the speech and religion cases might, at first blush, seem resolved by the fact that the Establishment Clause is special, insofar as it effectively acts as a limitation on government speech by prohibiting the government from promoting religious values. The same is not true of other values, such as democracy or patriotism, which the government is free to endorse and thus presumably to inculcate in students. But this difference in itself does not explain why the Free Speech Clause can be modified in the school context in order to inculcate values, while the Establishment Clause must remain fully operational in the school context, unless there is some difference between bending constitutional rights as a means to achieve a legitimate objective and bending constitutional rights in order to achieve objectives that would otherwise be impermissible. In other words, if inculcating values were truly a constitutionally privileged goal, one would be hard pressed to explain why it is permissible to truncate student speech rights as a means to inculcate certain values but not permissible to truncate student Establishment Clause rights in order to inculcate a particular set of values; it is no answer to say that the Constitution permits the former but does not allow the latter, because the Constitution prohibits abridging speech as much as it prohibits the government from endorsing religious values.

Even if there were an argument for allowing rights to be modified only when doing so is necessary as a means to achieving a legitimate end (rather than as necessary to achieve an end that is otherwise prohibited), the Court's Establishment Clause cases seem to prohibit the use of religious exercises to achieve the presumably legitimate end of inculcating morality.[388] The only use of religious materials, such as the Bible or Ten Commandments, im-

---

[387] See *Tinker*, 393 U.S. at 509; *Hazelwood*, 484 U.S. at 272–73.
[388] See, e.g., Abington Sch. Dist. v. Schempp, 374 U.S. 203, 223–24 (1963).

plicitly endorsed by the Court is an educational one: Religion and religious materials can be studied as an academic subject.[389]

The way to reconcile the cases is to recognize, as I suggested earlier, that the Court has not endorsed the inculcation of values as a privileged goal in itself, despite some loose language to the contrary in recent student speech cases. Rather, the speech cases that approve of the school's ability to inculcate values, as discussed above with regard to *Pico*, are best understood as providing insulation from challenge for the numerous academic decisions that school officials and teachers must make.[390] Decisions about which courses to teach, which topics to cover, which books to assign, which lessons to emphasize, all require content-based and viewpoint-based decisions, which in turn will inevitably reflect and promote particular values. If schools were prohibited from inculcating any values whatsoever, these academic decisions themselves would be subject to constant challenge, on the ground that schools were impermissibly promoting particular values.

Conceptualizing the inculcation of values as a protective shield around academic decisions makes the religion and speech cases fall into a fairly coherent pattern. As for the religion cases, one explanation for why religious values cannot be promoted is that the Court has not really accepted the idea that schools should have free rein to inculcate values. Similarly, that religion itself apparently cannot be used to inculcate secular values, such as morality, but can be studied as an academic subject, further suggests that—at the very least—the inculcation of values does not occupy the same privileged status as the promotion of academic knowledge. As for the speech cases, the Court has endorsed the inculcation of values when doing so is connected to a curricular exercise, but it has limited the ability of schools to inculcate values for their own sake. It has, for instance, prohibited schools from requiring students to affirm beliefs with which they disagree (at least when doing so does not serve an educational purpose), and it has limited the authority of schools to censor student speech outside of curricular activities.[391] In short, the school officials' authority is at its apex and the

---

389 See id. at 225; see also Edwards v. Aguillard, 482 U.S. 578, 593–94 .
390 See supra notes 59–77 and accompanying text.
391 See *Hazelwood*, 484 U.S. at 271–72; *Barnette*, 319 U.S. at 631 & n.12.

students' rights at their nadir when schools are pursuing academic goals.

The next issue involving some apparent tension among the cases is that of access to and exit from the public schools. The Court has protected some minimal rights of access to public schools: *Plyler* struck down a law that allowed schools to exclude the children of illegal aliens, and *Goss* provided students minimal due process rights when facing a disciplinary suspension. The Court has also protected the right of parents to remove their children from public schools: *Pierce* protected the rights of all students to attend private rather than public schools, and *Yoder* recognized the right of Amish parents with religious objections to remove their children from school after completion of the eighth grade.

At the same time, however, the Court has been quite reluctant to do any more than police the doors of public schools in order to allow students to enter and to exit. Thus, while protecting access to public schools, the Court has refused to guarantee a substantive level of education to those within public schools. Similarly, the Court has protected students facing temporary expulsion from schools, but it has refused to provide procedural (or substantive) protections to students facing corporal punishment within schools. And while it has recognized the right of parents with religious objections to remove their children entirely from public schools, it has thus far declined to recognize the right of parents with religious objections to remove their children from particular classes within public schools.

The Court thus appears willing to police access to schools but reluctant to interfere with the educational process within schools. One way to understand these cases is to recognize that the government acts in a different capacity when actually educating students than it does when deciding who should be educated and where. In deciding who should have access to or be compelled to attend its institutions, the government is acting more in a regulatory capacity than an institutional one. That is, decisions about access to and exit from institutions involve questions of general regulation of private behavior rather than decisions about the internal operation of the institutions themselves. The regulatory decisions about access and exit, moreover, do not themselves involve educational or academic considerations, but rather social considerations of who deserves to receive a public education and who has a right to decline public education. If we posit that the Court is willing to defer to the government only when it is acting in its capacity as educator, rather than in its capacity as regulator, the cases themselves are quite consistent and coherent. Put differently, it makes sense and is consistent with my thesis that the Court would be more willing to impose normal constitutional restraints upon the government when it is making general regulatory decisions.[392]

Race and gender cases, it bears mentioning, may best be understood as straddling the fault line between government as educator and government as regulator.[393] This is because it is possible to view race and gender-based policies primarily as general regulatory decisions about who should attend school with whom. When considered from this perspective, it is unlikely that courts would defer to government decisions, because deciding as a matter of general equity whether one group of students should attend school with another does not involve the exercise of any academic expertise to which courts might defer. It is also possible, however, to view such policies as related to the educational process itself, insofar as policies like racial integration or single-sex classes can, at least theoretically, be defended on pedagogical and academic grounds. As suggested earlier, the fate of single-sex schools and voluntary integration efforts may rest on just which of these perspectives courts choose to adopt.

The last issue that involves some tension among the cases concerns the contrary ways in which the Court has characterized public schools. In some cases, most notably the recent student

---

[392] An analogy to prison might be helpful. In deciding who belongs in prison, the government is obviously required to adhere to standard constitutional restraints upon its authority. But in operating prisons, the government is granted a great deal of deference, which includes loosening constitutional restraints that limit its authority outside of these institutional contexts. See, e.g., Turner v. Safley, 482 U.S. 78, 89 (1987) (establishing a deferential standard to assess prisoners' constitutional rights).

[393] Borrowing from Robert Post, one way to describe race and gender cases is to say that they straddle the line between managerial and democratic domains. As Post explains, in managerial domains, institutions are given deference to achieve instrumental objectives, whereas in democratic domains, the government's authority is more restrained. See Post, supra note 345, at 249–55. Determining the proper boundaries between the two domains can be quite difficult, as Post himself recognizes and as the race and gender cases demonstrate. See id. at 247–55.

speech and search cases, the Court has characterized schools as unique institutions.[394] The Court has accordingly demonstrated little concern in such cases that the constitutional standards established might spill over to other contexts. The Court did not seem worried in *Hazelwood*, for example, that allowing schools to censor student newspapers might provide ample precedent for allowing the government to censor local or national newspapers.

In other cases, however, the Court has characterized the schools as representative institutions, suggesting that the rules established in the school context would create a strong precedent for applying similar rules in other contexts. In *Rodriguez*, for example, the Court expressed great concern that establishing a fundamental right to education would necessarily establish strong and perhaps irresistible pressure to recognize fundamental rights to food and shelter.[395] Similarly, in *Barnette*, the Court suggested that allowing schools to compel students to affirm a belief with which they disagree would provide authority to the government generally to compel speech outside of the school context.[396] Still other cases, most notably the Court's desegregation and gender cases, rest on the assumption that the constitutional standards that apply within the school will also apply outside of the school—that is, there is no hint whatsoever in these cases that constitutional standards should be relaxed in light of the school environment.[397]

I suggest that the Court's differing characterizations of public schools reflect society's long-standing ambivalence about the nature of public schools. Schools have simultaneously been conceived as unique institutions, designed primarily to nurture and educate students in an environment that is intentionally separated and insulated from society, and as representative institutions, whose mission is to reflect and perhaps recreate the larger society in which they operate.[398] To say that the Court's cases reflect these distinct and somewhat contradictory views of public schools, how-

[394] See, e.g., *Acton*, 515 U.S. at 655–57 (describing the special nature of public schools); *Hazelwood*, 484 U.S. at 266–67 (same).

[395] See San Antonio Indep. Sch. Dist. v. Rodriguez, 411 U.S. 1, 37 (1973).

[396] See *Barnette*, 319 U.S. at 641–42 (arguing, *inter alia*, that "[t]hose who begin coercive elimination of dissent soon find themselves exterminating dissenters").

[397] See supra notes 171–225 and accompanying text.

[398] See, e.g., Ravitch, supra note 16; The Great Debate, Education Week, Apr. 21, 1999, at 1; see also infra notes 407–15 and accompanying text.

ever, is not to say that the Court itself has been inconsistent or incoherent in its expressed visions of public schools.

To the contrary, the Court's characterization of public schools has varied depending on the particular function of the policy being reviewed. When reviewing policies that are related to the academic function of schools, the Court has characterized schools as unique and has downplayed the possibility that constitutional standards applied in schools could easily be applied elsewhere. But when reviewing policies that do not advance an academic goal, the Court has characterized schools as similar to other institutions and other contexts and has either expressed concern or assumed that the constitutional standards applied in schools would apply outside of them as well.

Put differently, the Court's dual approach to public school cases reflects the dual nature of the schools themselves. Thus, when schools are acting to achieve goals that are unique to the institution of public schools, namely academic goals, the Court is willing to treat the institution as unique and mold constitutional standards to fit the context. On the other hand, when states, schools, or local governments are acting to achieve goals that are not unique to the institution, such as promoting or inhibiting racial or gender equality, refusing to equalize the opportunities of the poor, or attempting to coerce affirmance of patriotic values, the Court is unwilling to treat schools as unique or to tailor constitutional standards to take account of the school context.[399] Not only are these differing characterizations and approaches consistent with my positive thesis; as I shall explain directly below, they are also defensible as a normative matter.

III. Assessing the Court's Approach

Although my primary goal in this Article is to generate a positive theory regarding the Court's public school's cases, it seems worthwhile considering, at least briefly, whether the approach I have described is normatively attractive. Assuming, then, that my positive theory is accurate and that the Court's school cases do turn on an academic/social distinction, it remains to inquire whether this

[399] See, e.g., Missouri v. Jenkins, 515 U.S. 70, 88–90 (1995); *Rodriguez*, 411 U.S. at 37; *Barnette*, 319 U.S. at 641–42.

distinction is a useful and sensible guide to decisionmaking.[400] After offering a general, pragmatic defense of the Court's approach, I will describe and try to answer two possible critiques.

A. A General Defense of the Court's Approach

My defense rests on two assertions that (not surprisingly) strike me as reasonable but are open to dispute. First, public schools could not operate effectively if students could exercise all of their constitutional rights to the fullest extent—in other words, to the extent that they may exercise those rights outside of school. To take the most obvious example, classes simply could not be taught effectively if a classroom were considered the legal equivalent of a park and students were free to say or read whatever they liked. Second, educating students is sufficiently important to justify truncating constitutional rights that interfere with that goal. For example, if forced to choose between ensuring that students are able to learn the lessons teachers have selected for them and allowing students full freedom to speak and select their own lessons, I would argue that the former objective should prevail. To those who disagree with either assertion, what follows will surely fail to convince. But to those who find both propositions reasonable, the Court's approach in school cases will likely seem at least defensible.

If we accept that school officials may be justified in limiting students' constitutional rights in order to ensure the safe and effective operation of public schools, the obvious question becomes: Under what circumstances should constitutional rights be limited? It seems clearly unreasonable to provide education officials carte blanche to truncate constitutional rights. I gather that few, for example, would agree that school officials should be able to discriminate against black or female students, promote Catholicism, and arbitrarily suspend students provided that such actions are limited to the school context. At the very least, teachers and

---

[400] For those who remain unpersuaded by my positive account, this Part can be read as an argument in defense of the academic/social distinction itself rather than as a defense of the Court's actual approach. For the sake of clarity, when I refer to the "Court's approach" in this Part, it is to the approach as I have described it—namely, an approach that distinguishes between academic and social goals and privileges the former.

administrators should have to justify their actions and policies as related to the business and goals of public education.

To reach a reasonable balance between educational goals and student rights, therefore, one must distinguish the true "business" of the public schools from goals that fall outside of that sphere. And it is here, I believe, that the Court's cases reveal a defensible principle of separating the academic from the social functions of public schools. The principle is defensible because the academic function of public schools is what makes them unique as an institution. The one characteristic that all public (and private) schools share is that they are designed to teach students a body of knowledge and to impart academic and vocational skills. Take away everything else—all the extracurricular activities, all the socialization efforts, all the efforts to achieve broader social goals—and leave the academic programs, and one still has a school.[401] Without any academic programs, by contrast, there is simply not a school. This is not to deny that the social functions performed by public schools are important and pervasive. It is simply to suggest that social goals can be and are pursued by other institutions—and that they need not be pursued within public schools.

If the academic function of schools is what makes schools unique as institutions, and if we agree that achieving academic goals is of vital importance, it makes some sense that policies designed to enhance or protect academic goals should be treated more deferentially. Conversely, to the extent that a school is attempting to achieve a social goal, the less unique it is an institution and the more similar it is to other institutions and governmental programs. It would seem to follow that the same constitutional limitations that apply in other contexts to check government action should apply where the school is simply one avenue for achieving broader societal goals. Were this not the case, and were non-academic programs and goals able to trump constitutional rights, if nothing else

[401] Indirect support for this proposition is found in state court decisions defining the right, guaranteed by state constitutions, to an adequate education. These decisions define the right in academic terms and do not suggest at all that an adequate education requires the achievement of particular social or socialization goals. See, e.g., Rose v. Council for a Better Educ., 790 S.W.2d 186, 212 (Ky. 1989); McDuffy v. Secretary of Exec. Office of Educ. 615 N.E.2d 516, 524 (Mass. 1993); Claremont Sch. Dist. v. Governor, 703 A.2d 1353, 1359 (N.H. 1997).

it would be difficult to justify confining such rules to the school setting. If schools could promote religion, for example, or take race into account to achieve the social benefits of greater integration, why not allow other institutions or government programs to do the same?[402]

In short, the Court's approach can be defended, at least generally, on the grounds of necessity. Schools need some constitutional room in order to achieve their goals, and the Court needs to ensure that students do not shed all of their constitutional rights at the schoolhouse door. A defensible way to resolve this dilemma is to identify the core, universal function of schools, and to use this function as a guide to determine the circumstances in which schools will be granted deference. Selecting the academic function of schools as a guidepost certainly can be criticized, as I will explain below. But surely it is a reasonable solution to the very real dilemma that public schools present to courts and policymakers alike.

B. Answering Critiques of the Court's Approach

There are at least two different ways to critique the Court's approach. First, one could argue that the categories of academic and social are easily blurred, such that what the Court deems academic could easily be labeled social or vice-versa. To the extent the categories are not stable and determinate, they obviously will not be useful guides to courts or policymakers. Worse still, to the extent the categories can be manipulated, they can serve to mask rather than reveal the substantive choices being made by the Court in public school cases.

This critique is a formidable one, but it is not unanswerable. To begin, core academic functions, like teaching students a particular skill or conveying knowledge about a traditional academic topic, seem easily distinguishable from social functions like increasing educational opportunities for African-American or female students. The categories themselves, therefore, are not completely indeterminate. Of course, there have been and will be cases that test the boundaries of the categories, where it will be unclear

[402] Cf. San Antonio Indep. Sch. Dist. v. Rodriguez, 411 U.S. 1, 37 (1973) (asking how, if a fundamental right to education were recognized, the Court could refuse to recognize a fundamental right to food or shelter).

whether a school is trying to accomplish an academic or social goal, or both. Removing objectionable library books may viewed as connected to the academic function of selectively presenting information to students, or it may be viewed as an unjustified, naked attempt to further a social goal of inculcating students with officially approved values and viewpoints. Similarly, random drug testing of student athletes may serve both to prevent drug-related disruptions of the learning process, an academic goal, and simply to reduce teenage drug use, a social goal that transcends any academic concerns.[403]

Yet the difficulty of assigning some policies to one category or the other should not be surprising; all categories are imprecise at the edges. All categories are therefore somewhat manipulable. The real test of these categories thus may not lie in the realm of hypothetical issues that press at the edges or pose difficult taxonomic questions, but rather in the Court's actual treatment of the cases. Although true Court cynics may never be convinced, to me the Court's performance in past school cases is sufficiently coherent and consistent to conclude that the categories are meaningful and useful.

To highlight just two examples: Many who read the Court's religion cases contend that the Court is hostile toward religion and suggest that this factor, more than any other, explains the Court's cases.[404] This view, however, is simply untenable when one considers the Court's treatment of aid to religious schools: While the Court's approach overall is perhaps best described as wayward, the Court has shown an increasing willingness to allow public funds to

[403] See Vernonia Sch. Dist. 47J v. Acton, 515 U.S. 646 (1995), discussed supra note 120 and accompanying text.

[404] See, e.g., Frederick Mark Gedicks, Public Life and Hostility To Religion, 78 Va. L. Rev. 671, 671 & n.3 (1992) (stating, "[t]he United States Supreme Court's Religion Clause opinions are widely perceived to be hostile to religion," and collecting sources). Some dissenting Justices have also accused members of majority opinions of being hostile toward religion. See, e.g., Santa Fe Indep. Sch. Dist. v. Doe, 120 S. Ct. 2266, 2283–88 (2000) (Rehnquist, J., dissenting); County of Allegheny v. ACLU, 492 U.S. 573, 655 (1989) (Kennedy, J., concurring in part and dissenting in part) (arguing that majority's "view of the Establishment Clause reflects an unjustified hostility toward religion, a hostility inconsistent with our history and our precedents"); Wallace v. Jaffree, 472 U.S. 38, 85 (1985) (Burger, C.J., dissenting) (arguing that the majority opinion "manifests not neutrality but hostility toward religion").

flow to religious schools.[405] At the same time, however, the Court has consistently refused to allow any religious exercises to take place within public school classrooms. It is hard to explain this divergence on the ground that the Court is hostile toward religion; if it were, surely there would be some doctrinal way to prevent financial aid from flowing to religious schools. This in turn suggests that the Court has a particular view about religion in *public* schools and, as I have argued, the Court's view seems to be that promoting religion is inconsistent with the academic function of those schools.

Similarly, if the Court's decisions were not concerned with the academic functions of schools, but were really just *sub rosa* attempts to give school officials maximum deference to inculcate values—as many commentators suggest—it is hard to understand *Pierce* and *Yoder* or the distinctions drawn by the Court in its student speech cases. Why would the Court allow students, through *Pierce* and *Yoder*, to exit the public school system for private schools or home instruction by a religious community if values inculcation were the real driving force behind the Court's decisions? Why would the Court draw a distinction, in *Hazelwood*, between speech restrictions in curricular and extracurricular activities if values inculcation were a privileged goal? And why would the Court, in *Barnette*, limit the ability to inculcate values by prohibiting schools from compelling affirmance of the political beliefs represented by the flag and the pledge of allegiance?[406]

Again, this is not to deny that the categories are somewhat flexible and that some of the cases could have been decided differently. It is also not to deny that the Court makes value judgments, sometimes controversial ones, about the relationship between particular

[405] See, e.g., Mitchell v. Helms, 120 S. Ct. 2530 (2000) (overruling earlier decisions and upholding federal aid to religious schools); Agostini v. Felton, 521 U.S. 203 (1997) (overruling earlier decisions and allowing public school teachers to provide remedial education to children on the premises of private, religious schools); Zobrest v. Catalina Foothills Sch. Dist., 509 U.S. 1 (1993) (allowing the expenditure of public funds to support sign-language interpreters in parochial schools). See generally McCarthy, supra note 231, at 154 (arguing that in the last decade, the Supreme Court seems to be "reviving and perhaps expanding the 'child benefit' rationale to uphold government aid to sectarian schools"); Laura S. Underkuffler, Vouchers and Beyond: The Individual as Causitive Agent in Establishment Clause Jurisprudence, 75 Ind. L.J. 167, 171–79 (2000) (discussing the Court's cases regarding aid to sectarian schools).

[406] For discussion of and citation to these cases, see supra notes 37–48 (*Barnette*), 97–107 (*Hazelwood*), 265–70 (*Yoder*), 279–86 (*Pierce*) and accompanying text.

policies and academic goals. The connection between academics and randomly testing student athletes for drug use, for example, is sufficiently tenuous that one might well object to the Court's defense of the policy on academic grounds. My only point is that the categories themselves are capable of imposing some restraints on the Court's decisions and that the Court itself seems to take the categories seriously.

Although the Court's purported distinction between the social and academic functions of public schools may indeed be a workable and supportable one, there may still be reason to question the distinction from the perspective of educational history or educational philosophy. A second way to critique the Court's approach is thus to accept that the Court takes the categories seriously but to question the categories themselves. As a matter of history, schools have always performed socializing functions, and many would contend that these tasks are as important as the academic function of public schools.[407] Similarly, many educational philosophies stress the importance of preparing students for their lives as adults by providing not only analytical training but also the social skills and habits needed to become productive and responsible members of a democratic society.[408] Still others have viewed schools as the vehicle by which society can be recreated in a more perfect and just form.[409]

---

[407] See, e.g., Tyack, supra note 15, at 363-68 (describing the common school movement and compulsory school laws as resting on reformers' hopes to use "the powers of the state to intervene in families and to create alternative institutions of socialization"). See generally Cremin, supra note 15, (providing a brief history of values education); Joel S. Moskowitz, The Making of the Moral Child: Legal Implications of Values Education, 6 Pepp. L. Rev. 105, 107–17 (1978) (same).

[408] See, e.g., Amy Gutmann, Democratic Education 22–46 (1987) (arguing that schools should cultivate "democratic virtue" among students by preparing them to "participat[e] in democratic politics, to choos[e] among (a limited range of) good lives, and to shar[e] in the several subcommunities, such as families, that impart identity to the lives of its citizens"); Sherry, supra note 5, at 157 (arguing that education should "prepare children to become *responsible* and *deliberative* citizens in a *diverse* republic of *rights*," by ensuring that children learn "moral character, critical thinking, and cultural literacy").

[409] This view is most famously associated with John Dewey, one of the most influential American philosophers in the early twentieth century, who remains an important figure in the philosophy of education. See Robert B. Westbrook, John Dewey and American Democracy, at xiv (1991). Dewey viewed education as a process of "reconstruction," involving the "constant reorganizing or reconstructing of experience." John Dewey, Democracy and Education 89 (1922). This process would not only lead to "better habits" among students, see id. at 92, but could also be used

There thus may be persuasive normative arguments, based on tradition or philosophy, as to why it is unwise to place higher constitutional roadblocks in the way of schools desirous of accomplishing social goals.

At the same time, however, it is instructive to consider that debates about the various social goals of public schools are long-running and diverse. There are many who strongly oppose values inculcation or socialization efforts by public schools, as well as efforts to use schools as agents of social change.[410] There thus exists vast disagreement about the propriety of inculcating values in general, debates over which values should be inculcated, and disagreement about the desirability of using schools to promote such social goals as racial or gender equality. Those who harbor strong feelings about the nature and goals of public schools will likely believe that the Court should endorse their particular vision of public schooling—hence the numerous law review articles critiquing the Court for not implementing the author's favored education philosophy.[411]

But it may be that privileging the academic function of schools, as opposed to endorsing particular social goals, is a judicial move that taps into a wide, if abstract consensus about public schools. There is probably greater support, in other words, for the abstract proposition that schools should have the authority to ensure that

---

to reconstruct society outside of schools. See Lawrence A. Cremin, The Transformation of the School: Progressivism in American Education 1876–1957, at 118 (1961) (arguing that Dewey saw the school as a "lever of social change"). See generally Dupre, supra note 5, at 65–67 (discussing the social reconstruction model of education and Dewey's education philosophy).

[410] For an argument that children should have greater protection from inculcation and that liberal education should ensure that schools are unable to inculcate in children "an uncritical acceptance of *any* conception of the good life," see Bruce Ackerman, Social Justice in the Liberal State 163 (1980). See also id. at 162 (arguing that schools should foster "a cultural environment in which the child may define his own ideals with a recognition of the full range of his moral freedom"). For an argument that parents should have greater authority to direct their children's education and to protect them from exposure to ideas and values offensive to the parents, see Gilles, supra note 5, at 940–42 (arguing that "the project of developing a mandatory democratic education for every child is profoundly misconceived" and "that the state should defer to parents' educational decisions"); see also Stephen Arons, Compelling Belief: The Culture of American Schooling 189–221 (1983) (arguing that parents should be able to assert on their children's behalf a First Amendment right to be free from educational indoctrination).

[411] See, e.g., Dupre, supra note 5; Gilles, supra note 5; Sherry, supra note 5.

teachers can teach and students can learn than there is for any particular social goal that schools might perform.[412] This is not to say that particular academic or curricular decisions will never generate controversy, nor is it to suggest that the social functions that schools perform are unimportant. It is only to suggest that, in the absence of any way to identify those social functions that *should* or *must* be performed by schools, privileging only the academic function of schools at least serves as a way to limit the reasons for intruding upon students' constitutional rights to ones that most of us in the abstract can accept as valid.

Interestingly, in this way the Court's approach in public school cases may be the inverse of the approach that Cass Sunstein has described as prevalent in modern cases. Sunstein suggests that many of the Court's recent cases are characterized by incompletely theorized agreements, where the Court agrees on a result but not on any deep theoretical reason behind the result.[413] Doing so, Sunstein argues, is a good strategy to limit the occasion and scope of disagreements, as Justices, like most of us, will encounter more controversy when hashing out first principles and touching upon deeply held beliefs. In the public school cases, the opposite dynamic seems to be at work: Most of the Justices, like most citizens, seem to agree that the primary purpose of schools is to educate students. It is in translating that primary, abstract goal into concrete cases where the real disagreements arise—over such issues as the relevance of prayer or a moment of silence to educational goals, or the proper characterization of the school library, or the necessity of dispensing with a requirement of individualized suspi-

---

[412] Surveys of parents tend to support this proposition. One recent survey revealed, for example, that parents believe that schools should focus on teaching the basics, maintaining order within the schools, and insuring students' safety. See Steve Farkas & Jean Johnson, Time to Move On: African-American and White Parents Set an Agenda for Public Schools (Public Agenda 1998). The same survey revealed that African-American parents, by an 80% to 9% margin, say that the bigger priority for schools should be to raise achievement rather than focus on achieving more diversity and integration. Id. at 31. See generally Joseph Viteritti, Choosing Equality: School Choice, the Constitution and Civil Society 11–14 (1999) (discussing survey results).

[413] See Cass R. Sunstein, Incompletely Theorized Agreements, 108 Harv. L. Rev. 1733, 1739–43 (1996); Cass R. Sunstein, One Case At a Time: Judicial Minimalism on the Supreme Court, at xi–xii, 3–23 (1999).

cion for student drug searches.[414] And, again, I would not try to argue that the Court's translation of an abstract principle into concrete results is neutral, value free, or unassailable—only that it is defensible.

CONCLUSION

This Article takes a first step towards assessing the Court's public schools jurisprudence. It is also a step that departs from the conventional wisdom about the Court's efforts in the educational arena. I have resisted the argument, made by many commentators, that the Court has endorsed or adopted an overarching theory of education. In particular, I have taken issue with the pervasive suggestion in the literature that the Court has exalted and privileged the goal of values inculcation as the *raison d'être* of public schools. I have instead argued that the Court's cases reflect a more modest aim of distinguishing between the academic and social functions of schools. In addition to my main goal of using this distinction to formulate a positive theory of the Court's cases, I have also suggested that the distinction is at least defensible normatively.

With all of that said, I recognize that room remains for alternative interpretations of these cases. I thus end the Article with three suggestions about how it might be of some use to academics and advocates who agree with my positive theory and to those who harbor doubts. First, those advocates who agree with my positive theory and who are interested in advancing particular educational policies should focus their research and arguments on demonstrating how those desired policies advance academic goals. Those interested in single-sex classes or schools, for example, would do well to couch their arguments in academic terms, and to focus research on the academic benefits of single-sex education. Those

[414] Cf. Dan Kahan, The Secret Ambition of Deterrence, 113 Harv. L. Rev. 413, 483–84 (1999). Kahan argues that courts and citizens alike defend their views about criminal law in terms of deterrence as a means of avoiding more controversial idioms. In this sense, deterrence is an example of an abstract principle that lessens conflicts over the law; people can agree in the abstract that deterrence is a proper goal of criminal punishment and avoid more controversial claims about additional objectives of the criminal law. See id. A related phenomenon occurs in the school cases, insofar as defending school policies in terms of their relationship to academics is a way of avoiding more controversial claims about the policies.

interested in pursuing racial or socioeconomic integration should follow a similar path.

Second, those advocates who doubt the accuracy of my positive theory should at least be able to rely on this Article's insight that some constitutional rights but not others have been curtailed in the school setting. One strategy to advance particular education policies would be to press at this discrepancy and to argue in favor of more uniform deference to school officials. For example, one could contend that the Court's student search cases modify student Fourth Amendment rights in order to allow schools to pursue the social goal of deterring drug use. One could then argue that there is no principled reason to preclude school officials from pursuing the equally valid social goal of increasing interracial understanding, even if this requires modifying student equal protection rights. In either case, so the argument would go, schools should be given deference to pursue goals that school officials believe are important.

Finally, I would hope that this Article generates further discussion about the Court's public schools jurisprudence. As I mentioned at the outset, these cases offer a rich area of study. They provide insight into the Court's conception of public schools and also serve as a good example of how constitutional rules develop within and around institutions. As a result, these cases should be of interest not only to academics who study public schools but also to those more broadly interested in understanding how constitutional rights operate in different institutional settings.[415] The Court's public schools jurisprudence, in short, provides an excellent source of material for those interested in such questions as whether and why certain rights change in different institutional contexts—questions that ultimately could shed light on both the nature of various institutions as well as the nature of constitutional rights themselves.

[415] For recent works in this genre, see, for example, Neil K. Komesar, Imperfect Alternatives: Choosing Institutions in Law, Economics, and Public Policy (1994); Post, supra note 345; Frederick Schauer, Principles, Institutions, and the First Amendment, 112 Harv. L. Rev. 84 (1998).

POLICY STATEMENT

CORPORAL PUNISHMENT IN SCHOOLS

Approved by Council, June 1988

Corporal punishment is a discipline method in which a supervising adult deliberately inflicts pain upon a child in response to a child's unacceptable behavior and/or inappropriate language. The immediate aims of such punishment are usually to halt the offense, prevent its recurrence and set an example for others. The purported long-term goal is to change the child's behavior and to make it more consistent with the adult's expectations. In corporal punishment, the adult usually hits various parts of the child's body with a hand, or with canes, paddles, yardsticks, belts, or other objects expected to cause pain and fear.

In the United States, nine states explicitly bar corporal punishment in their school: New York, New Jersey, Massachusetts, Vermont, Rhode Island, New Hampshire, Maine, Hawaii and California. Certain large municipal school districts also prohibit this form of discipline: St. Louis, Atlanta, New Orleans, and Minneapolis. Similar legislation is pending in Ohio, Michigan, Wisconsin and Alaska. The American Academy of Child and Adolescent Psychiatry opposes the use of corporal punishment and supports legislation outlawing its use. Research on corporal punishment has shown that it may be harmful. Many other methods of discipline are effective in promoting self-control, eliminating undesirable behaviors and promoting desired behaviors in children.

Corporal punishment signals to the child that a way to settle interpersonal conflicts is to use physical force and inflict pain. Such children may in turn resort to such behavior themselves. They may also fail to develop trusting, secure relationships with adults and fail to evolve the necessary skills to settle disputes or wield authority in less violent ways. Supervising adults who will fully humiliate children and punish by force and pain are often causing more harm than they prevent.

The American Academy of Child and Adolescent Psychiatry opposes the use of corporal punishment in schools and takes issue with laws in some states legalizing such corporal punishment and protecting adults who use it from prosecution for child abuse. The Academy joins with the National Congress of Parents and Teachers, the American Medical Association, the National Education Association, the American Bar Association, the American Academy of Pediatrics, and other groups calling for an end to this form of punishment.

JOURNAL OF ADOLESCENT HEALTH 1992;13:240–246

SOCIETY FOR ADOLESCENT MEDICINE

Corporal Punishment in Schools

A Position Paper of the Society for Adolescent Medicine

Definition

Corporal punishment refers to intentional application of physical pain as a method of changing behavior. It includes a wide variety of methods such as hitting, slapping, punching, kicking, pinching, shaking, choking, use of various objects (wooden paddles, belts, sticks, pins, or others), painful body postures, use of electric shock, use of excessive exercise drills, or prevention of urine or stool elimination (1).

Historical Perspective

In the United States, corporal punishment has been a conventional method in disciplining children and youth since our colonial times (2,3). Only during the past 20 years has there emerged a growing outcry condemning such practices with school children (4,5).

In 1972 the American Civil Liberties Union (ACLU) and the American Orthopsychiatry Association sponsored a formal conference on this subject (2). At that time, only two states (Massachusetts and New Jersey) legally banned corporal punishment in schools. In 1974, the American Psychological Association passed a formal resolution banning corporal punishment in schools and established the Task Force on Children's Rights, further dealing with this issue. A National Education Association report was published during this decade which denounced corporal punishment in schools and officially recommended that it be abolished (2).

In 1987, a formal organization named the National Coalition to Abolish Corporal Punishment in Schools developed. This coalition included the National Center on Child Abuse Prevention, the American Academy of Pediatrics, the American Bar Association, the American Medical Association, the Parent-Teacher's Association, the National Education Association, the Society for Adolescent Medicine, and over 20 other groups who were united in their efforts to ban the practice of physically punishing children and youth in school. This coalition has continued an active movement, with national and local meetings, newsletters, articles in various publications, and other means designed to cultivate public awareness regarding this important issue (4,5).

Corporal punishment in schools has been proscribed in Europe, (including Eastern Europe), as well as in Israel, Japan, and other countries. One can trace the roots of corporal punishment in the United States to England, which remains the only European nation legally allowing it. In 1979, Sweden further advanced the rejection of corporal punishment in schools by banning physical punishment by parents, as well (6).

In 1867, New Jersey became the first state in the United States to legally ban such disciplinary action in schools. Other states which have subsequently passed a legal ban include California, Hawaii, Maine, Massachusetts, Michigan, Nebraska, New Hampshire, New York, Rhode Island, Vermont and Wisconsin, in addition to the District of Columbia (5,7,8). In other states (Alaska, Connecticut, Iowa, Minnesota, North Dakota, South Dakota, Oregon, and Virginia) there are state board of education directives and/or local school precepts repudiating corporal punishment (5). Current estimates suggest this ban includes over 200 cities (including 30 or more large urban regions) and many school districts by the action of local school boards or other local restrictions (5,9).

Incidence

Yet, 30 states continue to authorize corporal punishment in their schools. Though estimating that this problem has been underreported by two to three times, there were over 1 million occurrences identified in the 1986–1987 school year with 10,000–

1054-139X/92/$5.00

Published by Elsevier Science Publishing Co., Inc., 655 Avenue of the Americas, New York, NY 10010

20,000 students requesting subsequent medical treatment (4,5,7). Hyman et al. (10) note that there are about 1.5 million reported cases of physical punishment in school each year, but calculate the actual number to be at least 2–3 million.

The highest incidence tends to be in the south and southwest (particularly Florida, Texas, Arkansas, Alabama, Mississippi, Tennessee, Oklahoma, Georgia, and Kentucky), while the lowest is in the northeast, where a number of states have outlawed this (1,5,7,11). In 1984, 1 in 2,000 students in Utah and Connecticut received corporal punishment, compared with 1 in 8 Arkansas students (7). Current studies indicate that physical punishment is more common in grades kindergarten through 8 (versus high school), in rural schools (versus urban), in boys (versus girls), and in disadvantaged children (versus middle-class and upper-class Caucasians) (1,4,5, 7,11).

Au Courant Corpus Juris Milieu

A major obstacle to establishing a universal ban on corporal punishment is the current popular opinion in the United States that it is legally permissible to apply physical punishment to children in school. The common law since before the American Revolution has provided that, although teachers may use reasonable force to discipline children, any excessive or unreasonable force will subject the educator to either criminal liability or a civil claim for personal injuries. Due in part, no doubt, to the inability of students to interest overburdened prosecutors and police forces in filing criminal actions against teachers for alleged assaults, various attempts have been made by recipients of corporal punishment to expand their common law rights to the level of constitutional claims. These attempts have met with limited success (1,8,12,13).

In 1975, the United States Supreme Court concluded that the due process provisions of the Fourteenth Amendment require that students are entitled to a hearing prior to any prolonged ejection from school for disciplinary reasons (14). In the landmark case of *Ingraham v. Wright* (15), 2 years later, questions of students' constitutional rights in a disciplinary setting were again considered. Specifically, the Court considered two questions; 1) whether the reprimand-induced paddling of two male students violated their Eighth Amendment right to be free from "cruel and unusual punishment," and 2) whether the action violated their Fourteenth Amendment right to due process; i.e., their right to a hearing before the infliction of punishment.

The Court answered both questions in the negative declaring that the Eighth Amendment proscription against cruel and unusual punishment is designed to protect those charged and/or convicted of a crime, rather than students in a school disciplinary setting. Second, the Court held that the common law remedies of civil actions and criminal liability adequately protected the students' Fourteenth Amendment due process rights. The Court noted that the school milieu is an open organization with sufficient public surveillance to minimize the chance of abuse of children.

The Court in *Ingraham* specifically left open the question of whether and under what circumstances corporal punishment of a student might give rise to an independent federal cause of action to vindicate substantive rights under the due process clause. Since *Ingraham*, several Appeals Courts have proceeded through the opening provided by the Supreme Court and have remanded for trial, cases in which students alleged violations of their substantive due process rights. In *Hall v. Tawney* (16), the Fourth Circuit Court defined this as "the right to be free from state intrusions into the realm of personal privacy and bodily security through means so brutal, demeaning, and harmful as literally to shock the conscience of a court." The Tenth Circuit Court has agreed with *Hall* stating that "we believe that *Ingraham* requires us to hold that, at some point, excessive corporal punishment violates the pupil's substantive due process rights (17) (remanding for trial a case in which a 9-year-old girl was held up by her ankles and hit with a board on the front of her legs until they bled, resulting in a permanent scar). Agreeing with the Fourth and Tenth Circuits, the Eighth Circuit established a 4-step test to be used in determining whether particular conduct has resulted in violation of a student's substantive due process rights (18).

Nevertheless, the burden of establishing a substantive due process violation, regardless of which circuit's definition is used, is a very difficult burden to meet. Generally speaking, it would be easier to prove a criminal case of assault and battery than to prove that a teacher has violated a student's substantive due process rights in a particular school disciplinary action.

An example is a Texas case involving two girls (ages 5 and 6 years) who were struck three times across their buttocks because their teacher saw them giggling in a hall. In that case, the Federal Appeals Court ruled that there was no due process violation with excessive corporal punishment, because plaintiffs could turn to Texas common law. On March 6, 1989, the United States Supreme Court denied a review of this Texas case (8). Studies consistently note that Texas is one of the states having a high rate of corporal punishment. For example, in 1973, over 3,000 paddlings per month were given in Dallas schools, some only because the student did not address the teacher as "sir" or for incorrect spelling (7).

Thus, the attempts to expand students' common law rights by invoking the Constitution have met with limited, and generally, unsatisfactory results. Using the court system to prove that corporal punishment has been excessive remains difficult. The punished minor always has the burden of proof to show that punishment in a particular case was excessive, rather than requiring the involved school official to show that the punishment was reasonable under the circumstances (19).

Is Corporal Punishment a Positive Disciplinary Method?

There remains a strong undercurrent of opinion in the United States favoring corporal punishment in schools, and such advocates include various fundamental churches, the National Association of Secondary School Principals, and the American Federation of Teachers (20,21). A 1985 poll (20) revealed that such punishment is acceptable to 47% of the American population and 60% of school officials (teachers, administrators, board members). Current research (20,21) notes that adults (parents and teachers) who were physically punished as children are more supportive of this than those who were not.

Advocates for corporal punishment in schools feel, as noted by the *Ingraham* court decision, that it is an efficacious technique of training and discipline (2,22,23). According to this opinion, these children are better controlled, learn appropriate appreciation for authority, develop better social skills as well as improved moral character, and learn to better discipline themselves. Those with this conclusion often feel that our teachers do not have proper classroom order and that, for many students, physical punishment is the only technique left to preserve academic control. If this technique is thus removed, there will be greater disciplinary difficulty in our schools and reduced teacher security (2,21,23). Because current legal and popular opinion suggest it is acceptable for parents to physically punish their children, it is thus fully acceptable for school officials, who substitute for parents during school hours, to exercise this method as well (24). Such reasoning leads to the spurious conclusion that schools have a moral and legal obligation to physically discipline minors. There is also a specious qualification to such arguments, that corporal punishment is only used as a "last resort" when all else has failed (2).

The Case Against Corporal Punishment

It is the conclusion of the Society for Adolescent Medicine that corporal punishment is an ineffective method of discipline and has major deleterious effects on the physical and mental health of those inflicted (25). There is no clear evidence that such punishment effectuates more discipline or better control in the classroom (7,8,22,23). Physically punishing children has never been shown to enhance moral character development, increase the student's respect for teachers or other authority figures in general, intensify the teacher's control in class, or even protect the teacher (1,2,4,19). Such children, in our view, are being physically and mentally abused and there are no data actually demonstrating that such victims develop enhanced social skills or self-control skills (1,3,10). Current research concludes that corporal punishment is not always a method of last resort, and that there is not an increase in violence in schools which reject use of this technique. There are many effective alternatives to corporal punishment, and it is possible for school authorities to learn them and for children to benefit from such techniques (1,5,11,20,21,23).

Current research in behavior modification concludes that using positive reinforcement techniques that reward appropriate behavior is more efficacious and long lasting than methods utilizing aversive techniques. Punishment is based on aversive technology and produces very limited results (26). A student may cease acting up in one class only to continue in others. Such an individual learns the wrong message, one of avoidance or escape of getting caught or negative ways of eluding detection for wrong doing (27). This student apprehends techniques which actually lead to reduced self-control, with futile behavior characterized by more acting out, school absence, malingering, recidivism, and overt academic revocation (5,7,10,11,19–21,28).

Research notes that corporal punishment constructs an environment of education which can be described as unproductive, nullifying, and punitive. Children become victims, and trepidation is introduced to all in such a classroom. There is a limited (if any) sense of confidence and security, and even those children who are witness to such abuse are robbed of their full learning potential (22,24,26, 28,29). Students who are witnesses or victims of such abuse can develop low self-esteem, magnified guilt feelings, and the acquisition of anxiety symptoms; such results can have baneful results in the psychosocial and educational development of the students (24–27,30). When studies look at the milieu of these classrooms, one finds that all are subject to less, not more, learning. The nurturing of open communication, so vital to effective education, is severely spoiled in such aversive settings.

Hyman et al. (2,11,20) persistently assert that approximately one-half of students who are subjected to severe punishment develop an illness called Educationally Induced Post-Traumatic Stress Disorder (EIPSD). In this disorder, there is symptomatology analogous to the Post-Traumatic Stress Syndrome (PTSS). As with PTSS, EIPSD can be identified by a varying combination of symptoms characteristic of depression and anxiety. This mental health imbalance is induced by significant stress; with EIPSD the stress is the inflicted punishment. Such victimized students can have difficulty sleeping, fatigue, feelings of sadness and worthlessness, suicidal thoughts, anxiety episodes, increased anger with feelings of resentment and outbursts of aggression, deteriorating peer relationships, difficulty with concentration, lowered school achievement, antisocial behavior, intense dislike of authority, somatic complaints, tendency for school avoidance, school drop-out, and other evidence of negative high-risk adolescent behavior (23,24). This is consistent with research noting that punished children become more rebellious and are more likely to demonstrate vindictive behavior, seeking retribution against school officials and others in society (5). Such punishment can result in what is termed *operant aggression* (in which there is a direct verbal or physical attack against the punishment source). The intent is to destroy or immobilize that source to prevent delivery of further punishment. *Elicited aggression* can also result in verbal and physical attacks; however, the aggression may be directed toward others in the environment, even those who are not the source of the original punishment. The intent is simply to destroy or immobilize anything that might cause delivery of additional punishment (27,31).

Patterson's extensive research on aggressive behavior and the coercive family process concludes that an aversive consequence may also elicit an aggressive reaction and accelerate ongoing coercive behavior (28,29). This proponent of social learning theory further adds that children who experience aggressive acts are more likely to counterattack. These victims of aggressive acts eventually learn via *modeling* to initiate aggressive interchanges. These events perpetuate the use of aggressive acts and train children how to behave as adults. They learn to control unwanted behavior through the use of coercive techniques (28,29).

Children and adolescents can also be physically damaged by such punishment. Advocates of corporal punishment note it should be proportioned out in limited doses, based on the offense and without attempt to physically harm; however, this is often not the case, and many students are hurt. Apologists for aversive discipline suggest that the punishment must produce instant discomfort and must surprise the victim as soon as possible after the identified violation (26,27). Corporal punishment, however, does not often meet such standards, as punishment in excess of the infraction may occur, and repetition quickly eliminates the element of surprise. As noted previously (vida supra), at least 10,000–20,000 American students needed medical treatment after becoming victims of corporal punishment in their school environments during the 1986–1987 school year (4,5,7). Medical complications may prevent students from returning to school for days, weeks, or even longer. Reported medical findings include abrasions, severe muscle injury, extensive hematomas, whiplash damage, life-threatening fat emboli, severe arm or leg nerve injury (including fractures), brain hemorrhage, and others (including death!) (5,7,10,19).

The Promotion of the Wrong Message: Violence

The use of corporal punishment in schools promotes a very precarious message—that violence is an acceptable phenomenon in our society. It sanctions the notion that it is meritorious to be violent toward our children, thereby devaluing them in society's eyes (9,19). It encourages children to resort to violence because they see their authority figures or substitute parents using it. It also sanctions the use of physical violence by parents toward their children. Parents are not trained to use alternatives to corporal punishment and encouraging them to hit their children is a dangerous message to promote in our violent society. Many parents were abused themselves as children, and this will only worsen the violence our children must face. The result is that we are harming our children in teaching them that violence is acceptable, especially against the weak, the defenseless, the subordinate—a message which will negatively effect generations yet unborn. Violence is not acceptable and we must not support it by sanctioning its use by such authority figures as school officials (23). We must develop and maintain a nonviolent temperament and orientation toward our children (7).

Alternatives to Corporal Punishment

An important technique in maintaining classroom control is to develop a milieu of effective communication, in which the teacher displays an attitude of respect for the students. School officials can exhibit cordiality to students and an attitude that they generally enjoy working with children in the academic setting. Students must be taught in an environment that clearly states they are valued and understood. The emphasis is on positive educational exchanges between teachers and students, not futile, contentious, win-lose contests.

Teachers can learn sound blueprints regarding student motivation and nonviolent techniques of classroom control. It is critical to present educational material which is stimulating to the pupils and is aimed at their ability levels. Some students do need alternative academic courses, and these should be offered. All students (and their parents) should be carefully involved in decision making about school issues affecting them, including educational goals and disciplinary rules. Schools should have peer support programs which utilize techniques such as Rap Groups and Sociodrama to encourage acceptable behavior. The lack of parental involvement in the education of their children is cited by teachers as one of the major causes of current classroom disciplinary difficulty (32).

Behavior modification techniques for classroom control can be effectively utilized by school officials (33–37). Inappropriate behavior can be reduced by using *extinction*. This technique removes or eliminates the reinforcers which maintain the inappropriate actions (23,26,27,28,31). A variety of nonviolent disciplinary techniques can be taught and utilized, such as soft verbal reproofs or social isolation in addition to the persistent use of rewards (as love, praise, and attention by the teacher) for appropriate behavior (1,20,35–39). Such methods can be powerful, compelling tools, changing unacceptable behavior, and helping the locus of control become placed within the student in this model.

It is critical that our teachers receive as much support and training as possible in their efforts to maintain effective classroom control without resorting to violent techniques. Such training should include instructions on the deleterious short- and long-term consequences of corporal punishment. Schools should have an ample supply of counselors, especially for younger children. Schools need to have in-school suspension facilities, while avoiding use of large classroom sizes. Schools' policies need to allow for a wide variety of teaching and disciplinary methods which deemphasize the necessity for corporal punishment. The input of parents and students into such policies is critical to its overall success. An effective relationship must be developed between school officials, parents, and students to develop sensible rules which have appropriate consequences when infractions inevitably occur.

There is much that can be done at local and state levels to advocate the ban of corporal punishment in schools. Various court rulings have noted that corporal punishment in schools is an issue that can be resolved by state law and/or local district policies. Individuals can join various groups to evaluate their local and state climates in this regard (5,7). Banning corporal punishment at the local level has evolved from various effective strategies, such as civil suits against local schools using corporal punishment, promotion of publicity about such schools, and comparing the computerized corporal punishment rates of some schools. There is evidence that public opinion is gathering against such punishment. A survey report in 1989 noted that 61% of 1250 questioned adults disapproved of corporal punishment in schools, versus 51% in 1968 (40).

Summary Position

The Society for Adolescent Medicine concludes that corporal punishment in schools is an ineffective, dangerous, and unacceptable method of discipline. The use of corporal punishment in the school reinforces the notion that physical aggression is an acceptable and effective means of eliminating unwanted behavior in our society. We join many other national organizations recommending that it be banned and urge that nonviolent methods of classroom control be utilized in our school systems (5,7,22,41,42). We must abandon such a technique which overtly promotes more violence on our children.

References

1. Bauer GB, Dubanoski R, Yamanchi LA, et al. Corporal punishment and the schools. Educ Urban Soc 1990;22:285–99.
2. Hyman IA, McDowell E, Rains B. Corporal punishment and alternatives in the schools: An overview of theoretical and practical issues in National Institute of Education: Proceedings: Conference on Corporal Punishment in Schools: A National Debate, February 18–20, 1977, U.S. Government Printing Office, 729 222/565, 1977.
3. Herman DM. A statutory proposal to prohibit the infliction of violence upon children. Family Law Quarterly 1985;19:1–52.
4. 1986–1987 Elementary and Secondary Civil Rights Survey, National Summary of Projected Data. Washington, DC: Office of Civil Rights, U.S. Department of Education, 1987.
5. Poole, SR, Ushkow, MC, Nader PR, et al. The role of the pediatrician in abolishing corporal punishment in schools. Pediatrics 1991;88:162–7.
6. Olson DA. The Swedish ban of corporal punishment. Brigham Young University. Law Review 1984;447–56.
7. Moelis CS. Banning corporal punishment: A crucial step toward preventing child abuse. Child Legal Rights 1988;9:2–5.
8. Frazier HC. Corporal and capital punishment of juveniles. Med Law 1990;9:996–1004.
9. Block N, Fathman R. Convincing state legislatures to ban corporal punishment. Children's Legal Rights Journal 1988; 9:21–24.
10. Hyman IA, Zelikoff W, Clarke J. Psychological and physical abuse in the schools: A paradigm for understanding post-traumatic stress disorder in children and youth. J Traumatic Stress 1988;1:243–66.
11. Hyman IA, Irwin A, Lally D. Discipline in the 1980's: Some alternatives to corporal punishment. Children Today 1982; 11:10–13.
12. *Thrasher v. General Casualty*, 732 Supp 966, W.D. Wis (1990).
13. English A. Treating adolescents: Legal and ethical considerations. Med Clin North Amer 1990;74:1097–112.
14. *Goss v. Lopez*, 419 U.S. 565 (1975).
15. *Ingraham v. Wright*, 430 U.S. 651, 662 (1977).
16. *Hall v. Tawney*, 621 F. 2d 607 (4th Cir, 1980).
17. *Garcia v. Meira*, 817 F. 2d. 650 (10th Cir, 1987).
18. *Wise v. Pea Ridge School District*, 855 F. 2d. 560 (1988).
19. Reitman A. Corporal punishment in schools—The ultimate violence. Child Legal Rights 1988;9:6–13.
20. Hyman IA. Eliminating corporal punishment in schools: Moving from advocacy research to policy implementation. Child Legal Rights 1988;9:14–20.
21. Ciminillo LM. Discipline: The school's dilemma. Adolescence 1980;15:1–12.
22. Lynch JB. The human touch: Discourse on corporal punishment, in the work book of the National Conference to Abolish Corporal Punishment in Schools, August 17–19, 1988. (NCACPS, 750 Brooksedge Blvd., Suite 107, Westerville OH 43081.)
23. Dubanoski RA, Inaba M, Gerkewicz BA. Corporal punishment in schools: Myths, problems, and alternatives. Child Abuse Negl 1983;7:271–8.
24. Reinholz LK. A practical defense of corporal punishment in the schools, in National Institute of Education: Proceedings: Conference on Corporal Punishment in Schools: A National Debate, February 18–20, 1977, U.S. Government Printing Office, 729 222/565, 1977.
25. Garrison EG. Psychological maltreatment of children: An emerging focus for inquiry and concern; American Psychologist 1987;42:157–9.
26. Bongiovani AF. A review of research on the effects of punishment: Implications for corporal punishment in schools, in National Institute of Education: Proceedings: Conference on Corporal Punishment in Schools: A National Debate, February 18–20, 1977, U.S. Government Printing Office, 779 222/565, 1977.
27. Mallot RW, Whaley DL. Psychology Kalamazoo, MI: Behaviordelia Publishers, 1981:125–33.
28. Patterson GR. The aggressive child: Victim and architect of a coercive system. In Marsh EJ, Hamerlynck LH, Handy LC, eds. Behavior Modification and Families. New York: Brunner/Mazel, 1976:267–316.
29. Patterson GR. Coercive family process. Eugene, Oregon: Castalia Publishing, 1982.
30. Hart SN, Brassard MR. A major threat to children's mental health: Psychological maltreatment. American Psychologist 1987;42:160–5.
31. Skinner BF. Science and human behavior. New York, McMillan, 1961.
32. Wilson FC. A look at corporal punishment and some implications of its use. Child Abuse Negl 1982;6:155–64.
33. Zimbardo PG. Psychology and life. Glenview, IL: Scott, Foresman, 1988.
34. WE Brown, Payne T. Policies/practices in public school disciplines. Academic Therapy 1988;23:297–301.
35. Sulzer-Azaroff B, Mayer GR. Achieving educational excellence. New York, Holt, Rinehard, and Winston, 1986.
36. Sulzer-Azaroff B, Mayer GR. Applying behavior analysis procedures with children and youth. New York, Holt, Rinehard, and Winston, 1977.
37. Wolfgang CH, Glickman CD. Solving disciplinary problems: Strategies for classroom teachers. Boston, Allyn and Bacon, 1980.
38. Jones VF, Jones LS. Responsible classroom discipline: Creating positive learning environments and solving problems. Boston, Allyn and Bacon, 1981.
39. Carkhuff RR, Berenson PH, Pierce RM. The skills of teaching: Interpersonal skills. Amhurst, MA: Human Resource Development Press, 1973.
40. Schulman, Ronca and Bucuvalas, Inc. Public Attitudes And Actions Regarding Child Abuse And Its Prevention. National survey prepared for the National Committee for Prevention of Child Abuse; Chicago, IL: 1989.
41. Committee on School Health, American Academy of Pediatrics. Corporal punishment in schools. Pediatrics 1986; 73:258.

42. Committee on School Health, American Academy of Pediatrics. Corporal punishment in schools. Pediatrics 1991; 88:173.

Prepared by Ad Hoc Corporal Punishment Committee

1. Donald E. Greydanus, M.D.
   Professor of Pediatrics and Human Development
   Michigan State University
2. Helen D. Pratt, Ph.D.
   Assistant Professor Pediatrics and Human Development
   Michigan State University
3. Samuel E. Greydanus, III, JD
   Private Law Practice
   Boston, Massachusetts
4. Adele D. Hofmann, M.D.
   Professor of Pediatrics
   University of California—Irvine
5. C. Richard Tsegaye-Spates, Ph.D.
   Professor and Chairperson
   Department of Psychology
   Western Michigan University

Corporal Punishment in America's Public Schools and the U.N. Convention on the Rights of The Child: A Case for Nonratification

ANDRE R. IMBROGNO *

Abstract

The United States remains one of the few industrialized nations which continues to permit corporal punishment in their public schools. In recent years, opponents of corporal punishment have argued strongly in favor of the United States' ratification of the U.N. Convention on the Rights of the Child, a treaty which contains several provisions prohibiting the use of corporal punishment on children. Ratification of this treaty appears unlikely. Even if ratification were to occur, reliance upon international law to undo the long-standing and well-entrenched practice of corporal punishment in America's schools would not only prove ineffective, but could also produce undesirable consequences. A new norm rejecting corporal punishment in America's public schools may yet emerge, but only by changing popular attitudes at the community and state level.

I. Introduction

Currently, the only state-sanctioned corporal punishment [1] in the United States exists in our public schools. Approximately half of the states permit their elementary and secondary schools to use reasonable corporal punishment in the disciplining of students. [2] Schools in these states exercise this disciplinary right

* Law clerk for Justice Francis E. Sweeney of the Ohio Supreme Court; J.D., The Ohio State University, 1999; B.A., The Ohio State University, 1995. The author dedicates this article to the memory of his father, Professor Salvatore Imbrogno, Ph.D.

1. Just what "corporal punishment" is, is variously described. However, the several definitions one finds in the literature all contain essentially the same elements. Corporal punishment is aptly described as "the use of physical force with the intention of causing a child to experience pain, but not injure, for the purpose of correction or control of the child's behavior." MURRAY A. STRAUS, BEATING THE DEVIL OUT OF THEM: CORPORAL PUNISHMENT IN AMERICAN FAMILIES 4 (1994).

2. Those states that prohibit the use of corporal punishment in their public schools have eliminated the practice by statute or state regulation. *See* Susan H. Bitensky, *Spare the Rod, Embrace Our Humanity:*

with some regularity. The United States Department of Education's most recent estimates put the number of school-administered instances of corporal punishment at over 600,000 per year. [3] The United States remains one of only a few industrialized nations which permit corporal punishment in their schools. [4]

At the same time, respect for the rights of children appears to be growing throughout the world. The United Nations Convention on the Rights of the Child [5] (hereinafter "Convention"), which contains several provisions either explicitly or implicitly prohibiting the use of corporal punishment on children, [6] has been ratified by 191 nations, making it the most quickly and universally ratified human rights treaty yet. [7] Although some have argued strongly in favor of the treaty's ratification in the United States, ratification appears unlikely. Even if ratification were to occur, reliance upon international law as a means of undoing the long-standing practice of corporal punishment in America's schools is seriously misplaced. A new norm rejecting corporal punishment may yet emerge, but only by changing attitudes at the community and state level.

II. The U.N. Convention on the Rights of the Child

The drafters of the Convention were drawn from every region of the world with the goal of ensuring that all cultures and legal systems were represented in the drafting process. [8] The United States was itself an active participant in the ten-year-long drafting process and is a signatory to the Convention. [9] Nevertheless, the United States remains one of only two nations that have not

---

Toward a New Legal Regime Prohibiting Corporal Punishment of Children, 31 U. MICH. J.L. REFORM 353, 353 n.4 (1998) (canvassing the laws of individual states regarding corporal punishment in the schools). All fifty states permit the parental use of reasonable corporal punishment in the disciplining of children.

3. OFFICE FOR CIVIL RIGHTS, U.S. DEPARTMENT OF EDUCATION, 1990 ELEMENTARY AND SECONDARY SCHOOL RIGHTS SURVEY 1 (1993). The distribution of reported incidences is not uniform nationwide. Southern states have proportionately higher rates of corporal punishment than their Northern counterparts. *See* IRWIN A. HYMAN, READING, WRITING AND THE HICKORY STICK: THE APPALLING STORY OF PHYSICAL AND PSYCHOLOGICAL ABUSE IN AMERICAN SCHOOLS 57-62 (1990).

4. *See Hearing on Corporal Punishment: Hearings on H.R. 1522 Before the Subcommittee on Select Education of the House Committee on Education and Labor*, 102d Cong., at 70 (1992) (statement of Hon. Major R. Owens) ("Almost every other industrialized country in the world has already prohibited corporal punishment, and by federal legislation. Corporal punishment is still used only in the U.S., South Africa, part of Canada, and . . . the outback region of Australia, among developed countries in the world.").

5. G.A. Res. 44/25, 44 U.N. GAOR, Supp. No. 49, at 165, U.N. Doc. A/44736 (1989).

6. *See, e.g., id.* at arts. 19.1, 37(a), and 28.

7. *See* Susan Kilbourne, *Opposition to U.S. Ratification of the United Nations Convention on the Rights of the Child: Responses to Parental Rights Arguments*, 4 LOY. POVERTY L.J. 55, 55 (1998).

8. *See* Rebeca Rios-Kohn, *The Convention on the Rights of the Child: Progress and Challenges*, 5 GEO. J. ON FIGHTING POVERTY 139, 141 (1998).

9. Signing a treaty does not impose a duty to meet the treaty's requirements. *See* Vienna Convention on the Law of Treaties, Jan. 20, 1987, art. 18, 115 U.N.T.S. 331.

formerly ratified the Convention.[10] The Convention's protections extend to every human being below the age of eighteen, unless the applicable national law sets a younger age of majority.[11]

The Convention is exceedingly comprehensive in nature. "The Convention's uniqueness stems from the fact that it is the first legally binding instrument that incorporates the full range of human rights for children . . . thus giving all rights equal emphasis."[12] The substantive articles of the Convention recognize a wide-range of civil rights and freedoms for children, including the right to a name,[13] a nationality,[14] freedom of expression,[15] privacy,[16] and life.[17] The Convention also recognizes a right of children to such things as an adequate standard of living,[18] health services,[19] and education.[20] Protective rights in the Convention insulate children from economic[21] and sexual exploitation,[22] cruel treatment,[23] arbitrary separation from their families,[24] and abuses in the criminal justice system.[25]

The Convention's proscription of corporal punishment can be gleaned from those provisions dealing with the abuse and neglect of children. For instance, Article 19(1) provides, in part, that "States Parties shall take all appropriate . . . measures to protect the child from *all forms* of physical . . . violence . . . while in the care of parent(s), legal guardian(s), or *any other person who has the care of the child.*[26]

Similarly, Article 28(2) provides, in part, that "States Parties shall take . . . measures to ensure that school discipline is administered in a manner consistent with the child's human dignity and in conformity with the . . . Convention."[27] The United Nations Committee on the Rights of the Child has advised that this

10. Somalia is the other non-ratifying nation. It should be noted that Somalia does not have an internationally recognized government and, accordingly, is unable to ratify at this time.

11. Convention on the Rights of the Child, *supra* note 5, at art. 1.

12. Marc D. Seitles, *Effect of the Convention on the Rights of the Child Upon Street Children in Latin America: A Study of Brazil, Colombia, and Guatemala*, 16 IN PUB. INTEREST 159, 166 (1997).

13. Convention on the Rights of the Child, *supra* note 5, at art. 7(1).

14. *Id.*

15. *Id.* at art. 12(1).

16. *Id.* at art. 16(1).

17. *Id.* at art. 6(1).

18. *Id.* at art. 27(1).

19. *Id.* at art. 24(1).

20. *Id.* at art. 28(1).

21. *Id.* at 32(1).

22. *Id.* at art. 34.

23. *Id.* at art. 37.

24. *Id.* at art. 9(1).

25. *Id.* at art. 37.

26. *Id.* at art. 19(1) (emphasis added).

27. *Id.* at art. 28(2).

provision of the Convention is intended to outlaw the use of corporal punishment in schools.[28]

III. Corporal Punishment: Background

Corporal punishment of children, both in the home and the schools, has deep historical roots in the United States. Although empirical research on corporal punishment's effects on children is inconclusive, the possible effects of corporal punishment continue to be extensively debated by academicians. Properly framed, any debate about corporal punishment in the public schools must address both its deep historical roots and the ambiguity surrounding its effects.

A. History of Corporal Punishment in the United States

Corporal punishment in American homes and schools is a well-entrenched tradition.[29] Commentators commonly point to religion as one source of this entrenchment.[30] The Bible clearly sanctions corporal punishment,[31] and other religious and moral teachings likewise approve of the threat and use of force in the disciplining of children.[32] "Based upon religious authority, many believed that children were inherently evil and that beating was an effective method of driving the devil from them."[33] This view may still retain some currency. Irwin Hyman, a professor of school psychology who has written extensively on corporal punishment, argues that the devil theory remains an important basis for corporal punishment if even a fraction of those 66% of Americans who report that they believe in the devil also believe that pleasure is the work of the devil and that good character can be forged through pain and humility.[34]

28. *See* Susan H. Bitensky, *The Child's Right to Humane Discipline Under the U.N. Convention on the Rights of the Child: The Mandate Against All Corporal Punishment for Children*, 4 LOY. POVERTY L.J. 47, 52 (1998); Concluding Observations: Zimbabwe, CRC/C/15 Add. 55, at para. 18 (June 7, 1996); Concluding Observations: United Kingdom, CRC/C/15 Add. 34, at para. 31 (Feb. 15, 1995); Concluding Observations: Canada, CRC/C/15 Add. 37, at para. 25 (June 20, 1995).

29. *See* IRWIN A. HYMAN & JAMES H. WISE, CORPORAL PUNISHMENT IN AMERICAN EDUCATION: READINGS IN HISTORY, PRACTICE, AND ALTERNATIVES 23 (Irwin A. Hyman & James H. Wise eds., 1979).

30. *See* Gertrude J. Williams, *Social Sanctions for Violence Against Children: Historical Perspectives*, *in* CORPORAL PUNISHMENT IN AMERICAN EDUCATION: READINGS IN HISTORY, PRACTICE, AND ALTERNATIVES 25, 29-30 (1979); Leonard P. Edwards, *Corporal Punishment and the Legal System*, 36 SANTA CLARA L. REV. 983, 987 (1996).

31. *See, e.g.*, *Proverbs* 13:24 ("He that spareth the rod hateth his son, but he that loveth him chasteneth him"); *Proverbs* 29:17 ("Correct thy son, and he shall give thee rest; yea, he shall give delight unto thy soul"); *Proverbs* 22:15 ("Foolishness is bound in the heart of a child; but the rod of correction shall drive it far from him").

32. *See* Edwards, *supra* note 30, at 987.

33. *Id.*

34. HYMAN, *supra* note 3, at 32.

During colonial times, corporal punishment was thought to be both a desirable and necessary instrument for restraining sin and immorality in children.[35] Most immigrants who came to America in the eighteenth and nineteenth centuries brought with them a tradition of corporal punishment.[36] The latter part of the nineteenth century and the early 1900's witnessed a trend toward formal schooling away from home and the concomitant creation of a new source of corporal punishment - the public school teacher and administrator.[37]

While the amount and severity of corporal punishment has decreased in the twentieth century, corporal punishment remains an integral component of both the American family[38] and the American school.[39] While the support for corporal punishment in America's schools is the most equivocal, "[m]any teachers and a large percentage of the public believe that, just as parents must have the right to use corporal punishment 'when necessary,' teachers also need a similar right to maintain discipline and order in schools."[40]

Today, the existence of corporal punishment depends upon decisions made by policymakers at a level no broader than the state. Where state law prohibits schools from employing corporal punishment, local school administrators are, of course, prohibited from utilizing this form of discipline. Local school officials retain no discretion on the matter. However, states which permit corporal punishment either do not address the issue in their legislative codes or, if permitting the practice by statute, draft the statute in permissive, as opposed to mandatory terms, allowing, but not requiring, schools to utilize physical force in disciplining their students.[41] In either case, whether a state chooses to allow corporal punishment under the common law or by statute, local school administrators retain the discretion to prohibit the practice in their schools.

B. Effects of Corporal Punishment Upon the Child

Social science research on the effects of teacher-imposed corporal punishment is largely inconclusive.[42] The absence of conclusive empirical research on the subject has by no means reduced the intensity surrounding the academic

35. *See id.*; Ingraham v. Wright, 430 U.S. 651, 660 (1977) (noting that "[t]he use of corporal punishment in this country as a means of disciplining school children dates back to the colonial period").

36. *See* Edwards, *supra* note 30, at 988.

37. *See id.* at 990.

38. National surveys reveal that almost all American parents utilize corporal punishment in disciplining their children at some point from infancy through the teenage years. *See* STRAUS, *supra* note 1, at 21-24.

39. *See supra* text accompanying note 2.

40. STRAUS, *supra* note 1, at 111.

41. *See* Jon M. Bylsma, *Hands Off! New North Carolina General Statutes Section 115C-390 Allows Local School Boards to Ban Corporal Punishment*, 70 N.C. L. REV. 2058, 2059 (1992).

42. *See* Edwards, *supra* note 30, at 990.

debate about corporal punishment. The arguments on both sides of the debate are legion and passionately held.

Those who favor corporal punishment in America's schools point to the salutary effects corporal punishment is thought to have on discipline and order. Anthony Bongiovanni notes that, in recent years, we have witnessed an increase in concern over the perceived lack of discipline in American schools, and with it, increased calls for the use of corporal punishment to deal with recalcitrant students. [43] Although research indicates that the use of corporal punishment may in fact have precisely the opposite effect, [44] there are those in America's public schools who insist that the deterrent value of corporal punishment is self-evident. [45]

Related to the argument that corporal punishment has a deterrent effect, and based largely on the same assumption, are other arguments offered in support of corporal punishment. It is sometimes argued that corporal punishment teaches children to learn to obey and to respect authority [46] and builds students' character. [47] Proponents also suggest that corporal punishment is consistent with "the right of all students to receive an education, uninterrupted by a single, individual, disruptive student." [48] And some insist that corporal punishment is a desirable alternative to arguably more draconian punishments like suspension. [49]

Of course, corporal punishment continues to find support in religion and the notion that the practice is divinely ordained. [50] Finally, proponents of corporal punishment assert that corporal punishment is an inherent right of the parent

43. Anthony F. Bongiovanni, *An Analysis of Research on Punishment and its Relation to the Use of Corporal Punishment in the Schools*, *in* CORPORAL PUNISHMENT IN AMERICAN EDUCATION: READINGS IN HISTORY, PRACTICE, AND ALTERNATIVES 351, 351 (1979).

44. *See* Irwin A. Hyman, *A Social Science Analysis of Evidence Cited in Litigation on Corporal Punishment in the Schools*, *in* CORPORAL PUNISHMENT IN AMERICAN EDUCATION: READINGS IN HISTORY, PRACTICE, AND ALTERNATIVES 394, 397 (1979) (noting that "[t]here is research evidence that the infliction of pain often results in operant and elicited aggression which is counter-productive in terms of 'important educational interests' ").

45. *See, e.g.*, Lansing K. Reinholz, *A Practical Defense of Corporal Punishment in the Schools*, *in* CORPORAL PUNISHMENT IN AMERICAN EDUCATION: READINGS IN HISTORY, PRACTICE, AND ALTERNATIVES 342 (1979) (At the time of publication, author was a school administrator in Burlington, Vermont.).

46. *See* Edwards, *supra* note 30, at 990.

47. *See id.*

48. Reinholz, *supra* note 45, at 346.

49. *See id.* at 343.

50. *See supra* notes 30-34 and accompanying text.

and, through the doctrine of *in loco parentis*,[51] teachers and school administrators as well.[52]

A number of social scientists assert that corporal punishment, in addition to being morally offensive, is ineffective and can have harmful effects on children. A number of researchers link corporal punishment to increased violence on the part of the recipient during both childhood and adulthood.[53] Corporal punishment may legitimize violence in the eyes of the child.[54] Put differently, corporal punishment and aggression may be linked through "social learning" - children simply imitate the aggressive behavior of the individual inflicting the punishment upon them.[55] Indeed, because corporal punishment is administered by authoritarian figures such as parents and teachers - individuals the child is taught to respect and emulate - corporal punishment may have a particularly strong "social learning" effect. Corporal punishment has also been linked to juvenile delinquency and adult criminal behavior, often of a violent nature.[56] Corporal punishment has been associated with diminished occupational and economic achievement on the part of those who experience it during childhood.[57]

Criticism of corporal punishment is grounded largely in its perceived psychological impact on children. A few studies suggest that corporal punishment can create in children feelings of alienation, depression, and suicidal ideation that last long into adulthood.[58] Opponents urge that corporal punishment generates in children feelings of rage and indignation which cannot be expressed because of the fear that further punishment will result.[59] The child's response, it is argued, is to repress[60] his or her feelings.[61] Among the long-term consequences of this repressed anger may be aggressiveness, the

51. *See* Vernonia Sch. Dist. v. Acton, 515 U.S. 646, 655 (1995) (noting that "for many purposes 'school authorities act *in loco parentis*'") (quoting Bethel Sch. Dist. No. 403 v. Fraser, 478 U.S. 675, 681-684 (1986)); Kelly Frels, *Corporal Punishment - 1975 Style*, 42 NOLPE SCHOOL L.J. 149, 149 (1975) ("Teachers and administrators of public schools stand in some degree '*in loco parentis*' to the students."). *See also* Reinholz, *supra* note 45, at 342-343.

52. *See* Edwards, *supra* note 30, at 991.

53. *See* STRAUS, *supra* note 1, at 101.

54. *See id.*

55. *See* STRAUS, *supra* note 1, at 111. *See also* MARK G. YUDOF ET AL., EDUCATIONAL POLICY AND THE LAW 334 (3d ed. 1992) (noting that "[s]tudents learn about accepted norms by observing the actions of others, particularly as those actions have an impact on their day-to-day lives") (citing AMY GUTMANN, DEMOCRATIC EDUCATION 88-94 (1987)).

56. *See* STRAUS, *supra* note 1, at 107-110.

57. *See id.* at 140-142.

58. *See id.* at 142-144 (discussing alienation). *See generally* Murray A. Straus, *Corporal Punishment of Children and Adult Depression and Suicidal Ideation*, *in* COERCION AND PUNISHMENT IN LONG-TERM PERSPECTIVES 59 (Joan McCord ed., 1995).

59. *See* Bitensky, *supra* note 28, at 48-49.

60. "Repression" is the mental force responsible for actively keeping an individual from consciously acknowledging his potentially threatening or anxiety-provoking memories and feelings. *See* WILLIAM

inability to empathize, and a tendency toward either authoritarianism, or unquestioning obedience.[62]

Both sides of the corporal punishment debate offer compelling theories in defense of their positions, and both sides defend their respective views with passion. The state-by-state approach to corporal punishment which now exists permits the practice in at least some jurisdictions. As a result, it is, today, corporal punishment's critics that most vocally assert their views. An overview of America's corporal punishment jurisprudence explains this group's recent attempts to invoke United Nations' law to rid America's homes and schools of this practice. A meaningful obstacle to the use of corporal punishment is not likely to come from the federal and state courts, at least not any time soon.

IV. Corporal Punishment and the Courts

An examination of the courts' treatment of school discipline issues reveals a long history of judicial deference to local officials with respect to corporal punishment and other disciplinary matters. This deference notwithstanding, some civil actions have met with a measure of success. However, for a variety of reasons, the elimination, or wide-spread reduction, of corporal punishment through judicial action is not likely. While parental choice is, at least arguably, a fair resolution to the corporal punishment debate, for judicial and moral reasons, it is an unattractive solution from the standpoint of corporal punishment's strongest opponents.

A. Deference to Local Officials

In a series of decisions since 1969,[63] the United States Supreme Court has invited judicial scrutiny of school district disciplinary decisions. At the same time, the Court has consistently articulated in these cases a rule of substantial deference to decisions made by locally elected school officials. The Supreme Court's seminal decision on corporal punishment is *Ingraham v. Wright*,[64] handed down by the Court in 1977.

BUSKIST & DAVID W. GERBING, PSYCHOLOGY: BOUNDARIES AND FRONTIERS 504 (1990). Repression is an important element of Sigmund Freud's theory of personality. *See id.* at 503-504.

61. *See* Bitensky, *supra* note 28, at 49.

62. *See id.*

63. Academicians suggest that the Supreme Court's development of a school discipline jurisprudence can be traced to its 1969 decision in Tinker v. Des Moines Indep. Sch. Dist., 393 U.S. 503 (1969), wherein the Court held that the suspension from school of two secondary school students for wearing black arm bands in protest of the Vietnam War violated the students' First Amendment rights of free speech. *See, e.g.*, David M. Pedersent, *A Homemade Switchblade and a Bent Fork: Judicial Place Setting and Student Discipline*, 31 CREIGHTON L. REV. 1053, 1064-1065 (1998).

64. 430 U.S. 651 (1977).

In *Ingraham*, the Supreme Court held that the Eighth Amendment's Cruel and Unusual Punishment Clause does not apply to corporal punishment imposed as discipline in public schools. Although the Court found a liberty interest implicated, due process did not require notice and a hearing prior to the imposition of corporal punishment. [65] In the Court's view, the openness of the public schools, the supervision of these schools by the community, and the legal constraints on corporal punishment imposed under the common law and criminal law obviated the need for the constitutional protections sought by the students in this case. [66]

Underlying the Court's decision in *Ingraham* was its perception of corporal punishment as an issue best left to local educational policymakers. According to the Court, imposing additional constitutional safeguards would unduly intrude into areas of educational responsibility that rest primarily with local school authorities. [67] As David Pedersent notes, the *Ingraham* Court's quoting of Justice Black's concurring opinion in *Powell v. Texas* [68] is revealing: [69]

> [T]his Nation is too large, too complex and composed of too great a diversity of peoples for any one of us to have the wisdom to establish the rules by which local Americans must govern their local affairs. The constitutional rule we are urged to adopt is not merely revolutionary - it departs from the ancient faith based on the premise that experience in making local laws by local people themselves is by far the safest guide for a Nation like ours to follow. [70]

The *Ingraham* Court also recognized that extensive due process protections would burden, to an unacceptable extent, the use of corporal punishment as a disciplinary measure. [71] The Court acknowledged that the elimination of corporal punishment would be welcomed by many Americans; it stressed, however, that the decision to eliminate corporal punishment was not its to make. [72] According to the Court, "when such a policy choice may result from this Court's determination of an asserted right to due process, rather than from the normal processes of community debate and legislative action, the societal costs cannot be dismissed as insubstantial." [73]

---

65. *See id.*
66. *See id.* at 678.
67. *See id.* at 682.
68. 392 U.S. 514 (1968).
69. Pedersent, *supra* note 63, at 1069-1070.
70. Ingraham, 430 U.S. at 670-671 n.39 (quoting Powell v. Texas, 392 U.S. 514, 547-548 (1968) (Black, J., concurring)).
71. *Id.* at 662, 680.
72. *See id.* at 681.
73. *Id.* at 681.

The Supreme Court's deference to local officials in matters of school discipline extends beyond the corporal punishment issue to other educational matters having substantial constitutional implications, including search and seizure and free speech.[74] Repeatedly in its opinions the Supreme Court expresses deference to local authorities, quoting with approval its opinion in *Epperson v. Arkansas*,[75] wherein the Court stated "[j]udicial interposition in the operation of the public school system of the Nation raises problems requiring care and restraint. . . . By and large, public education in our Nation is committed to the control of state and local authorities."[76]

Research indicates that the tone of deference established by the Supreme Court is reflected in judicial decisions from the lower federal courts and the states.[77] A study by David Pedersent examined a wide variety of student discipline cases handed down by lower federal and state courts since 1995.[78] Pedersent writes that "[i]t is apparent from a review of these cases that the lower federal courts and the state courts have generally taken to heart the admonition of the . . . Supreme Court to grant deference to decision-making of local school officials."[79] In three-fourths of the cases examined, the courts either decided the case in favor of the school district or, for those cases in which school officials were not directly involved, in favor of a decision that would give school officials greater discretion in school discipline matters.[80]

B. Available Causes of Action

The Eighth Amendment, which after *Ingraham* provides only minimal protection against corporal punishment, is not the only constitutional vehicle by which to challenge the practice in court. Other possible causes of action include substantive due process, equal protection, and free exercise of religion under

74. *See, e.g.*, New Jersey v. T.L.O., 469 U.S. 325 (1985) (holding that the Fourth Amendment's prohibition on unreasonable searches applies to searches carried out by school officials, but that the standard for authorizing searches in the public schools is less rigorous than that in the criminal law context); Bethel Sch. Dist. v. Fraser, 478 U.S. 675, 681 (1986) (holding that a school district's three-day suspension of a student who gave a speech laden with sexual innuendo did not violate the student's free speech rights, and recognizing the core function of school officials to instill in students "habits and manners of civility as values in themselves conducive to happiness and as indispensable to the practice of self government in the [United States]"); Vernonia Sch. Dist. 47J v. Acton, 515 U.S. 646, 665 (1995) (upholding the validity of a school district's student athlete drug policy which authorized suspicionless random urinalysis drug testing, and noting that "[w]hen the government acts as guardian and tutor the relevant question [under the Fourth Amendment] is whether the search is one that a reasonable guardian and tutor might undertake").

75. 393 U.S. 97 (1968).

76. *Id.* at 104. *See, e.g.*, Goss v. Lopez, 419 U.S. 565, 578 (1975); Board of Curators of the Univ. of Mo. v. Horowitz, 435 U.S. 78, 91 (1978).

77. *See, e.g.*, Pedersent, *supra* note 63, at 1081-1083.

78. *Id.*

79. *Id.* at 1082-1083.

80. *See id.* at 1083.

the First Amendment. First Amendment challenges have not yet been brought. The other causes of action have met with varying degrees of success in recent years. However, as a basis for eliminating corporal punishment from the nation's public schools, each has severe limitations.

One question left open by the Supreme Court's decision in *Ingraham* was whether or under what circumstances corporal punishment of a public school child will give rise to an independent federal cause of action to vindicate substantive rights under the Due Process Clause of the Fourteenth Amendment. [81] The federal courts of appeals are not of one mind on this question. [82] Even in those circuits that recognize a substantive due process claim for unreasonable corporal punishment, the existence of the claim does little to placate corporal punishment's harshest opponents because the claim generally requires corporal punishment so excessive that it "shocks the conscience." [83] While providing a separate federal claim, in most cases the substantive due process claim will not cover acts of punishment not already prohibited under state criminal law or actionable under state common law.

Those bringing civil rights actions for the discriminatory application of corporal punishment face similar challenges in establishing their claims. The issue of discrimination is hardly academic in nature. Studies have demonstrated that "[p]roportionately, black children are subjected to corporal punishment many times oftener than white or Asian children in almost every school district in the nation." [84] Although this equal protection issue has not been frequently litigated, one federal court recently held that a claim for discriminatory imposition of corporal punishment brought under the federal civil rights law [85] states a valid cause of action. [86] However, as this same court noted, it is well-established that the Constitution is not violated solely because a state action has a racially disproportionate impact. Plaintiff must demonstrate a racially discriminatory intent or purpose. [87] African-American school children thus face a substantial evidentiary burden in these civil rights actions.

---

81. The Ingraham Court explicitly declined to address this substantive due process question. Ingraham, 430 U.S. at 659 n.12.

82. *Compare* Fee v. Herndon, 900 F.2d 804 (5th Cir. 1990) (holding that "injuries sustained as a result of corporal punishment irrespective of their severity do not implicate the Due Process Clause if the forum state provides adequate post-punishment civil or criminal remedies for students to vindicate any legal transgressions"), *with* Garcia v. Miera, 817 F.2d 650 (10th Cir. 1987) (holding that "corporal punishments that are inflicted on students and that are so grossly excessive as to be shocking to the conscience violate substantive due process rights without regard to adequacy of remedies").

83. *See, e.g., id.*

84. HYMAN, *supra* note 3, at 74.

85. 42 U.S.C. §§ 1981 & 1983 (1994).

86. Coleman v. Franklin Parish Sch. Bd., 702 F.2d 74 (5th Cir. 1983).

87. *See id.* at 77; Village of Arlington Heights v. Metropolitan Housing Dev. Corp., 429 U.S. 252, 264-265 (1976); Washington v. Davis, 426 U.S. 229, 240-241 (1976).

One possible cause of action which has not yet been brought by opponents of corporal punishment, but which could meet with some success, is one based on the First Amendment's religion clauses. While current religious doctrine overwhelmingly supports the practice of corporal punishment, some new-thought religions and even parts of the Bible itself advocate compassion toward children.[88] Although case law addressing the relationship between the First Amendment and corporal punishment is scarce, it appears that at least some courts will entertain First Amendment challenges to state-mandated bans on corporal punishment. These decisions could, perhaps, be analogized to cases involving state-sanctioned imposition of corporal punishment.

For instance, in *North Valley Baptist Church v. McMahon*,[89] a religious group operating a preschool challenged the constitutionality of California's Child Care Facilities Act, which, *inter alia*, prohibited corporal punishment in child care facilities. Although the court ultimately upheld the statute, it noted that where a group's religious beliefs mandate corporal punishment, a state-imposed burden on the practice could run afoul of the First Amendment's Free Exercise Clause.[90] The problem for the plaintiffs in *McMahon* was that they failed to show that corporal punishment was mandated by their religious beliefs.[91]

There is no apparent reason why such a holding could not be analogized to genuinely held religious *opposition* to corporal punishment.[92] However what makes this First Amendment action a poor vehicle for the eradication of corporal punishment is the fact that few contemporary religions oppose corporal punishment. Therefore, few challenges to corporal punishment are likely to be brought on these grounds. Indeed, corporal punishment finds considerably more support in religion than it does opposition.[93]

---

88. *See* Williams, *supra* note 30, at 30.

89. 696 F. Supp. 518 (E.D. Cal. 1988), *summarily aff'd*, 893 F.2d 1139 (9th Cir. 1990).

90. McMahon, 696 F. Supp. at 531. *Cf.* Mozert v. Hawkins County Bd. of Educ., 827 F.2d 1058, 1070 (6th Cir. 1987) (holding that "the requirement that public school students study a basal reader series chosen by the school authorities does not create an unconstitutional burden under the Free Exercise Clause when the students are not required to affirm or deny a belief or *engage . . . in a practice prohibited . . . by their religion*") (emphasis added).

91. McMahon, 696 F. Supp. at 531-532.

92. Of course, religious objection to corporal punishment is not consonant with mainstream religious thought. This fact, however, should not preclude those religious objections from being recognized under the First Amendment. While religious beliefs must be sincerely held, they "need not be acceptable, logical, consistent, or comprehensible to others in order to merit First Amendment protection." *See* Thomas v. Review Bd. of Ind. Employ. Sec. Div., 450 U.S. 707, 714 (1981).

93. *See supra* notes 30-34 and accompanying text.

C. Parental Choice

A number of school districts, by local rule, permit individual parents to determine whether their children will be subject to corporal punishment. Although there is a basic fairness underlying this approach to the controversial issue of corporal punishment, courts have shown an unwillingness to recognize a constitutional basis for this compromise. Again, as with the corporal punishment issue more generally, this parental choice model has its roots in local political processes, as opposed to federal law.

In one of the few cases addressing the issue of parental choice, *Baker v. Owen*,[94] plaintiff parents had told local school officials that they did not want their child subjected to corporal punishment. The parents' wishes notwithstanding, the child was given two licks with a drawer divider that was just slightly thicker than a ruler. While the court accepted the parents' argument that the Fourteenth Amendment embraces the right of a parent to determine and choose between means of discipline of children, that right was overborne by the countervailing and greater state interest in maintaining school discipline.[95] Two years later in *Ingraham*, the Supreme Court put its imprimatur on the *Baker* holding when it cited its summary affirmation of *Baker* for the proposition that "parental approval of corporal punishment is not constitutionally required."[96]

Thus, while the parental choice model is an expedient, and perhaps fundamentally fair, manner in which to deal with the corporal punishment controversy, it can do little to satisfy corporal punishment's strongest opponents. At bottom, the existence of parental choice is the end result of decisions made by local officials and, without a grounding in federal law, is vulnerable to all the vagaries of such decisionmaking. Moreover, to the extent corporal punishment is a moral issue, as many urge, an approach that allows the practice to continue,

94. 395 F. Supp. 294 (M.D. N.C. 1975) (three judge court), *summarily aff'd*, 423 U.S. 907 (1975).

95. *See id.* at 299. The court's decision is consistent with the model of school power prevailing today. That model, often equated with the *in loco parentis* doctrine, takes a broad view of school power as independent from the parent and grounded in the state's power to educate and discipline children. *See supra* note 51 and accompanying text; Ann Proffitt Dupre, *Should Students Have Constitutional Rights? Keeping Order in the Public Schools*, 65 GEO. WASH. L. REV. 49, 91-92 (1996). Indeed, in contrast to the delegation model of school power, which posits that school authority flows exclusively from an explicit or implicit delegation of authority from parents, a model which views school authority as rooted in the state's independent power to educate and discipline is more consistent with today's compulsory education laws. *See* Ingraham, 430 U.S. at 662.

96. *Id.* at 662 n.22. The Fourth Circuit had occasion to revisit the Baker decision in Hall v. Tawney, 621 F.2d 607 (4th Cir. 1980). In rejecting plaintiffs' argument that the paddling of their child violated their right to determine the means by which she could be disciplined, the Fourth Circuit pointed to the Baker decision, the Supreme Court's affirmation of that decision, and its own view that "[t]he state interest in maintaining order in the schools limits the rights of particular parents unilaterally to except their children from the regime to which other children are subject." *Id.* at 610.

even as against only those children whose parents expressly allow it, is an unacceptable resolution of the issue.[97]

Undoubtedly, those opposed to the use of corporal punishment in America's public schools have been frustrated by the deference the federal and state courts have shown local school administrators, the overall inadequacy of judicial action, and the deficiencies of the parental choice model. Compounding this frustration is the uneven treatment the issue has received in the states, as a number of jurisdictions continue to allow corporal punishment in their public schools. Accordingly, those opposed to the practice have, in recent years, increasingly looked to the Convention, hopeful that ratification will jettison corporal punishment from America's public schools.

V. The Convention: Challenges to Ratification and Enforcement

Opponents of corporal punishment in America's public schools have urged for United States ratification of the Convention. As noted, the United States remains one of only two nations which have not ratified the Convention.[98] Although this fact subjects the United States to a measure of political pressure both at home and abroad, ratification still faces significant, countervailing obstacles.[99]

The Convention's proscription of corporal punishment is clearly inconsistent with American historical tradition, mainstream religion, and judicial doctrine. Corporal punishment's long history and biblical grounding pose substantial obstacles to ratification. At the same time, the divided expert opinion on the subject does little to create any sense of urgency among those political actors weighing ratification.

The courts have erected still another obstacle to ratification. The Supreme Court, the lower federal courts, and the state courts have, by and large, minimized the constitutional implications surrounding school discipline, deferring to local officials, and through them, parents. As stated, this deference has served to define school discipline as a matter of largely local concern. To engraft upon corporal punishment, a matter of school discipline, law formu-

97. It is for these same political and moral reasons that our current system, which, in states where corporal punishment is allowed, permits local school administrators to set their own policies on the issue, is unsatisfactory to those opponents of corporal punishment currently lobbying for the Convention's ratification.

98. *See supra* note 10 and accompanying text.

99. Whatever the reason for nonratification of a treaty, in the absence of ratification, international law generally holds that the nonratifying country is under no duty to observe any of the treaty's requirements. *See* Sanford J. Fox, *Beyond the American Legal System for the Protection of Children's Rights*, 31 FAM. L.Q. 237, 244 (1997). Accordingly, the rights defined in a treaty that has not been signed by the United States do not belong to the people of this country. *See id.*

lated at the level of nations is a bold step; it is one bound to be met with some level of resistance not only from corporal punishment's strongest supporters, but also from those for whom personal ambivalence about the practice makes local management of the issue appear the reasonable course.

There are, then, substantial obstacles to ratification. Even if ratification were to occur, these obstacles give the United States Senate considerable incentive to limit the effects ratification will have upon domestic law. Indeed, the Senate has several mechanisms available to it by which it can ratify a treaty while simultaneously ensuring that it has little domestic impact. These mechanisms produce a kind of "qualified ratification." As a practical matter, they operate to ensure that ratification has little more than symbolic force.

For example, ratification of human rights treaties like the Convention is often accompanied by the imposition of several impediments to domestic enforcement. [100] In the past, when the United States has ratified a human rights treaty, it has usually been on the condition that the treaty does not furnish a rule of decision to be applied in domestic litigation. [101] As a result, the provisions of the treaty are not self-executing. [102] Put another way, the provisions of the treaty cannot be invoked in the courts. [103] The treaty will have domestic legal effect only if the treaty is later implemented by domestic legislation. [104]

The device of "reservations" is another means by which the Senate can ensure that a ratified treaty will not be domestically enforceable. "Upon ratifying a treaty, a country may declare that it chooses not to accept all of the duties imposed by the treaty." [105] The result of a reservation is the same as if the United States did not ratify the reserved part of the treaty. [106] A reservation precludes domestic enforcement of that provision reserved. [107] Thus, the Convention could be ratified with the United States entering a reservation on those provisions prohibiting corporal punishment. The United States thus retains the right to emasculate some or all of the Convention's provisions.

In sum, there exist numerous potential obstacles to the Convention's ability to outlaw corporal punishment as a matter of United States law. The forces of tradition, religion, and legal doctrine urge for nonratification or qualified ratification of the Convention. That said, unqualified ratification of the Con-

100. *See id.* at 244-246.

101. *See id.* at 244-245.

102. *See id.* at 245.

103. *See id.*

104. *See id.* In effect, the doctrine of self-execution of treaties nullifies operation of the Supremacy Clause in regard to human rights treaties. *See id.*

105. *Id.*

106. *See id.*

107. As an example, by entering a reservation to Article 6 of the Covenant on Civil and Political Rights, the United States was able to avoid assuming an obligation to ban the execution of juvenile offenders. *See id.*

vention is not so unrealistic that its consequences are not worth considering along with an alternative to ratification.

VI. The Consequences of Ratification and an Alternative

At least some of the Convention's proponents have expressed contentment with the symbolic rewards that some Senate action falling short of full, unqualified ratification would produce. For example, Susan Bitensky, a proponent of ratification, writes that "because the Convention legitimizes the idea of prohibiting corporal punishment of children, it may be instrumental in the gradual creation of a new norm in the United States disfavoring this form of discipline." [108] The hope is that "[t]he development of a new norm may, in turn, set the stage for domestic legal reform." [109]

This optimism is misplaced. Where, as with ratification of the Convention, the law is being used to deliver a disputed moral message, the result is likely to be, not the creation of a new norm, but rather a further polarization of the opposing views on corporal punishment along with a general denigration of law enforcement. Certain realities surrounding the issue of corporal punishment - the religious grounding, the divided expert opinion, and the history of local community control over the issue - make the question of corporal punishment in America's public schools a question that must be resolved at that level of government closest to the people. If a "new norm" rejecting corporal punishment is to take hold, it must be developed through the changing of attitudes at the grassroots level rather than from the top-down imposition of international law.

A. The Consequences of Ratification

We commonly think of moral legislation as an expression of society's collective feeling of revulsion toward particular acts. [110] Occasionally, however, "it is not consensus that is expressed [through moral legislation] but rather the symbolic interim victory of one set of contending forces or interests over another." [111] Because popular opinion on the issue of corporal punishment is more or less equally divided, ratification of the Convention would constitute an example of the latter - an interim victory for one of two contending forces. Unqualified ratification of the Convention, while not likely, is at least conceivable. Its effects are, therefore, worth considering.

108. Bitensky, *supra* note 28, at 52-53.

109. *Id.* at 53.

110. *See* Morris R. Cohen, *Moral Aspects of the Criminal Law*, 49 YALE L.J. 987, 1017 (1940).

111. Joseph Gussfield, *On Legislating Morals: The Symbolic Process of Designating Deviancy*, 56 CALIF. L. REV. 54, 58-59 (1968).

Before turning to the consequences of ratification, it may be wise to first consider how moral legislation could even be passed without public consensus. The short answer is that it is unusual, but not impossible. There are some issues on every legislative agenda so technical, uncontroversial, or of such limited impact that they affect or interest only a narrow segment of the population. Under these circumstances, consensus is largely unnecessary. Moral issues, however, are unlikely to fall into this category of issues. Some consensus will normally be necessary to pass moral legislation. [112] The Convention may be an exception to this general rule. International law, and the Convention in particular, pose problems for the consensus model of moral legislating.

At work in the context of the Convention are international pressures normally absent from the legislation process. What nation, for example, wants to be associated with Somalia, as the only nations that have failed to ratify a human rights treaty? Adding to the international embarrassment is the irony that the United States was a key participant in the drafting process.

Moreover, the nature of the interests affected, when combined with the level at which ratification occurs, also works to promote ratification without national consensus. At bottom, ratification would affect the interests of individual parents. Specifically, ratification would burden parents' ability to decide for themselves whether the physical disciplining of their children by school teachers and administrators is good public policy. This parental choice is reflected in the larger community's decision to allow or disallow such discipline in their public schools. These parental interests, however, are poorly mobilized to affect legislation at a national level. Supreme Court deference to parents and local officials in all matters pertaining to the child have ensured that rarely, if ever, would parents have to defend their interests beyond the boundaries of their own local school districts or states.

Furthermore, parents' interest in school discipline is not one that will generate much fervor even among those at risk of having the interest burdened. Parents who favor corporal punishment in their schools are not united by the

112. Consensus is even more important today as more and more groups are becoming mobilized and are making a difference politically. The classic instances of moral legislation in the past - for example, temperance - pitted politically powerful groups against weaker groups - e.g., Protestant versus Catholic, rural versus urban, native versus immigrant, and middle versus lower class. *See id.* at 59. Although the political playing field is not, today, completely level, there now exist more mobilized groups with more political influence than ever before. *See* TOM ADAMS, GRASS ROOTS: HOW ORDINARY PEOPLE ARE CHANGING AMERICA 8-9 (1991) (noting that, by organizing groups of like-minded people, ordinary citizens "are getting results and are attracting more people [to their causes] each day"); ADVISORY COMMISSION ON INTERGOVERNMENTAL RELATIONS, THE TRANSFORMATION IN AMERICAN POLITICS: IMPLICATIONS FOR FEDERALISM 242-243 (1986) (noting that the latter half of the twentieth century has witnessed the "vast proliferation of minority factions" and that "there are vastly more organized interests today than ever before"). Information-age technologies will continue to provide interests with increasingly efficient, low-cost means by which to organize and lobby key political decisionmakers. *See* WILLARD C. RICHAN, LOBBYING FOR SOCIAL CHANGE 62-65 (2d ed. 1996).

same kind of human rights mantra that emotionally unites those who are opposed to the practice. Although those who favor corporal punishment can find support for their position in religion, not all parents who favor corporal punishment base their preference on the Bible. Given the religious diversity that exists in this country, even within the Protestant sect for example, religion can serve only to divide parents, not to unite them in opposition to ratification. In a sense, religion generates too much emotion. All of this acts to create a situation in which ratification of the Convention, in effect an act of moral legislating, can, at least conceivably, occur without national consensus on the fundamental moral question involved - the propriety of corporal punishment in America's schools. Again, ratification is by no means likely, but it is not impossible.

Ratification without consensus would likely be a hollow victory for the Convention's proponents, at least with respect to those states which currently allow corporal punishment in their public schools, which, in fact, are the only systems that concern supporters of the Convention. This is true even if ratification occurs without qualification and the Convention is made directly enforceable in the courts of the United States. Many question the ability of the courts to vindicate fundamental rights in the face of significant popular opposition.[113] For the most part, the courts are practically powerless to insure that their decisions are supported by local administrative officials, which means that courts are largely dependent on popular support to implement their decisions.[114] "[C]ourts are . . . only modestly endowed with coercive capabilities - adequate, perhaps, for dealing with recalcitrant individuals, but probably insufficient for bringing large groups or powerful institutions into line."[115]

Law enforcement pays a price for the legislating of morals without popular consensus. Where popular support for a law is absent, the law is unlikely to be regularly enforced and is even less likely to be obeyed. Classic instances of the failure of moral legislation, unsupported by popular consensus, are the prohibition fiasco and today's anti-adultery laws. The moral message intended to be communicated by the law is contradicted by the absence of compliance and enforcement; "for while the public sees the conduct condemned in words, it also sees in the dramatic absence of [compliance and enforcement] that it is not condemned in deed."[116]

113. *See, e.g.*, Stuart A. Sheingold, The Politics of Rights: Lawyers, Public Policy, and Political Change 116 (1974).

114. *See* Gerald N. Rosenberg, The Hollow Hope: Can Courts Bring About Social Change 336 (1991).

115. Sheingold, *supra* note 113, at 8.

116. Sanford H. Kadish, Blame and Punishment 23 (1987).

Moreover, the spectacle of popular nullification of the government's commands has an unhealthy effect on law enforcement generally.[117] "It tends to breed cynicism and an indifference to . . . [legal] processes which augment tendencies toward disrespect for those who make and enforce the law."[118] As social and legal historian E.P. Thompson once noted, "[t]he essential precondition for the effectiveness of law, in its function as ideology, is that it shall display an independence from gross manipulation."[119] Similarly, those in the contemporary communitarian[120] movement urge that "[s]uccessful policies are accepted because they are recognized as legitimate, rather than imposed."[121]

That proponents of ratification overlook the potentially deleterious consequences of ratification is understandable. For those opposed to corporal punishment, the practice is not only ineffective and irrational, it is also immoral. For many, corporal punishment implicates fundamental human rights. Framed in this way, there is little room for debate. Few legal questions, however, lend themselves to such dogmatism. This is especially true in the area of education law, where a number of different values and rights are commonly in tension. Corporal punishment alone, for example, implicates issues of religion, parental rights, children's rights, and federalism. The confusion in this area is exacerbated by the inconclusive social science research on the subject.

Under these circumstances, the question of whether corporal punishment is to be permitted in America's public schools should, as the courts have suggested, be left to the evolving standards of the local communities. A new norm in opposition to corporal punishment may yet emerge, or it may not. What is key is that if opponents of the practice are intent on waging a war for the hearts and minds of the American public on this issue, they will have to fight individual battles at the grassroots level, changing attitudes and laws one community at a time. Reliance on the Convention is likely to produce only a short-lived symbolic victory destined to degenerate into a disrespected legal nullity.

---

117. *See id.*

118. *Id.*

119. E.P. THOMPSON, WHIGS AND HUNTERS: THE ORIGIN OF THE BLACK ACT 263 (1975).

120. Communitarianism is a contemporary political and social philosophy that emphasizes moral consensus; persuasion as opposed to imposition; the social dimension of human existence; and the responsibilities that must be borne by citizens, individually and collectively. *See* THE RESPONSIVE COMMUNITARIAN PLATFORM: RIGHTS AND RESPONSIBILITIES preamble, *in* THE ESSENTIAL COMMUNITARIAN READER (Amitai Etzioni ed., 1998). Communitarianism also emphasizes policymaking and policy-implementation through the smallest social and political institutions available. *See id.*

121. *Id.*

B. An Alternative to Ratification: Changing Attitudes at the Grassroots Level

The roots of corporal punishment in America's schools exist at the micro level of American society and politics. Because educators stand in the place of parents, [122] the practice is linked to the family, the most basic unit of society. Moreover, as noted, corporal punishment has roots in religion, one of the most private of human affairs. Finally, decades of judicial deference to local officials and parents with respect to this and other matters of education create the legitimate expectation among the public that policy change in this area will be the product of local political processes. Accordingly, if a new norm rejecting corporal punishment is to emerge, it must be forged not through international law, the most global level of policymaking available to humankind, but through the changing of individual attitudes at the local, grassroots level. This need for grassroots change is a product of the process by which society defines - i.e., labels - human behaviors.

Opponents of corporal punishment often equate the practice with child abuse or other forms of physical violence condemned by society. For instance, in an article supporting ratification of the Convention, Susan Bitensky draws an analogy between child abuse, wife beating, and corporal punishment. [123] Such statements beg the ultimate question of whether corporal punishment in America's public schools is good or bad policy. In those jurisdictions in which reasonable corporal punishment is still permitted, should it now be criminalized just as spousal abuse has been criminalized? Is corporal punishment a form of child abuse or is it properly distinguishable? In equating corporal punishment with child and spousal abuse, opponents of corporal punishment convey their bare opinions on these questions, but do little more.

On its face, the analogy between corporal punishment, spousal abuse, and child abuse is not a particularly compelling one. Corporal punishment is readily distinguishable, for example, by the purpose underlying the practice. Corporal punishment is largely intended to foster conformity and is carried out, at least ostensibly, for the benefit of the child. Spousal and child abuse, in contrast, are more gratuitous forms of violence which reflect the pathology of the abuser rather than the needs of the recipient.

More importantly, those who equate corporal punishment with child abuse, spousal abuse, and other acts recognized by society as deviant must confront the reality that their views are remarkably out of sync with those of the larger

122. *See supra* note 51 and accompanying text.

123. Bitensky, *supra* note 28, at 52. *See also* David B. Friedman & Alma S. Friedman, *Pediatric Considerations in the Use of Corporal Punishment in the Schools*, *in* CORPORAL PUNISHMENT IN AMERICAN EDUCATION: READINGS IN HISTORY, PRACTICE AND ALTERNATIVES 337, 340 (Irwin A. Hyman & James H. Wise eds., 1979); STRAUS, *supra* note 1, at 81-97.

society. After all, every state in the United States allows the use of reasonable corporal punishment by parents, and half of these states permit the practice in their public schools. Indeed, one would be hard-pressed to find even an ardent advocate of corporal punishment who supports child abuse. Society draws a clear distinction between corporal punishment and these acts of domestic abuse.

By and large, our society defines child/spousal abuse and corporal punishment differently, reserving the label "deviant" for the former, but not the latter. [124] "Deviancy" is socially defined and is a fluid concept. [125] Today's accepted behavior may be tomorrow's deviancy. Those who urge that corporal punishment is akin to child or spouse abuse must really be arguing for a redefining of corporal punishment as deviant behavior.

Although spousal abuse and corporal punishment are by no means perfectly analogous, the history of spousal abuse in the United States can tell us quite a bit about this process of redefinition. Until fairly recently, spousal battering was viewed as falling within the private sphere of the family and largely beyond the law's reach. [126] The "problem" of battering and the social and legal construct of the "battered woman" did not exist in this country until the woman's movement identified it. [127] Through the years, the battered woman's movement has played a critical role in providing services for battered women, lobbying state governments for legal remedies to end the violence, and, perhaps most importantly, developing public education efforts to change perceptions about battering. [128]

Through the efforts of the feminist leaders behind the battered woman's movement, spousal abuse was redefined as deviant behavior. With this redefining came a plethora of state civil and criminal remedies addressing the plight of battering victims. [129] It was only after attitudes about spousal abuse were

124. The distinction was recognized by the Supreme Court in the Ingraham decision. In that decision, the Court stressed the fact that students who have been subject to physical force which exceeds the bounds of reasonableness, crossing the line from corporal punishment to abuse, have a variety of civil and criminal remedies available to them. Ingraham, 430 U.S. at 678. It should be noted, however, that to a large extent the available civil remedies are illusory, as school systems and their teachers enjoy varying degrees of immunity from suit. In addition, any lawsuit would occur after the punishment had actually been imposed. The punishment cannot be undone in a subsequent proceeding. *Id.* at 695 (White, J., dissenting).

125. *See generally* HOWARD S. BECKER, OUTSIDERS: STUDIES IN THE SOCIOLOGY OF DEVIANCE (1973); EMILE DURKHEIM, THE DIVISION OF LABOR IN SOCIETY (1984); Daniel Patrick Moynihan, *Defining Deviancy Down*, *in* CONSTRUCTIONS OF DEVIANCE: SOCIAL POWER, CONTEXT, AND INTRODUCTION 25 (Patricia A. Adler & Peter Adler eds., 1994).

126. *See* Elizabeth M. Schneider, *The Violence of Privacy*, *in* THE PUBLIC NATURE OF PRIVATE VIOLENCE 36, 43 (Martha Albertson Fineman & Roxanne Mykitiuk eds., 1994).

127. *See id.* at 40.

128. *See id.* at 43.

129. Civil remedies include restraining orders and orders of protection designed to promote the physical separation of the battering husband from his victim. Criminal statutes typically provide for the arrest of

changed at the state level that the federal government addressed domestic violence in the Violence Against Women Act of 1994,[130] putting a national gloss on policy which emerged in the states.[131]

For corporal punishment to be effectively banished from America's public schools, the practice must experience a similar redefining. The process should begin not with the imposition of international law on local schools, but rather, with the changing of individual attitudes at the local community level. Neither the redefining of corporal punishment, nor any other social undertaking for that matter, should be assigned to an institution that is larger than necessary to do the job.[132] What can be done at the local and state level should not be passed on to the federal or international level.[133] The creation of a new norm rejecting corporal punishment in America's public schools must be the product of a process of redefinition that takes place one community and state at a time.

Of course, from the standpoint of corporal punishment's opponents, it appears more efficient to wage and win one battle in the United States Senate than fifty in the states. In the long run, however, the efficient course may not produce the best substantive results for opponents of corporal punishment. Without the hearts and minds of a majority of Americans behind it, the quick, efficient victory achieved through ratification of the Convention is likely to be an empty one at best.

VII. Conclusion

The Convention's ratification faces significant obstacles in the United States. Corporal punishment's deep historical roots, its biblical underpinning, the ambiguous academic debate surrounding it, and the history of local control over the practice make unqualified ratification of the Convention unlikely. The fact that half of the states retain corporal punishment in their public schools is ample proof of the absence of popular consensus on this issue.

Ratification in the absence of popular consensus could come with untoward consequences, as this moral legislation would exist as law, but law without the public support necessary to give it effect. Proponents of the Convention hope

batterers, either for the violent act itself or for violation of a restraining order. These civil and criminal remedies are, to one degree or another, available in every state. *See id.* at 42.

130. 42 U.S.C. § 13981.

131. The Violence Against Women Act establishes a new federal civil right to be free from crimes of violence motivated by gender. The Act also makes available to victims of gender-based violence a number of civil remedies which can be secured by victims in the courts of the United States. *See also* Doe v. Doe, 929 F. Supp. 608 (D. Conn. 1996) (upholding the Violence Against Women Act as a permissible constitutional exercise of congressional authority under the Commerce Clause).

132. *See* The Responsive Communitarian Platform, *supra* note 120, preamble.

133. *See id.*

that ratification will, at a minimum, lead to the emergence of a new norm disfavoring the practice of corporal punishment. What is more likely, however, is that this top-down policymaking will only harden opposing positions on this controversial issue.

A new norm rejecting corporal punishment in America's public schools may yet emerge; but it will have to emerge by changing public attitudes, one local community at a time. This will require from opponents of corporal punishment considerable time, energy, and effort. There exists, in ratification, a simpler approach to what these individuals view as the "problem" of corporal punishment, but there exists no simpler solution.

PARENS PATRIAE IN THE MARKETPLACE OF IDEAS
Limitations of Freedom of Expression in the Public Schools

Jonathan K. Parker
CHARLESTON SOUTHERN UNIVERSITY

One of the major responsibilities of the public schools is to develop in students the capacity for self-governance within the context of a pluralistic society. In order to carry out this responsibility, though, schools must exercise extensive guidance and control over students—actions that are intuitively counterproductive to the development of autonomy, which is a necessary prerequisite for self-governance.

In numerous decisions involving free expression in the schools, the courts have referred to the schools as "marketplaces of ideas" in which different ideologies and viewpoints compete for the attention of students. At the same time, the courts have often invoked the doctrine of *parens patriae* as a justification for the authority that school officials have over students.

This essay will examine the tension between the doctrine of *parens patriae* and the notion that public schools are marketplaces of ideas in the context of a variety of venues of student expression. The venues examined will include speech in general, racially and sexually harassing speech, dress, Internet access, student publications, and community service requirements. School officials are then cautioned to use restraint in exercising the doctrine of *parens patriae*. While it is necessary for schools to function in an orderly manner and for teachers to be able to exercise control over their classrooms, students need to have opportunities to openly express controversial viewpoints and to become informed and active participants in the democratic process.

Parens Patriae

The doctrine of *parens patriae*, the idea that the state is the ultimate "father" or guardian of all children, has given school authorities virtually unlimited power over children in school settings. Although parents have a fundamental right to direct the upbringing of their children, they also have a corresponding responsibility to provide for their children's physical and mental well-being. When they fail to fulfill their duty to their children, the state (under the authority of *parens patriae*) is expected to intervene.

This doctrine began to take shape during the late 1800s and early 1900s. Previously, children were typically viewed as chattel property, possessing few, if any, rights and having no direct relationship to the state. As various laws regarding children began to be enacted during the Progressive Era (particularly those restricting child labor and requiring school attendance), children were seen as having duties to the general good of society (Tyack, James, and Benavot 1987). The responsibility for inculcating these duties fell to school authorities, and this inculcative function began to be seen as a principal goal of schooling. In addition, the maintaining of discipline and order in the schools was seen as the primary means by which to accomplish this goal (Lane 1995).

Although *parens patriae* established children as legal entities, it denied them the choice, autonomy, and self determination that the First Amendment guaranteed adults. While it afforded children protection from unscrupulous or uncaring adults, it provided no protection from the almost tyrannical power of the state to subject them to almost limitless regulation:

> During school hours a teacher is authorized to subject youngsters to regulation of the minutest details. A schoolteacher's control approaches total power. Unless students comply, unless they show up at a particular school, attend a particular class, behave in particular ways, complete particular tasks, and reach a particular level of skill at doing them, then teachers may reduce their grades, humiliate them, extend their school day, withhold their

Jonathan K. Parker has recently been appointed dean of the School of Education at Charleston Southern University in South Carolina. Previously, he served as director of Teacher Education at Huntington College in Indiana. He has published articles on accreditation issues in teacher education and is currently working on a longitudinal study of male elementary teachers.

> diplomas, and, in the last resort, initiate criminal proceedings against them and their parents for attempting to flee the school house....Students live under the threats of teachers, and teachers are authorized to bring those threats to bear on any wayward defiance of their regime. (Muir 1986, 110)

This authorization to use virtually any means necessary to maintain order and discipline in the schools even extended to the ability to control students' basic bodily functions. The state Supreme Court of Alabama recently refused to review an appellate decision that upheld such authority. In this case, a judge ruled that a teacher and school officials were immune from a lawsuit that had been filed when a teacher refused to allow a child who was suffering from diarrhea to use the rest room during class. The judge maintained that school officials may exercise "discretionary functions" in controlling student behavior ("High Court" 1997, 14).

The School as a Marketplace of Ideas

> The vigilant protection of constitutional freedoms is nowhere more vital than in the community of American schools....The classroom is peculiarly the "marketplace of ideas." The Nation's future depends upon leaders trained through wide exposure to that robust exchange of ideas which discovers truth "out of a multitude of tongues, [rather] than through any kind of authoritative selection." (*Keyishian v. Board of Regents of University of State of New York*, 385 U.S. 589, 603 [1967])

In contrast to the doctrine of *parens patriae*, the idea of the school as a marketplace of ideas requires a very different perspective regarding the legal status of school children. In the 1960s in cases like *Keyishian* (quoted above) and *Tinker v. Des Moines Independent Community School District* (393 U.S. 503, 506 [1969]), the Supreme Court began to assert the idea that schools must begin training students in the democratic processes that allow us to be self-governing. The Court reasoned that if students are to become active participants in a democratic and pluralistic society, then it is important for them to have opportunities to hear and express a variety of political viewpoints while at school. This perspective is in keeping with research on the reasoning capabilities of young adolescents: they are able to maturely conceptualize civil liberties and are able to apply those conceptualizations in concrete situations (Helwig 1995).

In establishing First Amendment rights for students, the Court also established the idea that students have fundamental rights (beyond the right to an education) that must be respected by school authorities. Educators could no longer enjoy absolute authority over students as they had under *parens patriae*. Regarding student expression, schools could continue to have broad discretionary powers to regulate students except when it is clear that the expression is "pure speech," that is, not clearly associated with the school, not harmful to other students, or not inciting a substantial disruption or material interference to the functioning of the school.

General Speech

The supremacy of the *parens patriae* doctrine over all speech except for that which can be designated as "pure" was clearly articulated in *Bethel School District No. 403 v. Fraser* (106 U.S. 3159 [1986]). In this case, a high school student made a nominating speech in a school assembly that employed rather graphic sexual metaphors in extolling the qualifications of a particular candidate for student office. In the Supreme Court's review of the case, it was affirmed that school officials' mandate to "establish standards of civic and mature conduct" under the authority of *parens patriae* outweighed student rights of free expression, even in the context of a "political" speech. This was in stark contrast with the Court's insistence that political speech among adults be afforded absolute protection even if it is lewd and immature (*Hustler Magazine v. Falwell*, 485 U.S. 46 [1988]).

Racially and Sexually Harassing Speech

Schools have particularly broad powers to regulate speech that is either racially or sexually harassing. In March 1994, the United States Department of Education's Office for Civil Rights adopted a "Notice of Investigative Guidance on Racial Incidents and Harassment against Students." The notice stated that if verbal harassment is to the degree that a student cannot benefit from the educational services of a school district and the district does not stop the harassment, the district can be found in violation of Title VI of the U.S. Education Code (Stern 1994).

Although there have been cases at the college level in which overly broad and vague racial and/or sexual harassment policies have been overturned by the courts,[1] policies at the K–12 level have not yet been challenged except in the court of public opinion. One well-publicized case was that of a kindergarten boy who was suspended from school for planting a kiss on the cheek of a girl in his class. In this case, school officials were humiliated into developing a sexual harassment policy that took into account the age and sexual maturity of the parties involved.

Dress

Although *Tinker* related directly to a school dress issue (students were suspended for wearing black armbands to protest the conflict in Vietnam), the Supreme Court made it clear that school authorities were well within their purview to regulate student dress. Only in those cases where a particular expression through dress could reasonably be construed as "pure speech," such as the wearing of armbands to protest war, could students assert their First Amendment rights. In all other cases, it has been clear that school authorities have broad powers to regulate student dress. In recent years, schools have utilized these powers to a greater extent than in the past. Two trends in the regulation of student dress have been the outlawing of gang-related attire and mandates for school uniforms.

Two recent court decisions illustrate the rather tricky legal ground that school authorities tread when trying to regulate gang-related attire. In one, a district court ruled that a dress code prohibiting earrings was constitutional provided the school district established a rationale for the policy. Because the school district was able to document gang-related activity in and around the schools and to show that earrings were a part of gang attire, the prohibition was allowed. However, in another instance, a school district was not able to document gang activity in its elementary and middle schools so its prohibition of professional and college sports-team attire was allowed only at the high school level where the documentation was sufficient (Lane, Swartz, Richardson, and Van Berkum 1994).

A more effective means of dealing with problems associated with student dress has been to mandate the wearing of uniforms. When school districts have taken this tack, they have not had to provide any rationale other than linking the mandate with the furtherance of the educational mission of the district. Because mandatory uniform policies deprive all students of their freedom of expression equally, the courts have tended to defer to the discretion of school officials. In the one case that has reached the courts, a mandatory, no opt-out uniform policy in Maricopa, Arizona, was upheld in district court in 1995. Experts in this area have warned, however, that in the future, federal courts may require "actual evidence that uniforms enhance the learning environment" (Paliokas, Futrell, and Rist 1996, 35).

Internet Access

As more and more schools have connected to the Internet, the potential for misuse of this access has become a major concern for educators in a number of areas. Students might access Web sites or chat rooms that are sexually explicit. One student, showing a sexually explicit Web page to another student, might make the school vulnerable to charges of sexual harassment (Tenopir 1995). Students might also misuse electronic mail—for example, sending harassing messages to a teacher or another student. Finally, students may unknowingly link up with sexual predators who are known to prowl cyberspace (Frazier 1995).

Schools have responded to these concerns in a variety of ways. The least restrictive approach has been for a school to develop a technology code of conduct. Students are given individual accounts for access to the Internet that are routinely monitored. If a student misuses his or her account, Internet privileges are lost for a period of time (Frazier 1995). Another approach has been for schools to use blocking software. These programs, such as Cybersitter™ from Solid Oak Software, have the capacity to screen out any Web site, newsgroup, or chat line "that focuses on topics such as adult or sexual issues, illegal activities, bigotry, racism, drugs, or pornography." [2] In addition to restricting access to sites that have been put on a "bad sites list" (often updated daily), this software will screen out objectionable text from e-mail or from Web sites, newsgroups, or chat lines that have not been blacklisted.

While many public libraries and schools are already installing blocking software on their computer systems, some civil libertarians are attempting to "block the blocking." Some claim:

> Important information—such as how to conduct a self-examination for breast cancer—would be blocked by the software, which looks for key words, such as "breast," to determine whether a World-Wide Web site is pornographic.[3]

It is likely that the courts will support those schools that install blocking software on their systems. In cases involving the selection of curriculum materials, the courts have consistently sided with schools when they have decided not to purchase certain books for the library or to exclude particular materials in the curriculum. Since the information accessed by school computer systems can easily be construed as "curriculum materials," it is pretty much a foregone conclusion that blocking software will be able to restrict both student speech and student access to information over the Internet.

Student Publications

The question of what students could or could not publish in school-sponsored publications was somewhat unclear until 1988. In that year, the Supreme Court granted school officials sweeping power to control student expression in *Hazelwood School District v. Kuhlmeier* (108 U.S. 562 [1988]). In this case, a high school principal forbade the publication of two articles that were about to appear in the student newspaper. One discussed pregnancy among students while the other interviewed students who were children of divorced parents. The court reasoned that the principal's actions were justified because of "legitimate pedagogical concerns" and because this was "associative speech"—that is, speech that the school had some official association with as opposed to the "pure speech" of the black armbands in the *Tinker* case.

Although student publications in schools had often been subject to prior review previous to *Hazelwood* (Salomone 1994), this ruling made it clear that school authorities have complete control over any student speech that can be construed as being in association with the school. The enormous impact that this ruling potentially has on chilling student expression and compromising student understanding of democracy was apparent to some legal experts at the time. In a stinging dissent, Justice Brennan wrote:

> [This kind of censorship] is particularly insidious [from a high school principal] to whom the public entrusts the task of inculcating in its youth an appreciation for the cherished democratic liberties that our Constitution guarantees—what the majority lost sight of in its ruling was that the primary mission of public schools is to prepare young people for life as adults under a government that has vested its citizens with enormous individual responsibilities. To teach them that their school officials may censor is to teach them that government may censor. It prepares them to expect and accept somebody telling them what they may know and what they may say. (*Hazelwood School District v. Kuhlmeier,* 108 U.S. 562 [1988])

Religious Expression

Most litigation concerning religion in the schools has focused on what teachers and school officials may not promote in terms of religious expression. For example, in *Abington School District v. Schempp* (374 U.S. 203 [1963]), officially sanctioned school prayers were forbidden, and in *Lemon v. Kurtzman* (403 U.S. 602 [1971]) attempts by Rhode Island and Pennsylvania to subsidize instruction in non religious subjects at parochial schools were prohibited. However, recent guidelines developed by the Department of Education give students a fair degree of latitude in religious expression:

> Schools may not forbid students acting on their own from expressing their religious views solely because they are of a religious nature....This means that students can pray voluntarily in a non-disruptive manner, say grace over lunch, have a Bible at school and read it in study hall, and express their religious beliefs in their homework, artwork, and other written and oral assignments when appropriate to the lesson. In addition, during non-instructional time, student religious groups can meet on school grounds when other non-curriculum clubs meet. Students may also distribute religious literature on the same terms as other non-curriculum related student literature is distributed. (Riley 1995, 6)

This does not mean, however, that religious students have carte blanche to use school resources for proselyting purposes, particularly at the elementary level. In two recent cases, students were not allowed to use an oral presentation or "show and tell" time as a platform for expressing religious beliefs. Using precedent established in *Hazelwood,* the courts in both these cases indicated that the schools had a "legitimate pedagogical concern" in restricting the exposure of elementary age students to the religious beliefs of other students (Bjorklun 1994).

Community Service Requirements

More and more school districts are utilizing community service as a graduation requirement. In 1990, Bethlehem (Pennsylvania) School District adopted a community-service graduation requirement of sixty hours for high school students. Students could choose from a variety of social service providers or develop their own program. In 1993, two students sued, claiming that the requirement violated their First Amendment free speech rights because they were being forced to express altruism. They claimed it also violated the Thirteenth Amendment guarantee against involuntary servitude. The district and appellate courts ruled in favor of the school district, indicating that although the students were required to perform community service, they were not required to believe in altruism. The courts also noted that a "civic duty" exception to the Thirteenth Amendment allows for mandatory participation in military service and public works projects (Bittner 1994).

Conclusion

Are the schools truly marketplaces of ideas, or has *parens patriae* so compromised student free expression that the voters and leaders of tomorrow are not developing the skills necessary for participation in a free and democratic society? While it is imperative that school officials have the power and authority to operate schools in an orderly manner, it seems that recent trends in the abrogation of student First Amendment rights may have gone too far. It seems reasonable that school authorities should be able to impose dress and grooming standards on students, but to require all students in a district to wear uniforms seems to go beyond what is necessary to maintain a safe learning environment in schools. A more reasonable approach may be to designate certain schools in a district as "academies" in which students are required to wear uniforms. In this situation parents would be able to choose whether or not their children will wear uniforms.

It also seems reasonable for schools to have some control over student use of the Internet. However, schools need to be diligent in making sure that students have access to all information that is not prurient in nature. It is also important that schools not restrict student communication over the Internet (via e-mail, chat-rooms, or newsgroups) that is merely controversial or political.

The new guidelines regarding religious expression are a positive step, and the recent rulings regarding religious expression at the elementary level are probably a legitimate utilization of the *parens patriae* principle. However, the almost limitless authority of school officials to quash racially or sexually harassing speech and to require community service for graduation is cause for some concern. The First Amendment protects bigots and sexists, and the involuntary servitude imposed by community service requirements is really more akin to slavery than to the draft: there is no "national emergency" that requires drafting students into the ranks of community service volunteers. School authorities at the K–12 level need to be just as careful as post-secondary educators in crafting policies regarding racially and sexually harassing speech that are not so vague and overly broad that they transcend common sense. They also should carefully consider whether the goals attained by requiring community service for graduation are worth the cost of trampling on students' First and Thirteenth Amendment rights even if the courts have given them the authority to do so.

Looking beyond whether or not the principle of *parens patriae* is unduly restricting student speech, a greater concern may be the general lack of civic training that takes place in public schools. It seems that most students deal with the Constitution and the Bill of Rights as abstract documents in discrete units of study in history or political science classes. Students seldom get the chance to examine cases like *Tinker* or *Fraser* or *Hazelwood* and grapple with the free speech issues they have engendered. Is it, therefore, surprising that young adults are as politically apathetic as they seem to be? If we are really serious about using the schools to prepare students to be active participants in the democratic processes that have kept our country vibrant and free for the past two hundred years, then it is time that we make an effort to infuse civic education throughout the curriculum and find ways to get students excited about participating in the political process.

NOTES

[1] For example, in *Doe v. University of Michigan* (721 F. Supp. 852, 856 [E.D. Mich. 1989]), a federal court ruled that the racial and sexual harassment policy of the University of Michigan was both overly broad and vague. Vague language included "stigmatize" and "victimize." In *Iota XI Chapter of Sigma Chi Fraternity v. George Mason University* (993 F. 2d 43 [4th Cir. 1993]), it was found that sanctions against a fraternity for an "ugly woman contest" violated students' free speech rights.

[2] Quoted from "Cybersitter™ Advertisement" at «http://www.solidoak.com/cysitter.htm».

[3] See "Libraries and Schools Face New Rules on Internet Use" by Jeffrey R. Young at «http://www.chronicle.com/che-data/internet.dir/newres.dir/newres.htm».

WORKS CITED

Bittner, Marie. "The Constitutionality of Public School Community Service Programs." *The Clearing House* 68 (November/December 1994): 115–117.

Bjorklun, Eugene C. "Show and Tell, the Establishment of Religion, and Freedom of Speech." *West's Education Law Quarterly* 3 (January 1994)): 1–10.

Frazier, Max K. "Caution: Students on Board the Internet." *Educational Leadership* 53 (October 1995): 26–27.

Helwig, Charles C. "Adolescents' and Young Adults' Conceptions of Civil Liberties: Freedom of Speech and Religion." *Child Development* 66 (February 1995): 152–166.

"High Court Refuses to Revive Lawsuit in Bathroom-Pass Case." *Education Week* (22 January 1997): 14.

Lane, Kenneth E., Stanley L. Swartz, Michael D. Richardson, and Dennis W. Van Berkum. "You Aren't What You Wear." *American School Board Journal* 181 (March 1994): 64–65.

Lane, Robert Wheeler. *Beyond the Schoolhouse Gate.* Philadelphia: Temple University Press, 1995.

Muir, William K. "Teachers' Regulation of the Classroom." In *School Days, Rule Days,* edited by David L. Kirp and Donald N. Jensen, 110–127. Philadelphia: Falmer Press, 1986.

Paliokas, Kathleen L., Mary H. Futrell, and Ray C. Rist. "Trying Uniforms on for Size." *American School Board Journal* 183 (May 1996): 32–35.

Riley, Richard. "Common Ground on Religion. From the Desk of the Secretary of Education." *Teaching PreK–8* 26 (October 1995): 6.

Salomone, Rosemary C. "The Impact of *Hazelwood v. Kuhlmeier* on Local Policy and Practice." *NASSP Bulletin* 78 (December 1994): 47–61.

Stern, Ralph D. "Hate Speech: Political Correctness v. the First Amendment." Paper presented at the annual meeting of the National Organization on Legal Problems of Education, San Diego CA (November 1994). ERIC Document Reproduction Service No. ED 378 695.

Tenopir, Carol. "Internet Issues in Reference." *Library Journal* 120 (1 October 1995): 28, 30.

Tyack, David, Thomas James, and Aaron Benavot. *Law and the Shaping of Public Education, 1785–1954.* Madison: University of Wisconsin Press, 1987.

BEHIND THE SCENES IN IOWA'S GREATEST CASE: WHAT IS NOT IN THE OFFICIAL RECORD OF *TINKER V. DES MOINES INDEPENDENT COMMUNITY SCHOOL DISTRICT*

*John W. Johnson**

TABLE OF CONTENTS

I. INTRODUCTION[1]

I am very pleased to be here this morning to say a few words about *Tinker v. Des Moines Independent Community School District*[2] which, even after thirty years, is still the United States Supreme Court's leading decision on student rights. As many of you know, the *Tinker* case is studied in law schools, in colleges of education, in a variety of courses at universities, high schools, and even elementary schools. It is frequently alluded to in the Iowa press and is even brought up occasionally in casual conversations. No less an authority than "the nation's newspaper," *USA Today*, has bestowed the sobriquet of "Iowa's greatest

---

* Professor and Head of the Department of History at the University of Northern Iowa, Cedar Falls, Iowa.

1. This Article was adapted from an address at the Belin Lamson McCormick Zumbach & Flynn Constitutional Law Symposium held at Drake University Law School on October 9, 1999. Portions of the text of that address appeared previously in published form. *See* JOHN W. JOHNSON, THE STRUGGLE FOR STUDENT RIGHTS: *TINKER V. DES MOINES* AND THE 1960S (1997); John W. Johnson, *"Dear Mr. Justice": Public Correspondence with Members of the Supreme Court*, J. S. CT. HIST. 2, 101-12 (1997). Permission to draw from these publications for this Article has been granted by the University Press of Kansas and the *Journal of Supreme Court History*.

2. Tinker v. Des Moines Indep. Community Sch. Dist., 393 U.S. 503 (1969).

case" upon the polite demonstration of a handful of Des Moines young people in the 1960s that brought constitutional protections to the nation's students.[3]

Iowans' fascination with *Tinker* goes beyond familiarity. There is, I believe, an almost proprietary relationship that residents of the Hawkeye State have with *Tinker*. While performing the research for my book, *The Struggle for Student Rights*,[4] and in talking to readers since the book's publication, I have been impressed by how many Iowans remember the case, know something about the litigants or their attorneys, or just recall what the Des Moines schools were like in the 1960s. *Tinker* is not only Iowa's greatest case; it is Iowa's favorite case. Last year, when Governor Tom Vilsack was soliciting suggestions for a new state motto, I considered proposing the following: "Iowa: Home of Corn, Hogs, and *Tinker v. Des Moines*."

Over this past summer, after accepting the kind invitation to deliver this address, I pondered what aspects of *Tinker* to share with you. I decided not to say much about the facts in the dispute—the story of the armband episode is, after all, fairly well-known—especially to this audience. I have also elected not to assess the place of *Tinker* in American law—that is the focus of other sessions at this symposium, in which individuals more knowledgeable than I regarding education law will comment upon where *Tinker* fits in the state and country's legal tapestry. Rather, I have decided to tell some stories—three of them to be exact—about what I believe are intriguing dimensions of the black armband case that did not make it into the official legal record. Historians, I believe, tender some of their best contributions to public discourse when they unearth nuggets of novel detail or insight about topics previously thought to be well-mined.

II. THE OVERLOOKED LITIGANT

Quite appropriately, most accounts of the armband case that have appeared in the press or in law journals have focused attention upon John or Mary Beth Tinker.[5] However, there was a third named plaintiff, a very interesting young man named Christopher Eckhardt. Because there were two Tinkers and only one Eckhardt among the named plaintiffs, the short title of the case, as determined by the Clerk of the District Court for the Southern District of Iowa, became *Tinker v. Des Moines*—not *Eckhardt v. Des Moines*.[6]

---

3. Wayne Beissert & Tony Mauro, *Cases Across USA Help Shape Law*, USA TODAY, May 22, 1987, at 9F.

4. *See* JOHNSON, *supra* note 1.

5. *See id.* at 182-85, 189.

6. Dan Johnston, the attorney who represented the Tinkers and Christopher Eckhardt, also played a role in selecting the short title for the case. He listed the names of John and Mary Beth Tinker before that of Christopher Eckhardt on the Complaint. Interview with Dan Johnston,

Once the armband dispute officially became the "*Tinker* case," attention flowed toward John and Mary Beth rather than Christopher. The name Tinker was easier to pronounce and spell than Eckhardt, and it lent itself easily to various plays on words such as "Tinkering with *Tinker*." Moreover, the Tinker brother and sister combination made this a warm-hearted family story further enhanced by the fact John and Mary Beth's younger siblings, Hope and Paul (elementary school students in 1965), also wore armbands to school.[7] In addition, Mary Beth was the most photographed of the three plaintiffs.

Because the Tinker last name was the one that most people familiar with the case recognized, it was John and Mary Beth who, in later years, were asked to make appearances, accept awards, and talk about the case to sympathetic audiences, not Chris Eckhardt. These considerations reinforced the name "Tinker" in the public mind and obscured the name "Eckhardt." Even the cover of my own book carries the familiar UPI photograph of John and Mary Beth Tinker; the editor and I simply could not locate a good picture of the Tinkers *and* Chris Eckhardt. To redress the balance, I want to tell you some things about Chris Eckhardt this morning that do not derive from the official record of the case. Thus, the first story I wish to "submit for your approval"—as Rod Serling used to say on his popular mid-1960s television show "The Twilight Zone"—can be titled "The Overlooked Litigant."[8]

Chris Eckhardt was fifteen and a sophomore at Des Moines's Theodore Roosevelt High School in late 1965.[9] At the time of the armband case, Chris's father was a clinical psychologist and a faculty member at the College of Osteopathic Medicine and Surgery in Des Moines.[10] His mother was the Des Moines chapter president of the Women's International League for Peace and

---

Attorney for *Tinker* plaintiffs in Des Moines, Iowa (May 17, 1994) [*hereinafter* Johnston Interview].

7. *See* JOHNSON, *supra* note 1, at 26.

8. A longer account of the role of Christopher Eckhardt in the black armband case will appear in John W. Johnson, *The Overlooked Litigant in* Tinker v. Des Moines Independent Community School District, *in* TIME TO RECLAIM (Sandra Van Burkleo et al., forthcoming 2000). Unless otherwise noted, the portrait of Chris Eckhardt in this paper is drawn from the following: Telephone Interview with Christopher Eckhardt, *Tinker* plaintiff (May 4, 1994) [*hereinafter* Christopher Eckhardt Interview]; Telephone Interview with Margaret Eckhardt, mother of *Tinker* plaintiff (May 4, 1994) [*hereinafter* Margaret Eckhardt Interview]; and from clippings and mementos of Christopher Eckhardt provided to the author.

9. JOHNSON, *supra* note 1, at 9.

10. *Id.* at 9-10.

Freedom.[11] His parents were active in the 1960s in the same small Des Moines "peace community" that included the Reverend and Mrs. Tinker.[12]

As was the case with the Tinker children, Chris was exposed to liberal politics throughout his formative years.[13] His mother recalls Chris as a young boy joining her for speeches and meetings with various civil rights advocates who came to Des Moines.[14] Included among these visitors were black Georgia politician Julian Bond and John Howard Griffin, the author of *Black Like Me*.[15] Chris had also accompanied his parents on a number of civil rights marches in the middle 1960s.[16] At the November 1965 anti-Vietnam War March on Washington that provided the inspiration for the Des Moines armband demonstration the following month, Chris carried a sign that read "Follow the Geneva Accords of 1954."[17] At Roosevelt he helped form what he describes as a "political action discussion group" which brought public figures to school to talk with interested students.[18] Chris and his parents were members of Des Moines's First Unitarian Church,[19] and Chris was later vice president of the Unitarian Youth League.[20]

As a high school student, Chris was a busy young man. He maintained about a B+ academic average and was an elected representative to student government.[21] He was a member of the track team, had won fishing and weight lifting trophies, and would later be voted "most likely to succeed" in his class.[22] He also was voted the student with the cleanest locker.[23] Outside of school he was a Boy Scout, a youth leader at church, had a paper route, and a lawn-mowing and snow-shoveling business.[24] Dan Johnston, the attorney for the armband wearing students, characterized young Chris as a "regular kid."[25]

There was, however, a puckish side to Chris.[26] During his Roosevelt High years he was a member of what he describes as a group of about thirty male

---

11. *Id.* at 10.
12. *Id.*
13. *Id.*
14. *Id.*
15. *Id.*
16. *Id.*
17. *Id.*
18. *Id.*
19. *Id.*
20. *Id.*
21. *Id.*
22. *Id.*
23. *Id.*
24. *Id.* at 10-11.
25. Johnston Interview, *supra* note 6.
26. JOHNSON, *supra* note 1, at 11.

students who called themselves the "All Center Bums."[27] They hung out together after school and on weekends in an apartment they rented in downtown Des Moines.[28] At school assemblies they sat in their own section of the auditorium and refused to cheer for the Roosevelt athletic teams or to rise for the National Anthem.[29]

On the day before the December 1965 armband demonstration, word circulated in various Des Moines schools that a protest of some sort was imminent.[30] Chris recalls that gym teachers and coaches at Roosevelt were upset at the possibility of a protest against the Vietnam War.[31] Instead of conducting calisthenics to the chant of "Beat East High"—as was usually the case—he recalled that the gym teachers on that day encouraged students to substitute the phrase "Beat the Vietcong."[32] The coaches at Roosevelt also made it known that students wearing armbands to class were communist sympathizers and that they, as coaches and teachers, could not be held responsible for what might happen to students who demonstrated such a lack of patriotism.[33] Confirmation of this indirect threat took place after gym class on Wednesday when Chris and a friend were confronted by a group of angry male students who screamed at them: "If you [wear armbands tomorrow] . . . you'll find our fists in your face and our foot up your ass."[34]

On Thursday, December 16, 1965, Chris Eckhardt and a friend were driven to school by Chris's father.[35] Under his winter coat Chris was wearing a cocoa-

---

27. *Id.*

28. *Id.*

29. *Id.*

30. Christopher Eckhardt Interview, *supra* note 8.

31. *Id.* Although the media generally portrayed the demonstration as an "antiwar protest," the Tinkers, Christopher Eckhardt, and the other participating students were not necessarily against the Vietnam War. JOHNSON, *supra* note 1, at 4, 19. They maintained that they wore their armbands for two reasons: to mourn the casualties in the Vietnam War—American and Vietnamese—and to promote an extension of the anticipated "Christmas truce" in the War so as to encourage peace talks between the belligerents. *Id.* at 68.

32. Christopher Eckhardt Interview, *supra* note 8. The Roosevelt High football coach, Donald Prior, stated the chant "Beat the Vietcong" sprang from the students themselves as a form of "spontaneous combustion." Stephen Seplow, *Dispute over High School Chant of 'Beat Vietcong'*, DES MOINES REG., Dec. 20, 1965, at 1. Prior indicated that he saw no reason to stop the chanting because the boys were just "proving their Americanism." *Id.*

33. JOHNSON, *supra* note 1, at 8.

34. *Id.*

35. Unless otherwise indicated, the events of December 16, 1965, related here were drawn either from the Christopher Eckhardt Interview and the Margaret Eckhardt Interview, or from the federal district court testimony of Chris Eckhardt in the Transcript of *Tinker v. Des Moines Independent Community School District*, 258 F. Supp. 971 (S.D. Iowa 1966) (No. 7-1810-C-1) (located in the office of the Iowa Civil Liberties Union, Des Moines, Iowa).

colored sports jacket with a black armband of about one and one-fourth inches in width pinned to one of his sleeves.[36] Chris went immediately to his locker, removed his winter coat to reveal the armband, and then he proceeded to the principal's office to turn himself in.[37] As he saw it, he was engaging in an act of peaceful civil disobedience, that is, intentionally breaking a rule that he believed to be unjust and submitting to punishment so as to test the legality of the rule.[38] On his way to the principal's office Chris was confronted by the captain of the football team who attempted to rip the armband off his jacket.[39] After a brief scuffle, the football player left Eckhardt with words to the effect that he had better take the armband off in the principal's office or he would come looking for him.[40]

Shortly after this tense encounter, Chris arrived in the school's administrative office suite and proceeded to cool his heels for about forty-five minutes during which time various students filed by the glass enclosed office and taunted him with caustic remarks like "you're dead."[41] Eventually, Don Blackman, the Vice-Principal of Roosevelt, summoned Chris to an inner office.[42] Blackmun informed Chris that wearing a black armband violated school policy and asked him to remove it.[43] Chris refused, explaining that he was engaging in an act of civil disobedience by intentionally violating what he felt was an illegal policy.[44] Chris and Blackman talked for several more minutes; Chris persisted in his refusal to remove the armband.[45] At some point in the conversation, Velma Cross, the "girls' advisor" at Roosevelt joined Blackmun and Eckhardt.[46] She proceeded to tell Chris that he was "too young to have opinions."[47] She also told him that, if he was suspended, he could look for another high school to attend because they did not want him back at Roosevelt.[48]

Once it became clear that Chris was not going to follow the order to remove the armband, Blackman called his mother.[49] Mrs. Eckhardt said that she was aware that Chris had worn the armband that morning and that she felt he had

---

36. JOHNSON, *supra* note 1, at 16.
37. *Id.*
38. *Id.*
39. *Id.* at 16-17.
40. *Id.*
41. *Id.* at 17.
42. *Id.*
43. *Id.*
44. *Id.*
45. *Id.*
46. *Id.*
47. *Id.*
48. *Id.*
49. *Id.* at 18.

the right to wear it at school.[50] Blackman informed her that Christopher would be suspended if he did not remove the offending piece of cloth.[51] She responded by saying, "So be it," and Chris was suspended and sent home.[52] A few weeks later the suspensions of Chris, Mary Beth, and John Tinker, and two other students were upheld by the Des Moines School Board after two very contentious meetings.[53]

Chris's memories of what transpired in the aftermath of his suspension are illustrative of the risks and rewards that accrue to someone who takes an unpopular stand. He recalls occasions on which he was harassed by being called a "communist" or a "peace boy."[54] The Eckhardt family also kept a file of the letters and postcards on the armband affair that they received in the late 1960s.[55] For example, one letter addressed to Chris's parents contained a typed statement on the danger of communist subversion of America's youth allegedly perpetrated by leftist educators.[56] At points in this letter where "educators" or "professors" were mentioned, the anonymous sender had added the phrase "& parents."[57] Another postcard addressed to the Eckhardts read in part: "It seems that someone needs to psychoanalysis [sic] you two parents for what you are putting your children thru. . . . I'd do a lot of thinking about this . . . because it looks like your [sic] going to have a Harvey Lee Oswald [sic] on your hands . . . . Also, if your wife doesn't like this country then she can always go back to England and Germany . . . ."[58]

Not all of the mail Chris Eckhardt received was condemnatory. In January 1966 he received a letter from a Princeton, New Jersey rabbi who identified himself as a former student in the Des Moines public schools.[59] The rabbi's letter read in part: "I was filled with admiration for your sensitivity. It . . . requires a great deal to identify . . . with the suffering of one's 'enemies'. . . . I was [also] inspired by your courage. It is not easy, in these times, to affirm basic human values."[60]

---

50. *Id.*
51. *Id.*
52. *Id.*
53. *See id.* at 31-47.
54. *Id.* at 57.
55. The letters and postcards mentioned in these paragraphs are from the clippings and mementos of Christopher Eckhardt provided to the author from his family.
56. JOHNSON, *supra* note 1, at 57.
57. *Id.*
58. *Id.*
59. *Id.* at 58.
60. *Id.*

Chris Eckhardt has led a varied and interesting life since he wore his arm band to school in December 1965. He was elected to the Roosevelt High student council during his junior year in school, but he also continued as a member of the All Center Bums.[61] During the remainder of his high school years he had occasional disagreements with authorities. For example, he was arrested on a Des Moines sidewalk in March 1968 for throwing a snowball at a policeman.[62] When Eckhardt gave his name to the arresting officer, the reaction was: "Oh yeah, we know about you. We talk about you down at the office sometimes. You're that armband kid, you're that troublemaker."[63]

Eckhardt took his first college courses at Mankato State University in 1968.[64] Since then he has attended a number of other colleges—including Drake University—and held a variety of jobs. His employment résumé includes: selling life insurance, producing cable television programs, publishing a peace-oriented newspaper, and working for state governments in corrections and social services.[65] In 1978 he ran unsuccessfully for the Des Moines School Board—the same body that had upheld his school suspension thirteen years earlier.[66] In 1994, his persistence in college finally paid off with his receipt of a baccalaureate degree in political science from the University of South Florida.[67] Eckhardt says that his future portends more education, either in law school or graduate study in history. When I last checked, Chris was still living in Florida.

III. THE RELUCTANT JUSTICE

The second story I want to relate concerns the curious route that *Tinker* followed to get to the United States Supreme Court and finally to emerge from the pen of Justice Abe Fortas. I call it "The Reluctant Justice."

Shortly after their suspensions, the affected students and their parents filed a complaint in the United States District Court for the Southern District of Iowa.[68] After a hearing in the summer of 1966, Judge Roy Stephenson found in

---

61. *Id.* at 204.
62. *Id.*
63. *Id.*
64. *Id.* On September 18, 1998, Mankato State University underwent a name change and is now Minnesota State University, Mankato. *Minnesota State University, Mankato—A Brief History & Profile* (last modified Sept. 14, 1998) <http://www.mankato.msus.edu/dept/univops/history/>.
65. JOHNSON, *supra* note 1, at 204.
66. *Id.*
67. *Id.*
68. Complaint, Tinker v. Des Moines Indep. Community Sch. Dist., 258 F. Supp. 971 (S.D. Iowa 1966) (No. 7-1810-C-1) (located in the office of the Iowa Civil Liberties Union, Des Moines, Iowa).

favor of the Des Moines School District.[69] The Tinkers and Chris Eckhardt appealed Judge Stephenson's ruling.[70] In 1967, the case was argued twice before the Court of Appeals for the Eighth Circuit.[71] The second hearing before an en banc panel of the appeals court in the circuit resulted in a 4-4 split.[72] Supreme Court rules dictate that a tie vote does not disturb a lower federal court ruling.[73] In late 1967, Dan Johnston and the litigants decided to seek United States Supreme Court review of the armband prohibition.[74] Johnston and joint counsel for the American Civil Liberties Union petitioned for a writ of certiorari.[75] In early 1968, the nation's highest court, without explanation, granted the writ of certiorari thus enabling the case to come before the United States Supreme Court in oral argument in the following October Term.[76]

Published orders of certiorari never indicate which Justices vote for a petition. Occasionally one or two strong-minded Justices will file a written dissent to a granting of certiorari, thus revealing their own preferences. There were no written dissents to the granting of certiorari in the *Tinker* case, so at the time the votes on the petition for certiorari were unknown. However, years after the fact, the private papers of several of the *Tinker* Court Justices were made available to scholars,[77] revealing the breakdown of certiorari votes in the *Tinker* case was five in favor of hearing the case: William Brennan, William O.

---

69. Tinker v. Des Moines Indep. Community Sch. Dist., 258 F. Supp. at 973, *aff'd*, 383 F.2d 988 (8th Cir. 1967), *rev'd*, 393 U.S. 503 (1969).

70. Tinker v. Des Moines Indep. Community Sch. Dist., 383 F.2d 988 (8th Cir. 1967).

71. *Id.* at 988.

72. *See id.*

73. *See generally* Laird v. Tatum, 409 U.S. 824, 837-38 (1972) ("The disqualification of one Justice raises the possibility of an affirmance of a judgment below by an equally divided court. The consequence attending such a result is of course, that the principal of law presented by the case is left unsettled."); *see also* Arizona v. United States Dist. Court, 459 U.S. 1191, 1191 (1983) (citing 28 U.S.C. § 2109).

74. Tinker v. Des Moines Indep. Community Sch. Dist., 383 F.2d 988 (8th Cir. 1967), *petition for writ filed*, 36 U.S.L.W. 3323 (U.S. Jan. 17, 1968) (No. 1034).

75. *See id.*

76. Tinker v. Des Moines Indep. Community Sch. Dist., 383 F.2d 988 (1967), *cert. granted*, 390 U.S. 942 (1968).

77. I have reviewed the private Supreme Court Papers on *Tinker* in the collections of Hugo L. Black (Box 409), William Brennan (Box 416), Thurgood Marshall (Box 532), William O. Douglas (Box 1430), and Earl Warren (Box 385)—all in the Manuscript Division, Library of Congress, Washington, D.C. *See generally* JOHNSON, *supra* note 1, at 165-69, 190-94 (discussing personal notes of the Justices, as well as letters received by Justices regarding the *Tinker* case). For Abe Fortas's thoughts on *Tinker*, I have relied principally on LAURA KALMAN, ABE FORTAS: A BIOGRAPHY 186-290 (1990). Kalman's account is drawn mainly from the Abe Fortas Supreme Court Papers in the Yale University Archives.

Douglas, Thurgood Marshall, Potter Stewart, and Earl Warren; and four against: Hugo Black, Abe Fortas, John Marshall Harlan, and Byron White.[78]

Given their well-known positions on civil liberties issues, the certiorari alignment of the nine members of the Warren Court in *Tinker* was predictable but with two exceptions. As consistent supporters of civil liberties in past constitutional decisions, the negative votes on certiorari of Justices Black and Fortas are puzzling. Justice Black would later dissent in the *Tinker* case, thus explaining in cold print why he was against the students' appeal from the start.[79] But Justice Fortas would end up writing the majority opinion in favor of Christopher Eckhardt and the Tinkers.[80]

How could Justice Fortas vote against hearing the case, thus affirming the previous verdict for the school district, and then later write the landmark opinion to overturn the school district's position? That is a very interesting question that the record of the case does not answer. Had Fortas's position on certiorari prevailed in March 1968, the Supreme Court would have refused to hear the *Tinker* appeal, Fortas would not have written his majority opinion in the case, and the lower federal court rulings against the student litigants would have persisted.

Some background on Justice Fortas might be instructive at this point.[81] Abe Fortas had been an outstanding law student at Yale University in the early 1930s.[82] There, he had come under the crusading influence of law professor and later Supreme Court colleague, William O. Douglas.[83] In the 1930s, Fortas served in two of Franklin Roosevelt's New Deal agencies.[84] From 1940 until his 1965 appointment to the Supreme Court, Fortas operated as a high-powered Washington lawyer.[85] In 1948, Fortas's legal brilliance and political savvy helped Lyndon Johnson prevail in a disputed election to the United States Senate.[86] Thereafter, LBJ regarded Fortas as a close friend and adviser. Fortas was a strong supporter of individual rights. As a lawyer, he successfully defended a small-time crook in the leading right to counsel case, *Gideon v.*

---

78. Certiorari Tally Sheet for *Tinker v. Des Moines Indep. Community Sch. Dist.*, (Mar. 1, 1968) (Box 384) Supreme Court Papers of Earl Warren, Manuscript Division, Library of Congress, Washington, D.C. *See generally* JOHNSON, *supra* note 1, at 165 (discussing tally sheets found in the Justices' papers).

79. *See* Tinker v. Des Moines Indep. Community Sch. Dist., 393 U.S. 503, 515-26 (1969) (Black, J., dissenting).

80. *See id.* at 504-14.

81. *See generally* KALMAN, *supra* note 77 (providing the profile of Justice Fortas).

82. *Id.* at 15.

83. *Id.* at 18.

84. *Id.* at 29-30.

85. *Id.* at 186-87.

86. *Id.* at 200-02.

Wainwright.[87] On the Supreme Court, Justice Fortas's best known decision was probably *In re Gault*,[88] the case which established that juveniles have rights in courts of law.[89] In short, on the record, Justice Fortas should have been a clear vote in favor of granting certiorari in *Tinker* and over-turning the district court ruling against the students. But the actual story is more complicated.

At the time of the vote on the certiorari petition, Justice Fortas was not convinced that the First Amendment entitled members of the judiciary to second guess the discipline imposed by school administrators unless the record of a case showed "clear discrimination or clear abuse."[90] Fortas expressed his uncertainty by writing "this is a tough case" on one of his clerk's memoranda.[91]

The best explanation for Fortas's shift from the certiorari vote to the vote on the merits of the case stems from the Justice's friendship with President Johnson and a simple matter of timing.[92] When the certiorari vote was taken in March 1968, Fortas's friend and patron was in the White House and under siege by antiwar protesters.[93] However, when the case was ready for decision in February 1969, Johnson was no longer president.[94] So Fortas's vote defending the rights of protesters was not politically embarrassing to his old friend.[95]

The appeal in *Tinker* was argued before the Supreme Court on November 12, 1968, just a few days after the 1968 presidential election that would bring Richard Nixon to the White House and help free Abe Fortas to follow his natural judicial instincts. Nevertheless, Fortas's close questioning of Dan Johnston at the Oral Argument caused the young lawyer for the students to wonder about Fortas's inclinations.[96]

Johnston began his presentation to the United States Supreme Court with a reference to the evolution case, *Epperson v. Arkansas*,[97] decided earlier that day.[98] He noted that the case he was arguing and *Epperson* both dealt with the rights of individuals in the nation's public schools.[99] The difference was that

---

87. Gideon v. Wainwright, 372 U.S. 335 (1963).
88. *In re* Gault, 387 U.S. 1 (1967).
89. *Id.* at 55-59.
90. KALMAN, *supra* note 77, at 287-88.
91. *Id.* at 287.
92. JOHNSON, *supra* note 1, at 128.
93. *Id.*
94. *Id.* at 129.
95. *Id.*
96. Johnston Interview, *supra* note 6.
97. Epperson v. Arkansas, 393 U.S. 97 (1968).
98. Transcript of Oral Argument at 3, Tinker v. Des Moines Indep. Community Sch. Dist., 393 U.S. 503 (1969) (No. 1034).
99. *Id.*

Epperson concerned academic freedom for public school faculty, while the *Tinker* case dealt with the rights of students to express their political concerns symbolically.[100] Justice Fortas interrupted to make sure that Johnston was not saying that *Tinker* was a First Amendment Establishment Clause case.[101] Johnston quickly acquiesced to this clarification, indicating that *Tinker* was a First Amendment case "in the sense of expression of view," not a dispute involving religious worship.[102] Johnston later recalled that, given Fortas's quibble, he sensed he "was in trouble right away, right out of the box."[103] "According to Johnston's surmise, several Justices had not yet decided how they would vote on the armband case and, therefore, Fortas was [anxious] to emphasize that *Epperson* and *Tinker* were different kinds of cases—the former involving freedom of religion and the later being a free-speech case."[104] Following this exchange, Fortas did not have much to say for the remainder of the oral argument.

The conference at which the Justices discuss a case just argued is a highly secret affair. However, once again the papers of the Justices, later available to scholars, can reveal much about judicial thinking on key past decisions. The conference at which *Tinker* was discussed was held on Friday, November 15, 1968, three days after the oral argument.[105] Various Justices' notes indicate that Byron White dominated the discussion.[106] A phrase in Thurgood Marshall's notes of the conference's deliberations summarized White's position: "[The school district has] not done a good job [of demonstrating that the armbands were disruptive] and therefore [should] loose [sic]."[107] "White was also troubled that the Des Moines School District's prohibition order, by banning armbands from entire school campuses and not just classrooms, was too broad."[108]

Justices Abe Fortas and Thurgood Marshall "both indicated in the conference that they 'could go with Byron'—that is, favor reversal on the narrow

---

100. *Id.*
101. *Id.*
102. *Id.* at 3-4.
103. Johnston Interview, *supra* note 6.
104. JOHNSON, *supra* note 1, at 152.
105. This account of the conference on *Tinker* is drawn from the Supreme Court Papers of William Brennan (Box 416), William O. Douglas (Box 1430), Thurgood Marshall (Box 532), and Earl Warren (Box 385)—all in the Manuscript Division, Library of Congress, Washington, D.C. *See* JOHNSON, *supra* note 1, at 163-69 (detailing *Tinker* conference proceedings); KALMAN, *supra* note 77, at 287-88 (highlighting Fortas's rule in opposing certiorari to *Tinker* and then writing the opinion).
106. JOHNSON, *supra* note 1, at 167-68.
107. *Id.*
108. *Id.*

ground suggested by White."[109] "Marshall, after mentioning his inclination, said little. Fortas was more voluble: he stated that school authorities must control their schools, but they must also have a compelling justification for restricting the free expression of students [at] school functions."[110] For Justice Fortas, there was insufficient justification shown in the record for the restrictions instituted by the school district.[111] To Justice Fortas, any disruption caused by the armband wearing students was minimal and did not warrant the preemptive ban on armbands decreed by the school district.[112]

Because Justice White dominated the conference discussion on *Tinker*, why did he not write the opinion? Given the absence of clear evidence in the papers of the Justices, and given the fact, as far as I know, that Chief Justice Warren—the assigner of the opinion—never commented on this issue, no definite answer can be advanced. However, some speculation is in order.[113]

In the assignment of opinions, one consideration of the assigning Justice is to distribute as evenly as possible the writing of the Court's majority opinions.[114] As the Court's second most junior Justice, Justice Fortas was due a few more opinions in the 1968-1969 term.[115] Also, the Chief Justice may have felt that Justice Fortas, an able negotiator, could do a better job of holding together the majority than the more strong-willed White.[116] In addition, Justice Fortas's judicial philosophy was more consonant with the dominant pro-civil liberties tenor of the Warren Court than was White's judicial philosophy.[117] Finally, it is possible Chief Justice Warren selected Justice Fortas for this opinion because he had already established himself as the Court's "expert" on children's rights with his opinion two terms earlier in *In re Gault*.[118]

At the time *Tinker* was being reviewed by the Supreme Court, the man who would ultimately write the majority opinion was undergoing serious personal difficulties.[119] Abe Fortas had been nominated by LBJ in June 1968 to

---

109. *Id.*
110. *Id.*
111. *Id.*
112. Tinker v. Des Moines Indep. Community Sch. Dist., 393 U.S. 503, 508-09 (1969).
113. JOHNSON, *supra* note 1, at 168.
114. *Id.*
115. *Id.*
116. *Id.*
117. *Id.*
118. *Id.*; *see In re* Gault, 387 U.S. 1 (1967).
119. *See generally* BRUCE ALLEN MURPHY, FORTAS: THE RISE AND FALL OF A SUPREME COURT JUSTICE 477-526 (1988) (discussing Fortas's ethical problems and ensuing resignation); KALMAN, *supra* note 77, at 319-58 (discussing Fortas's defensive stance against personal attacks made on him).

replace the retiring Earl Warren as Chief Justice.[120] It turned out to be an ill-starred nomination. As a lame duck president, Johnson did not possess the political clout to get his old friend's appointment through the Senate confirmation hearings.[121] The hearings, when they did take place, became a battleground for republican criticisms of the Great Society. In addition, Fortas's financial relationship with a wealthy businessman brought his ethics as a Justice into question, thus further undermining his prospects for confirmation as Chief Justice.[122] A month before the *Tinker* appeal was argued, intense political pressure forced LBJ to withdraw Fortas's nomination for the Chief Justiceship.[123] Attacks on Fortas's ethics would continue during the time the *Tinker* case was under review. Just over two months after the announcement of the *Tinker* opinion, the unrelenting criticism would force Fortas to resign from the Court thus cutting short a promising judicial career.

IV. THANK YOU, JUSTICE BLACK

The third and final story I submit to you is titled, with just a little bit of tongue-in-cheek, "Thank you, Justice Black."[124] The legal papers of Supreme Court Justices occasionally contain some fascinating examples of the views of Americans in the form of letters addressed to the Justices. These letters offer an unsystematic but vivid measure of the public's concerns about sensitive national issues. Normally the letters on a particular case are addressed to the Justice writing the majority opinion. However, an impassioned dissent may also precipitate substantial correspondence.

By far the greatest number of letters to the Supreme Court in the aftermath of *Tinker* were addressed to Justice Hugo Black,[125] the Court's senior member in 1969 who wrote a stinging dissent in *Tinker*.[126] Justice Black was one of the Court's most liberal members from the 1930s through the mid-1960s. As he passed into the twilight of his judicial career, however, he became increasingly intolerant of certain forms of expression.[127] It was Black, after all, who

---

120. MURPHY, *supra* note 119, at 273.

121. *Id.* at 287.

122. *See generally id.* at 502-06 (discussing Fortas's involvement with this businessman).

123. *See id.* at 525.

124. A more extensive discussion of the letters to Justice Black in the aftermath of *Tinker* is in *Johnson*, *supra* note 1, at 101-12. *See also* JOHNSON, *supra* note 1, at 190-94 (discussing some of the 260 letters in Justice Black's legal papers).

125. JOHNSON, *supra* note 1, at 191.

126. *See* Tinker v. Des Moines Indep. Community Sch. Dist., 393 U.S. 503, 515-26 (1969) (Black, J., dissenting).

127. Basically, Black did not believe that "symbolic speech" deserved the same First Amendment protection as "pure speech." *See* Cohen v. California, 403 U.S. 15, 27 (1971) (Black,

complained in *Tinker* that the dictum "children are to be seen not heard" had sadly gone out of fashion in the 1960s.[128]

The legal papers of Justice Black in the Library of Congress include 260 letters relating to the *Tinker* case.[129] All but eight of these letters expressed agreement with Black's views.[130] A fair assumption is that Black's impassioned defense of order and traditional values struck a chord among many Americans troubled by what they perceived as the turmoil in the nation's schools—and perhaps American society generally—in the late 1960s. A majority of the letters praised Justice Black for his opinion in *Tinker*.[131] A California lawyer, for instance, wrote: "Your dissent . . . in the Des Moines, Iowa, High School case was one bright ray of sunshine that brought hope and encouragement to the hearts of millions of Americans. I salute you and encourage you to continue your battle for righteousness and sanity."[132] A woman from a small town in Kentucky conveyed similar sentiments: "Thank you and let me again say you are a man among men and a true and loyal American. Oh! Lord, how I wish there were more like you, we would have a much better world to live in."[133]

A number of letters to Justice Black came from appreciative secondary school personnel.[134] For example, a school counselor from Augusta, Georgia wrote: "As a counselor in a junior high school, I appreciate and admire your stand angrily dissenting in the Iowa Students' case."[135] She later stated that more discipline is necessary in the schools, not less.[136] Then she continued: "Maybe if your fellow Justices could sit where I sit for one day, a reversal of the present decision would be made."[137] In a similar vein, a superintendent from Glasgow, Missouri wrote:

J., dissenting); Adderley v. Florida, 385 U.S. 39, 44-48 (1966); Cox v. Louisiana, 379 U.S. 536, 577-78 (1965) (Black, J., dissenting).

128. Tinker v. Des Moines Indep. Community Sch. Dist., 393 U.S. at 522 (Black, J., dissenting).

129. JOHNSON, *supra* note 1, at 191.

130. *Id.*

131. *Id.*

132. Letter from Paul J. Henry to Hugo L. Black (Feb. 25, 1969) (Box 409); *see* JOHNSON, *supra* note 1, at 191. A copy of this letter was also found in the Papers of William O. Douglas, Manuscript Division, Library of Congress, Washington, D.C. (Box 1430); *see* JOHNSON, *supra* note 1, at 191.

133. Letter from L.H. Henderson to Hugo L. Black (Mar. 14, 1969) (Box 409); *see* JOHNSON, *supra* note 1, at 191.

134. JOHNSON, *supra* note 1, at 192.

135. *Id.*

136. *Id.* at 197.

137. Letter from Mrs. Marian C. Bentley to Hugo L. Black (Feb. 27, 1969) (Box 409); *see* JOHNSON, *supra* note 1, at 197.

> We wish to applaud you on your recent dissent . . . . Every day we witness this very obvious lack of respect for authority exercised by the young people we come in contact with in our school system . . . . Again we thank you for taking a stand and want you to know there are other people who agree with you and support you.[138]

The superintendent's letter was signed by twenty-two members of his school system, including principals, teachers, counselors, secretaries, and even the "cafeteria manager."[139]

Justice Black's dissent had suggested that many of the problems in American schools—at both the secondary and college levels—stemmed from weaknesses in the American family and in society in general. Most of those writing him favorable letters shared this conviction.[140] Like Black, they blamed an all too pervasive "permissiveness."[141] A man from Catonsville, Maryland wrote:

> Far too many youths today are, to quote an old popular song, "Runnin' Wild." Permissiveness seems to be the name of the game . . . . One hears quite a bit about lack of communication between parent and child. I say Hogwash! When I was a youngster, my mother had a very good means of communication. It was called "Hairbrush." And I seldom failed to get the message.[142]

A Springfield, Illinois physician also commended Black for his battle against permissiveness: "[Y]ou speak eloquently my feelings and those of so many of my countrymen whose responsibility it is to keep our cities, counties, and states strong and effective against this new sweeping plague of permissiveness over the entire United States."[143] He continued: "I'm sick and intolerant of permissive parents, permissive teachers, permissive law enforcement agencies, permissive legislators, and permissive courts. And I am particularly disappointed and ashamed of the many permissive Supreme Court decisions which have been coming down in recent years."[144]

---

138. *See* JOHNSON, *supra* note 1, at 197.

139. Letter from Jesse E. Walters, et al. to Hugo L. Black (Feb. 27, 1969) (Box 409); *see* JOHNSON, *supra* note 1, at 197.

140. *See* JOHNSON, *supra* note 1, at 197.

141. *Id.*

142. Letter from Arthur V. Watkins to Hugo L. Black (Feb. 28, 1969) (Box 409); *see* JOHNSON, *supra* note 1, at 197.

143. Letter from Jack R. Baldwin to Hugo L. Black (Feb. 24, 1969) (Box 409); *see* JOHNSON, *supra* note 1, at 197.

144. *See* JOHNSON, *supra* note 1, at 197.

All of the Justices receive unsigned letters from time to time.[145] Most of these are probably from harmless cranks, but some threaten injury.[146] Justice Black received a handful of anonymous letters shortly after the *Tinker* decision was announced.[147] One that appeared to support his position is still disturbing—especially when read thirty years later in the aftermath of the 1999 killings at Columbine High in Littleton, Colorado. It stated in part: "You don't have to worry about the laws breaking down. We are organizing a secret club to bring criminals to justise [sic]. We won't dress any different but will FIX all trouble makers in our school. Everyone says we are helpless but we know different."[148] The postscript read: "There are 8 of us."[149]

Of the handful of letters in the Black Papers critical of the Alabama Justice's dissent in *Tinker*, a common theme was that, if free expression was in fact constitutionally protected in a democracy, there should be free expression in the institutions primarily responsible for democratic education, that is, the nation's public schools. For example, a man from California wrote to ask "How are we to prepare our young people to become full and responsible citizens if they are not allowed to experience the opportunity to exercise, peacefully, the rights of citizenship?"[150] Another correspondent, identifying himself as a high school teacher with a special interest in constitutional law, submitted two similar queries:

> How are we to expect our young to assume responsibility and participate in our society constructively and meaningfully if we condemn and restrict them by standards we do not condone for ourselves? If they are to be prohibited from expressing their concerns within the institutions in which they spend a great portion of their productive hours, institutions which purport to prepare them to think and to function effectively in the rest of society, where and when then are they to learn responsibility and constructive effectiveness?[151]

Of the eight letters critical of Justice Black's *Tinker* dissent available in the Library of Congress's collection of judicial papers, Black's hand-scrawled notes

---

145. *Id.* at 193.
146. *Id.*
147. *Id.*
148. *Id.*
149. Letter from Anonymous to Hugo L. Black (no date) (Box 410); *see* JOHNSON, *supra* note 1, at 193.
150. Letter from David M. Peterson to Hugo L. Black (Feb. 26, 1969) (Box 410); *see* JOHNSON, *supra* note 1, at 194.
151. Letter from Joseph E. Andrews to Hugo L. Black (Feb. 25, 1969) (Box 410); *see* JOHNSON, *supra* note 1, at 194.

indicated that only one should receive a reply.[152] Perhaps Justice Black found it easier to thank his supporters than to respond directly to his critics.

V. CONCLUSION

In conclusion, let me address the question that has no doubt occured to many of you, "What do these three stories, concerning what is not in the official record of *Tinker*, tell us about constitutional law?" At the risk of oversimplifying, let me suggest the following answers. My first story, "The Overlooked Litigant," provides a good example of the homily that great Supreme Court cases can, and frequently do, emerge from the activities of average people—in this instance a person routinely omitted from discussions of "his own" case. The second story, "The Reluctant Justice," tells us that no matter how much we feel we know about Supreme Court decision-making, behind-the-scenes activities of the Justices, once revealed, can present us with some surprises. And the third story, "Thank you, Justice Black," tells us that the American public occasionally engages in a hidden but very stirring dialogue with members of the nation's highest judicial body.

Over the remainder of this symposium we will be hearing a great deal about the importance of *Tinker*. I look forward to the insights and analysis offered by the legal experts. But I also look forward to hearing some more good stories.

152. Letter from Hugo L. Black to Joseph E. Andrews (Mar. 4, 1969) (Box 410); *see* JOHNSON, *supra* note 1, at 194.

Schools as Intellectual and Moral Associations

*Bruce C. Hafen**

I. Introduction: Education and the Importance of Intellectual and Moral Associations

In one of his remarkable insights about the role of mediating structures in American democracy, Tocqueville wrote that certain voluntary associations nurture the formation of those "habits of the heart" that he called "mores."[1] By mores, Tocqueville meant "the whole moral and intellectual state of a people,"[2] particularly the ennobling attitudes that restrain individualism's destructive, acquisitive appetites and that develop each citizen's sense of personal and civic virtue. The institutions that best cultivate mores are "intellectual and moral associations," which differ from associations formed primarily for "political and industrial" ends. For Tocqueville, "nothing . . . more deserves attention than the intellectual and moral associations."[3] The "mores" formed in such places are "one of the great general causes responsible for the maintenance of a democratic republic in the United States."[4] Indeed, "[t]here have never been free societies without mores."[5]

By their very nature, "intellectual" and "moral" knowledge must be both *taught* and *learned*, not merely legislated. Hence, institutions of learning play a crucial role in a democratic society because they teach not only the skills that enable personal development, but also the skills that enable democracy's own meaningful continuity.[6] To this end, American schools have

---

* Provost and Professor of Law, Brigham Young University.

1. ALEXIS DE TOCQUEVILLE, DEMOCRACY IN AMERICA 287 (J.P. Mayer ed. & George Lawrence trans., Anchor Books 1969) (1966). Robert Bellah and his colleagues drew on this phrase for the title of their book, *Habits of the Heart*, which reviewed the state of individualistic attitudes in middle class American society. ROBERT N. BELLAH ET AL., HABITS OF THE HEART (1985).
2. TOCQUEVILLE, *supra* note 1, at 287.
3. *Id.* at 517.
4. *Id.* at 287.
5. *Id.* at 590.
6. *See generally* Bruce C. Hafen, *Developing Student Expression Through Insti-*

historically been concerned with three different categories of "mores." Using Tocqueville's terminology, I will call the first of these categories the "intellectual" or cognitive mores. Category I includes basic literacy and numeracy, along with the political, economic and other general knowledge required to exercise the duties of self-governance. Without such education, democratic masses are unable to make responsible electoral choices and then hold their elected leaders accountable under the theory of the Social Contract.

Within the more value-oriented "moral" sphere, I see two rather distinct additional categories—matters of moral "principle" and matters of moral "preference." Category II, matters of moral *principle*, includes universal values that all citizens must understand and accept as conditions of social survival in a free society, such as honesty, tolerance, civic loyalty, and some degree of personal responsibility. From the acceptance of such values comes each citizen's willingness to obey the unenforceable. Without that willingness to exercise self enforcement at some threshold level, democracy cannot flourish, or even survive.

Category III, matters of moral *preference*, includes personal choices that can have significant moral—and social—implications, but that will naturally vary from one person to another. For example, I would include here the development of the value systems that shape one's sense of life's meaning, allowing the pursuit of such subjective personal choices as career direction or religious orientation.

To illustrate the distinction I draw between principle and preference, consider the example of parental choice in educating one's children. As a matter of moral *principle* (Category II), every parent should ensure that his or her child obtains a rudimentary education in compliance with state compulsory school laws. However, as a matter of moral *preference* (Category III), parents are free to send their children to either a public school or a private school. Some private schools, as distinguished from public schools, may have a religious orientation consistent with parental religious preferences. A parent may regard a given private school's orientation as an essential ingredient in teaching her child an appropriate cosmic framework for understanding life's meaning. Because public schools rarely enter the

---

tutional Authority: Public Schools As Mediating Structures, 48 OHIO ST. L.J. 663 (1987).

sphere of moral preference in the sense in which I am using that term, parents who send their children to public schools must pursue alternative means for teaching their children the sense of personal meaning found within Category III's concern with cosmic frameworks. American society and the United States Supreme Court have balanced these issues of principle and preference by acknowledging the right of parents to direct the education of their children in accordance with each parent's personal philosophy of life and education, so long as that choice also satisfies fixed, general standards of educational achievement, as well as standards prohibiting child abuse and neglect.

By educating the nation's children in both the intellectual and moral spheres, American schools perform an indispensable "mediating" function between the public and private sectors of our national life as well as the public and private dimensions of each individual's life.

> A school aspires to be a bridge between the private world of the individual and the public world of society, helping each individual to realize his own autonomous sense of self while simultaneously inducting him into membership in the democratic community. He [or she] thus learns to give as well as to take from the wellsprings of a free culture. To fulfill such contradictory but lofty purposes, the school as [a] mediating institution must itself be a paradoxical construct, belonging both to the private world of the family and to the public world of the state. Thus a school must reflect *both* institutional authority and personal autonomy, private values and public virtues, excellence and equality, neutrality and advocacy.[7]

Against this background, I offer only a modest and general observation: if schools are to perform their mediating role in democratic society, legally based policy making should acknowledge and broadly support the institutional authority schools need in order to teach students in all three categories, subject to the principle of church/state separation in public schools. In what follows, I will suggest a few ideas that pursue this policy end.

II. Selected Historical Developments in American Schools

A review of certain historical developments illustrates how

7. *Id.* at 728-29.

courts and legislatures sometimes confuse the three categories in ways that weaken both intellectual and moral development.[8] For example, in the two categories of moral education, we must more clearly respect the distinction between matters of principle and matters of preference. One extreme to avoid in this regard is the approach that makes all choices within the moral sphere a matter of principle, leaving no room for matters of moral preference. This result can follow from excessive control by the public side of a school's mediating network, as illustrated by the totalitarian state that seeks to impose a monolithic order of meaning on each citizen's view of his or her life. Another extreme to be avoided is the approach that regards all moral choices as matters of preference. This attitude relativizes all of the issues having moral or ethical underpinnings by making every moral choice appear to be a matter of personal preference. Only by avoiding such extremes can a democratic society maintain schools that produce a citizenry that is "educated" in both the intellectual and moral sense. A brief review of the history of schools in America will provide the basis for a few comments on these observations.

A. *Public and Private Schools*

Let us first consider the public school heritage. In general, the center of policy gravity for American schools has, over time, moved from the private sphere toward the public sphere. American public schools originated in the colonial period at the most local levels of neighborhood and family, as reflected in the well established—but now somewhat less clear—traditions of local control and funding from local tax revenues. Indeed, as the concept of *in loco parentis* suggests, public schools were originally extensions of the home. Because local communities were once far more culturally homogeneous than are many communities today, this approach often allowed local communities to treat their local moral preferences as matters of moral principle.

Throughout much of the nineteenth century, the widespread acceptance of Protestant attitudes created a blurring of the line between moral principle and moral preference on a national scale.[9] However, increasing numbers of Catholic im-

8. As I will suggest toward the end of this paper, the newly emerging democracies of Eastern Europe and the former Soviet Union also need their own sources of authoritative master/apprentice tutoring. *See infra* part IV.

9. *See generally* Hafen, *supra* note 6, at 675 (discussing the development of

migrants found themselves unwilling to blend their distinctive religious values into the Protestant-flavored melting pot of American schools. As a result, Catholic families established alternative schools that reflected their moral preferences while at the same time honoring the most basic principles of educational quality and democratic ideals. Nonetheless, some Protestant majorities had difficulty accommodating this degree of deviation from their notion of moral principles in education, even to the degree of urging state compulsory school laws that required attendance at public schools.

In 1925, the Supreme Court struck down such a law in Oregon, thereby reinforcing the distinction between principle and preference.[10] Once parochial and other private schools have complied with the most basic expectations of Category I (intellectual foundations) and Category II (universal personal values), the Court said these schools are free to pursue Category III (moral preference). "The child is not the mere creature of the State; those who nurture him and direct his destiny have the right, coupled with the high duty, to recognize and prepare him for additional obligations."[11] These "additional obligations" include the privately chosen personal value systems of Category III.

B. *Desegregation and Schools as State Agents*

In 1954, through the vehicle of *Brown v. Board of Education*,[12] the Supreme Court cast American public schools in a leading role in the nation's struggle to desegregate a racially divided society. The schools' relatively successful response to this challenge reflected the best tradition of mediating structures, as the schools undertook the arduous task of *teaching* a new "habit of the heart" to American society. In so doing, the schools were operating within the meaning of Category II, conveying the expectations of a newly reinforced universal value—the elimination of racism. At the same time, the degree of judicial and political power required to sustain the desegregation movement also moved the schools further away from the local and private spheres toward the megastructure role we associate with the federal government. By casting the schools

---

the American school system).

10. Pierce v. Society of Sisters, 268 U.S. 510 (1925).
11. *Id.* at 535.
12. 347 U.S. 483 (1954).

more sharply into the role of a state actor, the Court made it more difficult for the schools to engage in the shaping of students' lives in other ways.

This momentum continued as the Bill of Rights began being applied to the school context in due process, search-and-seizure, and other cases during the 1960s and 1970s.[13] Schools increasingly seemed more like typical state agents than representatives of the parental role. It soon became more difficult to think of schools as institutions that should mediate between the private sphere and the megastructures of government because the schools in some sense had become part of the megastructure.

C. Church / State Issues

The next major chapter in the story of American schools involved the church/state cases that began with the school prayer and bible reading cases of the 1960s.[14] In an important sense, these cases proceeded from the Category II "universal" premise that the state should not interject itself into the purely personal value realm of Category III. However, the experience of the last generation has produced a body of evidence suggesting that both school personnel and the public have exaggerated the meaning of the church/state cases in two aberrational ways that are mutually reinforcing and harmful.

One of these aberrations is the incorrect assumption that the Court's prohibition of religious worship and its concern with state aid to parochial schools also means that schools should not be involved in Category II moral education at all, but should confine themselves solely to the intellectual realm of Category I. The other, related aberration is the belief that the same degree of laissez-faire pluralism that characterizes the state's regulation of personal choices of Category III should also characterize the way schools treat the moral issues of Category II. The effect of this attitude is to relativize values that were once considered normative because of their universal application. Taken together, these aberrational interpretations blur the distinctions among all three categories in confusing and unsettling ways.

---

13. *See, e.g*, Goss v. Board of Educ., 373 U.S. 683 (1963).

14. Wallace v. Jaffree, 472 U.S. 38 (1985); School Dist. v. Schempp, 374 U.S. 203 (1963); Engel v. Vitale, 370 U.S. 421 (1962).

In an illustration of how matters of moral principle can be relativized to become matters of personal preference, educational researcher Gerald Grant has documented "a shift of profound dimensions" in the emergence of a "new adversarial and legalistic character" in urban public schools since the 1960s.[15] One effect of this shift is that "[a]dult authority is increasingly defined by what will stand up in court."[16] And in a related vein, school personnel "are no longer sure that they know what is right, or if they do, that they have any right to impose it."[17] This attitude is influenced not only by the fear of litigation, but also by the prevailing belief among teachers and administrators that "children are adults capable of choosing their own morality as long as they do not commit crimes."[18] To the extent that such beliefs are accepted by schools, those schools will be unable to teach the moral habits of the heart traditionally located within Category II.

D. The Anti-authoritarian Revolution

Another recent chapter from the history of American education, the "student revolutions" of the 1960s, illustrates how a passion for personal preference can also undermine the schools' ability to teach even the intellectual elements of Category I. That revolutionary period questioned the legitimacy not only of governmental megastructures, but the legitimacy of all institutional authority structures, public or private.[19] Among this movement's most pervasive themes was its questioning of authority in any form, including the place of authority in educational processes and organizations. "The radical critique shook public confidence in the schools and in traditional teaching methods by portraying the schools as enemies of true learning and instrumentalities of social control."[20] Thus, the movement "openly opposed the self-discipline, order, and respect for reason that educational institutions rely on."[21] This basic rejection of authority posed a special challenge to education, not

---

15. Gerald Grant, *The Character of Education and the Education of Character*, AM. EDUC., Jan.-Feb. 1982, at 37, 41.
16. *Id.*
17. *Id.* at 42.
18. *Id.* at 44.
19. For further development of this theme, see Hafen, *supra* note 6, at 677-81.
20. *Id.* at 679.
21. DIANE RAVITCH, THE TROUBLED CRUSADE: AMERICAN EDUCATION, 1945-1980 200 (1983).

only in its moral dimensions but also in its Category I intellectual dimensions because "[e]ducation . . . is by its nature an exercise in authority . . . since the teacher presumably seeks to impart something that the student does not know or cannot do."[22]

The issue of authority reveals the paradoxical nature of public school education. Schools "mediate" between the private and public sphere, preparing children to move from the private world of childhood to the public world of responsible citizenship. We commonly regard mediating institutions as "voluntary associations," whose role is to maximize personal liberty—and to maximize the social stability that nourishes personal liberty—in a free society. Yet the "voluntary" association we call a public school operates under the mandate of "compulsory" school laws. This may seem like an impossible contradiction until we realize that children have a particular problem with the paradox of authority: because they lack actual as well as legal capacity, children have a special need to submit themselves—even by the force of compulsory laws—to the yoke of educational demands in order to develop their own capacity for autonomous action. This is not at all unusual, since mediating institutions typically ask individual citizens to yield some degree of short-term personal freedom for the sake of long-term communitarian values. Thus, by challenging the legitimacy of all authoritarian processes and institutions, the revolutionary era called into question not only the way schools function, but the way any intermediate institution functions.

III. Institutional Authority and the Student Expression Cases

Let us explore this problem using the Supreme Court's student expression cases as illustrations because these cases clearly display the conflict between institutional authority and student freedom. In addition, the development of this line of cases introduces some recent and significant attempts by the Court to restore the capacity of public schools to perform their mediating functions in the intellectual as well as in the moral categories.

Until 1986, the Court's experience in the student expres-

22. Diane Ravitch, *The Continuing Crisis: Fashions in Education*, 53 AM. SCHOLAR 183, 189 (1984).

sion area was concerned primarily with protecting the individual first amendment rights of students. For example, in the 1943 "flag salute" case, the Court held that a public school could not compel students who were Jehovah's Witnesses to pledge allegiance to the American flag because such compulsion has a coercive effect on religious beliefs.[23] And in the 1969 case of *Tinker v. Des Moines Independent Community School District*,[24] the Court protected the right of public school students to wear black armbands in a peaceful protest against the Vietnam War. *Tinker* held that schools may not discipline students for either actual or symbolic expression unless such expression is manifestly disruptive.[25] This seemingly unqualified holding left lower courts in considerable doubt about the right of schools to control curriculum-related expression that was not disruptive.

In 1982, a plurality of the Court held in *Board of Education v. Pico*[26] that students have a right to receive information, which right can limit the discretion of a school board to direct the arbitrary removal of books from school libraries. However, the Court also implicitly acknowledged that school boards have wide latitude in determining what books to order in the first instance and in exercising non-arbitrary control over curricular matters.[27]

This ongoing extension of protection for individual student interests came to an end in 1986, when the Court held in *Bethel School District v. Fraser*[28] that a school could discipline a student for giving a vulgar speech in a student assembly. This opinion reaffirmed in relatively broad terms the schools' obligation to teach citizenship values and to act *in loco parentis*. However, the opinion left some room for doubt whether this limitation on student speech would apply to circumstances other than offensive vulgarity.

Those doubts were removed by *Hazelwood School District v. Kuhlmeier*,[29] in which the Court held that a public school may regulate the content of a school newspaper produced by students in a journalism class. The basis for this holding was

---

23. West Virginia State Bd. of Educ. v. Barnette, 319 U.S. 624, 642 (1943).
24. 393 U.S. 503 (1969).
25. *Id.* at 505-06.
26. 457 U.S. 853, 869-72 (1982) (plurality opinion).
27. *Id.* at 863-72.
28. 478 U.S. 675, 685-86 (1986).
29. 484 U.S. 260, 273 (1988).

the Court's recognition that schools may control any school-sponsored expressive activity, not only within the traditional curriculum but in any circumstances that are or may be perceived as being school-sponsored.[30] This decision resolved many post-*Tinker* doubts by limiting the *Tinker* rule to private student speech that occurs outside school-sponsored activities. It also reinforced the principle of what might be called institutional academic freedom, a principle that is crucial to sustaining the functions of the "intellectual and moral associations" to which Tocqueville referred.[31] Let us consider the connection between these cases and that principle.

Certain features of the student expression cases are related to declines in the ability of schools to educate their students—not that the cases themselves directly reduced the schools' educational effectiveness; rather, *Tinker* was the child of an overall environment that challenged the institutional authority of schools. I have summarized elsewhere certain ways in which declining institutional authority in public schools since the 1960s has apparently contributed to reductions in student academic achievement.[32] As just one example, the empirical studies of James Coleman and his colleagues have established strong connections between the exercise of institutional authority and student performance in both academic and behavioral dimensions.[33] In both public and private schools, student achievement improves when schools maintain strong disciplinary policies, homework expectations, and attendance requirements. Reductions in school authority are most damaging to the educational attainments of disadvantaged students. In addition, students perceive firm disciplinary requirements as not only more effective, but also more fair.[34]

In some ways, the suspicions about school authority reflected in such cases as *Tinker* and *Pico* arose not from evidence that schools were actually damaging students by authoritative interventions, but from the growing ideological belief that because schools are part of the governmental megastructure, they should not intervene in students' lives, whether in intellectual

30. *Id.* at 271-73.
31. Bruce C. Hafen, Hazelwood School District *and the Role of First Amendment Institutions*, 1988 DUKE L.J. 685.
32. Hafen, *supra* note 6, at 684-88.
33. JAMES S. COLEMAN ET AL., HIGH SCHOOL ACHIEVEMENT: PUBLIC, CATHOLIC, AND PRIVATE SCHOOLS COMPARED (1982).
34. *See* Hafen, *supra* note 6, at 686-87.

or behavioral realms. This belief had been reinforced by the schools' emerging role as agents of the political state in the enforcement of national desegregation policies, as well as by the perceived doubt that the church/state cases seemed to cast on the schools' right to provide moral instruction of any kind.

Yet, despite the proper legal characterization of schools as state actors, the very nature of education places schools in a mediating role between each student and the larger community in ways that distinguish schools from any other state agency.

> Public education seeks affirmatively to teach the capacity to enjoy first amendment values—to mediate between ignorance and educated expression. [This] is a process that invites intrusion, requires authoritarian paternalism, and depends upon the exercise of unsupervisable discretion. There must be legal protection against clearly harmful abuse of this flexibility, but without some strong influence from those apparent enemies of personal autonomy in the educational process, little serious education is possible. Traditional first amendment jurisprudence was never designed to deal with governmental action of this kind, because the original cases arose in contexts involving adults and were concerned only with when to limit governmental action, not with how to encourage it toward such complex ends as educational development.[35]

The *Fraser* and *Hazelwood* cases have now sent the very important signal that schools can actually *foster* and *nourish* the underlying values of the First Amendment—such as free inquiry, personal expression, and participatory democracy—by authoritatively but affirmatively directing educational processes, not just by staying out of students' way. This is because students who lack education also lack the capacity for meaningful participation in the democratic experiment. Freedom of expression has two meanings—freedom *from* restraints, and the capacity *for* self-expression. Schools can heighten students' capacity *for* self-expression by providing them with effective educational tools—which, experience shows, must often be authoritatively imposed. Teachers and schools may and should also elect non-directive methods that distinctly lack authority or that place a premium on student initiative or student criticism of authority. But the methods chosen, according to *Hazelwood*, are matters of educational philosophy, not matters

35. *Id.* at 669.

of constitutional law. All of this suggests that a child's right to be educated can be more substantial than a child's right to be left alone. In education as in family life, we do not serve the long range interests of children when our civil liberties-based jurisprudence has the effect of abandoning children to their "rights."

The underlying theory of the *Hazelwood* case is that the institutional autonomy of schools can play a significant role in developing students' educated capacities; therefore, by recognizing the "institutional freedom" of a school, courts can in certain circumstances promote rather than retard the underlying purposes of the First Amendment. This assumes, of course, that a school so protected will shoulder its heavy burden of teaching well.

One year prior to its *Hazelwood* decision, the Court had recognized this fact about such "intellectual and moral associations" as schools and churches in *Corporation of the Presiding Bishop v. Amos*,[36] in which Justice Brennan stated in his concurring opinion that, "[s]olicitude for a church's ability to [engage in its own self-definition] reflects the idea that furtherance of the autonomy of religious organizations often furthers individual religious freedom as well."[37] In other words, a mediating institution needs protection from state intrusion not only to protect its purely institutional interests, but also to protect the right of its members to draw upon its institutional role as a carrier and developer of personal meaning. "The first amendment must therefore protect not only individual writers, but newspapers; not only religious persons, but churches; not only individual students and teachers, but schools."[38]

Given the value of Tocqueville's ideas about what "intellectual and moral associations" can do for both individuals and society, the ideal school would teach its students effectively in all three categories: I, intellectual knowledge and skills; II, universal moral principles; and III, a basis for finding personal meaning in life. A private religious school that maintains rigorous educational and intellectual standards is theoretically more likely than other institutions to fulfill this aspiration because such a school teaches the "mores" inherent within *each* category, perhaps integrating all three categories together. This re-

---

36. 483 U.S. 327 (1987).
37. *Id.* at 342 (Brennan, J., concurring).
38. Hafen, *supra* note 31, at 704-05.

sembles the ancient mythical model by which the young child learns *all* of life's meaning at the feet of a wise master of all knowledge. Public schools in the early part of American history approached a realization of educational goals in all three categories, but before long it was clear that state authority should not be employed to supersede parental prerogatives in directing the development of children's personal life orientation in Category III.

This recognition of the need to remove public schools from Category III took the first step in limiting schools' authority to teach "mores." The natural momentum of historical development, especially in recent years, has continued to limit schools' authority. For example, our longstanding skepticism about state involvement in Category III has now been transferred to a more recent skepticism about state involvement in Category II. If American society's pluralism makes it inappropriate for a school to teach *particular* religious and moral values, we can easily begin to believe that same pluralism also makes it inappropriate to teach *general* moral values—especially in a day when we increasingly, and unwisely, associate all moral codes and assumptions with particular ethnic and class-oriented backgrounds.

Having now moved to the point that school personnel "are no longer sure they know what is right, or if they do, that they have any right to impose it,"[39] we may begin to doubt not only a school's right to teach principles of character or citizenship, but also its right to assert institutional authority in the teaching of Category I intellectual and cognitive principles. The pre-*Hazelwood* student expression cases reflected these doubts. The extreme expression of this educational philosophy found a voice in the anti-authoritarian revolutions of the 1960s and 1970s, as illustrated by A.S. Neill's *Summerhill* school. Neill believed that "a child is innately wise and realistic. If left to himself without adult suggestion of any kind, he will develop as far as he is capable of developing."[40]

The view that schools as mediating institutions should not authoritatively intervene in children's minds and lives at any point along the entire spectrum from Category I to Category III essentially rejects Tocqueville's idea that individual citizens—children or otherwise—need the institutional constraint

39. Grant, *supra* note 15, at 42.
40. A.S. NEILL, SUMMERHILL: A RADICAL APPROACH TO CHILD REARING 4 (1960).

of being *taught* the "habits of the heart" that are essential for democratic success and continuity. With *Fraser* and *Hazelwood*, the Supreme Court has slowed the momentum that was moving toward this extreme conclusion, but the Court's decisions have not been well-received in the scholarly literature.[41] Whether American schools will build upon these cases and current public unhappiness with public education to reverse the historical tide remains very much an open question.

IV. IMPLICATIONS FOR THE NEW DEMOCRACIES

In the meantime, one wonders what the current vacuum of authority in Eastern Europe and the former Soviet republics will mean for the development of the civilizing habits and knowledge without which democracy cannot take deep and permanent root in those countries. As noted above, we have devalued educational authority in the United States by a gradual process that has continually extended both our skepticism about state authority and our commitment to the individual right to be left alone. The collapse of excessively authoritarian regimes has similarly—yet very suddenly—devalued authority in the newly emerging democracies, which predictably promotes anti-authoritarian attitudes. In either case, it is natural to expect a continual and at times intense distrust of any authoritarian practice or institution, whether in a government agency or in a quasi-public or even private institution.

A friend of mine spoke recently with an educational leader in an Eastern European university. The educator asked my friend to recommend a qualified professor from the United States who might come to his university and give a series of lectures on moral philosophy. The source of this interest was the educational leader's belief that his country has no more crucial challenge than to develop the seedbed in which individual citizens—old as well as young—can learn to be self-governing, not only politically and economically, but morally and even spiritually.

Will abstract lectures on moral philosophy exact from an audience the voluntary willingness to sacrifice self-interest in favor of the public good? What is the source of the personal

41. *See, e.g.*, J. Marc Abrams & S. Mark Goodman, *End of an Era? The Decline of Student Press Rights in the Wake of* Hazelwood School District v. Kuhlmeier, 1988 DUKE L.J. 706; Richard L. Roe, *Valuing Student Speech: The Work of the Schools as Conceptual Development*, 79 CAL. L. REV. 1271 (1991).

commitment to obey the unenforceable? I ask those questions not only about the new democracies, but about the educational wellsprings of American democracy. Tocqueville's answer to such questions was clear:

> Among laws controlling human societies there is one more precise and clearer, it seems to me, than all the others. If men are to remain civilized or to become civilized, the art of association [especially the art nurtured by intellectual and moral associations] must develop and improve among them at the same speed as equality of conditions spreads.[42]

Mary Ann Glendon observed that no institutions have appeared that take the place of the families, neighborhoods, workplace associations and religious associations that teach the skills essential to sustaining democratic societies. As a result, "paradoxically, liberal democratic welfare states seem to require the maintenance in their midst of value-generating institutions that are not necessarily organized on liberal principles. Yet, perversely, the liberal state and the free market seem to undermine the social supports upon which they rest."[43] She then quotes Francis Fukuyama, who wrote that "liberal principles have had a corrosive effect on the values predating liberalism that are needed to sustain strong communities, and thereby on a liberal society's ability to be self-sustaining . . . . Successful political modernization thus requires the preservation of something premodern within its framework."[44]

One of the "pre-modern" values upon which liberalism has a corrosive effect is the value of authority in the necessarily authoritarian process of education. A school is in this sense a strikingly pre-modern institution—pre-modern not only because its processes may require "compulsory" attendance for children, but paradoxically, because it is only by submitting to the authoritative direction of teachers that young people learn the skills, attitudes, and understandings without which they cannot successfully sustain the operation of a democratic society. As Eva Brann has written, "A school is not the world. And yet it is *a* world, a small republic of the intellect within the politi-

42. TOCQUEVILLE, *supra* note 1, at 517.
43. Mary A. Glendon, *Individualism and Communitarianism in Contemporary Legal Systems: Tensions and Accommodations*, 1993 B.Y.U. L. REV. 385, 416.
44. *Id.* & n.68.

cal community."[45] Thus a school is the place in which democracy is spiritually created and matured before its students enter the temporal place of free markets and the marketplace of ideas, once they have developed through arduous learning and effort the skills needed for truly autonomous action. To prematurely thrust students—or societies—onto this stage of total freedom is to put at risk not only their personal survival but the survival of the society their collective presence creates.

V. CONCLUSION

So how do democracies, old and new, learn these pre-modern survival skills? They need not only constitutions and blueprints, but teachers; not only stock markets and parliaments, but apprenticeships and *schools* of all kinds. The prescription for building a successful democracy may be like the prescription for other forms of knowledge that are essentially matters of *skill*, like building a Stradivarius violin: the prescription does not—and cannot—exist fully in writing. As Michael Polanyi has explained:

> *[T]he aim of a skilful [sic] performance is achieved by the observance of a set of rules which are not known as such to the person following them.*
>
> . . . .
>
> An art which cannot be specified in detail cannot be transmitted by prescription, since no prescription for it exists. It can be passed on only by example from master to apprentice. This restricts the range of diffusion to that of personal contacts, and we find accordingly that craftsmanship tends to survive in closely circumscribed local traditions. Indeed, the diffusion of crafts from one country to another can often be traced to the migration of groups of craftsmen . . . . [And] while *the articulate contents of science* are successfully taught all over the world in hundreds of new universities, *the unspecifiable art of scientific research* has not penetrated to many of these . . . . Without the opportunity offered to young scientists to serve an apprenticeship in Europe, and without the migration of European scientists to the new countries, research centres overseas could hardly ever have made much headway.
>
> It follows that an art which has fallen into disuse for the period of a generation is altogether lost. There are hundreds

45. EVA T.H. BRANN, PARADOXES OF EDUCATION IN A REPUBLIC 146 (1979).

> of examples of this to which the process of mechanization is continuously adding new ones. These losses are usually irretrievable. It is pathetic to watch the endless efforts—equipped with microscopy and chemistry, with mathematics and electronics—to reproduce a single violin of the kind the half-literate Stradivarius turned out as a matter of routine more than 200 years ago.
>
> *To learn by example is to submit to authority. You follow your master because you trust his manner of doing things even when you cannot analyse and account in detail for its effectiveness. By watching the master and emulating his efforts in the presence of his example, the apprentice unconsciously picks up the rules of the art, including those which are not explicitly known to the master himself. These hidden rules can be assimilated only by a person who surrenders himself to that extent uncritically to the imitation of another. A society which wants to preserve a fund of personal knowledge must submit to tradition.*[46]

The educational process of transmitting the prescription for modern, liberal democracy from one generation to another is impossible without submission in some degree to that pre-modern and anti-liberal principle of authority—not the unlimited and brutal authority of a "master" toward a slave, but the limited and nurturing authority of a "master" toward an apprentice. There was a time when we called this "anti-liberal" process a "liberal education." The educational process—even when authoritatively imposed—still has a fundamentally liberating effect.

46. MICHAEL POLANYI, PERSONAL KNOWLEDGE: TOWARDS A POST-CRITICAL PHILOSOPHY 49, 53 (1962) (emphasis in last paragraph added).

LIBERTY AND AUTHORITY: TWO FACETS OF THE INCULCATION OF VIRTUE

STANLEY INGBER

I. INTRODUCTION: CONFLICTING PERSPECTIVES

A. Tinker *in Context*

Adolescence is a time of rebellion, growth, change, and the beginning of meaningful self-awareness. It is not suprising, therefore, that the 1960s, which constituted the adolescent period of the baby-boomer generation, was noted for its lack of commitment to discipline, obedience and deference to authority.[1] It was a time remembered more for political and cultural conflict, urban chaos, civil rights battles, free speech movements on university campuses, and, perhaps most of all, the national divide over the Vietnam War. The 1960s was an era during which the value of order—of deference to authority—was challenged profoundly, to the great chagrin of those who view order as an imperative in a civilized society.

This era of turmoil is the context in which one must understand the Supreme Court's decision in *Tinker v. Des Moines Independent Community School District*,[2] the twenty-fifth anniversary of which decision this Symposium commemorates. In *Tinker*, the Supreme Court struck down a school regulation prohibiting the wearing of black armbands to protest the Vietnam War. In sweeping language, the Justices declared their rejection of the proposition that students "shed their constitutional rights to freedom of speech or expression at the schoolhouse gate."[3]

In an age when claims of liberty were embraced increasingly while those heralding authority were deemed suspect, one would have been most

---

 James Madison Endowed Chair in Constitutional Law, Drake University. B.A. 1969, Brooklyn College; J.D. 1972, Yale Law School.

[1] The 1960s created a "new mood," displacing "social complacency" with a "clamor for bold leadership in all areas of American life." ROBERT WEISBROT, FREEDOM BOUND: A HISTORY OF AMERICA'S CIVIL RIGHTS MOVEMENT 18 (1990). This "new mood" was based in part on the "restless idealism of the postwar baby-boom generation that was just coming of age." *Id.*

[2] 393 U.S. 503 (1969).

[3] *Id.* at 506.

surprised had the Court ruled that students were totally devoid of First Amendment protections.[4] Indeed, as Professor Bruce Hafen, my colleague in this symposium, has noted, the facts of *Tinker* provided an ideal setting for the affirmation of students' free speech interests.[5] The students wore black armbands peacefully and with their parents' consent, their symbolic expression addressed what likely was the most important political issue of the day, and their statement did not contest educational policy; it was more akin to a personal conversation among students concerning public issues, a conversation that neither intruded upon the work of the schools, nor implied any official endorsement.[6]

The language of the Court's opinion, however, initially appeared to be significantly more far-reaching than the aforementioned facts warranted. Committed to the position that state-operated schools were forbidden from serving as little "enclaves of totalitarianism" in which school officials possessed "absolute authority over their students,"[7] the Court held that the state could not confine students to the expression of only officially approved sentiments.[8] Noting the need to foster intellectual traits consistent with those required of a democratic polity, the majority emphasized the role of education in providing a participatory forum for the exchange of ideas, a forum crucial in the training of future leaders.[9] Essentially, the classroom was to serve as a "marketplace of ideas."[10] Thus, school officials could not prohibit expression on the basis of an "undifferentiated fear or apprehension of disturbance,"[11] but could do so only on the basis of "facts which might reasonably have led school authorities to forecast substantial disruption of or material interference with

---

[4] Indeed, earlier cases had already demonstrated that free speech claims were potentially valid in public school environs. *See, e.g.*, West Virginia State Bd. of Educ. v. Barnette, 319 U.S. 624 (1943) (prohibiting schools from compelling students to salute American flag).

[5] Bruce C. Hafen, Hazelwood School District *and the Role of First Amendment Institutions*, 1988 DUKE L.J. 685, 688 [hereinafter Hafen, Hazelwood].

[6] *Id.*

[7] *Tinker*, 393 U.S. at 511.

[8] *Id.*

[9] *Id.*, at 512. The Court emphasized that such training required "wide exposure to that robust exchange of ideas which discovers truth 'out of a multitude of tongues, [rather] than any kind of authoritative selection.'" *Id.* (alteration in original) (citation omitted) (quoting Keyishian v. Board of Regents, 385 U.S. 589, 603 (1967)). The Court appeared to be merging free speech arguments grounded in the community's interest in character building with those based on an uninhibited "search for truth." For a discussion of the multi-faceted functions of rights claims generally and free speech claims specifically, see *infra* notes 73-91 and accompanying text.

[10] *Tinker*, 393 U.S. at 512.

[11] *Id.* at 508.

school activities. . . ."[12]

Such language understandably was disconcerting to those who believed that order and obedience to authority are necessary prerequisites for effective learning.[13] *Tinker* engendered fear of anarchy, of schools in utter disarray as students questioned the decisions and disobeyed the directives of educational officials and professionals. Envisioning educational institutions increasingly beleaguered by students "running loose, conducting break-ins, sit-ins, lie-ins and smash-ins,"[14] Justice Black cried out in dissent, "I . . . disclaim . . . that the Federal Constitution compels the teachers, parents, and elected school officials to surrender control of the American public school system to public school students."[15]

Tinker may not have caused the cataclysmic results feared by Justice Black, but the decision did portend difficulty for many school officials. If their authority were constrained by student free speech rights, what limit could be placed upon students' disregard of efforts to establish a given level of order and decorum in the schools? If free speech rights meant that students could choose their own beliefs, at what juncture would schools be prohibited from requiring the acceptance of certain information or from inculcating certain values? Would every effort to impose authority be open to defiance, leading to litigation if disciplinary action were taken? Under such a regime, how could schools educate? Were there no longer any *givens* or *truths*? As one scholar lamented during this period of institutional uncertainty, school personnel "are no longer sure that they know what is right, or if they do, that they have any right to impose it."[16]

Most assuredly, much obedience and deference to authority is necessary for schools to function effectively.[17] In fact, Bruce Hafen has

---

[12] *Id.* at 514.

[13] *See, e.g., id.* at 522 (Black, J., dissenting) (arguing that purpose of public schools is to teach children through use of order and discipline).

[14] *Id.* at 525 (Black, J., dissenting).

[15] *Tinker*, 393 U.S. at 526 (Black, J., dissenting).

[16] Gerald Grant, *The Character of Education and the Education of Character*, AM. EDUC., Jan.-Feb. 1982, at 37, 42. Bruce Hafen attributes this self-doubt in educational professionals to the development of a pluralistic society:

> If American society's pluralism makes it inappropriate for a school to teach particular religious and moral values, we can easily begin to believe that same pluralism also makes it inappropriate to teach general moral values—especially in a day when we increasingly, and unwisely, associate all moral codes and assumptions with particular ethnic and class-oriented backgrounds.

Bruce C. Hafen, *Schools as Intellectual and Moral Associations*, 1993 B.Y.U. L. REV. 605, 617 [hereinafter Hafen, *Schools*].

[17] In fact, some published studies suggest that academic achievement improves when schools maintain strong disciplinary policies, homework expectations, and attendance requirements. *See,*

gone so far as to insist that "*only by submitting* to the authoritative direction of teachers [can] young people learn the skills, attitudes, and understandings without which they cannot successfully sustain the operation of a democratic society."[18] The importance of education in inculcating values and, thereby, integrating children into their normative community was recognized by the Court in the landmark civil rights decision *Brown v. Board of Education.*[19] *Brown* described education as government's most important duty precisely because "it is a principal instrument in awakening the child to cultural values."[20]

Despite its importance, however, education through the exercise of authority and the insistence upon obedience is risky business. Given the universality of compulsory education in America,[21] state-sponsored education necessarily raises important questions about government's proper role in controlling thought and expression and, thereby, in molding character in a democratic society. An abusive government might use schools to induce captive[22] and immature children uncritically to accept values that support and enhance the status quo.[23] Such government action

---

e.g., JAMES S. COLEMAN ET AL., HIGH SCHOOL ACHIEVEMENT: PUBLIC, CATHOLIC, AND PRIVATE SCHOOLS COMPARED 186-87 (1982).

[18] Hafen, *Schools,supra* note 16, at 619 (emphasis added).

[19] 347 U.S. 483 (1954).

[20] *Id.* at 493. The policy of inculcating community values through education has ancient and respected roots in Western thought. Plato, for instance, proposed censoring the stories that teachers told so that children would not assimilate "opinions for the most part contrary to those that we shall think it desirable for them to hold when they are grown up." PLATO, THE REPUBLIC, bk. II, ch. VII, at 177 (Paul Shorey trans., 1930). Aristotle believed that legislators could produce good citizens by instilling in them virtuous habits from childhood. *See* ARISTOTLE, THE NICOMACHEON ETHICS, bk. II, ch. I, at 71 (Harris Rackam trans., 1939). This notion that instilling morality—building character—is a vital function of education has continued into modern times. *See, e.g.*, DESIDERIUS ERASMUS, THE EDUCATION OF A CHRISTIAN PRINCE 212-13 (L. Born trans., 1936); JOHN LOCKE, SOME THOUGHTS CONCERNING EDUCATION 90 (R. Quick ed., 1913). The attitude regarding character enhancement has thrived in the United States. *See* Ambach v. Norwick, 441 U.S. 68, 76-77 (1979) (asserting that education is foundation of citizenship, preparing children for public responsibility, professional training, and cultural appreciation). One hundred and fifty-five years ago de Tocqueville observed: "In the United States politics are the end and aim of education." Richard L. Berkman, *Students in Court: Free Speech and the Functions of Schooling in America*, 40 HARV. EDUC. REV. 567, 569 (1970) (citation omitted) (quoting Alexis de Tocqueville).

[21] Since 1918, all states have required that children within a specified age group attend school. ROBERT M. O'NEIL, CLASSROOMS IN THE CROSSFIRE 59 (1981).

[22] Of course, in Pierce v. Society of Sisters, 268 U.S. 510, 525 (1925), the Court recognized a parent's right to place her child in a private school. That right, however, may have little significance for a parent who cannot afford private education or who independently values the social interaction of public education.

[23] Mark G. Yudof, *Library Book Selection and the Public Schools: The Quest for the Archimedean Point*, 59 IND. L.J. 527, 540 (1984) [hereinafter Yudof, *Library Book Selection*].

may severely undermine the ability of individuals to judge independently and intelligently. Consequently, schools easily might subvert the very core justifications of the First Amendment.[24]

The dilemma of public education is thus manifest. Because few institutions affect young, impressionable personalities as profoundly as do our schools,[25] we as a community are justifiably concerned that our educational program should promote the "right" skills and values for the development of an individual capable of contributing in a meaningful way to our community. Yet by authorizing schools to develop this "right" environment, we leave our children highly vulnerable to "village tyrants"[26] who might pervert the education process. Under the guise of properly educating the young, government could predispose children to accept and defer to authority while passively adopting prevailing values and current attitudes.[27] The school system, consequently, epitomizes the tension between liberty and authority.

B. Tinker's *Aftermath*

Over the twenty-five years since *Tinker*, many have questioned whether the Court's response to this tension was too one-sided, too supportive of liberty.[28] Although *Tinker* has never been overruled, its

---

"The power to teach, inform, and lead," cautions Provost Yudof, "is also the power to indoctrinate, distort judgment, and perpetuate the current regime." Mark G. Yudof, *When Governments Speak: Toward a Theory of Government Expression and the First Amendment*, 57 TEX. L. REV. 863, 865 (1979) [hereinafter Yudof, *When Governments Speak*].

[24] As Stephen Arons warns: "If the government were able to use schooling to regulate the development of ideas and opinions by controlling the transmission of culture and the socialization of children, freedom of expression would become a meaningless right. . . . " STEPHEN ARONS, COMPELLING BELIEF: THE CULTURE OF AMERICAN SCHOOLING 206 (1983).

[25] In fact, in many ways public schools are an indoctrinator's dream. *See* Steven Shiffrin, *Government Speech*, 27 UCLA L. REV. 565, 647 (1980). First, attendance is compulsory, and students lack the independent knowledge or psychological sophistication necessary to evaluate critically what their teachers tell them. Second, public schools can disguise their message as highly valued "education" rather than less trustworthy propaganda. Third, the adult teacher's authority and seemingly vast fund of knowledge will likely impress the children. Finally, teachers reward and punish students according to how well they learn the lesson of the day. *See* Yudof, *When Governments Speak*, *supra* note 23, at 875.

[26] West Virginia State Bd. of Educ. v. Barnette, 319 U.S. 624, 638 (1943).

[27] *Cf.* Robert D. Kamenshine, *The First Amendment's Implied Political Establishment Clause*, 67 CAL. L. REV. 1104, 1104 (1979) (proposing that courts interpret First Amendment to prohibit political establishment in order to alleviate government's power to indoctrinate citizens).

For an exhaustive work on the subject of government's role as communicator and educator, see MARK YUDOF, WHEN GOVERNMENT SPEAKS: POLITICS, LAW AND GOVERNMENT EXPRESSION IN AMERICA (1983).

[28] *See, e.g.*, Hafen, *Schools*, *supra* note 16, at 613 ("This seemingly unqualified holding left lower courts in considerable doubt about the right of schools to control curriculum-related

significance has been severely eroded, perhaps as a reaction to this criticism. The legal trend is unmistakably toward increasing deference to the decisions of school administrators.[29] By providing First Amendment rights to students only "in light of the *special characteristic of the school environment*,"[30] *Tinker* essentially sowed the seeds of its own virtual demise. The italicized language above easily justifies judicial reluctance to second-guess the day-to-day judgments rendered by those represented as uniquely trained and experienced in educating our young.[31] If, for example, alternative educational philosophies support greatly differing degrees of student participation and creative inquiry, on what basis are courts to choose and mandate one approach over another? Judges may understandably question whether their legal training adequately qualifies them to determine the "educational suitability"[32] of various teaching techniques and materials. Judges, therefore, may feel ill-equipped to police public education.[33] Supervising compliance with a decree to desegregate is one thing, but regularly reviewing the orchestration of the school environment is quite another.

Two Supreme Court cases illustrate the extent to which emphasis has

---

expression that was not disruptive.").

[29] *See* Stuart L. Leviton, *Is Anyone Listening to Our Students? A Plea for Respect and Inclusion*, 21 FLA. ST. U. L. REV. 35, 38 (1993) (discussing use of lower court rhetoric to support increasing deference to school administrators and resulting narrowing of students' rights); *see also* Roger J.R. Levesque, *International Children's Rights Grow Up: Implications for American Jurisprudence and Domestic Policy*, 24 CAL. W. INT'L L.J. 193, 208 (1994) (discussing trend of U.S. courts to limit rights of students by deferring to discretion of school administrators).

[30] *Tinker*, 393 U.S. at 506 (emphasis added).

[31] For a discussion of the societal threat posed by those claiming that their expertise insulates their judgment from societal review, see *infra* text accompanying notes 179-86 and note 183. *See also* Stanley Ingber, *Socialization, Indoctrination, or the "Pall of Orthodoxy": Value Training in the Public Schools*, 1987 U. ILL. L. REV. 15, 34-37 [hereinafter Ingber, *Socialization*] (questioning educators' insistence on choosing curricula because of claims of specialized training and experience).

[32] "Educational suitability" was deemed by the Court as an acceptable criterion for a school board to use when determining whether a given book review could remain in the school library. Board of Educ. v. Pico, 457 U.S. 853, 857 (1982) (plurality opinion). In *Pico*, the Court imposed constitutional limits on a school board's discretion to remove books from junior and senior high school libraries. *Id.* at 869. Although such removals are found unlawful when based on "narrowly partisan or political" motivations, deletions are "perfectly permissible" when based on determinations of educational suitability. *Id.* at 870-71. Educational suitability, however, may be even harder for a jurist to identify than is obscenity. Yet when discussing obscenity, one Justice confessed that all he could state with assurance was that "I know it when I see it." Jacobellis v. Ohio, 378 U.S. 184, 197 (1964) (Stewart, J., concurring).

[33] *E.g.*, Epperson v. Arkansas, 393 U.S. 97, 114 (1968) (Black, J., concurring) (asserting that courts lack ability to supervise "the curriculum of every public school in every hamlet and city in the United States").

again been placed on upholding the authority of school officials when these officials are confronted by student speech activities. In *Bethel School District No. 403 v. Fraser*,[34] the Court upheld a three-day suspension of a high school student who used "an elaborate, graphic, and explict sexual metaphor" while delivering a speech before a school assembly to nominate a fellow classmate for a student government position.[35] Although the Court repeatedly spoke of public education's role in inculcating "'fundamental values necessary to the maintenance of a democratic political system,'"[36] it recognized that First Amendment freedoms nevertheless had to be "balanced against the society's countervailing interest in teaching students the boundaries of *socially appropriate behavior*."[37] More importantly, the majority concluded that "[t]he determination of what manner of speech in the classroom or in the school assembly is inappropriate properly rests with the school board."[38] Most telling in *Bethel* was the Court's acceptance of the proposition that learning obedience to authority was fundamental to the initiation of the child into the community and to her preparation for citizenship.[39]

Bethel left uncertain whether this constraint on student expression applied to contexts beyond that of offensive vulgarity.[40] The Court clarified this issue two years later in *Hazelwood School District v. Kuhlmeier*.[41] In *Hazelwood*, the Court relied on *Bethel* to affirm school officials' broad authority over all school-sponsored expressive activities.[42] The school newspaper at Hazelwood East High School was part of a journalism course which was a "regular classroom activit[y]" for which the students received academic credit.[43] The journalism teacher exercised considerable control over the newspaper, including selecting its editors, setting publication dates, editing stories, and assigning story ideas.[44] The

---

[34] 478 U.S. 675 (1986).

[35] *Id.* at 677-78.

[36] *Id.* at 683 (quoting Ambach v. Norwick, 441 U.S. 68, 77 (1979)).

[37] *Id.* at 681 (emphasis added). This language paved the way for school boards to consider enacting speech codes either prohibiting hateful comments or mandating political correctness. Although I find this conclusion troubling, there is an extent to which I believe *Bethel*'s rationale compelling. *See infra* text accompanying notes 261-69.

[38] *Bethel*, 478 U.S. at 683.

[39] *Id.* ("The process of educating our youth for citizenship in public schools is not confined to books, the curriculum, and the civics class; schools must teach by example the shared values of a civilized social order.").

[40] Hafen, *Schools*, *supra* note 16, at 613.

[41] 484 U.S. 260 (1988).

[42] *Id.* at 266-67.

[43] *Id.* at 268.

[44] *Id.*

school principal reviewed every issue prior to publication.[45] When the principal excised two pages from the newspaper after performing a pre-publication review, three student staff members sued, alleging that their First Amendment rights had been violated.[46] The principal defended his actions on the grounds that the deleted pages contained two articles—one describing the experiences of pregnant students, the other discussing the impact of divorce on students at the school—that impinged on the privacy rights of parents and pregnant students.[47] Using language that swept significantly beyond that necessary to uphold the principal's actions, the Court proclaimed that "educators do not offend the First Amendment by exercising editorial control over the style and content of student speech in school-sponsored expressive activities so long as their actions are *reasonably related to legitimate pedagogical concerns*."[48]

Hence, *Hazelwood*, together with *Bethel*, establishes a huge category of student speech to which *Tinker* no longer applies: "school-sponsored expressive activities."[49] Neither case, however, questioned *Tinker*'s insistence that schools are to prepare students for self-governance as members of a democratic polity. Instead, they portrayed their holdings as creating the structure and order needed to educate and create the enlightened citizenry whose existence is a prerequisite to self-government.[50] They adhered to the belief, expressed earlier by Justice Powell, that "[l]egal restrictions on minors . . . may be important to the child's chances for the full growth and maturity that make eventual participation in a free society meaningful and rewarding."[51]

Unfortunately, the *Hazelwood* Court failed to properly consider the

---

[45] *Id.* at 269.

[46] *Hazelwood*, 484 U.S. at 263-64.

[47] *Id.* at 274-75. The principal made this argument even though the pregnant students had agreed to discuss their experiences, and the article used fictitious names. *Id.* at 263. The principal's concern was that, because there were few pregnant students, the personal information in the article would reveal the identity of the students. *Id.* at 274.

[48] *Id.* at 273 (emphasis added).

[49] *Hazelwood*, 484 U.S. at 273.

[50] The relationship between democracy and education was understood clearly by our nation's founding generation. Thomas Jefferson, for example, concluded that "illuminat[ing] the minds of the people" was the most effective means of preventing those with power—even in the best of governmental forms—from "perverting it into tyranny." Thomas Jefferson, *Bill for the More General Diffusion of Knowledge* (1779), *quoted in* EVA T.H. BRANN, PARADOXES OF EDUCATION IN A REPUBLIC 40-41 (1979).

[51] Bellotti v. Baird, 443 U.S. 622, 638-39 (1979). Similarly, Professor Hafen stated that "children have a special need to submit themselves . . . to the yoke of educational demands in order to develop their own capacity for autonomous action." Hafen, *Schools*, *supra* note 16, at 612.

fact that children gain more than information and skills from school. They also learn socially accepted patterns of behavior and role expectations. Thus, beyond authority and obedience, students also must be exposed to liberty—the experience of liberty—if they are to be forged into contributing members of a democratic polity. The paradox in granting liberty to children stems from the realization that society must indoctrinate children so that they may be capable of autonomy. The centrality of this paradox to the mission of education has been forgotten in recent years.

II. THE SUBTLETIES OF LIBERTY

Appreciating the importance of preparing children to experience liberty, without condemning order, requires a subtle understanding of liberty in general. Yet one's understanding of liberty may be influenced by the ideological perspective used when analyzing the concept.

A. *Two Alternative Political Perspectives: An Historical Approach*

Even during our nation's founding era, many political leaders recognized the interplaying roles of autonomy, responsibility and obedience in the development of liberty.[52] Embraced in this recognition was the insight that liberty or freedom could too easily degenerate into what eighteenth-century thinkers called license or licentiousness.[53] Licentiousness, it was feared, could threaten the very existence of the new nation by sapping its economic and political strength, "leaving its people too weak

---

[52] *See* DAVID N. MAYER, THE CONSTITUTIONAL THOUGHT OF THOMAS JEFFERSON 148-49 (1994) (discussing James Madison's concerns of preserving will and autonomy of majority).

[53] Jeremiah Atwater, the first president of Middlebury College, cautioned the assembled Vermont legislature in 1801 that "[l]iberty, if considered as a blessing, must be taken in a qualified sense. The freedom which it implies, must be a limited, not [an] absolute freedom . . . for the very idea of government always supposes some restraint." Jeremiah Atwater, *A Sermon*, *in* 2 AMERICAN POLITICAL WRITING DURING THE FOUNDING ERA: 1760-1805, at 1170, 1172 (Charles S. Hyneman & Donald S. Lutz eds., 1983). John Locke, one of the inspirations for the American experiment with republican government, wrote that "[f]reedom . . . is not . . . [a] liberty for every one to do what he lists, [or] to live as he pleases." JOHN LOCKE, TWO TREATISES OF GOVERNMENT 301-02 (Peter Laslett ed., critical ed. 1960) (3d ed. 1698). Benjamin Rush, a noted Philadelphia doctor and educator, commented in 1787: "In our opposition to monarchy, we forgot that the temple of tyranny has two doors. We bolted one of them by proper restraints; but we left the other open, by neglecting to guard against the effects of our own ignorance and licentiousness." Benjamin Rush, An Address (1787), *quoted in* FORREST MCDONALD, NOVUS ORDO SECLORUM: THE INTELLECTUAL ORIGINS OF THE CONSTITUTION 3 (1985). For a contemporary perspective on the interrelationship between liberty and responsibility, see LAWRENCE M. MEAD, BEYOND ENTITLEMENT: THE SOCIAL OBLIGATION OF CITIZENSHIP 43 (1986) ("Those who are free of responsibility for themselves cannot be free to make their own way in society.").

and dissolute to repel corruption from within or invaders from without."[54] Thus, the compelling challenge of the age "was to make authority and liberty compatible."[55]

To respond to this challenge, Americans drew on two competing visions of social order. One vision, embodied by the liberal tradition of the Enlightenment[56] and embraced by the federalists,[57] emphasized the individualism of people acting in society, and examined how social institutions rest on and constrain individual preferences.[58] Each person was viewed as a distinct unit.[59] Autonomy and separation were emphasized; relationships among individuals were secondary.[60] According to this tradition, the purpose of the community was simply to give individuals the needed security (i.e. freedom) to pursue their private interests. So viewed, liberty was the extent to which the individual, once assured of this minimum level of security, was left unrestricted by the state.[61]

The alternative vision, drawing on the tradition of civic republicanism,[62] emphasized the essential social nature of individuals. This

---

[54] Suzanna Sherry, *Without Virtue There Can be No Liberty*, 78 MINN. L. REV. 61, 62-63 (1993).

[55] JAY FLIEGELMAN, PRODIGALS AND PILGRIMS, THE AMERICAN REVOLUTION AGAINST PATRIARCHAL AUTHORITY 1750-1800, at 14 (1982).

[56] *See* 1 PETER GAY, THE ENLIGHTENMENT: AN INTERPRETATION, THE RISE OF MODERN PAGANISM 3-27 (1966) (discussing intellectual climate of European Enlightenment giving birth to views of many American political thinkers of era).

[57] *See* THE FEDERALIST PAPERS (Clinton Rossiter ed., 1961).

[58] This analysis of the liberal tradition is drawn primarily from LOUIS HARTZ, THE LIBERAL TRADITION IN AMERICA (1955) and C.B. MACPHERSON, THE POLITICAL THEORY OF POSSESSIVE INDIVIDUALISM: HOBBES TO LOCKE (1962).

[59] Theorists emphasizing our separateness included: THOMAS HOBBES, LEVIATHAN 110 (Liberal Arts Press ed., 1958) (1651) ("The condition of man . . . is a condition of war of every one against every one . . . ."); JOHN LOCKE, TWO TREATISES OF GOVERNMENT 296 (Peter Laslett ed., 1967) (3d ed. 1698) ("[A]ll men are naturally in [the] State [of nature], and remain so, till by their own consent they make themselves Members of some Politick Society . . . ."). For an account of the central role of individualism in the seventeenth century English thought that shaped Western political philosophy, see MACPHERSON, *supra* note 58.

[60] DAVID A.J. RICHARDS, THE MORAL CRITICISM OF LAW 51 (1977); MICHAEL J. SANDEL, LIBERALISM AND THE LIMITS OF JUSTICE 133 (1982).

[61] Accordingly, public liberty was viewed as synonymous with individual liberty. GORDON S. WOOD, THE CREATION OF THE AMERICAN REPUBLIC, 1776-1787, at 63 (1969); Stanley N. Katz, *Thomas Jefferson and the Right to Property in Revolutionary America*, 19 J.L. & ECON. 467, 482 (1976). Because the interest of the community was equated with the aggregate of individual interests, the prosperity of the nation increased in conjunction with increased freedom of individuals to pursue their own desires.

[62] *See* J.G.A. POCOCK, THE MACHIAVELLIAN MOMENT: FLORENTINE POLITICAL THOUGHT AND THE ATLANTIC REPUBLICAN TRADITION 462 (1975); CAROLINE ROBBINS, THE EIGHTEENTH-CENTURY COMMONWEALTHMAN: STUDIES IN THE TRANSMISSION, DEVELOPMENT, AND CIRCUMSTANCES OF ENGLISH LIBERAL THOUGHT FROM THE RESTORATION OF CHARLES II UNTIL

perspective—embraced most fully by the anti-federalists who feared large, impersonal and powerful government[63]—rejected the individualism of the Enlightenment and focused instead on republican theorists dating back to ancient Greece and the Italian city-states.[64] Republicanism perceived people as gaining an understanding of their lives from participation and interaction with others in a social world that they jointly created.[65] Consequently, the assumption was that people were shaped by the institutions in which they functioned; the central theme was connection rather than autonomy.[66] Society preceded the individual, for self-knowledge was possible only with reference to the social matrix within which individuals found themselves.[67] Institutions of social life, therefore, were important because they forged the character of citizens.[68] It was the responsibility of these institutions to promote "civic virtue"—a capacity to overcome private passion, or appetite, in public decision-

---

THE WAR WITH THE THIRTEEN COLONIES (1959); GARRY WILLS, EXPLAINING AMERICA: THE FEDERALIST (1981); WOOD, *supra* note 61.

[63] *See generally* HERBERT J. STORING, WHAT THE ANTI-FEDERALISTS WERE FOR (Murray Dry ed., 1981). Although, the "home" of republican thought in American constitutionalism may have been in the work of the anti-federalists, *see* Cass R. Sunstein, *Beyond the Republican Revival*, 97 YALE L.J. 1539, 1547 (1988), many republican themes existed in federal thought as well. H. Jefferson Powell, *Reviving Republicanism*, 97 YALE L.J. 1703, 1705 (1988). The philosophical distinction between the federalists and anti-federalists was not one of total opposition but one of emphasis and degree. *See* Linda K. Kerber, *Making Republicanism Useful*, 97 YALE L.J. 1663, 1666-67 & n.13 (1988).

[64] *See* Richard A. Epstein, *Modern Republicanism—Or the Flight from Substance*, 97 YALE L.J. 1633, 1634 (1988).

[65] According to this tradition, "man was by nature a political being, a citizen who achieved his greatest moral fulfillment by participating in a self-governing republic." Gordon S. Wood, *Classical Republicanism and the American Revolution*, 66 CHI.-KENT L. REV. 13, 23 (1990).

[66] Theoretical works accepting this social nature of humanity included: ADAM FERGUSON, AN ESSAY ON THE HISTORY OF CIVIL SOCIETY 4 (Duncan Forbes ed., 1966) (1767) (arguing that "[m]ankind are to be taken in group[s], as they have always subsisted" and that "[t]he history of the individual is but a detail of the sentiments and thoughts he has entertained in the view of his species"); DAVID HUME, A TREATISE OF HUMAN NATURE 485 (L.A. Selby-Bigge ed., 1967) ("'Tis by society alone [man] is able to supply his defects, and raise himself up to an equality with his fellow-creatures. . . .'").

[67] *See* Paul W. Kahn, *Reason and Will in the Origins of American Constitutionalism*, 98 YALE L.J. 449, 517 (1989) ("[A]s a member of a particular discursive community, the individual simultaneously creates both his own individual identity and that of the community.").

[68] This perspective insisted that we each define and understand ourselves through personal attachments. We acquire our values through the interplay of innumerable influences of family, friends, neighbors, church, schools, cultural figures, and others. *See* Duncan Kennedy, *The Structure of Blackstone's Commentaries*, 28 BUFF. L. REV. 209, 211-12 (1979). Human individuality is formed through processes of language, thought, and feeling, which naturally and necessarily include other persons.

making.[69] A virtuous citizenry was one that had learned from its institutions that the public good differed from the aggregate of private preferences.[70] For such a citizenry, liberty consisted of a process of seeking and structuring a shared *telos*, consisting of a common value system for citizen and community.[71] The quintessential public institutions were those that allowed individuals to *experience* liberty through an ongoing process of self-determination.[72]

B. *The Constitutional Concept of "Right"*

Given these differing conceptions of liberty,[73] it is significant that it was the anti-federalists (rather than the federalists), with their commitment to this republican orientation, who were the force that galvanized support for the inclusion of a Bill of Rights in the United States Constitution.[74] Viewing society as a teacher—a molder of character—rather than just a

---

[69] As one pair of scholars remarked, "Good republican government might transform individuals; good liberal (Lockean) government merely protected them." DANIEL A. FARBER & SUZANNA SHERRY, A HISTORY OF THE AMERICAN CONSTITUTION 13 (1990).

[70] A virtuous citizen had an independent mind and a willingness to use it for the good of the community. Virtue meant taking responsibility for oneself and one's community. Virtue also meant letting reason control passion, and letting long-term community interests override selfish individual wants. Citizens in a virtuous republic deliberated rationally about what would best serve the interests of the community. For republicans, governmental decisions were not mere responses to private interests, but were efforts to decide upon and implement communal values. *See* JOSEPH VINING, LEGAL IDENTITY 13-33 (1978). Rather than Locke, the philosophical emphasis was on Rousseau, *see* JUDITH N. SHKLAR, MEN AND CITIZENS: A STUDY OF ROUSSEAU'S SOCIAL THEORY 104 (1969) (discussing Rousseau's preoccupation with republican governments), Machiavelli, *see generally* POCOCK, *supra* note 61, and Aristotle, *see* ERNEST BARKER, THE POLITICAL THOUGHT OF PLATO AND ARISTOTLE 295 (1959) (describing Aristotle's concept of citizenship as participation in political decision-making).

[71] *See* Paul Brest, *The Fundamental Rights Controversy: The Essential Contradictions of Normative Constitutional Scholarship*, 90 YALE L.J. 1063, 1109 (1981); *see also* JANE J. MANSBRIDGE, BEYOND ADVERSARY DEMOCRACY 26-28 (1980) (describing development of common interests in political community); CAROLE PATEMAN, PARTICIPATION AND DEMOCRATIC THEORY 1-21 (1970) (commenting on political and communal values of democratic society).

[72] *See* HANNA ARENDT, ON REVOLUTION 248-55 (1963); DAVID HELD, MODELS OF DEMOCRACY 186-220 (1987). For republicans, individual fulfillment came from "sharing in a collective autonomy, a collective freedom and glory." HANNA PITKIN, FORTUNE IS A WOMAN: GENDER AND POLITICS IN THE THOUGHT OF NICCOLO MACHIAVELLI 81 (1984).

[73] Isaiah Berlin's distinction between "negative" and "positive" liberty captured the essential difference between liberty under individualism, as embraced by the federalists, and liberty under republicanism, as embraced by the anti-federalists. Isaiah Berlin, *Two Concepts of Liberty*, *in* FOUR ESSAYS ON LIBERTY 118, 118-35 (1969).

[74] *See* STORING, *supra* note 63, at 64 ("It is often said that the major legacy of the Anti-Federalists is the Bill of Rights.").

regulator of conduct,[75] the anti-federalists believed that the proposed Constitution inadequately accounted for this character-building role. An important component of their argument for a federal bill of rights was the role they hoped the document would play in providing the political and moral education necessary for the development of a virtuous citizenry.[76]

This history should cause us to question the common contemporary perception that constitutional rights are designed solely to secure the interests of individuals, most commonly the interest of personal autonomy, by respecting individual choice.[77] A more subtle comprehension of these rights reveals that they may serve multiple purposes. Of course, in order for a right to be enforced through litigation, some individual must be privileged to claim it. Nevertheless, rights not only encompass individualistic values but those that are interpersonal or communal as well.[78] The individual, therefore, may possess that right only, or at least partially, in an agency or fiduciary capacity, thus, protecting the interests of others or the polity in general.

The multifarious functioning of constitutional rights is clearly apparent in the context of the First Amendment right to free speech. The argument

---

[75] Anti-federalist Melancton Smith captured this spirit when he said:

> Government operates upon the spirit of the people, as well as the spirit of the people operates upon it—and if they are not conformable to each other, the one or the other will prevail. . . . Our duty is to frame a government friendly to liberty and the rights of mankind, which will tend to cherish and cultivate a love of liberty among our citizens.

Melancton Smith, Address Delivered in the Course of Debate by the Convention of the State of New York on the Adoption of the Federalist Constitution (June 21, 1788), *reprinted in* 6 THE COMPLETE ANTI-FEDERALIST 155, 160-61 (Herbert J. Storing ed., 1981).

[76] One anti-federalist insisted that a bill of rights would provide "the first lesson of the young citizens becoming men, to sustain the dignity of their being." 5 THE COMPLETE ANTI-FEDERALIST, *supra* note 75, at 273.

[77] *See, e.g.*, LAURENCE H. TRIBE, AMERICAN CONSTITUTIONAL LAW § 15-1, at 1302 (2d ed. 1988); Cass R. Sunstein, *Deregulation and the Hard-Look Doctrine*, 1983 SUP. CT. REV. 177, 187 (1983). Most contemporary "rights-based" theories of constitutional law are centered around concern for upholding individual action. *See, e.g.*, Ronald Dworkin, *Liberalism*, *in* PUBLIC AND PRIVATE MORALITY 113, 127 (Stuart Hampshire ed., 1978) (arguing that liberalism supposes that individuals must be free to choose own vision of "good life").

The seminal defense of rights theory is contained in RONALD DWORKIN, TAKING RIGHTS SERIOUSLY (1977). An assessment of the role of rights theory can be found in Peter Westen, *The Rueful Rhetoric of "Rights"*, 33 UCLA L. REV. 977, 977-78 (1986) ("The language of 'rights' has become the rhetoric of choice in our society for asserting moral and legal claims.").

[78] *See* Seth F. Kreimer, *Allocational Sanctions: The Problem of Negative Rights in a Positive State*, 132 U. PA. L. REV. 1293, 1389 (1984) (contending that constitutional rights protect values other than individual choice); Kathleen M. Sullivan, *Unconstitutional Conditions*, 102 HARV. L. REV. 1415, 1490 (1989) (stating that "constitutional liberties . . . do not simply protect individual rightholders piecemeal").

against censorship is often stated in terms of autonomy, and attributes to free speech an overriding purpose of respecting and protecting an individual's absolute freedom of thought and conscience necessary to promote self-realization and self-expression.[79] Speech, however, is not the only means by which these autonomy-based interests can be served. They may be furthered through virtually all voluntary conduct, including one's choice of profession, dress, and consumer goods.[80] Consequently, a recognition of the social importance of free speech is necessary to explain why speech has been singled out for constitutional protection.

The often-used metaphor of the "marketplace of ideas" encapsulates the interpersonal or systemic interests of free speech, resting as much on its importance to the receiver of any message as it does to the communicator.[81] This perspective of free speech interests has two component parts. The first assumes that a process of robust debate, if uninhibited by governmental interference, will lead to the discovery of truth, or at least to the best perspectives on solutions for social problems.[82] The second component emphasizes the social value of an informed citizenry acting as sovereign overseeing governmental action.[83] Proponents of this latter

---

[79] Some commentators assert that autonomy is the singular—or at least the primary—justification for free speech. *See, e.g.*, Charles Fried, *The New First Amendment Jurisprudence: A Threat to Liberty*, 59 U. CHI. L. REV. 225, 233 (1992); Martin H. Redish, *The Value of Free Speech*, 130 U. PA. L. REV. 591, 593 (1982).

[80] "An individual may develop his faculties . . . from trading in the stock market, following his profession as a riverport pilot, working as a barmaid, engaging in sexual activity, playing tennis, rigging prices or in any of thousands of other endeavors." Robert H. Bork, *Neutral Principles and Some First Amendment Problems*, 47 IND. L.J. 1, 25 (1971); *see also* Cass R. Sunstein, *Free Speech Now*, 59 U. CHI. L. REV. 255, 303-04 (1992).

[81] *See, e.g.*, Board of Educ. v. Pico, 457 U.S. 853, 866-68 (1982) (emphasizing student's "right to receive information and ideas"); Red Lion Broadcasting Co. v. FCC, 395 U.S. 367, 390 (1969) (claiming that interests of recipients of speech rather than that of communicator are paramount for First Amendment purposes). The core insight of the *Red Lion* case, which upheld the FCC's Fairness Doctrine against constitutional attack by broadcasters, was that the interest in legally protected private autonomy from government is not always connected with the interest of democratic self-governance. *Id.* at 392-93.

[82] Although this classic image of competing ideas and robust debate dates back to English philosophers John Milton, *see* John Milton, *Aeropagitica* (London 1644), *in* THE PROSE OF JOHN MILTON 265 *passim* (J. Max Patrick ed., 1967), and John Stuart Mill, *see* JOHN STUART MILL, ON LIBERTY 15-71 (Elizabeth Rapaport ed., 1978), Justice Holmes first introduced this concept into American jurisprudence in his 1919 dissent to Abrams v. United States, 250 U.S. 616 (1919), stating that "the best test of truth is the power of the thought to get itself accepted in the competition of the market." *Abrams*, 250 U.S. at 630 (Holmes, J., dissenting).

[83] *See* Kenneth L. Karst, *Equality as a Central Principle in the First Amendment*, 43 U. CHI. L. REV. 20, 23-25 (1975). *See generally* Vincent Blasi, *The Checking Value in First Amendment Theory*, 1977 AM. B. FOUND. RES. J. 523, 529-44 (1977) (stating that free expression is check against abuse of official power).

conception insist that the best decisions can be reached in a democracy only if the citizenry is fully aware of the issues involved, the options available, and the interests or values at stake.[84]

Yet for many, these interpersonal or systemic functions of free speech do not explain the need to safeguard extremist or hateful communication such as the anti-semitic message of the Nazis. Few, for example, were willing to credit the Nazis who wished to march through Skokie, Illinois,[85] with expanding the menu of views from which individuals choose their truths.[86] Such a strong commitment to free speech may be more fully explained by another set of interests—communal interests. Through our legal response to speech activity, we create a social identity that reflects and embodies the aspirations and values of the community. The protection of the Skokie march thus can be viewed as a collective, self-disciplinary exercise in communal tolerance.[87]

The communal interest in free speech, therefore, need not be based on the skeptic's fear of the fallibility of governmental attempts to identify truth. Rather, it is based on a desire to nurture certain character traits in the polity. Free speech seeks to make people courageous, resilient, and tolerant. It attempts to create a polity willing to stake confidence and resolve against deviance and dissent, one that is unafraid to hear the worst that can be said about its own moral and cognitive situations.[88] So

---

[84] *See, e.g.*, ALEXANDER MEIKLEJOHN, FREE SPEECH AND ITS RELATION TO SELF-GOVERNMENT 88 (1948) (asserting that First Amendment's primary purpose is to give every voting citizen fullest possible understanding of problems with which members of self-governing society must deal).

[85] *See* National Socialist Party of Am. v. Village of Skokie, 434 U.S. 1327 (1977) (denying stay); National Socialist Party of Am. v. Village of Skokie, 432 U.S. 43 (1977) (per curiam); Collin v. Smith, 578 F.2d 1197 (7th Cir.), *stay denied*, 436 U.S. 953, *and cert. denied*, 439 U.S. 916 (1978). *See generally* David Goldberger, *Skokie: The First Amendment Under Attack by its Friends*, 29 MERCER L. REV. 761, 772 (1978) (stating that commitment to Bill of Rights can be "peeled away, one supporting group at a time").

[86] Holmes argued that all views, even those we detest, need to be given the opportunity to *succeed* in the marketplace. *See* Gitlow v. New York, 268 U.S. 652, 672-73 (1925) (Holmes, J., dissenting). Unsurprisingly, the Jewish community of Skokie questioned why the arguments of anti-semitism and genocide should be offered such an opportunity. For many, the contention that unrestricted expression of the precepts of Nazism must be protected because we cannot know whether such ideas are actually false is both unpersuasive and offensive. *See* DONALD A. DOWNS, NAZIS IN SKOKIE: FREEDOM, COMMUNITY AND THE FIRST AMENDMENT 32 (1985) (estimating that ACLU lost 30,000 members—15% of its total membership—and $500,000 per year in contributions because of defense of Nazis' right to march through Skokie).

[87] *See* LEE C. BOLLINGER, THE TOLERANT SOCIETY 198-200 (1986).

[88] Thus, free speech presently builds character through both the experience of communicating and that of reacting to communication. In the very act of talking, values such as power, enlightenment, skill, affection, respect, health and well-being are latently shaped and shared. Social structures that foster active involvement can cultivate qualities essential to a democratic society,

viewed, the emphasis of the First Amendment shifts from the value of the speech, as represented by the interpersonal interest in information exchange, to the value of the response, as represented by the communal interest in tolerance.[89] Tolerance becomes a means through which society communicates and affirms its own principles, thereby creating a sense of community.[90] The deep structure of this character-based argument, therefore, is collectivist and communitarian, rather than individualistic.

C. *The Importance of Intermediary Institutions*

Despite the availability of this more subtle, holistic approach to liberty, the civic republican language of community has all but disappeared from the lexicon of rights.[91] Instead, the rhetoric of liberal political philosophy—a philosophy which posits individuals capable of freely choosing among values without constraint—provides the bedrock from which our modern commitment to liberty, including free speech, arises.[92]

---

qualities such as self-confidence, inquisitiveness, and a willingness to question authority. *See* PATEMEN, *supra* note 71, at 45-66 (examining positive correlation between participation and sense of political efficacy).

But perhaps of even greater importance, a strong doctrine of free expression has its greatest effect on the character of those who possess the power to control speech. They are required to be more tolerant and respectful of individual integrity, more open to change, and more accustomed to, or less fearful of, challenge.

[89] *See* Suzanna Sherry, *An Essay Concerning Toleration*, 71 MINN. L. REV. 963, 976 (1987) (describing contribution of scholarship of Lee Bollinger in understanding value of free speech).

[90] *See* Lee C. Bollinger, *Free Speech and Intellectual Values*, 92 YALE L.J. 438, 460 (1983) (noting community is created and defined through tolerance). In this light, it is revealing to compare the opinion of Justice Holmes in Gitlow v. New York, 268 U.S. 652, 672-73 (1925) (Holmes, J., dissenting), emphasizing the importance of offering even extremist speech a chance to *succeed* in the marketplace, with that of Justice Brandeis in Whitney v. California, 274 U.S. 357, 372 (1927) (Brandeis J., concurring). In this landmark opinion, Justice Brandeis cautioned that "repression breeds hate . . . ." *Id.* at 375. This phrase can be read as a double-entendre. Brandeis was concerned not only with the hate experienced by dissidents, but also with the hate experienced by those with power to punish dissent. The passage is not primarily about consequences or tactics; it is about character. For Brandeis, tolerance was an act of civic courage. *See* Vincent Blasi, *The First Amendment and the Ideal of Civic Courage: The Brandeis Opinion in* Whitney v. California, 29 WM. & MARY L. REV. 653, 691 (1988) ("The courageous attitude, Brandeis asserts, is that of receptivity to new arrangements and new ways of thinking.").

[91] There has been, however, somewhat of a revival of republican philosophy in present social theory. *See, e.g.*, Symposium, *The Republican Civil Tradition*, 97 YALE L.J. 1493 (1988) (symposium on civil republicanism).

[92] *See* Suzanna Sherry, *Civic Virtue and the Feminine Voice in Constitutional Adjudication*, 72 VA. L. REV. 543, 544-45 (1986) (asserting that present paradigm of political and moral philosophy is individualist). For many, individualism is the foundation upon which our constitutional commitment to free speech is built. *Id.* "Individualism lies at the very core of American culture," writes one group of scholars. ROBERT N. BELLAH ET AL., HABITS OF THE HEART: INDIVIDUALISM AND COMMITMENT IN AMERICAN LIFE 142 (1985). "We believe in the

But by asserting that individuals are independent and self-sufficient originators of their own ideas and beliefs—that they exist free of cultural context—the individualist perspective denies the community's role in both shaping and reflecting an individual's values.[93] Thus, individualism provides an unrealistic account of our moral existence; individuals cannot be separated from the community in which they reside.[94]

Yet even with this realization of the importance of "community," the concept is problematic in today's large and heterogeneous state. The community which now structures the individual's sense of self and dominates the process of character building can no longer be equated with the state. Today, the obligation of character development essentially falls on intermediate level institutions or social groupings situated somewhere between the isolated individual and the distant, and often abstract, state.[95] These groups and institutions, such as civic and voluntary organizations, social and recreational clubs, churches, workplaces, schools, families and neighborhoods, with their face-to-face interplay among members, serve as

---

dignity, indeed the sacredness, of the individual. Anything that would violate our right to think for ourselves, judge for ourselves, make our own decisions, live our lives as we see fit, is not only morally wrong, it is sacrilegious." *Id.*

[93] *See* MACPHERSON, *supra* note 58, at 263-64; David A.J. Richards, *Sexual Autonomy and the Constitutional Right to Privacy: A Case Study in Human Rights and the Unwritten Constitution*, 30 HASTINGS L.J. 957, 976 (1979) (discussing foundation of constitutional morality).

[94] In spite of our best efforts, we can never truly extricate ourselves from the influence of our cultural milieu. As historian Isaiah Berlin notes:

> For am I not what I am, to some degree, in virtue of what others think and feel me to be? When I ask myself what I am, and answer: an Englishman, a Chinese, a merchant, a man of no importance, a millionaire, a convict—I find upon analysis that to possess these attributes entails being recognized as belonging to a particular group or class by other persons in my society, and that this recognition is part of the meaning of most of the terms that denote some of my most personal and permanent characteristics. I am not disembodied reason. Nor am I Robinson Crusoe, alone upon his island. It is not only that my material life depends upon interaction with other men, or that I am what I am as a result of social forces, but that some, perhaps all, of my ideas about myself, in particular my sense of my own moral and social identity, are intelligible only in terms of the social network in which I am . . . an element.

Berlin, *supra* note 73, at 155.

[95] An early commentator on American society was struck by the abundance and importance of these intermediate institutions. 2 ALEXIS DE TOCQUEVILLE, DEMOCRACY IN AMERICA 114-28 (Phillips Bradley ed., 1945). "Americans of all ages, all conditions, and all dispositions constantly form associations." *Id.* at 114. Justice Brennan heralded voluntary associations as "critical buffers between the individual and the power of the State." Roberts v. United States Jaycees, 468 U.S. 609, 619 (1984). Bruce Hafen has also written extensively of the importance of intermediate institutions, what he calls "mediating institutions." Bruce C. Hafen, *Developing Student Expression Through Institutional Authority: Public Schools As Mediating Structures*, 48 OHIO ST. L.J. 663, 696 (1987) [hereinafter Hafen, *Developing Student Expression*].

the situs of a majority of those experiences which give moral and intellectual meaning to our world.[96] They are the true bases and bear the primary responsibility for social integration and the formation of ideals and beliefs.[97] Essentially, character development is the responsibility of an individual's interactive community.

Thus, character-building depends on lessons gained in the interplay of daily life. Without day-to-day opportunities for meaningful participation in microsettings, people will not develop the relevant skills and attitudes desirable within the community, and may lack a sense of their ability to make a difference in broader political arenas.[98] It is, therefore, the

---

[96] *See* Grant McConnell, *The Public Values of the Private Association*, *in* NOMOS XI: VOLUNTARY ASSOCIATIONS 147, 149 (J. Roland Pennock & John W. Chapman eds., 1969) (noting that private associations "build norms and patterns of behavior"); Richard B. Stewart, *Organizational Jurisprudence*, 101 HARV. L. REV. 371, 380-84 (1987) (describing alternative normative conceptions of intermediate organizations) (reviewing MEIR DAN-COHEN, RIGHTS, PERSONS, AND ORGANIZATIONS: A LEGAL THEORY FOR BUREAUCRATIC SOCIETY (1986)).

If we are to recognize the importance of these intermediate groups in relation to character building, we also must be aware of the danger. The more one's sense of self is tied to one's role in these institutions that incorporate face-to-face contact, the more coercive pressure to conform these groups exercise. Consequently, for some, these small "governing" units represent the greatest danger to individual liberty. *See* THE FEDERALIST NO. 10, at 77-79 (James Madison) (Clinton Rossiter ed., 1961) (expressing fear of coercive power of small groups).

[97] These small-scale institutions can serve as "private boot camps for citizenship . . . serv[ing] not as havens for the dominant culture, but as vehicles for teaching the primacy of the common good, writ small." Kathleen M. Sullivan, *Rainbow Republicanism*, 97 YALE L.J. 1713, 1720 (1988). Some urge that, because of the opportunities for greater participation, feelings of attachment, and common purpose, these smaller associations can give their members a sense of interdependence in the creation of the meanings that give life to the institution. Thus, they can provide the experience of acting for the public good. *See* Gerald E. Frug, *Cities and Homeowners Associations: A Reply*, 130 U. PA. L. REV. 1589, 1600-01 (1982).

[98] *See* Stanley Ingber, *Rediscovering the Communal Worth of Individual Rights: The First Amendment in Institutional Contexts*, 69 TEX. L. REV. 1 (1990) [hereinafter Ingber, *Rediscovering*].

> What [most people] fail to recognize is that for most Americans those contexts of greatest First Amendment protection [voting, participation in protest marches, demonstrations, picketing, and leafletting] are tangential to their daily lives. Most of us probably would feel sheepish if the degree to which we take advantage of and experiance the opportunity to express our opinions or exercise independent thought were assessed. Mark Twain's notorious comment regarding the practical impact upon individuals of our present legal protection of speech behavior retains its sting: "It is by the goodness of God that in ourt country we have those three unspeakably precious things: freedom of speech, freedom of conscience, and the prudence never to practice either of them."

Id. at 49 (footnotes omitted) (quoting MARK TWAIN, FOLLOWING THE EQUATOR 196 (1987)). A system which protects speech only in contexts experienced by few will have little effect on character the development of the citizenry. *See also* Suzanna Sherry, *Responsible Republicanism: Educating for Citizenship*, 62 U. CHI. L. REV. 131, 192 (1995) (discussing importance of First Amendment freedoms in "education for republican citizenship").

structure society imposes upon day-to-day intercourse that creates the habits of interaction, socializes proper role expectations, and communicates subtly but powerfully those values for which the community stands.[99] Each of us are constructed by the social setting in which we find ourselves, determining our attitudes towards such factors as hierarchy, expertise, creativity and independence.[100]

Consequently, we must give considerable attention to the vital lessons learned in these mundane contexts, for I believe that it is within these settings that character is actually built and values inculcated. If responsible freedom cannot be fostered in these day-to-day contexts, then a political community built on civic virtue and courage is an impossible dream.[101] Intermediate institutions are integral to the fulfillment of First Amendment concerns; they serve both as the boot camp and the front line in the effort to forge the character of a democratic polity.[102]

Unfortunately, this insight is missing from the Supreme Court's recent willingness to minimize free speech experiences in public school settings—settings vital to the creation of who we are as individuals, and what we care and stand for as a community.

III. Education for Citizenship

A. *Children and Liberty*

If constitutional rights presently are based on the rhetoric of individualism,[103] it is not surprising that the individual interests encompassed by

---

[99] Other authors have recognized the character-building or communal value of communicative freedom. *See, e.g.*, BOLLINGER, *supra* note 87; Sherry, *supra* note 92. They see First Amendment jurisprudence as playing a largely educative role. Through our legal response to speech activity, they believe we create a social identity that reflects and embodies the aspirations and values of the community. *See* MEIKLEJOHN, *supra* note 84, at 58 ("The Supreme Court, we have said, is and must be one of our most effective teachers. It is, in the last resort, an accredited interpreter to us of our own intentions.").

[100] *See* Paul Brest, *Further Beyond the Republican Revival: Toward Radical Republicanism*, 97 YALE L.J. 1623, 1628 (1988) ("[T]he methods or habits of 'constitutional thinking' likely cannot be developed on the spur of the moment.").

[101] The values a community hopes its citizens exude, therefore, must be embodied in the community's institutional arrangements. Consequently, it is submitted that if we exclude institutional settings from First Amendment coverage, the concept of a society founded on virtuous, popular participation is likely to remain unfamiliar and foreign, perforce making its attainment unrealistic. If we are trained in our daily lives quietly to accept authority or, alternatively, enthusiastically to wield authority, we cannot expect to create a polity capable of anything other than acceptance of an entrenched status quo.

[102] *See* Sullivan, *supra* note 97, at 1720.

[103] *See supra* text accompanying note 92.

the First Amendment fare poorly in school settings. Given that individualism posits persons capable of choosing among values without constraint from others or the state, children surely constitute the "Achilles heel of liberal ideology."[104] For children, the communal role in character-building is incontrovertible[105] because children are not born with a community allegiance or a particular cultural orientation.[106] Society must teach values, thereby molding character, if children are to have conceptions of the public good as adults. Although the initial source of a child's self-perception lies with the home and family, once the child begins to attend school, a major initiative passes beyond the family to the educational institution.[107] Consequently, many commentators argue that education's inherent indoctrinative character leaves the First Amendment with no legitimate role in our public schools.[108]

One may not simply gloss over the importance of liberty for children, however, by insisting that because they lack the facility to choose in an intelligent, rational, and independent manner, children fail to possess "that full capacity for individual choice which is the presupposition of First Amendment guarantees."[109] Regardless of whether one accepts an

---

[104] Shiffrin, *supra* note 25, at 647. Others echo Shiffrin's characterization. *See, e.g.*, Larry Alexander, *Liberalism as Neutral Dialogue: Man and Manna in the Liberal State*, 28 UCLA L. REV. 816, 855 (1981).

[105] Even libertarian John Stuart Mill, in discussing liberty as autonomy, recognized children as a necessary limit upon his philosophy. MILL, *supra* note 82, at 9. Little remains of the concept of unrestrained choice, however, if the educational process may socialize children for 18 years with the intent of forging "good citizens."

[106] Yodof, *Library Book Selection*, *supra* note 23, at 531.

[107] *See* Jules Henry, *Attitude Organization in Elementary School Classrooms*, *in* READINGS IN THE SOCIAL PSYCHOLOGY OF EDUCATION 254 (Werrett W. Charters & Nathaniel L. Gage eds., 1963) (stating that classroom "does not merely sustain attitudes . . . created in the home, but reinforces some, de-emphasizes others, and makes its own contribution"). As children get older, their peer community and the pop-media culture will also have an effect.

[108] *See, e.g.*, JOSEPH TUSSMAN, GOVERNMENT AND THE MIND 51-85, 167 n.29 (1977) (concluding that state's "teaching power" involves inducting children into community, rendering notions of children's free speech and state ideological neutrality irrelevant); David A. Diamond, *The First Amendment and Public Schools: The Case Against Judicial Intervention*, 59 TEX. L. REV. 477 (1981) (contending that schools' indoctrinative function precludes recognizing First Amendment rights for children); Brian A. Freeman, *The Supreme Court and First Amendment Rights of Students in the Public School Classroom: A Proposed Model of Analysis*, 12 HASTINGS CONST. L.Q. 1, 24 (1984) (asserting that classroom dialogue facilitates learning process which includes "value inculcation," instead of forum for free trade of ideas); Stephen R. Goldstein, *The Asserted Constitutional Right of Public School Teachers to Determine What They Teach*, 124 U. PA. L. REV. 1293 (1976) (stating that scope of indoctrinative interests in public education precludes in-class activities contrary to wishes of school authorities).

[109] Ginsberg v. New York, 390 U.S. 629, 649-50 (1968) (Stewart, J., concurring). The argument goes further still, claiming that children need to be protected from the consequences of

individual or communitarian perspective on the value of speech conduct, this view begs two fundamental questions: (1) How can young adults autonomously choose among competing options if they have had little prior experience with such choice? and (2) How can individuals as adults exemplify the civic virtues of public-spiritedness, participation, and tolerance if their experiences during their most formative years inhibit such traits? Both the individualist and communitarian goals of free speech are unattainable if societal institutions are structured so as to cultivate interactive habits in children which are inconsistent with the needs of a democratic polity.[110] Students who receive nothing but predigested ideas throughout their childhood cannot miraculously transform into autonomous, free-thinking individuals upon reaching adulthood.

Public institutions, of course, are established to fulfill specified societal needs; schools are established to educate the young. They must be given the tools and freedom to efficiently fulfill that mission. Part of that mission, however, is the preparation of students for induction into a democratic polity. Regardless of the students' readiness for autonomy, our communitarian goals require that they be exposed to free speech experiences in an environment capable of promoting civic virtue, of character building. Therefore, we must structure our schools so that they may succeed not only in the education *of* citizens but also in the education of students *for* citizenship.[111]

B. The Mission of Education

Citizens who lack education also lack the capacity for meaningful participation in a democracy. Even during the founding era of the eighteenth-century, many writers and speakers stressed the necessity of education, recognizing that an ignorant people cannot sustain freedom.[112]

---

their own poor choices. *See* Bellotti v. Baird, 443 U.S. 622, 635 (1979) (commenting that children "lack the experience, perspective, and judgment to recognize and avoid choices that could be detrimental to them"); *see also* Bruce C. Hafen, *The Learning Years: A Review of The Changing Legal World of Adolescence*, 81 MICH. L. REV. 1045, 1048-49 (1983) [hereinafter Hafen, *The Learning Years*] (noting that limitations on choice are "form of protection for minors . . . against their own immaturity and against their vulnerability to exploitation by others").

[110] Thus, Professor Hafen acknowledges that despite his belief that infants and young children totally lack the capacity for self-governance, "[a]dolescence . . . is another matter." Hafen, *The Learning Years*, *supra* note 109, at 1045.

[111] *See* Sherry, *supra* note 54, at 77 (distinguishing between education "for" citizenship and education "of" citizens).

[112] In 1782, Zabdiel Adams preached that "[a]n ignorant people will never long live under a free government. They will soon become slaves." Zabdiel Adams, An Election Sermon (1782), *in* 1 AMERICAN POLITICAL WRITING DURING THE FOUNDING ERA: 1760-1805, *supra* note 53,

Thus, education of citizens—education intended to inform and to create certain skills, including those of communication and comprehension—is indispensable to the fostering and nourishing of the underlying values of the First Amendment.[113] Students must gain the capacity to enjoy these free speech values. They must "receive knowledge," and to do so they may well have to accept the authority of their teachers.[114]

To accomplish these goals, schooling certainly requires a degree of order and discipline.[115] Without it, students may well be denied the "right" to an effective education. Based on this need to educate citizens, Professor Hafen concludes that "courts should presume the constitutional validity of rational decisions by public school officials that implicate educational matters, both curricular and extracurricular."[116] This presumption is "grounded in interests associated with students' right to be taught the values underlying the [F]irst [A]mendment."[117]

As previously stated, however, schools are responsible not only for education *of* citizens but also for education *for* citizenship.[118] Schools invariably teach values.[119] Thus, Professor Hafen also appreciates that

---

at 539, 555. In 1799, Samuel Knox wrote that "[i]gnorance . . . has ever been the parent and stupid nurse of civil slavery . . . ." Samuel Knox, *An Essay On the Best System of Liberal Education*, *in* ESSAYS ON EDUCATION IN THE EARLY REPUBLIC 271, 288 (Frederick Rudolph ed., 1965). Joel Barlow noted in 1801 that "[i]gnorance is everywhere . . . an infallible instrument of despotism." Letter II from Joel Barlow to His Fellow Citizens of the United States: On Certain Political Measures Proposed to Their Consideration (1801), *in* 2 AMERICAN POLITICAL WRITING DURING THE FOUNDING ERA: 1760-1805, *supra* note 53, at 1099, 1121.

[113] *See* Hafen, *Developing Student Expression*, *supra* note 95, at 669 ("Public education seeks affirmatively to teach the capacity to enjoy first amendment values--to mediate between ignorance and educated expression.").

[114] Professor Hafen, in fact, describes education as "necessarily [an] authoritarian process." Hafen, *Schools*, *supra* note 16, at 619. He further concludes that the "widespread reduction of institutional authority in public schools over the past generation is statistically correlated with the recently publicized declines in the academic achievement of American students." Hafen, Hazelwood, *supra* note 5, at 700.

[115] *See* New Jersey v. T.L.O., 469 U.S. 325, 350 (1985) ("Without first establishing discipline and maintaining order, teachers cannot begin to educate their students.").

[116] Hafen, *Developing Student Expression*, *supra* note 95, at 664.

[117] *Id.*

[118] *See supra* text accompanying note 111. Although the Supreme Court often mentions democratic citizenship as one goal of education, *see, e.g.*, Bethel Sch. Dist. No. 403 v. Fraser, 478 U.S. 675, 681 (1986); Board of Educ. v. Pico, 457 U.S. 853, 864 (1982), there has been little or no careful consideration of what an education for citizenship might entail.

[119] Even schools wishing to avoid "value-training" inevitably teach values. Curricular choices, such as whether to supply a wood-working shop or to hire a music teacher, convey delicate value judgments about the purpose of education. Having students read Gabriel Garcia Marquez's novel, *One Hundred Years of Solitude*, rather than Geoffrey Chaucer's *Miller's Tale*, communicates something about the value of multiculturalism. The very pedagogical style and procedural environment of the classroom (through students' day-to-day interpersonal experiences with

schools must commit themselves to initiating students into the normative culture of our community by transmitting "fundamental civic and moral virtues such as integrity, cooperation, self-reliance, and responsibility."[120]

Still, a problem exists. Although value transmission is essential for preparing the student for citizenship, if such indoctrination is too successful, it threatens the development of a democratic personality. Controlling the system of value transmission is "a hallmark of totalitarianism."[121] Thus, any effort to indoctrinate "official" values[122] is in tension with our designs to have a democratic polity.[123] The desire to induct children into their community "must be tempered by the realization that much of what society achieves depends on individuals who do not or will not conform to the prevailing wisdom."[124]

Herein lies the dilemma. Society must indoctrinate children so they may be capable of independent, critical thought. Paradoxically, education

---

teachers, administrators, and other children) instills value positions on matters such as the respect due authority, the worth of creative or critical thinking, and the tolerance due opposing opinions. *See* MARSHALL MCLUHAN, UNDERSTANDING MEDIA: THE EXTENSIONS OF MAN 7 (1964) (suggesting that medium itself may be most significant message); *see also* Galles, *A Basement Tour of the Ivory Tower*, GAINESVILLE SUN, June 9, 1989, at 13A (contending that classroom experiences, rather than formal curricula, provide most significant school lessons). A value-neutral system is simply inconceivable.

[120] Hafen, *Developing Student Expression*, *supra* note 95, at 700. Clearly, this was part of the pressure behind the Court's positions in both *Hazelwood* and *Bethel*. *See* Hazelwood Sch. Dist. v. Kuhlmeier, 484 U.S. 260, 273 (1988) (deferring to school official's decision when reasonably related to legitimate pedagogical concerns); *Bethel*, 478 U.S. at 681 (confirming school's role in "teaching students the boundaries of socially appropriate behavior"). For a fuller review of both cases, see *supra* text accompanying notes 34-51.

[121] PETER L. BERGER & RICHARD J. NEUHAUS, TO EMPOWER PEOPLE: THE ROLE OF MEDIATING STRUCTURES IN PUBLIC POLICY 6 (1977) (discussing alternative methods to provide "welfare-state services").

[122] *Webster's Third New International Dictionary* defines "indoctrinate" as follows: "to cause to be impressed and usu. ultimately imbued (as with . . . partisan or sectarian opinion, point of view, or principle) . . .: cause to be drilled or otherwise trained (as in a sectarian doctrine) and usu. persuaded . . . ." WEBSTER'S THIRD NEW INTERNATIONAL DICTIONARY 1153 (1971). Implicit in the concept of indoctrination is the sense that the individual has been restricted in her ability to perceive new ideas and to appreciate perspectives contrary to the point of view with which she has been "imbued."

[123] Freedom of speech presupposes that the beliefs and opinions that individuals form are not the product of deliberate efforts to shape and condition those beliefs to conform with official policy. To allow officials to inculcate values is to admit that free speech protects expression only so long as the speaker has been conditioned to say what those in authority accept. In a society of such preconditioned speakers, freedom of speech is virtually irrelevant. *See supra* notes 22-27 and accompanying text (noting schools may be used as forum to induce children into adopting values that enhance status quo); *see also* text accompanying notes 103-11 (noting that schools play role of indoctrinating students with values, which may suppress individual choice).

[124] Yudof, *Library Book Selection*, *supra* note 23, at 530.

must promote autonomy while simultaneously denying it by shaping and constraining present and future choices.[125]

Resolving this dilemma requires a re-evaluation of the school's mission as value inculcator. Schools inevitably play a crucial role in the process by which the young are inducted into society.[126] But this induction process must ensure that the adults it produces see themselves as worthy and capable of participating meaningfully in an ongoing process of collective self-determination. Consequently, if schools are to fulfill their mission of educating youths for citizenship, the norms embodied in the First Amendment also must be transmitted. The very impressionability of children makes it vital that community institutions inculcate within the young the free speech values which are crucial to the promotion of a democratic personality. Schools must support free speech not because of any concern over autonomy, but because of our communal interest in character development.[127]

Accepting this character-building interest, public institutions must recognize that certain virtues are public goods to be nurtured. Under any set of social conditions, American democracy will be the poorer if our public institutions do not foster communal support and indoctrinate the values of individual dignity, creativity, mutual respect, inquisitiveness, civic and intellectual courage, and the willingness (on occasion) to question authority.[128] Through the experiences of conveying and reacting to communication, individuals—under a free speech regime—can be socialized

---

[125] *See* ROBERT M. HARE, DECISIONS OF PRINCIPLE, PHILOSOPHY AND EDUCATION 72, 85 (Israel Scheffler ed., 1958); Yudof, *Library Book Selection*, *supra* note 23, at 528 (noting education both promotes and denies autonomy by shaping and constraining one's choices); *cf.* EDMUND BURKE, REFLECTIONS ON THE REVOLUTION IN FRANCE, *reprinted in*, SELECTED WRITINGS OF EDMUND BURKE 343, 350-54 (W.J. Bate ed., 1960) (noting paradox in fact that freedom of choice was necessary for "legal existence of the sovereign magistry" while at same time laws dictated that king must hold crown by succession).

[126] Indeed, public schools may be "the primary vehicle for transmitting 'the values on which our society rests.'" Plyler v. Doe, 457 U.S. 202, 221 (1982) (quoting Ambach v. Norwick, 441 U.S. 68, 76 (1979)).

[127] People must be socialized to think critically and independently if we wish to deter what Lee Bollinger referred to as the "obedient mind," a mind unable to think for itself. BOLLINGER, *supra* note 87, at 247. Despite Professor Hafen's antipathy to judicial enforcement of student free speech claims, *see* Hafen, *Developing Student Expression*, *supra* note 95, at 664 (recommending deference to most decisions of school officials), he appreciates that "[a]s holders of inchoate rights of democratic citizenship, students have a high stake in the development of their own critical powers to act in the future as sovereign citizens." *Id.* at 707.

[128] I believe this idea is to a great extent what Justice Brandeis had in mind in his opinion in Whitney v. California, 274 U.S. 357, 377 (1927) (Brandeis, J., concurring) (relating to governmental system fostering "courageous, self-reliant men"), *overruled on other grounds*, Brandenburg v. Ohio, 395 U.S. 444 (1969).

to think (and then to act) critically, independently, and tolerantly.[129]

The task for schools, therefore, is to instill within children a belief that society promotes and appreciates diverse views, independent inquiry, critical thought, and public debate. To inculcate children with the belief that individuals who resist becoming indoctrinated with all of the mores of a society are valuable to that society is not an easy task. To do so, public schools not only must intone the rhetoric of free speech, they must act and structure themselves to give credibility to their statements.[130] Children are unlikely to internalize the values of civic virtue if their schools appear to systematically trivialize or ignore such values. Consequently, the public recognition of First Amendment rights for students serves a necessary pedagogical function.[131]

But in schools, as in other institutions, the claims of order compete with the claims of freedom. Certainly education requires some degree of discipline within the institution.[132] But a student who is taught in an environment where opposing views are suppressed to emphasize discipline and order gets improper signals regarding democratic values and personal self-awareness.

Consequently, to fulfill their inculcative functions, schools must offer the *experience* of expressive liberties. It is through the experience of making particular independent decisions that children develop the capacity for making them generally.[133] "Being mature takes practice," reminds

---

[129] For an earlier, more extensive discussion of the character-building implications of free speech experiences, see *supra* note 88.

[130] Schools that extol the virtues of free speech but then restrict expression institutionally are actually teaching children powerful lessons about what rights really mean: "Watch what I do, not what I say."

[131] *See* John H. Garvey, *Children and the First Amendment*, 57 TEX. L. REV. 321, 344-47 (1979) (justifying free speech for children in terms of its educational function).

[132] *See* Eva-Lotta Jansson, *Disciplinean Issue at Center but Some Say District Troubles are Typical Rather than a Substantial Concern*, KAN. CITY STAR, June 22, 1995, at 1 (discussing problems of student discipline and behavior in one school district); Shannon D. Murray, *Hammond Teachers Plan Uniform Approach to Discipline at Overcrowded School*, BALTIMORE SUN, July 30, 1995, at 10C (noting one school's response to increased disobedience ranged from verbal reprimand to detention for using vulgar language and insulting other students). Unquestioningly, order has deteriorated so severely in some schools that a significant emphasis on discipline is warranted in these settings. Even in such environments, however, students will be better prepared to be contributing members of society if their schools also convey the importance of liberty, and indicate that there exist appropriate times and means responsibly to question authority.

[133] Hafen, *Developing Student Expression*, *supra* note 95, at 696. The issue, thus, is focused more on character development than autonomy. *Cf.* Rogers M. Smith, *The "American Creed" and American Identity: The Limits of Liberal Citizenship in the United States*, 41 W. POL. Q. 225, 247 (1988) ("Freedom should not be understood to mean simply a lack of hindrance in doing

Franklin Zimring.[134] "To know this is to suppose [one] justification for extending privileges in public law . . . to those who have not yet reached full maturity."[135] It is also through experience, rather than rhetoric, that students see and come to understand the way authority responds to nonconformity in our society. Thus, schools must be aware of the vital lessons they teach concerning the interplay of power, status, independence, and inquisitiveness.

Education for citizenship is a complicated task. It requires children to be socialized into the norms of society while remaining free to question or even abandon them.[136] It demands that while teaching children what they need to know (i.e., education of citizens), a process that necessitates a degree of order and obedience to authority, they also must be taught the value of, and skills needed for, questioning authority. Both liberty and authority are essential to the inculcation of virtue. Consequently, the question we must answer is: how should schools be structured to convey our commitment to, and the importance of, both of these seemingly conflicting values?

IV. Some Practical Implications

The mission of public education—consisting of both the education of citizens and the education for citizenship—is formidable. Elsewhere I have depicted this effort as an "ideological enigma":[137]

> Schools are asked simultaneously to respect and nurture both the communal and individual aspects of the human spirit. Schools invariably shape children's attitudes through selectively exposing them to ideas and perspectives, thereby predisposing them to accept certain established views as adults. Yet, while indoctrinating the child, schools also ostensibly exist to equip each child with the skills and self-confidence necessary to allow him to reflect critically upon the values with which he is being socialized. The school system, consequently, epitomizes the tension between the focus of liberal political theory on individual autonomy and the community's need to sustain and perpetuate itself.[138]

Because of this "tension," public schools historically have been the stage

---

what we will. It means valuing and exercising our capacities for reflective self-direction and choosing ways of life that preserve and enhance those capacities for all.").

[134] FRANKLIN E. ZIMRING, THE CHANGING LEGAL WORLD OF ADOLESCENCE 89 (1982).

[135] *Id.*

[136] HARE, *supra* note 125, at 85.

[137] Ingber, *Socialization*, *supra* note 31, at 94.

[138] *Id.* at 94-95.

of passionate struggles and conflicts.[139] Interestingly, this conflict most often has not been over the lofty and potentially conflicting goals of education.[140] Rather, it has concerned the question of how these goals are to be attained[141]—how schools should function and be structured, and who should monitor their success. In turning to these practical problems, let us first consider whether (and if so, how) we can create an educational environment that supports order and obedience while encouraging critical thought and the questioning of authority.

A. *A Divided Educational Program*

One would think the various components of the educational program—the classroom, the library, extra-curricular activities and others—would be structured to reinforce the efforts to fulfill common educational goals. The problem is that we have identified goals which may not, in all contexts, be consistent with each other. Developing virtue requires both an obedience to authority and experiences of independent, critical thought; the latter are sometimes at odds with authority. Perhaps the answer is to artificially divide the educational program, dedicating part to one perspective on the interplay between obedience and independence, and the other to an alternative perspective.[142]

1. *Board of Education v. Pico*: An Illustrative Case

This suggestion about artificially dividing the educational program, although perhaps not revolutionary, seems the only way to understand cases such as *Board of Education v. Pico*.[143] In *Pico*, the Supreme Court

---

[139] *See id.* at 40-47 (discussing historical conflicts over selection of school texts for students).

[140] For example, my writing has differed markedly with that of Professor Hafen over the need for courts to recognize and uphold student free speech claims. *Compare* Hafen, Hazelwood, *supra* note 5, at 685 (praising *Hazelwood* decision for reinforcing institutional authority of schools) *with* Ingber, *Rediscovering*, *supra* note 98, at 83-84 (criticizing *Hazelwood* as giving school officials too much deference in controlling student speech). Yet, when Professor Hafen describes "helping each individual to realize his own autonomous sense of self while simultaneously inducting him into membership in the democratic community" as part of education's mission, Hafen, *Developing Student Expression*, *supra* note 95, at 728, I can do nothing but concur.

[141] For example, Professor Hafen has expressed his concern that efforts to uphold individualism were excessive and had taken their "toll on community and institutional continuity, especially with respect to . . . institutions [such as schools]." Hafen, *Developing Student Expression*, *supra* note 95, at 703.

[142] Undoubtedly, no aspect of the educational program can be exclusively devoted to either perspective. Degrees of both obedience and independence must exist in all contexts to avoid imbuing either subservience or self-centeredness. However, differing contexts can *emphasize* one perspective over another.

[143] 457 U.S. 853 (1982) (plurality opinion).

found that the First Amendment restricts the power of school officials to indoctrinate students. Specifically, the Court imposed constitutional limits on a school board's discretion to remove books from junior and senior high school libraries.[144] The Court was highly fragmented;[145] nonetheless, a clear majority held that a boundary exists beyond which school authorities cannot venture to indoctrinate children with community values.[146]

Writing for the plurality,[147] Justice Brennan found that the school board in *Pico* had violated the student's "'right to receive information and ideas.'"[148] Brennan distilled this right from the "role of the First Amendment . . . in affording the public access to discussion, debate, and the dissemination of information and ideas."[149] This role, he concluded, applied equally to public schools: "[J]ust as access to ideas makes it possible for citizens generally to exercise their rights of free speech and press in a meaningful manner, such access prepares students for active and effective participation in the pluralistic, often contentious society in which

---

[144] *Id.* at 871-72.

[145] The nine Justices filed seven separate opinions. *Id.* at 854-55.

[146] *See Pico*, 457 U.S. at 871-72 (plurality opinion) (determining that U.S. Constitution limited school board's otherwise broad discretion to remove books from libraries); *id.* at 879-80 (Blackmun, J., concurring) (agreeing that First Amendment restricted school board's authority to remove books from library); *id.* at 883 (White, J., concurring) (agreeing that U.S. Constitution limited school board's removal of books).

[147] The plurality consisted of Justices Brennan, Marshall and Stevens. *Id.* at 854.

[148] *Id.* at 867 (quoting Stanley v. Georgia, 394 U.S. 557, 564 (1969)). Arguably, the Court had recognized a right to receive information in many different contexts. *See* Virginia State Bd. of Pharmacy v. Virginia Citizens Consumer Council Inc., 425 U.S. 748, 756-57 (1976) (holding that consumers have right to receive information through price advertisements by pharmacists); Kleindienst v. Mandel, 408 U.S. 753, 762-65 (1972) (recognizing right of university officials to hear Marxist lecturer, but decided on other grounds); Red Lion Broadcasting Co. v. FCC, 395 U.S. 367, 377-80 (1969) (stating that radio listeners have right to ideologically balanced broadcasts); *Stanley*, 394 U.S. at 577 (addressing right to receive obscenity in home); Lamont v. Postmaster Gen., 381 U.S. 301 (1965) (discussing addressee's right to receive Communist publication in mail); Martin v. City of Struthers, 319 U.S. 141, 143 (1943) (considering right to receive handbills and pamphlets).

Despite these cases, the plurality opinion seemed to depart from prior court doctrine. Before *Pico*, the Supreme Court had predicated the "right to know" upon the speaker's right to speak. *Virginia Citizens Consumer Council, Inc.*, 425 U.S. at 757 ("If there is a right to advertise, there is a reciprocal right to receive the advertising . . . ."). In other words, the right to know merely protected the speaker's right to communicate with a willing listener. Authors, editors, and publishers have no similar right requiring public schools to choose and distribute their books. A "right to know" may prevent the government from unreasonably blocking the flow of information. This right, however, certainly does not require the state affirmatively to aid speakers in reaching potential recipients. *See* Garvey, *supra* note 131, at 374 (noting that right to know does not place obligation on state to provide information to children).

[149] *Pico*, 457 U.S. at 866 (quoting First Nat'l Bank v. Bellotti, 435 U.S. 765, 783 (1978)).

they will soon be adult members."[150] Thus, Brennan found that a student's right to receive ideas was inherent in the justifications used to support the free speech guarantee generally.

The problem with this approach is that it neglects the very purpose of public schools. A right to receive ideas is essentially inconsistent with the inculcative function of public school education,[151] a function which even Justice Brennan acknowledged as legitimate.[152] "Selectivity" is essential to any school system. The plurality's view of education, taken to its logical conclusion, would prohibit school boards from making even curricular decisions—decisions which inherently compel choices of inclusion and exclusion.

Justice Brennan was not oblivious to the conceptual difficulties that a "right-to-know" in public schools created. He revealed his discomfort by seeking to impose certain limits on this newly articulated right, including a distinction between the classroom and the school library.[153] He stated that value inculcation might justify a school board's absolute control over the curriculum, but that such control was inappropriate in the school library's atmosphere of unrestricted inquiry.[154]

Distinguishing between the classroom and the library has some surface appeal.[155] The classroom is prescriptive by nature, as evidenced by its requirements of compulsory attendance and uniform curriculum. Curriculum choices necessarily hinge upon the limited time and resources available to the school system, and the need for students to use the same textbook in a given course. The library, however, is different. Schools do not compel students to use it. Its stacks may contain works beyond the standard curriculum, where students can pursue individualized interests. Consequently, the voluntary library seems more consistent with the

---

[150] 457 U.S. at 868.

[151] *See* Yudof, *Library Book Selection*, *supra* note 23 (asserting that schooling enterprise requires board's ability to choose textbooks and courses). The dissenting Justices in *Pico*—Burger, Rehnquist, Powell, and O'Connor—emphasized this apparent conflict between the plurality's First Amendment perspective and the long accepted goal of public education to train values. *See, e.g.*, *Pico*, 457 U.S. at 889 (Burger, C.J., dissenting) (stressing that in order to inculcate students with necessary values, school board must have discretion to decide appropriateness of materials for school); *id.* at 914 (Rehnquist, J., dissenting) (noting that concept of students' rights of access to information in schools is contrary to nature of education as inculcative).

[152] *See Pico*, 457 U.S. at 864 ("We have . . . acknowledged that public schools are vitally important . . . as vehicles for 'inculcating fundamental values' . . . ." (quoting Ambach v. Norwick, 441 U.S. 68, 76-77 (1979)).

[153] *Pico*, 457 U.S. at 869.

[154] *Id.*

[155] *See* Yudof, *Library Book Selection*, *supra* note 23 (noting "different attributes" of classrooms and libraries).

hub-bub of the marketplace than does the compulsory classroom.[156] Unlike the classroom, the library poses no risk of exposing students to viewpoints they find disturbing or undesirable. A library book will be read only by those who seek it out.[157]

Despite these favorable points, Brennan's distinction between the classroom and the library remains unconvincing. Viewing a school library as a place of *bounded* student inquiry under the school authorities' direction is no more unreasonable than viewing it as a place of broad, self-directed student exploration. If the public school system in its entirety may inculcate ideas, surely school libraries may contribute to that process.[158] The plurality severs the library from the goals of the educational venture generally. Although some may prefer its approach, the plurality fails to justify it as a constitutional requirement.

Thus, it simply is not illogical to choose to integrate the library into the public school system's process of value inculcation. Our normal predilections are to treat logically indistinguishable cases consistently. Consistency loses its appeal, however, when it produces less beneficial, rather than more beneficial, outcomes.[159] In such situations, inconsistency can have an affirmative value.[160]

---

[156] Minarcini v. Strongsville City Sch. Dist., 541 F.2d 577, 582-83 (6th Cir. 1976) (noting that library rather than classroom is "mighty resource in the free marketplace of ideas") (citing Abrams v. United States, 250 U.S. 616 (1919) (Holmes, J. dissenting)).

[157] Society, therefore, need not protect children from the library in the same way that it might need to protect the child from unsolicited vulgarity over the radio. *See* FCC v. Pacifica Found., 438 U.S. 726, 749-50 (1978) (noting that children may be exposed to vulgarity over radio against their wishes and without warning).

[158] Board of Educ. v. Pico, 457 U.S. 853, 878 (1982) (Blackmun, J. concurring). The plurality appears to have equated the public school library, which may reasonably be perceived as an adjunct to the educational system, with the entrepreneur bookseller, who has no similar responsibility.

[159] *See* RALPH WALDO EMERSON, *Self-Reliance*, *in* ESSAYS 45, 57 (1904) ("A foolish consistency is the hobgoblin of little minds, adored by little statesmen and philosophers and divines.").

[160] Logic, simply, may not be the only constitutionally valid criterion for making distinctions. Lee Bollinger, for example, in his article on regulating mass media, argues that although, for First Amendment purposes, electronic broadcasting and the print media are indistinguishable, a "powerful rationality" exists for treating the two mediums differently—regulating the electronic media more restrictively than is constitutionally permitted for its print media analogue. Lee C. Bollinger, Jr., *Freedom of the Press and Public Access: Toward a Theory of Partial Regulation of the Mass Media*, 75 MICH. L. REV. 1, 2-3 (1976). He concludes:

> What the Court has never fully appreciated is that the very similarity of the two major branches of the mass media provides a rationale for treating them differently. By permitting different treatment of the two institutions, the Court can facilitate realization of the benefits of two distinct constitutional values, both of which ought to be fostered: access in a highly concentrated press and minimal governmental intervention. Neither

The public school system, as represented by *Pico*, was such a case. As character-building institutions aimed at fostering a virtuous, democratic polity, schools must inculcate both the importance of authority and the value of liberty. By accepting an otherwise *illogical* distinction between the classroom and the library—thus treating potentially like things differently—the Court resolved the dilemma of promoting contending norms simultaneously by "dividing" the school program into two theoretical units, with one serving a broad indoctrinative function and the other exhorting a student's right to receive a broad spectrum of information.[161] Both liberty and authority received public affirmation.

2. Other Points of Division

Although *Pico* divides the education program between the curriculum and the library, others have suggested alternative points.[162] In fact, the

---

> side of the access controversy emerges victorious. The Court has imposed a compromise—a compromise, however, not based on notions of expediency, but rather on a reasoned, and principled, accommodation of competing first amendment values.

Id. at 36. By treating like things differently, the Court, at least partially, achieves two inconsistent goals that otherwise could not be realized simultaneously.

[161] The library is an ideal place to fulfill this latter role, thereby allowing schools to avoid the appearance of imposing official orthodoxy upon our youth. First, overt ideological screening of library books will more likely appear as the "book burning" that we equate with repressive governments. Libraries and book stores play a crucial role in our culture and are closely intertwined with the history and tradition behind freedom of speech and the press. Although one may distinguish the function of a grade school library from that of a bookstore or a general library open to the public-at-large, *see supra* note 156 and accompanying text, the distinction is subtle, and not necessarily easily conveyed. On the other hand, society more fully equates the classroom with the training of youth and the inculcation as performed by the family. *See, e.g.*, Vernonia Sch. Dist. v. Acton, 115 S. Ct. 2386, 2391 (1995) ("[T]eachers and administrators of . . . schools stand in loco parentis over children entrusted to them."). Official control of library materials, therefore, strikes closer to the core of First Amendment rhetoric and threatens the perception of individual choice and liberty.

[162] One education-law scholar, Stephen Goldstein, argues that what we are confronting is two differing conceptual models of education—one prescriptive and the other analytic. Stephen Goldstein, *Reflections of Developing Trends in the Law of Student Rights*, 118 U. PA. L. REV. 612, 614 (1970). While recognizing that these polar models signify only "theoretical paradigm[s] that never exist in pure form," he then divides education not spatially (as in *Pico*) but rather, chronologically. *Id.* He views pre-college public education as essentially prescriptive, involving a passive student absorbing furnished information and accepted truths, and college and post-graduate studies as analytic, where student and teacher engage each other as active participants in the search for truth. *Id.* By dividing the educational process into two totally distinct phases, Goldstein attempts to find a compromise between authoritative inculcation and the development of the ability to think critically.

Yet after analysis, Goldstein's effort at a chronological division must be rejected. Smothering grade school children in orthodox values may preclude independence in college, since truly successful inculcation inevitably colors future working and thinking habits. More troubling, however, is that those students who never attend college will totally miss an education that

interplay of *Tinker* and *Hazelwood* creates a new partition between the domain of authority and that of independent choice. As described by Professor Hafen, "*Hazelwood* now draws a . . . distinction between a student's private speech, which remains eligible for protection under *Tinker*, and her expression through official school channels, which *Tinker* no longer protects."[163] A case once viewed as an effort to structure an environment which would serve as a "forum crucial in the training of future leaders"[164] has been relegated to a position of protecting "private student interpersonal communication in such places as school yards and cafeterias."[165] Furthermore, both *Hazelwood* and *Tinker* itself limit the protection of student speech to conversation topics not directly challenging school policies or confronting school authorities.[166] The domain of critical, independent thought—an intellectual trait essential to a virtuous democratic personality—has become limited indeed. If, during the adolescence of the baby-boomer generation (the 1960s), we leaned strongly toward rebellion, growth and change, then during the middle-age of that same generation (the 1980s and 90s), the overwhelming emphasis is respect for authority and deference to the judgment of "professional experts."

Both distinctions—that of private versus institutionally-sponsored speech and that of institutionally-oriented versus institutionally-unrelated speech—are most unfortunate if our educational mission includes, as I believe it should, an effort to publicly support, promote experiences of, and inculcate First Amendment norms. Once we acknowledge the necessity of inculcating the free speech virtues of participation and tolerance as part of education's central mission of character development, there is something insidious about relegating free speech experiences to contexts unsponsored by the educational institution. One would think inculcation would demand a *public showing* of institutional commitment to free speech values. To deny such values in all school sanctioned activities—the classroom, the

---

promotes free inquiry. Thus, we cannot so easily discount the primary and secondary school student's role in educational decisions.

For another more flexible effort to account for a child's increasing readiness for exposure to liberty experiences as she grows older, see Hafen, *Developing Student Expression*, *supra* note 95, at 696.

[163] Hafen, Hazelwood, *supra* note 5, at 689.

[164] Tinker v. Des Moines Indep. Community Sch. Dist., 393 U.S. 503, 511 (1969).

[165] Hafen, *Developing Student Expression*, *supra* note 95, at 728.

[166] The Court in *Tinker* stressed that the students' actions "neither interrupted school activities ***nor sought to intrude in the school affairs*** or the lives of others." *Id.* at 514 (emphasis added). *Hazelwood* continued to emphasize the need for deference to school official determinations which are "reasonably related to legitimate pedagogical concerns." Hazelwood Sch. Dist. v. Kuhlmeier, 484 U.S. 260, 273 (1988).

school newspaper, school produced plays, etc.—demonstrates vividly the insincerity of any rhetorical claims of the importance of free speech to the molding of a democratic personality. The grudging acceptance of independent, critical thought in contexts viewed as irrelevant to the educational mission thereby explicitly excludes from that mission the virtues embodied in the First Amendment.[167]

Even more troubling is the inference that *Tinker*'s impact should be limited to its facts. Unlike *Bethel* and *Hazelwood*, the student communication prohibited in *Tinker* was unrelated to any school concern; it merely happened to take place on school grounds. To confine *Tinker*'s significance to institutionally-unrelated speech, however, would be both ironic and counterproductive. Such a limitation opens the school to discussions of only those issues unconnected to the educational environment.[168] Reason would support an opposite policy.[169] One would think the classroom (as involved in *Tinker*) would serve *least well* as a forum for discussing matters extraneous to the course.[170]

More importantly for purposes of the character-enhancing role of free speech experiences, the distinction between institutionally-oriented and institutionally-unrelated expression is not merely unjustified, it is also dysfunctional.[171] To teach students that they are free to speak only as

---

[167] Thus, I strongly disagree with Professor Hafen's attempt to develop a continuum of school activities as a method for analyzing free speech claims, with the classroom curriculum at one extreme and private intercommunication at the other. Hafen, *Developing Student Expression*, *supra* note 95, at 728. For Hafen, the stronger the educational content of the activity, the more it falls on the curricular side of the continuum and the less open it is to free speech claims. *Id.* But Hafen is ignoring the inculcative, character-building function of education. (Or, at the very least, he is describing the myopic view of the *Hazelwood* Court.) It is precisely in these "educational" contexts that the child learns what the public school and, assumedly, society itself value and what they do not. This is the vital lesson that most concerns me.

[168] Examples of speech left unprotected would include a student's rejection in a history class of the portrayal of Thomas Jefferson—an owner of slaves—as a defender of freedom, criticism of an officially prescribed dress code, or the protestation of a decision to discontinue music training as a cost-saving measure.

[169] *Cf.* Brown v. Louisiana, 383 U.S. 131, 141-43 (1966) (holding that protest held in municipal library was constitutionally protected precisely because library itself was focus of expressive activity).

[170] As Justice Stevens aptly noted: "Any student of history who has been reprimanded for talking about the World Series during a class discussion of the First Amendment knows that it is incorrect to state that a 'time, place, or manner restriction may not be based upon either the content or subject matter of speech.'" Consolidated Edison Co. v. Public Serv. Comm'n, 447 U.S. 530, 544-45 (1980) (Stevens, J., concurring) (quoting majority's opinion at 536).

[171] Elsewhere, I have argued similarly against the Court's effort in Connick v. Myers, 461 U.S. 138 (1983), to categorize speech according to differing degrees of protection afforded when evaluating the free speech rights of public employees. Ingber, *Rediscovering*, *supra* note 98, at 58. The Court's requirement in *Connick* that protected statements must involve "matters of

long as their message is tangential to their institutional environment is to give a lesson in subservience rather than in participation and civic courage.[172] To tell school officials that, as speech regulators, they need permit only student comments that are consistent with, or at least unthreatening to, their "expert" perception of proper pedagogy or educational suitability is to convey nothing to officials (or students) about the importance of tolerance. Instead, such an approach cultivates a respect for elitism and hierarchy. Any effort to instill the intellectual and interpersonal habits of civic virtue must focus considerable attention on the structuring of our educational institutions. The character-building lessons learned through the experience of communicating with others, and responding to the communication of others, are not dependent upon the subject matter of the expression.[173]

---

public concern," 461 U.S. at 147, would make sense if the First Amendment were concerned only with the interpersonal or systemic interests of free speech as a means of developing an informed citizenry. But the requirement is flawed when one also considers the communal component of free speech. The character-enhancing lessons of free speech learned through the experience of communicating and regulating communication of others are not dependent on the subject matter of the communication. In *Connick*, where the plaintiff was dismissed for complaining about intra-office policies, 461 U.S. at 141, the employee learned that questioning authority and attempting to retain some measure of control over a vital part of one's life (i.e. one's work environment) is a risky enterprise. Ingber, *Rediscovering*, *supra* note 98, at 58. Her supervisor, in turn, learned that those in positions of power can suppress challenges to authority. *Id.* Clearly, the employee is not encouraged to embrace the value of self-governing participation, nor is her supervisor encouraged to embrace that of tolerance.

Finally, there is something discomforting about government agency supervisors, or even courts, determining whether or not a particular matter is one of public concern. "Whenever a governmental institution decides that a given fact . . . is not a fitting topic for public discussion nor relevant to any issue of public concern, it is essentially imposing an ideological perspective . . . . " Stanley Ingber, *Rethinking Intangible Injuries: A Focus on Remedy*, 66 CAL. L. REV. 772, 845 (1985) [hereinafter Ingber, *Rethinking Intangible Injuries*]; *cf.* Walter Weyrauch, *Law as Mask—Legal Ritual and Relevance*, 73 CAL. L. REV. 699, 709 (1978) (discussing judge's role in deciding what is relevant in trial as reflecting "prevailing value judgments" of society of which judge is part).

[172] Such was the fear that Justice Brennan expressed in his *Hazelwood* dissent. Hazelwood Sch. Dist. v. Kuhlmeier, 484 U.S. 260, 284 (1988) (Brennan, J., dissenting).

[173] Perhaps this realization led Professor Meiklejohn to abandon his distinction between public and private speech. Initially, he insisted that only public speech deserved First Amendment protection. *See* MEIKLEJOHN, *supra* note 84, at 24-25. Subsequently, however, he found the distinction difficult to maintain. He finally was compelled to conclude that "novels and dramas and paintings and poems" also fell within the ambit of free speech protection. Alexander Meiklejohn, *The First Amendment is an Absolute*, 1961 SUP. CT. REV. 245, 257. Essentially, Meiklejohn had come to understand that the First Amendment protected not only the development of political values but also anything that goes into the making of a good political actor. The Court, occasionally, also has suggested this insight. *See, e.g.*, Abood v. Detroit Bd. of Educ., 431 U.S. 209, 231 (1977) (suggesting that expression concerning philosophical, social, artistic, economic, literary, and ethical matters is entitled to full First Amendment protection).

B. *Rethinking Divisions and the Role of the Judiciary*

1. The Meaning of Efficiency

The Court in *Bethel* unquestionably is correct when it states that "[t]he process of educating our youth for citizenship in public school is not confined to books, the curriculum, and the civic class."[174] It is equally true that all components of the educational program—curriculum, library and extra-curricular activities, such as student publications, election assemblies and performing arts programs—may be structured and called upon to contribute to the efficient fulfillment of the educational mission. The problem is defining that mission. Efficiency is a concept that takes on meaning only in relation to substantive goals.[175]

Given our constitutional mandate, our educational goals should not be limited to imparting to children useful information and transmitting to them the cultural norms of the past. Our educational institutions also must accept their responsibility for promoting democratic virtues in order to further the communal goal of building the character necessary for a democratic polity. Authority and obedience may aid the efficient pursuit of some of our goals, but if free speech is neglected in the day-to-day contexts so central to the character-forging experiences of our impressionable youth, we risk breeding caution and stifling initiative, thereby fostering only the virtue of obedience.[176] Thus, along with their ability to achieve our prescriptive goals for education, schools must be structured to offer experiences in which authority can be challenged and norms questioned if they are to further the virtues of participation and tolerance, and help to fulfill our polity-developing goals. Somewhere within the official structure of our schools, we must promote the experience of free speech values, and nowhere may we obviously and formally denigrate them.[177]

---

[174] Bethel Sch. Dist. No. 403 v. Fraser, 478 U.S. 675, 683 (1986).

[175] *See* Mario J. Rizzo, *The Mirage of Efficiency*, 8 HOFSTRA L. REV. 641 (1980).

[176] Outside of educational contexts, courts have evaluated the impact on free speech goals of regulations intended efficiently to aid the state's effort at maintaining litter-free streets and freely circulating traffic . *See, e.g.*, Heffron v. International Soc'y for Krishna Consciousness, Inc., 452 U.S. 640, 654 (1981) (holding that only if "alternative forums for the expression of . . . protected speech exist" may state regulate distribution and sale of literature at state fair to further efficient crowd flow); Schneider v. State, 308 U.S. 147, 162 (1939) (rejecting ban on leafletting intended to prevent littering).

[177] The importance of public schools in the development of a democratic polity explains why the rejection of student free speech claims cannot be justified simply as time, place and manner restrictions. *See* Cox v. New Hampshire, 312 U.S. 569, 576 (1941) (developing time, place and

2. A Question of Trust and Symbolism

a. Deference to Expertise

Some scholars agree that schools should provide experiences promoting student initiative and criticism of authority, yet still insist that courts should reject student free speech claims.[178] Essentially, these critics believe that, although such opportunities may be good pedagogy, their existence, timing, and frequency are matters of educational philosophy left to educational officials and professionals. Consequently, these opportunities should not be compelled by courts as constitutional mandates.[179] This position of judicial deference, often accepted by jurists, represents a deep-seated discomfort with the competence of courts to second-guess decisions of alleged school experts.[180] Because the courts lack special knowledge of proper pedagogy for our schools, they should avoid reviewing policies made by those who claim expertise and are immersed in the educational settings.[181]

Claims of expertise, however, should not be a talisman that magically insulates a group's judgment from review.[182] On the contrary, the very immersion of educational specialists into the mire of conflicts they are to resolve should call into question the advisability of deference. Individuals accustomed to wielding power cannot readily see issues from the perspec-

---

manner doctrine). A student who claims a right of access to a particular book, for example, may be reminded that despite the book's absence from the school library, it remains available at the public libraries and local bookstores. A student prohibited from denouncing a school dress code during a school assembly may well be able to state the same complaint in a public park across the street from the school yard. Obviously, if First Amendment claims are to be recognized, the rationale cannot be truly a right of access to information or to communicate one's thoughts. Rather, the concern must be for the values that schools ought to be inculcating and the character traits they ought to be forging. For those purposes, access or opportunity away from the school is irrelevant. *But see* Hafen, *Developing Student Expression*, *supra* note 95, at 724 (noting that under Supreme Court doctrine child wishing to express herself in ways prohibited at school continues to have "entire off-campus world" at her disposal). For further discussion of this point, see *infra* text accompanying notes 184-88.

[178] *See, e.g.*, Hafen, *Schools*, *supra* note 16, at 615.

[179] *Id.*

[180] *See* Board of Curators v. Horowitz, 435 U.S. 78, 90 (1978) (asserting that educational specialists, rather than courts, should make decisions requiring academic judgment).

[181] Hafen, *Developing Student Expression*, *supra* note 95, at 699 (stating that schools must be protected from "second-guessing by the courts when educational issues are at stake").

[182] Burton Bledstein has studied the dangers of professionalism and the claims of expertise generally. He concludes by cautioning his readers to beware of the "arrogance, shallowness, and potential abuses . . . by . . . individuals who justify their special treatment and betray society's trust by invoking professional privilege, confidence and secrecy." BURTON J. BLEDSTEIN, THE CULTURE OF PROFESSIONALISM 334 (1976).

tive of those who are the subjects of their authority. Judges, of course, are not immune from this disability,[183] nor are they necessarily wiser or more beneficent than other bureaucrats. But at least the controversies they are asked to resolve do not involve individuals questioning judicial authority and then asking tolerance of the court.[184] The immersion of educators in the institutional setting of public schools likely makes their authority in such settings a fundamental source of self-image. Relying on them to tolerate the questioning of their judgment by students (i.e. underlings) may be a highly unrealistic expectation.[185] Because judges are detached from the controversy, they have less at stake and may be more willing to consider the character-building significance embedded in the First Amendment's provisions. Given the risk of petty tyrants, some measure of judicial oversight of public school decision-makers is essential to motivate them to consider the communal worth of recognizing constitutional claims. Consequently, continued judicial deference to school official discretion denigrates First Amendment values. If our voiced commitment to develop the intellectual attributes of a democratic polity is not to ring hollow, a meaningful and visible degree of judicial review of public school decisions is imperative.

b. Confirming Free Speech Rhetoric: An Illustration

Such a demonstration of public commitment, however, does not require the courts to be in the business of micro-managing our schools by reviewing each and every educational decision.[186] It is sufficient that courts review school officials' decisions and acknowledge students' speech

---

[183] As Thomas Grey has noted, judges are simply "officials given more job security than other civil servants. . . . They are comfortably middle-of-the-road, senatorially confirmable lawyer-politicians. . . . [U]nder the robes, federal judges are ordinary members of the comfortable classes." Thomas C. Grey, *The Constitution as Scripture*, 37 STAN. L. REV. 1, 23-24 (1984).

[184] Courts have been unsympathetic to parties who claim the right to question judicial authority through disobedience, although similar questioning of legislative authority has been upheld. *Compare* Shuttlesworth v. Birmingham, 394 U.S. 147, 160-61 (1969) (Harlan, J., concurring) (asserting that one should be able to act on his belief in unconstitutionality of prior restraint on speech and ignore restraint, rather than being compelled to seek review by court) *with* Walker v. Birmingham, 388 U.S. 307, 317-19 (1967) (holding that, despite questionable constitutional validity of injunction against street parades, affected individuals were obligated to apply to courts for dissolution of injunction rather than simply to disobey it).

[185] Gerald E. Frug, *The Ideology of Bureaucracy in American Law*, 97 HARV. L. REV. 1276, 1334 (1984) (insisting that bureaucratic self-policing is not credible).

[186] Justice Black, in his concurrence in Epperson v. Arkansas, 393 U.S. 97 (1968), essentially made this point. *Id.* at 114 (Black, J., concurring) (insisting that courts lack wherewithal to supervise "every public school in every hamlet and city in the United States").

rights with sufficient frequency to retain the credibility of our claimed commitment to First Amendment values. Courts also must react to those occasional "outrageous" cases where the conflict between our free speech rhetoric and public school reality is simply too blatant.[187]

Again, *Pico* may help to illustrate this point.[188] Justice Brennan, in articulating a students' "right to know," carefully limited the restriction on school board discretion to situations where the board removed library books, rather than simply never acquiring them in the first place.[189] Given that limited resources obviously prohibit schools from acquiring every book published, this distinction between the acquisition and removal of books appears sensible.

Upon closer analysis, however, the distinction seems totally inconsistent with any notion of a student's right to know. The student suffers the same loss of perspectives regarding exposure to new ideas whether the school removes the books or initially rejects them.[190] Either way, selective exposure may shape children's attitudes. The "right-to-know" surely does not depend on whether school officials read a book and officially reject its perspectives after, rather than before, its purchase.

Justice Blackmun's concurrence in *Pico*, however, clarifies the significance of this distinction. Blackmun saw the constitutional issue differently from the plurality. According to the Justice, the state could emphasize certain values or subjects, and even inculcate community perspectives, as long as it did not "attempt to shield students from certain ideas that officials find politically distasteful."[191] The issue was not whether students had access, but whether the board's act symbolically stigmatized the rejected book, author or perspective. Under his approach, schools, consistent with their function of inculcating values, could support one point of view while critically evaluating and rejecting an alternative. Only by condemning an idea—by officially labeling it as beyond the pale

---

[187] Wilson v. Chancellor, 418 F. Supp. 1358 (D. Or. 1976), illustrates an overt conflict with constitutional symbols that required court intervention. In *Wilson*, a high school teacher who had invited a series of outside speakers to address his political science class challenged a school board order prohibiting political guest speakers. *Id.* at 1361. The board issued its order after speeches by a Democrat, a Republican, and a member of the John Birch Society, but before a scheduled speech by a Communist. *Id.* The content and timing of the order made it obvious that the board's purpose was to prevent student access to, and to stigmatize, a specific political perspective. *Id.* at 1364. The Oregon district court held the order unconstitutional, stating that it unreasonably infringed on the student's right to know. *Id.*

[188] *See supra* text accompanying notes 143-54.

[189] Board of Educ. v. Pico, 457 U.S. 853, 862 (1982).

[190] *See* Diamond, *supra* note 108, at 516; Garvey, *supra* note 131, at 372.

[191] *Pico*, 457 U.S. at 882 (Blackmun, J., concurring).

of free discussion and scrutiny—would schools violate the Constitution.

Justice Blackmun thus identified the symbolic importance of the Court's distinction. The issue did not involve access to expression, or even whether the government may actually control and indoctrinate. Instead, the issue was whether there existed the *appearance* of governmental manipulation and repudiation of First Amendment values.[192] Refusal to purchase a book merely makes that book one of innumerable others that the school has not acquired.[193] Removal, on the other hand, singles out a book for disapproval. This kind of purge is more inimical to the First Amendment because it dramatically communicates official disapproval of the condemned work in a way that failing to acquire a book normally does not. Again, since both failure to acquire and removal prevent a student from reading a particular work in the school library, the issue is clearly one of symbols rather than access.[194]

Thus, the Court intervened in *Pico* because the school board's effort to manipulate students to conform to board members' political and social tastes was simply too flagrant—too reminiscent of the "book burning" we

---

[192] With exemplary candor, Justice Blackmun noted the importance of appearances, confessing:

> I also have some doubt that there is a theoretical distinction between removal of a book and failure to acquire a book. But as Judge Newman [of the Second Circuit] observed [in his concurrence to the lower Second Circuit decision], there is a profound practical and evidentiary distinction between the two actions: "removal, more than failure to acquire, is likely to suggest that an impermissible political motivation may be present. There are many reasons why a book is not acquired, the most obvious being limited resources, but there are few legitimate reasons why a book, once acquired, should be removed from a library not filled to capacity."

Id. at 878 n.1 (Blackmun, J., concurring) (quoting Pico v. Board of Educ., 638 F.2d 404, 436 (2d Cir. 1980), *aff'd*, 457 U.S. 853 (1982)).

[193] Thus, to make a constitutional case, a teacher or student would have the difficult—if not impossible—task of proving that the school was not purchasing a book because the librarian or school board found its content objectionable.

[194] Judge Newman, of the Second Circuit, clearly addressed in his *Pico* opinion the central importance of symbolism in the school board's actions:

> The symbolic effect of a school's action in removing a book solely because of its ideas will often be more significant than the resulting limitation upon access to it. The fact that the book barred from the school library may be available elsewhere is not decisive. What is significant is that the school has used its public power to perform an act clearly indicating that the views represented by the forbidden book are unacceptable. The impact of burning a book does not depend on whether every copy is on the fire. Removing a book from a school library is a less offensive act, but it can also pose a substantial threat of suppression.

Pico, 638 F.2d at 434 (Newman, J., concurring).

equate with repressive governments.[195] The Court was obliged to uphold constitutional symbols and aid the process of inculcating First Amendment values. The risks of excessive judicial involvement in public schools were, however, also obvious to the Court. Much of *Pico*, therefore, may be explained as an effort to uphold constitutional appearances while limiting judicial intrusion to only those cases in which appearances are most in jeopardy.

c. Motivating Tolerance and Constitutional Sensitivity

As I stated earlier, when courts refrain from questioning any decision labeled "pedagogical" by school officials, they have acceded to the judgment of educational professionals and their claims of expertise.[196] Relying on such individuals to exhibit the virtue of tolerance and to promote that of questioning authority is unrealistic when it is their very authority that is being contested.[197] Consequently, self-policing is no more credible when practiced by school authorities than when practiced by anyone else in society. Yet judicial deference must assume that just this form of self-regulation will take place.

Occasional judicial intervention when First Amendment values appear most in jeopardy offers students a degree of proof of the importance their community attaches to the democratic virtues of participation, critical thought, and tolerance. The potential of judicial oversight, however, does more than confirm the importance of free speech norms to students as they are inducted into our democratic polity. It also motivates school officials to consider and to exhibit the democratic virtue of tolerance. If school officials know that courts will involve themselves, at least in extreme cases, they may have sufficient reason to regard seriously their responsibility for both nurturing and exhibiting the civic virtues of a democratic polity and refrain from acting precipitantly.[198]

Furthermore, the very possibility of judicial oversight has a disciplinary effect on the sorts of measures or regulations that school officials can

---

[195] *See supra* note 161 (discussing reasons libraries, compared to classrooms, are well suited to symbolize schools' recognition of free speech values).

[196] *See supra* text accompanying notes 178-85 and note 182 (discussing dangers of deferring to claims of expertise).

[197] *See supra* text accompanying note 185 (noting that it is unlikely that educators will tolerate students' questioning of their judgment).

[198] *See* Yudof, *Library Book Selections*, *supra* note 23, at 553; *see also* James v. Board of Educ., 461 F.2d 566, 575 (2d Cir.), *cert. denied*, 409 U.S. 1042 (1972). The Second Circuit stressed its belief that the very threat of judicial involvement would temper school board abuse. *Id.* For some, this possibility was the most significant contribution of *Pico*. *See* Comment, Board of Education v. Pico: *The Supreme Court's Answer to School Library Censorship*, 44 OHIO ST. L.J. 1103, 1124 (1983).

propose or enforce because of the potential need to present publicly the rationale for these actions.[199] When positions must be defended by argument and reason, they are not likely to be justified in terms of self-interest. The requirement of appeal to public-oriented reasons may increase the probability that public-oriented actions will be taken in the end.[200] The risk associated with the more visible process of decision-making involved in a judicial critique of state proffered rationales heightens the likelihood of such pressures. Thus, a convergence is possible—and necessary—between the adjudicatory process, by which some limited number of conflicts are resolved, and promoting civic virtues throughout the corridors of government, including those of our public schools.[201]

The greatest influence of intermittent judicial intervention, therefore, may be on the method and content of the deliberations of school boards and officials. As such, the constitutional limits posed may serve an important function even if these limits do appear poorly defined,[202] mostly symbol-

---

[199] Several constitutional theorists posit a conception of constitutional review that features precisely this process of public explanation and discussion. *See, e.g.*, ALEXANDER M. BICKEL, THE SUPREME COURT AND THE IDEA OF PROGRESS 91 (1970) (depicting constitutional decisions as part of national conversation); Eugene V. Rostow, *The Democratic Character of Judicial Review*, 66 HARV. L. REV. 193, 208 (1952) (referring to judicial discussion of problems as "a vital element in the community experience through which American policy is made"); *see also* Owen M. Fiss, *Foreword: The Forms of Justice*, 93 HARV. L. REV. 1, 14 (1979) ("The task of a judge . . . should be seen as giving meaning to our public values and adjudication as the process through which that meaning is revealed or elaborated.").

[200] Tocqueville suggested as much. *See* JOHN STUART MILL, *Tocqueville on Democracy in America*, *in* ESSAYS ON POLITICS AND CULTURE 187, 223-24 (1962); *see also* WILLIAM N. NELSON, ON JUSTIFYING DEMOCRACY 94-130 (1980) (emphasizing public deliberation as value of democracy); JON ELSTER, SOUR GRAPES: STUDIES IN THE SUBVERSION OF RATIONALITY 35-42 (1983) (critically discussing this view). Of course, it would be a mistake to exaggerate the extent of this effect. Self-interest motivations may merely be concealed; the requirement of deliberation can invite hypocrisy. Even hypocrisy, however, may create feelings of guilt that, in turn, may act as a constraining factor. Stanley Ingber, *The Interface of Myth and Practice in Law*, 34 VAND. L. REV. 309, 353-56 (1981).

[201] Thus, the aim of occasional judicial intervention is not increased litigation. The most important character-building lessons are not those gained from isolated judicial decisions. Rather, these lessons are learned from the way educational institutions handle conflict generally. Judicial oversight serves its function best when it motivates all parties—teachers, administrators, parents, and students—to seek methods of conflict resolution, other than courts, which promote the development of those attributes conducive to a democratic polity. *See infra* note 202 (discussing similar point); *see also* Ingber, *Rediscovering*, *supra* note 98, at 93-97 (considering judicial role in encouraging decisional processes consistent with "structural due process").

[202] The amorphous and incomplete nature of the rules which the courts have designed for the public schools provides institutional flexibility but also imposes a high level of institutional uncertainty and insecurity. These indeterminate precepts do supply the means, however, for courts to confront those "outrageous" cases while avoiding the need to thrust themselves into all of the multitudinous conflicts that may arise daily in our public schools. *See supra* text

ic,[203] and self-enforced.[204] Cases such as *Tinker* and *Pico*, by interjecting a constitutional element into educational matters, may do more than simply make school board members aware of the risk of litigation.[205] Hopefully, they also imbue board members and the community they represent with a different sense of their educational role and responsibility, a sense that recognizes the importance of inculcating an appreciation for tolerance and independent, critical thought—as well as for authority—in a process of educating for citizenship.

3. Imprecise Divisions

a. Messages of Exclusion

Earlier, I suggested the possible need to divide the educational program, dedicating part to experiences fostering the virtues of order and authority, and part to those instilling the virtues of liberty, including independent, critical thought and tolerance.[206] Such a division, I mentioned, hopefully would demonstrate the cultural importance given to these virtues (thus facilitating the process of inculcation) while allowing students to practice the differing skills required for virtuous citizenship.

---

accompanying note 183-85 (discussing court deference to educational experts).

[203] Thurmond Arnold, critiquing the role of symbolism in government, cogently exclaimed: "Almost all human conduct is symbolic. Almost all institutional habits are symbolic. The symbols are everywhere inconsistent. Society is generally more interested in standing on the side lines and watching itself go by in a whole series of different uniforms than it is in practical objectives." THURMOND ARNOLD, THE SYMBOLS OF GOVERNMENT 17 (1935).

[204] Yudof, *Library Book Selection*, *supra* note 23 (making same point).

[205] Some concern for litigation may not be bad. School boards (and other school officials) may avoid the cost and potential embarrassment of lawsuits if they encourage all parties of interest to enter the deliberative process early, and listen to all positions with respect and consideration. The heart of democratic government is a sense shared by all that their particular interests, prejudices, and diverse characteristics are brought to bear on the decision-making process. *See* ARNOLD, *supra* note 203, at 34 (recognizing that government must give diverse groups at least symbolic recognition and respect for worth of differing precepts when writing, "the function of law is not so much to guide society, as to comfort it"). Regardless of the decision reached, all concerned will more likely accept the result if no affected group feels alienated from the decision-making process. *See, e.g.*, Loewen v. Turnipseed, 488 F. Supp. 1138, 1152-53 (N.D. Miss. 1980) (suggesting that school boards should be prevented from functioning unless they provide method to be heard for those affected by board decisions). School boards, reading these decisions, should feel pressure to solicit, rather than ignore or deprecate, the views of various affected groups. Such pressure and the behavior it promotes are consistent with the virtues of a democratic polity—virtues that schools should inculcate by deed as well as by word.

[206] *See supra* text accompanying note 142. I also cautioned, at that point, against the possible misconception that any part of the education program could be *exclusively* devoted to any one pattern of experiences. *See supra* note 142.

More recently, I attempted to limit judicial intrusion upon school affairs to only that number of occasions needed to publicly reaffirm our society's commitment to First Amendment values, especially where the conflict between free speech rhetoric and public school reality is so glaring as to threaten the credibility of our resolve.[207]

Fulfilling the purpose I have set for judicial oversight, however, likely hinders our ability to maintain a clear division regarding which aspect of the educational program will concentrate on which component of civic virtue. Divisions cannot be precise because the messages conveyed can be profoundly different as one varies the circumstances from which they emerge.

For example, an analysis of court decisions would suggest that although school boards must be cautious in removing books from a school library, the latitude they have in determining what books to order initially is considerable.[208] Yet the very justification that supports this distinction between removing and obtaining a book compels it to remain obscure. The issue at stake in these library cases, as revealed earlier,[209] was not informational access for students. Rather, it was whether an idea had been officially condemned as beyond the pale of free discussion and scrutiny. This stigmatization—this badge of infamy—simply is more obvious when books are removed than when they *merely* are not purchased. This situation, however, might not always be the case.

Consider a situation where the school board publicly announces that it is determined never to buy a work written by a homosexual or one that portrays homosexuality in a positive light. Such action communicates, as clearly as any book removal, that the views of homosexuals, or a favorable perspective on homosexual life, are so unacceptable—so "beyond the pale"—as to be unworthy of even the slightest consideration.[210] It is this

---

[207] *See supra* text accompanying notes 186-87.

[208] *See* Board of Educ. v. Pico, 457 U.S. 853, 863-72 (1982) (plurality opinion).

[209] *See supra* text accompanying notes 191-94.

[210] Justice Rehnquist recognized the possibility of such a situation in his dissent in *Pico*, rejecting the distinction between initial purchases and the removals of school library books. *Pico*, 457 U.S. at 916-17 (Rehnquist, J., dissenting). If the issue was public visibility, he reasoned, "a school board's public announcement of its refusal to acquire certain books would have every bit as much impact on public attention as would an equally publicized decision to remove the books." *Id.* Justice Rehnquist is clearly right. His only error is in his conclusion that once we recognize that book removals and acquisitions cannot be theoretically distinguished, the only option for courts is to refrain from oversight of public school library policies altogether. The alternative, quite obviously, in those situations where the basis for nonacquisition is sufficiently well known to make the purchase/removal distinction unconvincing, is to dismiss the distinction and condemn both deeds.

official message of exclusion, rather than any concern about access or the ability to categorize the deed as one of removal rather than of nonacquisition,[211] that justifies judicial intervention in order to reinforce symbolically our conception of individual integrity[212] and our commitment to tolerance as a civic virtue.[213]

b. Curriculum and Classroom Activities

Analysis of the importance, for First Amendment purposes, of messages of exclusion emanating from public schools is illuminating but complicated. It brings into question some understandings about the importance of order and authority in divisions of the educational process where these values normally are assumed to reign supreme. Both jurists and scholars have generally agreed that the judgment of school boards concerning the curriculum[214] (except where that judgment implicates

---

[211] The distinction between removal and nonacquisition is essentially a surrogate means for noting the presence of such a message of exclusion. In reality, given the need for routine decisions as to which books the schools initially should purchase, no need normally exists to publicize a decision not to purchase any given book. The decision to remove a book already purchased, however, is likely to be sufficiently exceptional to require, if noticed, some public explanation. *See supra* text accompanying notes 192-94 and note 192 (recognizing practical, evidentiary significance of book removals compared to purchases).

[212] Earlier, I noted that under the republican political theory an individual cannot be understood outside of her communal interactive context. *See supra* text accompanying notes 65-73. Because of their inculcative role, schools, perhaps more than other institutions, implicitly accept this perspective. But for those persons committed to liberal individualism, *see supra* text accompanying notes 56-61, a reference to the First Amendment as a limitation on indoctrination by public schools serves to protect the *appearance* of promoting individual integrity. In this vein, and given the present primacy of liberal political philosophy, *see supra* text accompanying note 92, elsewhere I have asserted:

> Public acceptance of the myth of individual autonomy and the value neutral state imparts an aura of legitimacy and authority to government. Although obvious discrepancies exist between this myth and the reality of value inculcation, full public awareness of these discrepancies could threaten the legitimacy of governmental decision making. Preserving the myth thus is crucial to continued social stability. Preservation requires that the public perceives no systematic manipulation of the individual's perspective by processes of indoctrination or socialization.

Ingber, *Socialization*, *supra* note 31, at 71-72 (footnotes omitted). The values of the First Amendment thus serve important functions both under individualism and under civic republicanism. For one, they legitimate government; for the other, they promote character--building and civic virtue.

[213] Although official messages of exclusion always should be judicially suspect, I conclude below that they are sometimes justified. *See infra* note 218. The questions to be asked are, of course, what are the standards of justification, and who shall enforce them.

[214] Decisions overtly as diverse as *Tinker*, *Pico* and *Hazelwood* appear to agree that curricular judgments of school officials are virtually absolute (excluding those implicating separation of church and state). *See* Hazelwood Sch. Dist. v. Kuhlmeier, 484 U.S. 260, 271 (1988)

separation of church and state)[215] and the judgment of teachers concerning the use and substance of classroom discussions[216] are not subject to judicial second-guessing. Student liberty claims seem least compelling (and, thus, least likely to gain judicial support) when they are directed at these issues or contexts.[217] Yet understanding the proper judicial/constitutional grounds for discomfort over messages of exclusion may necessitate reconsideration of this general belief in an unbridled commitment to authority when dealing with these issues. Upon reflection, the very concept of academic freedom,[218] which is at times judicially enforced,[219] represents a limitation upon the supremacy of order and

---

(determining that educators are entitled to exercise significant control over "activities [that] may fairly be characterized as part of the school curriculum"); Board of Educ. v. Pico, 457 U.S. 853, 869 (1982) (plurality opinion) ("[School Board members] might well defend their claim of absolute discretion in matters of *curriculum* . . . ."); *see also* Tinker v. Des Moines Indep. Community Sch. Dist., 393 U.S. 503, 514 (1969) (stressing fact that student petitioners had not "interrupted school activities nor sought to intrude in the school affairs"). Many scholars concur. *See, e.g.*, Hafen, *Developing Student Expression*, *supra* note 95, at 728 (noting that student free speech claims are least likely to obtain judicial approval when directed at classroom curriculum); Diane Ravitch, *The Continuing Crisis: Fashions in Education*, 1984 AM. SCHOLAR 183, 193 (expressing doubt as to whether academic curriculum can be democratized "without cheapening it").

[215] *See, e.g.*, Edwards v. Aguillard, 482 U.S. 578 (1987) (holding unconstitutional state law requiring teaching of "creation science" whenever theory of evolution is taught); Epperson v. Arkansas, 393 U.S. 97 (1968) (striking down state law prohibiting public school teachers from teaching evolution).

[216] *See, e.g.*, *Hazelwood*, 484 U.S. at 271 (recognizing authority of teachers to control student expression to assure other students learn intended lesson); *Tinker*, 393 U.S. at 514 (emphasizing that students' act of protest, although taking place within classroom, was not directed at school or its personnel and, as silent demonstration, did not interrupt class); Hafen, *Developing Student Expression*, *supra* note 95, at 728 (minimizing legal significance of student free speech claims in classroom).

[217] Needless-to-say, school boards or teachers, without judicial insistence, could decide for their own institutional or pedagogical reasons to encourage participation of students, and other school community members, in curricular deliberations and in the structuring of norms of classroom discussion.

[218] The initial concept of academic freedom grew out of a German university setting. It included the "idea of 'convincing' one's students, of winning them over to the personal system and philosophical views of the professor . . . ." Walter P. Metzger, *The German Contribution to the American Theory of Academic Freedom*, *in* 1 EMERSON, HABER AND DORSEN'S POLITICAL AND CIVIL RIGHTS IN THE UNITED STATES 806 (4th ed. 1976). American academic opinion has not condoned fully this pedagogical approach. *Id.* For a comprehensive history of academic freedom in this country, see RICHARD HOFSTADTER & WALTER P. METZGER, THE DEVELOPMENT OF ACADEMIC FREEDOM IN THE UNITED STATES (1955).

[219] Regarding the constitutional basis of academic freedom, the Supreme Court generally has confined itself to a few "eloquent but isolated statements." THOMAS EMERSON, THE SYSTEM OF FREEDOM OF EXPRESSION 616 (1971). These statements always are made in reference to more traditional constitutional doctrines. Thus, the Court has at various times derived academic freedom from free speech, due process, the rule against vagueness in statutory language, and the

authority even when dealing with curricular matters.

A school board, intent on conveying information and inculcating norms valued by its members, rightfully would insist upon the authority to determine what to exclude, as well as what to include, in the school's curriculum.[220] Nevertheless, courts have distinguished curricular inclusions from exclusions, acknowledging greater school board control over minimum, rather than maximum, curriculum content. Teacher discharge cases illustrate this pattern. The courts have permitted the school board to discharge a teacher to assure that the board's own chosen material was transmitted to the student, but have prohibited a discharge that was grounded in an effort to assure that the material was transmitted *to the exclusion of competing perspectives*.[221] Only in the latter situation has the dismissal communicated an official rejection of specific information or perspectives. Only then has the board sent a message of exclusion and intolerance for the community, including students, to hear.

Consequently, the doctrine of academic freedom is best explained not as a constitutional entitlement of the teacher per se, but as a mechanism for restricting the school system's ability to impose uniform values upon a captive and impressionable audience.[222] It prevents the school board from communicating to the students, through the spectacle of a teacher's discharge, the importance of subservience and the danger of independent,

---

rule against established religion. *Id.* at 610. For some relevant cases upholding academic freedom claims, see *infra* notes 221-22.

[220] "[E]ducation may be viewed as providing certain inputs to students with the decision of what not to communicate being equally as significant as that of what to communicate." STEPHEN R. GOLDSTEIN & E. GORDON GEE, LAW AND PUBLIC EDUCATION 108 (1974); *see* Board of Educ. v. Pico, 457 U.S. 853, 914 (Rehnquist, J., dissenting) ("Determining what information *not* to present to the students is often as important as identifying relevant material.").

[221] *See* Kingsville Indep. Sch. Dist. v. Cooper, 611 F.2d 1109 (5th Cir. 1980) (protecting teacher's right to include controversial material relevant to prescribed curriculum even when forbidden to do so by superiors); *see also Developments in the Law—Academic Freedom*, 81 HARV. L. REV. 1045, 1098 (1968) (theorizing that minimum, but not maximum standards, are inherent in concept of compulsory education). *Compare* Palmer v. Board of Educ., 603 F.2d 1271, 1273 (7th Cir. 1979) (permitting discharge of teacher who refused to teach "patriotic ceremonies"), *cert. denied*, 444 U.S. 1026 (1980) *with* Russo v. Central Sch. Dist. No. 1, 469 F.2d 623 (2d Cir. 1972) (protecting teacher's right to sit silently and not participate while another teacher conducted class flag ceremonies), *cert. denied*, 411 U.S. 932 (1973).

[222] Most court decisions on academic freedom ground themselves in the belief that independent thinking by teachers is needed to cultivate students' capacity for critical and independent thought through exposure to a diversity of views. *See* Keyishian v. Board of Regents, 385 U.S. 589, 603 (1967); Wieman v. Updegraff, 344 U.S. 183, 194-98 (1952) (Frankfurter, J., concurring); Cary v. Board of Educ., 427 F. Supp. 945, 949 (D. Colo. 1977), *aff'd*, 598 F.2d 535 (10th Cir. 1979); Albaum v. Carey, 283 F. Supp. 3, 10-11 (E.D.N.Y. 1968); *see also* TUSSMAN, *supra* note 108, at 58-59.

critical thought. Such a lesson would be inconsistent with the necessity to educate for citizenship, and to enhance the character of a democratic polity.

The classroom component of this argument is somewhat more difficult to document. Instead, let me address your educated instincts. In 1987, the Supreme Court rejected, as being in violation of the Establishment Clause, Louisiana's attempt to require instruction in "creation science" whenever the theory of evolution was taught.[223] Does the prohibition of a school system from teaching "scientific creationism" equally permit a teacher's silencing of a student who, consistent with the normal pattern of student discussion,[224] wishes to state her concern over evolution's deviation from the biblical account of the creation of humankind? There seems something quite different between a public school's inability to promote a specific religious belief,[225] and a public school teacher's authority to banish from his classroom as unworthy of comment—as beyond the pale[226]—a perspective held by people of good will within the community. The difference may be one between preventing schools from fostering religious beliefs within students and allowing teachers to officially denigrate those same beliefs when expressed by children in their classes.[227] Thus, even the classroom must be structured to avoid the blatant besmirching of First

---

[223] Edwards v. Aguillard, 482 U.S. 578, 597 (1987).

[224] Thus, I am excluding from my question the student who decries the instructor or other students, who screams, or who refuses to yield the floor after the accustomed limit on a single student's speaking time has elapsed.

[225] The Court in *Aguillard* found Louisiana's purpose in requiring the teaching of "creation science" to be the advancement of a particular religious belief. 482 U.S. at 593.

[226] This argument cannot be taken too far. Some perspectives really may be beyond the pale: for example, one supporting the sexual abuse of children. In the process of defining ourselves as a community, some values become so entrenched and widely accepted in our cultural community that they are no longer subject to serious debate. At this point they become part of our "civil religion," *see* Robert N. Bellah, *Civil Religion in America*, 96 DAEDALUS 1 (1967) (introducing term "civil religion" into modern lexicon), and their antithesis comes to reside *outside* the universe of culturally conceivable options. *See* Ingber, *Rediscovering*, *supra* note 98, at 1517-20 (trying to capture this concept through image of "community agenda of alternatives"). The value of protecting children from sexual abuse has likely reached such a position in contemporary America. Thus, silencing the classroom expression of a contrary perspective is unlikely to even raise a judicial eyebrow. The same cannot be said with respect to the status of the cultural debate over the origin of humankind and the significance of the biblically-based perspective. Defining the boundary of our "universe of culturally conceivable options" may sometimes appear self-evident; at other times, it may constitute the most difficult decision that school officials and, at times and in due course, courts, must make.

[227] Silencing such beliefs is a violation of both the Free Speech and Free Exercise Clauses. *See* Widmar v. Vincent, 454 U.S. 263, 277 (1981) (finding that concept of free speech was violated in university's refusal to provide facilities to student group wishing to use them for religious worship and discussion, while generally making those facilities available to other student groups).

Amendment values.

c. Extra-Curricular Activities

As shown, even the curricular and classroom components of public education may be *judicially* compelled at times to communicate the virtues of liberty.[228] Nevertheless, these components remain most dependent on the alternative virtues of order and authority. A reasonable pedagogical theory that educators might choose perceives the grade-school classroom as prescriptive by nature, and identifies curriculum choices as hinging upon the limited time and resources of the school system and the requirement that students use the same textbooks in a given course.[229] Consequently, when evaluating the degree of judicial oversight properly directed toward extra-curricular activities, one finds that some activities are virtually part of the classroom curriculum, demanding much the same emphasis on order and authority. Others, however, can—and likely should—proceed quite effectively without this emphasis and with a greater recognition of the cultural significance of liberty.[230] Under the latter set of circumstances, if liberty is denied unnecessarily, it communicates to students the undesirable message of institutional indifference or societal disregard for liberty-oriented virtues. This message is most disquieting given our alleged

---

[228] *See supra* text accompanying notes 214-27.

[229] *See supra* text following note 152; *see also* Yudof, *Library Book Selection*, *supra* note 23, at 547 (stressing educational limitations of classroom). Other pedagogical perspectives reject these perceptions. Beginning with John Dewey, some education theorists have stressed the communitarian significance of the child's role in his own education. *See* JOHN DEWEY, DEMOCRACY AND EDUCATION 393 (1916); *see also* Lawrence Kohlberg & Rochelle Mayer, *Development as the Aim of Education*, 42 HARV. EDUC. REV. 449, 494 (1972) (agreeing with Dewey's view and asserting "that all children . . . are 'philosophers' intent on organizing their lives into universal patterns of meaning"). For such theorists, education must be participatory.

Despite this conflict, one should recall Justice Holmes' famous dissent in Lochner v. New York, 198 U.S. 45, 74-76 (1905), noting that "[t]he Fourteenth Amendment does not enact Mr. Herbet Spencer's Social Statics." *Id.* at 75 (Holmes, J., dissenting). If Holmes is correct, there would seem no greater justification for interpreting the Constitution to impose John Dewey's educational viewpoint. *See* DEWEY, *supra*. Educators may choose the pedagogical theory they prefer as long as they do not apply it in ways which communicate and inculcate denigration of values of liberty. The communal interests of free speech cannot permit this.

[230] This portion tracks the contextual standard for protecting speech employed in Grayned v. City of Rockford, 408 U.S. 104 (1972). In *Grayned*, the Court sustained an ordinance barring certain demonstrations near schools after questioning "whether the manner of expression [was] basically incompatible with the normal activity of a particular place at a particular time." *Id.* at 116. Under a "basic incompatibility" test, the nature or mission of the institution initially dictates whether the regulation is appropriate. *See* International Soc'y for Krishna Consciousness, Inc. v. Lee, 505 U.S. 672 (1992). If the communicative pattern is compatible with the institution's continued effective functioning, then *tolerance* should be exercised and *participation* encouraged.

attempt to inculcate democratic values as part of the community's educational mission.

Thus, not all extra-curricular activities justify equal degrees of judicial deference to the judgment of educational professionals. The Court's lack of this understanding in *Hazelwood* is more troubling than its precise holding. Because the school newspaper at issue was a graded classroom assignment of a journalism course,[231] it arguably was subject to the same school and faculty oversight as any other classroom assignment. The Court, however, did not limit itself to these facts. Instead, it gave educators carte blanche control over the content of all "school-sponsored" student speech whenever a pedagogical explanation was possible. The phrase "school sponsored" appears to be defined so broadly as to include any student communication relevant to, and delivered during, a school--authorized activity.[232] This definition not only encompasses classroom expression, but also student speech associated with all extra-curricular activities. As previously suggested, this perception extends judicial deference too far.[233] It allows schools, with the imprimatur of constitutionality, to be structured to enforce subservience to an unrelenting authority. The lessons taught in such an environment are antithetical to those needed to habituate civic virtue.

Contemplating a different type of extra-curricular activity helps demonstrate the unfortunate consequences of the Court's ruling. Given the Justices' apparent indifference to the precise facts of *Hazelwood*, one can only assume the Court would reach the same conclusion in a case involving a student newspaper that was not associated with any journalism course, but was produced by students on school grounds as an on-going project of an offically-recognized extra-curricular journalism club with a faculty advisor. Under such circumstances, however, I would argue that the greater detachment of the student paper from the school curriculum and, therefore, its greater symbolic similarity to the press generally, make official silencing[234] of the paper much more damaging to our goal of forging a

---

[231] For a review of the factual details of the *Hazelwood* conflict that occurs in Hazelwood Sch. Dist. v. Kuhlmeier, 484 U.S. 260 (1988), see *supra* text accompanying notes 43-47.

[232] *Hazelwood*, 484 U.S. at 271-74. Again we see the irony of a free speech interpretation that only protects expression which is irrelevant to the context in which it is delivered. *See supra* text accompanying notes 164-67. It seems that, if anything, such circumstances actually *increase* the justification for requiring the speech to be taken elsewhere, where it may be equally, if not more, effective.

[233] *See supra* text accompanying notes 164-70.

[234] I use the word "silencing" rather than "censoring" to reduce any bias in my argument. If the school's action can be seen as consistent with the proper educational mission of our public schools, than the action cannot rightfully be labeled "censorship."

democratic polity.

To fortify the argument that greater official recognition of the liberty virtues is both possible and mandated in my "reformulated" *Hazelwood* context, we need only consider the Court's response to the educational conflicts that developed in the wake of its decision in *Widmar v. Vincent*.[235] In *Widmar*, the Court held that a public university, while directed by the Establishment Clause to avoid promoting religion, was *required* by the Free Speech Clause to provide religious groups equal access to the university's "open forum."[236] Prompted by uncertainty about the extent of *Widmar's* application to elementary and secondary schools, Congress enacted the Equal Access Act of 1984.[237] The Act prohibits public secondary schools which have established a "limited public forum" from denying a student religious group permission to meet on school premises during non-instructional time.[238]

Despite the statute, school officials at Westside High School, a public secondary school in Omaha, Nebraska, refused to allow students to form a Christian club, which would have joined the thirty other student groups already approved as after-school extra-curricular activities.[239] In *Board of Education of the Westside Community Schools v. Mergens*,[240] the Supreme Court found that the school's action violated the Equal Access Act,[241] and that the Act, to the extent that it provided public school facilities to student groups intending to use them for religious purposes, did *not* violate the Establishment Clause.[242] Much of the Court's opinion focused on whether a "limited public forum" existed at the school[243] and

---

[235] 454 U.S. 263 (1981).

[236] *Id.* at 269. The Court rejected the university's claim that granting access would imply school sponsorship of the religious groups involved or of their practices. *Id.* at 274.

[237] 20 U.S.C. § 4071 (1988).

[238] *Id.* § 4071(a). The Equal Access Act states that "[a] public secondary school has a limited open forum whenever such school grants an offering to or opportunity for one or more noncurriculum related student groups to meet on school premises during non-instructional time." *Id.* § 4071(b). The statute is not limited by its terms to protecting religious groups. *Id.* § 4071(a). It also prohibits public schools which receive federal financial assistance from denying student groups access on the basis of the "political, philosophical or other content of speech [likely to be engaged in at the group's] meetings." *Id.*

[239] *See* Board of Educ. v. Mergens, 496 U.S. 226, 231-33 (1990) (plurality opinion).

[240] *Id.* at 226.

[241] *Id.* at 247.

[242] *Id.* at 253. Specifically, Justice O'Connor stated that "[a]lthough the Act permits 'the assignment of a teacher, administrator, or other school employee to the meeting for custodial purposes,' such custodial oversight of the student-initiated religious group, merely to ensure order and good behavior, does not impermissibly entangle government in the day-to-day surveillance or administration of religious activities." *Id.*

[243] *Mergens*, 496 U.S. at 234-47.

on the substance of Establishment Clause doctrine.[244] The Court also analyzed what constituted "school-sponsored expressive activities" within extra-curricular activities.[245] We will concentrate on this latter aspect of the opinion since the term, as used in *Mergens*, appears to have a significantly narrower meaning than it had in *Hazelwood*.

Westside's school board had adopted a policy covering student groups and organizations that heralded them as a "vital part of the total education program as a means of developing good citizenship, wholesome attitudes, good human relations, knowledge and skills."[246] Notwithstanding the obvious effort of the board (totally consistent with the philosophy of *Hazelwood*) to integrate all extracurricular activities into the common educational missions of information presentation, skills development and value inculcation, the *Mergens* Court not only refused to defer to the board's curricular judgment, but adamantly rejected it.[247] Yet the board's policy hardly was indefensible, its pedagogical approach hardly unheard of.[248] Despite its reasonableness, the Court recognized that the Congressional attempt, through the Equal Access Act, to demonstrate our nation's support for, and desire to promote, experiences of expressive liberty in our schools would be totally defeated if the board's holistic understanding of education were approved.[249] The board's approach would mandate an emphasis on order and authority in *all* extra-curricular meetings and functions equivalent to that which is justified in the classroom, thereby smothering efforts to stress independence and tolerance in any school activity.

---

[244] *Id.* at 247-53.

[245] *Id.* at 249-52.

[246] *Id.* at 231 (quoting Board Policy 5610).

[247] *Mergens*, 496 U.S. at 243-45. The Court stated: "To the extent that petitioners contend that 'curriculum related' means anything remotely related to abstract educational goals . . . we reject that assignment." *Id.* at 244. The Court then adopted the language of the Court of Appeals, indicating that

> [a]llowing such a broad interpretation . . . would make the [Act] meaningless. A school's administration could simply declare that it maintains a closed forum and choose which student clubs it wanted to allow by tying the purposes of those student clubs to some broadly defined educational goal. At the same time the administration could arbitrarily deny access to school facilities to any unfavored student club on the basis of the content of the speech of that group.

Id. at 244-45 (quoting Board of Educ. v. Mergens, 867 F.2d 1076, 1078 (8th Cir. 1989), *aff'd*, 496 U.S. 226 (1990)).

[248] *See supra* text accompanying notes 158-70 (recognizing logic of choosing to fully integrate varying school components into common and consistent enterprise of value inculcation).

[249] Board of Educ. v. Mergens, 496 U.S. 226, 244-45 (1990).

Thus, as in *Pico*,[250] the Court marked an educationally important, if not a logical, division among extra-curricular activities, relegating some to the domain of authority and others to that of liberty. Using a clearly different understanding of "curriculum" than had the board, the Justices in *Mergens* found that some officially-recognized, after-school activities were curriculum-related and that others were not.[251] For those clubs or groups not adequately tied to the curriculum, the student expressive activities associated therewith were understood properly as "permit[ted]" by the school rather than "endorse[d]" or "support[ed]."[252] *Tolerating* speech activities was different from *sponsoring* them.[253] Even the requirement that each student organization, in order to be officially recognized, have a faculty sponsor present at its meetings was insufficient to turn student expression into institutional expression.[254] If school officials feared others might erroneously conclude that the communication of students in officially permitted expressive activities equaled school-sponsorship, they needed only to publicly disavow the connection.[255] For some extra-curricular activities, the virtues of liberty—tolerance, participation and independent thought—were to come to the fore, thus adding another dimension to the school's effort to educate for citizenship.[256]

---

[250] Board of Educ. v. Pico, 457 U.S. 853 (1982).

[251] *Mergens*, 496 U.S. at 239-41. The Court defined "curriculum related" to include any student group of which

> the subject matter of the group is actually taught, or will soon be taught, in a regularly offered course; if the subject matter of the group concerns the body of courses as a whole; if participation in the group is required for a particular course; or if participation in the group results in academic credit.

Id. at 239-40.

[252] *Id.* at 250 (stating "proposition that schools do not endorse everything they fail to censor").

[253] *Id.* at 252 ("Although a school may not itself lead or direct a religious club, a school that *permits* a student-initiated and student-led religious club to meet after school . . . does not convey a message of state approval or endorsement of the particular religion.") (emphasis added).

[254] *Id.* at 252-53.

[255] *Mergens*, 496 U.S. at 251.

[256] *Mergens*, of course, involved the interpretation of a statute. Too broad a definition of "curricular-sponsored expressive activities" would have defeated the Congressional purpose in enacting the legislation. Congressional attempts to ensure both liberty and authority experiences in our schools, however, deserve no greater judicial support than does the Constitution's character-building goals to which I have referred so often. *See supra* text accompanying notes 88-90. In fact, as explained earlier, *see supra* text accompanying notes 235-38, the Equal Access Act was an effort to extend to secondary schools the constitutional principles announced in Widmar v. Vincent, 454 U.S. 263 (1981). Consequently, I have no difficulty extending the Court's analysis in *Mergens* to constitutional challenges, such as those involved in Hazelwood Sch. Dist. v. Kuhlmeier, 484 U.S. 260 (1988).

My conclusion that a *Hazelwood*-type situation (as earlier reformulated[257]) should be decided in a manner more consistent with that of *Mergens* is augmented by my sympathy for the efforts of the *Hazelwood* student journalists. These high school students were not acting in an immature or unprofessional manner. If the political issue of the day during *Tinker*'s 1960s was the Vietnam War, then the defining political and cultural issues of the 1980s and 1990s well might involve divisions and concerns relating to abortion, teen pregnancy, sexual harassment and abuse, and parental responsibility. The articles deleted from the student paper in *Hazelwood* were sincere attempts to consider the impact of these issues upon the students of the school, from those students' perspective. When responsible efforts to confront the real-life problems of today's adolescents are silenced as too sensitive for publication, those affected are likely to equate their experience with official disregard of free-speech values, rather than with an attempt to secure needed school decorum in the face of childish student behavior. Such lessons "teach youth to discount important principles of our government as mere platitudes."[258] Students rightfully would perceive such silencing as an act of "censorship."[259]

Precisely because of the reasons which cause me to sympathize with the *Hazelwood* student journalists, I find the *Bethel* decision[260] more compelling. The use of the sexual metaphor in the student's nominating speech *was* juvenile and may well have conflicted with the school's mission of teaching the limits of socially appropriate discourse. Inculcation of civic virtue may necessitate public disapproval of vulgarity during a school assembly.

To take such a posture, however, requires reconsideration of the position I have long held: that the First Amendment should not "indulge . . . the facile assumption" that one can somehow separate the substance and form of speech.[261] "Speakers often choose words," I have written, "not only for their cognitive content but for their emotive force.

---

[257] *See supra* text accompanying notes 231-34.

[258] West Virginia State Bd. of Educ. v. Barnette, 319 U.S. 624, 637 (1943).

[259] I believe the use of the label has now been proven appropriate. *See supra* note 234.

[260] *See supra* text accompanying notes 34-39.

[261] *See, e.g.*, Ingber, *Socialization*, *supra* note 31, at 65-66; Stanley Ingber, *The Marketplace of Ideas: A Legitimizing Myth*, 1984 DUKE L.J. 1, 32-36. The quoted phrase comes from Justice Harlan's opinion in Cohen v. California, 403 U.S. 15, 26 (1971), in which the Court held that the First Amendment protects a person's right to wear a jacket bearing the words "Fuck the Draft" in a courthouse corridor. More fully, Harlan warned: "[W]e cannot indulge in the facile assumption that one can forbid particular words without also running a substantial risk of suppressing ideas in the process. Indeed, governments might soon seize upon the censorship of particular words as a convenient guise for banning the expression of unpopular views." *Id.*

Unconventional terminology used to convey unpopular ideas may be essential to communicate the intensity with which the speaker holds his perspective."[262]

When writing these words, I was still of the opinion that liberal political philosophy properly provided the foundation of our constitutional commitment to free speech. My conception of free-speech rights, therefore, focused on their importance in furthering the goal of individualism to promote autonomy and, relatedly, their interpersonal function of promoting a "marketplace of ideas."[263] More recently, I have come to view as of equal, if not superior importance, the communal value of free speech in fostering civic virtue and the democratic polity based upon it.[264] This more subtle conception of rights—including individual, systematic and communal components—was presented earlier.[265] Also suggested was the proposition that, when dealing with children, the significance of free speech relates more to the communal interest of character development than to the individual's concern for the protection of autonomy, an autonomy that children do not yet fully possess.[266] When dealing with adults, therefore, for whom the securing of autonomy is of great import, free speech demands that much significance be given to the individual's choice of wording, with all of its nuances and shadings. For children, however, especially in their role of student, where the inculcation of civic virtue is the strongest justification for recognizing free-speech claims, promoting a capacity to overcome private passion or appetite in public decision-making is likely more consistent with First Amendment goals. Consequently, one can approve of the monitoring of vulgar language in a school assembly, as in *Bethel*,[267] to promote a preferred level of social discourse without simultaneously conferring upon the state the power to control the language

---

[262] Ingber, *Socialization*, *supra* note 31, at 65. Justice Brennan stressed this point in FCC v. Pacifica Found., 438 U.S. 726, 750-51 (1978) (holding that FCC may regulate radio broadcasts that use indecent but not necessarily obscene language). In his dissent, Justice Brennan insisted:

> The idea that the content of a message and its political impact on any who might receive it can be divorced from the words that are the vehicle for its expression is transparently fallacious. A given word may have a unique capacity to capsule an idea, evoke an emotion or conjure up an image.

Id. at 773 (Brennan, J., dissenting).

[263] *See* Ingber, *Socialization*, *supra* note 31, at 15, 47-48.

[264] *See generally* Ingber, *Rethinking Intangible Injuries*, *supra* note 171 (discussing importance of free speech as it relates to community interaction in general).

[265] *See supra* text accompanying notes 73-90.

[266] *See supra* notes 103-11 and accompanying text.

[267] Bethel Sch. Dist. v. Fraser, 478 U.S. 675 (1986).

of public debate generally.[268]

4. An Overall Perspective

Apparently, not a single aspect of the education process can separate itself from education's inculcative mission. The inculcation of virtue, a process upon which our founding generation depended for the success of our nation,[269] requires an appreciation for the value of both liberty and authority. That appreciation realistically can be obtained only if students—the youth of our nation—simultaneously become habituated to the roles of order and authority and of tolerance and independence through experiences that give credence to the proclaimed virtues of each. One difficulty faced by schools which makes them such complex and fragile institutions is that experiences of some of these virtues can overshadow the experiences of others.[270] Yet, experiences of all are necessary for the molding of the virtuous, democratic personality.

Dividing the educational process into separate components, each accentuating a different set of virtues, is of some help. It is a blunt

---

[268] This distinction may be of greatest significance when school boards attempt to use vulgarity as a reason to remove a book from a public school's library. A student told that she must delete vulgarity from her school assembly address is still able to repackage her message to convey some, if not all, of her meaning. Any loss in substance due to the change in form may be outweighed by the training in preferred styles of social discourse. When a book is removed for vulgarity, however, there is no opportunity for rephrasing, and the author's message is fully removed from the school. This difference, when added to the symbolic communication of school library book removals as described earlier, *see supra* text accompanying notes 191-94, cautions against the "facile assumption" that substance and form can be separated in the library context.

[269] Sherry, *supra* note 54, at 68-70.

[270] Here lies the hopefully implicit limitation of Professor Hafen's assertion that "regulation can *protect* adolescents even as it restricts them as a way to help them *learn* by their own experience as their normal developmental processes unfold." Hafen, *The Learning Years*, *supra* note 109, at 1061. Certainly, students need order and authority if they are to obtain the information and information-gathering skills needed to be informed as adults. In addition, students sometimes must be protected even from themselves because they do not yet possess personalities with sufficient maturity to avoid risks of their own making. *Id.* at 1048-49 ("[L]imitations on choice rights represent a form of protection for minors because they protect minors against their own immaturity and against their vulnerability to exploitation by others."). But if we protect them to the point that they do not experience the need to tolerate diversity, the thrill of independent thought, and the empowerment gained by questioning authority, then we shall have protected them to the point where they have *learned* the character traits of conformity and subservience.

Although public schooling requires us to admit that cultures do and should constrain, we must not equate cultural influence with cultural domination. The socialization process within the schools must appear to inculcate a tradition that we acknowledge to be unfinished or incomplete. ALASDAIR C. MACINTYRE, AFTER VIRTUE 207 (1981). Society must perceive inculcation as neither too successful, nor too efficient. The system must remain ostensibly pervious—leaving a space for liberty to reign.

instrument, however, needing further refinement to avoid institutional communications that "outrageously" denigrate any of these values. There is little chance that school officials or education professionals will act to discredit the school's commitment to order and authority, for these values provide those individuals with their institutional status. But to ensure that their actions do not impinge upon the believability of their liberty-supportive and tolerance-supportive rhetoric, a credible threat of judicial oversight must exist.[271] Even if exercised solely for egregious cases, judicial intervention in defense of free speech norms can both motivate greater sensitivity of those norms by educators and provide public proof of the sincerity of the community's belief in liberty's importance to otherwise potentially skeptical students. Such a demonstration may help accomplish the difficult task of indoctrinating children with the belief that individuals who resist becoming wholly indoctrinated are highly valuable to society. And so the educational enigma continues.

V. ADDENDUM

The desk at which I sat while writing this Article is only a few miles away from the various sites associated with the *Tinker* conflict. In fact, in Des Moines, the case virtually has become part of the community's folklore.[272] This glorification of *Tinker* happened despite my belief that the sweeping language used by the Court to ensure that our schools inculcate the virtues of liberty frightened educators and led to a judicial backlash. As a result of this backlash, the virtues of order and authority have been reestablished as supreme in virtually all aspects of the official

---

[271] Thus, although the Supreme Court appears to have embraced the position of *Hazelwood*, 484 U.S. at 272-73, I cannot accept what Professor Hafen characterizes as his "modest and general observation" that courts, subject to the principle of separation of church and state, should defer expansively to judgments of educational institution authorities. Hafen, *Schools*, *supra* note 16, at 607. An assurance of deference may undermine Professor Hafen's own encouragement that schools, on occasion, "elect non-directive methods that distinctly lack authority or that place a premium on student initiative or student criticism of authority." *Id.* at 615.

[272] A few years ago, for example, many of the principals of Tinker v. Des Moines Indep. Community Sch. Dist., 393 U.S. 503 (1969), came back to Des Moines to participate in a "Visiting Scholars" program at Roosevelt High School, one of the schools where students wore armbands. The first evening, a public discussion about the events leading to the decision and its effect over the years, was held in the school's auditorium. *See School Report*, DES MOINES REG., Apr. 27, 1992, at 9A. The following day, the *Tinker* students (and their former attorney) spent time at the school talking with their present-day counterparts. Mary Challender, *Three Who Took a Stand See Results of Effort*, DES MOINES REG., May 9, 1992, at 3M. A day after their departure, the *Des Moines Register* had an editorial praising their courage and their role as defenders of free speech. Dennis Ryerson, *Reflecting on the Tinker Case*, DES MOINES REG., May 10, 1992, at 3E.

educational process.[273] It appears that *Tinker* has been left to reign in contexts such as the cafeteria and school yard as well as other areas where the speech involves private interpersonal communications among students which neither are incorporated into, nor impact upon, the educational mission. The residual significance of *Tinker*, therefore, has little to do with the need to recognize a place for inculcating tolerance, participation, and independent, critical thought—the virtues of liberty—in the planning of our school structure.

Still, *Tinker* provides students with some expressive rights that did not exist as clearly prior to the decision. The domain of private speech and that of noninterruptive demonstrations of views not directly challenging school policy would seem to remain—for whatever that is worth—within the decision's continuing sphere of protection. But even here, twenty-five years after *Tinker*, school officials still may not have heard or understood *Tinker*'s message regarding the importance of preparing students for, and habituating them to, both the glory and responsibility of liberty.

Thirty miles up Interstate 35 from the scenes of *Tinker* is the city of Ames, Iowa, an academic community housing Iowa State University. Just last year an issue arose at Ames Middle School where four eighth-graders were suspended for a day for wearing T-shirts designed to protest what they perceived as sexism within their community.[274]

The newspaper account of the story goes something like this: For over a year and without any institutional objection, a number of Ames Middle School boys had been wearing T-shirts to school bearing the logo of a restaurant chain known as Hooters.[275] The shirts portray owl eyes peering out from Os in the word "Hooters". The shirts carry slogans such as "More than a mouthful."[276] The sexual innuendo is obvious.

Some girls at the school did not think the trumpeting of a message about women's breast sizes from boys' garments was the most collegial

---

[273] There is one exception, however. Although presented initially only as a plurality view, the restrictions on library book removals set forth in Board of Educ. v. Pico, 457 U.S. 853 (1982), presumably remain in force.

[274] Douglas Burns, *Four Students Suspended Over T-Shirt Controversy*, DAILY TRIB., Apr. 20, 1994, at A1; Thomas R. O'Donnell, *Kids Air Thoughts on T-Shirt Flap*, DES MOINES REG., Apr. 27, 1994, at 1M.

[275] In May of 1994, the national restaurant chain settled a sexual harassment lawsuit filed by six of its waitresses. All Hooters waitresses are required to wear Hooters T-Shirts—often cropped or knotted—and short shorts. The dress code had been an issue in the lawsuit, but terms of the settlement were not disclosed. *Sexual Harassment Suits at Hooters Are Settled*, STAR TRIB., May 11, 1994, at 1B.

[276] Burns, *supra* note 274, at A2; *Teen Girls Crow Back at Sexism*, PLAIN DEALER, June 21, 1994, at 1E [hereinafter *Teen Girls Crow*].

move in coeducation. So as both a spoof and a protest, the girls designed and produced their own T-shirts sporting a picture of a rooster and accompanied by the word, "Cocks."[277] The back of the shirt carried the slogan "Nothing to crow about."[278] Before wearing their shirts to school, however, the girls approached the principal for permission.[279] *He denied it.*[280] Some students wore the shirts anyway, and when a few refused to obey the principal's order that they remove them or turn them inside out, the principal suspended them.[281]

Given Ames' location, no one should have been surprised when the local paper, *The Daily Tribune*, published an editorial criticizing the school's actions that quoted at length from *Tinker*.[282] The editorial reminded school officials that "'students are entitled to freedom of expression of their views,'" that "'schools may not be enclaves of totalitarianism,'" and that "'students may not be . . . confined to the expression of those sentiments that are officially approved.'"[283] Recognizing that the entire skirmish was not a public relations bonanza for the school, administrators organized a forum to discuss the incident and the related issues of free speech and sexual harassment.[284] During the forum, the students defending the prohibited action were poised and articulate. The history teacher who moderated the forum voiced his pride in the girls.[285] The Assistant Superintendent of Schools lauded them as "thoughtful young people" who had been "beautiful through this."[286] The principal even conceded that he may have been wrong.[287]

How did the school then show its support to these "thoughtful young people" who, despite institutional discouragement, had practiced the virtues

---

[277] Burns, *supra* note 274, at A1.

[278] *Id.*

[279] The girls actually asked permission! At the very moment of their resolve, they still sought approval of the institutional authority. Somehow I doubt that the boys even considered such deference before wearing their shirts.

[280] *Teen Girls Crow*, *supra* note 276, at 1E.

[281] *Id.* One may be curious about why the principal saw the need to ban the wearing of the girls' T-shirt for even a day, when the boys had been freely wearing T-shirts parodying women's breasts for over a year without raising any official concern.

[282] *Editorial: Controversial T-Shirts, Message Are Harmless*, DAILY TRIB., Apr. 26, 1994, at A10 (quoting Tinker v. Des Moines Indep. Community Sch. Dist., 393 U.S. 503, 511 (1969)) [hereinafter *Editorial: Controversial T-Shirts*].

[283] *Id.*

[284] Thomas R. O'Donnell, *Ames Officials Cluck at Students' T-Shirts*, DES MOINES REG., Apr. 22, 1994, at 1M.

[285] Rekka Basu, *Girls Give a Hoot About Free Speech*, USA TODAY, June 9, 1994, at 11A.

[286] *Editorial: Controversial T-Shirts*, *supra* note 282, at A10.

[287] *Teen Girls Crow*, *supra* note 276, at 1E.

of participation and independent, critical thought? How did it correct this error and portray support for tolerance rather than intolerance? It banned *both* T-shirts.[288] Someone clearly had missed *Tinker*'s message.[289] Or perhaps that message simply has been washed away in the history of the last twenty-five years.

[288] *Id.*

[289] The students were not the ones missing the message. For example, one of the girls involved said, "We wanted to make people talk and think about [the sexist implications of the Hooters T-shirts]. . . . We wanted them (the Hooters shirts) to be socially unacceptable rather than legally unacceptable." Basu, *supra* note 285, at 11A (quoting student).

Guarding the Treasure: Protection of Student Religious Speech in the Classroom

*Chad Allred**

I. Introduction

In February 1996, New Jersey first-grader "Z.H." was rewarded for his reading skills. Z.H.'s teacher, Ms. Oliva, allowed students reaching a certain reading proficiency to read a book of their own choosing to the rest of the class.[1] Z.H. chose to read "A Big Family," a story adapted from Genesis included in *The Beginner's Bible*.[2] "However, because of its religious content, Ms. Oliva did not allow Z.H. to read the story to the class. Instead, although the other students were allowed to read their nonreligious stories to the class, he was allowed to read the story only to Ms. Oliva."[3] After unsuccessfully requesting that Z.H. be allowed to read his story to the class, Z.H. and his mother filed suit against the local Board of Education and the State Department of Education alleging a violation of "Z.H.'s rights to Freedom of Expression under the First Amendment."[4] The district court granted the defendants' motions for judgment on the pleadings.[5] The Court of Appeals for the Third Circuit affirmed without comment.

While it is pleasing to recall that students and teachers do not lose their constitutional rights at the schoolhouse gate,[6] we know that students and teachers do not enjoy their constitutional rights as fully within the schoolhouse as when they are outside of it. Within the

---

* J.D., University of Texas School of Law; Associate, Ellis, Li & McKinstry PLLC, Seattle. The author would like to thank Brandon Bennett, Prof. Douglas Laycock, Kyle D. Netterfield, Fernando Rodriguez, and Andrew J. Toles for their thoughtful comments on earlier drafts, and Randi J. Allred for her unflinching support.

1. C.H. *ex rel.* v. Oliva, 990 F. Supp. 341, 346 (D.N.J. 1997), *aff'd*, 166 F.3d 1204 (3d Cir. 1998) (hereinafter C.H. v. Olivia). "The material was subject to review by Ms. Oliva to ensure that it would be suitable in length and complexity for first grade students." *Id.* at 346 n.2.
2. *Id.*
3. *Id.* at 347.
4. *Id.*
5. *Id.* at 356.
6. *See* Tinker v. Des Moines Indep. Community Sch. Dist., 393 U.S. 503, 506 (1969).

American schoolhouse, the robust freedoms of religious exercise and of speech are restricted. *C.H. v. Oliva* highlights the difficulty of determining how tight this restriction must be, especially when the conduct at issue is not only within the schoolhouse, but within the elementary school classroom.

Freedom of speech was clearly important to the framers of our Constitution and has remained a valued freedom over the past two centuries. It is understandable that Z.H.'s family would sense that something had gone awry when Z.H. was not allowed to read his story. Although Z.H. does have a right to some protected speech within the classroom setting, it is also clear that the framers valued religious liberty. Part of their plan to protect this liberty was the Establishment Clause of the First Amendment—an effort to leave religious choices within the hands of citizens and out of the reach of government. Thus, it is understandable that the school district may have seen it as the district's constitutional duty to prohibit Z.H. from reading his story. Moreover, it is understandable that many parents would expect the school district to prohibit Z.H.'s presentation, believing that the Constitution preserves the freedom to send their children to public school without fear that the children will be coerced or proselytized. This tension between the Free Speech Clause and the Establishment Clause is not new. Part of the reason why the tension lingers is the lack of clear standards. Judges and attorneys, not to mention students, parents, and teachers, are left to wonder if and when one clause has priority over the other and what the standards are for making such a decision.

Accepting *Oliva* as a paradigm example, this Article attempts to ease the Free Speech Clause-Establishment Clause tension in the context of student religious speech within the public classroom. In Part II, momentarily leaving the Establishment Clause aside, this Article evaluates the degree of freedom which Z.H. and student speakers like him have to speak within the elementary school classroom and asserts that where student expression is not school-sponsored and does not occur in a "nonpublic" forum, *Tinker v. Des Moines Independent Community School District*[7] governs the scope of protection for this expression. In Part III, this Article examines the Establishment Clause defense to determine whether it acts to prohibit religious speech such as Z.H.'s and argues that, guided by *Capitol Square Review &*

---

7. *Id.*

Advisory Board v. Pinette,[8] courts should not apply the Establishment Clause to student religious expression in the classroom.

This Article makes two observations, both in Parts II and III, that have received insufficient attention in the academic literature and in the courts. First, students in public school classrooms are "captive speakers." Due to compulsory attendance laws, students are "captive" not only when hearing speech, but also when they wish to speak. Adhering to the First Amendment means protecting not only captive listeners, but also captive speakers. Second, in the face of the potential misperception of students that their school endorses the speech of a fellow student, teachers have an extraordinary opportunity to simultaneously disclaim endorsement and teach the fundaments of religious liberty. Rather than treating students as static and incapable of distinguishing between state-sponsored and private religious expression, teachers should explain the distinction, along with the importance the Constitution assigns to religious expression.

II. FREE SPEECH WITHIN THE CLASSROOM WALLS

The first issue of importance is whether, aside from the Establishment Clause, Z.H. had the right to speak freely in his classroom. If he did not have this right—if the school district could curtail his speech for reasons unrelated to the Establishment Clause—the issue of whether the Establishment Clause may restrict student religious speech in the classroom is irrelevant.[9]

In *Tinker v. Des Moines Independent Community School District*, the Supreme Court considered the right of junior high and high school

---

8. 515 U.S. 753 (1995).

9. *See, e.g.*, DeNooyer v. Livonia Pub. Sch., 799 F. Supp. 744, 754 n.8 (E.D. Mich. 1992), *aff'd*, 12 F.3d 211 (6th Cir. 1993), *cert. denied*, 511 U.S. 1031 (1994) (not reaching the Establishment Clause issue after deciding second-grader's right to speak was not infringed).

Establishment Clause analysis would also be unnecessary if Z.H. colorably alleged a violation of the Free Exercise Clause. Although the *Oliva* court stated that "the complaint clearly alleges deprivation of rights secured by the Constitution—Free Exercise of Religion," the Free Exercise Clause apparently was not directly at issue in the case. *Oliva*, 990 F. Supp. at 352. Because Z.H. had a freedom of speech claim—one constitutional provision that provided him with at least a facial right to religious expression—it is unimportant for the purpose of this article whether he could make a Free Exercise claim as well.

The questioned conduct in *Oliva* might be protected by both the Free Speech Clause and the Free Exercise Clause. The Supreme Court and commentators alike agree that these two clauses somewhat overlap. *See Pinette*, 515 U.S. at 767-68 (plurality opinion); Bd. of Educ. of Westside Community Sch. v. Mergens, 496 U.S. 226, 250 (1990); Douglas G. Laycock, *Religious Liberty as Liberty*, 7 J. CONTEMP. LEGAL ISSUES 313, 348-52 (1996). However, some commentators suggest that the Free Exercise Clause provides no protection for religious speech that is not otherwise provided by the Free Speech Clause. *See* William P. Marshall, *Religion as Ideas: Religion as Identity*, 7 J. CONTEMP. LEGAL ISSUES 385, 392-404 (1996).

students to wear black armbands at school in order to protest the hostilities in Vietnam.[10] The Court held that the students had the right to wear the armbands at school and that the school authorities could prohibit speech only when they could reasonably "forecast substantial disruption of or material interference with school activities."[11] Conduct that "materially disrupts classwork or involves substantial disorder or invasion of the rights of others is, of course, not immunized by the constitutional guarantee of freedom of speech."[12]

The Court stated:

> The school officials banned and sought to punish petitioners for a silent, passive expression of opinion, unaccompanied by any disorder or disturbance on the part of petitioners. There is here no evidence whatever of petitioners' interference, actual or nascent, with the school's work or of collision with the rights of other students to be secure and to be let alone. Accordingly, this case does not concern speech or action that intrudes upon the work of the schools or the rights of other students.[13]

But the Court clarified that its holding did not apply only to silent expression:

> Any departure from absolute regimentation may cause trouble. Any variation from the majority's opinion may inspire fear. Any word spoken, in class, in the lunchroom, or on the campus, that deviates from the views of another person may start an argument or cause a disturbance. But our Constitution says we must take this risk, and our history says that it is this sort of hazardous freedom—this kind of openness—that is the basis of our national strength and of the independence and vigor of Americans who grow up and live in this relatively permissive, often disputatious, society.[14]

Nearly twenty years after *Tinker*, in *Hazelwood School District v. Kuhlmeier*, the Supreme Court considered the extent to which school officials can exercise control over the contents of a high school newspaper produced as part of the school's journalism class.[15] The Court distinguished the case from *Tinker* primarily in two ways. First,

---

10. *Tinker*, 393 U.S. at 504.
11. *Id.* at 514.
12. *Id.* at 513.
13. *Id.* at 507.
14. *Id.* at 508-09 (citing Terminiello v. Chicago, 337 U.S. 1 (1949)).
15. 484 U.S. 260, 262 (1988). Specifically, the school principal banned certain articles concerning divorce and pregnancy from the newspaper. *Id.* at 263-64.

the Court found that the school newspaper was not a "public forum."[16] "Accordingly, school officials were entitled to regulate the contents of [the newspaper] in any reasonable manner. It is this standard, rather than our decision in *Tinker* that governs this case."[17] Second, the *Hazelwood* Court asserted that *Tinker* sets forth the standard for appropriately punishing *student* speech, but not "for determining when a school may refuse to lend *its* name and resources to the dissemination of student expression."[18]

The Court explained:

> The question whether the First Amendment requires a school to tolerate particular student speech—the question that we addressed in *Tinker*—is different from the question whether the First Amendment requires a school affirmatively to promote particular student speech. The former question addresses educators' ability to silence a student's personal expression that *happens to occur* on the school premises. The latter question concerns educators' authority over school-sponsored publications, theatrical productions, and other expressive activities that students, parents, and members of the public might reasonably perceive to bear the imprimatur of the school. These activities may fairly be characterized as part of the school curriculum, whether or not they occur in a traditional classroom setting, so long as they are supervised by faculty members and designed to impart particular knowledge or skills to student participants and audiences.[19]

Thus, the *Hazelwood* Court indicated that the standard it applied is appropriate (and the *Tinker* standard is inappropriate) where the speech in question (1) occurs in a nonpublic forum and (2) is school-sponsored.[20]

---

16. *Id.* at 267-70. *See infra* Part II.A. (discussion of forum analysis). The *Tinker* Court made no mention of forum analysis.

17. *Id.* at 270 (citing Perry Educ. Ass'n v. Perry Local Educators' Ass'n, 460 U.S. 37, 46 (1983)).

18. *Hazelwood*, 484 U.S. at 277-78 (emphasis added).

19. *Id.* at 270-71 (emphasis added). The Court found that banning the articles in the school newspaper was constitutionally permissible. *Id.* at 276.

20. It is arguable that these two factors are merely two aspects of one inquiry. That is, where an expression is school-sponsored, the location or program in which the expression occurs is not a public forum. Likewise, whatever speech occurs within a nonpublic forum at a school is sponsored by the school. *See* Ruti Teitel, *The Unconstitutionality of Equal Access Policies and Legislation Allowing Organized Student-Initiated Religious Activities in the Public High Schools: A Proposal for a Unitary First Amendment Forum Analysis Test*, 12 HASTINGS CONST. L.Q. 529 (1986).

A. *Forum Analysis*

One's right to speak is subject to numerous qualifications depending on the *content* of the speech.[21] Additionally, the level of protection that speech receives depends upon the *location* of the speaker.[22] The government may curtail private speech depending upon whether the speaker is on government property, what type of government property it is, and the degree of control the government has exercised over access to the property. Under the Supreme Court's "forum analysis," courts decide whether the government property or program at issue is a traditional public forum, a designated public forum, or a nonpublic forum.

A "traditional public forum" is a place "which by long tradition or government fiat ha[s] been devoted to assembly and debate."[23] Thus, the government generally does not establish traditional public fora. Instead, these fora are recognized by the long-held traditions and common practice that surround them. The classic examples of this type of fora are parks and sidewalks.[24] The government may restrict private speech in a traditional public forum on the basis of the speech's content, but only to serve a compelling state interest that the restriction is narrowly drawn to achieve.[25]

In contrast to a traditional pubic forum, a "designated public forum" (also called a "limited public forum") is government property that the government has effectively "open[ed] for indiscriminate public use for communicative purposes."[26] Hence, unlike a traditional public forum, the government must actively create a designated public

---

21. The State may curtail, or not protect, speech that is imminently dangerous (*see, e.g.*, Brandenburg v. Ohio, 395 U.S. 444 (1969); Edwards v. South Carolina, 372 U.S. 229 (1963)); distinctly commercial (*see, e.g.*, Bd. of Trustees of State Univ. of New York v. Fox, 492 U.S. 469 (1989)); or of decidedly low value (*e.g.*, obscenity).

22. *See, e.g.*, Cornelius v. NAACP Legal Defense & Educ. Fund, 473 U.S. 788 (1985); Hague v. Committee for Indus. Org., 307 U.S. 496 (1939).

23. *Perry*, 460 U.S. at 45; *see also Cornelius*, 473 U.S. at 800 (finding the purpose of this type of forum to be the "free exchange of ideas").

24. *See, e.g.*, Lamb's Chapel v. Center Moriches Union Free Sch. Dist., 508 U.S. 384, 391 (1993).

25. *See Cornelius*, 473 U.S. at 800; *Perry*, 460 U.S. at 45.

26. *Lamb's Chapel*, 508 U.S. at 392; *see also Hazelwood*, 484 U.S. at 267 ("[T]he government does not create a [designated] public forum by inaction or by permitting limited discourse, but only by intentionally opening a nontraditional forum to public discourse."); *Cornelius*, 473 U.S. at 817 (Blackmun & Brennan, JJ., dissenting) (defining this type of public forum as "government property which the government has opened for use as a place for expressive activity for a limited amount of time, or for a limited class of speakers, or for a limited number of topics"); *Perry*, 460 U.S. at 45.

forum. As with a traditional public forum, the government may impose a content-based restriction on speech in a designated public forum only if the restriction serves a compelling state interest and is narrowly drawn to achieve that end.[27]

A "nonpublic forum" (also called a "closed forum") is property that the government has not opened to the public.[28] The government need not have a compelling state interest in order to regulate speech in a nonpublic forum, but subject matter and speaker distinctions must be "reasonable in light of the purpose served by the forum and [must be] viewpoint neutral."[29]

The *Hazelwood* Court said that *Tinker* did not apply because the forum at issue, the school newspaper, was a nonpublic forum.[30] According to the reasoning in *Hazelwood*, in cases involving student expression, the courts must determine whether the location (or program) in which the speech occurred is a nonpublic forum. Several courts have declined to make this determination (or have made it implicitly)—treating forum analysis as irrelevant to student expression on school grounds.[31] This treatment makes sense because there is no question as to whether the student speakers have the right to be at the school.[32] As constitutional scholar Douglas Laycock asserts:

---

27. *See Cornelius*, 473 U.S. at 800; *Perry*, 460 U.S. at 45.

28. *See Cornelius*, 473 U.S. at 819 (Blackmun & Brennan, JJ., dissenting) (defining a nonpublic forum as "property that is not compatible with general expressive activity").

29. *Lamb's Chapel*, 508 U.S. at 393 (quoting *Cornelius*, 473 U.S. at 806).

30. *Hazelwood*, 484 U.S. at 267-70.

31. *See* Seamons v. Snow, 84 F.3d 1226, 1237 (10th Cir. 1996) (applying *Tinker* after deciding student speech about hazing incident was not school-sponsored); Burch v. Barker, 861 F.2d 1149, 1159 (9th Cir. 1988) (challenge to school district policy requiring approval of all student-written material prior to distribution at high school); Phillips v. Anderson County Sch. Dist. Five, 987 F. Supp. 988, 492-94 (D.S.C. 1997) (applying *Tinker*); Duran v. Nitsche, 780 F. Supp. 1048, 1053 n.3 (E.D. Pa. 1991) ("The court recognizes the emerging line of cases holding that public forum analysis is not appropriate in all free speech/public school cases. These cases have intimated that public forum concepts are not applicable when the speech is not school sponsored.") (citation omitted), *order vacated, appeal dism'd*, 972 F.2d 1331 (3rd Cir. 1992); Slotterback v. Interboro Sch. Dist., 766 F. Supp. 280, 290 (E.D. Pa. 1991) ("Because *Tinker* merely involved students' personal expression during school hours in a place where the students were entitled to be, *Tinker* and factually similar cases have nothing to do with a school's status as a public forum."); Rivera v. East Otero Sch. Dist. R-1, 721 F. Supp. 1189, 1193 (D. Colo. 1989) ("[W]hether or not a school campus is available as a public forum to others, it is clear that the students, who of course are required to be in school, have the protection of the First Amendment while they are lawfully in attendance."); Muller v. Jefferson Lighthouse Sch., 98 F.3d 1530, 1546 (7th Cir. 1996) (Rovner, J., concurring).

32. Justice O'Connor and Justice Brennan have recognized this point:

> There may be important differences between cases in which citizens have a legal right to be present on government property and those in which "citizens claim a right to enter government property for the particular purpose of speaking." Douglas Laycock, *Equal Access and Moments of Silence: The Equal Access Status of Religious Speech by Private*

> When citizens claim a right to enter government property for the particular purpose of speaking, it is relevant to ask whether other speakers have been allowed the same privilege, or whether the property is particularly appropriate for speech. The various versions of the public forum doctrine address these questions. But public forum analysis is irrelevant when access is not an issue. When citizens are going about their business in a place they are entitled to be, they are presumptively entitled to speak.[33]

Laycock's assertion is consistent with the Supreme Court's use of public forum analysis. In *Hazelwood* there was no question as to whether the students were allowed access to the school. The issue centered around the scope of their access to the school newspaper. It was the school newspaper, not the school itself, that the Court found to be a nonpublic forum.[34] Moreover, before the Court decided whether the students had the right to publish the specific articles censored by the principal, it considered whether the students had any right at all to "speak" through the newspaper.[35] That is, before the Court decided that school officials were justified in restricting the challenged articles, the Court decided the threshold question of whether the students had an independent right of access to the newspaper. The Court concluded that the students did not—their access to the newspaper was at the indulgence of the school district.[36]

In *Lamb's Chapel v. Center for Moriches Union Free School District*, a church sued a school district, alleging that the district violated the Constitution by denying the church access to school facilities for a religious-oriented film series on child-rearing, when the facilities were otherwise available during nonschool hours for social, civic, recreational, and political uses.[37] As in *Hazelwood*, the Court engaged in forum analysis, but only after it concluded that the

---

> *Speakers*, 81 NW. U. L. REV. 1, 48 (1986), *cited in* Board of Airport Comm'rs of Los Angeles v. Jews for Jesus, Inc., 482 U.S. 569, 573 (1987) (O'Connor, J.). In the former class of cases—into which the instant case falls—the Court has recognized that when citizens are going about their business in a place they are entitled to be, they are presumptively entitled to speak. *See* Jamison v. Texas, 318 U.S. at 416.

United States v. Kokinda, 497 U.S. 720, 744 n.2 (1990) (Brennan, J., dissenting) (holding that Post Office sidewalk was not traditional public forum and that Postal Service regulations prohibiting solicitation on Post Office premises did not violate Free Speech Clause).

33. Laycock, *supra* note 32, at 48. *But see DeNooyer*, 799 F. Supp. at 752 ("The Supreme Court has not made the 'use' versus 'access' distinction.").

34. *Hazelwood*, 484 U.S. at 268-70.

35. *See id.* at 269 (noting that the students' assertion that "they could publish 'practically anything'" in the newspaper was unfounded).

36. *See id.*

37. 508 U.S. at 387-89.

plaintiffs had no right to access the district's property apart from the district's "opening" of the property.[38]

In *Rosenberger v. University of Virginia*, a student organization that published a Christian newspaper challenged the university's refusal to disperse funds to the group from the Student Activity Fund (SAF), a fund created by the university to pay for a broad range of extracurricular student activities.[39] University policy allowed several of the student groups recognized as Contracted Independent Organizations (CIOs) to get the SAF reimbursement.[40] While the plaintiff student group, Wide Awake Productions, had become a CIO, the university had denied the group SAF funding.[41] As in *Hazelwood* and *Lamb's Chapel*, the Court used forum analysis.[42] But once again, this analysis was appropriate only because the plaintiffs did not have a right to access the university programs apart from the right granted by the university.[43]

Whereas in *Hazelwood*, *Lamb's Chapel*, and *Rosenberger*, the plaintiffs asserting freedom to speak had no independent entitlement to enter and speak upon the property (or program) in issue, this was not the situation in *Tinker*.

> Because students were indisputably entitled to be on the school grounds, the only question in *Tinker* was whether the school had a constitutionally sufficient reason to suppress their speech. The Court's requirement that the school show a material and substantial interference with the educational function is addressed to that question.[44]

Unlike in *Hazelwood*, *Lamb's Chapel*, and *Rosenberger*, where the defendants had the right to ban entrance by the plaintiffs (and others)

---

38. *Id.* at 391 ("[T]he [School] District need not have permitted after-hours use of its property for any of the uses" allowed by state law). The Court found that since the school district allowed groups with other perspectives on family values and child-rearing to use the facilities, the district had committed viewpoint discrimination and, thus, it was unconstitutional to exclude the church from using the facilities. *Id.* at 394-97.

39. 515 U.S. 819, 823-24 (1995).

40. *Id.* at 823.

41. *Id.* at 825.

42. *Id.* at 829-30. As in *Lamb's Chapel*, the Court actually based its decision upon viewpoint discrimination. *Id.* Viewpoint discrimination is unconstitutional even in a nonpublic forum. *See supra* note 29 and accompanying text.

43. *See id.* at 823 ("CIO status is available to any group the majority of whose members are students, whose managing officers are full-time students, and that complies with certain procedural requirements.").

44. Laycock, *supra* note 32, at 48.

to the government property, the *Tinker* plaintiffs were actually compelled to be on the government property.

Even if sympathetic to the idea of rejecting forum analysis in cases where students speak on *school grounds* generally, forum analysis proponents may charge that student speech in the *classroom* is a category unto itself. While students may have some leeway to "go about their business" during lunch, passing periods, and recreation times, they are not at such leisure in the classroom. In the classroom, students are to be actively learning and participating in a program led by the teacher. Forum analysis proponents may assert that this is not a time for broad discourse, religious or otherwise—especially in an elementary school.

This assertion is mostly, but not completely, accurate. While the student in the classroom and the student on the playground both have unquestioned access to their locations, the student in the classroom does not have the same liberty to speak as does the one on the playground. This is no reason, however, to engage in forum analysis; to the contrary, it is a reason to apply *Tinker*, where the appropriate standard for determining the degree of protection for the speech is to inquire whether the speech in question materially and substantially interferes with the educational function. The standard is responsive to the educational setting: Speech that is not substantially disruptive on the playground may very well be substantially disruptive in the classroom. Under *Tinker*, school officials can censor the latter, but not the former. In both scenarios, though, school officials must be able to substantiate their forecast of disruption.[45] Unfounded fears do not justify censorship in the classroom any more than they do on the playground.[46]

---

45. *See Tinker*, 393 U.S. at 509 ("[U]ndifferentiated fear or apprehension of disturbance is not enough to overcome the right to freedom of expression.").

46. In *Settle v. Dickson County School Board*, a ninth-grade teacher assigned her class a four-source research paper, requiring only that each paper topic be "interesting, researchable and decent." 53 F.3d 152, 153 (6th Cir. 1995). A student sued under the Free Speech Clause when the teacher refused to accept a research paper entitled "The Life of Jesus Christ" and gave the student a "zero" for failing to write on another topic. *Id.* Applying the *Tinker* standard, and asking whether the topic of Jesus materially disrupted classwork or involved substantial disorder, would have made *Settle* a case easily decided for the plaintiff. Instead, applying a categorical "classroom" rule, and based on the flawed conclusion that the *Hazelwood* Court found the school newspaper to be an "open forum," (*cf. Hazelwood*, 484 U.S. at 268-70 (finding that the newspaper was not a public forum)), the *Settle* court concluded that "[w]here learning is the focus, as in the classroom, student speech may be even more circumscribed than in the school newspaper or other open forum." *Settle*, 53 F.3d at 155.

B. *School Sponsorship*

A second issue to consider in determining whether to apply *Tinker* or *Hazelwood* is whether the speech was sponsored by the school. Importantly, the *Hazelwood* Court acknowledged that there is speech that merely "happens to occur" at school.[47] An example of this speech, the Court noted, was the wearing of armbands by the *Tinker* students in the classroom.[48] The Court contrasted this "happening" with "activities that students, parents, and members of the public might *reasonably* perceive to bear the imprimatur of the school."[49] An example of school-sponsored speech is a publication or a theatrical production.[50] By the Court's reasoning, nonschool-sponsored and school-sponsored student expression are two distinguishable situations that call for two different standards. The distinction would be meaningless if one of the scenarios swallowed the other. Despite how little we may know about the parameters of each category, we know definitely that neither category encompasses the other. Thus, even if parents, members of the public, or fellow students were to perceive that *Tinker*-like student expression is sponsored by the school, this perception would not be reasonable and *Tinker*, rather than *Hazelwood*, should control the extent to which school officials may regulate student expression. Even so, three further concerns merit discussion.

1. Compulsory Attendance

Some argue that the fact that students are compelled by law to be in the classroom creates *per se* school sponsorship of whatever speech occurs there.[51] Yet the *Hazelwood* Court showed that this conclusion is incorrect. Despite compulsory school attendance, the Court said that student expression that merely "happens" at school is not sponsored

---

47. *Hazelwood*, 484 U.S. at 271.

48. *Id.*

49. *Id.* (emphasis added).

50. *Id.*

51. *See, e.g.*, Ira C. Lupu, *To Control Faction and Protect Liberty: A General Theory of the Religion Clauses*, 7 J. CONTEMP. LEGAL ISSUES 357, 371 (1996) ("In those school settings accompanied by compulsory attendance requirements, state-sponsored religious exercises infringe the religious liberty of those coercively required to attend. With or without coercion, neutrality is impossible in these settings; majority religion and favored sects will always dominate the enterprise."); Leah Gallant Morgenstein, Note, *Board of Education of Westside Community Schools v. Mergens: Three "R's" + Religion = Mergens*, 41 AM. U. L. REV. 221, 230 n.50 (1991) ("Compulsory attendance laws, the impressionability of young students, and the potential perception of school sponsorship combine to make the public school a sensitive forum for equal access considerations.").

by the school.[52] Indeed, the Court's example of a nonschool-sponsored expression—the students wearing armbands in *Tinker*—occurred in a classroom full of students compelled to be in that classroom.[53] While compulsory attendance may be problematic in other ways,[54] it is not a reason to treat all student speech within the classroom as school-sponsored speech.

2. Aggregate Number of Speakers

Some also might argue that a school sponsors student expression when the aggregate number of speakers from a particular viewpoint is especially high. That is, when the vast majority of a classroom expresses the same ideas, the school sponsors that expression de facto. Admittedly, as a practical matter, a standard more stringent than the *Tinker* standard might be desirable where, for example, eighteen of twenty third-graders in a Texas school read Bible stories during their respective turns to "show and tell." The substantial disruption standard might be insufficient to completely protect the lone Buddhist student in the class. This scenario is problematic on a personal and social level, which I address below.[55] However, this scenario is not problematic on the constitutional level.

As a constitutional matter, the Free Speech Clause protects *each* student speaker. The protection is an individual right. It would be unreasonable[56] to diminish an individual student's protection because he sought to exercise his right in close proximity of time or space to other students exercising the same right. For example, we would not say that people protesting as a group deserve less Free Speech protection because they might persuade or intimidate those against whom they protest. Moreover, reducing speakers' protection because they all come from one viewpoint would be a form of viewpoint discrimination, a clear violation of the Free Speech Clause.[57]

---

52. *Hazelwood*, 484 U.S. at 271.

53. *See Tinker*, 393 U.S. at 516 (Black, J., dissenting) ("Here the constitutional right to 'political expression' asserted was a right to wear black armbands during school hours and at classes.").

54. *See infra* Part II.D. (discussion of captive audience) and Part III (discussion of Establishment Clause).

55. *See infra* Part II.C. (discussion of emotional harm to young listeners).

56. *See Hazelwood*, 484 U.S. at 271 ("expressive activities that students, parents, and members of the public might reasonably perceive to bear the imprimatur of the school").

57. *See Rosenberger*, 515 U.S. at 829. This is not to mention the administrative difficulty of the school deciding when several speakers come from "one" viewpoint.

As the *Hazelwood* Court noted, a finding of school sponsorship may be based on a reasonable perception by students.[58] The schools are in a great position to clarify for students what is or is not sponsored by the school. Even if there is a large number of speakers with the same viewpoint, a teacher can explain in simplified terms that the Constitution protects each student's right to speak.

3. Age

A third concern is that, because of their youth and immaturity, elementary school children often mistake "pure" student expression for school-sponsored student expression. As the *Oliva* court noted,

> At this age [first grade], it is quite reasonable to assume that these children could have been easily confused whether or not Z.H.'s teacher merely let Z.H. read his book, or if she approved of its message. Presenting the book to the teacher for approval was part of the standard procedure of that class activity; consequently, the books that were allowed to be read were those approved by the teacher. It is likely that some first-grade students would not fully understand all of the reasons why something could be unsuitable for use in a school activity and could instead believe that the books Ms. Oliva allowed to be read were those books that she liked or those with which she personally agreed.[59]

This concern is intensified when it is combined with the above two concerns. When especially *young* students are *compelled* to be at school and *many student speakers* express the same view, it may be even more likely that listening students misperceive that the speakers' expression is sponsored by the school.

It is important to remember, however, that this perception of school sponsorship is based on confusion and *mis*understanding. The erroneous perception of a young child, or anyone for that matter, cannot transform speech that happens at school into speech that the school promotes and stands behind. The perception would be inaccurate and unreasonable.[60] There is no reason to allow the

---

58. *Hazelwood*, 484 U.S. at 271.

59. *Oliva*, 990 F. Supp. at 355. *See also DeNooyer*, 799 F. Supp. at 747 (defendants argued "that second graders might not have the maturity to understand the context in which the [Christian] song was presented, that the students might assume that the School District endorsed the message of the song").

60. If not instructive or clarifying, it is at least interesting to note the *Hazelwood* Court's ambiguity, in a mere four sentences, as to what constitutes "school-sponsored" student expression. First, the Court says that it is not "a student's personal expression that happens to occur on the school premises." *Hazelwood*, 484 U.S. at 271. Rather, it includes "expressive activities that

subjective perception of one child (or of several children) to define the scope of the constitutional right of another child.

Moreover, as previously noted, school officials, above all, are in an extraordinary position to curb erroneous perception. Schools can clarify for students what expression is or is not sponsored by the school. Teachers can explain that a plurality of opinions and beliefs exist in the world, especially in our country, and even in the classroom. There is no reason for this fundamental lesson of civics not to take root in the elementary school. Justice Brennan made this point sharply in his dissent in *Hazelwood*:

> The sole concomitant of school sponsorship that might conceivably justify the distinction that the Court draws between sponsored and nonsponsored student expression is the risk "that the views of the individual speaker [might be] erroneously attributed to the school." Of course, the risk of erroneous attribution inheres in any student expression, including "personal expression" that, like the armbands in *Tinker*, "happens to occur on the school premises." Nevertheless, the majority is certainly correct that indicia of school sponsorship increase the likelihood of such attribution, and that state educators may therefore have a legitimate interest in dissociating themselves from student speech.
>
> But "[e]ven though the governmental purpose be legitimate and substantial, that purpose cannot be pursued by means that broadly stifle fundamental personal liberties when the end can be more narrowly achieved." Dissociative means short of censorship are available to the school. It could, for example, require the student activity to publish a disclaimer, . . . or it could simply issue its own response clarifying the official position on the matter and explaining why the student position is wrong.[61]

C. *Age as an Independent Objection to Tinker*

Even if a court were to conclude that the student speech at issue occurred in something other than a nonpublic forum and that the speech was not school-sponsored, there is an objection to applying the *Tinker* standard in the elementary school context that is independent of the concern that young children are more likely to misperceive school sponsorship. The concern is that student speakers may

---

students, parents, and members of the public might reasonably perceive to bear the imprimatur of the school." *Id.* Thus, it is only reasonable perception that can render expression "school-sponsored." Yet, "[e]ducators are entitled to exercise greater control over [school-sponsored] student expression to assure . . . that the views of the individual speaker are not erroneously attributed to the school." *Id.*

61. *Hazelwood*, 484 U.S. at 288-89 (Brennan, J., dissenting) (citations omitted).

emotionally harm student listeners.[62] The court in *Muller v. Jefferson Lighthouse School* expressed this concern in the midst of discussing whether the student speech occurred in a public forum:

> Declaring the elementary school classroom, hallway, or playground forums for unfettered student communication would require either a severe incursion into the critical educational mission of the elementary school or a substantial contraction of the First Amendment protections afforded speech in a public forum. Perhaps both. But neither alteration is necessary on the facts before us. In a public forum, the Christian can tell the Jew he is going to hell, or the Jew can tell the Christian he is not one of God's chosen, no matter how that may hurt. But it makes no sense to say that the

---

62. A variation on this theme is represented by *Baxter v. Vigo County Sch. Corp.*, in which an elementary school student alleged that she had a right under *Tinker* to wear confrontational T-shirts (stating, *e.g.*, "Unfair Grades," "Racism"). 26 F.3d 728, 730, 736 (7th Cir. 1994). The court held that the school principal had qualified immunity. *Id.* at 738; *see also* Harless v. Darr, 937 F. Supp. 1339, 1350 (S.D. Ind. 1996) (finding school officials immune from constitutional challenges to the officials' prohibiting elementary school student from passing out religious tracts at school). The court based its reasoning upon the fact that the plaintiff "was at least seven years younger than the youngest student in *Tinker*." *Baxter*, 26 F.3d at 738.

> [G]iven the indications in [*Bethel School District v. Fraser*, 478 U.S. 675 (1986),] and [*Hazelwood*] that age is a relevant factor in assessing the extent of a student's free speech rights in school, in addition to the dearth of caselaw in the lower federal courts, we are unable to conclude that the Baxters have demonstrated that the right [the principal] is alleged to have violated was "clearly established."

Id. Yet the court's analysis is confused. First, the court quoted the *Fraser* Court's statement that "[i]t does not follow . . . that simply because the use of an offensive form of expression may not be prohibited to adults making what the speaker considers a political point, the same latitude must be permitted to children in public school." *Id.* (internal quotation marks omitted) (quoting *Bethel Sch. Dist.*, 478 U.S. at 682). Yet, this is consistent with *Tinker*. While an adult may be allowed a measure of offensiveness in his speech, *Tinker* curtails similar speech by a student when it substantially disrupts the classroom.

Second, the *Baxter* court quoted the *Hazelwood* Court's statement that "a school must be able to take into account the emotional maturity of the intended audience in determining whether to disseminate student speech on potentially sensitive student topics." *Baxter*, 26 F.3d at 738 (internal quotation marks omitted) (quoting *Hazelwood*, 484 U.S. at 272). Yet the *Hazelwood* Court was addressing the standard for regulating *school-sponsored* speech. The *Baxter* court offers no analysis of how it perceived—or how the plaintiff's fellow students reasonably could have perceived—the plaintiff's confrontational T-shirts to be sponsored by the school.

As the *Baxter* court alludes, some courts and commentators are concerned that young students are not sufficiently mature to handle a broad freedom to speak. *See* Jay Alan Sekulow et al., *Proposed Guidelines for Student Religious Speech and Observance in Public Schools*, 46 MERCER L. REV. 1017, 1072 (1995). Yet maturity is not a prerequisite to free speech protection. Under the First Amendment, it is assumed initially that all Americans, even students, enjoy free speech protection. "[N]othing in the [F]irst [A]mendment postpones the right of religious speech until high school." *Baxter*, 26 F.3d at 738 (quoting Hedges v. Wauconda Community Sch. Dist. No. 18, 9 F.3d 1295, 1298 (7th Cir. 1993)). This Article, and cases such as *Tinker* and *Hazelwood*, wrestle with where to draw the lines of protection of student speech, based not on the maturity of the speaker, but upon the competing rights of those whom the speaker affects.

> overly zealous Christian or Jewish child in an elementary school can say the same thing to his classmate, no matter the impact. Racist and other hateful views can be expressed in a public forum. But an elementary school under its custodial responsibilities may restrict such speech that could crush a child's sense of self-worth.[63]

The court's conclusion controls its analysis. Finding that classrooms are "forums for unfettered student communication" cannot be right, the court says, because this "could crush a child's sense of self-worth," a presupposed constitutional evil. Yet, as precious as a child's self-worth is and as much as it should be protected, damage to a child's self-worth is not necessarily equivalent to material and substantial disruption of the educational environment. While the *Muller* court concludes that it never makes sense to allow "the overly zealous" child to tell another that he is going to hell (i.e., "no matter the impact"), in *Tinker* the Supreme Court made clear that, for the sake of the First Amendment, those within the schoolhouse may have to experience some measure of "the discomfort and unpleasantness that always accompany an unpopular viewpoint."[64]

Still, one might assert that there is doctrinal support for valuing a child's emotional health above another child's right to speak. For example, while the courts protect symbolic speech under the First Amendment, they do not protect violent acts that may very well also be symbolic speech.[65] Short of actual violence, "fighting words" are not protected.[66] Yet *Tinker* itself accounts for excessive intimidation by student speakers. If one student's statement that another is going to hell is part of an open and peaceful exchange, under *Tinker*, the speech likely should be protected. If, however, the statement disrupts the class, *Tinker* addresses the situation.

> [T]he *Tinker* standard is flexible enough to account for the differences in maturity between elementary school and older children. Given their youth, it is more likely that unrestricted speech in any given circumstances would be more likely to "substantially disrupt" the school's normal operation where younger students are involved. But this does not mean that school officials need not have

63. Muller v. Jefferson Lighthouse Sch., 98 F.3d 1530, 1539-40 (7th Cir. 1996) (holding that a school district code requiring predistribution review and nonschool-endorsement disclaimer on materials was constitutional).

64. *Tinker*, 393 U.S. at 509.

65. *See* H.C. HUDGINS, JR. & RICHARD S. VACCA, LAW AND EDUCATION: CONTEMPORARY ISSUES AND COURT DECISIONS 414-15 (4th ed. 1995).

66. NAACP v. Claiborne Hardware Co., 458 U.S. 886, 927 (1982) (citing Chaplinsky v. New Hampshire, 315 U.S. 568, 572 (1942)).

facts on which to base their fear of disruption before restricting speech.[67]

D. *Captive Audience Exception*

Just as there is a concern about student age that is independent of the concern about school sponsorship, there is an independent concern about compulsory attendance.[68] The concern is that the *listening* students may not want to hear the expression of student speakers. Admittedly, part of maturing and learning social skills is encountering people and expression that we either dislike or with which we disagree. Yet one usual option for the "unreceptive listener" is to physically distance oneself from the speaker or the speech. If it is an obnoxious phone salesman, we can hang up the phone. If it is a disagreeable pastor, we can leave the pew. If it is an aggressive protester, we can walk away. When we do not have the option to remove ourselves from speech coming our way, the courts have often held that the speech is not protected by the First Amendment.[69]

In the classroom, students usually do not have an opportunity to remove themselves from expression they dislike or with which they disagree. Because they are compelled to be in the classroom, they must endure whatever speech occurs there. Some may argue that this is reason to apply a "captive audience" exception to free speech protec-

---

67. Sekulow, et al., *supra* note 62, at 1072. As of yet, there are no "decisions of the Courts of Appeals applying *Tinker*-based speech right to the elementary school setting." *Muller*, 98 F.3d at 1538. *But see* Johnston-Loehner v. O'Brien, 859 F. Supp. 575, 580-81 (M.D. Fla. 1994) (applying *Tinker* where elementary school student challenged school district policy "requiring that students obtain the review and approval of school officials prior to distributing any written material").

Phillips v. Anderson County School District Five demonstrates how courts can apply *Tinker* effectively. 987 F. Supp. 488 (D.S.C. 1997). In *Phillips*, a middle school student alleged that he had a right to wear a jacket that looked like the Confederate battle flag. *Id.* at 490. The middle school's student body was about three-fourths white and one-fourth black, and in the five years prior to the time that school officials prohibited the plaintiff from wearing his jacket, the school had experienced at least five incidents of violence or near violence caused by student display of a Confederate flag. *Id.* The court concluded as a matter of law that school officials had a reasonable basis for determining that the plaintiff's jacket would likely result in another substantial disruption at the school. *Id.* at 493.

68. *See supra* Part II.B.1.

69. Frisby v. Schultz, 487 U.S. 474, 487 (1988) ("The First Amendment permits the government to prohibit offensive speech as intrusive when the 'captive' audience cannot avoid the objectionable speech."); Charles R. Lawrence III, *If He Hollers Let Him Go: Regulating Racist Speech on Campus*, 1990 DUKE L.J. 431, 456 ("Courts have held that offensive speech may not be regulated in public forums such as streets and parks where a listener may avoid the speech by moving on or averting his eyes, but the regulation of otherwise protected speech has been permitted when the speech invades the privacy of the unwilling listener's home or when the unwilling listener cannot avoid the speech.").

tion in the classroom—one that allows schools great latitude in regulating student speakers when they speak to unreceptive classmates.[70] Looking at the listeners alone, and assuming that they are, in fact, "unreceptive,"[71] the argument seems persuasive.

Yet one cannot look at the listeners alone. Unlike the speakers in the traditional "captive audience" cases, in the classroom, the speakers are also compelled to be there.[72] Whereas the phone salesman, the pastor, and the protester have thousands of people to whom they can express themselves, the student speaker, compelled to be in school six to eight hours a day, does not have that option. If he is to express himself at all during those six to eight hours, the student speaker will have to do it in the classroom. Thus, the classroom is unlike virtually any other place of expression: the listener has no escape and the speaker has no other forum for expression. If one student wants to speak and another does not want to hear it, one must budge.

Three reasons, taken together, justify the combination of applying the *Tinker* standard and not applying a captive audience exception in this context. First, the right to freedom of speech (or the right to have the government not impede free speech) is specifically enumerated in absolute terms.[73] Even if on a practical basis we cannot accept the absolute nature of the Free Speech Clause,[74] the absolute language should carry weight.[75] In contrast, the captive audience exception is

---

70. *See Muller*, 98 F.3d at 1541 ("Children in public schools are a captive audience that school authorities acting in loco parentis may protect.") (internal quotation marks omitted) (quoting *Bethel*, 478 U.S. at 684); *but cf.* Seamons v. Snow, 84 F.3d 1226, 1236 (10th Cir. 1996) (in discussing substantive due process: "Compulsory attendance laws for public schools, however, do not create an affirmative constitutional duty to protect students from the private actions of third parties while they attend school.").

71. This requirement could be the source of administrative difficulty. In captive audience cases, the exception to free speech protection is based upon a finding that the listeners are not receptive. Even if one accepts that the captive audience exception ought to apply in this context, it does not necessarily follow that the school should be able to "apply" the exception without first verifying that the listening students are unreceptive, as opposed to genuinely interested or, at least, willing to listen.

72. *See* Sekulow, et al., *supra* note 62, at 1019.

73. U.S. CONST. amend. I.

74. Justice Black often attempted to stick to the absolutist sense of the text. But even Justice Black found this approach unworkable. *See, e.g.*, *Tinker*, 393 U.S. at 515 (Black, J., dissenting). *See also* John M. Beahn, *Reno v. ACLU: The Communications Decency Act Hits a Red Light on the Information Superhighway*, 47 CATH. U. L. REV. 333, 333 (1997) ("Although the language of the First Amendment appears absolute, the Supreme Court never has held the First Amendment to confer an absolute right to free speech.").

75. Douglas Laycock, *Notes on the Role of Judicial Review, the Expansion of Federal Power, and the Structure of Constitutional Rights*, 99 YALE L.J. 1711, 1745 (1990) (book review) ("The proper standard for implied exceptions to absolute rights should be something like the compelling interest test. An implied exception to a textually absolute right should be an extraordinary thing.

a court-made adjustment to the Free Speech Clause.[76] While the exception makes sense where the speaker has other places for expression,[77] no such leeway exists in the classroom. To accommodate the unreceptive listener effectively would require placing the scope of the student speaker's right to speak within the listener's discretion. Any lack of receptivity by a fellow student would act as a prohibition of the speaker's right to speak while at school—the captive audience would be allowed the "heckler's veto." In this situation, it is reasonable that the constitutional clause, rather than the exception, should prevail.

Second, unreceptive listeners have the tool of counterspeech. Where this opportunity exists, counterspeech, rather than prohibition of the original speech, is the better option.[78] Unreceptive listeners can employ counterspeech to protect themselves, to defend truth, and to dilute speech with which they disagree. In contrast, if the captive audience exception were applied, student speakers would be left with no comparable tool to balance the situation. They would have to dilute their speech enough to not elicit an "unreceptive" response from a fellow student.

Third, the *Tinker* standard itself mitigates unfairness to unreceptive listeners. It is likely that in situations in which listeners will be genuinely unreceptive (*e.g.*, where the speech is unusually loud or aggressive), the speech in question will be substantially disruptive, especially in an elementary school classroom.[79] If regular listeners

---

We have learned from experience that 'no law' cannot literally mean no law. But 'no law' should mean hardly any law—as few laws as possible.").

76. Arguably, it is merely the proper interpretation of what the Free Speech Clause actually means.

77. *See, e.g.*, *Frisby*, 487 U.S. at 484-87 (finding that city ordinance limiting speech served narrowly tailored government interest and that captive audience exception was applicable where "ordinance permits the more general dissemination of a message" and "preserves ample alternative channels of communication"). Additionally, the captive audience exception is more favored when the unwanted speech invades the listener's home, "the last citadel of the tired, the weary, and the sick." Madsen v. Women's Health Ctr., Inc., 512 U.S. 753, 775 (1994) (internal quotation marks omitted) (quoting *Frisby*, 487 U.S. at 484).

78. *See, e.g.*, Waters v. Churchill, 511 U.S. 661, 672 (1994) ("Under the First Amendment there is no such thing as a false idea, the fitting remedy for evil counsels is good ones." (internal quotation marks omitted) (citing Gertz v. Robert Welch, Inc., 418 U.S. 323, 339 (1974)); Whitney v. California, 274 U.S. 357, 375 (1927) (Brandeis, J., concurring)); Washington v. Vote No! Comm., 135 Wash. 2d 618, 626, 957 P.2d 691, 696 (1998) ("Instead of relying on the State to silence false political speech, the First Amendment requires our dependence on even more speech to bring forth truth.") (citations omitted).

79. *See* Sekulow, et al., *supra* note 62, at 1072.

(*i.e.*, outside the school setting) had the protection *Tinker* affords, the captive audience exception would be less needed.[80]

Some may argue that counterspeech will be of no help in the hands of elementary school children—they are too young to effectively counter another's speech.[81] But surely one youngster can effectively counter the speech of another youngster. On average, both will be equally youthfully inarticulate, disorganized, and rambling. Some may also argue that counterspeech will be ineffective where there is a large aggregate number of same-viewpoint speakers. While this is worthy of concern, counterspeech from a lone dissenter can be effective. In particular, if several speakers share the same viewpoint, the veracity of their claims can be dealt with singularly. It is only one viewpoint that must be opposed. The real discomfort here is the intimidation that the lone dissenter might face. *Tinker* will curb part of that intimidation. Any intimidation that exists beyond the scope of the *Tinker* standard is part of the cost of the Free Speech Clause.[82]

E. *Applying Tinker to Oliva*

One might ask whether applying *Tinker*, instead of *Hazelwood*, would actually make a difference. Would the *Tinker* standard allow for greater student religious speech within the classroom? On the doctrinal level, the answer is yes.[83] Under *Tinker*, school officials can prohibit student speech only when they "forecast substantial disruption of or material interference with school activities" or an "invasion of the rights of others."[84] Under *Hazelwood*, "[i]t is only when the decision to censor a school-sponsored publication, theatrical production, or other vehicle of student expression has no valid educational purpose that the First Amendment is so 'directly and sharply implicate[d],' as

80. *See Frisby*, 487 U.S. at 486 ("The type of picketers banned by the [city] ordinance generally do not seek to disseminate a message to the general public, but to intrude upon the targeted resident, and to do so in an especially offensive way. Moreover, even if some such picketers have a broader communicative purpose, their activity nonetheless inherently and offensively intrudes on residential privacy. The devastating effect of targeted picketing on the quiet enjoyment of the home is beyond doubt.").

81. *See, e.g.*, *Muller*, 98 F.3d at 1538 ("The 'marketplace of ideas,' an important theme in the high school student expression cases, is a less appropriate description of an elementary school, where children are just beginning to acquire the means of expression.").

82. *See supra* note 62 and accompanying text.

83. The words "allow for" are important here. The argument here is not that if courts apply *Tinker* to student speech in the classroom a greater quantum of student religious speech will result. Rather, it is that the First Amendment protects an individual's right to speak, if he so chooses, and that *Tinker* better protects that choice.

84. *Tinker*, 393 U.S. at 513-14.

to require judicial intervention to protect students' constitutional rights."[85]

In review, *Oliva* also demonstrates the effect of *Tinker*. The first decision to be made is whether *Tinker* or *Hazelwood* applies. If the student speech occurs in a nonpublic forum and is sponsored by the school, *Hazelwood* applies. If not, *Tinker* applies. The *Oliva* court quoted the *Hazelwood* statement that "school facilities may be deemed to be public forums only if school authorities have 'by policy or by practice' opened those facilities 'for indiscriminate use by the general public,' or by some segment of the public, such as student organizations."[86] The court then summarily concluded that "[i]t is clear that Z.H.'s school and classroom were not public forums."[87] The only support the court relied upon was "the fact that Z.H.'s teacher reserved the right to inspect and reject each child's reading selection before it was presented to the class."[88]

The court's reasoning is flawed. There is, in fact, no elementary school classroom that is open for "indiscriminate use by the general public." Where the issue is whether a member of the public has a right to speak in the school, this fact is important. In cases such as *Oliva*, however, the issue is the degree of freedom a *student* has to speak. As discussed above, when a person is in a place he is entitled—or compelled—to be, *as to that person*, the place cannot reasonably be considered a "closed forum."[89]

Even if student expression occurs in a nonpublic forum, as the *Oliva* court concluded, the expression still must be school-sponsored in order for *Hazelwood* to apply. Yet the *Oliva* court gave no consideration to the issue of school sponsorship before applying the *Hazelwood* standard.[90] While later in the opinion, the court did discuss potential misperception by Z.H.'s classmates,[91] the court offered no explanation of why this perception would be reasonable or why Ms. Oliva, in Justice Brennan's words, could not have employed the "[d]issociative means short of censorship [that were] available to the school."[92]

---

85. *Hazelwood*, 484 U.S. at 273 (citation omitted).
86. *Oliva*, 990 F. Supp. at 352 n.16 (quoting *Hazelwood*, 484 U.S. at 267).
87. *Id.* at 352 n.16.
88. *Id.*
89. *See supra* Part II.A.
90. *See Oliva*, 990 F. Supp. at 352-53.
91. *See supra* Part II.B.3.
92. *Hazelwood*, 484 U.S. at 289 (Brennan, J., dissenting).

Assuming that the *Oliva* court should have applied *Tinker*, what would be the result of doing so? According to the court, "because of its religious content, Ms. Oliva did not allow Z.H. to read the story to his class."[93] Is this reason sufficient under *Tinker*? One can argue that issues of religion often profoundly divide people, and that it is likely that a religious story would offend another student to the extent that classroom activities could be substantially disrupted. Yet the *Tinker* Court stated that

> [i]n order for . . . school officials to justify prohibition of a particular expression of opinion, [they] must be able to show that [their actions were] caused by something more than a mere desire to avoid the discomfort and unpleasantness that always accompany an unpopular viewpoint. Certainly where there is no finding and no showing that engaging in the forbidden conduct would "materially and substantially interfere with the requirements of appropriate discipline in the operation of the school," the prohibition cannot be sustained.[94]

Ms. Oliva made no determination that Z.H.'s speech would cause a material or substantial disruption. Rather, "Z.H. was not allowed to read the book to his classmates during class time because it was The Bible, a religious book that constitutes the very foundation for a number of, but obviously not all, religions."[95] Ms. Oliva banned Z.H.'s speech to avoid the discomfort that accompanies a potentially divisive viewpoint—an impermissible act according to the Supreme Court in *Tinker*.[96]

---

93. *Oliva*, 990 F. Supp. at 347.

94. *Tinker*, 393 U.S. at 509 (citation omitted). The Court further proclaimed that

> undifferentiated fear or apprehension of disturbance is not enough to overcome the right to freedom of expression. Any departure from absolute regimentation may cause trouble. Any variation from the majority's opinion may inspire fear. Any word spoken, in class, in the lunchroom, or on the campus, that deviates from the views of another person may start an argument or cause a disturbance. But our Constitution says we must take this risk.

Id. at 508. *See also* Hsu v. Roslyn Union Free Sch. Dist. No. 3, 85 F.3d 839, 872 (2d Cir. 1996) ("[A]llowing the Walking on Water Club to guarantee that three of its prayer leaders will be Christians does not constitute 'substantial and material interference' with the School's mission of educating and disciplining.").

95. *Oliva*, 990 F. Supp. at 354.

96. This is not to mention that banning the Bible, or religious books generally, from the reading program was likely viewpoint discrimination, itself a violation of the Constitution. *See Rosenberger*, 515 U.S. at 829.

III. THE ESTABLISHMENT CLAUSE

During the discussion of the Free Speech Clause, undoubtedly many readers waited for the other shoe to drop. Even if *Tinker* should apply in cases such as *Oliva*, and student speech such as Z.H.'s should be protected under *Tinker*, one must still take account of the Establishment Clause.

Courts and commentators agree that the Establishment Clause restricts government action.[97] Thus, for example, if Microsoft began including in Windows 98 a screen saver that displays Bible verses, many of the computer users "compelled" to use Windows 98 might not like the screen saver, but they would have no Establishment Clause claim based on the inclusion of the Bible verses. The Establishment Clause cannot reach Microsoft's expression because the expression is private and not "of" the government. In order for the Establishment Clause to apply to a situation, it must be one in which the government acts.

The difficulty in the context of religious expression in the classroom is deciding when the expression is, in fact, private and when it is of the government. The Establishment Clause does not reach the former; it greatly limits the latter. When a teacher or school official speaks about religion or in a religious mode (*e.g.*, prayer), the Establishment Clause clearly is at issue because the government, through its agent, has spoken. Then the question for the court becomes whether this government speech constitutes an "establishment"—*i.e.*, whether the Clause is violated. Since it is obvious that applying one of the Supreme Court's Establishment Clause tests[98] is the task at hand, a court need not go through the mental exercise, much less the written exercise, of noting that the government has acted.

How should courts assess the constitutionality of religious expression *by a student*? Like Microsoft's expression, the student expression is made by a private citizen, not a government agent. Nevertheless, some courts reason that if the school permits student religious speech, that act of permission may violate the Establishment Clause.[99] In assessing the validity of this approach, it is useful to

---

97. *See Pinette*, 515 U.S. at 766 (plurality); *id.* at 779 (O'Connor, J., concurring).

98. *See* Ingebretsen v. Jackson Pub. Sch. Dist., 88 F.3d 274, 278-79 (5th Cir. 1996), *cert. denied*, 117 S. Ct. 388 (1996) ("The Fifth Circuit has identified three tests that the Supreme Court has used to determine whether a government action or policy constitutes an establishment of religion": the Lemon, coercion, and endorsement tests).

99. *See, e.g.*, *Oliva*, 990 F. Supp. at 353 (discussing "endorsement" concerns).

first take note of both the text of the First Amendment and how the framers of the Constitution viewed religious liberty.

A. *The First Amendment Text*

The First Amendment states: "Congress shall make no law respecting an establishment of religion, or prohibiting the free exercise thereof; or abridging the freedom of speech. . . ."[100] The first relevant observation is that the text states, "*Congress* shall make no law." While the Supreme Court long ago decided that the Fourteenth Amendment makes the First Amendment equally effective upon state governments,[101] it is important to remember that it is government action with which the amendment is concerned.

Second, the First Amendment does not designate any priority among the Establishment, Free Exercise, and Free Speech Clauses. As a purely textual matter, each clause has equal weight and it is reasonable that each clause has a function independent from the other First Amendment clauses.

Third, the First Amendment text does not indicate what the term "speech" encompasses. However, it is clear that "speech" includes religious speech. Speech does not lose the protection of the Free Speech Clause because the speech is religious.[102] Moreover, because the First Amendment text directs that Congress shall make no law prohibiting the free exercise of religion, speech that is part of the free exercise of religion is twice protected, once by the Free Speech Clause and once by the Free Exercise Clause.[103]

Fourth, as with the word "speech," the text does not clarify the meaning of "establishment." "Establishment" often connotes something permanent or institutionalized,[104] and some have argued that the Establishment Clause prohibits only founding a national religion or preferring one religious sect over another.[105] Others have

---

100. U.S. CONST. amend. I.

101. Cantwell v. Connecticut, 310 U.S. 296, 303 (1940).

102. *Pinette*, 515 U.S. at 760 ("a free-speech clause without religion would be *Hamlet* without the prince").

103. Douglas Laycock, *Freedom of Speech That Is Both Religious and Political*, 29 U.C. DAVIS L. REV. 793, 796 (1996); *see also supra* note 9.

104. *See* WEBSTER'S THIRD NEW INTERNATIONAL DICTIONARY 778 (1986).

105. Chief Justice Rehnquist has asserted that

> [i]f one were to . . . construe the [First] [A]mendment in the light of what particular "practices . . . threaten those consequences which the Framers deeply feared; whether, in short, they tend to promote that type of interdependence between religion and state which the First Amendment was designed to prevent," one would have to say that the First Amendment Establishment Clause should be read no more broadly than to prevent

argued that the Clause forbids any law that even tends toward an "establishment."[106]

B. *The Framers' View of Religious Speech*

"Religious speech is central to the First Amendment because religion is central to the First Amendment."[107] The framers made religion central to the First Amendment because of their considered commitment to religious liberty.[108] This commitment grew out of three primary realizations. First, government attempts to suppress unpopular religious views had caused vast suffering in Europe and, though to a lesser degree, in the colonies.[109] Second, religious beliefs are of unparalleled importance to the individual. Thus, it is best to leave religion in the hands of those who care about it most: individuals themselves.[110] Third, religious beliefs ultimately are of little

---

> the establishment of a national religion or the governmental preference of one religious sect over another.

Wallace v. Jaffree, 472 U.S. 38, 100 (1985) (Rehnquist, J., dissenting) (quoting Abington Sch. Dist. v. Schempp, 374 U.S. 203, 236 (1963) (Brennan, J., concurring)).

106. In refuting Chief Justice Rehnquist's view, Justice Souter has asserted that "[t]he Framers repeatedly considered and deliberately rejected such narrow language and instead extended their prohibition to state support for 'religion' in general." Lee v. Weisman, 505 U.S. 577, 614 (1992) (Souter, J., concurring).

> Some commentators have suggested that by targeting laws respecting "an" establishment of religion, the Framers adopted the very nonpreferentialist position whose much clearer articulation they repeatedly rejected. Yet the indefinite article before the word "establishment" is better seen as evidence that the Clause forbids any kind of establishment, including a nonpreferential one. If the Framers had wished, for some reason, to use the indefinite term to achieve a narrow meaning for the Clause, they could far more aptly have placed it before the word "religion."

Id. at 615 (citations omitted). *See also* Akhil Reed Amar, *The Bill of Rights as a Constitution*, 100 YALE L.J. 1131, 1157 (1991).

How one answers the question of what the Establishment Clause prohibits does not alter the first two of the above observations: the First Amendment restricts government action and it gives no priority to any one of its clauses. However, one's answer may very well affect the third observation: the First Amendment protects religious speech. If the Establishment Clause prohibits only some sort of national religion or preference among sects, religious speech may not be very problematic. For example, Z.H.'s speech alone, even if promoted by his teacher, would not nationalize religion. On the other hand, if the Establishment Clause requires the government to be neutral toward religion—to neither encourage nor discourage religion—religious speech, if promoted by the government, is problematic.

107. Laycock, *supra* note 103, at 797.

108. *See* Laycock, *supra* note 9.

109. *Id.*; *see also* Engel v. Vitale, 370 U.S. 421, 432 (1962) ("[A] purpose of the Establishment Clause rested upon an awareness of the historical fact that governmentally established religions and religious persecutions go hand in hand.").

110. Laycock, *supra* note 9, at 317; *see also Engel*, 370 U.S. at 432 ("The Establishment Clause thus stands as an expression of principle on the part of the Founders of our Constitution that religion is too personal, too sacred, too holy, to permit its 'unhallowed perversion' by a civil

importance to civil government—problems due to lack of national religious uniformity pale in comparison to those that arise from attempts to impose such uniformity.[111] Because of their commitment to religious liberty, the framers believed that to the extent that any class of speech is worth protecting, religious speech is clearly within that class.

In light of the framers' high valuation of religious speech because of its religious content, the framers would have contradicted themselves if they had restricted it more than other sorts of high-value speech *because of* religious speech's nonsecular content. That is, if religious speech is highly valuable, it may be as restricted as other high-value speech, but not for the very reason for which it is thought valuable. Moreover, if the framers sought to protect religious liberty in order to avoid the suffering that usually attends the government imposition of religious uniformity, it would be counterproductive to allow less religious speech than other high-value speech. Likewise, because the framers thought that religion matters most to individuals and that it is not worthwhile for government to impose religious uniformity, it would not make sense to write an amendment that first doubly protects religious speech—through the Free Exercise and Free Speech Clauses—but then simultaneously voids the right to engage in that speech.

C. Distinguishing Private Speech from Government Speech

1. Recent Cases

The Supreme Court's most recent effort to distinguish private and government expression under the Establishment Clause is *Capitol Square Review & Advisory Board v. Pinette*.[112] In *Pinette*, the review board charged with regulating public access to the plaza surrounding the Statehouse in Columbus, Ohio, denied an application by the Ku Klux Klan to place an unattended cross in the plaza for two weeks during the Christmas holidays.[113] Looking to the Free Speech Clause, a majority of the Court found that when the KKK applied to erect the cross, it sought to engage in "constitutionally protected expression" and that the Statehouse plaza was a "full-fledged public forum."[114] The majority began its analysis by stating bluntly that

---

magistrate.").

111. *See* Laycock, *supra* note 9, at 317.

112. 515 U.S. 753 (1995).

113. *Id.* at 758.

114. *Id.* at 761.

the KKK's religious display was "private expression,"[115] but it did not explain how it reached this conclusion. The Court did explain that it viewed the case before it as being like *Lamb's Chapel v. Center for Moriches Union Free School District*[116] and *Widmar v. Vincent*,[117] in that in all three cases "[t]he State did not sponsor [the speaker's] expression."[118] A plurality in *Pinette* refused to apply any Establishment Clause test to the KKK's challenged speech, finding neither "expression by the government itself," nor "government action alleged to discriminate in favor of private religious expression or activity."[119]

There are two primary differences between *Pinette* and *Oliva*. First, the speech in *Oliva* was a book rather than a symbol. Second, the location of the speech in *Oliva* was a public school classroom rather than state capitol grounds. The first distinction is of little consequence. There is no indication in *Pinette* that the Court's analysis would have differed significantly had the form of speech been different.[120] The second distinction matters. One might argue that allowing Z.H. to read his story would violate the Establishment Clause because those who would have received the speech were a captive audience—students forced to attend school; whereas in *Pinette*, those who saw the cross were free to come and go from the capitol grounds.

In *Lee v. Weisman*, the Supreme Court considered a public high school student's challenge to a school district policy that allowed principals to invite clergy to offer prayers at middle school and high school graduations.[121] The Court held that a religious exercise may not be "conducted at a graduation ceremony where, as we have found, young graduates who object are induced to conform."[122] The Court's holding was controlled, in part, by a finding of compulsory attendance: "Even for those students who object to the religious exercise, their attendance and participation in the state-sponsored

115. *Id.* at 760.

116. 508 U.S. at 384 (holding that school district violated church members' Free Speech rights by denying church access to district's facilities based solely on viewpoint church wished to present).

117. 454 U.S. 263 (1981) (holding that public university violated Free Speech Clause by excluding student religious group from facilities open to other student groups).

118. *Pinette*, 515 U.S. at 763.

119. *Id.* at 764.

120. *See id.* at 786 (Souter, J., concurring) ("When an individual speaks in a public forum, it is reasonable for an observer to attribute the speech, first and foremost, to the speaker, while an unattended display (and any message it conveys) can naturally be viewed as belonging to the owner of the land on which it stands.").

121. 505 U.S. at 581.

122. *Id.* at 599.

religious activity are in a fair and real sense obligatory."[123] The Court's holding was equally dependent upon its finding that

> [s]tate officials direct[ed] the performance of a formal religious exercise . . . The government involvement with religious activity in this case is pervasive, to the point of creating a state-sponsored and state-directed religious exercise in a public school. . . . [F]rom a constitutional perspective it is as if a state statute decreed that the prayers must occur.[124]

The pervasive government involvement stemmed from the fact that the school principal "decided that an invocation and a benediction should be given" and "chose the religious participant"; both choices were "attributable to the State."[125]

Four years after *Lee*, in *Ingebretsen v. Jackson Public School District*, the Fifth Circuit considered an appeal from a district court's decision to enjoin enforcement of Mississippi's School Prayer Statute, which allowed prayer at compulsory and noncompulsory school events.[126] Similar to the *Lee* Court's finding of extensive government involvement, the *Ingebretsen* court found that "[t]he statute will inevitably involve school officials in determining which prayers are 'nonsectarian and nonproselytizing' and in determining who gets to say the prayer at each event."[127] The court also noted more than once that "students will be a captive audience that cannot leave without being punished by the state or School Board for truancy or excessive absences."[128]

In contrast to *Pinette*, where the plurality did not even apply one of the Establishment Clause tests, the courts in *Lee* and *Ingebretsen* tested for, and found, an Establishment Clause violation. How is this contrast reconciled? One possible answer is that *Lee* and *Ingebretsen*

---

123. *Id.* at 586.

124. *Id.* at 586-87.

125. *Id.* at 587. *See also* American Civil Liberties Union of New Jersey v. Black Horse Pike Regional Bd. of Educ., 84 F.3d 1471 (3d Cir. 1996) (en banc) (student-initiated prayer at graduation violates the Establishment Clause).

126. 88 F.3d 274, 277 (5th Cir. 1996). Specifically, "[t]he district court enjoined enforcement of the statute in its entirety with the exception of the portion which permits prayers to take place at graduation ceremonies in accordance with *Jones v. Clear Creek Indep. Sch. Dist.*, 977 F.2d 963, 972 (5th Cir. 1992) (Jones II)." *Id.* at 278.

The statute at issue read in part: "[I]nvocations, benedictions or nonsectarian, nonproselytizing student-initiated prayer shall be permitted during compulsory or noncompulsory school-related student assemblies, student sporting events, graduation or commencement ceremonies and other school-related events." *Id.* at 277.

127. *Id.* at 279.

128. *Id.* at 279-80.

involved public schools, while *Pinette* did not. Yet, presumably, adults and children in the general public (*i.e.*, those who might see the cross in *Pinette*) are equally as protected as students in public schools. More accurately, whatever "establishment" the Establishment Clause prohibits, the Clause applies equally in and out of the public schools. But the school/nonschool answer does strike near another more plausible answer: *Lee* and *Ingebretsen* involved captive audiences, while *Pinette* did not. The *Pinette* plurality did not refer to the lack of a captive audience. Rather the plurality stated that "[r]eligious expression cannot violate the Establishment Clause where it (1) is purely private and (2) occurs in a traditional or designated public forum, announced and open to all on equal terms."[129]

However, this does not mean that the captive audience answer is without merit. Perhaps the *Pinette* Court would have engaged the Establishment Clause had the case involved a captive audience. It is hard to imagine how a captive audience could have existed in *Pinette*, given the open nature of the state capitol grounds upon which the religious expression occurred. But, for illustration, we might vary the *Pinette* facts. First, suppose that the religious expression consisted of a group of "speakers" with hand-held crosses rather than a large, free-standing cross. With this variation, the *Pinette* holding should remain the same: the government merely "watches on," but neither speaks itself nor discriminates in favor of the speech. Second, suppose further that the capitol grounds were extremely crowded (*e.g.*, on the Fourth of July) and that because of the extreme crowd many of the people "receiving" the religious expression were effectively unable to distance themselves from the expression. Now a captive audience might exist. Does the *Pinette* holding change? If it does change—if the Establishment Clause is now at issue—something more fundamental has also changed: the government has become a speaker or a promoter of the speech.

Thus, we should ask whether the existence of a captive audience transforms what would otherwise be private expression into government expression. In our present *Pinette* example, it is arguable that the speakers have less protection for their speech in the face of a captive audience.[130] Yet the government (the review board) *acts* no more

129. *Pinette*, 515 U.S. at 770. As to the students compelled to be there, classrooms cannot be considered nonpublic fora. *See supra* Part II.E. Rather, as to those students, the classrooms are "open to all on equal terms." If a classroom were not open to all on equal terms—*e.g.*, if Z.H.'s teacher allowed Z.H. to command the class's attention, but allowed no other student to do the same—the Establishment Clause would clearly be at issue.

130. *See supra* Part II.D.

when the audience is captive than it does when the audience is not captive. Captive audience or not, the review board merely holds open the plaza for public use, accepts applications by public users, and processes those applications based upon criteria such as safety and sanitation.[131] With no further government action in our captive audience version of *Pinette* than in the actual *Pinette* case, there is no reason to test for an Establishment Clause violation in our example when the plurality did not do so in *Pinette*. Captive audience does not mean government expression.

2. Government-Created Captive Audience?

Many will argue, however, that the above example differs greatly from cases such as *Oliva*, because in the latter cases the government itself creates the captive audience via compelled classroom attendance. Where the government makes an audience captive by force of law, the argument goes, religious speech directed at that audience implicates the Establishment Clause. Yet in most cases like *Oliva*, the party claiming an Establishment Clause violation does not challenge the government's compulsory attendance law. Rather, the party takes compulsory attendance as a given and challenges the school's allowance of religious speech or conduct within the classroom.[132]

Because the Establishment Clause is implicated only if the government acts, we should ask whether compulsory attendance is sufficient to make religious expression in the classroom "attributable to the State."[133] This question is similar to one addressed above in the discussion of the Free Speech Clause: Does compulsory attendance in the classroom create *per se* school sponsorship of whatever speech occurs there?[134] In that context, the answer is no; compelled class-

---

131. *See Pinette*, 515 U.S. at 757-58.

132. *See, e.g.*, *Oliva*, 990 F. Supp. at 353 (discussing "endorsement" concerns).

133. *Lee*, 505 U.S. at 587.

134. *See supra* Part II.B.1. The difference between the two questions is this: Under the Free Speech Clause, we ask whether compulsory attendance *allows* school officials the discretion to censor student speech for any valid educational purpose (*see Hazelwood*, 484 U.S. at 273), as opposed to regulating the speech only when the officials forecast that the speech will substantially disrupt or materially interfere with school activities or invade the rights of others (*see Tinker*, 393 U.S. at 513-14). Under the Establishment Clause, we ask whether compulsory attendance *requires* school officials to censor student speech that is religious.

In the Free Speech discussion, the question was also asked whether the fact that a listener is "unreceptive" should create an exception to speech protection in the classroom. *See supra* Part II.D. The answer is no. Of course, regarding the hypothetical drawn from *Pinette* (not a classroom setting), the traditional captive audience exception might well apply. That is, a court might not reach the Establishment Clause because it decides that the speakers' protection is limited when speaking to the unreceptive listeners.

room attendance does not necessarily mean school sponsorship. The reasoning for this answer is based, in part, on the Supreme Court's recognition in *Hazelwood* that some student expression merely "happens to occur" in the classroom, as opposed to being sponsored by the school.[135]

While the *Hazelwood* Court made its assertions in the context of the Free Speech Clause, it is reasonable that the Court's analysis should also apply in the Establishment Clause context. That is, despite compulsory attendance, there is at least some student speech in the classroom not attributable to the government—speech that should not implicate the Establishment Clause. However, one might argue that while compulsory attendance should not be enough to create "government sponsorship" in the Free Speech context, it should be enough under the Establishment Clause. There are at least two rationales for this argument.

a. A Broad Reading of the Establishment Clause

The first rationale is that the Establishment Clause is concerned with *any tendency* toward an establishment of religion, and when the government compels classroom attendance and then allows religious speech or conduct there, an establishment of religion is begun. This justification is flawed. Even if the Establishment Clause prohibits the slightest move toward establishing religion, we are still left with the difficulty of determining the meaning of "establishment." The solution under the present rationale would be simply to prohibit religious speech and conduct in the classroom. That is, although we are not sure what an establishment of religion looks like, we can probably avoid it through categorical prophylactic measures. Yet, in contrast to the uncertainty regarding "establishment," we do know that religious speech and conduct are valued under our Constitution.[136] It is inconsistent with the Constitution to root out any trace of religion.

b. Maximum Liberty

One might also assert that finding "government sponsorship" under the Establishment Clause based solely on compulsory attendance (and not doing so under the Free Speech Clause) is consistent with maximizing individual liberty. That is, while finding government

---

135. *See Hazelwood*, 484 U.S. at 270-71. It is noteworthy that this recognition is secondary to the recognition that there is, in fact, private student expression in the school setting, as opposed to only government-sponsored student expression.

136. *See supra* parts III.A-B.

sponsorship under the Free Speech Clause means *less* protection for the student speaker, finding government sponsorship under the Establishment Clause means *more* protection for all students against the State getting into the religion business. Yet the latter would maximize liberty in only one scenario: if it were agreed that religious speech and conduct are oppressive and undesirable. Even if finding government sponsorship based upon compulsory attendance basically eradicated religion in the classroom, this outcome is justified because courts would be protecting citizens against a bad thing. But it is far from agreed that religion is undesirable. To the contrary, the framers in the 1790s and the federal courts in the years since have accorded religion high priority. Indeed, the Constitution protects religious practice via the Free Exercise Clause and the Free Speech Clause. The effect of "easily" finding government sponsorship is to transform the Establishment Clause's function from preventing the establishment of religion to that of prohibiting religion.

c. *Government Action Required*

To find that the government acts when student speech occurs in a classroom in which the government has compelled attendance misassigns responsibility for the speech. When the government compels attendance, it clearly acts. This action, like any government action, should be subject to Establishment Clause scrutiny. Yet the fact that the government acts by compelling attendance does not mean that no student speaks unless prompted by the government. Even though the government compels attendance in the classroom, it does not have control over all that is spoken there.[137] Nor should it be "charged" with control over all that is spoken there. The effect of charging the government with this control would be to make any religious speech occurring in the classroom subject to the full force of the Establishment Clause. Students would have no more right to religious speech than a government agent (*e.g.*, the class teacher) would have. In effect, the classroom would be a "religion-free" zone. The classroom, where our public school children spend the better part of the day for 170 days a year, would become a place from which religion is banished instead of a place where religion is cherished. This result would contradict the framers' belief that religious discourse is valuable

137. For example, teachers often place broad requirements on the type of expression required to fulfill an assignment. *See, e.g.*, *Oliva*, 990 F. Supp. at 346 (teacher allowed students "to read a book of their own choosing to the rest of the class").

and it would prioritize the Establishment Clause above the Free Speech Clause, despite the lack of textual support for this priority.

This result is additionally problematic because it contradicts one of the framers' core intents for the Establishment Clause: preventing the imposition of uniformity in religious belief. The Clause should protect students and others from the government deciding the most important issues in life. As a corollary, it should not preempt citizens' independent ability to prevent the government from deciding these issues. That is, the Clause should not silence speakers who counter the government's position on what the speakers believe to be issues of vital importance.[138] Yet this is what happens when a court calls student speech in a compulsory attendance classroom "government action." By being assigned responsibility for student religious speech—which is then restricted by the Establishment Clause—the government silences religious speakers. There must be student religious expression in the classroom that is private, neither the product of government action nor sponsored by the government.

This conclusion is consistent with both *Lee* and *Ingebretsen*. While each court found an Establishment Clause violation where attendance was compelled, each court's holding also depended upon the conclusion that the religious speech was "state-sponsored" and "state-directed."[139] In *Lee*, this result was due to the finding that a government agent, the school principal, decided that prayers should be given and then chose who should give those prayers.[140] This government action was equivalent to a statute prescribing prayer.[141] In *Ingebretsen*, the government-sponsorship stemmed from the inevitability of school officials having both to distinguish sectarian and nonsectarian prayers and to choose who would pray.[142] If either court had considered compulsory attendance *alone* sufficient to create government sponsorship, then once the court noted the compulsory attendance, it could have foregone further reasoning as to why it found government sponsorship.

138. *See* Sekulow, et al., *supra* note 62, at 1020 ("To deny students the right to express views contrary to those the state wishes to impose would turn the public schools into indoctrination centers in which students would be force-fed only that which the state wanted them to hear. School officials, in effect, would be prescribing orthodoxy.").

139. *See Lee*, 505 U.S. at 586-87; *Ingebretson*, 88 F.3d at 279.

140. *Lee*, 505 U.S. at 587.

141. *Id.* at 586-87.

142. *Ingebretsen*, 88 F.3d at 279.

D. The Endorsement Test

Some disagree with the assertion that the Establishment Clause should not even be an issue in cases involving student religious speech in the classroom. They argue that if the government has not acted problematically, applying the Establishment Clause will reveal this truth. In *Pinette*, four Justices chose to forego Establishment Clause analysis.[143] Four of the other five Justices applied a version of the "endorsement test."[144] Justice O'Connor, joined by Justices Breyer and Souter, asserted that "the endorsement test asks the right question . . . even where a neutral state policy toward private religious speech in a public forum is at issue," and found no constitutional violation.[145] Justices Ginsburg and Stevens did find a violation.[146] Under the endorsement test, "[e]very government practice must be judged in its unique circumstances to determine whether it constitutes an endorsement or disapproval of religion."[147] At first blush, it may seem that this test addresses what this Article wrestles with in Part III: whether the government "acts" when it allows student religious expression in the classroom. Yet the endorsement test is an unacceptable test to apply to speech such as Z.H.'s.

In *Pinette*, Justice O'Connor emphasized that she is unlikely "to come to a different result from the plurality where truly private speech is allowed on equal terms in a vigorous public forum that the government has administered properly."[148] Her disagreement with the plurality resulted from her belief "that an impermissible message of endorsement can be sent in a variety of contexts, not all of which involve direct government speech or outright favoritism."[149] For example, Justice O'Connor noted, the distinction between government speech endorsing religion and private speech endorsing religion made

143. *Pinette*, 515 U.S. at 753 (Chief Justice Rehnquist and Justices Kennedy, Scalia, and Thomas).

144. *See id.* at 772 (O'Connor, J., concurring, joined by Souter & Breyer, JJ.) (applying endorsement test); *id.* at 783 (Souter, J., concurring, joined by O'Connor & Breyer, JJ.) (same); *id.* at 799 (Stevens, J., dissenting) (same). Justice Ginsburg based her brief opinion on the assumption that "the aim of the Establishment Clause is genuinely to uncouple government from church." *Id.* at 817 (Ginsburg, J., dissenting) (citing Everson v. Board of Educ., 330 U.S. 1, 16 (1947)).

145. *Pinette*, 515 U.S. at 772 (O'Connor, J., concurring).

146. *Id.* at 797 (Stevens, J., dissenting); *id.* at 817 (Ginsburg, J., dissenting).

147. County of Allegheny v. American Civil Liberties Union, Greater Pittsburgh Chapter, 492 U.S. 573, 624-25 (1989) (O'Connor, J., concurring) (citations omitted).

148. *Pinette*, 515 U.S. at 775 (O'Connor, J., concurring).

149. *Id.* at 774.

by the plurality in *Board of Education of Westside Community Schools v. Mergens*[150] was dependent, in part, upon concluding that "secondary school students are mature enough and are likely to understand that a school does not endorse or support student speech that it merely permits on a nondiscriminatory basis."[151] Justice Souter made the same point, noting that in *Widmar v. Vincent*,[152] "[i]t was relevant that university students 'should be able to appreciate that the University's policy is one of neutrality toward religion,' that students were unlikely, as a matter of fact, to 'draw any reasonable inference of University support from the mere fact of a campus meeting place.'"[153] Thus, Justices O'Connor and Souter indicated that where school students do not understand that their school does *not* support student religious speech, but merely permits it on a nondiscriminatory basis, the Establishment Clause imposes upon the government an affirmative obligation "to take steps to avoid being perceived as supporting or endorsing a private religious message."[154]

Assuming that in *Oliva*-like cases the elementary school students do not understand that their school does not endorse the private religious message, what "steps" can school officials take to adhere to the endorsement test interpretation of the Establishment Clause? One option would be for schools to refrain from compelling classroom attendance either altogether or during periods of private religious expression. This option, however, surely would be unpopular and would raise a number of administrative difficulties. A second option is for the class teacher to censor the private religious message.

Does the Establishment Clause mandate censoring students? Justice O'Connor's and Justice Souter's concurrences in *Pinette* are not decisive on this point, but they seem to indicate that (1) if students misperceive endorsement,[155] and (2) no other options exist, the Establishment Clause imposes an "affirmative obligation" to avoid the misperception.[156] This result is unfortunate, one might argue, but it

---

150. 496 U.S. 226 (1990) (holding that the Equal Access Act does not violate the Establishment Clause).

151. *Pinette*, 515 U.S. at 774-75 (internal quotation marks omitted) (quoting *Mergens*, 496 U.S. at 250 (plurality)); *see also id.* at 788 (Souter, J., concurring) (quoting same passage from *Mergens*).

152. 454 U.S. 263 (1981) (holding that public university violated Free Speech Clause by excluding student religious group from facilities open to other student groups).

153. *Pinette*, 515 U.S. at 791 (Souter, J., concurring) (quoting *Widmar*, 454 U.S. at 274 n.14).

154. *Id.* at 777 (O'Connor, J., concurring).

155. *See supra* notes 148-54 and accompanying text.

156. *Pinette*, 515 U.S. at 777 (O'Connor, J., concurring).

is, especially in the context of the elementary school classroom, merely a part of the price that must be paid for a constitutional guarantee that the government will not impose religious uniformity.

Yet adopting the second option (censoring the religious expression) is more than unfortunate; it is wrong for reasons addressed above and revisited here. First, it is wrong because it allows the Establishment Clause to trump the Free Speech Clause so that although the religious speaker's expression is protected by the Free Speech Clause,[157] it is then muted by the Establishment Clause. There is no textual support for this subordination of the Free Speech Clause.

Second, and related, the result is wrong because it relegates private religious speech—usually considered high-value speech—to a level of less protection than other private high-value speech. For example, while a student is allowed to give a nondisruptive presentation about his trip to the Libertarian National Convention, he is not allowed to read a story out of Genesis. This devaluation of religious speech contradicts the framers' support for religious liberty and the First Amendment's double protection for religious speech.

Third, it is unreasonable to make the scope of one citizen's constitutional right subject to the erroneous perception of another citizen.[158] To do so belies the very conception of a constitutional right as a civil liberty of the highest order, curtailed only in the most pressing of circumstances.

Some will argue that these three assertions fall short because of the unique context of the topic at hand: one involving young, impressionable, immature individuals. The Establishment Clause is perhaps most needed by vulnerable elementary school students. Yet no court or

---

157. This assumes that the student expression is permissible under the *Tinker* standard, as detailed in Part II.

158. Chief Justice Burger addressed this issue in his dissent in *Bender v. Williamsport Area School District*:

> The Court of Appeals agreed that the Establishment Clause prohibited [the student-initiated club] from meeting on school premises because to allow it to meet could have been misinterpreted by other students as active state support of religion. Under that analysis, because an individual's discussion of religious beliefs may be confused by others as being that of the State, both must be viewed as the same. Yet the several commands of the First Amendment require vision capable of distinguishing between state establishment of religion, which is prohibited by the Establishment Clause, and individual participation and advocacy of religion which, far from being prohibited by the Establishment Clause, is affirmatively protected by the Free Exercise and Free Speech Clauses of the First Amendment. If the latter two commands are to retain any vitality, utterly unproven, subjective impressions of some hypothetical students should not be allowed to transform individual expression of religious belief into state advancement of religion.

475 U.S. 534, 553 (1986) (Burger, C.J., dissenting).

commentator has explained persuasively why the Free Speech Clause is not also needed by elementary school students. That is, why are the "captive speakers" not at risk, as well? Although young and articulate, elementary school students are entitled to express their views about the fundamental issues of life and to resist an educational environment devoid of religious explanations of reality. It is the case that young citizens *equally* need, and deserve, the rights afforded by *both* the Establishment Clause and the Free Speech Clause. It is also the case that, unlike in any other context, in the public school classroom, there is no room for either right to "budge."

E. A Better Option

In addition to either waiving compulsory attendance or censoring private student speech, there is a third option for school officials faced with misperception by student listeners: teaching. Justice Brennan pointed to this option in his *Hazelwood* dissent: "Dissociative means short of censorship are available to the school."[159] Rather than viewing the relationship between the Establishment Clause and the Free Speech Clause as a "zero sum game" (where a gain for one clause is necessarily a loss for the other) educators and lawyers alike would do well to view the "tension" as an opportunity for an overall gain in understanding. Even in the elementary school classroom, a teacher can begin to explain the fundaments of religious liberty. For example: "Each family chooses what religion, if any, it will follow. The school doesn't interfere with that. Not everyone believes what Z.H. believes, but the school doesn't take sides. This story is important to Z.H., and whether we agree or disagree with him, we're going to listen to him politely."

For those such as Justices O'Connor and Souter, who believe the Establishment Clause requires the government to take affirmative "steps to avoid being perceived as supporting or endorsing a private religious message,"[160] this type of disclaimer should be sufficient. If cases such as *Oliva* require Establishment Clause scrutiny—a conclusion with which this Article disagrees—the scrutiny must be of the government action, not the student speech. If the Establishment Clause requires a remedy, the burden of the remedy should fall on the school: an earnest attempt to correct misperception should be enough. It is doctrinally untenable to ban otherwise protected student speech just because the school is unsuccessful in curing misunderstanding.

159. *Hazelwood*, 484 U.S. at 289 (Brennan, J., dissenting).
160. *Pinette*, 515 U.S. at 777 (O'Connor, J., concurring).

For those such as the Justices in the *Pinette* plurality, a "teaching disclaimer" by the school, in the name of the Establishment Clause, will be doctrinally unnecessary. Yet this group would have no constitutional objection to the practice. The practical benefits of the disclaimer would be more religious liberty and better understanding by students.

In *Oliva*, the speech at issue was "private"—*i.e.*, Z.H.'s speech, not the government's. Although Z.H.'s proposed expression occurred in a classroom in which he and his classmates were compelled to be, the classroom and the reading program were open and accessible to all the students in the classroom. With no valid reason to attribute Z.H.'s speech to the government, the Establishment Clause should not have curtailed protection provided by the Free Speech Clause. At most, the Establishment Clause required only that Ms. Oliva disclaim endorsement by the school.

IV. CONCLUSION

Cases such as *C.H. v. Oliva* are difficult because they involve tension within the First Amendment that is not easily resolved by text, history, or logic. Both parties wave the banner of religious liberty and both parties point to the First Amendment to justify their claims. The proper first step of analysis in these cases, however, is not specific to religious liberty. The first step is to determine whether the protection afforded to the student's speech (religious or not) is broad enough to make unconstitutional the school officials' restriction of the speech. If the scope of protection is not broad enough, the school officials' restriction is permissible and there is no colorable need for Establishment Clause analysis.

Under *Hazelwood*, if student expression occurs in a "nonpublic forum" and is sponsored by the school, school officials can reasonably regulate the expression for any educational purpose. If not, under *Tinker*, officials can censor the speech only if they reasonably forecast that the expression will lead to a substantial disruption, a material interference with the educational function, or an invasion of the rights of others. While a public school classroom certainly is not open for indiscriminate use by the public, as to the students compelled by law to be in the classroom, the classroom is not a nonpublic forum because there is virtually no restriction upon these students' access to the classroom.

Similarly, under *Hazelwood*, student expression that merely happens to occur at school is not "school-sponsored." This result is not changed by the presence of compulsory attendance, a large number of speakers with the same viewpoint, or the young age of elementary school students. School sponsorship is dependent upon a reasonable perception that the expression bears the school's imprimatur. None of this is to say that students have free reign in the classroom. To the contrary, the *Tinker* standard—substantial disruption—will be met more easily in the classroom than, for example, on the playground, where it is hard to disrupt an educational function. The *Tinker* standard will also be met more easily in the elementary school than in secondary schools, given that self-discipline is more rare among younger students.

The second fundamental step of analysis in cases such as *Oliva* is specific to religious liberty. When school officials restrict student religious speech in the classroom in a way that is impermissible under *Tinker*, the question becomes whether the Establishment Clause justifies the officials' actions. Because the Establishment Clause restricts only government action, in order to violate the Clause, student religious expression (or the promotion of it) must somehow be attributable to the government. While the Supreme Court and federal appellate courts have found Establishment Clause violations where compulsory attendance and government sponsorship exist, these courts have not found that compulsory attendance necessarily creates government sponsorship. Moreover, such a finding would make all student classroom speech attributable to the government and, hence, subject to being prohibited by the Establishment Clause. Testing for a violation via the "endorsement test" would lead to a similar result if that test is interpreted to give weight to the *mis*perception of student listeners.

By devaluing religious speech and potentially creating a "religion free" public classroom, each of these approaches would contradict the intent of the framers of the Constitution and the First Amendment text. The better approach is suggested by the plurality in *Pinette*, which held that religious expression cannot violate the Establishment Clause when it is private and occurs in a forum open to all on equal terms. Where school officials merely allow student religious speech in the same manner that they allow other (*i.e.*, "secular") speech, the Establishment Clause is not implicated.

The First Amendment should flourish as fully as possible in the public elementary school classroom. While students (and their parents) undoubtedly deserve the Amendment's protection against religious indoctrination, the Amendment protects only against indoctrination by the government. Simultaneously—and perhaps equally as vital to resisting government indoctrination—the First

Amendment allows students to make their own attempts at persuasion by expressing their beliefs about matters of fundamental concern. By applying *Tinker*, courts can allow this high-value, private proselytizing, while ensuring that the expression does not unduly disrupt the educational environment. By following *Pinette*, courts can guard against eradicating private religious expression in the classroom.

An Alternative Approach to the Fourth Amendment in Public Schools: Balancing Students' Rights with School Safety*

I. INTRODUCTION

A public school student, on his way to class, enters the school building through an exterior doorway. There is a bulge protruding from the student's jacket which is noticed by a teacher monitoring the hallways.[1] Acting on impulse, the teacher approaches the student and grabs him. The teacher then reaches underneath the student's jacket for the bulge and finds a . . . .

Statistics show that students in the United States collectively bring nearly 135,000 guns to school everyday.[2] Data suggests that twenty percent of our nation's high school students bring some type of weapon to school at least once a month.[3] Statistics also "show 'alarming increases' in drug use by students in grades six through twelve."[4] As weapons, violence, and drugs in

* I would like to express appreciation to my wife for her patience and support, Scott Cameron for his encouragement and guidance, and Brett Tolman and Trent Nelson for their helpful suggestions and feedback.

1. This scenario was inspired by the case *Juan C. v. Cortines*, 647 N.Y.S.2d 491 (App. Div. 1996), *rev'd on other grounds*, 679 N.E.2d 1061 (N.Y. 1997).

2. *See* Deborah Austen Colson, *Safe Enough to Learn: Placing an Affirmative Duty of Protection on Public Schools Under 42 U.S.C. § 1983*, 30 HARV. C.R.-C.L. L. REV. 169, 170 (1995) (citing ROBERT L. MAGINNIS, FAMILY RESEARCH COUNCIL, VIOLENCE IN THE SCHOOL HOUSE: A 10-YEAR UPDATE 3 (1994)).

3. *See id.*; *see also* Steve Friess, *Poll Shows Teens Living Healthier*, LAS VEGAS REV.-J., Jan. 25, 1998, at 1B (reporting that of 1464 randomly chosen Nevada high school students, 21% said they had brought a weapon to school in the past thirty days); Leslie Ansley, *Many Teens Feel Unsafe in School*, USA TODAY, Aug. 13, 1993, at 01A (according to write-in survey "about half" of 65,193 teens in grades six through twelve knew someone who carried a weapon to school).

4. Andrew Mollison, *Officials Huddle Today Over Rising Drug Use by Young Kids Getting High: Use of Heroin, Crack Cocaine, LSD, Inhalants and Marijuana by 12-to 17-Year-Olds Reported on the Increase*, ATLANTA CONST., Nov. 1, 1995, at A7; *see* Larry Craig, *Clinton's Failing War on Drugs*, GOV'T PRESS RELEASE, Nov. 7, 1997, *available in* 1997 WL 12104713 (reporting the University of Michigan's "Monitoring the Future" survey to show that nearly one out of twenty high school seniors and one in every thirty tenth graders use marijuana *daily*); John W. Gonzales, *State Appeals to Parents as Study Says Kids Dabbling More in Drugs*, HOUSTON CHRON., Jan. 11, 1998, at 1

public schools continue to be a problem,[5] situations like the one above will become more prevalent.[6] Though what is found in the student's possession may lessen any public discomfort over the teacher's actions,[7] under current Supreme Court precedent,[8] this

---

(reporting that the Texas Commission on Alcohol and Drug Abuse biennial survey of 107,000 secondary students found that "nearly two-thirds . . . used illicit substances . . . in the previous year. . . . Use [of marijuana] among eighth-graders has tripled in five years"); *Pride: Illicit Drug Use in Junior High Continues to Rise*, ALCOHOLISM & DRUG ABUSE WKLY., Nov. 3, 1997, at 3, *available in* 1997 WL 9026822 ("The most surprising finding in the [10th annual Parents' Resource Institute for Drug Education (PRIDE)] survey is the across-the-board increase in illicit drug use by youngest students, ages 11 to 14 . . . .").

5. *See* New Jersey v. T.L.O., 469 U.S. 325, 339 (1985) ("Maintaining order in the classroom has never been easy, but in recent years, school disorder has often taken particularly ugly forms: drug use and violent crime in the schools have become major social problems.").

6. *See, e.g.*, France Griggs, *Grim Truth: Preventing a Paducah Impossible*, CINCINNATI POST, Dec. 3, 1997, at 1A (reporting that the Cincinnati Public School District projects it will conduct 33% more searches of students in 1998 than in 1997).

7. At the core of the Fourth Amendment debate in public schools are two issues, safety and privacy. One may have strong feelings about public schools being safe places and find the confiscation of contraband to be a lofty goal, no matter what the costs. Such feelings are exemplified in the newspaper article titled *Ruling Leaves Our Schools at Risk*. Eliot Spitzer & Dennis Saffran, *Ruling Leaves Our Schools at Risk*, TIMES UNION (Albany), Feb. 9, 1997, at E2 (supporting legislation making the reasonableness of a search of a public school student irrelevant in a school disciplinary hearing when a dangerous weapon is found). On the other hand, strong feelings may arise over violations of students' privacy rights, as noted in this newspaper headline, *Strip Searches of Students Anger Parents in Oregon*. Lauren Dodge, *Strip Searches of Students Anger Parents in Oregon*, FORT WORTH STAR-TELEGRAM, Feb. 1, 1998, at 13 (quoting comments from several parents outraged over the strip search of their children). These competing concerns, and striking the appropriate balance between them, are the focus of this Comment.

8. In *New Jersey v. T.L.O.*, 469 U.S. 325 (1985), the Court held that the legality of a search of a student would depend "on the reasonableness, under all the circumstances, of the search." *Id.* at 341. The reasonableness of a search is determined by answering the following questions: "[F]irst . . . 'whether the . . . action was justified at its inception,' second, whether the search as conducted 'was reasonably related in scope to the circumstances which justified the interference in the first place.'" *Id.* (quoting Terry v. Ohio, 392 U.S. 1, 20 (1968)).

The Court proceeded to provide meaning to these phrases for their application in the school setting:

> Under ordinary circumstances, a search of a student by a teacher or other school official will be "justified at its inception" when there are reasonable grounds for suspecting that the search will turn up evidence that the student has violated or is violating either the law or the rules of the school. Such a search will be permissible in its scope when the measures adopted are reasonably related to the objectives of the search and not excessively intrusive in light of the age and sex of the student and the nature of the infraction.

Id. at 341-42 (footnotes omitted).

search is likely a violation of the student's Fourth Amendment right[9] to be free from "unreasonable searches and seizures."[10]

In criminal proceedings, the constitutional guarantees of the Fourth Amendment are protected by the exclusionary rule, which requires that evidence obtained during an illegal search[11] or seizure[12] be suppressed from the corresponding adjudicatory proceeding.[13] The Supreme Court has concluded that the Fourth

---

9. In the juvenile delinquency proceeding which the fact scenario is based on, the court made the factual finding that "'the outline of the gun was not visible'" to the person conducting the search, and the slight bulge underneath the jacket "was not in any particular shape or form and was not remotely suspicious." Juan C. v. Cortines, 647 N.Y.S.2d 491, 492 (App. Div. 1996), *rev'd on other grounds*, 679 N.E.2d 1061 (N.Y. 1997). Subsequently, the juvenile court found the search to be unreasonable, suppressed the gun, and dismissed the juvenile delinquency petition. *See id.*

Other cases seem to support the conclusion that this scenario is a violation of the reasonableness standard. In *Cales v. Howell Public Schools*, 635 F. Supp. 454 (E.D. Mich. 1985), the court held that the search by a school official was illegal as the search was not justified at its inception.

> This court does not read *T.L.O.* so broadly as to allow a school administrator the right to search a student because that student acts in such a way so as to create a reasonable suspicion that the student has violated some rule or law. Rather, the burden is on the administrator to establish that the student's conduct is such that it creates a reasonable suspicion that a specific rule or law has been violated and that a search could reasonably be expected to produce evidence of that violation.

Id. at 457; *see also In re* Appeal in Pima County Juvenile Action, 733 P.2d 316 (Ariz. Ct. App. 1987) (holding no reasonable suspicion for principal to search student since the principal had no personal knowledge regarding the boy's conduct and received no report creating a reasonable suspicion that drugs would be found).

10. U.S. CONST. amend. IV. The Fourth Amendment provides:

> The right of the people to be secure in their persons, houses, papers, and effects, against unreasonable searches and seizures, shall not be violated, and no Warrants shall issue, but upon probable cause, supported by Oath or affirmation, and particularly describing the place to be searched, and the persons or things to be seized.

Id.

11. In the school setting, "[a] student search is an attempt [by school officials] to gain access to any item that is shielded from public view and located in a protected place or thing. . . . Virtually any attempt to find or discover something hidden from public view will be considered a search in the school setting." JON M. VAN DYKE & MELVIN M. SAKURAI, CHECKLISTS FOR SEARCHES AND SEIZURES IN PUBLIC SCHOOLS 2-1 to 2-2 (1998).

12. "[A] seizure is any governmental action which materially interferes with a student's possessory interests in personal property. In the school setting something is seized when school officials confiscate or take it away from a student." *Id.* at 6-1 (citing United States v. Jacobsen, 466 U.S. 109, 113 (1984)).

13. *See, e.g.*, State v. Young, 216 S.E.2d 586, 590 (Ga. 1975) (defining the exclusionary rule as "'a judicially-created remedy designed to safeguard Fourth Amendment rights generally through its deterrent effect, rather than a personal constitutional right of the party aggrieved.'" (quoting United States v. Calandra, 414

Amendment's exclusionary rule does not bar illegally seized evidence in every instance,[14] but the Court has not determined whether the appropriate remedy for violation of the student's Constitutional rights in a public school disciplinary proceeding[15] is the exclusionary rule.[16] Consider, for instance, how the exclusionary rule might apply in the situation posed at the beginning of this Comment. Let us assume that the teacher finds a gun bulging from the student's jacket. The student is brought before the school disciplinary board, facing discipline for bringing a weapon onto school grounds. Most likely the student would move to have the gun excluded from the hearing as inadmissible evidence. For this to occur, the board must first find that there was a search or seizure, that the search or seizure was unconstitutional, and that the exclusionary rule precludes the board from considering the illegally seized evidence.[17] If the board answers these questions affirmatively, then the exclusionary rule would bar admission of the fruits of the illegal search, the gun, as evidence in the hearing. Most likely, this would leave only the teacher's testimony that she saw a bulge in the student's jacket as evidence of the student bringing a weapon onto

---

U.S. 338, 348 (1974))). *See generally infra* Part II.B.

14. *See infra* Part II.C.

15. A public school disciplinary proceeding is synonymous with a "[p]ublic school administrative disciplinary hearing[; both terms refer to] whatever internal adjudicative-investigative forum the public school employs to determine the appropriate disciplinary response to a student's violation of a school regulation." Kathleen K. Bach, Note, *The Exclusionary Rule in the Public School Administrative Disciplinary Proceeding: Answering the Question After* New Jersey v. T.L.O., 37 HASTINGS L.J. 1133, 1134 n.5 (1986).

16. At the outset, it should be noted that this Comment deals exclusively with the situation where the search or seizure is conducted by school authorities (rather than the police or school authorities acting in conjunction with the police) and the evidence seized is sought to be used in a school disciplinary hearing rather than in a criminal or juvenile delinquency proceeding.

Some jurisdictions have held that the exclusionary rule should apply to exclude the fruits of unlawful school searches conducted by school officials from criminal trials and delinquency proceedings. *See, e.g.*, State v. Mora, 330 So. 2d 900 (La. 1975), *vacated for clarification*, 423 U.S. 809 (1975). Other courts have determined that the rule should not apply in these instances. *See, e.g.*, State v. Lamb, 224 S.E.2d 51 (Ga. Ct. App. 1976).

17. It is important to distinguish between the restrictions placed on searches by the Fourth Amendment and the remedies for violation of the Fourth Amendment. In *New Jersey v. T.L.O.*, 469 U.S. 325 (1985), the Supreme Court established the standard by which school officials are to conduct searches. *See* discussion *supra* note 8. This Comment deals with the remedies available when a school official violates the standards for searches, set forth by the Court in *T.L.O.*

school grounds. Thus, the student would not be punished for bringing the gun to school.

This example raises a difficult question: What is the proper balance between a school's duty to provide a safe learning environment and its duty to protect the privacy afforded students under the Fourth Amendment? Currently, courts, and school districts taken to court, have two options: either to apply or not to apply the exclusionary rule in the school disciplinary hearing. This Comment will explain why these narrow options fail to achieve a satisfactory balance between school safety and students' rights and will explore an alternative approach, which if implemented, would both protect students' rights and further school safety.

Part II of this Comment begins with a synopsis of the constitutional rights afforded students in public schools. This Part also focuses on application of the exclusionary rule in criminal proceedings and looks at Supreme Court cases addressing the issue of whether the exclusionary rule should apply to contexts outside of the criminal setting. Part II concludes with a capsulation of those cases addressing the issue of whether the exclusionary rule applies to school administrative hearings.

Part III provides the arguments and policies both in favor of, and against, applying the exclusionary rule in school administrative disciplinary hearings. Part IV offers an alternative approach to the exclusionary rule in the school administrative hearing, based on proposed policy guidelines. The model policy will be analyzed in light of the arguments for and against the exclusionary rule. This analysis will show how the vast majority of concerns, expressed by both sides, are satisfied under the model policy. Additionally, Part IV focuses on the incentives for, and benefits accruing to, school districts that implement a form of the suggested proposal. This Comment concludes in Part V that the proposed approach achieves a more satisfactory balance of the competing interests than would either applying or not applying the exclusionary rule to school disciplinary hearings.

II. THE CONSTITUTION AND THE STUDENT

A. *The Public School Student's Constitutional Rights*

The doctrine *in loco parentis*[18] encompasses the common law view of the legal status of minors in the public school setting. Under this doctrine, school officials stand in place of parents during school hours, assuming both the authority and responsibility of the parents in disciplinary actions against the student.[19] The doctrine's foundation rests on the premise that individual constitutional rights mature only when one reaches the state-defined age of majority.[20]

The Supreme Court initially departed from the common law view in *Tinker v. Des Moines Independent Community School District*[21] by striking down a school regulation as a violation of the student's First Amendment rights, which are not "shed . . . at the schoolhouse gate."[22] The Court held that for "school officials to justify prohibition of a particular expression of opinion," it must show that such expression would "'substantially interfere with the requirements of appropriate discipline in the operation of the school.'"[23] The Court has expanded those constitutional rights not "shed at the schoolhouse gate" beyond the First Amendment. In *Goss v. Lopez*,[24] the Court held that in order to satisfy due process requirements, a student, who is to be suspended for 10 days or less, must be given oral or written notice of the charges, and if denied, the student must receive an explanation of the evidence the authorities have and an opportunity to present his or her side of the story.[25] Ten years later in *New Jersey v. T.L.O.*,[26] the Court recognized a student's Fourth

---

18. *See generally* 59 AM. JUR. 2D *Parent and Child* § 75 (1996) (defining the term *in loco parentis*).

19. *See T.L.O.*, 469 U.S. at 336 ("Teachers and school administrators, it is said, act *in loco parentis* in their dealings with students: their authority is that of the parent, not the State, and is therefore not subject to the limits of the Fourth Amendment." (citing R.C.M. v. Texas, 660 S.W.2d 552 (Tex. App. 1983))).

20. *See* Planned Parenthood v. Danforth, 428 U.S. 52, 74 (1976).

21. 393 U.S. 503 (1969).

22. *Id.* at 506.

23. *Id.* at 509 (quoting Burnside v. Byars, 363 F.2d 744, 749 (5th Cir. 1966)).

24. 419 U.S. 565 (1975).

25. *See id.* at 581.

26. 469 U.S. 325 (1985). Though the Court was originally faced with the issue of whether the exclusionary rule should apply to evidence illegally seized by school officials in a criminal prosecution, the Court answered the question of what standard was to be applied to school searches and seizures under the Fourth Amendment. The Court in

Amendment right to be free from "unreasonable searches and seizures" by school officials. In reaching this holding, the Court found that school officials were state agents and could not "claim the parents' immunity from the strictures of the Fourth Amendment."[27] The Court noted that "'the concept of parental delegation' [*in loco parentis*] as a source of school authority is not entirely 'consonant with compulsory education laws.'"[28]

The Supreme Court, faced with balancing the "schoolchild's legitimate expectation of privacy" with the "school's . . . legitimate need to maintain an environment in which learning can take place," concluded that a lesser standard than probable cause should apply in the school setting.[29] The Court held that the legality of a search by school officials should be based on its "reasonableness, under all the circumstances."[30] The Court reasoned that such a standard would "spare teachers and school administrators the necessity of schooling themselves in the niceties of probable cause and permit them to regulate their conduct according to the dictates of reason and common sense."[31]

In its application of the reasonableness standard to the facts of *T.L.O.*, the Court held that the search was reasonable and therefore did not address the remedies for violation of students' Fourth Amendment rights.[32]

B. *Origins of the Exclusionary Rule*

The debate among members of the Supreme Court concerning the exclusionary rule "has always been a warm one."[33] Under

---

T.L.O. was similarly faced with "accommodat[ing] the interests protected by the Fourth Amendment and the interest of the States in providing a safe environment conducive to education in the public schools." *Id.* at 332 n.2.

27. *Id.* at 337. "In carrying out searches and other disciplinary functions pursuant to such policies, school officials act as representatives of the State, not merely as surrogates for the parents . . . ." *Id.* at 335.

28. *Id.* at 336 (quoting Ingraham v. Wright, 430 U.S. 651, 662 (1977)). *See infra* note 101 for discussion on compulsory education (or compulsory attendance) laws.

29. *T.L.O.*, 469 U.S. at 340.

30. *Id.* at 341. See discussion *supra* note 8 for the Court's elaboration on application of the "reasonableness, under all the circumstances" standard in the public school setting.

31. *Id.* at 343. *But see id.* at 354, 365-66 (Brennan, J., concurring in part and dissenting in part) (criticizing the Court's adoption of the "reasonableness" standard "whose only definite content is that it is *not* the same test as the 'probable cause' standard").

32. *See id.* at 343-48.

33. United States v. Janis, 428 U.S. 433, 446 (1976). "Except for the unanimous

the common law, if the tendered evidence was relevant, "the method of obtaining it was unimportant"[34] for purposes of admissibility, and the remedy for breach of a defendant's Fourth Amendment rights was an action for damages.[35] Today, the exclusionary rule bars the admission of illegally seized evidence in criminal cases at both the state and federal levels.[36]

In *Weeks v. United States*[37] the Supreme Court held that the Fourth Amendment prohibited the use of evidence secured through an illegal search and seizure in a federal criminal prosecution.[38] Reflecting on the history of the amendment, the Court noted that the framers' intent in drafting the Fourth Amendment was to stop the unreasonable searches and seizures then permitted under the general warrants issued by government authority and sanctioned by the writs of assistance.[39] The Court advanced two arguments for application of the exclusionary rule. First, allowing unlawfully seized evidence to be used against a citizen accused of a crime nullifies the citizen's right to be free from "unreasonable searches and seizures" rendering the Fourth Amendment of "no value."[40] Second, those charged with upholding the Constitution cannot sanction "unwarranted practices destructive of rights secured by the Federal Constitution."[41]

In 1949, the Supreme Court in *Wolf v. Colorado* declined to impose the exclusionary rule as a matter of due process requirements through the Fourteenth Amendment to the States.[42]

---

decision . . . in *Weeks v. United States*, the evolution of the exclusionary rule has been marked by sharp divisions in the Court. Indeed, *Wolf*, *Lustig*, *Rochin*, *Irvine*, *Elkins*, *Mapp*, and *Calandra* produced a combined total of 27 separate signed opinions or statements." *Id.* at 446 n.15.

34. Olmstead v. United States, 277 U.S. 438, 462-63 (1928).

35. *See id.*; Wolf v. Colorado, 338 U.S. 25, 32 n.1 (1949) (listing state court decisions and state statutes providing civil and criminal remedies against the searching law enforcement official or issuer of the search warrant), *overruled by* Mapp v. Ohio, 367 U.S. 643 (1961).

36. *See Mapp*, 367 U.S. at 657.

37. 232 U.S. 383 (1914).

38. *See id.* at 398. However, there is some debate as to whether the case held only that evidence illegally seized could be returned to its rightful owner even if this made the evidence unavailable for trial. *See* Lawrence Crocker, *Can The Exclusionary Rule Be Saved?*, 84 J. CRIM. L. & CRIMINOLOGY, 310, 313 (1993). In *Silverthorne Lumber Co. v. United States*, 251 U.S. 385 (1920), the Court definitively held illegally seized evidence inadmissible in a prosecution in federal court.

39. *See* United States v. Chadwick, 433 U.S. 1, 7-8 (1977); *Weeks*, 232 U.S. at 390.

40. *Weeks*, 232 U.S. at 394.

41. *Id.* at 392.

42. 338 U.S. 25, 31 (1949) ("[I]n practice the exclusion of evidence may be an

Twelve years later in *Mapp v. Ohio*, the Court reversed *Wolf* and imposed the exclusionary rule upon the States.[43] Though judicial integrity was the Supreme Court's theory backing the exclusionary rule in *Mapp*,[44] the Court has more recently asserted that the exclusionary rule was "designed to safeguard Fourth Amendment rights . . . through its deterrent effect."[45] That is, the rule exists "to remove incentives for the government to engage in any future conduct that is either technically or intentionally unconstitutional."[46]

C. *The Exclusionary Rule Outside the Criminal Trial*

Because the exclusionary rule is viewed as a deterrent rather than a form of redress, it has not been interpreted to apply in all adjudicatory proceedings.[47] While it is obvious that the exclusionary rule applies in state and federal criminal prosecutions, it is less clear, with a few exceptions, where else the exclusionary rule applies. The rule has been held not to apply to collateral criminal proceedings, such as grand jury proceedings,[48] nor does the rule bar collateral use of the illegally seized evidence, such as for impeachment purposes.[49] The Court has also held that illegally seized evidence is admissible in deportation hearings,[50] and civil tax litigation[51] but shall be excluded in forfeiture proceedings.[52] Originally, the Court utilized

---

effective way of deterring unreasonable searches, [but] it is not for this Court to condemn as falling below the minimal standards assured by the Due Process Clause a State's reliance upon other methods which, if consistently enforced, would be equally effective."), *overruled by* Mapp v. Ohio, 367 U.S. 643 (1961).

The division among the members of the Court was, to some degree, based on the issue of whether the exclusionary rule was mandated by the Fourth Amendment, or rather a judicially created rule. *See Wolf*, 338 U.S. at 39-40 (Black, J., concurring) ("[T]he federal exclusionary rule is not a command of the Fourth Amendment but is a judicially created rule of evidence . . . ."). *But see id.* at 48 (Rutledge, J., dissenting) ("The view that the Fourth Amendment *itself* forbids the introduction of evidence illegally obtained in federal prosecutions is one of long standing and firmly established." (emphasis added)).

43. 367 U.S. 643 (1961).
44. *See id.* at 646-50.
45. United States v. Calandra, 414 U.S. 338, 348 (1974).
46. *Id.* at 347.
47. *See, e.g.*, VAN DYKE & SAKURAI, *supra* note 11, at 7-2.
48. *See Calandra*, 414 U.S. at 354.
49. *See* United States v. Havens, 446 U.S. 620, 627-28 (1980).
50. *See* INS v. Lopez-Mendoza, 468 U.S. 1032 (1984).
51. *See* United States v. Janis, 428 U.S. 433 (1976).
52. *See* One 1958 Plymouth Sedan v. Pennsylvania, 380 U.S. 693 (1965).

a multi-factored test to determine whether the proceeding was "quasi-criminal" in nature, thus justifying the application of the exclusionary rule.[53] More recently the Court has utilized a balancing test to determine whether the rule should apply in a particular proceeding.

1. *The quasi-criminal test*

In *One 1958 Plymouth Sedan v. Pennsylvania*, the Supreme Court held that evidence seized in the course of an illegal search of an automobile must be excluded in a proceeding for forfeiture of the automobile.[54] The Court classified the forfeiture proceeding as "quasi-criminal" based upon a two-prong inquiry: (1) whether the proceeding's objective is "to penalize for the commission of an offense against the law"[55] and (2) whether the penalty rendered would be a greater punishment than criminal prosecution.[56] Comparing the potential criminal and civil sanctions, the Court found that the forfeiture of the car, valued at $1000, would be greater than the maximum $500 penalty defendant could be liable for under the criminal law. The Court concluded that it would be "anomalous" to require the exclusion of illegally seized evidence in the criminal proceeding but not in the forfeiture proceeding.[57]

2. *The balancing test*

Though some courts have continued to apply the quasi-criminal test to determine whether the exclusionary rule should apply to a particular proceeding,[58] other courts have questioned the test's continued viability in light of more recent Supreme Court precedent.[59] Thus a new test has emerged.

---

53. *See id.*
54. *See id.*
55. *Id.* at 700.
56. *See id.* at 701.
57. *See id.*
58. *See* James v. Unified Sch. Dist. No. 512, 899 F. Supp. 530 (D. Kan. 1995); Jones v. Latexo Indep. Sch. Dist., 499 F. Supp. 223 (E.D. Tex. 1980); Smyth v. Lubbers, 398 F. Supp. 777 (W.D. Mich. 1975), discussed *infra* Part II.D.
59. *See, e.g.*, Morale v. Grigel, 422 F. Supp. 988 (D.N.H. 1976).

> Following the invitation of . . . *Plymouth Sedan* lower courts applied the exclusionary rule to civil proceedings. While not overruled, th[is] case[] ha[s] been severely undermined by recent Supreme Court decisions upholding a tax assessment based upon illegally seized evidence, *Janis*, and allowing the

To determine whether the exclusionary rule should be applied in a civil proceeding under this newest test, the Court balances the benefits of applying the exclusionary rule to the proceeding against the societal costs flowing from the application of the rule.[60] The balancing test has most recently been used by the Court to conclude that the exclusionary rule does not apply in civil tax litigation nor in deportation hearings. In *United States v. Janis*, the Court held that the exclusionary rule did not prohibit the Internal Revenue Service from using evidence illegally obtained by the Los Angeles Police Department in a civil tax assessment.[61] In its balancing analysis, the Court concluded that the costs of excluding the unlawfully seized evidence from the federal civil proceeding outweighed the "sufficient likelihood" that the rule would deter the conduct of state police.[62] Because this case dealt with evidence obtained by one agency but used by another, the Court left undecided the question of whether the exclusionary rule should apply in a civil proceeding against an "intrasovereign" violation of the Fourth Amendment;[63] that is where the party conducting the illegal search is also the party seeking to have the evidence admitted at the adjudicatory proceeding. The Court answered this question eight years later in *INS v. Lopez-Mendoza*.[64]

In *Lopez-Mendoza*, the Court addressed the issue of whether the exclusionary rule should apply in a deportation hearing, so as to exclude evidence illegally seized by Immigration and Naturalization Service ("INS") officials.[65] Applying the same balancing test applied in *Janis*, the Court held that the exclusionary rule did not apply to INS "intrasovereign" violations of the Fourth Amendment.[66] Though the deterrent effect of the exclusionary rule is greater in "intrasovereign" violations, the

---

Government to propound questions based upon illegally seized evidence to a grand jury witness, *Calandra*.

Id. at 1000 (citations omitted).

60. *See* United States v. Janis, 428 U.S. 433, 454 (1976).
61. *See id.*
62. *Id.* at 454.
63. *See id.* at 455-56 & n.31.
64. 468 U.S. 1032 (1984).
65. *See id.*
66. *See id.* at 1051.

Court noted factors which weakened the deterrent effect the rule would have under the circumstances.[67]

The "most important" factor, in the Court's view, was that the INS "has its own comprehensive scheme for deterring Fourth Amendment violations by its officers."[68] The INS's scheme included the following procedures to safeguard Fourth Amendment rights: (1) "rules restricting stop, interrogation and arrest practices"; (2) "instruction and examination in Fourth Amendment law" for new agents and "periodic refresher courses" for others;[69] and (3) "procedure[s] for investigating and punishing immigration officers who commit Fourth Amendment violations."[70] Persuaded by these factors, the Court held that the societal costs of applying the rule outweighed its benefits and declined to extend the protection of the exclusionary rule in such a proceeding.[71]

D. *Federal Court Precedent Addressing Application of the Exclusionary Rule in the School Disciplinary Setting*

Whether the exclusionary rule should apply in the school disciplinary setting has been addressed in federal court on multiple occasions.[72] Three federal district courts have held that the exclusionary rule should apply in the school disciplinary hearing to assure protection of the student's constitutional rights.[73] In

---

67. The Court noted that immigration judges and the attorneys that practiced before them were not well-versed in Fourth Amendment law and that the deterrent value of the exclusionary rule in a deportation proceeding "is undermined by the availability of alternative remedies." *Id.* at 1045.

68. *Id.* at 1044-45.

69. *Id.*

70. *Id.*

71. *See id.* at 1050 ("By all appearances the INS has already taken sensible and reasonable steps to deter Fourth Amendment violations by its officers, and this makes the likely additional deterrent value of the exclusionary rule small.").

72. State courts have addressed the issue as well, though less frequently. The most recent state decision addressing the issue is the highly publicized case *Juan C. v. Cortinez*, 647 N.Y.S.2d 491 (App. Div. 1996), *rev'd on other grounds*, 679 N.E.2d 1061 (N.Y. 1997). *Juan C.* is the first case in which a state constitution was held to bar illegally seized evidence from a school disciplinary hearing. For an insightful look at the case and its procedural history, see Mai Lihn Spencer, Note, *Suppress or Suspend: New York's Exclusionary Rule in School Disciplinary Proceedings*, 72 N.Y.U. L. REV. 1494 (1997).

73. *See* Jones v. Latexo Indep. Sch. Dist., 499 F. Supp. 223 (E.D. Tex. 1980); Smyth v. Lubbers, 398 F. Supp. 777 (W.D. Mich. 1975); Caldwell v. Cannady, 340 F. Supp. 835 (N.D. Tex. 1972).

Smyth v. Lubbers, college officials found marijuana while conducting a search of plaintiffs' rooms without a warrant or consent.[74] The court conducted its analysis under the "quasi-criminal" test[75] and found that since violation of the regulation required proof that the criminal law had been violated and that "the punishment in fact imposed by the College is more severe than that likely to be imposed by any state or federal court for the same offense,"[76] the district court concluded that it would be "anomalous here, too, not to apply an exclusionary rule."[77]

Similarly in *Jones v. Latexo Independent School District*, six students were suspended from school as a result of a search utilizing a dog trained to detect drugs, which located drug paraphernalia in the students' possession.[78] The court found the search unconstitutional and was faced with deciding whether the exclusionary rule should keep the illegally seized evidence out of the school disciplinary hearing.[79] While the *Jones* court referenced *Janis*, it found the situation in *Janis* "quite unlike" that presented before it.[80] Using the "quasi-criminal" test, the district court found that plaintiffs "suffered a penalty as a result of the illegal searches carried out by defendants . . . [and though] the punishment imposed [expulsion] was non-criminal in nature, it was . . . a deprivation rather than merely the restitution of monies wrongfully retained, as in *Janis*."[81] On this basis the court found that the exclusionary rule should apply. Finally, in *Caldwell v. Cannady*, the court, with little analysis, held that precedent required the school board to exclude evidence that had been obtained unconstitutionally.[82]

More recently, the federal courts addressing the issue have declined to extend the exclusionary rule to school disciplinary

---

74. 398 F. Supp. at 781.

75. *See* discussion *supra* Part II.C.1.

76. *Smyth*, 398 F. Supp. at 794 (weighing two year suspension from college against one year probation with the possibility that the charges would be dismissed if the probation was not violated).

77. *Id.* The court also focused on the fact that application of the exclusionary rule was the only effective way to protect students' constitutional rights since damages, only recoverable from those acting in bad faith, would provide little deterrence. *See id.*

78. 499 F. Supp. 223, 227 (E.D. Tex. 1980).

79. *See id.* at 237-38.

80. *Id.* at 238.

81. *Id.*

82. 340 F. Supp. 835, 839 (N.D. Tex. 1972).

hearings.[83] In *James v. Unified School District No. 512*, a student expelled from high school for possession of a firearm on campus alleged a violation of his constitutional rights and sought injunctive relief that would allow him to take exams and attend school the following year.[84] Addressing the issue of whether illegally seized evidence should be barred from the school disciplinary hearing, the court noted that "case law does not prohibit using the fruits" of a Fourth Amendment violation in school disciplinary hearings.[85] Rather than utilizing the balancing test, the court relied, to some degree, on Tenth Circuit precedent that the exclusionary rule was applicable in civil cases that could be characterized as "quasi-criminal."[86] The *James* court cited two cases[87] and without further analysis held that "[s]chool disciplinary hearings are not 'quasi-criminal' proceedings" and "plaintiff . . . cannot avail himself of the exclusionary rule in this context."[88]

Most recently, the Eighth Circuit addressed the issue in *Thompson v. Carthage School District*.[89] In *Thompson*, the court relied heavily on *United States v. Janis*, *INS v. Lopez-Mendoza*, and the balancing test.[90] The court found that the societal cost of excluding the evidence would be very high since application of

---

83. *See* Thompson v. Carthage Sch. Dist., 87 F.3d 979 (8th Cir. 1996); James v. Unified Sch. Dist. No. 512, 899 F. Supp. 530 (D. Kan. 1995).

84. 899 F. Supp. at 532.

85. *Id.* at 533.

86. *See id.* at 533-34 (citing Savina Home Indus. v. Secretary of Labor, 594 F.2d 1358, 1363 (10th Cir. 1979) (holding exclusionary rule applicable in OSHA administrative hearing)).

87. *See* Nash v. Auburn Univ., 812 F.2d 655 (11th Cir. 1987); Herbert v. Reinstein, 1994 WL 587095, at *5 (E.D. Pa. 1994), *rev'd*, 70 F.3d 1255 (3d Cir. 1995).

88. *James*, 899 F. Supp. at 534. From *James*, it appears that the *Plymouth Sedan* "quasi-criminal" test is dispositive regarding applicability of the exclusionary rule since the court did not attempt to balance the societal costs or benefits of application of the rule. However, other courts subscribe to the notion that the *Plymouth Sedan* test is only the first of two steps in determining whether the exclusionary rule applies. "[T]he exclusionary rule . . . [applies] if the proceeding can be characterized as 'quasi criminal' and if the invocation of the rule would outweigh the costs to society under *Janis*." Pike v. Gallagher, 829 F. Supp. 1254, 1265 (D.N.M. 1993) (footnote omitted). Although *Pike* utilized the "quasi-criminal" test as another factor in its balancing test, it conceded that it was "unclear if the Supreme Court requires a threshold finding that the nature of the civil proceeding is 'quasi-criminal' or if the nature of the proceeding is merely one factor in applying the *Janis* balancing test." *Id.* at 1265 n.6 (footnotes omitted).

An additional alternative is that the *Plymouth Sedan* test has been subsumed by the balancing test. *See* discussion *supra* note 59.

89. 87 F.3d 979 (8th Cir. 1996).

90. *See supra* Part II.C.2.

the rule would "frustrate[] the critical governmental function of educating and protecting children" by preventing the discipline of those students who disrupt the educational process or endanger others.[91] The Eighth Circuit also concluded that "[a]pplication of the exclusionary rule would require suppression hearing-like inquiries inconsistent with the demands of school discipline."[92]

Weighing the benefits of the exclusionary rule, the court focused on the rule's deterrent effect and whether it would in fact deter Fourth Amendment violations in the school setting.[93] Noting that the exclusionary rule would have a strong deterrent effect, because it was an intrasovereign violation, the court proceeded to distinguish the case from *Lopez-Mendoza*. The court first noted that unlike INS agents and illegal immigrants, students and school officials do not have an adversarial relationship but rather a "'commonality of interests'"[94] and "'[t]he attitude of the typical teacher is one of personal responsibility for the student's welfare'" and education.[95] Second, the court noted that children's legitimate privacy expectations were somewhat limited at school.[96] The court concluded that under these circumstances there is little need for the deterrent effect afforded by the exclusionary rule and any deterrent effect that application of the exclusionary rule would provide could "not begin to outweigh the high societal costs of imposing the rule."[97] The court thus concluded that the exclusionary rule did not apply to the school disciplinary proceeding.

As these cases demonstrate, the federal courts are in a conundrum, not only as to whether or not the exclusionary rule should apply in school disciplinary hearings, but also whether the appropriate test to determine whether the rule applies is the balancing test or the "quasi-criminal" test. Uniformity among the federal courts in this area of the law is lacking, and it is

---

91. *Thompson*, 87 F.3d at 981.

92. *Id.*

93. *See id.*

94. *Id.* (quoting New Jersey v. T.L.O., 469 U.S. 325, 350 (1985) (Powell, J., concurring)).

95. *Id.* (quoting New Jersey v. T.L.O., 469 U.S. 325, 350 (1985) (Powell, J., concurring)).

96. *See id.*

97. *Id.* at 982.

unlikely that the Supreme Court will address the issue any time soon, if at all.[98]

III. ARGUMENTS FOR AND AGAINST THE EXCLUSIONARY RULE

An exploration of arguments on both sides of the battle over the exclusionary rule in school administrative hearings serves two functions. First, it provides the reader with an overview of the issues and concerns regarding applying or not applying the rule. Second, these arguments provide a checklist by which to evaluate the proposal articulated in Part IV of this Comment. That is, the proposal will be analyzed and evaluated against the concerns expressed by both sides to exemplify its superiority to the exclusionary rule in the school disciplinary hearing.

A. *Arguments Against Applying the Exclusionary Rule*

1. *Compromised school safety*

As was touched on previously, a monumental concern of applying the exclusionary rule to school disciplinary hearings is that the rule would compromise school safety.[99] Before exploring the arguments as to how the rule would compromise school safety, it may be helpful to understand why school safety is held in such high regard legally, as well as socially.

As Justice Powell noted in *T.L.O.*, the "special characteristics of elementary and secondary schools . . . make it unnecessary to afford students the same constitutional protections granted adults and juveniles in a nonschool setting."[100] For example, all fifty states require compulsory school attendance.[101] Because

98. *See* L. Goering, *Constitutional Law: Privacy Penumbra Encompasses Students in School Searches*, 25 WASHBURN L.J. 135, 146 n.82 (1985) (noting a possible reason for not deciding whether the exclusionary rule should have applied in *T.L.O.* was because there were not enough Justices to get rid of it).

99. For an illustration of this concern in a slightly different context, see *Thompson*, 87 F.3d at 981, where the court began with a hypothetical situation where the application of the exclusionary rule barred the expulsion of a high school student who had confessed to the murder of his classmate, because the student was not read his Miranda Rights prior to giving his confession. The court concluded: "We doubt any parent would compromise school safety in this fashion." *Id.*

100. New Jersey v. T.L.O., 469 U.S. 325, 348 (1984) (Powell, J., concurring).

101. *See* Donald L. Beci, *School Violence: Protecting Our Children and the Fourth Amendment*, 41 CATH. U. L. Rev. 817, 821 (1992); *see, e.g.*, ALA. CODE § 16-28-3 (1987) (requiring attendance for children ages 7 to 16); IDAHO CODE § 33-202 (Supp. 1992) (requiring children age 7 to 16 to attend school); 105 ILL. COMP. STAT. ANN. 5/26-1 (West

states require school attendance, even over parental objection,[102] the state and the school have a "moral duty to maintain student discipline and to protect children from violence that occurs while they are attending the very schools to which the state has bound them to attend."[103] Another special characteristic of public schools is the legal duty placed upon the state to protect students.[104] This duty comes from two sources: (1) state statutes and school board regulations,[105] and (2) the *in loco parentis* doctrine, under which teachers and school administrators may be held liable for their failure to act when a student is in danger in the school setting.[106] Against this backdrop, and in light of common sense, it is easy to see why student safety is of such high concern.

Opponents of the exclusionary rule argue that its application in the disciplinary setting would compromise school safety in numerous ways. First, application of the rule to disciplinary hearings, through its suppression of credible evidence, may prohibit the school from expelling or suspending a "dangerous" student, which would frustrate the protection of children by preventing discipline "of [those] students who disrupt education or endanger other students."[107] Second, allowing a student who is perceived as "dangerous" to continue to attend the public school would possibly cause other students, school officials and parents to feel threatened and less safe at school.[108] Third, al-

---

1993) (requiring compulsory attendance for children ages 7 to 16); WASH. REV. CODE ANN. § 28A.225.10 (West 1997) (requiring compulsory attendance for children ages 8 to 18).

102. *See* Prince v. Massachusetts, 321 U.S. 158 (1944).

103. Beci, *supra* note 101, at 821; *see T.L.O.*, 469 U.S. at 350 ("[T]he school has the obligation to protect pupils from mistreatment . . . .").

104. *See* Gordon J. v. Santa Ana Sch. Dist., 208 Cal. Rptr. 657, 666 (Ct. App. 1984) ("[W]e do not discount their sincere and accurate emphasis on the duty of the school administration to protect law abiding students from delinquents among them . . . .").

105. *See T.L.O.*, 469 U.S. at 336 ("[P]ublic school officials . . . act in furtherance of publicly mandated educational and disciplinary policies."); *see, e.g.*, IDAHO CODE § 33-512(4) (1997) (charging school officials with duty to protect health of pupils); NEB. REV. STAT. § 28-1204.03(5) (1997) ("Schools have a duty to protect their students and provide an environment which promotes and provides an education in a nonthreatening manner."); N.J. STAT. ANN. § 18A:25-2 (West 1997) (providing school officials with authority to prevent disorderly conduct by students).

106. *See* Beci, *supra* note 101, at 823. For analysis and argument that under certain circumstances school teachers and officials should have a federal constitutional duty to protect students from violence, see Colson, *supra* note 2.

107. Thompson v. Carthage Sch. Dist., 87 F.3d 979, 981 (8th Cir. 1996).

108. *See Gordon J.*, 208 Cal. Rptr. at 667 (noting that the costs of implementing

lowing a student caught "red handed" to go unpunished for breaking school rules would send a message to other students that they can break the rules and get away with it. Such a result would undermine the discipline of students and thereby frustrate the education and protection of children.[109] Finally, application of the exclusionary rule would have a "chilling effect on effective disciplinary enforcement."[110] That is, school officials would refrain from searching students because of their concern that the results of the search would be suppressed. By foregoing such a search, the school official will not be able to discipline the students, and more importantly may fail to take needed action to protect other students from harm.[111]

2. *More cumbersome adjudication*

Another argument against the exclusionary rule is that application of the rule would create "more cumbersome adjudication" by requiring additional hearings, to determine if evidence should be suppressed, that are inconsistent with the demands of school discipline.[112] The rationale behind this theory is that the exclusionary rule and its implementation in the disciplinary proceeding would divert valuable educational and administrative resources from the educational process.[113]

---

the exclusionary rule include "damage to the morale of parents and teachers, [which cost] is too dear").

109. *See* Anne Proffitt Dupre, *Should Students Have Constitutional Rights? Keeping Order in the Public Schools*, 65 GEO. WASH. L. REV. 49, 51-52 (1996). Professor Dupre, a public school teacher prior to entering law school, remarks:

> Parents of diverse social and economic backgrounds, white and black, wealthy and middle class, are removing their children from public schools due to concerns about order and safety. . . . The chaos that has overtaken many of our public schools did not happen overnight. Serious discipline problems do not arise spontaneously in a school. They creep in as children realize that schools are unwilling or unable to take disciplinary action for lesser conduct. Each time that misconduct by an individual student went unquestioned because the teacher or principal was afraid that it did not meet the . . . standard[s] set forth by the Supreme Court we took one more step toward the turmoil that exists in the public school community today.

Id.

110. Spencer, *supra* note 72, at 1538.

111. *See* New Jersey v. T.L.O., 469 U.S. 325, 350 (1984) ("The primary duty of school officials is the education and training of young people. Without first establishing discipline and maintaining order, teachers cannot begin to educate the student.").

112. *Thompson*, 87 F.3d at 981.

113. *See* Bach, *supra* note 15, at 1165.

3. *The exclusionary rule does not deter constitutional violations in the school setting*

The final argument is that in the school setting, the exclusionary rule does not fulfill its purpose, to deter state actors from violating the constitutional rights of its citizens,[114] to such a degree so as to warrant its application. Proponents of the rule recognize that the relationship being dealt with in the school setting is an "intrasovereign" one, and that this in and of itself would likely have a strong deterrent effect on the actor. However, the anti-exclusionary rule camp argues that the special characteristics of our public schools weaken this argument substantially. First, the relationship between the student and the school official is quite unlike the relationship where the exclusionary rule initially was applied, between law enforcement officials and criminal suspects.[115] The teacher's goal is to educate, encourage and help their students, far different from that of a police officer's goals to thwart and apprehend suspected criminals. Since no accurate empirical data exists as to whether the exclusionary rule actually works in the criminal setting,[116] the student-teacher relationship casts even more doubt upon the rule's deterrent effects among this type of nonadversarial relationship.

A corollary argument is that since a school official's primary duty is not law enforcement, the official will have less training in search and seizure law and therefore may, in good faith, not know that a search is illegal, or even be aware of the consequences of the exclusionary rule. Under these circumstances, the exclusionary rule would not provide any deterrence. Additionally, because of the intense pressure placed on school officials to protect students from the threat of drugs and weapons, "school officials are not likely to be deterred by the exclusionary rule and are more likely to engage in a search simply to dispel

---

114. *See supra* notes 45-46.

115. *See Thompson*, 87 F.3d at 981. ("School officials . . . are not law enforcement officers. They do not have an adversarial relationship with students.").

116. *See* United States v. Janis, 428 U.S. 433, 450-52 (1976) ("[A]lthough scholars have attempted to determine whether the exclusionary rule in fact does have any deterrent effect, each empirical study on the subject, in its own way, appears to be flawed."); *see also* Dallin H. Oaks, *Studying the Exclusionary Rule in Search and Seizure*, 37 U. CHI. L. REV. 665 (1970) (concluding that no effective quantitative measure of the exclusionary rule's deterrent efficacy had been devised).

their fears that students are in possession of such harmful items."[117]

B. Arguments in Favor of the Exclusionary Rule

1. The rule's deterrent effect

The major rationale advanced for adoption of the exclusionary rule in the school disciplinary setting is the same rationale advanced for its application in the criminal setting, its deterrent effect.[118] The idea behind the exclusionary rule is that school officials will be deterred from violating students' constitutional rights if they know that the results of their illegal search will not be available in the corresponding adjudication. Advocates of the rule feel that "[a] strong deterrent is needed to prevent random" or harassing searches of schoolchildren and their belongings.[119]

Compulsory attendance laws[120] give further support to the argument in favor of the application of the exclusionary rule. Since students are required to attend public schools, the students' rights should be provided the utmost protection in a place where they are legally bound to be and in a setting which calls for "constant submission to authority."[121] This protection, the argument goes, will be best provided by the exclusionary rule because the relationship is an intrasovereign one.[122] Also, this camp advances the notion that the exclusionary rule is likely to be more effective in the school setting than in the criminal setting because the community and administration involved in this setting are smaller.[123] Individuals in the school system conducting illegal searches are more likely to be reprimanded for unconstitutional behavior because a school's administration is smaller, more intimate and capable to act more quickly than the criminal justice system.

---

117. Myron Schreck, *The Fourth Amendment in the Public Schools: Issues for the 1990s and Beyond*, 25 URB. LAW. 117, 155 (1993).

118. *See* Bach, *supra* note 15, at 1146.

119. Spencer, *supra* note 72, at 1523.

120. *See* discussion *supra* notes 100-02 and accompanying text.

121. Spencer, *supra* note 72, at 1523.

122. *See supra* note 63 and accompanying text.

123. *See* Spencer, *supra* note 72, at 1525.

> [A] school official receives greater feedback about his disciplinary activities. Unlike the three-tiered criminal justice system, the school's administrative disciplinary process frequently occurs entirely within the school or the local school district. Far less bureaucratic compartmentalization impedes the flow of relevant information. Moreover, the school adjudication is far more expeditious than a criminal proceeding. As a result, feedback on the propriety and consequences of search activity is more immediate and relevant, even though the offending searcher may not, beyond giving testimony, participate personally in the adjudication.[124]

2. *Only viable alternative to protect students' rights*

Another argument that this group advances is that without the exclusionary rule there is currently no viable alternative to ensure the protection of students' rights.[125] An alternative frequently suggested to replace the exclusionary rule in deterring illegal searches and seizures is lawsuits against the authority who conducted the search or seizure. Under 42 U.S.C. § 1983 individuals can sue state officials, including school districts and individuals,[126] in federal court for violation of rights secured by the United States Constitution or federal laws.[127]

---

124. Bach, *supra* note 15, at 1165-66.

125. *See, e.g.*, Jones v. Latexo Indep. Sch. Dist., 499 F. Supp. 223, 239 (E.D. Tex. 1980) ("Failure to apply the exclusionary rule would leave school officials free to trench upon the constitutional rights of students without restraint or fear of adverse consequences."); Morale v. Grigel, 422 F. Supp. 988, 1001 (D.N.H. 1976) ("The Supreme Court has basically left students remediless for Fourth Amendment violations in the federal courts.").

126. *See, e.g.*, Monell v. New York City Dep't of Soc. Servs., 436 U.S. 658 (1978). However, a § 1983 action may not be brought against a state or state agency. *See, e.g.*, Will v. Michigan Dep't of State Police, 491 U.S. 58 (1989):

127. *See* Beci, *supra* note 101, at 827. A § 1983 action may provide either injunctive relief, where there is a clear pattern of conduct by school officials violating constitutional rights on an ongoing basis, *see, e.g.*, Rizzo v. Goode, 423 U.S. 362 (1976), or compensatory damages, if the violations are isolated incidents. *See, e.g.*, Bivens v. Six Unknown Named Agents of the FBI, 403 U.S. 388 (1971).

> A school official is liable, under 42 U.S.C. § 1983, to a wronged student only if he knew or reasonably should have known that the action he took within his sphere of official responsibility would violate the constitutional rights of the student affected, or if he took the action with the malicious intention to cause a deprivation of constitutional rights or other injury to the student.

Wood v. Strickland, 420 U.S. 308, 322 (1975).

In theory this approach holds promise, but in the school context the option is practically foreclosed. Generally, young people lack the resources necessary to commence costly affirmative litigation,[128] or the students may not even be aware that their rights have been violated or that a damage remedy exists.[129] As well, "attorneys are probably not enthusiastic about taking such cases, given that they are lengthy, complex and have little likelihood of success."[130] Nor is the law very favorable to the student as school authorities enjoy some immunity under state statutes and students can only recover by showing that the official acted in bad faith.[131] All these factors lead to the conclusion that suits against the offending official are not realistic; one commentator concludes that the exclusionary rule remains the only "effective means of informing school officials of their Fourth Amendment mistakes and assuring that such errors are not repeated."[132]

3. *Judicial and administrative integrity*

Another concern regarding not applying the exclusionary rule is the importance of judicial and administrative integrity in the context of school disciplinary settings.[133] "The 'imperative of judicial integrity' generally refers to the need for the judiciary to refrain from associating itself with and thus apparently approving of the government's use of illegally obtained evidence in a criminal prosecution."[134] The essential aim of this concern is to maintain respect for and trust in the law and those individuals charged with enforcing the law. Because schools are characterized as "the central socializers of American children" the concern for integrity is particularly significant.[135] As the Supreme Court

---

128. *See* Smyth v. Lubbers, 398 F. Supp. 777, 794 (W.D. Mich. 1977).

129. *See* Spencer, *supra* note 72, at 1528.

130. *Id.*; *see* Irene Merker Rosenberg, *A Door Left Open: Applicability of the Exclusionary Rule to the Juvenile Court Delinquency Hearings*, 24 AM. J. CRIM. L. 29, 41 (1996) ("Recovery for Fourth Amendment violations is difficult, damages are not high, young people tend not to make good witnesses, and attorneys may well decline to prosecute such actions." (footnote omitted)).

131. *See, e.g.*, *Smyth*, 398 F. Supp. at 794.

132. *See* Rosenberg, *supra* note 130, at 42.

133. *See supra* notes 45-46 and discussion in text, noting that this was a past rationale under Supreme Court precedent.

134. Bach, *supra* note 15, at 1150 (quoting Elkins v. United States, 364 U.S. 206, 222 (1960) (Stewart, J., concurring)).

135. Spencer, *supra* note 72, at 1531.

remarked, "[t]he vigilant protection of constitutional freedoms is nowhere more vital than in the community of the American schools."[136] Keeping our public schools free "from the taint of illegal, unconstitutional behavior is of paramount importance."[137] The lesson that those in a position of authority must themselves obey the rules is especially important in the controlled setting of a public school, where students are, for the most part, at the mercy of school officials and "struggle to find consistency in the rules, rewards, and punishment systems."[138] Young people are very impressionable and school officials are expected to be role models. Justice Stevens comments:

> The schoolroom is the first opportunity most citizens have to experience the power of government. Through it passes every citizen and public official, from schoolteachers to policemen and prison guards. The values they learn there, they take with them in life. One of our most cherished ideals is the one contained in the Fourth Amendment: that the government may not intrude on the personal privacy of its citizens without a warrant or compelling circumstances.[139]

Application of the exclusionary rule to the school disciplinary proceeding would "make[] an important statement to young people that 'our society attaches serious consequences to a violation of constitutional rights,' and that this is a principle of 'liberty and justice for all.'"[140]

Similarly, those parents and students who see or experience racial discrimination or misconduct on the part of the school officials will lose faith in a system that benefits from such misconduct.

> Most educators consider the shaping of character to be the school's primary task. While a child must learn to conform his behavior to societal rules and to respect the rights of others, it

---

136. Shelton v. Tucker, 364 U.S. 479, 487 (1960).

137. Spencer, *supra* note 72, at 1532 (footnotes omitted).

138. *Id.* at 1534-35.

139. New Jersey v. T.L.O., 469 U.S. 325, 385-86 (1985) (Stevens, J., concurring in part and dissenting in part).

140. *Id.* at 374 (Stevens, J.,concurring in part and dissenting in part) (quoting Stone v. Powell, 428 U.S. 465, 492 (1976) and 36 U.S.C. § 172 (1994) (pledge of allegiance)).

is also true that a child must learn that others, including adults, must also conform to these rules.[141]

The importance of maintaining judicial integrity is bolstered by the special relationship the school has with the local community.[142]

> Each school site has intensely local and personal affiliations. Local school boards usually are elected bodies which must be responsive to local community pressures. The typical school-community relationship promotes the free flow of information, by means of student reporting or regular public meetings, about the daily activities and disciplinary policies of the school.[143]

IV. AN ALTERNATIVE APPROACH

In brief summation, public school students have been afforded Fourth Amendment rights under the Federal Constitution to be free from unreasonable searches and seizures by school officials.[144] The lower courts have split on whether the exclusionary rule is the appropriate remedy for violation of such rights.[145] As has been shown, there are valid concerns as to why the exclusionary rule should or should not be applied in the school disciplinary setting.[146] The following alternative approach bridges the gap between these competing interests by (1) protecting students' rights, (2) providing a safe learning and working environment for students and school officials, and (3) provid-

---

141. Bach, *supra* note 15, at 1162-63.

142. *Cf.* Ingraham v. Wright, 430 U.S. 651, 670 (1977). Justice Powell made the following statement, in the context of the Eighth Amendment, regarding the relationship between the school and the local community:

> The schoolchild has little need for the protection of the Eighth Amendment. Though attendance may not always be voluntary, the public school remains an open institution . . . and at the end of the school day, the child is invariably free to return home. Even while at school, the child brings with him the support of family and friends and is rarely apart from teachers and other pupils who may witness and protest any instances of mistreatment. The openness of the public school and its supervision by the community afford significant safeguards against the kinds of abuses from which the Eighth Amendment protects the prisoner.

Id.

143. Bach, *supra* note 15, at 1163.

144. *See* New Jersey v. T.L.O., 469 U.S. 325, 341 (1985).

145. *See supra* Part II.D.

146. *See supra* Part III.A-B.

ing school districts with much needed direction in Fourth Amendment jurisprudence.

This proposed approach is based upon a two-prong theory. First, to effectively deter constitutional misconduct on the part of teachers and school administrators, school officials must be educated about the rights of school children as articulated by the Supreme Court. Second, if the student's rights are violated, the offending school official "must suffer some negative consequence as a direct result of the misconduct."[147] The following is a model proposal[148] which provides a framework to achieve the goals of this approach:

> § 1. Standard. No student shall be searched unless the school official reasonably suspects that evidence violating the law or school policy will be found in a particular place. The scope of such search is not to exceed the search's original objective and the method of the search shall not be excessively intrusive in light of the nature of the suspected infraction and the age and sex of the student.
>
> § 2. Training and Education. New school officials shall receive instruction and examination in search and seizure law, and all other school officials receive refresher courses on a yearly basis.

---

147. Harry M. Caldwell & Carol A. Chase, *The Unruly Exclusionary Rule: Heeding Justice Blackmun's Call to Examine the Rule in Light of Changing Judicial Understanding About Its Effects Outside the Courtroom*, 78 MARQ. L. REV. 45, 67 (1994).

148. This language is suggested as a starting point for fashioning new policy and/or enhancing existing policy and is based upon federal case law. State law should be considered in adding to or supplementing this language as should the special circumstances of your school district. For instance, Louisiana requires that school officials obtain a warrant before conducting a search. *See* State v. Mora, 307 So. 2d 317 (La. 1975), *vacated for clarification*, 423 U.S. 809 (1975). As well, the exclusionary rule is the appropriate remedy in a school disciplinary hearing for violation of a student's rights under Article 1, Section 12 of the New York Constitution. *See* Juan C. v. Cortines, 647 N.Y.S.2d 491 (App. Div. 1996), *rev'd on other grounds*, 679 N.E.2d 1061 (N.Y. 1997).

Additionally, the proposed language addresses only suggested policy. If such a policy were implemented, its success would depend to a great extent on the policy being translated into procedures to specifically guide school officials through the process. There are numerous resources offering practical and detailed instruction on compliance with search and seizure law in public schools. For a concise and somewhat unique approach, see JOHN H. DISE ET AL., SEARCHES OF STUDENTS, LOCKERS AND AUTOMOBILES (Crisis Intervention Series, 1994). For a more comprehensive approach, see VAN DYKE & SAKURAI, *supra* note 11.

§ 3. Reporting Procedure. All searches or seizures conducted by school officials are to be reported within a reasonable time to the appropriate school district administrator for review.[149]

§ 4. Violations. Those individuals found to violate any of the standards articulated in § 1 may be subject to any or all of the following disciplinary action: additional training and education under § 2, administrative leave, suspension of pay, or other disciplinary action found to be an effective deterrent.

§ 5. Notice. School officials shall provide regular notification to students and parents of the school's disciplinary policies and procedures.

A. *Origins of the Proposal*

Before providing an analysis of the proposal, the origins of the proposal and its sections should be explained. The proposal is intended to be used by school districts as a model comprehensive scheme to deter Fourth Amendment violations by school officials. The proposal contains all the factors which the Supreme Court found to be "most important" in refusing to apply the exclusionary rule to an INS deportation hearing in *Lopez-Mendoza*.[150]

Section 1 is essentially the reasonableness standard, established by the Supreme Court in *New Jersey v. T.L.O.*, used to determine the legality of searches and seizures of students by school officials in public schools.[151] Section 2 provides for the instruction and examination of school officials in Fourth Amendment law. Section 3 addresses the procedures for reporting and investigating searches or seizures conducted by school officials. The proposal's bite is found in section 4, which contains the deterrence strategy. School officials who commit Fourth Amendment violations are subject to different types of disciplinary action, the purpose behind the discipline being to deter future violations of section 1 of the proposal. Section 5 of the proposal was included to create dialogue about the proposal, and the broader issue of constitutional rights, between students, par-

149. For examples of search and seizure report forms see VAN DYKE & SAKAI, *supra* note 11, at 11-1 to 11-4.

150. INS v. Lopez-Mendoza, 468 U.S. 1032, 1048 (1984); *see generally supra* Part II.C.2.

151. *See* New Jersey v. T.L.O., 469 U.S. 325, 341-42 (1985).

ents, teachers, and school officials. Enactment and compliance with each of these sections by a school district would essentially negate the need for the exclusionary rule in the school disciplinary hearing.[152]

B. The Rationale Behind the Proposal

To evaluate the model proposal against the concerns expressed in Part III, the fact scenario at the beginning of this Comment will be utilized. Once again, assume that the teacher finds a gun on the student. If the exclusionary rule applies, the gun is inadmissible at the disciplinary hearing, and the student's Fourth Amendment rights are protected. However, the costs and fears of applying the rule, articulated by those opposing the exclusionary rule in Part III.A, may come to fruition. On the other hand, if the exclusionary rule does not apply, then school safety and discipline has not been undermined, yet the student's rights are violated and left unprotected, as there are no negative consequences for violation of these rights.

Now assume that the student and teacher were in a school district that had implemented the proposed policy in this Comment. Under the strictures of the policy, namely the education and training requirement, there is a greater likelihood that the search of the student would have been conducted in a constitutional manner. However, even the best training programs will not be one hundred percent effective in deterring all illegal searches and seizures. Therefore, assume that the teacher searches the student in a manner which is inconsistent with section 1 of the policy and finds a gun. Pursuant to section 2, the teacher contacts the appropriate administrative official and tells her about the search of the student and finding the gun. The administrative official then reviews the circumstances of the search with the student and other relevant parties. If the administrative official has reason to believe that section 1 of the policy has been violated, then a hearing will be conducted to answer two questions: (1) whether the teacher's search of the student violated section 1 of the policy and (if question one is answered affirmatively), (2) in light of the circumstances surrounding the teacher's search, as well as the teacher's past conduct regarding searches, what should be the appropriate conse-

152. *See* discussion *infra* Part IV.B.

quences for the teacher under section 4 of the policy for the violation of section 1. Along with this investigation and hearing, the student will be involved in a disciplinary hearing before the school disciplinary board. Rather than excluding the gun from the hearing to protect the student's rights, this disciplinary process is utilized to protect students' rights, and the student faces the appropriate consequences for bringing a gun to school.[153]

This alternative method is superior to the exclusionary rule in the school administrative hearing because it meets the vast majority of concerns voiced by both camps over the exclusionary rule.[154]

1. *Meeting the concerns of the anti-exclusionary rule camp*

The primary concern of the anti-exclusionary rule camp is that the exclusionary rule makes public schools less safe by suppressing reliable evidence needed to discipline the student. Under the proposed policy, instead of reliable evidence being suppressed, the appropriate disciplinary action would be taken against the school official who conducted the illegal search. Therefore the safety concerns expressed against application of the exclusionary rule are alleviated, yet students' rights still have a viable means by which they are protected.

For instance, the student who brought the gun to school will be disciplined so that he or she is no longer a threat to the students and faculty at the school. Nor will students, parents or school officials fear coming to school or have concerns about a "dangerous student" being in attendance at the school. Because the gun-wielding student does not go unpunished, as he would under the exclusionary rule, other students' respect for the law and rules will not be undermined and the student body will be

153. One valid concern with the proposal is that it places the fox in charge of guarding the hen house. That is, what checks are there to make sure that the school officials will impose just discipline on other school officials found to violate section 1 of the policy? The first check is that school officials who do not impose discipline that effectively deters future violations run the risk of losing one of the key benefits of the proposal, advantage in litigation. A court will see through the mere adoption of the *Lopez-Mendoza* factors and mandate the exclusionary rule since the school district's tactics have not been an effective deterrent. Secondly, the student still has the option of bringing a § 1983 action to compensate for egregious or recurring violations of his or her Fourth Amendment rights. *See generally supra* notes 125-26 and accompanying text.

154. *See supra* Part III.A-B.

sent the clear message that those who break the rules will be held accountable for their actions, teachers and students alike.

Another argument advanced by the anti-exclusionary rule camp is that, under the balancing test, the exclusionary rule in the school setting would not provide enough additional deterrent effect on school officials to warrant its application. The proposed policy does not question this conclusion, but responds as follows. First, when the counterbalancing costs of the exclusionary rule, namely the decrease in school safety, are taken out of the balancing equation, courts would be more likely to apply the exclusionary rule in the school administrative hearing setting. The proposed policy to a large degree neutralizes the adverse costs of protecting Fourth Amendment rights. The additional deterrence provided by this proposal is less expensive, in terms of societal costs under the balancing test, than the cost of the exclusionary rule's added deterrent effect. In addition, unlike the exclusionary rule's all or nothing approach, the school district has greater latitude under the proposed policy to determine the best way to deter its officials from violating the student's constitutional rights. By tailoring the punishment to fit the crime, the degree of deterrence gained by implementation of this policy has the potential to be even greater than the degree of deterrence obtained under the rigid exclusionary rule.[155]

The final argument advanced by the anti-exclusionary rule camp is that the rule would create more cumbersome adjudications. As far as this concern is a valid one,[156] the proposed policy does not mitigate this concern. Under either deterrent scheme, the board must first decide whether the search or seizure was reasonable.[157] Unless there is no protection afforded students' constitutional rights, then this determination would always have to be made by the school disciplinary board. With this understanding, the question then becomes, which do we value more, the marginal cost of additional administrative functions or the protection of students' constitutional rights? Viewed in this

---

155. For instance, one can easily imagine a situation where the teacher's motivations to search the child are driven by something other than punishing the child through the school disciplinary process. If the exclusionary rule is the only deterrent, the rule will not effectively deter this type of unconstitutional behavior.

156. *See* Bach, *supra* note 15, at 1169 (arguing that this is not a valid concern).

157. *See* discussion *supra* note 8.

light, the additional resources required to conduct such investigations and hearings are of minimal cost.

2. Meeting the concerns of the pro-exclusionary rule camp

Next, it must be determined how the proposed policy stacks up against the pro-exclusionary rule camp. The concern is that without the exclusionary rule, there will be no effective deterrent to protect the students' rights. This author does not dispute that a § 1983 action, by itself, is not an effective deterrent, but advances the position that punishing directly those who violate the students' Fourth Amendment rights will provide at least as good a deterrent effect as the exclusionary rule, without the high societal costs,[158] as it provides for and allows a more flexible approach to deter offenders of the Fourth Amendment.[159] The main benefit of the proposed policy is that privacy rights are protected without the high costs associated with applying the exclusionary rule.

This proposed policy also successfully addresses the judicial integrity concern expressed by advocates of the rule. As previously noted, supporters of the exclusionary rule fear that students will lose respect for school officials and the law when they see an adult break the rules and go unpunished for this activity. The proposed policy teaches this lesson to students in a very direct way, as opposed to the exclusionary rule's imputation of punishment upon the illegal searcher through the suppression of evidence. The teacher will be reprimanded for violating the student's rights under section 4 of the proposed policy. Thus, the students will more directly and effectively learn the lesson that school officials must respect the law and the rights of school children.

---

158. *See* Caldwell & Chase, *supra* note 147, at 67 (concluding that police officers who violate the Fourth Amendment should suffer negative consequence as a direct result of their misconduct to be effectively deterred).

159. *See* discussion *supra* note 155 and accompanying text. One commentator has noted that "[s]chool administrators are better equipped than judges to develop policies that best meet their local educational goals." Karen M. Clemes, Note, Lovell v. Poway Unified School District: *An Elementary Lesson Against Judicial Intervention in School Administrator Disciplinary Discretion*, 33 CAL. W. L. REV. 219, 242-43 (1997). As well, amidst the "ever increasing task of maintaining school order," *id.* at 241, "schools should be given substantial constitutional leeway in carrying out their traditional mission of responding to particularized wrongdoing." *Id.* at 243.

An additional benefit of the proposed policy over the exclusionary rule is its consistency. Referring back to the hypothetical at the beginning of this Comment, assume that the teacher conducting the search finds nothing in the student's jacket. Even though nothing was found by the teacher, the search is still a violation of the student's constitutional rights. The exclusionary rule has no application in this scenario as there is no disciplinary hearing since the student was not breaking any of the school rules. Compare this result with the result under the proposed policy. Assuming the teacher is found to have violated section 1, the teacher will be subject to discipline under section 4. Not only does the proposed policy provide greater protection to students' constitutional rights, from the student's perspective it would seem more fair and consistent. It does not make sense that a teacher should be punished for violating a student's constitutional rights only when the student is culpable of violating school policy. This could easily be interpreted by students as providing a greater amount of protection to those students who are "less deserving of protection."

C. *Utility of the Proposed Policy*

> [A] peculiar strength[] of our form of government [is] each State's freedom to "serve as a laboratory; and try novel social and economic experiments." *No area of social concern stands to profit more from a multiplicity of viewpoints and from a diversity of approaches than does public education.*[160]

1. *The proposed policy as a sword*

Implementation of the proposed policy can be viewed as a sword to be wielded by school districts in two respects. First, in those jurisdictions that have determined the exclusionary rule does not apply, there is currently little incentive for school officials to obey the strictures of the Fourth Amendment. The fact that students' constitutional rights essentially go unprotected under current federal precedent should concern school officials, teachers, parents, and students. Adopting some form of the pro-

160. San Antonio Sch. Dist. v. Rodriguez, 411 U.S. 1, 50 (1973) (emphasis added) (footnote omitted) (quoting New State Ice Co., v. Liebmann, 285 U.S. 262, 280, 311 (1932) (Brandeis, J., dissenting)).

posed policy would symbolically and practically send the message to students and parents, as well as teachers and administrators, that students' constitutional rights are to be respected and will be protected.[161]

Second, implementation of the proposal by a school district would be a solemn cry for autonomy. Decisions concerning student discipline in public schools traditionally were made by officials at the state and local level.[162] Within the past three decades the federal courts have departed significantly from their traditional deference to state and local disciplinary decisions.[163] The Supreme Court's intervention in the day to day running of public schools "has made it more difficult for public schools to reclaim the order and discipline necessary to educate students."[164]

A school district which adopts a form of the proposed policy would be taking a large step toward preserving its own autonomy by limiting the need and or opportunity for courts to mandate school districts to conduct themselves in a manner according to the courts' bidding. The need for courts to intervene would decrease as implementation of the proposed policy would send a resounding signal to the courts regarding the capability and desire of local governments to take control and determine how best to meet their educational goals.[165]

2. *The proposed policy as a shield*

Implementing and following a policy similar to the one proposed by this Comment will provide school districts a shield to protect themselves from civil liability, conflicts or incidents damaging to the relationship and trust between the community and

---

161. Parents become upset when their children's consitutional rights are violated or perceived to be violated. *See* Dodge, *supra* note 7, at 13. ("They take it for granted that just because they are kids, they don't have rights."); Inara Verzemnieks & Chastity Pratt, *Hunt for Thief at Duniway Went Too Far*, PORT. OREGONIAN, Jan. 31, 1998, at B-1 (noting that school officials and police issued written apologies to students and parents for search that "went too far"); *NBC News Sunrise: Oregon Parents Protest Strip Searches of Their Daughters* (NBC television broadcast, Feb. 3, 1998), *text available in* 1998 WL 5280939 (noting protest by angry parents whose daughters were strip searched while in school).

162. *See* Bach, *supra* note 15, at 1134.

163. *See id.* at 1134-35 & n.9.

164. Dupre, *supra* note 109, at 49.

165. *See* Robert B. Harper, *School Searches, A Look into the 21st Century*, 13 MISS. C. L. REV. 293, 296 (1993); Clemes, *supra* note 159, at 242-43.

school, and unwanted precedent from the federal courts. First, school districts will protect themselves from liability under § 1983 suits, for which the school district might be required to pay money damages for egregious violations of a student's constitutional rights.[166] Implementation of the training elements of the proposed policy would properly educate school officials on how to conduct searches in a constitutional manner. Such a policy, if adhered to, would provide the school a shield from liability under § 1983.

As well, the school district would be protecting itself from another externality that comes with egregious or recurring violations of constitutional rights, namely community outrage.[167] The notice provision in the model policy (section 5) encapsulates the vision that those school districts adopting some form of the model policy will notify the local community and involve it in its endeavors to protect students' rights and ensure school safety.

Finally, the fact that a school district has its own training procedures and deterrence schemes in place is a critical element in the Supreme Court's analysis of whether the exclusionary rule should be applied in a noncriminal setting.[168] The proposed policy fulfills the same requirements that the Court found to be "most important" in *Lopez-Mendoza*. With the proposed policy in place, school districts facing litigation over whether the exclusionary rule should apply in the school setting would have a step-up over school districts without the proposed policy. In short, since the courts are to measure the exclusionary rule's deterrent effect at the margin, that is, application of the exclusionary rule must cause deterrence in addition to that which already arises by other means,[169] the proposed policy would shield a school district from being required to adopt the exclusionary rule.

---

166. There are benefits to merely having a clear policy. In at least one post-*T.L.O.* decision, a civil rights action against a school district withstood summary judgment in favor of the school district apparently because the district lacked a clearly stated policy prohibiting the type of unconstitutional search initiated by the school official. *See* Cales v. Howell Pub. Sch., 635 F. Supp. 454 (E.D. Mich. 1985).

167. *See* discussion *supra* note 161.

168. *See* discussion *supra* Part II.C.1.

169. *See* United States v. Janis, 428 U.S. 433, 453 (1975); Bach, *supra* note 15, at 1149.

V. CONCLUSION

"Education 'is perhaps the most important function' of government. and government has a heightened obligation to safeguard students whom it compels to attend school."[170] Public school students should be, and feel, safe in schools. They should be free from violence by other students as well as from unreasonable invasions of privacy by school officials. While the exclusionary rule seems to require one at the expense of the other, the alternative approach articulated in this Comment attempts to secure both the protection of the students' constitutional rights and the physical protection of members of the school community. The alternative approach maintains the flexibility and discretion needed to keep order in public schools. The proposed policy is in line with the Supreme Court's mandate that the policy should "neither unduly burden the efforts of school authorities to maintain order in their schools nor authorize unrestrained intrusions upon the privacy of school children,"[171] but rather maintain the appropriate balance.

J. Chad Mitchell

170. New Jersey v. T.L.O., 469 U.S. 325, 353 (1985) (quoting Brown v. Board of Educ., 347 U.S. 483, 493 (1954)).

171. *Id.* at 342-43.

CONSTITUTIONALIZATION OF SCHOOL DISCIPLINE: AN UNNECESSARY AND COUNTER-PRODUCTIVE SOLUTION

*Hon. J. Harvie Wilkinson III, First Panelist**

It is a great pleasure to be able to participate in the Symposium on Due Process and Public Education. I must say initially that I find it disheartening that so much of the debate over public education today concerns disciplinary problems. When you see a headline about the public schools today, you instinctively shudder and become concerned that someone has been shot at or assaulted. One day perhaps such incidents will be too commonplace even to merit a headline. School crime will become like street crime. Will anyone even notice?

I remember with an odd sort of nostalgia the sense of alarm that gripped American public education after the Soviet Union launched Sputnik I in 1957. At least we were concerned then about the quality of America's math and science curriculum. Today, the debate involves how to keep the weapons out of class. Schools should be a primary way out of a life of despair. Too often, they have now become scenes of despair.

Do we have a huge disciplinary problem? It is a question on which we would all award immediate summary judgment. The denial of a disciplinary crisis would not even survive a motion to dismiss.

The causes of social ills are rarely simple. Many different things have contributed to the problems besetting public education, and it may seem unfair to single out the law and the courts as the primary culprits. We must acknowledge, nonetheless, the long trend toward providing greater procedural protections for the young. It probably began in 1967 with the case of *In re Gault*,[1] which revolutionized due process in juvenile court proceedings. That decision had a profound impact upon students' rights and school discipline. In *Tinker v. Des Moines Independent Community School District*,[2] secondary students were held to have First Amendment rights to wear black armbands. In *Goss v. Lopez*,[3] students were provided with the right to notice and a brief hearing before being subject to even

---

* Circuit Judge, U.S. Court of Appeals for the Fourth Circuit.

1. 387 U.S. 1 (1967).

2. 393 U.S. 503 (1969).

3. 419 U.S. 565 (1975).

a short disciplinary suspension. In *Wood v. Strickland*,[4] school officials were afforded only qualified immunity from suit under section 1983.[5]

Subsequent Supreme Court decisions did decline to extend the Cruel and Unusual Punishments Clause to corporal punishment in public schools,[6] declined to mandate extensive hearings on academic as opposed to disciplinary suspensions,[7] and declined to extend the full protections of the Fourth Amendment Warrant Clause to searches of a student on school premises.[8] Even this latter set of cases, however, only underscored the increasing prevalence of education litigation of all types and varieties, much of it brought for the purpose of expanding the rights of students who attend public schools.

Litigation is what you and I do for a living. We tend not to be traumatized by it because we live with the uncertainties and inconveniences and anxieties associated with the courtroom every day. Litigation, however, is decidedly not what school teachers, principals, and school board members do for a living. They would prefer to devote their lives as professional educators to improving the minds and broadening the horizons of their students. They would not opt to spend their time fending off these same students either in the hallway or in court. Time in court is time out of the classroom. Answering depositions educates no one. A teacher or principal probably wants to be in court about as much as you and I want to be in a hospital. They would do anything to avoid it, and the most effective way of avoiding it is to become risk-averse.

It is all very well and good to say that qualified immunity will protect school officials in all but the most egregious cases. Litigation, however, is by its very nature unpredictable, and to suspend even an unruly student is to risk being sued. One does not get sued under section 1983, however, for being passive and doing nothing. A course of constant inaction may detract from the general quality of the educational environment, and it may degrade the public interest, but it spares the concerned school principal the prospect of an angry plaintiff in court.

Much of the impetus behind the student rights revolution has stemmed from a fear of the arbitrary exercise of discretion. School officials, it has been argued, are apt to make mistakes. We worry that maybe the wrong person will be punished, and due process is seen as a way to ensure fair and reflective decisions. It may have these virtues, but

---

4. 420 U.S. 308 (1975).
5. 42 U.S.C. § 1983 (1988).
6. Ingraham v. Wright, 430 U.S. 651 (1977).
7. Board of Curators v. Horowitz, 435 U.S. 78 (1978).
8. New Jersey v. T.L.O., 469 U.S. 325 (1985).

I wonder if in the school setting the most vigorous proponents of due process have paused to tally up the costs. The proper exercise of authority invariably involves the exercise of discretion. A society in which decisionmakers have been stripped of discretion will be bereft of necessary hierarchy and devoid of the essential ingredients of public order.

Inevitably in the course of daily life, every one of us must exercise discretion. Lawyers must exercise discretion, business executives must exercise discretion, plumbers and construction workers and hair stylists must exercise discretion. A society which lives in complete distrust of discretion is a society which courts paralysis.

One place where discretion must be exercised is in the upbringing of the young. We understand that parents and teachers are imbued as a general matter with a certain fund of life experience, knowledge, and maturity. Otherwise, why would we commit children to their charge? So when we say we need due process to curtail discretion, we fail to understand that discretion in the training of youth is both socially indispensable and pedagogically required.

I wonder, really, how great is the risk that principals and teachers will abuse this discretion. I remember one summer when I taught a course in remedial English to students in a public junior high school. It was not difficult to learn quickly who in that class was willing to learn, who would respond to patient individual attention, and who was absolutely bent on being disruptive. Teachers know who the troublemakers are. If anything, teachers give students chance after chance to learn and to cooperate. Sometimes, however, infractions simply have to be dealt with if the teacher is to maintain respect. To open up the prospect of judicial hindsight of all disciplinary action is to divest teachers and principals of their ability to take the steps necessary for classroom order and instruction to survive.

Now it is true that discretion in society is always bounded by rules. Is it necessary, however, for the rules in local schools to be established by the expansion of federal constitutional law? School authorities already labor under layer upon layer upon layer of rules. School principals promulgate rules; local school boards have rules; state boards of education have rules; state laws, both civil and criminal, provide rules. The real question is, when and where shall the rulemakers desist? Schools will not be bereft of due process in the absence of federal judicial oversight; school principals will not turn a deaf ear to a student with another side of the story to tell. Parents have a way of giving schools an earful if a child has been unjustly treated, or even if she has not.

A recent debate in Boston between the mayor, the school superintendent, and the school principals over expulsion hearings for violent and disruptive students was instructive. There was great disagreement among the parties over how expeditiously hearings should be scheduled and how formal the process should be, but no disagreement with the idea that hearings should be retained as a means of protecting students' due process rights.[9]

When we take the important step of constitutionalizing a problem such as student discipline, we do two things. First, we remove it from the hands of the democratic process and place it in the lap of the federal courts. A constitution of such pervasive reach can become an instrument of disenfranchisement. The second thing we do by constitutionalizing a problem is to indicate a preference for centralized rules and solutions over disparate state and local prescriptions. The degree to which we constitutionalize our differences of opinion has been hotly debated in the world of substantive due process. What I would suggest to you is that the balance between constitutionalization and democratization is no less vital an issue where procedural due process is concerned. The school discipline cases, I would suggest, are an area in which the dangers of constitutionalization should not be overlooked.[10]

I trust I need not belabor the point that too many constitutional obligations can place our public schools at a comparative disadvantage to private and parochial institutions. The public schools are in the market for top teaching talent, yet polls of public school teachers have invariably pointed to disciplinary problems as one reason why many public school teachers quit and why so many other teachers go to private or parochial schools or decide upon another career altogether.[11]

The problem of student discipline and, hence, of teacher retention and recruitment may be especially acute in schools that serve disadvantaged communities. It goes without saying that these are the very communities in which the promise of public education must burn brightest. Yet suits over student discipline have the potential of arming student plaintiffs with a sword and leaving educators, via qualified immunity, with a very limited shield. Every wrongdoer can always threaten courtroom action and thereby limit the exercise of authority to what is very difficult to assemble, *i.e.*, the air-tight case.

---

9. Diego Ribadeneira, *Harrison-Jones Orders Faster Expulsion Hearings*, BOSTON GLOBE, Apr. 3, 1992, Metro/Region, at 19.

10. *See* J. Harvie Wilkinson III, Goss v. Lopez: *The Supreme Court as School Superintendent*, 1975 SUP. CT. REV. 25 (Philip B. Kurland ed. 1976).

11. *See, e.g.*, Pamela Coyle, *Teachers' Stay Isn't For Long; Louisiana Study Cites Discipline Woes*, NEW ORLEANS TIMES-PICAYUNE, Oct. 24, 1994, at A1 (noting that a "study by the Louisiana Education Policy Research Center found discipline problems were the No. 1 reason that new teachers left their schools").

The ready availability of student causes of action places school authority not in the position of asserting itself, but in the continuing position of having to justify itself. In a school environment in which weapons are present, drugs are available, and assaults are commonplace, it is unwise to have authority placed on the defensive by the continuing prospect of litigation. The impulse to let the courts decide can undermine parental and educational authority to the serious detriment of an entire generation. A framework of pure legalism and excess constitutionalism shows scant promise of resolving the disciplinary problems of disadvantaged school districts or, indeed, of schools anywhere.

Rights are a precious thing in America, and I would be the last to want to give them up. But the rights of adolescents are not in all respects the same thing as the rights of adults, and it is sensible for society to insist that students grow gradually into their exercise. The Rights Revolution has emphasized the psychological impact upon students of a fear of rejection and a loss of entitlement. The Rights Revolution has failed, however, to communicate to future generations the full consequences of a neglect of responsibilities.

It is essential for the schools to teach the lesson of responsibilities. Responsibilities involve a corresponding respect for rights — not simply for one's own rights, but for the rights of others. Responsibilities go hand-in-hand with rights, and students ought to understand that the former must be learned before the latter may be enjoyed.

PROTECTING STUDENT RIGHTS PROMOTES EDUCATIONAL OPPORTUNITY: A RESPONSE TO JUDGE WILKINSON

*Nadine Strossen, Second Panelist**

The conference brochure states the following as the first question for discussion, and I am quoting, "What are the real-world consequences of due process decisions broadly expanding the right to challenge . . . the determinations of local public officials?" I am going to answer that question, but I am going to do so by focusing on its unstated but logically necessary counterpart question, namely, what are the real-world consequences of broadly expanding the power of local public officials to deprive individuals of life, liberty, or property without any procedural protections?

Judge Wilkinson has talked about the dangers of constitutionalization. I would like to focus on the dangers of the lack of constitutionalization, especially when we are considering public institutions, which, by definition, are unconstrained by market forces. Therefore, the only possible constraint on their abuse of power, their deprivation of individual liberty, is constitutional constraint. My points are broadly applicable to all of the specific subjects to be considered during this conference, not only the public schools.

I agree with Judge Wilkinson, of course, that we are witnessing frustrating problems throughout our society, including our schools — notably the distressing levels of violence and crime. But too many government officials and citizens, in their desperation to solve seemingly intractable problems, seek illusory quick fixes that will not, in fact, fix anything at all. And, as usual, the customary scapegoats are brought forward, namely, individual rights and the actions of those of us either practicing before the courts or the courts themselves, who seek to honor and enforce those individual rights.

Interestingly, Judge Wilkinson began his remarks by stating that there are many problems, many complex factors that feed into our current

---

* President, American Civil Liberties Union; Professor of Law, New York Law School.
For research assistance, the author thanks Thomas Hilbink, Dolly Voorhees, and Donna Wasserman. This article includes examples and authorities that Professor Strossen did not have time to include in her oral presentation. It does not, however, add any arguments or conclusions that Professor Strossen did not present at the conference.

disciplinary problems in the schools and in society at large. He noted that it was probably unfair to single out courts and laws, but then he proceeds to do exactly that.

It reminds me of something that Mark Twain once reportedly said: when the only tool you have available is a hammer, all problems start to look like nails. So, with due respect, I am not surprised that a judge and a lawyer would seek to focus on courts and laws, even though they do not afford the most important solution — if, indeed, any solution at all — to the problem of violence in our schools.

This band-aid approach is doubly flawed. It is both unprincipled and ineffective. That it is unprincipled to deny individual rights for the purported goal of promoting order or discipline, or some other social good, is apparently a fundamental tenet among Federalist Society members as well as among American Civil Liberties Union members. According to the conference brochure, a founding principle of the Federalist Society is "that the State exists to preserve freedom." Accordingly, the purpose of public schools, along with all other government institutions, is to preserve freedom and not to maintain order or anything else. Education is, indeed, an essential prerequisite for all citizens to be able to realize their equal rights under the law. It is "the great equalizer," in the words of the United States Department of Education.[1]

It is the special responsibility of federal courts in our governmental system to guarantee that other government institutions do not unjustly deprive citizens of their rights. This responsibility is particularly important when the victims of government abuses are relatively powerless. In the public schools, the victims of official abuses are among the most powerless members of our society. They are children and teenagers, many of whom are also poor, disabled, or members of racial minorities.

So, number one, denying liberty to these young people is an unprincipled approach to solving problems of discipline in the schools. Second, denying liberty is as ineffective a strategy as it is unprincipled. It reminds me of a sadly prophetic warning that Thomas Jefferson conveyed to James Madison more than 200 years ago:[2] "A society that will trade a little liberty for a little order will deserve neither and lose both." Indeed, this insight has proven painfully true in the context of the public schools.

Let me remind you of the minimal due process guarantees that the Supreme Court set out in *Goss v. Lopez*,[3] because I think they have been

1. *See* Brief of NAACP and Southern Christian Leadership Conference as Amici Curiae at 10–11, Goss v. Lopez, 419 U.S. 565 (1975) (citing Office of Education report entitled *Equality of Educational Opportunity*) [hereinafter "*Goss* Amicus Brief"].

2. *See* Editorial, *Factoring in Civil Rights*, MASS. LAW. WKLY., July 29, 1991, at 4.

3. 419 U.S. 565 (1975).

somewhat overblown in the paraphrasing we have heard. All that the Supreme Court required was that some notice of the charges against a student be provided. Notice could be given orally either before or after the suspension or discipline took place. Moreover, the only other thing the Court guaranteed was the right to respond to those charges informally. Again, the response could be given after the suspension. These are hardly earth shattering procedural guarantees. Experience shows that denying students even these minimal safeguards not only impairs their vital rights, but also makes no positive contribution to a sound educational environment.

To the contrary, experts agree that punishing students without procedural safeguards will increase any negative attitudes or behavior on the part of those students and will have a detrimental effect both on the school and ultimately on society at large. For example, the Teachers College at Columbia University conducted a study in 1970, at the threshold of the due process revolution.[4] This study demonstrates that before this revolution we had a crisis in our schools related to the absence of due process guarantees. This study, *Civic Education in a Crisis Age*, concluded:

> A large majority of the students feel they are regularly subjected to undemocratic decisions . . . and hence are becoming increasingly frustrated and alienated by school. Students are not forming a reasoned allegiance to a democratic political system, because they receive no meaningful experience with such a democratically oriented system in their daily lives in school. We must teach the viability of democratic modes of conflict-resolution, and win respect for these as just and effective.[5]

I would now like to amplify the core principles I have just outlined by making some specific points about the role of procedural due process in public school discipline. I will state all these points now, and then I will elaborate as much as time permits.

First, procedural safeguards are necessary to reduce unfair, arbitrary, and biased disciplinary measures. These measures have permanent adverse consequences for students. Second, procedural safeguards are necessary to reduce racial discrimination in administering school discipline. Third, even after the Supreme Court's decisions in *Goss* and other

4. *See Goss* Amicus Brief at 12 (citing DEAN MURPHY, CIVIC EDUCATION IN A CRISIS AGE: AN ALTERNATIVE TO REPRESSION AND REVOLUTION: SUMMARY OF A RESEARCH PROJECT TO DEVELOP OBJECTIVES FOR A NEW CIVIC EDUCATION CURRICULUM FOR AMERICAN SECONDARY SCHOOLS IN THE 1970S (1970)).

5. *Id.*

cases, public schools still often engage in unfair and arbitrary treatment of students, as well as racial discrimination, in meting out discipline. Fourth, it follows that, far from having too many procedural protections and rights, public school students do not have enough safeguards against arbitrary official conduct. Fifth, there is no evidence that harsh penalties do any good, either for the student who is punished or for others in the school community. On the contrary, much evidence suggests that harsh penalties are counterproductive, especially when unaccompanied by procedural safeguards. Sixth, respecting individual rights is even more important in the public schools than in society at large. Seventh, the notion that things would be better if only we could roll the clock back to the good old days before the procedural due process revolution reflects an inaccurate, romanticized notion of pre-due process reality. They were hardly good old days for many who only now have meaningful access to public education.

I will now briefly discuss several of these points. First, procedural safeguards are necessary to reduce arbitrary treatment. Judge Wilkinson asked how great is the risk that discretion will be abused by school officials. I can answer that unqualifiedly. It is not a risk; it is a certainty. The experience of those who worked in the public schools before the due process revolution demonstrated this.

A 1972 article in the *Journal of Law and Education* by two individuals who worked with the New York Civil Liberties Union's Students' Rights Project summed it up well. It explained that the pattern of arbitrary suspensions and expulsions revealed the fundamentally custodial attitude of the public schools toward children who are black or Puerto Rican and poor. It revealed a system of segregation so thoroughly refined that mere physical separation, Southern-style, was not necessary in order to maintain pervasive inequality. And it revealed that what had for years been characterized as a drop-out problem was

> in fact a push-out problem. . . . [A]lmost all [the complaints we received] involved procedural problems; the maze of mechanisms which the schools used to rid themselves of students who present difficult problems the schools are not prepared to meet or who do not fit the mold in which the schools operate.[6]

Second, and clearly related to my first point, procedural safeguards are necessary to reduce racial discrimination in the administration of discipline. In 1975, Mark Yudof, who is now the Provost at the University of

---

6. Ira Glasser & Alan H. Levine, *Bringing Student Rights to New York City's School System*, 1 J.L. EDUC. 213, 215–16 (1972).

Texas, wrote an article about the suspension and expulsion of black students from public schools entitled "Suspension and Expulsion of Black Students From the Public Schools: Academic Capital Punishment."[7] Along with nonacademic capital punishment, its academic counterpart has always been disproportionately meted out to members of racial minorities, particularly to young African-American males. It is no coincidence that *Goss* itself involved the sweeping, indiscriminate suspension of black students from Columbus, Ohio public schools for allegedly taking part in demonstrations following Black History Week.

In their amicus brief for *Goss*, the NAACP and the Southern Christian Leadership Conference reminded the Supreme Court that school officials who resisted racial desegregation consistently used suspensions and other disciplinary measures as an important tool of their resistance. Indeed, in prosecuting desegregation cases, the Justice Department sought and obtained court orders expunging students' suspension records and mandating procedural safeguards before any suspension. In short, history has shown that public school discipline without due process violates constitutional guarantees of both liberty and equality.

My third point is that, even after *Goss*, public schools still engage in much unfair and arbitrary treatment of students, and much racial discrimination, in meting out discipline. Recent surveys show that many schools ignore students' procedural protections and impose discipline in situations where it is clearly inappropriate, including where students are simply exercising their free speech rights.

The racially discriminatory pattern of school discipline persists, too. To give just one example from the many, many studies that have documented these patterns, recent surveys indicate that although black students constitute sixteen percent of the school population nationwide, they continue to receive almost twice as many suspensions, roughly thirty percent.[8]

These ongoing problems lead to my fourth point. Far from having too many procedural safeguards, public school students have too few safeguards against arbitrary official conduct. In fact, when the Court decided *Goss*, school officials did not criticize it, as the dissenting Justices predicted they would. On the contrary, the main criticism came from the

---

7. Mark G. Yudof, *Suspension and Expulsion of Black Students From the Public Schools: Academic Capital Punishment and the Constitution*, 39 LAW & CONTEMP. PROBS. 374 (Spring 1975).

8. Muriel Cohen, *U.S. Public Schools Suspend Blacks at Twice the Rate of Whites; But Massachusetts Group Reports that State Figures are Consistent with Enrollment*, BOSTON GLOBE, Dec. 12, 1988, at A56 (citing a study by the National Coalition of Advocates for Students).

civil liberties/civil rights community, which maintained that *Goss* did not provide enough protection for students' rights.

Experience since then has shown that criticism to be well-taken. For example, this was the conclusion of a 1993 empirical study of school districts across the country by Donald Stone.[9] In addition to finding that African-American students are suspended at a rate 250% higher than Caucasian students, the Stone study also found that, in general, suspension was overused and abused.[10] Stone therefore urged that suspension be used only as a last resort, only in emergency situations, and that, even then, it should be preceded with more extensive procedural due process guarantees than the Court had required in *Goss*, including an independent hearing officer. Interestingly, some recent studies of school disciplinary problems recommend enforcement of even more stringent limitations on measures such as suspension, reserving them for truly emergency situations.

With all due respect to the questioner during the previous discussion, I do not think that wearing green hair to school happens to present a real threat to the order and discipline of the school.[11] One might ask not why the ACLU was defending that student's right to express his views through green hair, but rather why the school was wasting taxpayers' resources and its energies in suggesting that somehow it was interfering with the educational process for him to do that.

In contrast to the *de minimis* nature of the school's concern, the student's interest was the preeminently important one of free expression on public issues. Green hair has been used to express messages of support for environmental causes and pacifism, as chronicled in the classic movie, *The Boy with Green Hair*. Thus, green hair is the counterpart of the black armbands that the Supreme Court held protected by public school student's First Amendment rights in its landmark ruling in *Tinker v. Des Moines School District*.[12]

Far from depriving school officials of their necessary discretion, as Judge Wilkinson intimated, *Tinker* affirmed school officials' power to suppress expression that constitutes a "material and substantial disruption" of the educational process. But just as the black armbands in *Tinker* constituted no such disruption, neither did the green hair in the more recent case.

---

9. Donald H. Stone, *Crime & Punishment in Public Schools: An Empirical Study of Disciplinary Proceedings*, 17 AM. J. TRIAL ADVOC. 351 (1993).

10. *Id.* at 366.

11. *See Panel I: Discussion*, 1 MICH. L. & POL'Y REV. 297, 301 (1996).

12. 393 U.S. 503 (1969). The ACLU also represented the students in the *Tinker* case.

My fifth point is that there is no indication that harsh penalties do any good, either for the student who was penalized or for others in the school community. To the contrary, many experts agree that suspension is counterproductive from both perspectives. For example, a 1994 book by Eric P. Hartwig and Gary M. Ruesch concluded:

> Although it seems that . . . suspension, expulsion, and other exclusionary processes may result in a more orderly school environment, the opposite appears to be more often true. Many students who have been excluded come back to the school environment at some point, and as a result of negative feelings, the school may become a convenient . . . object of revenge. 82% of individuals in prison today are high school dropouts.[13]

Likewise, another recent paper, by the Advocates for Children of New York, indicted all school disciplinary measures, such as suspension, which superficially focus on symptoms, and which alienate students from school:

> Suspensions inherently increase the chances that students will never complete their education. Suspended or expelled high school students often fail to return to school, joining the thousands of . . . public school students who drop out each year. When this occurs, the long-term costs to society far exceed the short-term cost of educating even the most difficult young people in the academic and social skills necessary for productive employment.[14]

Of course, ineffective as measures such as suspension are in any case, they are even more ineffective when meted out unfairly, without procedural safeguards. Any time "law and order" is perceived to be unfair, order breaks down. This point was made by Charles Silberman in his classic book, *Crisis in the Classroom*: "Careless punishment in the schools serves only to breed more defiance and destruction, which breeds more repression . . . especially when accompanied by arbitrariness, racial prejudice, assumption of student guilt and general disregard of individual rights."[15]

My sixth point is that respect for individual rights is even more important in the public schools than in society at large. One of the major

---

13. ERIC P. HARTWIG & GARY M. RUESCH, DISCIPLINE IN THE SCHOOL 42 (1994).

14. Diana M.T.K. Autin, *Prevention and Alternatives: Reducing Out-of-School Suspensions*, at 1 (1992) (position paper for Advocates for Children of New York) (on file with author).

15. CHARLES E. SILBERMAN, CRISIS IN THE CLASSROOM: THE REMAKING OF AMERICAN EDUCATION (1970).

reasons for this conclusion was well stated by Justice Robert Jackson. It ties in with a concern that was raised by Judge Wilkinson when he recognized that at some point we do have to give young people rights, and they have to learn how to exercise them responsibly. But how can they do that if we shelter them from the experience of responsibly exercising their rights? As Justice Jackson said, "[Public schools] are educating the young for citizenship. . . . [This] is reason for scrupulous protection of constitutional freedoms of the individual child by the public schools, if we are not to strangle the free mind at its source and teach youth to discount important principles of our government as mere platitudes."[16] Underscoring this point, the Supreme Court has declared, "The vigilant protection of constitutional freedoms is nowhere more vital than in the community of American schools."[17]

Seventh, and I am going to conclude on this point, this romanticized notion that we used to have good old days before the due process revolution is really an unfounded myth. In truth, the old days were not very good, especially for the large number of students who were not given any meaningful access to the so-called "public schools." I say "so-called" because many categories of students were wholly excluded from the public schools, including three-fourths of all minority students at that time. Yes, we have many problems today, but we are at least looking at a situation where we do have truly universal access to education. That is an important gain in terms of both freedom and equal educational opportunity.

One study that has been widely cited by opponents of the due process revolution supposedly shows that in 1940 the most serious problems in public schools were such trivial infractions as talking and gum-chewing, whereas in 1987 the most serious problems in public schools included drug and alcohol abuse, pregnancy, suicide, and violent crime. Putting aside the fact that this supposed study has no empirical foundation, the actual facts show that, in terms of health, safety, and educational opportunity, young people today are better off than their 1940 counterparts.

For example, in 1940, only 49% of all young people graduated from high school. Pregnant girls were kicked out. Handicapped, learning-disabled, and troubled students were warehoused away from public view, and 75% of all minority and low-income students were excluded altogether.

Today, by contrast, more than 90% of all teenagers are enrolled in high school and 75% graduate on time, with the largest gains coming

16. West Virginia State Board of Education v. Barnette, 319 U.S. 624, 637 (1943).

17. Shelton v. Tucker, 364 U.S. 479, 487 (1960).

from stressed populations: minorities, students with disabilities, pregnant girls, and low-income youngsters. Illiteracy today is one-fifth its 1940 level. College enrollment has quadrupled.

I am certainly not arguing that 1994 — anymore than 1940, 1975, or any other era — is a halcyon time in terms of public schools. To the contrary, much serious work needs to be done in the school system, not only to improve students' educational experiences but also to improve their basic rights. What I am saying, though, is that there is no correlation between *increased* student rights and *decreased* educational opportunities. Actually, the rights revolution has gone hand-in-hand with the unprecedented opening up of meaningful educational opportunities to all students, including many who were deprived of such opportunities in the past. Our ongoing challenge is to carry forward on the path lit by the Supreme Court's decision in *Brown v. Board of Education*[18] exactly forty years ago tomorrow, namely, to ensure the constitutional rights of all public school students, and to ensure that all of them receive equal and adequate educational opportunities.

---

18. 347 U.S. 483 (1954).

Acknowledgments

DeMitchell, Todd A. "'The Right to Direct the Upbringing of a Child.' Parent as Sovereign and the State as Educator: A Balance of Vital Interests", 6 *International Journal of Education Reform* pp. 368–376 (1997). Reprinted with the permission of *International Journal of Educational Reform.*

Garnett, Richard W., "Taking Pierce Seriously: The Family, Religious Education, and Harm to Children," Vol. 76 *Notre Dame Law Review* 109–146 (2000). Reprinted with permission. Copyright © 2000 by the *Notre Dame Law Review*, University of Notre Dame. The publisher bears responsibility for any errors.

Ross, William G., "The Contemporary Significance of Meyer and Pierce for Parental Rights Issues Involving Education," Vol. 34 *Akron Law Review* 177–207 (2000). Reprinted with the permission of the *Akron Law Review.*

Underkuffler, Laura S., "The Price of Vouchers for Religious Freedom," Vol. 78 *University of Detroit Mercy Law Review* 463–478 (2001). Reprinted with the permission of *University of Detroit Mercy Law Review.*

Lupu, Ira C., "The Increasingly Anachronistic Case Against School Vouchers," Vol. 13 *Notre Dame Journal of Law Ethics & Public Policy* 375–396 (1999). Reprinted with the permission of the Notre Dame Law School.

Brown, Lisa A. & Gilbert, Christopher, " Understanding the Constitutional Rights of School Children," Vol. 34 *Houston Lawyer* 40–45 (1997). Reprinted with the permission of the *Houston Lawyer.*

Ryan, James E., "The Supreme Court and Public Schools," Vol. 86 *Virginia Law Review* 1335–1433 (2000). Reprinted with the permission of the University of Virginia, School of Law.

American Academy of Child and Adolescent Psychiatry. "Policy Statement: Corporal Punishment in Schools" *American Academy of Child and Adolescent Psychiatry* (11 pages) (June 1988). Reprinted with the permission of Williams & Wilkins.

"Corporal Punishment in Schools: A Position Paper of the Society for Adolescent Medicine," *Journal of Adolescent Health*: 1992;

13:240–246. Reprinted with the permission of Elsevier Science, Inc. Copyright © 1992 by the Society for Adolescent Medicine.

Imbrogno, Andre R. "Corporal Punishment in America's Public Schools and the U.N. Convention on the Rights of the Child: A Case for Nonratification" Vol. 29 *Journal of Law and Education* 125–147 (2000). Reprinted with permission from *Journal of Law and Education*, Vol. 29, Issue 2, pp. 125–147.

Parker, Jonathan K, "*Parens Patriae* in the Marketplace of Ideas: Limitations of Freedom of Expression in the Public Schools," *Proteus: A Journal of Ideas*, Fall 1997, pp. 39–41. This article originally appeared in *Proteus: A Journal of Ideas*, Fall 1997, Shippensburg, PA 17257–2299. Copyright © 1997 by Shippensburg University. Reprinted with permission.

Johnson, John W. "Behind the Scenes in Iowa's Greatest Case: What Isn't in the Official Record of *Tinker v. Des Moines Independent Community School District,*" Vol. 48 *Drake Law Review* 473–490 (2000). Reprinted with the permission of Drake University Law School.

Hafen, Bruce C., "Schools as Intellectual And Moral Associations," 1993 *Brigham Young University Law Review* 605–621 (1993). Reprinted with the permission of Brigham Young University.

Ingber, Stanley, *"Liberty and Authority: Two facets of the Inculcation of Virtue,"* Vol. 69 St. John's Law Review 421–479 (1995). Reprinted with the permission of the St. John's Law Review.

Allred, Chad "Guarding the Treasure: Protection of Student Religious Speech in the Classroom," Vol. 22 *Seattle University Law Review* 741–780 (1999). Reprinted with the permission of Seattle University, School of Law.

Mitchell, J. Chad, Comment, "An Alternative Approach to the Fourth Amendment in Public Schools: Balancing Students' Rights with School Safety," Vol. 1998 *Brigham Young University Law Review* 1207–1240 (1998). Reprinted with the permission of Brigham Young University.

Wilkinson, III, Hon. J. Harvie, "Constitutionalization of School Discipline: an Unnecessary and Counter-Productive Solution," Vol. 1 *Michigan Law & Policy Review* 309–313 (1996). Reprinted with the permission of *Michigan Law Review.*

Strossen, Nadine, "Protecting Student Rights Promotes Educational Opportunity: A Response to Judge Wilkinson," Vol. 1 *Michigan Law & Policy Review* 315–323 (1996). Reprinted with the permission of *Michigan Law Review.*